Lecture Notes in Computer Science   10244

Commenced Publication in 1973
Founding and Former Series Editors:
Gerhard Goos, Juris Hartmanis, and Jan van Leeuwen

Khalid Saeed · Władysław Homenda
Rituparna Chaki (Eds.)

Computer
Information Systems and
Industrial Management

16th IFIP TC8 International Conference, CISIM 2017
Bialystok, Poland, June 16–18, 2017
Proceedings

 Springer

Editors
Khalid Saeed
Bialystok University of Technology
Bialystock
Poland

Władysław Homenda
Warsaw University of Technology
Warsaw
Poland

Rituparna Chaki
A.K. Choudhury School of Information
   Technology
University of Calcutta
Kolkata, West Bengal
India

ISSN 0302-9743   ISSN 1611-3349 (electronic)
Lecture Notes in Computer Science
ISBN 978-3-319-59104-9   ISBN 978-3-319-59105-6 (eBook)
DOI 10.1007/978-3-319-59105-6

Library of Congress Control Number: 2017941492

LNCS Sublibrary: SL3 – Information Systems and Applications, incl. Internet/Web, and HCI

Printed on acid-free paper

This Springer imprint is published by Springer Nature
The registered company is Springer International Publishing AG
The registered company address is: Gewerbestrasse 11, 6330 Cham, Switzerland

Preface

CISIM 2017 was the 16th of a series of conferences dedicated to computer information systems and industrial management applications. The conference was supported by IFIP TC8 Information Systems. This year it was held during June 16–18, 2017, in Bialystok, Poland, at the Faculty of Computer Science of Bialystok University of Technology.

In all, 85 papers were submitted to CISIM by researchers and scientists from a number of reputed universities in the Czech Republic, France, Germany, Hungary, India, Italy, Japan, Lithuania, Luxembourg, Malaysia, New Zealand, Poland, Portugal, South Korea, Tunisia, and USA. Most of the papers were of high quality. Each paper was assigned to at least two reviewers initially, and the accept decision was taken after receiving two positive reviews. In the case of conflicting decisions, another expert's review was sought for the respective papers. In total, about 200 reviews were collected from the referees for the submitted papers. In order to maintain the guidelines of Springer's Lecture Notes in Computer Science series, the number of accepted papers was limited. Furthermore, a number of electronic discussions were held between the Program Committee (PC) chairs and members to decide about papers with conflicting reviews and to reach a consensus. After the discussions, the PC chairs decided to accept for publication in the proceedings book the best 60 of the total submitted papers.

The main topics covered by the chapters in this book are biometrics, security systems, multimedia, classification and clustering, industrial management. Besides these, the reader will find interesting papers on computer information systems as applied to wireless networks, computer graphics, and intelligent systems.

There also was a Special Session on Engineering of Enterprise Software Products (organizers: Prof. Nabendu Chaki and Dr. Anirban Sarkar from University of Calcutta and National Institute of Technology Durgapur in India).

We are grateful to the four esteemed speakers for their keynote addresses. The authors of the keynote talks were Profs. Nabendu Chaki, University of Calcutta, India; Young Im Cho, Seoul University, South Korea; Mario Koeppen, Kyushu Institute of Technology, Japan; Witold Pedrycz, University of Alberta, Canada; Kenneth Regan, University at Buffalo (SUNY), USA. All the keynote abstracts are published in the proceedings.

We would like to thank all the members of the PC and the external reviewers for their dedicated efforts in the paper selection process, particularly Profs. Kateřina Slaninová, Debdutta Barmanroy, Jan Martinovič, and Pavel Moravec. We also thank the honorary chairs of the conference, Profs. Witold Pedrycz and Ryszard Tadeusiewicz. Special thanks are extended to the members of the Organizing Committee, both international and the local, and the team at Springer for their great efforts to make the conference a success. We are also grateful to Andrei Voronkov, whose EasyChair system eased the submission and selection process and greatly supported the compilation of the proceedings. The proceedings editing was managed by Jiří Dvorský (Technical University of Ostrava, Czech Republic), to whom we are indeed very grateful.

We hope that the reader's expectations will be met and that the participants enjoyed their stay in the beautiful city of Bialystok.

June 2017

Khalid Saeed
Władysław Homenda
Rituparna Chaki

Organization

Program Committee

Esref Adali	Istanbul Technique University, Turkey
Raid Al-Tahir	University of the West Indies, St. Augustine, Trinidad and Tobago
Aditya Bagchi	Indian Statistical Institute, India
Sambit Bakshi	National Institute of Technology Rourkela, India
Debdutta Barmanroy	CIEM, India
Anna Bartkowiak	Wrocław University, Poland
Sukriti Bhattacharya	University College of London, UK
Rahma Boucetta	National Engineering School of Gabes, Tunisia
Nabendu Chaki	University of Calcutta, India
Rituparna Chaki	University of Calcutta, India
Samiran Chattoppadhyay	Jadavpur University, India
Sankhayan Choudhury	University of Calcutta, India
Agostino Cortesi	Ca' Foscari University of Venice, Italy
Pierpaolo Degano	University of Pisa, Italy
Jirí Dvorský	VŠB-Technical University of Ostrava, Czech Republic
Pietro Ferrara	IBM T.J. Watson Research Center, USA
Miguel Ferrer	Universidad de Las Palmas de Gran Canaria, Spain
Manoj Gaur	Malaviya National Institute of Tech. Jaipur, India
Marina Gavrilova	University of Calgary, Canada
Raju Halder	Ca' Foscari University of Venice, Italy
Władysław Homenda	Warsaw University of Tech., Poland (Co-chair)
Khalide Jbilou	Université du Littoral Côte d'Opale, France
Flaminia Luccio	Ca' Foscari University of Venice, Italy
Jan Martinovič	VŠB-Technical University of Ostrava, Czech Republic
Pavel Moravec	VŠB-Technical University of Ostrava, Czech Republic
Romuald Mosdorf	Białystok University of Technology, Poland
Hien Thanh Nguyen	Ton Duc Thang University, Vietnam
Nobuyuki Nishiuchi	Tokyo Metropolitan University, Japan
Tadeusz Nowicki	Military University of Technology, Poland
Andrzej Pacut	Warsaw University of Technology, Poland
Jerzy Pejaś	WPUT in Szczecin, Poland
Jaroslav Pokorný	Charles University, Czech Republic
Piotr Porwik	University of Silesia, Poland
Jose Proenca	University of Minho, Portugal
Kenneth Regan	University at Buffalo (SUNY), USA
Khalid Saeed	Białystok University of Technology, Poland (Co-chair)
Anirban Sarkar	National Institute of Technology Durgapor, India

Rafał Scherer	Częstochowa University of Technology, Poland
Ewa Skubalska-Rafajłowicz	Wrocław University of Technology, Poland
Kateřina Slaninová	VŠB-Technical University of Ostrava, Czech Republic
Václav Snášel	VŠB-Technical University of Ostrava, Czech Republic
Zenon Sosnowski	Białystok University of Technology, Poland
Jarosław Stepaniuk	Białystok University of Technology, Poland
Marcin Szpyrka	AGH Kraków, Poland
Bay Dinh Vo	Ton Duc Thang University, Vietnam
Sławomir Wierzchoń	Polish Academy of Sciences, Warsaw, Poland
Michał Woźniak	Wrocław University of Technology, Poland
Sławomir Zadrożny	Polish Academy of Sciences, Warsaw, Poland

Additional Reviewers

Marcin Adamski	Białystok University of Technology, Poland
Piotr Artiemjew	University of Warmia and Mazury, Poland
Cezary Boldak	Białystok University of Technology, Poland
Katarzyna Borowska	Białystok University of Technology, Poland
Soumya Brata Saha	University of Calcutta, India
Pavla Dráždilová	VŠB-Technical University of Ostrava, Czech Republic
Dorota Duda	Białystok University of Technology, Poland
Wojciech Froelich	University of Silesia, Poland
Ekaterina Grakova	VŠB-Technical University of Ostrava, Czech Republic
Andrzej Chmielewski	Białystok University of Technology, Poland
Wiktor Jakowluk	Białystok University of Technology, Poland
Kateřina Janurová	VŠB-Technical University of Ostrava, Czech Republic
Agnieszka Jastrzebska	Warsaw University of Technology, Poland
Adam Klimowicz	Białystok University of Technology, Poland
Maciej Kopczynski	Białystok University of Technology, Poland
Michal Krumnikl	VŠB-Technical University of Ostrava, Czech Republic
Miloš Kudělka	VŠB-Technical University of Ostrava, Czech Republic
Marek Lampart	VŠB-Technical University of Ostrava, Czech Republic
Eliška Ochodková	VŠB-Technical University of Ostrava, Czech Republic
Walenty Oniszczuk	Białystok University of Technology, Poland
Antoni Portero	VŠB-Technical University of Ostrava, Czech Republic
Jyoti Prakash Singh	National Institute of Technology Patna, India
Francesca Pratesi	University of Pisa, Italy
Mariusz Rybnik	University of Białystok, Poland
Sangeet Saha	University of Calcutta, India
Bidyutbiman Sarkar	University of Calcutta, India
Soumya Sen	University of Calcutta, India
Ditipriya Sinha	University of Calcutta, India
Marek Tabędzki	Białystok University of Technology, Poland
Lukáš Vojáček	VŠB-Technical University of Ostrava, Czech Republic
Xiao Xiao	Tokyo Metropolitan University, Japan

Keynotes

Enterprise Modelling and Requirements Engineering Using i* Framework

Nabendu Chaki

Department of Computer Science and Engineering,
University of Calcutta, Kolkata, India
nchaki@cucse.org

Abstract. Goal Modelling techniques are used to identify and detect errors, conflicts, or issues that may arise in the later phases of the life-cycle. Early detection of errors between project goals helps in reducing the cost to a great extent. In our efforts to assess the advantages of applying model checking on goal models, we have used i* framework and developed the i*ToNuSMV tool.

The i* is one of the most complex multi-agent modelling frameworks. We have used it for requirements engineering. Actors and inter-dependencies between the Actors are said to be intentional for the i* framework. The i*ToNuSMV tool acts as a POC for the proposed Semantic Implosion Algorithm where we can feed i* models and temporal specifications as input and check whether the specifications are satisfied by the model.

The NuSMV model verifier runs in the back end to verify the specification and generates a counterexample if it fails to satisfy. The goal model reconciliation framework has been supplemented with an implementation road-map. Goal models and process models have completely different objectives and characteristics. The most crucial differential characteristic being the sequence-agnostic nature of goal models. In this perspective, it becomes necessary to spell out a mechanism for semantic effect annotation of goal models, and how these effects can be reconciled over the entire enterprise for performing different kinds of analysis.

The main motivation is to help designers and developers identify and rectify errors in the requirements phase itself, before the requirements are formally documented and specified.

Development of Knowledge Base Sharing Technologies for Cloud Service Robot

Young Im Cho

Deptartment of Computer Engineering,
Gachon University, Seongnam, South Korea
yicho@gachon.ac.kr

Abstract. Businesses related to artificial intelligence are forming ecosystems in areas such as the development of core technologies and the efficiency of jobs in enterprises. These technologies are expected to achieve sustained growth in the future. In the future, deep learning will be differentiated according to the level of practical use for each applicable field, and research and development will be needed from a long-term perspective. In terms of existing technologies, deep learning is an artificial neural network model, a field of machine learning, and is used for information collection, classification, prediction, recognition, and control functions in almost all industries including business. In terms of product specificity, it will be used to build robotic industry ecosystem such as infrastructure of cloud sourcing based on knowledge and intelligence data of robot in future by developing knowledge base sharing technology of service robot. In terms of commercialization status, deep learning technology is being used in speech recognition, image processing, autonomous driving car, artificial intelligence computer, virtual personal assistant, etc. Currently, the cloud robot industry does not have a common interface or communication standard between robots, unlike other computing industries. Since the operating system uses various operating systems such as Windows, Linux, RTOS, and Android, technology development is slowing down. Therefore, it is necessary to standardize not only the operating system but also the robot application, the common interface and the communication standard in order to promote the robot industrial technology and activate the robot software market. Currently, there are VWNS robot software frameworks such as OPRoS (Open Platform for Robotics Services) in Korea and ROS (Robot Operation System) in USA. The interfaces of application programs are standard of RoIS (Robot Interaction Service) and RLS (Robot Localization Service). However, since it is still in the development stage, it is necessary to build a common infrastructure that is more widespread and to standardize and globalize it. In this presentation, we will present technologies and standardization methods for knowledge base sharing in cloud service robots.

Social Optimization: Framework, Algorithms and Applications

Mario Koeppen

Department of Computer Science and Electronics,
Kyushu Institute of Technology, Kitakyushu, Japan
mkoeppen@ieee.org

Abstract. The efficient design, management and control of today's technological systems and solutions is to an increasing degree characterized by societal aspects. This also applies to the classical task of optimization as it appears now in new domains like group decision making, fair distribution, equity of resource sharing and we can find among the application domains communication networks, cloud computing, risk assessment, pattern recognition, computational security, collaborative and recommendation systems. These tasks can often not be expressed by simple function evaluations anymore. Relational mathematics, which is studied in mathematical economics and social choice theory, provides a rich and general framework and appears to be a natural and direct way to express corresponding optimization goals, to represent user preferences, to justify fairness criterions, or to valuate utility. The talk will have two main parts. In the first part, basic approaches from mathematical economics to the problemacy of fairness (in distribution and allocation) are recalled. It is followed by the presentation of a set of relations that are able to represent various aspects of fairness along with their motivation. Starting with the "classical" fairness relations maxmin fairness, proportional fairness and lexicographic maxmin, we can recover their mutual relationships and their design flexibility in order to define further relations, with regard to e.g. multi-resource problems, ordered fairness, self-weighted fairness, collaborative fairness, and fuzzy fairness. In the second part, we want to illustrate and demonstrate the application of these concepts to basic data processing and optimization tasks, especially in data mining, multi-agent systems, pattern recognition and performance comparison of metaheuristic algorithms. In this part we will also mention the tractability of larger-scaled problems by presenting algorithmic approaches by meta-heuristic algorithms derived from well-known evolutionary multi-objective optimization algorithms, as a side note also show that the No-Free-Lunch theorems do not apply to the proposed relational optimization.

Data Analytics: Selected Insights into Data Quality, Associations, and Information Granules

Witold Pedrycz

Department of Electrical and Computer Engineering,
University of Alberta, Edmonton, Canada
pedrycz@ee.ualberta.ca

Abstract. Data are the blood life of today's society. The diversity of data is enormous. The quality of data including their comprehensive and multifaceted characterization becomes of paramount importance and is central to further data analysis and processing.

In this presentation, we cover a suite of selected insights into data quality and elaborate on their quantification. The two central issues involving coping with incomplete data (invoking data imputation) and imbalanced data are discussed.

In addressing these issues and delivering algorithmically sound solutions, we advocate a central role of information granularity being played in dealing with the two above stated problems and yielding the results quantified in terms of information granules. With this regard to make the presentation self-contained, we include selected prerequisite material on Granular Computing, especially a discussion on designing information granules.

Revealing interpretable and conceptually stable associations (relationships) within data form another central item on the agenda of data analytics. We show how granular mappings engaging granular parameter spaces are developed and assessed. Associative relationships constructed in terms of granular bidirectional and multidirectional associative memories are investigated. We also develop granular autoencoders and stacked granular autoencoders.

Chess and Informatics

Kenneth Regan

Department of Computer Science and Engineering,
University at Buffalo, The State University of New York,
Albany, USA
regan@buffalo.edu

Abstract. Computer chess began as a field to investigate human cognition and the creation of artificial intelligences. It became instead a grand race to get the most out of computer hardware and software for brute-force searches that evolved into incredibly smart algorithmics. A modern program on a smartphone has been shown to trounce programs of a dozen years ago running on muscle machines with 50 times the power. Machines defeated the human champion at chess two decades ago and have now come to dominate us via deep learning at Go, our deepest hallowed game. The programs are arbiters of quality and optimality of move choices and strategy decisions whose authority is beyond almost all doubt. Paradoxically, this level of singularity may finally enable some of the original AI aims to be realized. Deep analysis of chess positions from human games reveals new kinds of 'laws of nature' and regularities of human performance. Several laws from mine and others' research will be exhibited and targeted to probe deeper problems of how we think, when and why we stop thinking, and how we process information.

Contents

Industrial Management and Other Applications

Various Aspects of Computer Security

Algorithms

Pattern Classification with Rejection Using Cellular Automata-Based Filtering

Agnieszka Jastrzebska[✉] and Rafael Toro Sluzhenko

Faculty of Mathematics and Information Science, Warsaw University of Technology,
ul. Koszykowa 75, 00-662 Warsaw, Poland
A.Jastrzebska@mini.pw.edu.pl, toror@student.mini.pw.edu.pl

Abstract. In this article we address the problem of contaminated data in pattern recognition tasks, where apart from native patterns we may have foreign ones that do not belong to any native class. We present a novel approach to image classification with foreign pattern rejection based on cellular automata. The method is based only on native patterns, so no knowledge about characteristics of foreign patterns is required at the stage of model construction. The proposed approach is evaluated in a study of handwritten digits recognition. As foreign patterns we use distorted digits. Experiments show that the proposed model classifies native patterns with a high success rate and rejects foreign patterns as well.

1 Introduction

Pattern recognition is an important branch of machine learning and data mining. In a typical pattern recognition scenario, we assume that there is a finite number of classes (categories) of patterns on which we want to form an automated mechanism that assigns appropriate class labels to patterns appearing on its input. The process of learning is based on an already labeled subset of patterns that we have at hand and we use to train the classifier. Ideally, we wish that the trained classifier will be able to recognize not only patterns used at the stage of training, but also new patterns that it had not seen before.

In this paper we address the problem of contaminated datasets, where apart from proper patterns, that we call *native patterns*, we have garbage patterns, so called *foreign patterns*. Processing of such dataset aims at:

- classifying native patterns and
- rejecting foreign patterns.

The problem of contaminated datasets is especially valid when we are collecting pattern samples in an out-of-lab environment. It may happen that preprocessing mechanisms (image binarization, gray-scale transformation, filtering, segmentation, etc.) do not perform well and we obtain incorrect patterns. Foreign patterns contaminate the dataset as they do not belong to any proper class. Moreover,

K. Saeed et al. (Eds.): CISIM 2017, LNCS 10244, pp. 3–14, 2017.
DOI: 10.1007/978-3-319-59105-6_1

we cannot assume that foreign patterns are known at the stage of classifier construction. Thus, the main idea behind this approach is to develop a generic foreign pattern rejection mechanism that will allow us to reject a broad variety of samples of different kind.

In this paper we introduce a novel approach for classification with foreign pattern rejection based on the formalism of cellular automata. The method is suited for image recognition. The phase of model construction is based entirely on native data, so no knowledge about foreign patterns is needed to build the classifier. This makes the model applicable to real-world scenarios, where the origin of any foreign pattern is typically unknown. The proposed method is tested in an empirical study of handwritten digits recognition. As foreign patterns we use distorted digits. It shall be mentioned that patterns come in various forms: images, sound or voice recording, etc. and there are two approaches to process them: either by using the original pattern format or by employing feature vectors (features are numbers describing original patterns). In our method we operate on images (original pattern format).

The paper is structured as follows. Section 2 presents the background knowledge on foreign elements detection. Section 3 presents the concept of cellular automata in the context of pattern recognition. Section 4 covers the proposed method for native image classification with foreign pattern rejection. Section 5 is devoted to experimental evaluation of the proposed model. Section 6 concludes the paper.

2   Literature Review

Popular mechanisms for pattern recognition reinforced with foreign pattern rejection process data in form of feature vectors. In this branch of studies we find two groups:

– one in which the training phase is based on synthesized foreign patterns, and
– methods that are based on native patterns only.

The first stream of research assumes that foreign patterns form separate class(es) and we shall be able to describe them in a way analogical to the way how we describe native patterns. In the training process we learn how to distinguish between foreign class(es) and native class(es). Among studies following this line of thought we find, for instance [2,4].

The second group of methods does not assume that foreign patterns form class(es). Therefore, these rejection mechanisms are trained on native patterns only. As an example of such a method we may give a centroid-based approach, whose goal is to locate a determined number of centroids in the data and using the notion of distance determine areas around centroids that should be occupied by native patterns only. If a pattern resides outside of the area close to a centroid, it gets rejected. Particular implementations of this approach are documented in [11,12]. Another well-known method for foreign element rejection based on native patterns only is the one-class SVM, also called ν-SVM, or novelty detection SVM. For a more in-depth elaboration on this method one may consult [13,15]. The one-class SVM detects soft boundaries of a set that we pass on to its input. As a consequence, we are able to asses which elements surely belong to this class and which of them do not.

In this paper we propose an approach to foreign pattern rejection that is not based on features vectors, but on images. Filters are the most similar approach to the method presented in this paper. A typical application of filters is to suppress, reconstruct or enhance certain characteristics of an image. Standard filters reduce noise in an image (like mean filter, median filter, smoothing filters, speckle removal filters), normalize content of an image, detect and/or enhance edges in an image. For a comprehensive reference to image processing one may consult [3]. In the presented approach we apply sets of automata rules that in fact act as a collection of filters and they alter images. On top of that, we provide a simple additional decision algorithm that assigns class labels and rejects foreign patterns. Importantly, rules are developed based on training set of images what distinguished this method from "classical" filters.

The literature presents a few cellular automata-based approaches to pattern recognition, including methods reported in [8,10]. On the other hand, formalism of cellular automata as concept allows for substantial implementation flexibility and therefore at the current development stage we see greater similarity of our approach to filters rather than to the methods described in the cited papers.

3   Cellular Automata

An **Automaton** is a self-operating machine or software algorithm which follows a determined sequence of operations in order to process some input data. Analogously, a **Cellular automaton** can be understood as a software algorithm which follows a determined set of **rules** that prescribe changes to the input data. Another definition of this concept can be found in *Cellular Automata for Pattern Recognition* [14]:

> "*Cellular Automata (CA) are spatiotemporal discrete systems* [9] *that can model dynamic complex systems* [14]."

Simulation. A simulation of such algorithm would take place in a grid, i.e. a big rectangle with cells in it, like a matrix. In there, cells would be constantly evaluated and their colors (formally called **states**) modified, and such change would be determined by the rules that were previously defined before running the simulation. A rule tells the automaton where to look for and what to do with a given cell if such rule is satisfied. From the automaton perspective, a cell has two important properties:

1. a **state** that is subject to changes at any given time, and
2. a **neighborhood** of surrounding cells, whose states are considered as important as the state of the cell itself.

Rules. A rule r_i is a statement applied to a single cell, which consists of a condition and an action to be taken when such condition is satisfied, where i denotes the index of such rule within its corresponding rule set. Usually, the condition takes into consideration the current state of a given cell and the states of its neighbors. If satisfied, the target cell might potentially change its current state, depending on what the matched rule dictates. In the application, 8 different rules were designed to work with a 3×3 neighborhood and their goal is to detect any type of edge an image could have. The general purpose of each rule is to find live cells and, if the rule is matched, switch their states to dead. At the end of such operation, the results will yield clearly defined edges of live cells for any image, which will allow the program to compute a series of statistics based on this result and store them for the label generation stage. The patterns shown in Fig. 1 represent the rules used by this program. In order to find a match, it is enough for a rule to find the exact combination of states at the desired positions. This means that it is not a problem if there are more live cells than needed in a neighborhood, as long as the ones that are required to be in that particular state fulfill that requirement. This approach has been named *Partial Pattern Match*.

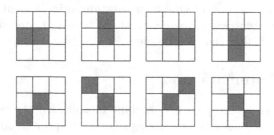

Fig. 1. Rules used by the program for finding edges in images.

4   Patterns Recognition Using Cellular Automata

4.1   Image Sets

The program works with different types of image sets, where each one plays its own role within the modeling and classification processes. These sets constitute the input to the cellular automaton algorithm.

Training Set. A training set is a set of image samples that belong to C different classes and are used by the program for learning. Based on these samples, a classification model is created that is later used by the application for classifying different test images and verifying the quality of such model.

Validation Set. A validation set is a set of image samples that belong to C different classes and are used for tuning up the parameters of a classifier. At the end of the training phase, a validation set is used in order to compare the performance of the algorithm and avoid over-fitting of its parameters. Such set of images is used for improving the classification model and assigning the appropriate scores to each class label. It is a middle-step between the actual training and the testing phases.

Test Set. A test set (also called *hold-out set*) is a collection of sample images that are used only to assess the performance of a fully-trained classifier. A test set is used for evaluating the relationships that were discovered by the application and check if such relationships hold true.

4.2   The Algorithm

The goal for the cellular automaton is to take each subset of the input training set, analyze each image by applying the aforementioned rules and compute a series of statistics based on the cells that did not change with respect to the total number of dead cells that conform the actual shape in the image and were affected by a particular rule. This applies to every next image from the given collection. Each rule in the rule set is applied one time (if a given cell matches its criteria) and results of that single transition for each cell are recorded separately. Based on the collected information, decision rules are generated. These rules tell the system how to classify a test input image based on a range of the form:

$$min\{S_{C_i}\} \leq S_{r_i} \leq max\{S_{C_i}\}$$

where:

$min\{S_{C_i}\}$ - the lowest interval value for an image belonging to a class C_i, where
    i denotes the index of the given class within the set of all classes
$min\{S_{C_i}\}$ - the highest interval value for an image belonging to a class C_i, where
    i denotes the index of the given class within the set of all classes
S_{r_i} - the actual statistic computed for the given test image after applying a rule r_i

Such set of decision rules needs to be validated and eventually refined before it is used on test sets.

In order to avoid potentially imprecise image classifiers, a validation set is required for adjusting the already defined classification model and verifying its utility. The validation set consists of a collection of images that need to be classified by the automaton without knowing to which class they originally belong. The procedure for such classification is the same as in the **Automaton** subsection, with the difference that statistics for these unknown images are not stored anymore, instead, they are used for assigning labels to those images based on the already generated decision rules.

The steps for the classification model validation are as follows (for every image in the validation set):

Part 1:

1. Apply a rule to an image
2. Count how many cells remained in live state after applying the rule
3. Compute a statistic S_j of the number of cells that stayed alive and the type of rule that led to such result for a given image, where j corresponds to the index of the given statistic within the set of all statistics for a given class.
4. Use the statistic S_j to assign a class label L_C to the image based on the decision rules
5. Store information about the assignment in a table
6. Repeat the same procedure for every next image in the current subset.

Part 2:

7. Check if the image was assigned the correct class label C_{L_i}, where i denotes the index of the given label from the set of all labels that were generated for the given class
8. Count how many classifications where correct for a given rule set R_i, where i denotes the index of the rule set from the set of all rule sets
9. Store the score S_{R_i} of the result in a pair $\{R_i, S_{R_i}\}$
10. Repeat the same procedure for every next image in the current subset.

At the end, select a pair $\{R_i, S_{R_i}\}$ such that

$$S_{R_i} := \max\{S_{R_i}\}$$

Such rule set will be then defined as the best one for classifying images of a given class C_i. The system is now ready for analyzing test sets.

4.3   Testing the Classification Model

Once the classification model has been built, the next step is to test its efficiency by applying it to different test image sets. Classification of images is done following the steps below (for every image in the test set):

Part 1:

1. Apply a classifier to a test image
2. Count how many cells remained in live state after applying the classifier rule
3. Compare the number of cells that stayed alive and the type of rule that led to such result against the intervals that were defined by the label of the given classifier
4. If all the edge types match the given intervals, assign the classifier label
5. Store information about the assignment in a statistic S_j
6. Repeat the same procedure for every next image in the current subset.

Part 2:

Once the classification procedure is over, use the statistics to build a confusion table and present it as a summary of all the tests performed on a given test set.

5   Experiments

5.1   Experimental Settings

Image Preprocessing. Before running a training or testing routine, the program must ensure normalization of any image in a training/validation/test set. That is, each image must be properly scaled and converted to black and white. Preprocessing ensures comparability of different images in the imported sets, which in turn assures correctness of results. In general, it is assumed that every set will contain already normalized images, i.e. scaled, gray-scaled and cleared up. Nevertheless, a preventive local normalization shall be performed for any case. The aim of scaling is to resize each image to a standard, predefined size such that it has the same dimensions as the rest. Such resizing helps setting one common size to all the images in a set, i.e. the matrix size of each is the same. The standard dimensions used by the algorithm are 28×28 pixels, a size which does not implicate any quality loses in images of simple shape on a white background – such as handwritten digits – and helps the application to improve the image processing speed. Gray-scaling is applied in order to work with black and white images, whose shapes are better recognizable and their edges clearly defined.

Image Labeling. Image labeling is the process of deciding to which class an unknown image belongs. In order to take such decision, the program needs to apply the classification model it created based on the training and validation sets that were provided by the user. The final results will depend on the quality and quantity of the input data. Each predefined rule used by the application has its own, unique type. The type attribute helps the program detecting edges in images much easier, thus preventing potentially erroneous label assignments.

5.2   Data Sets

The experiment was based on a native dataset of handwritten digits taken from the MNIST database [7]. Some samples are illustrated in Fig. 2. The MNIST database holds approximately $1,000$ images of each digit, which makes a 10-class problem, leaving us with 10 unique class labels: $0, 1, \ldots, 9$. In order to train the classifier we took 200 samples of each native class for the training set, 200 samples of each native class for the validation set, and 300 samples of each class for the testing set. Naturally, training, validation, and testing sets of native patterns are disjoint.

For rejection mechanism testing purposes, we used datasets of distorted digits. Samples of foreign patterns are displayed in Fig. 3. Distorted digits were formed based on original MNIST images, from which we randomly selected 300 samples of each digit and applied various modifications. In total, foreign datasets were made of $3,000$ samples (analogously to the test set of native patterns).

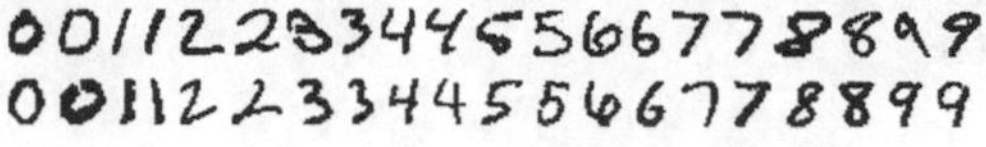

Fig. 2. Samples of native patterns (handwritten digits) from the MNIST database.

Fig. 3. Samples of foreign patterns – digits distorted with salt and pepper noise. From top to bottom: samples with few black pixels removed, samples with few black pixels removed and few black pixels added, samples with black pixels added.

5.3 Quality Evaluation

The case of pattern recognition with rejection requires dedicated quality measures. The following – very straightforward – notions are used:

- CC (Correctly Classified) – the number of correctly classified patterns, i.e. native patterns classified as native with correct class label,
- TP (True Positives) – the number of native patterns classified as native (no matter, into which native class),
- FN (False Negatives) – the number of native patterns incorrectly recognized as foreign,
- FP (False Positives) – the number of foreign patterns incorrectly recognized as native,
- TN (True Negatives) – the number of foreign patterns correctly recognized as foreign.

Quantities TP, FN, FP, and TN are widely used in different literature in the context of binary pattern recognition. This set of quantities is supplemented

Table 1. Quality measures for classification with rejection.

$$\text{Native Precision} = \frac{TP}{TP+FP} \qquad\qquad \text{Accuracy} = \frac{TP+TN}{TP+FN+FP+TN}$$

$$\text{Foreign Precision} = \frac{TN}{TN+FN} \qquad\qquad \text{Strict Accuracy} = \frac{CC+TN}{TP+FN+FP+TN}$$

$$\text{Native Sensitivity} = \frac{TP}{TP+FN} \qquad\qquad \text{Fine Accuracy} = \frac{CC}{TP}$$

$$\text{Foreign Sensitivity} = \frac{TN}{TN+FP} \qquad \text{Strict Native Sensitivity} = \frac{CC}{TP+FN}$$

$$\text{F–measure} = 2 \cdot \frac{\text{Precision} \cdot \text{Sensitivity}}{\text{Precision} + \text{Sensitivity}}$$

with another quantity: *Correctly Classified*, which allows a more versatile quality evaluation.

Based on the notions above: CC, TP, FN, FP and TN, we construct different measures, shown in Table 1.

5.4 Results

This subsection presents results of classification procedures performed on the different test sets mentioned above. Such results allow us comparing outcomes when the classification model is built, based on pattern (image) sets. We apply measures discussed in Sect. 5.3. Let us recall factors taken into account:

- Number of classes (Fixed: 10)
- Number of images in a test set (Fixed: 300 per class)
- Number of images in a training set (Fixed: 200 per class)
- Number of images in a validation set (Fixed: 200 per class).

Figure 4 illustrates quality measures computed from the classification with rejection procedures that were run against native handwritten digit datasets and foreign datasets of distorted digits.

In first place, let us look into the quality of native pattern acceptance. This could be evaluated by the Native Sensitivity, Native Precision, and Native F-measure. Native Sensitivity measures how many native patterns were accepted, and no knowledge about foreign pattern rejection is needed to compute it. Therefore, in Fig. 4, bars for this measure stay exactly the same for all the three foreign sets we have tested. The proposed method accepts native patterns extremely well: Native Sensitivity is on the level of 99.53%. Native Precision expresses a balance between accepted native patterns and all accepted patterns. The poorest Native Precision was achieved on the foreign set of distorted digits with few black pixels randomly removed. In this case, the Native Precision is equal 83.74%. The other two sets were rejected with much higher success rate. Native Precision for distorted images with randomly added black pixels and with randomly added and removed black pixels was equal to 99.27% and 98.06% respectively. The Native F-measure expresses a proportion between Native Sensitivity and Native Precision, and it joins those to measures together into a single factor. Therefore, it is very high for the set with black pixels added and with black pixels removed and for the set with black pixels added. It is lower for the set with black pixels removed, which is a consequence of a lower Native Sensitivity achieved for this dataset.

Strict Native Sensitivity measures the classification rate achieved by the classification/rejection model. It stays the same for all the foreign sets, as it only measures classification quality. The proposed mechanism works very well – it does not reject native patterns, and furthermore, it assigns correct class labels. The Strict Native Sensitivity is equal to 97.80%.

The Fine Accuracy parameter measures how – by adding a rejection mechanism – we can improve classification rates. Such rejection mechanism could be

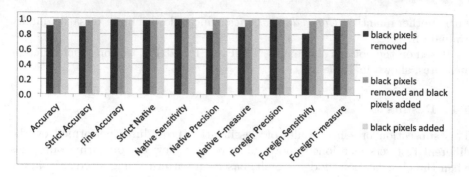

Fig. 4. Quality measures for classification with rejection for the native dataset of handwritten digits and foreign datasets of distorted handwritten digits.

useful when rejecting native patterns that would otherwise be misclassified if such rejection procedure didn't exist. The Fine Accuracy in our experiment was indeed higher than the Strict Native Sensitivity, which confirms that the rejection model rejects "difficult" native patterns that are hard to classify correctly.

Accuracy and Strict Accuracy express a balance between native pattern acceptance and foreign pattern rejection. In the case of the foreign dataset of digits that were distorted by removing few black pixels, for which the rejection was less successful, those two measures are relatively low: oscillating around 90%, whereas for the other two foreign datasets they are much higher (around 98%–99%).

Foreign Precision, Foreign Sensitivity, and Foreign F–measure evaluate the rejection quality achieved for tested foreign datasets. The Foreign Sensitivity and Foreign F–measures revealed clearly that the proposed mechanism works better if new, unexpected black pixels are disturbing recognized images. Let us recall that the studied distortions come from three variants of salt and pepper noise. Removing black pixels turned out to be more confusing for the automata. The Foreign F–measure was equal to 90.95% for the set with removed black pixels, 98.03% for the set with white pixels added and black pixels removed, and 99.40% for the foreign set with black pixels added.

6   Conclusion

In the paper we presented a novel approach to pattern recognition: classification of native patterns with foreign pattern rejection based on cellular automata. The proposed method was experimentally evaluated in a case study of handwritten digit recognition. As foreign patterns we used three datasets of distorted digits that were modified by adding different salt and pepper noise effects. Experimental results showed that the method, despite of its relative simplicity, has a very high success rate at native pattern classification and foreign pattern rejection.

If we compare our previous studies on feature-vector-based geometrical approaches to foreign pattern rejection reported in [1], we can say that the automata-based method introduced in this paper outperforms the geometrical model as it provides a better balance between native pattern acceptance and foreign pattern rejection. However, in order to popularize the proposed approach we need to extend the scope of experiments onto more challenging datasets, for instance for printed musical notation as reported in [5] to investigate how the proposed method works for imbalanced data.

In the future, we plan to take a full benefit of the cellular automaton formalism. The implemented and tested processing is so far very simple, because it is based on single automata transitions, making the implemented model more like a collection of filters than cellular automata itself. We believe that there is more to be achieved with the fully-developed cellular automata-based model, and that motivates us to continue further development of our project. Relative simplicity of the current implementation will become much more complicated in the process, but the model will get far more interesting from the theoretical point of view. An alternative path is to apply a different kind of automata instead, like for instance bipolar automata, in which processing is based on operations defined in [6].

Acknowledgements. The research is supported by the National Science Center, grant no. 2012/07/B/ST6/01501, decision no. DEC-2012/07/B/ST6/01501.

References

1. Ciecierski, J., Dybisz, B., Jastrzebska, A., Pedrycz, W.: A geometrical approach to rejecting option in pattern recognition problem. In: Saeed, K., Homenda, W. (eds.) CISIM 2015. LNCS, vol. 9339, pp. 231–243. Springer, Cham (2015). doi:10. 1007/978-3-319-24369-6_19
2. Desir, C., Bernard, S., Petitjean, C., Laurent, H.: One class random forests. Pattern Recogn. **46**, 3490–3506 (2013)
3. Gonzalez, R.C., Woods, R.E.: Digital Image Processing. Prentice Hall, Upper Saddle River (2008)
4. Hempstalk, K., Frank, E., Witten, I.H.: One-class classification by combining density and class probability estimation. In: Daelemans, W., Goethals, B., Morik, K. (eds.) ECML PKDD 2008. LNCS, vol. 5211, pp. 505–519. Springer, Heidelberg (2008). doi:10.1007/978-3-540-87479-9_51
5. Homenda, W., Optical music recognition: the case study of pattern recognition. In: Kurzyński, M., Puchała, E., Woźniak, M., Żołnierek, A. (eds) Computer Recognition Systems. Advances in Soft Computing, vol 30, pp. 835–842. Springer, Heidelberg (2005)
6. Homenda, W., Pedrycz, W.: Processing uncertain information in the linear space of fuzzy sets. Fuzzy Sets Syst. **44**(2), 187–198 (1991)
7. LeCun, Y., Cortes, C., Burges, C.: The MNIST database of handwritten digits. http://yann.lecun.com/exdb/mnist
8. Maji, P., Ganguly, N., Saha, S., Roy, A.K., Chaudhuri, P.P.: Cellular automata machine for pattern recognition. In: Bandini, S., Chopard, B., Tomassini, M. (eds.) ACRI 2002. LNCS, vol. 2493, pp. 270–281. Springer, Heidelberg (2002). doi:10. 1007/3-540-45830-1_26

9. Von Neumann, J.: Theory of Self-Reproducing Automata. University of Illinois Press, Champaign (1966)
10. Raghavan, R.: Cellular automata in pattern recognition. Inf. Sci. **70**(1–2), 145–177 (1993)
11. Shin, K., Abraham, A., Han, S.Y.: Enhanced centroid-based classification technique by filtering outliers. In: Sojka, P., Kopeček, I., Pala, K. (eds.) TSD 2006. LNCS, vol. 4188, pp. 159–163. Springer, Heidelberg (2006). doi:10.1007/11846406_20
12. Takci, H., Gungor, T.: A high performance centroid-based classification approach for language identification. Pattern Recogn. Lett. **33**, 2077–2084 (2012)
13. Vapnik, V.: The Nature of Statistical Learning Theory. Springer, New York (1995)
14. Wongthanavasu, S., Ponkaew, J.: Cellular automata for pattern recognition. In: Salcido, A. (ed.) Emerging Applications of Cellular Automata. InTech (2013)
15. Ypma, A., Duin, R.: Support objects for domain approximation In: Proceedings of ICANN 1998 (1998)

Distributed NVRAM Cache – Optimization and Evaluation with Power of Adjacency Matrix

Artur Malinowski and Paweł Czarnul$^{(\boxtimes)}$

Department of Computer Architecture, Faculty of Electronics,
Telecommunications and Informatics,
Gdańsk University of Technology, Gdansk, Poland
artur.malinowski@pg.gda.pl, pczarnul@eti.pg.gda.pl

Abstract. In this paper we build on our previously proposed MPI I/O NVRAM distributed cache for high performance computing. In each cluster node it incorporates NVRAMs which are used as an intermediate cache layer between an application and a file for fast read/write operations supported through wrappers of MPI I/O functions. In this paper we propose optimizations of the solution including handling of write requests with a synchronous mode, additional modes preventing data preloading from a file and synchronization on file close if the solution is used as temporary cache only. Furthermore, we have evaluated the solution for a real application that computes powers of an adjacency matrix of a graph in parallel. We demonstrated superiority of our solution compared to a regular MPI I/O implementation for various powers and numbers of graph nodes. Finally, we presented good scalability of the solution for more than 600 processes running on a large HPC cluster.

Keywords: NVRAM · Distributed cache · Graph processing · Performance optimization

1 Introduction

High performance computing (HPC) was always related to aiming at better and better hardware. At the beginning, it mainly involved building larger clusters with better CPUs. A breakthrough emerged with manycore processors, such as graphics processing unit (GPU) used for general purpose processing (e.g. NVIDIA CUDA, OpenCL), coprocessors designed especially for computations (e.g. Intel® Xeon Phi™, Epiphany architecture) or even specially designed CPUs (e.g. Sunway processors used in Sunway TaihuLight, the most powerful supercomputer in TOP500 list, June 2016 edition).

Apart from a processing unit, another essential component of computer architecture is memory. With memory the situation is much different. Typical improvement of RAM is based on a higher capacity and better parameters (e.g. higher frequency, lower latency) of next generation Double Data Rate

© IFIP International Federation for Information Processing 2017
Published by Springer International Publishing AG 2017. All Rights Reserved
K. Saeed et al. (Eds.): CISIM 2017, LNCS 10244, pp. 15–26, 2017.
DOI: 10.1007/978-3-319-59105-6_2

(DDR) RAM devices, while modern storage is always connected with superior SSDs. So far, no hardware device that would extend memory properties has acquired significant popularity.

Universal memory, that is only hypothetical for now, is one of possible candidates for breakthrough in memory technologies. Combining advantages of RAM (byte-level access, high speed and bandwidth, low latency) with advantages of SSD (large capacity and persistence) should definitely increase performance of many computer systems. Although not available on the market yet, many technologies are being researched to create a practical device and several of these seem to be promising [20]. Moreover, recent press reports suggest, that we can expect devices with parameters between NAND based memory (used in SSD) and DRAM soon [9,10]. In order to describe such memory in this paper, we would use the NVRAM term (non-volatile, random access memory) keeping in mind, that this memory is expected to have a byte-level access.

Full replacement of main memory and storage by a single, universal memory would probably trigger the need for redesigning the architecture of computing systems at multiple levels, but such a huge change cannot be expected to be introduced at once. Instead of this, we assume that first NVRAM devices would be used as complementary memory together with RAM and storage. For that reason, we decided to focus on possibilities coming from incorporating supplementary NVRAM devices into HPC platforms.

In 2016 we proposed the idea of NVRAM distributed cache located as an additional layer between a file system and a parallel distributed application [16]. The extension was transparent to the developer, because of its compatibility with the well-known Message Passing Interface (MPI) I/O API [18]. The motivation for this solution was improving performance and making the development process easier. Initial testing with a set of benchmarks gave promising results. Within this paper, we present further research on our MPI I/O NVRAM distributed cache. The research includes performance optimizations, as well as evaluation of the solution with a real life application – computing power of graph adjacency matrix. In fact, the application could be used e.g. for social network analysis or calculating shortest path lengths between multiple nodes simultaneously.

2   Related Work

In 2009, Kryder and Kim presented a set of thirteen emerging non-volatile memory technologies, that had a potential to replace NAND Flash by 2020 [14]. A report, published by Wong and Salahuddin in 2015, agrees on the candidates to the universal memory technology, but did not try to predict when real devices would appear on the market [20]. Scientist, that conduct research on magnetoresistive RAM (MRAM) [1,4], spin-transfer-torque MRAM (STT-MRAM) [15,19], or phase change memory (PCM) [2,23], suggest, that we can expect it soon.

3D XPoint^{TM} technology, announced by Intel® and Micron® in 2015 [9,10], is probably the closest to be used in production environment – first 3D XPoint^{TM} Intel® Optane^{TM} devices are expected in 2016 [11]. Comparison between NVMe

NAND SSD (nowadays the fastest SSDs) and a prototype of 3D XPoint^{TM} technology powered device gave promising results – the time to access a 4kB block from an application was reduced almost 7 times [6]. Unfortunately, at the moment of writing this paper, we do not have any more Intel® Optane^{TM} performance results.

Emerging memory technologies triggered research on architectures, algorithms, and applications that would benefit from properties of the new hardware. NVMcached, key-value cache for byte-addressable NVRAM, is an example – designing the system taking into consideration the new memory type allowed to improve performance up to 2.85 times [21]. Another exemplary research on this topic could be a log-structured file system NOVA [22], or our idea for checkpointing in NVRAM using the MPI One-sided API [5].

There are also solutions based on NVRAM related with speeding up I/O operations in HPC. Two papers concern Active NVRAM – a device that, apart from memory component, includes low power CPU [12,13]. Although the proposed architecture has potential benefits, computing units are not expected in first production devices. Another set of solutions use SSD devices. Systems like S4D-Cache [7] or SLA-Cache [8] significantly improve parameters of PFS, however, we believe that differences between typical SSD and byte-addressable NVRAM require more dedicated solutions.

3 Proposed Solution

3.1 NVRAM Distributed Cache Architecture

This section is a short summary of our previous research on NVRAM distributed cache. In a typical MPI application, MPI I/O is used in order to communicate with parallel file system (PFS). Figure 1 shows a difference between the classical approach and our solution. Instead of calling an MPI I/O implementation directly, an application uses NVRAM cache routines. This process is transparent to the programmer as the cache API is the same as MPI I/O API. NVRAM cache communicates with PFS through MPI I/O, which gives an instant support for many file systems.

We assume that each node is equipped with its own NVRAM device and it participates in a distributed cache. On each node a single thread, called a cache manager, is spawned – it is responsible for creation and management of its part of the cache. When a file is opened, it is split into equally sized parts, one for each cache manager. Then, the cache manager is responsible for prefetching its whole part of file (in the file opening phase), serving read, write and sync requests from the application, flushing all of the data into PFS (in the file closing phase). The main advantages of the extension, in comparison to typical solutions, are:

- low latency, caused by serving requests as fast as possible by omitting complicated data rearrangement algorithms,
- fully decentralized management with no communication between cache managers – cache parts are assigned at the beginning, so each application process knows exactly where data is,

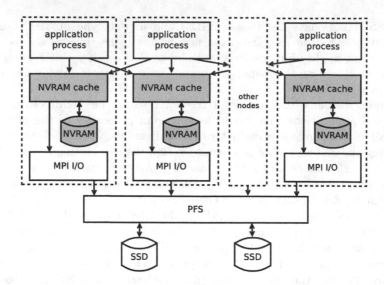

Fig. 1. Exemplary architecture of the solution for cluster nodes, components within a single node are inside dashed bracket. NVRAM cache layer marked with gray illustrates the difference between classical architecture and the one extended with NVRAM cache. Number of nodes in the solution is not limited.

– minimal meta-data – no cache blocks, no *fetched* flags (all data prefetched), no *dirty* flags (all data treated as dirty).

It is clear, that a significant overhead is introduced with prefetching the whole file and flushing it back in the end. Moreover, the solution is aimed at applications that access small chunks of data (gain from byte addressing of NVRAM) from spread file locations (no drawback from omitting staging algorithms). As it was shown in previous papers [16,17], for long running and data intensive HPC applications that operate on small data parts, our solution performs better than unmodified MPI I/O. In this paper, we want to evaluate it with an application that does not meet those criteria strictly.

Another important issue is connected with persistence of NVRAM. We have shown, that our solution could be used to prevent data from being damaged – a consistent state of the file could be recreated from the cache [17]. Although it allows to recover only from several failure types, its low overhead and ease of programming could be a solution complementary or even in some cases competitive to checkpointing.

3.2 Extension Optimizations

The most significant performance optimization applies to serving write requests. In the first version of the extension, a cache manager responded to the process in an asynchronous way, before the exact data was written into a device. Data consistency was provided by sequential processing of the cache manager thread.

Although such a strategy reduced the latency slightly when the number of requests was kept at a low level, it caused performance drop with more data-intensive applications. In most popular MPI implementations write requests started queuing in a cache manager, that caused unpredictable and huge growth of latency for successive requests. The solution based on changing communication into a synchronous version and sending a response after all the processing was done, fixed the performance drop.

Another optimization is connected with omitting unnecessary overhead in opening and closing a file. Introduced improvements rely on better support for three MPI_File_open access modes:

- MPI_MODE_CREATE: if the file does not exist, prevent from prefetching data,
- MPI_MODE_RDONLY: prevent from synchronization at file closing,
- MPI_DELETE_ON_CLOSE: prevent from synchronization at file closing.

In special cases like treating the file as a huge distributed shared memory, most of the cache overhead related to file opening and closing is avoided.

3.3   Graph Processing Application

The graph theory has many real world applications like obtaining social network properties (e.g. Facebook, Twitter), processing maps and locations (e.g. Google Maps, GPS based navigation systems), optimizing layout of connections (e.g. designing cellular network layout) or preparing some recommendations (e.g. Netflix, Google PageRank). A great deal of algorithms hidden behind those applications are computational demanding and without further optimization they will not be able to handle increasing volume of data. In this paper we propose how to extend a selected algorithm with our MPI I/O NVRAM distribute cache. As an exemplary algorithm we have chosen the transformation, that could provide multiple graph properties, among others:

- number of paths of length n that connect two vertices,
- shortest path lengths,
- number of triangles in the graph.

Many different data structures could be used for representation of graphs. The selected problem requires checking often whether two vertices are adjacent, so a representation that minimizes complexity of this operation would be beneficial. Complexity of such query in adjacency matrix is $O(1)$. Disadvantages of an adjacency matrix are irrelevant in the context of the selected algorithm. Slow adding or removing vertices is negligible because of constant size of a graph. Large memory consumption is unimportant since NVRAM distributed cache provides storage of size limited to the sum of all NVRAM capacities in a cluster. In our implementation, an adjacency matrix graph representation is used.

With an adjacency matrix, in order to search for walks of particular length between vertices, matrix multiplication could be used. Assuming A is the adjacency matrix, in the matrix A^n each element $a_{n(i,j)}$ represents the number of walks of length n connecting vertex i with vertex j. The idea is illustrated with the exemplary A, A^2 and A^3:

$$A = \begin{bmatrix} 0 & 1 & 1 & 0 \\ 0 & 0 & 1 & 0 \\ 0 & 0 & 0 & 1 \\ 1 & 1 & 0 & 0 \end{bmatrix}, \ A^2 = A \cdot A = \begin{bmatrix} 0 & 0 & 1 & 1 \\ 0 & 0 & 0 & 1 \\ 1 & 1 & 0 & 0 \\ 0 & 1 & 2 & 0 \end{bmatrix}, \ A^3 = A \cdot A \cdot A = \begin{bmatrix} 1 & 1 & 0 & 1 \\ 1 & 1 & 0 & 0 \\ 0 & 1 & 2 & 0 \\ 0 & 0 & 1 & 2 \end{bmatrix}.$$

From the above matrices one can read for instance:

- there are 2 paths of length 2 that connect vertex 4 with vertex 3 ($a_{2(4,3)} = 2$),
- the shortest path from vertex 3 to vertex 1 is 2 (smallest n where $a_{n(3,1)} > 0$ is 2),
- the number of triangles in the graph is 2 ($\frac{1}{3} \sum_{i=1}^{v} a_{3(i,i)} = 2$).

To calculate power of a matrix efficiently, in this application, communication-avoiding Cannon's algorithm is used [3].

4   Experiments

The MPI I/O NVRAM extension is designed for applications of specific properties. To benefit most from the extension, a data-intensive application should access small data chunks from spread locations and run long enough to compensate for the overhead for initialization and deinitialization. Implementation of an algorithm for graph adjacency matrix is an attempt of validating the extension with an application that does not strictly possess these properties. The application accesses larger data chunks at once from neighboring locations, what is especially convenient for parallel file systems we want to compete with. Within this section we want to prove, that proposed MPI I/O NVRAM distributed cache is beneficial for a wide range of applications by showing a case study of an application that does not meet our cache requirements.

4.1   Testbed Environment

The extension was tested on two clusters: Lap06 and K2 described in detail in Tables 1 and 2. Each node in Lap06 is equipped with an NVRAM hardware simulation platform, set to pessimistic values. Lower times would result in even better results for the NVRAM version. In contrast, K2 simulates NVRAM using tmpfs but its size allows to measure scalability.

4.2   Performance Tests

Calculating power of a matrix can have different real-world applications, including graph processing. For some of them, storing a final matrix is crucial (e.g. searching for the number of walks of a particular length), but other use it only as intermediate values (e.g. searching for the number of triangles). From the

Table 1. Lap06 and K2 clusters – hardware and software configuration

	Lap06	K2
Number of computing nodes	6	96
Number of PFS nodes	2	3
CPU	2 × Intel® Xeon® E5-4620, 2.20 GHz (2.60 GHz turbo)	2 × Intel® Xeon® E5345, 2.33 GHz
RAM	15 GB	8 GB
Network	40 Gb/s Infiniband	10 Gb/s Ethernet
Storage	SSD	HDD
NVRAM simulation	17 GB, hardware simulation	4 GB, tmpfs
MPI implementation	MPICH 3.2	
PFS	Orange-FS 2.8.7	

Table 2. NVRAM simulation platform parameters in Lap06 cluster

Additional latency to access the data	2000 ns
Time required to flush data on device	600 ns
Memory bandwidth	9.5 GB/s

perspective of MPI I/O, if the application does not need the final matrix stored on disk, MPI_MODE_DELETE_ON_CLOSE could be used in order to trigger additional optimizations. For that reason, most test cases are split into groups according to *delete on close* mode (on and off).

As the execution time does not depend on graph properties other than its size, for each test case we generated n nodes and connected each two nodes with the probability of 2%. All scenarios apply to low graph powers, so each value of the adjacency matrix is stored in a 1 byte cell, that results in the size of the final file equal to n^2 bytes.

Performance Optimizations. As stated in Sect. 3, handling of write requests with a synchronous mode was the most noticeable improvement over the previously proposed extension. Comparison of synchronous and asynchronous mode for graph processing application is presented in Fig. 2. Results show 30% reduction of application's execution time for small computed graph powers. Moreover, while increasing the power of a graph, the performance gain is greater.

Results with *Delete on Close* Mode Off. According to Fig. 3, execution time of the application grows linearly with the power. The greater the power of a matrix, the greater execution time and greater performance gain from the

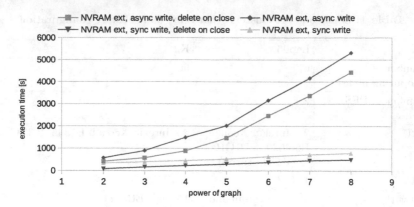

Fig. 2. Power of adjacency matrix, comparison between synchronous and asynchronous write. Values for fixed graph size (10 000 nodes) and different powers. Lap06 cluster.

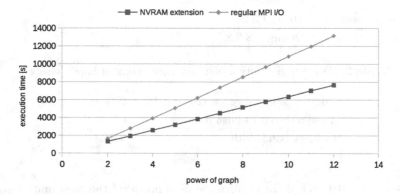

Fig. 3. Power of adjacency matrix, comparison between unmodified MPI I/O and proposed extension. Values for fixed graph size (20 000 nodes) and different powers. Lap06 cluster. *Delete on close* mode off.

NVRAM distributed cache. For example, with power of 2 the proposed extension is less than 20% faster than unmodified MPI I/O, while for larger powers it is more than 40% faster. Increasing performance gain is caused by overhead for initialization and deinitialization that is independent from the power.

Figures 4, and 5 present an exponential growth of execution time for different sizes of input graphs. Plots prepared for power of 2 show that for small powers with *delete on close* mode off the proposed extension is beneficial only for small input data. The chart with results of power of 8 is an example that for higher powers the NVRAM distributed cache is superior for each input size.

Results with *Delete on Close* Mode On. The *delete on close* mode allows to omit the phase of synchronization between the NVRAM distributed cache and the parallel file system. For that reason, execution time of an application is reduced, what is especially important for smaller powers. Figure 6 shows that

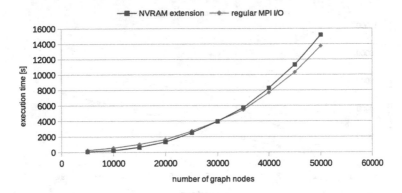

Fig. 4. Power of adjacency matrix, comparison between unmodified MPI I/O and proposed extension. Values for fixed power (2) and different graph sizes. Lap06 cluster. *Delete on close* mode off.

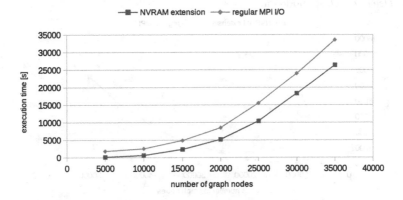

Fig. 5. Power of adjacency matrix, comparison between unmodified MPI I/O and proposed extension. Values for fixed power (8) and different graph sizes. Lap06 cluster. *Delete on close* mode off.

the proposed solution performs significantly better than the regular MPI I/O for powers starting with 2, while Fig. 7 proves, that the extension gives performance gain both for small and large size of input.

Scalability. Figure 8 illustrates a respectable scalability of the algorithm, as well as the proposed NVRAM cache. With an increasing size of a cluster environment, average load of a single node related to I/O operations is constant, because a higher number of I/O requests from computing nodes is handled by a higher number of cache managers. A typical PFS environment usually is not so flexible and in case of an unexpected heavy load requires hardware reconfiguration.

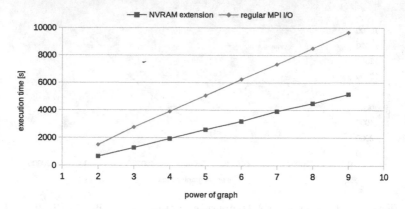

Fig. 6. Power of adjacency matrix, comparison between unmodified MPI I/O and proposed extension. Values for fixed graph size (20 000 nodes) and different powers. Lap06 cluster. *Delete on close* mode on.

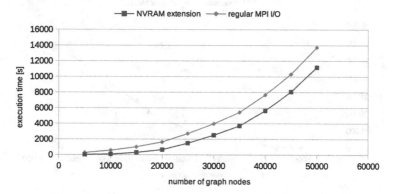

Fig. 7. Power of adjacency matrix, comparison between unmodified MPI I/O and proposed extension. Values for fixed power (2) and different graph sizes. Lap06 cluster. *Delete on close* mode on.

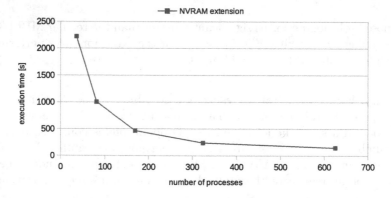

Fig. 8. Power of adjacency matrix, scalability. Values for fixed power (2) and fixed graph size (20 000 nodes). K2 cluster. *Delete on close* mode off.

5   Summary and Future Work

Motivation of this research was related to expected incorporation of emerging memory technologies in production devices soon, which was justified in the introduction and related work. Within this paper we described an optimized version of MPI I/O distributed cache supported by byte-addressable NVRAM. Then we focused on its evaluation with an application that computes powers of adjacency matrix using Cannon's algorithm. Presented results of experiments prove, that with the tested application our solution performed better than regular MPI I/O.

Our future plans include further optimization of the extension and its evaluation with a wider range of applications. Moreover, we also want to focus on the mechanism, that would allow to predict the benefit from our extension without actual running of an application.

Acknowledgments. The research in the paper was supported by a Grant from Intel Technology Poland.

References

1. Åkerman, J.: Toward a universal memory. Science **308**(5721), 508–510 (2005). http://science.sciencemag.org/content/308/5721/508
2. Alpert, A., Luo, R., Asheghi, M., Pop, E., Goodson, K.: Analytical model of graphene-enabled ultra-low power phase change memory. In: 2016 15th IEEE Intersociety Conference on Thermal and Thermomechanical Phenomena in Electronic Systems (ITherm), pp. 670–674, May 2016
3. Cannon, L.E.: A cellular computer to implement the Kalman Filter algorithm. Ph.D. Thesis. Montana State University (1969)
4. Dong, X., Wu, X., Sun, G., Xie, Y., Li, H., Chen, Y.: Circuit and microarchitecture evaluation of 3D stacking magnetic RAM (MRAM) as a universal memory replacement. In: 45th ACM/IEEE on Design Automation Conference, 2008 (2008)
5. Dorożynski, P., Czarnul, P., Malinowski, A., Czuryło, K., Dorau, Ł., Maciejewski, M., Skowron, P.: Checkpointing of parallel MPI applications using MPI one-sided API with support for byte-addressable non-volatile RAM. Procedia Comput. Sci. **80**, 30–40 (2016). International Conference on Computational Science 2016, ICCS 2016
6. Foong, A., Hady, F.: Storage as fast as rest of the system. In: 2016 IEEE 8th International Memory Workshop (IMW), pp. 1–4, May 2016
7. He, S., Sun, X.H., Feng, B.: S4D-cache: smart selective SSD cache for parallel I/O systems. In: 2014 IEEE 34th International Conference on Distributed Computing Systems (ICDCS), pp. 514–523, June 2014
8. He, S., Wang, Y., Sun, X.H.: Improving performance of parallel I/O systems through selective and layout-aware SSD cache. IEEE Trans. Parallel Distrib. Syst. **27**(10), 2940–2952 (2016)
9. Intel Corporation: Intel and Micron Produce Breakthrough Memory Technology. http://newsroom.intel.com/community/intel_newsroom/blog/2015/07/28/intel-and-micron-produce-breakthrough-memory-technology
10. Intel Corporation: Introducing Breakthrough Memory Technology. http://www.intel.com/content/www/us/en/architecture-and-technology/non-volatile-memory.html

11. Intel Corporation: Introducing Intel Optane Technology Bringing 3D XPoint Memory to Storage and Memory Products, https://newsroom.intel.com/press-kits/introducing-intel-optane-technology-bringing-3d-xpoint-memory-to-storage-and-memory-products/

12. Kannan, S., Milojicic, D., Talwar, V., Gavrilovska, A., Schwan, K., Abbasi, H.: Using active NVRAM for cloud I/O. In: 2011 Sixth Open Cirrus Summit (OCS), pp. 32–36, October 2011

13. Kannan, S., Gavrilovska, A., Schwan, K., Milojicic, D., Talwar, V.: Using active NVRAM for I/O staging. In: Proceedings of the 2nd International Workshop on Petascal Data Analytics: Challenges and Opportunities, PDAC 2011, pp. 15–22. ACM, USA (2011). http://doi.acm.org/10.1145/2110205.2110209

14. Kryder, M., Kim, C.S.: After hard drives - what comes next? IEEE Trans. Magn. **45**(10), 3406–3413 (2009). http://dx.doi.org/10.1109/TMAG.2009.2024163

15. Makarov, A., Sverdlov, V., Selberherr, S.: Magnetic tunnel junctions with a composite free layer: a new concept for future universal memory, pp. 93–101. Wiley Inc. (2013). http://dx.doi.org/10.1002/9781118678107.ch6

16. Malinowski, A., Czarnul, P., Dorożynski, P., Czuryło, K., Dorau, Ł., Maciejewski, M., Skowron, P.: A parallel MPI I/O solution supported by byte-addressable non-volatile RAM distributed cache. In: Position Papers of the 2016 Federated Conference on Computer Science and Information Systems, Annals of Computer Science and Information Systems, vol. 9, pp. 133–140. PTI (2016). http://dx.doi.org/10.15439/2016F52

17. Malinowski, A., Czarnul, P., Maciejewski, M., Skowron, P.: A fail-safe NVRAM based mechanism for efficient creation and recovery of data copies in parallel MPI applications. In: Grzech, A., Świątek, J., Wilimowska, Z., Borzemski, L. (eds.) Information Systems Architecture and Technology: Proceedings of 37th International Conference on Information Systems Architecture and Technology – ISAT 2016 – Part II. AISC, vol. 522, pp. 137–147. Springer, Cham (2017). doi:10.1007/978-3-319-46586-9_11

18. Message Passing Interface Forum: MPI: A message-passing interface standard version 3.1 (2015). http://www.mpi-forum.org/docs/mpi-3.1/mpi31-report.pdf

19. Wolf, S.A., Lu, J., Stan, M.R., Chen, E., Treger, D.M.: The promise of nanomagnetics and spintronics for future logic and universal memory. Proc. IEEE **98**(12), 2155–2168 (2010)

20. Wong, H.S.P., Salahuddin, S.: Memory leads the way to better computing. Nat. Nanotechnol. **10**, 191–194 (2015)

21. Wu, X., Ni, F., Zhang, L., Wang, Y., Ren, Y., Hack, M., Shao, Z., Jiang, S.: NVMcached: an NVM-based Key-Value Cache. In: Proceedings of the 7th ACM SIGOPS Asia-Pacific Workshop on Systems, APSys 2016, pp. 18:1–18:7. ACM, USA (2016). http://doi.acm.org/10.1145/2967360.2967374

22. Xu, J., Swanson, S.: NOVA: a log-structured file system for hybrid volatile/non-volatile main memories. In: 14th USENIX Conference on File and Storage Technologies (FAST 2016), pp. 323–338. USENIX Association, Santa Clara, February 2016

23. Zilberberg, O., Weiss, S., Toledo, S.: Phase-change memory: an architectural perspective. ACM Comput. Surv. **45**(3), 29:1–29:33 (2013). http://doi.acm.org/10.1145/2480741.2480746

Optimal Controlled Random Tests

Ireneusz Mrozek[✉] and Vyacheslav Yarmolik

Faculty of Computer Science, Bialystok University of Technology,
Wiejska 45A, 15-351 Bialystok, Poland
i.mrozek@pb.edu.pl, yarmolik10ru@yahoo.com
http://www.wi.pb.edu.pl

Abstract. Controlled random tests, methods of their generation, main criteria used for their synthesis, such as the Hamming distance and the Euclidean distance, as well as their application to the testing of both hardware and software systems are discussed. Available evidences suggest that high computational complexity is one of the main drawbacks of these methods. Therefore we propose a technique to overcome this problem. In the paper we propose the algorithm for optimal controlled random tests generation. Both experimental and analytical investigation clearly show the high efficiency of proposed solution especially for the multi-run tests with small number of iterations. The given tests can be applied for hardware and software testing but it seems they may be particularly interesting from the perspective of the effective detection of pattern sensitive faults in RAMs.

Keywords: Random tests · Controlled tests · Multi-run tests · Hemming distance · Euclidean distance · Pattern sensitive faults · RAM

1 Introduction

It is known that the testing problem is computationally most expensive and mathematically NP-complete [1,2]. The same time the complexity of the modern embedded systems is steadily growing. It is, therefore, important to consider how testing can be performed more effectively.

In case of single hard to detect faults that may have just a handful of unique tests in the entire search space there have been proposed probability based algorithms where new test vectors are generated based on the input probability correlation of previously unsuccessful test vectors [3].

In case of systems with limited number of inputs we can use exhaustive testing. However the exponential growth of the test length restricts the concept of the exhaustive testing to circuits with a limited number of inputs [4].

This paper was supported by grant S/WI/3/13 from Faculty of Computer Science at Bialystok University of Technology, Ministry of Science and Higer Education, Poland.

K. Saeed et al. (Eds.): CISIM 2017, LNCS 10244, pp. 27–38, 2017.
DOI: 10.1007/978-3-319-59105-6_3

Locally exhaustive [5] or pseudo exhaustive [6–8] testing is a concept to avoid the restricted number of inputs of the circuit under test. These approaches are the real alternatives to exhaustive testing. They allow for sufficiently reducing the number of the test vectors. It is possible by taking advantage of the fact that often many or all output variables depend only on a small subset of input variables [5].

As a good approximation of exhaustive and pseudo exhaustive testing the random testing have been widely used [9–12]. The advantages of random testing include its low cost, ease of implementation, ability to generate numerous test cases automatically, generation of test cases in the absence of the object specification and apart from these; it brings randomness into the testing process. Random testing and its variations have been extensively used and studied for both hardware and software systems. Unfortunately random testing is much less effective than other testing techniques such as equivalence partition testing, boundary value analysis testing [13].

Standard random testing does not exploit some information that is available in black box testing environment. Therefore controlled approach to random testing (Controlled Random Tests) may be used. One of the approaches for controlled random testing is Antirandom Testing [14]. Antirandom Testing is based on various empirical observations showing that many faults result in failures in contiguous areas of the input domain [15]. Therefore one way to improve the failure-detection effectiveness of random testing is somehow taking advantage of this fact. In this case each test vector is chosen such that its total distance from all previous vectors is maximum [14,16]. This approach has proved more efficient than random testing [14]. Unfortunately the basic antirandom method essentially requires enumeration of the input space and computation of distances for each potential input vector [14]. Therefore many modification of antirandom tests have been proposed [15–24]. But even for improved version of the method, very often computations become too expensive for real dimension N of the test vectors [25].

In this paper the efficiency of controlled random tests is investigated and validated. Unlike our parallel proposals presented in [26,27] where we focus on multiple controlled random tests consisting of r single controlled random tests, in this paper we investigate a single optimal controlled random test and we present the greedy-like algorithm for its generation. By optimal controlled random test we understand the set of test patterns where each pattern is chosen such that its total distance from all previous patterns is the greatest possible value. So, unlike the known solutions, our approach keeps the distances between the current and previous test patterns as large as possible. All the analytical results are validated through extensive simulation-based experiments.

This paper is divided into four more sections. Section 2 provides a brief overview of the principle concept behind Controlled Random Tests. Section 3 highlights the main idea of our algorithm. We analyze and discuss the experimental results in Sect. 4, and make a conclusion in Sect. 5.

2   Controlled Random Tests Investigations

The key feature of controlled random tests generation is the information, which can be obtained from the test and used for test patterns generation. There are numerous different useful approaches which exploited the information from the test itself [14,25,28]. For all this methods, considering the binary case, the next definitions can be done.

Definition 1. *Test (T) is a set of test patterns $\{T_0, T_1, T_2, \ldots, T_{q-1}\}$, where $T_i = t_{i,N-1}, t_{i,N-2}, \ldots, t_{i,2}, t_{i,1}, t_{i,0}$, with $t_{i,l} \in \{0,1\}$, and N is the size of patterns in bits.*

Definition 2. *Controlled Random Test $T = \{T_0, T_1, T_2, \ldots, T_{q-1}\}$ (CRT) is a test with randomly chosen the test patterns T_i, $i \in \{0, 1, 2, \ldots, q-1\}$, such that T_i satisfies some criterion.*

The first formally define approach for controlled random test generation have been presented in [14] by Y. Malaiya. The proposed approach was called antirandom testing, since selection of each test explicitly depends on the test patterns already generated. The next formal definition for antirandom tests have been used:

Definition 3. *Antirandom test (AT) is a test with a test pattern T_i, $i \in \{0, 1, 2, \ldots, q-1\}$, is chosen such that it satisfies some criterion with respect to all patterns $T_0, T_1, T_2, \ldots, T_{i-1}$ have been obtained before.*

To make each new pattern different compare with previously generated the Hamming and Cartesian distances as the measure of differences have been chosen, which can be defined as [14].

Definition 4. *The Hamming Distance $HD(T_i, T_j)$ (HD) between two binary vectors T_i and T_j is calculated as a weight $w(T_i \oplus T_j)$ (number of ones) of vector $T_i \oplus T_j$.*

$$HD(T_i, T_j) = w(T_i \oplus T_j) = \sum_{l=0}^{N-1} (t_{i,l} \oplus t_{j,l}). \tag{1}$$

Definition 5. *The Cartesian Distance $CD(T_i, T_j)$ (CD) between two binary vectors T_i and T_j is given by:*

$$
\begin{aligned}
\mathrm{CD}(T_i, T_j) &= \sqrt{(t_{i,0} - t_{j,0})^2 + (t_{i,1} - t_{j,1})^2 + \ldots + (t_{i,N-1} - t_{j,N-1})^2} \\
&= \sqrt{|t_{i,0} - t_{j,0}| + |t_{i,1} - t_{j,1}| + \ldots + |t_{i,N-1} - t_{j,N-1}|} \\
&= \sqrt{\mathrm{HD}(T_i, T_j)}.
\end{aligned} \tag{2}
$$

The antirandom testing scheme attempts to keep testing procedure as efficient as possible, taking into account the hypothesis that if two patterns have only a small distance between them then the sets of faults encountered by the two patterns is likely to have a number of faults in common. Conversely, if the distance between two patterns is large, then the set of faults detected by one is likely to contain only a few of the faults detected by the other [14,29]. For the set of more then two test patterns the next definitions have been proposed [14].

Definition 6. Total Hamming Distance *(THD)*, Total Cartesian Distance *(TCD) for any pattern T_i is the sum of its Hamming (Cartesian) distances with respect to all previous patterns $T_0, T_1, T_2, \ldots, T_{i-1}$.*

$$\text{THD}(T_i) = \sum_{j=0}^{i-1} \text{HD}(T_i, T_j), \qquad \text{TCD}(T_i) = \sum_{j=0}^{i-1} \text{CD}(T_i, T_j). \qquad (3)$$

Definition 7. Maximal Distance Antirandom Test *(MDAT) is a test such that each pattern T_i is chosen to make the total distance THD or TCD between T_i and patterns $T_0, T_1, T_2, \ldots, T_{i-1}$ maximal.*

The main properties of MHDAT and MCDAT are the following:

any permutation the patterns bits $t_{i,j}$ within the antirandom test T MHDAT (MCDAT) for all i patterns simultaneously will results in new MHDAT (MCDAT) antirandom test [14,29],

any MHDAT (MCDAT) will always contain complementary pair of patterns, i.e. T_{2k} will always be followed by T_{2k+1} which is complementary for all bits in T_{2k} where $k = 1, 2, \ldots,$ [14,29].

Above presented properties allow reducing the complexity of MHDAT (MCDAT) generation but, for general case, unfortunately the basic antirandom method essentially requires enumeration of the input space and computation of distances for each potential input pattern [14,29]. Even for improved version of the method computations, it becomes too expensive for real dimension N of the test patterns [16].

3   Optimal Controlled Random Test Generation

The key feature of controlled random test generation is the information obtained from the test and used for the current pattern T_i generation.

As shown in the previous section, the controlled random tests are generated based on a restricted number of metrics, including the Hamming distance between two patterns T_i and T_j ($\text{HD}(T_i, T_j)$), the Cartesian distance ($\text{CD}(T_i, T_j)$), the total Hamming distance for the next test pattern T_i ($\text{THD}(T_i)$), the total Cartesian distance ($\text{TCD}(T_i)$), the total Hamming distance for the test

T (THD(T)), and the total Cartesian distance (TCD(T)) [14,28,29]. These metrics are used for proposed greedy-like methods of controlled random test generation [14,16,25,28–30]. In all these algorithms, the best immediate, or local, solution has been taken to reach a globally optimal solution. The optimal choice at each stage based on simple metrics has been performed with the hope of finding the global optimum. The greedy-like algorithm was the only solution for controlled random test generation because it is faster than other optimization methods, like dynamic programming for example.

Based on the presented metrics, an optimal controlled random test (OCRT) will be constructed. Step by step, starting from one test pattern T_0, the consecutive patterns will be selected in terms of adopted earlier metrics according to the greedy-like algorithm.

At the beginning, the first test pattern T_0 is chosen as any arbitrary random N-bit binary vector out of 2^N possible. For example, let $T_0 = 000\ldots0$. This does not result in any loss of generality [14,16,28].

As the second pattern T_1, according to all metrics, an optimal value is the complement of T_0, then $T_1 = \overline{T}_0$, and $T = \{T_0, T_1\}$ for the previously adopted example $T_1 = 111\ldots1$. The optimality of this choice is supported by the maximal values of all metrics: HD(T_0, T_1) = THD(T_1) = THD(T) = N, and CD(T_0, T_1) = TCD(T_1) = TCD(T) = $\sqrt{N}$.

To obtain the third pattern T_2, the HD(T_i, T_j) and CD(T_i, T_j) measures cannot be used because the maximization of this value leads to the confusing result that $T_2 = T_0$. That is why, in our investigation, both characteristics will not be used. The same conclusion can be made for THD(T_i) and THD(T). It follows from the fact that for $T = \{T_0, T_1, T_2\}$, where $T_1 = \overline{T}_0$, any value of T_2 gives THD(T_2) = N and THD(T) = $2N$. It should be noticed that, even in cases $T_2 = T_0$ and $T_2 = T_1$, these metrics have the same values THD(T_2) = N and THD(T) = $2N$.

As the candidate for the third optimal pattern T_2, any pattern that satisfies to the next relations $T_2 \neq T_0$ and $T_2 \neq T_1$ can be chosen. For example, we take T_2 with HD(T_0, T_2) = Z, then HD(T_1, T_2) = $N - Z$. For Cartesian functions, the following results are TCD(T_i) = CD(T_0, T_2) + CD(T_1, T_2)=$\sqrt{Z} + \sqrt{N - Z}$, TCD(T)=CD(T_0, T_1) + CD(T_0, T_2) + CD(T_1, T_2) =$\sqrt{N} + \sqrt{Z} + \sqrt{N - Z}$. Then, maxTCD($T_i$) and maxTCD($T$) can be achieved as the solution $Z = N/2$ of the equation $\delta(\sqrt{Z} + \sqrt{N - Z})/\delta Z = 0$. For further investigation, suppose that N is an even number, so that, in our example, the first $N/2$ bits of pattern $T_2 = 000\ldots01111$ take the value 0, and the rest take value 1.

To summarize the third pattern construction, it is quite important to emphasize that, for our test $T = \{T_0, T_1, T_2\} = \{000\ldots0, 111\ldots1, 000\ldots0111\ldots1\}$, the next patterns (fourth, fifth, and so on) should be selected from the set of patterns with the weight $w(T_i) = N/2$ due to the maximum values of TCD(T_2) = $2\sqrt{N/2}$ and TCD(T) = $\sqrt{N} + 2\sqrt{N/2}$ for three pattern tests T. In this case, for new consecutive pattern T_i, the Hamming distances HD(T_i, T_0) and HD(T_i, T_1) have the values $N/2$, which allow for TCD(T_i) and TCD(T) maximization.

According to the previous discussion, as the potential fourth pattern, T_3 is the pattern with the weight $w(T_3) = N/2$ and should maximize the value of $\text{TCD}(T_3)$ and $\text{TCD}(T)$. The obvious solution exists, namely, $T_3 = \overline{T}_2$ and for our example $T_3 = 111\ldots1000\ldots0$.

The same result can be obtained based on the FAR algorithm [25]. According to this algorithm, using three previous patterns $T_0 = 000\ldots0$, $T_1 = 111\ldots1$ and $T_2 = 000\ldots0111\ldots1$, a centroid pattern will be obtained $C = c_{N-1}, c_{N-2}, \ldots, c_2, c_1, c_0 = 1/3, 1/3, 1/3, \ldots, 1/3, 2/3, 2/3, 2/3, \ldots, 2/3$. Thus, the FAR algorithm creates a binary centroid pattern $000\ldots01111$ [25]. At the final step of the FAR algorithm, a new anti-random pattern $T_3 = 111\ldots10000$ is constructed by complementing each bit of the binary centroid pattern.

For the pattern T_3, the total Cartesian distance is $\text{TCD}(T_3) = \sqrt{N} + 2\sqrt{N/2}$ and $\text{TCD}(T) = 2\sqrt{N} + 4\sqrt{N/2}$ for four pattern tests T.

This procedure can be generalized for the following steps. At all consecutive stages, the next pattern will be chosen to maximize two metrics $\text{TCD}(T_i)$ and $\text{TCD}(T)$. When pattern T_i with an even subscript number $i \in \{0, 2, 4, \ldots, 2k-2\}$ is chosen, the following relation should be true:

$$maxTCD(T_i) = i \times \sqrt{N/2}$$
$$maxTCD(T) = (i/2) \times \sqrt{N} + (i^2/2) \times \sqrt{N/2}. \tag{4}$$

The pattern with the even subscript i is chosen so that $\text{HD}(T_i, T_j) = N/2$ between pattern T_i and all previous patterns $T_j, j < i$. The pattern with an odd subscript $i \in \{1, 3, \ldots, 2k - 1\}$ is the complement value of the previous pattern with an even subscript (i.e., $T_i = \overline{T}_{i-1}$). Then, both metrics are

$$maxTCD(T_i) = \sqrt{N} + (i - 1) \times \sqrt{N/2}$$
$$maxTCD(T) = ((i + 1)/2) \times \sqrt{N} + ((i^2 - 1)/2) \times \sqrt{N/2}. \tag{5}$$

As an example, we take $N = 2^m$, then the number q of patterns within the OCRT $T = \{T_0, T_1, T_2, \ldots T_{q-1}\}$ equals $2(m + 1)$. For $m = 3$, OCRT consisting of $2(m + 1) = 2(3 + 1) = 8$ patterns with both metrics ($maxTCD(T_i)$ and $maxTCD(T)$ are presented in Table 1.

For the general case, the number OCRT patterns is calculated as $q = 2(\lceil log_2 N \rceil + 1)$, and the constructive algorithm for pattern generation is presented in [7].

The presented procedure of OCRT construction, based on the greedy-like algorithm, is the best solution that can be obtained according to the procedure of all known algorithms for *controlled random test* generation, namely, *anti-random test* generation [14], *fast anti-random test* generation [25], *orderly random test* construction [28], and numerous modifications, like the *maximal distance anti-random test*, *maximal Hamming distance test*, and so on.

To summarize, the optimal controlled random test generation (Algorithm 1) for construction of OCRT for $N = 2^m$ is proposed. By optimal controlled random test we understand the set of test patterns where each pattern is chosen such that its total distance ($\text{TCD}(T_i)$ and $\text{TCD}(T)$) from all previous patterns is the greatest possible value.

Table 1. Optimal controlled random test for $q = 8$.

T_i	$t_{i,7}$	$t_{i,6}$	$t_{i,5}$	$t_{i,4}$	$t_{i,3}$	$t_{i,2}$	$t_{i,1}$	$t_{i,0}$	$max\mathrm{TCD}(T_i)$	$max\mathrm{TCD}(T)$
T_0	0	0	0	0	0	0	0	0	–	–
T_1	1	1	1	1	1	1	1	1	$\sqrt{8}$	$\sqrt{8}$
T_2	0	0	0	0	1	1	1	1	$2\sqrt{4}$	$\sqrt{8} + 2\sqrt{4}$
T_3	1	1	1	1	0	0	0	0	$\sqrt{8} + 2\sqrt{4}$	$2\sqrt{8} + 4\sqrt{4}$
T_4	0	0	1	1	0	0	1	1	$4\sqrt{4}$	$2\sqrt{8} + 8\sqrt{4}$
T_5	1	1	0	0	1	1	0	0	$\sqrt{8} + 4\sqrt{4}$	$3\sqrt{8} + 12\sqrt{4}$
T_6	0	1	0	1	0	1	0	1	$6\sqrt{4}$	$3\sqrt{8} + 18\sqrt{4}$
T_7	1	0	1	0	1	0	1	0	$\sqrt{8} + 6\sqrt{4}$	$4\sqrt{8} + 24\sqrt{4}$

ALGORITHM 1. Construction of OCRT for $N = 2^m$

1. Initial matrix M with N columns and $q = 2(m+1)$ rows should be constructed based on the trivial divide and conquer algorithm [31]. The first row M_0 takes the value with N zeros, and the second row (M_1) is all ones. The consecutive rows with even subscripts $i > 0$ are the set of even number blocks, where half are all zero blocks and another half are all blocks with one. The next row with an odd subscript is the negation of the previous row with an even subscript (e.g., M_1 is complement of M_0). On each iteration of this algorithm, the current row of matrix M with an even subscript is constructed from the previous row with an even subscript, so that all its blocks are divided into two equal blocks, when the first new block is all zeros and the second is all ones.
2. Based on some permutations, the algorithm conducts column reordering for matrix M to obtain matrix M^*, which is called a mask vector matrix.
3. Randomly chosen N bits pattern P out of 2^N possible patterns is regarded as the first pattern $T_0 = P$.
4. Each new i-th pattern $T_1, T_2, T_3, \ldots, T_{2m+1}$ is the bit-wise exclusive or sum $T_i = P \oplus M_i^*$.
5. Repeat Step 4 until all $2(m + 1)$ patterns have been constructed.

It should be mentioned that column reordering for any matrix does not change the value of the Hamming distance between any two rows (patterns), which follows from the Eq. (1). We consider the random matrix M with three rows and four columns and the matrix M_1^* that is obtained by column reordering from the matrix M.

$$
\begin{array}{c}
M \\
\begin{array}{c|cccc}
 & C_1 & C_2 & C_3 & C_4 \\
\hline
T_0 & 0 & 0 & 1 & 0 \\
T_1 & 1 & 0 & 0 & 1 \\
T_2 & 1 & 1 & 0 & 0
\end{array}
\end{array}
\qquad
\begin{array}{c}
M_1^* \\
\begin{array}{c|cccc}
 & C_3 & C_4 & C_1 & C_2 \\
\hline
T_0^* & 1 & 0 & 0 & 0 \\
T_1^* & 0 & 1 & 1 & 0 \\
T_2^* & 0 & 0 & 1 & 1
\end{array}
\end{array}
$$

We notice that the value of the Hamming distance between any two rows of matrix M equals the distance between corresponding rows of matrix M_1^*:

$$HD(T_0, T_1) = HD(T_0^*, T_1^*) = 3,$$
$$HD(T_0, T_2) = HD(T_0^*, T_2^*) = 3$$
$$HD(T_1, T_2) = HD(T_1^*, T_2^*) = 2.$$

The same observation can be made for the operation used in Step 4 of Algorithm 1. Let us again consider the random matrix M, the random pattern T_r, and the matrix M_2^*, where each row is bit-wise exclusive of the corresponding row of matrix M and pattern T.

M	C_1	C_2	C_3	C_4
T_0	0	0	1	0
T_1	1	0	0	1
T_2	1	1	0	0

$T_r = 1\,0\,1\,1$

M_2^*	C_1^*	C_2^*	C_3^*	C_4^*
T_0^*	1	0	0	1
T_1^*	0	0	1	0
T_2^*	0	1	1	1

We again notice that the value of the Hamming distance between any two rows of matrix M equals the distance between the corresponding rows of matrix M_2^*:

$$HD(T_0, T_1) = HD(T_0^*, T_1^*) = 3,$$
$$HD(T_0, T_2) = HD(T_0^*, T_2^*) = 3$$
$$HD(T_1, T_2) = HD(T_1^*, T_2^*) = 2.$$

We conclude that Steps 2–4 of the Algorithm 1 do not affect the main characteristic of the test patterns generated in Step 1. However, at the same time, the above steps allow us to generate different sets of test patterns characterized by maximum distances between the patterns. We can use those patterns to effectively detect different sorts of faults, for example, pattern sensitive faults in RAM.

Now, as an example, we generate OCRT for $N = 2^m = 2^3$ using Algorithm 1,

Example 3.1. OCRT generating for $N = 2^m = 2^3$

1. Initial matrix M with $N = 8$ columns and $q = 8$ rows is constructed, so that $M_0 = 00000000$ and $M_1 = 11111111$. The new M_2 row is obtained from M_0

Table 2. Masks vector matrices M^* for $m = 3$

M_i^*	$t_{i,2}$	$t_{i,6}$	$t_{i,1}$	$t_{i,4}$	$t_{i,3}$	$t_{i,7}$	$t_{i,5}$	$t_{i,0}$
M_0^*	0	0	0	0	0	0	0	0
M_1^*	1	1	1	1	1	1	1	1
M_2^*	1	0	1	0	1	0	0	1
M_3^*	0	1	0	1	0	1	1	0
M_4^*	0	0	1	1	0	0	1	1
M_5^*	1	1	0	0	1	1	0	0
M_6^*	1	1	0	1	0	0	0	1
M_7^*	0	0	1	0	1	1	1	0

by the dividing it on two blocks: one with all zero code and the second with all ones, where M_3 is the complement value of M_2, The next rows of matrices M (M_4, ..., M_7) are obtained in the same way (see Table 1).

2. Mask vector matrices M^*, as a result of column reordering of M (Table 1) are presented in Table 2.
3. If the randomly chosen $N = 8$-bit pattern is $P = 01111010$, then $T_0 = P = 01111010$.
4. Each new i-th pattern $T_1, T_2, T_3, \ldots, T_7$ is the bit-wise exclusive or sum $T_i = P \oplus M_i^*$, where M_i^* is taken from Table 2.
5. All $q = 2(m + 1) = 8$ patterns for OCRT are presented in Table 3 with the corresponding values of the metrics.   ■

Table 3. OCRT patterns for $m = 3$

T_i	$t_{i,7}$	$t_{i,6}$	$t_{i,5}$	$t_{i,4}$	$t_{i,3}$	$t_{i,2}$	$t_{i,1}$	$t_{i,0}$	$max\text{TCD}(T_i)$	$max\text{TCD}(T)$
T_0	0	1	1	1	1	0	1	0	–	–
T_1	1	0	0	0	0	1	0	1	$\sqrt{8}$	$\sqrt{8}$
T_2	1	1	0	1	0	0	1	1	$2\sqrt{4}$	$\sqrt{8} + 2\sqrt{4}$
T_3	0	0	1	0	1	1	0	0	$\sqrt{8} + 2\sqrt{4}$	$2\sqrt{8} + 4\sqrt{4}$
T_4	0	1	0	0	1	0	0	1	$4\sqrt{4}$	$2\sqrt{8} + 8\sqrt{4}$
T_5	1	0	1	1	0	1	1	0	$\sqrt{8} + 4\sqrt{4}$	$3\sqrt{8} + 12\sqrt{4}$
T_6	1	0	1	0	1	0	1	1	$6\sqrt{4}$	$3\sqrt{8} + 18\sqrt{4}$
T_7	0	1	0	1	0	1	0	0	$\sqrt{8} + 6\sqrt{4}$	$4\sqrt{8} + 24\sqrt{4}$

The brief analyses demonstrate that the presented procedure can construct a set of OCRT depending on the initial pattern P. For the general case, the number of OCRT patterns is calculated as $q = 2(\lceil log_2 N \rceil + 1)$, and the algorithm for OCRT pattern generation is slightly different for the mask vector matrix generation.

The proposed algorithm seems to be efficient in terms of computation complexity. For any value of N, the most difficult procedure is the mask vector matrix (M) generation and performing column reordering to obtain M^*. Indeed, increasing N by two times needs only two additional rows for M. Then, the new M is constructed so that all N-bit rows for the previous M are extended to $2N$ bits using the simple doubling of all blocks with the same values 0 or 1 and adding two final rows $M_{2m-2} = 010101\ldots01$ and $M_{2m-1} = 101010\ldots10$.

4   Experimental Results

Finally, to confirm the proposed solution we have compared the coverage of several controlled random tests strategy (OCRT, pure antirandom tests [14], concatenated antirandom tests [14], STPG [22]) and random one in terms of

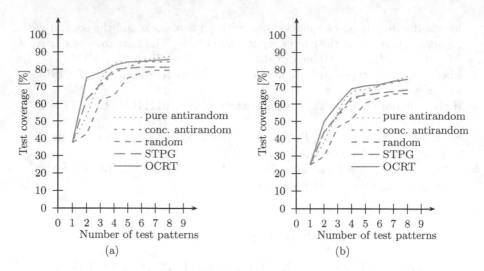

Fig. 1. The coverage of all arbitrary k out of N bits for different antirandom test schemes: (a) $k=3$ and $N=64$, (b) $k=4$ and $N=64$

number of generated binary combinations for all arbitrary k out of N bits. Using different methods, we had generated test sets consisting of eight test patterns and then we compared their coverage with each other. In the case of pure antirandom tests THD was used as a fitness function whilst concatenated antirandom vectors were employed from Example 7 in [14]. Due to the fact that the authors of STPG algorithm have not indicated how to determine the adding factors [22], a random value was used. The experiments have been done for $k = 3$ and $k = 4$. The obtained results are shown in the Fig. 1a and b. The x-axis represents the number of the test patterns, and the y-axis – the number (in percent) of binary combinations for all arbitrary $k = 3$ and $k=4$ out of $N = 64$ bits. For Fig. 1, we observe that all coverages curves rise sharply and them exhibits a smooth behavior. We observe high efficiency of OCRT especially for the first few patterns of the test. At the end of the test process OCRT gives us the same or slightly lower (see Fig. 1b) level of fault coverage as in case of pure antirandom patterns. The same time we should noted that OCRT is characterized by easier computational method in compare to other analyzed techniques. Most known antirandom techniques still need a lot of resources (strong CPU for computation of distances between vectors, additional memory to collect generated vectors, etc.) that may be unavailable in case of embedded systems and BIST technique.

5   Conclusions

In the paper a new approach called as Optimal Controlled Random Test has been introduced. It uses previously adopted metrics attempting to make all known Greedy like controlled random testing more effective. Unlike the known solutions the new approach keeps the distances $\mathrm{TCD}(T_i)$ and $\mathrm{TCD}(T)$ as large as possible. Both experimental and analytical investigation clearly show the high efficiency of proposed solution especially for the first few iterations of the multi-run test. However the OCRT has an obvious advantageous compare with all known methods. It is more efficient in terms of computation complexity.

References

1. Venkatasubramanian, M., Agrawal, V.D.: Failures guide probabilistic search for a hard-to-find test. In: 25th IEEE North Atlantic Test Workshop, NATW 2016, Providence, RI, USA, May 9–11, 2016, pp. 18–23 (2016)
2. Fujiwara, H., Toida, S.: The complexity of fault detection problems for combinational logic circuits. IEEE Trans. Comput. **31**(6), 555–560 (1982)
3. Venkatasubramanian, M., Agrawal, V.D.: A new test vector search algorithm for a single stuck-at fault using probabilistic correlation. In: IEEE 23rd North Atlantic Test Workshop, NATW 2014, Johnson City, NY, USA, May 14–16, 2014, pp. 57–60 (2014)
4. Tang, D., Woo, L.: Exhaustive test pattern generation with constant weight vectors. IEEE Trans. Comput. **32**, 1145–1150 (1983)
5. Furuya, K.: A probabilistic approach to locally exhaustive testing. Trans. IEICE (Trans. Inst. Electron. Inf. Commun. Eng.) **E72**(5), 656–660 (1989)
6. Kuhn, R.D., Okum, V.: Pseudo-exhaustive testing for software. In: Proceedings of the 30th Annual IEEE/NASA Software Engineering Workshop, Computer Society, pp. 153–158. IEEE, Washington, DC (2006)
7. Das, D., Karpovsky, M.: Exhaustive and near-exhaustive memory testing techniques and their BIST implementations. J. Electron. Test. **10**(3), 215–229 (1997)
8. Yarmolik, S.V.: Iterative near pseudoexhaustive random testing. Informatics **2**(26), 66–75 (2010)
9. Duran, J.W., Ntafos, S.C.: An evaluation of random testing. IEEE Trans. Softw. Eng. **10**(4), 438–444 (1984)
10. Grindal, M., Offutt, J., Andler, S.F.: Combination testing strategies - a survey. Technical report ISE-TR-04-05, GMU Technical report, July 2004
11. Seth, S., Agrawal, V., Farhat, H.: A statistical theory of digital circuit testability. IEEE Trans. Comput. **39**, 582–586 (1990)
12. Sosnowski, J.: Experimental evaluation of pseudorandom test effectiveness. In: Proceedings of 24th Euromicro Conference, Vasteras, Sweden, pp. 184–187. IEEE Computer Society (1998)
13. Reid, S.C.: An empirical analysis of equivalence partitioning, boundary value analysis and random testing. In: Proceedings of the 4th International Symposium on Software Metrics, Computer Society, pp. 64–73. IEEE, Washington, DC (1997)
14. Malaiya, Y.K.: Antirandom testing: getting the most out of black-box testing. In: Proceedings of 6th IEEE International Symposium on Software Reliability Engineering, ISSRE 1995, pp. 86–95. IEEE Computer Society (1995)
15. Chen, T.Y., Kuo, F.C., Merkel, R.G., Tse, T.H.: Adaptive random testing: the art of test case diversity. J. Syst. Softw. **83**, 60–66 (2010)
16. Wu, S.H., Jandhyala, S., Malaiya, Y.K., Jayasumana, A.P.: Antirandom testing: a distance-based approach. VLSI Des. **2008**, 1–2 (2008)
17. Feldt, R., Poulding, S.M., Clark, D., Yoo, S.: Test set diameter: quantifying the diversity of sets of test cases. In: 2016 IEEE International Conference on Software Testing, Verification and Validation, ICST 2016, Chicago, IL, USA, April 11–15, 2016, pp. 223–233 (2016)

18. Choi, E.H., Artho, C., Kitamura, T., Mizuno, O., Yamada, A.: Distance-integrated combinatorial testing. In: Proceedings of 27th International Symposium on Software Reliability Engineering (ISSRE 2016), Ottawa, Canada, pp. 93–104, October 2016

19. Mrozek, I.: Analysis of multibackground memory testing techniques. Int. J. Appl. Math. Comput. Sci. **20**(1), 191–205 (2010)

20. Mrozek, I., Yarmolik, V.N.: Antirandom test vectors for BIST in hardware/software systems. Fundam. Inform. **119**(2), 163–185 (2012)

21. Mrozek, I., Yarmolik, V.N.: Iterative antirandom testing. J. Electron. Test **28**(3), 301–315 (2012)

22. Yiunn, D., Bin A'ain, A., Khor, Ghee, J.: Scalable test pattern generation (STPG). In: 2010 IEEE Symposium on Proceedings of the Industrial Electronics Applications, ISIEA 2010, pp. 433–435, October 2010

23. Zhou, Z.: Using coverage information to guide test case selection in adaptive random testing. In: Computer Software and Applications Conference Workshops, pp. 208–213 (2010)

24. Yarmolik, V.N., Mrozek, I., Yarmolik, S.V.: Controlled method of random test synthesis. Autom. Control Comput. Sci. **49**(6), 395–403 (2016)

25. Mayrhauser, A., von, Bai, A., Chen, T., Anderson, C., Hajjar, A.: Fast antirandom (FAR) test generation. In: Proceedings of 3rd IEEE International Symposium on High-Assurance Systems Engineering, HASE 1998, pp. 262–269. IEEE Computer Society, Washington, DC (1998)

26. Mrozek, I., Yarmolik, V.: Methods of synthesis of controlled random tests. In: Saeed, K., Homenda, W. (eds.) CISIM 2016. LNCS, vol. 9842, pp. 429–440. Springer, Cham (2016). doi:10.1007/978-3-319-45378-1_38

27. Yarmolik, V.N., Mrozek, I., Yarmolik, S.V.: Controlled method of random test synthesis. Autom. Control Comput. Sci. **49**(6), 395–403 (2015)

28. Xu, S.: Orderly random testing for both hardware and software. In: Proceedings of the 2008 14th IEEE Pacific Rim International Symposium on Dependable Computing, Washington, DC, pp. 160–167. IEEE Computer Society (2008)

29. Wu, S.H., Malaiya, Y.K., Jayasumana, A.P.: Antirandom vs. pseudorandom testing. In: Proceedings of IEEE International Conference on Computer Design: VLSI in Computers and Processors, ICCD 1998, p. 221 (1998)

30. Xu, S., Chen, J.: Maximum distance testing. In: Asian Test Symposium, pp. 15–20 (2002)

31. Knuth, D.E.: The Art of Computer Programming: Sorting and Searching, vol. 3, 2nd edn. Addison Wesley Longman Publishing Co., Inc, Redwood City (1998)

Tabu Search and Greedy Algorithm
Adaptation to Logistic Task

Kamil Musiał, Joanna Kotowska, Dagmara Górnicka,
and Anna Burduk[✉]

Faculty of Mechanical Engineering, Wrocław University of Science
and Technology, Wybrzeze Wyspianskiego 27, 50-370 Wroclaw, Poland
{kamil.musial,joanna.kotowska,dagmara.gornicka,
anna.burduk}@pwr.edu.pl

Abstract. Distribution companies, in order to maintain a competitive advantage, must demonstrate not only the quality of the offered goods, but also the speed of execution of orders. This article deals with the allocation of the available capacity of transport during the transportation of goods between companies. Solving the problem of optimization is offered by the chosen methods of an artificial intelligence, such as Tabu Search algorithm, greedy algorithm and Tabu Search using the results of the greedy algorithm. The results were compared with the actual results of one of the Dutch distribution companies.

Keywords: Tabu search · Greedy · Optimization · VRP

1 Introduction

Nowadays distribution companies are required to manage such transport processes that the orders are delivered on time at the lowest possible cost. However, most of the decisions about the optimization problem is taken only on the basis of human beliefs. Such an approach, however, often result in skipping the best solution, while generating financial losses. A similar problem was observed in one of the Dutch distribution companies. This paper addresses the issue of possible use of available transport capacity during the transportation of products. Finding the most favorable solution to this type of problem is possible if using methods of linear programming. However, the specificity of distribution companies as well as a variety and often a large number of orders forces reduction of the time required for the calculation. Artificial intelligence methods gained more and more popularity in recent years in the search of solutions close to optimal in a relatively short period of time in different areas.

The vehicle routing problem (VRP) is undoubtedly one of the most studied combinatorial optimization problems in literature. It can be defined as the problem of designing routes for delivering vehicles of given capacities, to supply a set of customers with known locations and requests from a single depot [11, 12]. Routes for the vehicles are designed to minimize some objective such as the total distance traveled [7]. The VRP is NP-hard and therefore most of the literature has focused on heuristic

K. Saeed et al. (Eds.): CISIM 2017, LNCS 10244, pp. 39–49, 2017.
DOI: 10.1007/978-3-319-59105-6_4

solution methods [3–5, 8]. Vehicle routing problems exhibit an impressive record of successful meta-heuristic implementations [9].

Meta-heuristic algorithms can be applied on many kinds of decision problems without the need to transform them into mathematical formulations [1, 2, 9]. Tabu search is a meta-heuristic approach that guides a local heuristic search procedure to explore the solution space beyond local optimality [4–6]. One of the important characteristics is memory function, which can restrict some search directions for a more detailed local search and make it easier to leave local optimum solution. In tabu search, a tabu list is used to define search prohibition, and a move is a process that the algorithm uses to change the current solution to the new solution. In this research, the greedy randomization adaptive search procedures are adopted to generate alternative moves, and these dynamic moves are designed to control the search direction [10]. The idea of dynamic move range tends to reduce search space near a good move; otherwise, the search space is enlarged. The greedy design means that the best candidate move is compared with all tabu moves, and good moves are removed from the tabu list. The good moves refer to the moves that are better than the current best solution. During the simulation, vehicles' attributes and paths are assumed fixed [7].

2 Problem Description and Notation

The analyzed case concerns the Dutch company that distributes clothing stores in Denmark, Belgium and France. Various types of clothing are transported in cartons of a particular volume or on hangers with a volume depending on the type of clothing. 16 couriers is responsible for the carriage of goods. They have private cars with a specified maximum transport capacity. Each carrier supports the route assigned to him, without possibility to change it. Commodity turnover occurs rapidly, and transportation plans are adjusted up to date, depending on orders. Due to the pace of the generated orders there are situations where it is impossible to implement all of them, because it exceeds the available capacity of a transport. Then, the order of their execution determines the priority of the order (Table 1).

The "red" orders are implemented as first with the highest priority, "yellow" orders should be given higher priority than the "green" but they are not critical for the day.

The company is growing and thus the appropriate management of order is more challengeable. Solutions used before become insufficient when customers required speed when at the same time a number of packages and their sizes were rising. The desire to preserve the competitive advantage of the company requires optimizing the ways of transporting goods to contractors.

3 Characteristics of Optimization Model

3.1 Issue Analysis

Computer simulation of random solutions allows finding the optimum solution for these types of problems. The program introduced the actual data of relevant cases for

Table 1. Orders priority

Colors	Name	Case
Green	Normal	Date of implementing the order is relatively distant
Yellow	Increased	Order with a fixed time is required due to the fact it has been exceeded before for this particular client
		Delivering the order on time is crucial for the bigger purchase order to end successfully
		Implementation Deadline passes within 1 day
		There are expected difficulties in implementing of the order
Red	High	The contract is executed for a client with a personalized strategic agreement
		Exceeding the delivery time is associated with high financial penalty
		Order is executed again due to the error caused by the company
		The final term of the execution of the order passes that day

the ability to compare the results obtained with the solutions chosen by the company. The model was built on the given example of the existing distribution company. The data come from the actual procurement plan for the day. Table 2 shows a selected fragment of the couriers daily work summary.

Table 2. Daily summary excerpt

No.	Capacity [m³]	Amount of available orders [pcs]	Orders handled [pcs]	Used capacity [m³]	% of max capacity	Yellow orders [pcs]	Red orders [pcs]
1.	8	14	4	7.464	93.3	1 of 2	N/A
2.	12	22	8	10.72	89.33333	3 of 4	2 of 2
3.	13.5	11	8	12.94	95.85185	2 of 2	N/A
4.	9.2	23	5	9.161	99.57609	1 of 1	1 of 1
5.	18	17	12	17.664	98.13333	3 of 3	N/A
6.	22	12	12	13.413	60.96818	1 of 1	N/A
7.	14.4	15	14	14.37	99.79167	5 of 5	3 of 4
8.	11	8	8	9.926	90.23636	2 of 2	N/A
9.	9	14	6	8.527	94.74444	1 of 1	2 of 2
10.	14.3	15	10	14.066	98.36364	1 of 1	N/A
11.	14	6	6	3.826	27.32857	2 of 2	N/A
12.	7	11	7	6.841	97.72857	1 of 1	N/A
13.	12	16	8	10.384	86.53333	6 of 8	1 of 1
14.	7.2	11	5	6.955	96.59722	4 of 4	N/A
15.	16	21	10	14.482	90.5125	4 of 6	1 of 2
16.	11.4	12	6	10.58	92.80702	1 of 3	N/A
		228			94.86715	-8	-2

16 courier has from 6 to 22 contracts, in total – 228 contracts with an average volume of 1.145 m³, including 47 of the yellow priority and 12 with red priority. Capacities of cars is from 7 m³ to 16 m³. On that day 3 couriers had the volume of orders less than the maximum capacity of their cars. In this case, each of the test algorithms shows the optimal solution, and the percentage use of the available capacity of the car is not related to the type of optimization, and therefore these examples are not taken into account in further analysis.

3.2   Model Assumptions

The main function of the program was to establish the maximum utilization of the available capacity in the way the supply of goods is the most favorable. Constant limits assumed in the case are:

- the volume of garments in cartons,
- the volume of clothes on hangers,
- the maximum capacity of the transport courier car,
- the number of couriers.

Size volume introduced to the nearest 1 dm³ (1 L). In addition, the following assertions were made:

- routes are assigned to specific cars and couriers, there is no possibility of converting cars or route changes,
- mass of the goods is irrelevant, because the clothing is relatively lightweight and is not a critical factor in the present case,
- carriers cannot share orders between them,
- ruled out the possibility of making individual arrangements with couriers.

(Eg. returning for the remained orders in order to save the length of the route, at the expense of realization of the remaining orders later).

3.3   Introduced Optimization Parameters

For the purpose of the algorithm was introduced parameter "p", stating the importance of the group of contracts, adequately to the priority. After analyzing the results of a delivery the priorities have been assumed. The orders for the "red" parameter "p" accepts the importance of 1000, for the procurement of "yellow" 3 and for "green" contracts 1. Priority red are absolutely a priority, and giving priority to orders of yellow scales with a value of 3 enables to treat them in the first place, if it does not drastically reduce the use of space.

4   Considered Algorithms

For the considered case it was decided to use algorithms: Tabu Search, Greedy algorithm and a combination algorithm Tabu Search using the solution proposed by the greedy algorithm as a zero solution/start solution. The aim was to present the company calculation method allowing to find a solution in 5 s or less using a mid-range computer. This will allowing the company to freely modify orders and receive converted solutions in near real-time. The programming language used to create the algorithms is C++.

4.1 Tabu Search

Tabu Search is an algorithm that searches the space created from all possible solutions with a particular sequence of movements. Among them, there are taboo movements (forbidden). The algorithm avoids oscillation around the local optimum by storing information about proven solutions in the form of a list of taboos (TL). Tabu Search algorithm is a deterministic, in a contrast to e.g. the genetic algorithm. Treating the same data several times with the same Tabu Search algorithm will give the same results.

Algorithm **Tabu Search** (S_0, var S, max_m, max_iter)

Set S = S_0 and iter = 0
Repeat
        m = 0

        best = 0

        iter = iter + 1

            Repeat

                m = m+1

                Execute **Check_the_neighboring_solution** (S,S_m)

                Execute **Check_Tabu_list** (S,S_n)

                        if ($f(S_m)$ > best **then** (best = $f(S_m)$ and (m2= m))

            until (m = max_m)

        Execute **Add_to_Tabu_list** (S,S_{m2})

        S= S_{m2}

        If best > sol **then** sol = best
Until iter = max_iter

Analyzed problem can be reduced to a binary sequence:

$$1\ 1\ 0\ 0\ 1\ 0\ 1\dots$$

in which each bit corresponds to the order assigned to the courier. The value of "1" means that the courier undertakes the contract, the value of "0" that he rejects it. For example, the implementation of the five orders starts from the obtaining of the set of orders, described as a specified bit sequence, eg:

$$1\ 0\ 1\ 0\ 1.$$

Check the neighboring solution:
The algorithm checks all neighboring solutions (differing in one bit):

$$\begin{array}{ccccc}
1 & 0 & 1 & 0 & 0 \\
1 & 0 & 1 & 1 & 1 \\
1 & 0 & 0 & 0 & 1 \\
1 & 1 & 1 & 0 & 1 \\
0 & 1 & 1 & 0 & 1,
\end{array}$$

Check Tabu List:
The algorithm checks whether the transition between data solutions has already been made. If so, such a solution is skipped and then the best solution, according to the specified criterion, is chosen:

$$1\ 1\ 1\ 0\ 1$$

Add to Tabu List:
And adds it to a list of prohibited movements (TL): If a found solution is the best found so far, the algorithm remembers it as the solution algorithm. The algorithm then repeats the operation with specified number of times.

In the case of each bit represents the size of the contract [o]- order $[o_1, o_2.....o_n]$ and its priority $[p_1, p_2, p_3]$.

According to the assumptions (Sect. 3.2) capacity of transport vehicles for the route is strictly defined. The algorithm has a limit: the total volume of contracts multiplied by the bit value representing the order does not exceed the maximum capacity of the transport car V_{max}.

$$0o_1 + 1o_2 + 1o_3 + \cdots + 0o_n \leq V_{max} \tag{1}$$

Following this equation it is seen that the total volume of the selected orders cannot exceed the maximum available capacity of the car.

According to the adopted objective function (Sect. 3.2) criterion for choosing the best solution is the total volume of contracts multiplied by the priority values and by the priorities of the value of bits representing the order data.

$$F(c) = 0o_1p_1 + 1o_2p_2 + 1o_3p_3 + \ldots + 0o_np_n \rightarrow MAX \tag{2}$$

The algorithm was set to 100 iterations.

4.2 Greedy Algorithm

Greedy algorithm is a method of determining a solution by making a selection in each step. This means that the chosen solution is the one that seems to be the best at the moment. The rating is locally optimal but does not analyze if the data in the following steps will make sense. The greedy algorithm, like Tabu Search algorithm also does not guarantee finding the optimal solution.

Greedy method (o, p, V, V_max, o_number)

V = 0

Execute **Sort descending** (o,p)

Execute: **Add highest orders** (o,p,V_max)

Repeat:

      Execute: **Add next** (o,p,Vmax)

Untill (V = V_max) **or** (all orders added)

Sort descending:
In this issue algorithm multiplies the volume of each order by the value of its priority, and the sorts the results descending:

$$o_{1'}p_{1'} \geq o_{2'}p_{2'} \geq o_{3'}p_{3'} \geq \ldots \geq o_{n'}p_{n'} \tag{3}$$

Add highest orders:
Thereafter adds capacity orders from the highest sorted values until it reaches the maximum value, not exceeding the capacity of the car:

$$o_{1'} + o_{2'} + \ldots + o_{m'} \leq V_{max} \tag{4}$$

Add next:
When adding another order exceeds the permitted volume/overflow the car, then this solution is skipped, the next is added and the criterion of maximum capacity is checked. If:

$$o_{1'} + o_{2'} + \ldots + o_{m'} + o_{m+1'} > V_{max} \tag{5}$$

Then:

$$o_{1'} + o_{2'} + \ldots + o_{m'} + o_{m+2'} \leq V_{max} \tag{6}$$

The algorithm terminates when the available capacity will be used:

$$o_{1'} + o_{2'} + \ldots + o_{m'} = V_{max} \tag{7}$$

or when all the orders will be added or rejected.

$$o_{1'} + o_{2'} + \ldots + o_{m'} + o_{m+2'} + o_{m+5'} + o_{n-1'} + o_{n'} \leq V_{max} \tag{8}$$

4.3   Solution Combining Greedy Algorithm and Tabu Search

For the purposes of research a solution combining the above two methods is proposed. The third algorithm starts its operation in accordance with the specifics of the greedy algorithm. The solution obtained in this way is a set of an input data to the search algorithm according to the algorithm method Tabu Search. Functional diagram is shown in Fig. 1.

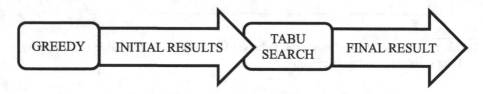

Fig. 1. Diagram of the combined algorithm

Combined algorithm presented in Fig. 1. has been analyzed regarding to the accuracy of this solution according to the accepted criterion in comparison with a simple algorithm Tabu Search and the number of iterations needed which affects the time needed for the program to turn the best result.

5   Analysis of the Results

Based on the assumptions pictured algorithms were developed for the analyzed case was. The use of analyzed algorithms to solve the optimization of a problem has been compared. Their effectiveness has been studied on the example of a real case of status orders for the one day in the analyzed company. Each of the algorithms proposed the most beneficial plan for the transport of distributed goods. The hardware used to make

Table 3. Summary of results of analyzed methods

Method	% of used capacity	Orders uncompleted yellow	Orders uncompleted red
Current	94,87	8/47	2/12
Tabu Search	99,29	0/47	0/12
Greedy	98,67	1/47	0/12
Tabu Search + Greedy	99,39	0/ 47	0/12

the computation is a medium-class laptop with processor Intel Core i5-430 m, 8 GB RAM and Windows 7 Professional, 64-bit Operating System. The results obtained, in terms of amount of completed priority orders and the use of available capacity is shown in Table 3 below.

Be analyzing the capacity of used cars it can be observed that each of the proposed method achieves better results than the current system of the company. The difference between the real solution, and the solutions suggested by the artificial intelligence methods in the use of available capacity is less than 5 percentage points, giving a real gain for the company. Couriers, selecting orders in accordance with their experience left 8 orders of yellow priority and 2 of red priority, which is unacceptable in this case. The solution proposed by the greedy algorithm leaves one order of yellow priority – this situation is acceptable. Algorithms, Tabu Search and Tabu Search enriched with solution of greedy algorithm allowed 100% accomplishment of the priority order.

As mentioned in Sect. 4.1 Tabu Search algorithm was set to 100 iterations – it analyzed 100 neighboring solutions and passed to the best.one. As can be seen in Table 4. simple Tabu Search algorithm achieved the best solution after maximum of 17 iterations. This means that if the number of iterations was reduced to 17 and accelerated search solutions around the 5-fold, in a given case, the results would be identical. Tabu Search algorithm starting from the solutions generated by the greedy algorithm needed at maximum 4 iterations to get the best solution. The number of the best iteration of "0" means that the input set of orders was not improved during 100 iteration - Tabu Search algorithm is not able to improve the solution proposed by the greedy algorithm. As shown in Table 2 modified Tabu Search algorithm showed the best use of the capacity of the car. The algorithm combining the greedy algorithm and Tabu Search is the best in terms of mentioned criteria and provides a good solution for the analyzed case and can give the company a real gain.

6   Summary

For the purpose of research, an algorithm which, by the use of available resources, allows to find the most beneficial way to transport distributed goods has been built. The results of the research conducted on the example of a real Dutch distribution company demonstrated the potential benefits that could be achieved by the use of the proposed methods. Each of them allows to achieve much better results than the current system of

Table 4. Summary of the best iteration

No.	Number of the best solutions	
	Tabu search with Greedy	Simple Tabu Search
1.	0	5
2.	4	15
3.	3	7
4.	0	8
5.	1	17
6.	0	12
7.	3	5
8.	2	12
9.	1	10
10.	2	14
11.	4	15
12.	4	16
13.	0	7

the company. The differences between the results achieved by the three tested algorithms are small. For the analyzed case, the most advantageous method proved algorithm combining operation methods of Greedy algorithm and Tabu Search.

References

1. Burduk, A., Musiał, K.: Genetic algorithm adoption to transport task optimization. In: Graña, M., López-Guede, J.M., Etxaniz, O., Herrero, Á., Quintián, H., Corchado, E. (eds.) ICEUTE/SOCO/CISIS -2016. AISC, vol. 527, pp. 366–375. Springer, Cham (2017). doi:10.1007/978-3-319-47364-2_35
2. Burduk, A., Musiał, K.: Optimization of chosen transport task by using generic algorithms. In: Saeed, K., Homenda, W. (eds.) CISIM 2016. LNCS, vol. 9842, pp. 197–205. Springer, Cham (2016). doi:10.1007/978-3-319-45378-1_18
3. Baldacci, R., Christofides, N., Mingozzi, A.: An exact algorithm for the vehicle routing problem based on the set partitioning formulation with additional cuts. Math. Prog. Ser. A **115**(2), 351–385 (2008)
4. Bożejko, W., Uchroński, M., Wodecki, M.: Parallel tabu search algorithm with uncertain data for the flexible job shop problem. In: Rutkowski, L., Korytkowski, M., Scherer, R., Tadeusiewicz, R., Zadeh, Lotfi A., Zurada, Jacek M. (eds.) ICAISC 2016. LNCS, vol. 9693, pp. 419–428. Springer, Cham (2016). doi:10.1007/978-3-319-39384-1_36
5. Glover, F., Laguna, M.: Tabu Search. Kluwer Academic Publishers, Norwell (1997)
6. Grabowski, J., Pempera, J.: New block properties for the permutation flow shop problem with application in tabu search. J. Oper. Res. Soc. **52**(2), 210–220 (2001)
7. Hu, T., Chen, L.: Traffic signal optimization with greedy randomized tabu search algorithm. J. Transp. Eng. **138**(8), 1040–1050 (2012)
8. Lysgaard, J., Letchford, N.A., Eglese, W.R.: A new branch-and-cut algorithm for the capacitated vehicle routing problem. Math. Program. **100**(2), 423–445 (2004)

9. Pacheco, J., García, I., Álvarez, A.: Enhancing variable neighborhood search by adding memory: application to a real logistic problem. Knowl. Based Syst. **62**, 28–37, (2014)
10. Resende, M., Ribeiro, C.: Greedy randomized adaptive search procedures. In: Glover, F., Kochenberger, G.A. (eds.) Handbook of Metaheuristics. International Series in Operations Research & Management Science, vol. 57, pp. 219–249. Springer, New York (2003)
11. Rudawska, A., Čuboňova, N., Pomarańska, K., Stanečková, D., Gola, A.: Technical and organizational improvements of packaging production processes. Adv. Sci. Technol. Res. J. **10**(30), 182–192 (2016)
12. Toth, P., Vigo, D.: Branch-and-bound algorithms for the capacitated VRP. In: The Vehicle Routing Problem, pp. 29–52. SIAM, Philadelphia (2001)

Evolutionary Algorithm for the Time-Dependent Orienteering Problem

Krzysztof Ostrowski[✉]

Faculty of Computer Science, Bialystok University of Technology, Bialystok, Poland
k.ostrowski@pb.edu.pl

Abstract. The Time-Dependent Orienteering Problem (TDOP) is a generalization of the Orienteering Problem where graph weights vary with time. It has many real life applications particularly associated with transport networks, in which travel time between two points depends on the moment of start. The paper presents an evolutionary algorithm with embedded local search operators and heuristic crossover, which solves TDOP. The algorithm was tested on TDOP benchmark instances and in most cases achieved optimal or near optimal results clearly outperforming other published methods.

Keywords: Time-dependent orienteering problem · Evolutionary algorithm · Metaheuristic · Local search operators

1 Introduction

The Orienteering Problem (OP) can be formulated on a graph in which each vertex has assigned a profit and each edge has a cost. The goal of the OP is to find a path between given points limited by total cost which maximizes total profit of visited vertices. The OP has many practical applications including tourist trip planning [14], transport logistics and others. For example in tourist trip planning each attraction (point of interest - POI) has some profit assigned. In this case the purpose is to find as attractive trip as possible with limited duration. It can by solved by OP algorithms.

In this paper the Time-Dependent Orienteering Problem (TDOP) [13] is tackled. TDOP is a generalization of OP in which graph weights (indentified with travel times) vary with time. In practical situations, usually travel time between two places depends on the moment of travel start. Examples of time-dependent networks are public transport networks (travel times determined by timetables) as well as other transport networks (travel times determined by time of a day and traffic). Determining most profitable paths in such networks (i.e. most attractive trips for tourists) comes down to solving TDOP.

To solve the TDOP author proposed an evolutionary algorithm with local search methods embedded. It was based on the algorithm which author developed for classic OP obtaining solutions close to optimal for benchmarks up to

© IFIP International Federation for Information Processing 2017
Published by Springer International Publishing AG 2017. All Rights Reserved
K. Saeed et al. (Eds.): CISIM 2017, LNCS 10244, pp. 50–62, 2017.
DOI: 10.1007/978-3-319-59105-6_5

a few hundred vertices [24]. Some modifications were applied to the algorithm: allowance of infeasible solutions (too long paths) in a population and adaptation of operators to time dependency.

The article is organized as follows. Literature review is presented in Sect. 2. Detailed mathematical problem definition is given in Sect. 3. In Sect. 4 there is a description of proposed evolutionary algorithm. Section 5 contains computational results of the algorithm and comparisons with other metaheuristics. Finally, in Sect. 6 conclusion and further research are included.

2 Literature Review

The Orienteering Problem was introduced by Tsiligirides [1]. The OP (and its generalizations) is an NP-hard optimization problem [2] and exact algorithms for OP can be very time-consuming for larger graphs. The exact algorithms usually applied for the OP are the branch-and-cut methods [5,7]. However, because of its computational difficulty, most OP papers are devoted to heuristics and metaheuristics. Various approaches were based i.a. on greedy and random- ized construction of solutions [1,2,17], local search methods [4,10], tabu search [6], ant-colony optimization [11] and genetic algorithms [8]. Author's previous OP research concentrated on development of evolutionary algorithms with local search operators, which proved successful on benchmark instances [18,22,24,25].

The Time-Dependent Orienteering Problem (TDOP) is relatively new and most of papers regarding TDOP were published in current decade. Most of them emphasize practical application of TDOP especially in transport networks. Fomin et al. [9] presented first approach to the problem - they proposed $(2 + \epsilon)$- approximation algorithm for TDOP. The problem version tackled in the arti- cle was simplified because each node had the same profit (equal to 1). LI [13] developed an exact method basing on dynamic programming and solved small instances of TDOP. He used discretized time and there were 1440 time states (number of minutes in a day). It was the first article about classic TDOP (nodes profits can be arbitrary).

The TDOP solutions can be practically used in networks of tourist attractions connected by means of public transport. A few papers concentrated on TDOP application in such networks. In paper [15] first such an application was presented - algorithm was tested on POI and public transport network of Tehran. The authors used a different name to the problem and routes utility was computed in a different way to classic OP but the problem was closely related to TDOP.

Garcia et al. [16] for the first time applied classic TDOP version in a public transport network - experiments were conducted on POI and public transport network of San Sebastian. Their solution also took into account time-windows and multiple paths (Time-Dependent Team Orienteering Problem with Time Windows). In order to solve the problem they used Iterated Local Search method (ILS). However, they used some simplifications: computations performed on aver- age daily travel time (first approach) and assumption of periodic public transport timetables (second approach).

Recently one of the first approaches which uses real time-dependent weights in public transport network was presented [23]. Experiments were conducted on POI and public transport network of Athens. Authors proposed 20 topologies and 100 tourist preferences combining into 2000 different test cases. Authors introduced two fast heuristics (TDCSCR and TDSlCSCR), which based on iterated local search and vertex clustering, and made comparisons with ILS.

Another solution of TDOP tested on real travel times of POI and public transport network (city of Bialystok) was proposed by the author of this paper [21]. The algorithm based on local search procedures and was tested in three variants which processed network weights in different ways. Time-dependent variant performed computation on real travel times, mean variant operated on static network of daily averaged travel times (like in approaches described above) and hybrid variant used information from both approaches.

Verbeeck et al. [19] developed new benchmark instances for TDOP. These networks model street traffic. The authors proposed ant-colony approach, tested it on mentioned benchmarks and compared with optimal solutions (obtained by them). The tested metaheuristic achieved high quality results in short execution time. Gunawan et al. [20] modified Verbeeck's benchmarks (discretization of time) and tested a few approaches: greedy construction, iterated local search (ILS), adaptive ILS and variable neighborhood descent. The best solutions were generated by adaptive ILS metaheuristic.

3 Definition of the Time-Dependent Orienteering Problem

Let $G = (V, E)$ be a directed, weighted graph. In this paper each weight between vertices i and j ($i, j \in V$) is identified with travel time between these vertices and is a function $w_{ij}(t)$ dependent on the moment of travel start t. Each vertex i has a nonnegative profit p_i and a nonnegative visit time τ_i. Given the time-dependent graph, moment of start t_0, time limit T_{max}, start and end vertices (s and e) the purpose of TDOP is to find a path from s to e starting at time t_0 which maximizes total profit of visited vertices and its total cost (travel time) does not exceed T_{max}. TDOP can be formulated as Mixed Integer Programming problem. Let x_{ij} is 1 iff a path contains direct travel from i to j and 0 otherwise. Let y_i is 1 iff a path contains vertex i and 0 otherwise. Let t_i be a time of arrival at vertex i - this function is defined only for vertices contained in a path. The purpose of TDOP is to maximize formula 1 without violating constraints given by formulas 2–8. Formula 2 limits total time budget. Formula 3 indicates that the path starts in s and ends in e. Constraint 4 means that each vertex can be visited only once while formula 5 is a relation between variables x and y. Formulas 6 and 7 are used to compute arrival times at visited vertices. Constraint 8 guarantees that there are no sub cycles.

$$max \sum_{i \in V} (p_i \cdot y_i) \tag{1}$$

$$t_e + \tau_e - t_0 \leq T_{max} \tag{2}$$

$$\sum_{j \in V} x_{sj} = \sum_{i \in V} x_{ie} = 1 \qquad (3)$$

$$\mathop{\forall}_{k \in V \setminus \{s,e\}} (\sum_{i \in V} x_{ik} = \sum_{j \in V} x_{kj} \leq 1 \qquad (4)$$

$$\mathop{\forall}_{i \in V} (y_i = max(\sum_{j \in V} x_{ij}, \sum_{j \in V} x_{ji})) \qquad (5)$$

$$t_s = t_0 \qquad (6)$$

$$\mathop{\forall}_{i \in V, j \in V} (x_{ij} = 1 \Rightarrow t_j = t_i + \tau_i + w_{ij}(t_i + \tau_i)) \qquad (7)$$

$$\mathop{\forall}_{S \subset V} (\sum_{i \in S} y_i < \sum_{i \in V} y_i \Rightarrow \sum_{i,j,\in S} x_{ij} < \sum_{i \in S} y_i) \qquad (8)$$

4 Proposed Algorithm Description

To solve the TDOP author proposed an evolutionary algorithm with local search methods embedded (during mutation), disturb operator, 2-point crossover and deterministic crowding as selection mechanism. Operators have two forms (random and heuristic) - their frequency and specificity are controlled by algorithm parameters. Infeasible solutions (too long paths) can be included in a population as well and they are penalized by fitness function. A path representation is used in the proposed algorithm - each gene in a chromosome is associated with visited vertex in a corresponding path. After random initialization of paths, procedures of crossover, selection, mutation and disturbance and applied repeatedly. Evolution terminates after N_g generations or earlier if there is no improvement in the last C_g generations. The result is the best feasible path obtained during algorithm run.

4.1 Evalutation

Let S be a path with total profit p_S and total cost (travel time) c_S. Fitness function of a feasible path (not exceeding T_{max}) is equal to its profit. If path S is too long its fitness is: $fitness(S) = p_S \cdot (\frac{T_{max}}{c_S})^k$. Fitness function decreases as solution is farther from feasibility boarder T_{max}. Parameter k is associated with penalty severity: larger values mean stronger penalties. Fitness function is adaptive: at the beginning $k = 1$ and every 10 generations there is a check - if more than α percent of individuals are infeasible then k is increased by 0.1.

4.2 Initialization

At the beginning initial population of P_{size} random paths is generated. Construction of each solution begins with adding start vertex s. Afterwards, random vertices are iteratively added at the end of the path as long as further insertions are possible without violating T_{max} constraint (including cost of traveling back to end vertex).

4.3 Crossover

During crossover $\frac{P_{size} \cdot c_p}{2}$ different pairs of parents are randomly selected from the population (c_p - crossover probability) and each pair undergoes crossover procedure. A specialized 2-point crossover operator was used. At the beginning an ordered set S of common vertices for both parents is determined. Vertices order in the set is the same as in first parent. Next, chromosome fragments between two successive vertices in S are exchanged and two offspring are created. If any duplicates appear in offspring individuals outside of exchanged fragments they are immediately removed. Crossover can be performed in two ways depending on how exchanged fragments are chosen. Random crossover variant chooses crossing points randomly while heuristic crossover maximizes fitness function of the fitter offspring (all exchange options are checked). Created offspring can exceed T_{max} limit. The probability of using heuristic crossover is indicated by parameter c_h while the probability of using random version is $1 - c_h$. In Fig. 1 there is an example of crossover.

parents

parent A: (**16**, 3, 7, **4**, 5, **9**, 12, 11, 14, **1**)

parent B: (**16**, 6, 8, 2, **4**, 13, 10, **9**, 15, **1**)

crossover variant I

child 1: (**16**, 6, 8, 2, **4**, 5, **9**, 12, 11, 14, **1**)

child 2: (**16**, 3, 7, **4**, 13, 10, **9**, 15, **1**)

crossover variant II

child 1: (**16**, 3, 7, **4**, 13, 10, **9**, 12, 11, 14, **1**)

child 2: (**16**, 6, 8, 2, **4**, 5, **9**, 15, **1**)

crossover variant III

child 1: (**16**, 3, 7, **4**, 5, **9**, 15, **1**)

child 2: (**16**, 6, 8, 2, **4**, 13, 10, **9**, 12, 11, 14, **1**)

Fig. 1. Example of 2-point crossover. Given two parents which have 4 common vertices (16, 4, 9, 1) there are three possible fragment exchanges between successive points. Variant I shows children created by fragments exchange between vertices 16 and 4, variant II is created by segments exchange between points 4 and 9 while variant III shows offspring individuals created by exchange of fragments between vertices 9 and 1.

4.4 Selection

In the algorithm no parent selection is used. Instead, survival selection is applied in the form of deterministic crowding [3]. After crossover procedure ends each offspring competes with one of its parents and the fitter individual is chosen to the next generation. To preserve population diversity competition is performed between more similar child-parent pairs. Pair arrangement is determined by distance measure. In this problem two distance measures are applied: edit distance (operations insert and delete) and cardinality of symmetric difference of vertex sets. The second is computed initially - if it suggests that child-parent pairs should be swapped then more complex procedure of edit distance is calculated.

4.5   Mutation

During mutation phase $P_{size} \cdot m_p$ individuals are randomly selected from the population (m_p is mutation probability). First, each chosen individual undergoes 2-opt procedure. This procedure tries to replace two non-adjacent edges in a path by two other edges in order to shorten the path as much as possible. Given a path $(v_1, v_2, ..., v_i, v_{i+1}, ..., v_j, v_{j+1}, ..., v_k)$ 2-opt procedure replaces edges (v_i, v_{i+1}) and (v_j, v_{j+1}) by edges (v_i, v_j) and (v_{i+1}, v_{j+1}) and reverses path fragment between v_{i+1} and v_j. The resulting path is:
$(v_1, v_2, ..., v_i, v_j, v_{j-1}..., v_{i+1}, v_{j+1}, v_{j+2}..., v_k)$.

Afterwards one vertex insertion or one vertex deletion is carried out. Probabilities of insertion and deletion are the same (0.5). Both insertion and deletion can be either random or heuristic (local search). Heuristic insertion from all possible non-included vertices (and all insertion places) chooses the option that maximizes ratio of vertex profit to path travel time increase. Random insertion chooses new vertex randomly but insertion place is chosen to minimize travel time increase. Heuristic deletion chooses the vertex that minimizes ratio of vertex profit to path travel time decrease. During mutation T_{max} limit can be exceeded. The ratio between local search and randomness is determined by parameter m_h (analogically to c_h in crossover phase).

4.6   Disturb

Disturb procedure can be perceived as a different type of mutation which causes bigger changes in routes. The operator chooses $P_{size} \cdot d_p$ individuals from the population (d_p is disturb probability). Each chosen individual is disturbed - a path fragment of random length (but containing at most 10 percent of all path vertices) is removed. Two types of disturb are possible: first version removes a random fragment of random length while heuristic version works analogically to deletion mutation - from all possible fragments of a given length it chooses the option minimizing ratio of fragment profit to path travel time decrease. Specificity of this operator is determined by parameter d_h.

4.7   Adaptation to Time Dependency

TDOP algorithm operates on time-dependent networks and for this reason each path modification is associated with recalculation of edge travel times after the modification point. This can be particularly time-consuming in case of heuristic operators. For this reason some modifications were applied to these parts.

Vertex insertion: After inserting new vertex all edge travel times after insertion place have to be recalculated. Insertion operators of the algorithm choose the best insertion place for an included vertex (minimizing travel time increase). Trying each insertion place and recalculating weights is time consuming. However, it is possible to determine the best insertion place in $O(N)$ run time (N - number of nodes in a path). The purpose of insertion is to minimize path travel time increase but it can be replaced by an equivalent goal of earliest possible arrival into the last vertex in a modified path. It can be computed in one loop over the path. In the i-th iteration we compare two arrival times into vertex i: one resulting from insertion new vertex directly before i and one resulting from best insertion place chosen so far. If current insertion place is better than previous best (arrival time into vertex i is earlier) we update our best choice.

2-opt: The purpose of 2-opt is to decrease path travel time as much as possible by edges replacement. Each edge exchange is associated with recalculating travel times in a large fragment of a path (part of it is reversed). In order to decrease execution time of 2-opt some modifications were applied - instead of time-consuming repeated recalculations of travel times the procedure tries to estimate total travel time of reversed path fragments. At first the initial travel time of the path (before changes) is divided into equal time intervals. Afterwards some reversed path fragments (starting at different times) are precomputed. Estimation is fast and base on finding an appropriate precomputed path (explanation in Fig. 2). Exact calculations are performed only if estimation signals that travel time can be shortened - it significantly reduces computations.

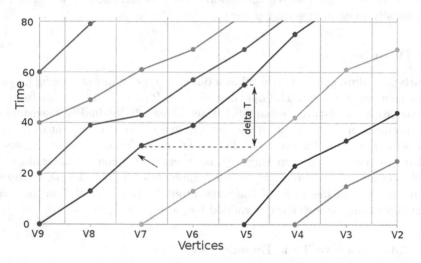

Fig. 2. Estimating travel time of reversed fragment of a path. The path is $(v_1, v_2, ..., v_{10})$ and it starts at time $t = 0$ and ends at time 80. Time was divided into $D = 4$ equal intervals and all possible vertices in reversed fragments are $v_9, v_8, ... v_2$. The figure can be treated as 2-dimensional array and in each cell there is a precomputed path fragment visiting a given vertex (determined by column) at a given time interval (determined by row). For example in order to estimate travel time of fragment (v_7, v_6, v_5) starting at time $t = 27$ we should find an appropriate column (v_7) and row (interval 20–40) and route fragment associated with it (pointed by arrow). Afterwards we compute the difference of arrival times between v_5 and v_7 (deltaT), which is the estimation.

5   Experimental Results

5.1   Parameters

Experiments were conducted on a computer with Intel Core i7 3.5 GHz processor and algorithms were implemented in C++. In Table 1 there are values of all parameters of proposed evolutionary algorithm. Population size was set to 100 or 30. The first population size ($P_{size} = 100$) is derived from original OP algorithm, which performed computations on larger networks. The smaller population size ($P_{size} = 30$) was introduced in order to reduce execution time in smaller TDOP instances. Parameters associated with generations were adjusted to population size - their values allow algorithm to fully converge. The remaining parameters of the algorithm were determined in a process of automatic tuning. The author used Parameters ILS [12] meta-algorithm to calibrate his method. The parameters of evolutionary algorithm were tuned on classic OP calibration instances but proved to be applicable to TDOP instances as well. More details about tuning can be found in one of author's previous papers on the OP [24].

Table 1. Parameters of the evolutionary algorithm

Param.	Value	Description	Param.	Value	Description
P_{size}	100/30	Population size	m_p	1	Mutation probab.
N_g	5000/1500	Max. generations number	c_p	1	Crossover probab.
C_g	500/150	Max. generations number without improvement	d_p	0.01	Disturb probab.
			m_h	1	Mutation heuristic coeff.
α	90	Max. percentage of infeasible solutions	c_h	0.8	Crossover heuristic coeff.
			d_h	0,8	Disturb heuristic coeff.

5.2   Test Instances

TDOP benchmark instances were introduced by Verbeeck et al. [19]. These test instances model street traffic. The benchmark authors introduced 7 networks containing 21–102 vertices. Maximum travel times (T_{max}) were between 5 and 14 hours and all paths started at 7 in the morning in node 1 and ended in last node: N. There are three classes of benchmark networks:

- Class I contains the smallest networks (21–32 vertices). These are original TDOP instances which were solved optimally by benchmark authors.
- Class II contains all benchmark networks - they were slightly modified so that optimal results were the same as in static OP network. Details in [19].

– Class III instances were developed from previous classes by applying time discretization in order to compare author's algorithm with Gunawan's metaheuristics [20]. Original start time was 7 am and time limit 14 h.

5.3 Results

The author tested the evolutionary algorithm (EVO) on these instances and compared it to optimal solutions, ant-colony metaheuristic (ACS) [19] and Adaptive ILS [20]. Gaps were expressed in percent and computed as $100 \cdot (1 - \frac{res}{opt})$ where *res* is result obtained by a metaheuristic (average from 30 runs in case of EVO) and *opt* is profit of optimal solution. Execution time is given in seconds.

In Table 2 results of class I instances are given: performance of two evolutionary algorithm versions (P_{size} of 100 and 30) is presented and compared to ACS and optimal solutions. EVO100 obtains optimal solutions for all test cases and is on average 0.8 percent better than ACS. The biggest obtained gap is over 4 percent. EVO30 is only 0.1 percent worse than EVO100 and is much faster. Only in one case EVO30 is much worse than EVO100 (over 1.5%).

Table 2. Results for class I instances. N is network size.

N	T_{max}	EVO100		EVO30		ACS	Opt.	N	T_{max}	EVO100		EVO30		ACS	Opt.
		Time	Gap	Time	Gap	gap	result			Time	Gap	Time	Gap	gap	result
32	5	0.8	0	0.1	0	0	115	21	9	0.6	0	0.1	1.5	0	260
32	6	1.0	0	0.1	0	0	135	21	10	0.7	0	0.1	0	0	310
32	7	1.1	0	0.1	0	0	160	21	11	0.7	0	0.1	0	0	340
32	8	1.2	0	0.1	0	2.2	185	21	12	0.8	0	0.1	0.2	0	375
32	9	1.4	0	0.1	0	0.5	210	21	13	0.9	0	0.1	0	0	425
32	10	1.6	0	0.2	0	0.4	230	33	5.5	0.8	0	0.1	0	4.3	370
32	11	1.6	0	0.2	0	0	250	33	6.5	0.9	0	0.1	0	0	420
32	12	1.8	0	0.2	0	1.9	270	33	7.5	1.1	0	0.1	0	4	500
21	5	0.5	0	0.1	0	0	100	33	8.5	1.2	0	0.1	0	2.9	560
21	6	0.5	0	0.1	0	0	150	33	9.5	1.4	0	0.1	0	1.9	620
21	7	0.6	0	0.1	0	0	195	33	10.5	1.6	0	0.1	0	0.3	650
21	8	0.6	0	0.1	0.3	0	220	33	11.5	1.8	0	0.2	0	1.2	690
									avg.	**1.0**	**0**	**0.1**	**0.1**	**0.8**	**322.5**

In Table 3 results of class II instances are presented. EVO100 again achieves optimal solutions for most test cases and average gap is close to 0 percent. On average it is 1.4 percent better than ACS and for some instances the difference is more than 5 percent. EVO100 clearly outperforms ACS especially in case of some larger instances. EVO30 is on average only 0.1 percent worse than EVO100 but for some of largest test cases (100–102 nodes) the difference are larger (0.5–1.1 percent). Execution time of proposed methods is also acceptable.

Table 3. Results for class II instances.

N	T_{max}	EVO100		EVO30		ACS	Opt.	N	T_{max}	EVO100		EVO30		ACS	Opt.
		Time	Gap	Time	Gap	gap	result			Time	Gap	Time	Gap	gap	result
32	5	0.9	0	0.1	0	0	135	100	5	2.3	0	0.3	0.5	0.8	486
32	6	1.0	0	0.1	0	0	165	100	6	2.7	0	0.3	0.1	1.7	590
32	7	1.3	0	0.1	0	0	185	100	7	4.5	0.2	0.4	0.3	2.5	679
32	8	1.3	0	0.1	0	0	210	100	8	4.0	0	0.5	0.4	4.5	771
32	9	1.5	0	0.1	0	0	240	100	9	5.0	0	0.7	0.6	4.2	853
32	10	1.7	0	0.1	0	1.5	260	100	10	6.1	0.02	0.8	1.1	3	932
32	11	1.7	0	0.2	0	0	275	100	11	6.4	0	0.9	0.2	0.9	1007
32	12	1.9	0	0.2	0	0	285	100	12	8.8	0	1.1	0.1	3	1083
32	13	1.9	0	0.2	0	0	285	100	13	7.9	0	1.2	0.1	1.7	1147
21	5	0.6	0	0.1	0	0	165	100	14	9.9	0	1.2	0.6	5.3	1198
21	6	0.7	0	0.1	0	0	200	64	6.5	2.6	0	0.3	0	0.3	870
21	7	0.6	0	0.1	0	0	225	64	7	2.9	0	0.4	0.04	0.6	930
21	8	0.7	0	0.1	0	0	275	64	8	3.4	0	0.4	0.1	0.9	1056
21	9	0.7	0	0.1	0	0	315	64	9	3.9	0	0.4	0	0.8	1152
21	10	0.8	0	0.1	0	0	375	64	10	4.5	0	0.5	0.02	1.1	1236
21	11	0.8	0	0.1	0	0	415	64	11	6.1	0	0.8	0.4	1.8	1308
21	12	0.8	0	0.1	0	0	440	64	12	6.2	0	0.7	0.01	1.5	1344
21	13	0.9	0	0.1	0	0	450	64	13	6.0	0	0.6	0	0	1344
33	5.5	0.9	0	0.1	0	0	430	64	14	6.1	0	0.6	0	0	1344
33	6.5	1.0	0	0.1	0	0	490	102	4	2.3	0	0.3	0	5.3	532
33	7.5	1.3	0	0.1	0	0	550	102	5	2.9	0	0.4	0	6.1	648
33	8.5	1.3	0	0.1	0	0	590	102	6	3.9	0	0.5	0.2	1.1	774
33	9.5	1.5	0	0.2	0	0	630	102	7	5.0	0	0.6	0	1.8	884
33	10.5	1.7	0	0.1	0	0	680	102	8	6.5	0	0.8	0.1	6.1	994
33	11.5	1.8	0	0.2	0	0	730	102	9	7.2	0	1	0.1	2.5	1090
33	12.5	1.9	0	0.2	0	1	770	102	10	7.7	0	1.1	0.01	3.1	1175
33	13.5	2.0	0	0.2	0	0.8	800	102	11	8.6	0	1.4	0	4.6	1251
66	5.5	1.5	0	0.2	0	0.3	580	102	12	9.6	0	1.3	0	3.2	1317
66	6	1.8	0.03	0.2	0.2	2.3	650	102	13	15.5	0.02	2	0.5	5.6	1368
66	7	2.5	0.04	0.3	0.3	1.6	770		**avg.**	**3.5**	**0.01**	**0.4**	**0.1**	**1.4**	**710.7**

In Table 4 results for class III instances are compared. The proposed method was compared with Gunawan's Adaptive ILS method (which achieved generally the best results among heuristics tested by them). Both versions of EVO are on average 1.7–2 percent better than Adaptive ILS and for most instances achieve optimal results or close to best known solutions (average gap 0.2–0.5 percent). EVO30 performance is generally slightly worse than EVO100 but it is about 1–1.5 percent worse than EVO100 for a few larger networks. Gunawan's heuristics had execution time limit of 1 second (this limit was also used in case of EVO30).

Table 4. Results for class III instances. Symbol d is discretization step (in minutes).

d	N	EVO100		EVO30		Ad.ILS	Best	d	N	EVO100		EVO30		Ad.ILS	Best
		Time	Gap	Time	Gap	gap	result			Time	Gap	Time	Gap	Gap	result
1	32	1.7	0	0.2	0.0	0.1 •	285	15	32	1.2	3.8	0.1	3.8	0	260
	21	0.8	0	0.1	0	0	450		21	0.6	0	0.1	0	2.5	405
	33	1.8	0	0.2	0	0.3	780		33	1.4	0.3	0.1	1.3	2.5	680
	100	16.4	0.1	1.0	0.6	8.4	1145		100	5.0	0.1	0.6	0.9	5.9	864
	66	6.7	0	0.8	0.2	1.0	1513		66	1.7	0	0.2	0	0.6	870
	64	7.9	0	0.8	0	0.5	1344		64	4.9	0	0.5	0.6	1.6	1254
	102	36.6	0.1	1.0	1.4	6.5	1372		102	9.3	0	1.0	0.5	4.5	1068
5	32	1.5	0	0.2	0	0	280	30	32	0.9	0	0.1	0.2	0	220
	21	0.7	0	0.1	0	2.2	450		21	0.5	0	0.0	0	0	355
	33	1.5	0	0.1	0	2.1	760		33	1.1	0	0.1	0	0	590
	100	9.3	0	1.0	0.6	7.6	1032		100	2.4	1.2	0.3	1.7	3.5	623
	66	3.2	0	0.4	0.3	1.0	1260		66	1.6	0	0.2	0	0.2	850
	64	6.1	0	0.6	0.5	2.9	1274		64	1.5	0	0.1	0	0	768
	102	14.4	0	1.0	1.5	6.8	1244		102	2.6	0.1	0.3	0.3	1.1	690
								avg.		**5.1**	**0.2**	**0.4**	**0.5**	**2.2**	**810.2**

6 Conclusions and Further Research

The experiments show that proposed evolutionary algorithm with memetic operators is an effective metaheuristic for the Time-Dependent Orienteering Problem (TDOP). The results obtained for TDOP benchmarks by the algorithm are optimal or close to optimal in most cases and are better than those obtained by other metaheuristics. Author's method, which was successfully used to tackle the classic Orienteering Problem (OP), achieved high quality results for TDOP benchmarks as well. Promising results suggest that proposed method should be adapted to other related problems. Therefore further research will concentrate on application of the algorithm for other problems from OP family i.e. variants with multiple paths (Team OP and Team TDOP) and with time-windows.

Acknowledgements. The author is grateful for support from the Polish Ministry of Science and Higher Education at the Bialystok University of Technology (S/WI/1/2014).

References

1. Tsiligirides, T.: Heuristic methods applied to orienteering. J. Oper. Res. Soc. **35**(9), 797–809 (1984)
2. Golden, B., Levy, L., Vohra, R.: The orienteering problem. Naval Res. Logistics **34**, 307–318 (1987)
3. Mahfoud, S.W.: Crowding and preselection revisited. In: Proceedings of the 2nd International Conference on Parallel Problem Solving from Nature (PPSN II), Brussels, Belgium, 1992, pp. 27–36, Elsevier, Amsterdam (1992)

4. Chao, I., Golden, B., Wasil, E.: Theory and methodology - a fast and effective heuristic for the orienteering problem. Eur. J. Oper. Res. **88**, 475–489 (1996)
5. Gendreau, M., Laporte, G., Semet, F.: A branch-and-cut algorithm for the undirected selective traveling salesman problem. Networks **32**(4), 263–273 (1998)
6. Gendreau, M., Laporte, G., Semet, F.: A tabu search heuristic for the undirected selective travelling salesman problem. Eur. J. Oper. Res. **106**, 539–545 (1998)
7. Fischetti, M., Salazar, J., Toth, P.: Solving the orienteering problem through branch-and-cut. Informs J. Comput. **10**, 133–148 (1998)
8. Tasgetiren, M.: A genetic algorithm with an adaptive penalty function for the orienteering problem. J. Econ. Soc. Res. **4**(2), 1–26 (2001)
9. Fomin, F.V., Lingas, A.: Approximation algorithms for time-dependent orienteering. Inf. Process. Lett. **83**, 57–62 (2002)
10. Vansteenwegen, P., Souffriau, W., Vanden Berghe, G., Oudheusden, D.V.: A guided local search metaheuristic for the team orienteering problem. Eur. J. Oper. Res. **196**(1), 118–127 (2009)
11. Schilde, M., Doerner, K., Hartl, R., Kiechle, G.: Metaheuristics for the biobjective orienteering problem. Swarm Intell. **3**, 179–201 (2009)
12. Hutter, F., Hoos, H.H., Leyton-Brown, K., Stutzle, T.: ParamILS: an automatic algorithm configuration framework. J. Artif. Intell. Res. **36**, 267–306 (2009)
13. Li, J.: Model and algorithm for time-dependent team orienteering problem. Commun. Comput. Inf. Sci. **175**, 1–7 (2011)
14. Vansteenwegen, P., Souffriau, W., Vanden Berghe, G., Van Oudheusden, D.: The city trip planner: an expert system for tourists. Expert Syst. Appl. **38**(6), 6540–6546 (2011)
15. Abbaspour, R.A., Samadzadegan, F.: Time-dependent personal tour planning and scheduling in metropolises. Expert Syst. Appl. **38**(10), 12439–12452 (2011)
16. Garcia, A., Vansteenwegen, P., Arbelaitz, O., Souffriau, W., Linaza, M.T.: Integrating public transportation in personalised electronic tourist guides. Comput. Oper. Res. **40**(3), 758–774 (2013)
17. Campos, V., Marti, R., Sanchez-Oro, J., Duarte, A.: Grasp with path relinking for the orienteering problem. J. Oper. Res. Soc. **156**, 1–14 (2013)
18. Koszelew, J., Ostrowski, K.: A genetic algorithm with multiple mutation which solves orienteering problem in large networks. In: Bădică, C., Nguyen, N.T., Brezovan, M. (eds.) ICCCI 2013. LNCS, vol. 8083, pp. 356–366. Springer, Heidelberg (2013). doi:10.1007/978-3-642-40495-5_36
19. Verbeeck, C., Sörensen, K., Aghezzaf, E.H., Vansteenwegen, P.: A fast solution method for the time-dependent orienteering problem. Eur. J. Oper. Res. **236**(2), 419–432 (2014)
20. Gunawan, A., Yuan, Z., Lau, H.C.: A mathematical model and metaheuristics for time dependent orienteering problem. Angewandte Mathematik und Optimierung Schriftenreihe AMOS 2014 (2014)
21. Ostrowski, K.: Comparison of different graph weights representations used to solve the time-dependent orienteering problem. Trends in Contemporary Computer Science, Podlasie 2014, pp. 144–154. Bialystok University of Technology Publishing Office (2014)
22. Zabielski, P., Karbowska-Chilinska, J., Koszelew, J., Ostrowski, K.: A genetic algorithm with grouping selection and searching operators for the orienteering problem. In: Nguyen, N.T., Trawiński, B., Kosala, R. (eds.) ACIIDS 2015. LNCS, vol. 9012, pp. 31–40. Springer, Cham (2015). doi:10.1007/978-3-319-15705-4_4

23. Gavalas, D., Konstantopoulos, C., Mastakas, K., Pantziou, G., Vathis, N.: Heuristics for the time dependent team orienteering problem: application to tourist route planning. Comput. Oper. Res. **62**, 36–50 (2015)
24. Ostrowski, K.: Parameters tuning of evolutionary algorithm for the orienteering problem. Adv. Comput. Sci. Res. **12**, 53–78 (2015)
25. Ostrowski, K., Karbowska-Chilinska, J., Koszelew, J., Zabielski, P.: Evolution-inspired local improvement algorithm solving orienteering problem. Ann. Oper. Res. (2016). doi:10.1007/s10479-016-2278-1

Optimalization of Parallel GNG by Neurons Assigned to Processes

Lukáš Vojáček[1]([✉]), Pavla Dráždilová[2], and Jiří Dvorský[2]

[1] IT4Innovations, VŠB - Technical University of Ostrava,
17. listopadu 15/2172, 708 33 Ostrava, Czech Republic
lukas.vojacek@vsb.cz

[2] Department of Computer Science, FEECS, VŠB - Technical University of Ostrava,
17. listopadu 15/2172, 708 33 Ostrava-Poruba, Czech Republic
{pavla.drazdilova,jiri.dvorsky}@vsb.cz

Abstract. The size, complexity and dimensionality of data collections are ever increasing from the beginning of the computer era. Clustering is used to reveal structures and to reduce large amounts of raw data. There are two main issues when clustering based on unsupervised learning, such as Growing Neural Gas (GNG) [9], is performed on vast high dimensional data collection – the fast growth of computational complexity with respect to growing data dimensionality, and the specific similarity measurement in a high-dimensional space. These two factors reduce the effectiveness of clustering algorithms in many real applications. The growth of computational complexity can be partially solved using the parallel computation facilities, such as High Performance Computing (HPC) cluster with MPI. An effective parallel implementation of GNG is discussed in this paper, while the main focus is on minimizing of interprocess communication. The achieved speed-up was better than previous approach and the results from the standard and parallel version of GNG are same.

Keywords: Growing neural gas · High-dimensional dataset · High performance computing · MPI

1 Introduction

The size and complexity of data collections are ever increasing from the beginning of the computer era, while the dimensionality of the data sets is rapidly increasing in recent years. Contemporary and especially future technologies allow us to acquire, store and process large high dimensional data collections. High dimensional data collections are commonly available in areas like medicine, biology, information retrieval, web analysis, social network analysis, image processing, financial transaction analysis and many others.

Clustering, considered the most important unsupervised learning problem, is used to reveal structures, to identify "natural" groupings of the data collections

K. Saeed et al. (Eds.): CISIM 2017, LNCS 10244, pp. 63–72, 2017.
DOI: 10.1007/978-3-319-59105-6_6

and to reduce large amounts of raw data by categorizing in smaller sets of similar items.

There are two main issues when clustering based on unsupervised learning, such as *Growing Neural Gas* (GNG) [9], is performed on vast high dimensional data collection:

1. The fast growth of computational complexity with respect to growing data dimensionality, and
2. The specific similarity measurement in a high-dimensional space, where the expected distance, computed by Euclidean metrics to the closest and to the farthest point of any given point, shrinks with growing dimensionality [2].

These two factors reduce the effectiveness of clustering algorithms on the above-mentioned high-dimensional data collections in many real applications.

The growth of computational complexity can be partially solved using the parallel computation facilities, such as *High Performance Computing* (HPC) cluster with MPI. Obviously, it is necessary to resolve technical and implementation issues specific to this computing platform. An effective parallel implementation of GNG is discussed in this paper, while the main focus is on minimizing of interprocess communication.

2 Artificial Neural Networks

2.1 Related Works

The methods based on Artificial Neural Networks (ANN) are highly computationally expensive. There are different approaches on how to improve effectivity of these methods. The one possibility is to improve computation. The authors of this paper [3] propose two optimization techniques that are aimed at an efficient implementation of the GNG algorithm internal structure. Their optimizations preserve all properties of the GNG algorithm. The first technique enhances the nearest neighbor search using a space partitioning by a grid of rectangular cells and the second technique speeds up the handling of node errors using the lazy evaluation approach.

The next possibility for how to improve effectivity methods based on ANN is parallelization. In the paper [4] the authors combine the batch variant of the GNG algorithm with the MapReduce paradigm resulting in a GNG variant suitable for processing large data sets in scalable, general cluster environments. The paper [16] is focused on the actualizations of neurons' weights in the learning phase of parallel implementation of SOM. There are two extremal update strategies. Using the first strategy, all necessary updates are done immediately after processing one input vector. The other extremal choice is used in Batch SOM – updates which are processed at the end of whole epoch and authors study update strategies between these two extremal strategies.

For parallelization is often use Graphics Processing Units (GPU). In the paper [1] authors present the results of different parallelization approaches to the

GNG clustering algorithm. They especially investigated the GPU and multi-core CPU architectures. Authors in the paper [12] explore an alternative approach for the parallelization of growing self-organizing networks, based on an algorithm variant designed to match the features of the large-scale, ne-grained parallelism of GPUs, in which multiple input signals are processed simultaneously. The paper [15] describes the implementation and analysis of a network-agnostic and convergence-invariant coarse-grain parallelization of the deep neural network (DNN) training algorithm. The coarse-grain parallelization is achieved through the exploitation of the batch-level parallelism. This strategy is independent from the support of specialized and optimized libraries. Therefore, the optimization is immediately available for accelerating the DNN training. The proposal is compatible with multi-GPU execution without altering the algorithm convergence rate.

2.2 Growing Neural Gas

The principle of this neural network is an undirected graph which need not be connected. Generally, there are no restrictions on the topology. The graph is generated and continuously updated by competitive Hebbian Learning [8,13]. According to the pre-set conditions, new neurons are automatically added and connections between neurons are subject to time and can be removed. GNG can be used for vector quantization by finding the code-vectors in clusters [7], clustering data streams [6], biologically influenced [14] and 3D model reconstruction [10]. GNG works by modifying the graph, where the operations are the addition and removal of neurons and edges between neurons.

To understand the functioning of GNG, it is necessary to define the algorithm. The algorithm described in our previous article [17] is based on the original algorithm [5,7], but it is modified for better continuity in the SOM algorithm. The description of the algorithm has been divided for convenience into two parts. Here is the Algorithm 1 which describes one iteration.

Remark. The notation used in the paper is briefly listed in Table 1.

3   Parallelization

In the paper [17] we have dealt with the parallelization of GNG. The following is a brief description of our parallelization algorithm.

After analysing the GNG learning algorithm we identified the one most time-consuming processor area. This part was selected as a candidate for the possible parallelization. The selected area are:

Finding BMU – this part of GNG learning can be significantly accelerated by dividing the GNG output layer into smaller pieces – distribution of neurons for effective parallelization. Each piece is then assigned to an individual computation process. The calculation of the Euclidean distance among the individual

Table 1. Notation used in the paper

Symbol	Description
M	Number of input vectors
n	Dimension of input vectors, number of input neurons, dimension of weight vectors in GNG output layer neurons
N	Current number of neurons in GNG output layer
N_{max}	Maximum allowed number of neurons in GNG output layer
n_i	i-th input neuron, $i = 1, 2, \ldots, n$
N_i	i-th output neuron, $i = 1, 2, \ldots, N$
e_{ij}	edge between neurons N_i and N_j for some $i, j = 1, \ldots, N$, where $i \neq j$.
E	set of all edges in GNG
G	undirected graph describing topology of GNG, $G(\{N_1, \ldots, N_N\}, E)$
t	Current epoch, $t = 1, 2, \ldots, T$
X	Set of input vectors, $X \subset \mathbb{R}^n$
$\boldsymbol{x}(t)$	Current input vector in epoch t, arbitrarily selected vector from set $X \boldsymbol{x}(t) \in X$, $\boldsymbol{x}(t) = (x_1, x_2, \ldots, x_n)$
$\boldsymbol{w_k}(t)$	Weight vector of neuron N_k, $k = 1, 2, \ldots, N \boldsymbol{w_k}(t) \in \mathbb{R}^n$, $\boldsymbol{w_k}(t) = (w_{1k}, w_{2k}, \ldots, w_{nk})$
N_{c_1}	The first Best Matching Unit (BMU_1), winner of learning competition
N_{c_2}	The second Best Matching Unit (BMU_2), the second best matching neuron in learning competition
$\boldsymbol{w_{c_1}}(t)$	Weight vector of BMU_1
$\boldsymbol{w_{c_1}}(t)$	Weight vector of BMU_2
l_{c_1}	Learning factor of BMU_1
l_{nc_1}	Learning factor of BMU_1 neighbours
e_i	Local error of output neuron N_i, $i = 1, 2, \ldots, N$
α	Error e_i reduction factor
β	Neuron error reduction factor
γ	Interval of input patterns to add a new neuron
a_{max}	Maximum edges age
a_{ij}	Age of edge e_{ij}
p	Number of processes
V_i	Set of neurons assigned to $Process_i$
V	Set of in the GNG

input vector and all the weight vectors to find BMU in a given part of the GNG output layer is the crucial point of this part of GNG learning. Each process finds its own partial BMU in its part of the GNG output layer. Each partial BMU is then compared with other BMUs obtained by other processes.

Algorithm 1. One iteration of the Growing Neural Gas algorithm

1. Find neurons BMUs neurons N_{c_1} and N_{c_2}.
2. Update the local error e_{c_1} of neuron N_{c_1}

$$e_{c_1} = e_{c_1} + \|w_{c_1} - x\|^2 \tag{1}$$

3. Update the weight vector w_{c_1} of neuron N_{c_1}

$$w_{c_1} = w_{c_1} + l_{c_1}(x - w_{c_1}) \tag{2}$$

4. For all neurons N_k where exists edge $e_{c_1 k}$ (N_{c_1} neighbourhood)
   (a) Update the weights w_k using l_{nc_1} learning factor

$$w_k = w_k + l_{nc_1}(x - w_k) \tag{3}$$

   (b) Increase age a_{kc_1} of edge $e_{c_1 k}$

$$a_{kc_1} = a_{kc_1} + 1 \tag{4}$$

5. If there is no edge between neurons N_{c_1} and N_{c_2}, then create such edge. If the edge exists, the age is set to 0.
6. If any edge has reached the age of a_{max}, it is removed.
7. If there is a neuron without connection to any edge, the neuron is then removed.
8. If the number of processed input vectors in the current iteration has reached the whole multiple of the value γ and the maximum allowed number of output neurons is not reached, add a new neuron N_{N+1}. The location and error of the new neuron is determined by the following rules:
   (a) Found neuron N_b(NBE) which has the biggest error e_b.
   (b) Found neuron N_c(NSE) among neighbours of neuron N_b and has the biggest error e_c among these neighbours.
   (c) Create a new neuron N_{N+1} and the value of w_n is set as:

$$w_{N+1} = \frac{1}{2}(w_b + w_c) \tag{5}$$

   (d) Creating edges between neurons N_b and N_{N+1}, and also between neurons N_c and N_{N+1}.
   (e) Removed edge between neurons N_b and N_c.
   (f) Reduction of error value in neurons N_b and N_c using the multiplying factor α. Error for neuron N_{N+1} is equal to the new error of neuron N_b.

Information about the BMU of the whole network is then transmitted to all the processes to perform the updates of the BMU neighbourhood.

Updates of weights – update weights of edges incident with N_{c1} it is quickly in the event that the neighboring nodes to N_{c1} are on a same process. This part can theoretically accelerate if we move adjacent nodes on a single process. Unfortunately, the transfer node for multidimensional data is very time consuming (test data have a dimension of 8000+).

A detailed description of our parallelization process is described in Fig. 1.

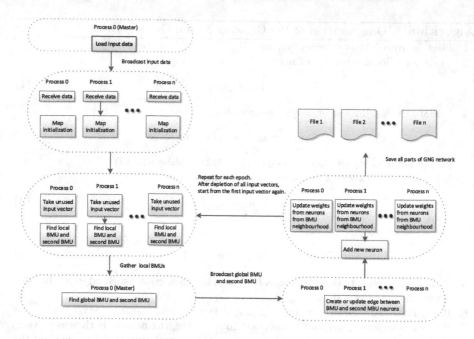

Fig. 1. Parallel algorithm

The parallelization of GNG learning was performed on an HPC cluster, using *Message Passing Interface* (MPI) technology. MPI technology is based on effective communication between processes. That means that one application can run on many cores. The application uses MPI processes which run on individual cores. The processes are able to send and receive messages and data, communicate etc. Detailed information about HPC and MPI technology is provided, for example, in [11].[1]

3.1 Distribution Neurons for Effective Parallelization

In the paper [17] we used Method 1 (the equal distribution of neurons), where new neurons are allocated to the process with the lowest number of neurons (see Fig. 2). The advantage of this distribution is constant workload processes. The disadvantage is increased communication between processes.

Our goal is to focus on reducing interprocessor communication by using the following methods for adding new neuron:

Method 2 The neurons are gradually added to the process, which currently does not contain a predetermined number of neurons ($\frac{N_{max}}{p}$). If one process is filled up so a new neuron is added to the next process (see Fig. 3).

---

[1] A specification of MPI is available on the web: http://www.mpi-forum.org/.

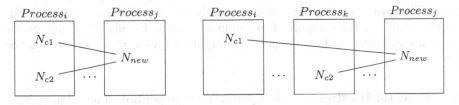

Fig. 2. Add the new neuron to the next free $Process_j$ by a cyclic way - Method 1.

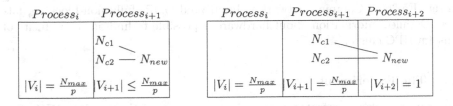

Fig. 3. Add the new neuron to the $Process_x$ by gradual way - Method 2.

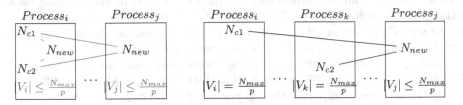

Fig. 4. Add the new neuron to the $Process_x$ where is N_{c1} or N_{c2} - Method 3.

Method 3 The start is similar to Method 1. If $|V_i| \geq 2 \; \forall i \leq p$ then add N_{new} to $Process_i$ where $(N_{c1} \in V_i$ and $|V_i| \leq \frac{N_{max}}{p})$ or add N_{new} to $Process_k$ where $(N_{c2} \in V_k$ and $|V_k| \leq \frac{N_{max}}{p})$ or add N_{new} to the next free $Process_j$ (see Fig. 4).

4 Experiments

4.1 Experimental Datasets and Hardware

One dataset was used in the experiments. The dataset was commonly used in Information Retrieval – *Medlars*.

Medlars Dataset. The Medlars dataset consisted of 1,033 English abstracts from a medical science[2]. The 8,567 distinct terms were extracted from the Medlars dataset. Each term represents a potential dimension in the input vector

---

[2] The collection can be downloaded from ftp://ftp.cs.cornell.edu/pub/smart. The total size of the dataset is approximately 1.03 MB.

space. The term's level of significance (weight) in a particular document represents a value of the component of the input vector. Finally, the input vector space has a dimension of 8,707, and 1,033 input vectors were extracted from the dataset.

Experimental Hardware. The experiments were performed on a Linux HPC cluster, named Anselm, with 209 computing nodes, where each node had 16 processors with 64 GB of memory. Processors in the nodes were Intel Sandy Bridge E5-2665. Compute network is InfiniBand QDR, fully non-blocking, fat-tree. Detailed information about hardware is possible to find on the web site of Anselm HPC cluster[3].

4.2   The Experiment

The experiment was oriented towards a comparison of the parallel GNG algorithm and parallel by modification by assignment to processes. The Medlars dataset was used for the experiment. A parallel version of the learning algorithm was run using 2, 8, 16, 24, 32 and 64 MPI processes. The records with an asterisk (*) represents the results for only one process i.e. this is the original serial learning algorithm and there is no network communication.

GNG parameters are the same for all experiments and are as follows $\gamma = 200$, $e_w = 0.05$, $e_n = 0.006$, $\alpha = 0.5$, $\beta = 0.0005$, $a_{max} = 88$, M $= 2021$, $\delta = 1500$. The achieved computing time is presented in Table 2.

Table 2. Computing time with respect to number of cores, standard GNG algorithm, dataset medlars

Cores	Computing time [mm:ss]		
	Method 1	Method 2	Method 3
1*	35:41		
4	09:36	10:28	10:41
8	06:59	06:25	06:52
16	05:53	06:18	06:37
24	07:29	05:33	05:35
32	07:42	07:13	07:17

As we can see from Table 2 and Fig. 5, the computing time depends on the number of used cores as well. With a growing number of processors, the computation effectiveness increases, and the computational time is sufficiently reduced (in the paper [17] we used Method 1).

---

[3] https://support.it4i.cz/docs/anselm-cluster-documentation/hardware-overview.

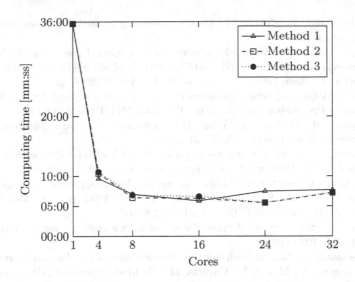

Fig. 5. Graph of computing time with respect to number of cores, standard GNG algorithm, dataset medlars

5   Conclusion

In this paper the parallel implementation of the GNG neural network algorithm is presented. The achieved speed-up was better than our previous approach. However, the effectiveness of a parallel solution is dependent on the division of the output layer. The authors introduced three different methods of neuron assignment to processes, where better acceleration for the new approaches was achieved. These approaches reached the best time but speed up is not too significant for the selected data set. Our methods are focusing on the different ways of assigning a new neuron in the GNG to processes for parallel computation.

In future work we intend to focus on the sparse date, use combinations of neural networks for improved result and improved acceleration.

Acknowledgement. This work was supported by The Ministry of Education, Youth and Sports from the Large Infrastructures for Research, Experimental Development and Innovations project "IT4Innovations National Supercomputing Center LM2015070" and by Grant of SGS No. SP2017/100 "Parallel processing of Big Data 4", VŠB-Technical University of Ostrava, Czech Republic.

References

1. Adam, A., Leuoth, S., Dienelt, S., Benn, W.: Performance gain for clustering with growing neural gas using parallelization methods. In: ICEIS, vol. 2, pp. 264–269 (2010)
2. Beyer, K., Goldstein, J., Ramakrishnan, R., Shaft, U.: When is "nearest neighbor" meaningful?. In: Database Theory 1999, vol. 1540, pp. 217–235 (1999)

3. FišEr, D., Faigl, J., Kulich, M.: Growing neural gas efficiently. Neurocomputing **104**, 72–82 (2013)
4. Fliege, J., Benn, W.: MapReduce-based growing neural gas for scalable cluster environments. In: Perner, P. (ed.) MLDM 2016. LNCS(LNAI), vol. 9729, pp. 545–559. Springer, Cham (2016). doi:10.1007/978-3-319-41920-6_43
5. Fritzke, B.: A growing neural gas network learns topologies. In: Advances in Neural Information Processing Systems 7, pp. 625–632. MIT Press (1995)
6. Ghesmoune, M., Lebbah, M., Azzag, H.: A new growing neural gas for clustering data streams. Neural Netw. **78**, 36–50 (2016)
7. Holmström, J.: Growing neural gas experiments with GNG, GNG with utility and supervised GNG. Master's thesis, Uppsala University, 30 August 2002
8. Martinetz, T.: Competitive hebbian learning rule forms perfectly topology preserving maps. In: Gielen, S., Kappen, B. (eds.) ICANN 1993, pp. 427–434. Springer, London (1993). doi:10.1007/978-1-4471-2063-6_104
9. Martinetz, T., Schulten, K.: A "neural-gas" network learns topologies. Artif. Neural Netw. **1**, 397–402 (1991)
10. Orts-Escolano, S., Garcia-Rodriguez, J., Serra-Perez, J.A., Jimeno-Morenilla, A., Garcia-Garcia, A., Morell, V., Cazorla, M.: 3D model reconstruction using neural gas accelerated on GPU. Appl. Soft Comput. **32**, 87–100 (2015)
11. Pacheco, P.: Parallel Programming with MPI, 1st edn. Morgan Kaufmann, Burlington (1996)
12. Parigi, G., Stramieri, A., Pau, D., Piastra, M.: A Multi-signal variant for the GPU-based parallelization of growing self-organizing networks. In: Ferrier, J.-L., Bernard, A., Gusikhin, O., Madani, K. (eds.) Informatics in Control, Automation and Robotics. LNEE, vol. 283, pp. 83–100. Springer, Cham (2014). doi:10.1007/978-3-319-03500-0_6
13. Prudent, Y., Ennaji, A.: An incremental growing neural gas learns topologies. In: Proceedings of the 2005 IEEE International Joint Conference on Neural Networks, IJCNN 2005, vol. 2, pp. 1211–1216 (2005)
14. Sledge, I., Keller, J.: Growing neural gas for temporal clustering. In: Proceedings of the 19th International Conference on Pattern Recognition, ICPR 2008, pp. 1–4 (2008)
15. Tallada, M.G.: Coarse grain parallelization of deep neural networks. SIGPLAN Not. **51**(8), 1:1–1:12 (2016)
16. Vojáček, L., Dráždilová, P., Dvorský, J.: Self organizing maps with delay actualization. In: Saeed, K., Homenda, W. (eds.) CISIM 2015. LNCS, vol. 9339, pp. 154–165. Springer, Cham (2015). doi:10.1007/978-3-319-24369-6_13
17. Vojáček, L., Dvorský, J.: Growing neural gas – a parallel approach. In: Saeed, K., Chaki, R., Cortesi, A., Wierzchoń, S. (eds.) CISIM 2013. LNCS, vol. 8104, pp. 408–419. Springer, Heidelberg (2013). doi:10.1007/978-3-642-40925-7_38

Methodology for the Development of Accessible User Interfaces Based on Meta-Model Transformations: The Case of Blind Users

Lamia Zouhaier[✉], Yousra Bendaly Hlaoui, and Leila Jemni Ben Ayed

Laboratory LaTICE Higher School of Sciences
and Technologies of Tunis University of Tunis, Tunis, Tunisia
zouhaier.lamia@yahoo.fr

Abstract. We propose a generic approach for the adaptation of user interfaces to the accessibility context. This approach is based on the Model-Driven Engineering MDE. Thus, we adapt any kind of UI to the accessibility context based on a generic adaptation process. We are based on meta-model transformations parametrized with the context of accessibility. The proposed approach generates modality-based UI adapted to each disability. We have developed an accessibility context related to the type of disability, the used platform, the user identity and his/her situation, the surrounded environment and modelled into ontology. The metamodel transformations were based on mapping rules implemented by the Kermeta language.

1 Introduction

The intelligent devices have enhanced the life of the humanity targeting all categories of users. These platforms vary considerably in their properties as the screen size, the resolution and the interaction devices [13]. That is why adapting a user interface (UI) for various user devices is still one of the most interesting topics. In addition, adapting an UI to the user's disability remains the most interesting problem of the accessibility of interactive systems. Users with disabilities usually experience barriers when they interact with UIs which are not adequately adapted to their needs [12, 24].

Unfortunately, no effective solution has been proposed considering the context of accessibility related to people with disabilities. This context is defined as a combination of the disability profile of the user, the physical environment of the used computing platform and the user mobility situation. Therefore, we have developed an accessibility context related to the user disability profile, the used platform, the user identity, his/her mobility situation and his/her surrounded environment [22].

In this paper, we present a generic approach for the adaptation of any type of UI to the user context of accessibility [24]. This solution has to be generic in order to allow the re-usability and to consider all kind of disability. Furthermore,

K. Saeed et al. (Eds.): CISIM 2017, LNCS 10244, pp. 73–84, 2017.
DOI: 10.1007/978-3-319-59105-6_7

instead of building an adaptation process for each given UI model, we develop a unique adaptation process getting as input the UI meta-model. To ensure this genericity, we are based on the Model Driven Engineering (*MDE*) [15].

Therefore and based on the MDE principals, our approach is defined of a series of meta-model transformations between different UI models. Thus, we propose a PIM (Platform Independent Model) to PIM transformation representing the abstract adaptation process which adapts any kind of UI model to the disability profile of current user. This transformation provides as output an adapted UI model to the user disability profile. To ensure the genericity of this process, we define all categories of user disability profiles with an ontology. As ontologies [2, 23] are used to specify and manipulate any kind of knowledge [22]. Hence, the proposed transformation are defined by a set of mapping rules between non adapted UI metamodel and adapted UI metamodel using the user accessibility profile ontology as a parameter. That is why, we have considered these mapping rules as adaptation rules.

Once the adapted UI is provided, we perform a PIM to PSM (Platform Specific Model) transformation. This transformation consists of a specific adaptation process of the user disability profile adapted UI model to provide an adapted UI model to the execution platform. This output is not only adapted to the given user disability profile but also is adapted to the interaction modalities of the used execution platform [25]. The interaction modalities (vocal, graphic, multimodal (vocal and graphic), tactile, gestural) depend on the kind of the user disability. This dependence is specified in our approach by a relationship between the user disability profile ontology and the technical context ontology. This relationship allows in the PIM to PSM transformation the right selection of the convenient and the effective mode of the interaction between the user with disabilities and their execution platform. In the PIM to PSM transformation, we have respected the accessibility norms such as the norm *WCAG2.0* [7, 10] and the norm *ISO 9241-171* [9] using their directives in our mapping rules [26].

The remainder of the paper is organized as follows. In Sect. 2, we provide an overview of some related works dealing with accessibility of UI. The third section is a description of the proposed approach. Section four is dedicated to focus on the adaptation process and the specific transformation. The fifth section is an illustration of the proposed approach and sixth one represents an evaluation of this approach. Finally, in the conclusion section, we present some concluding remarks and future work.

2   Related Works

Several MDE approaches [3, 4, 17, 18, 20] have been proposed in the adaptation of the UIs. They have considered, in their adaptation process, only the user preferences and the platform technical context without considering the user accessibility context.

Some of UI context adaptation approaches [1, 6] have considered the accessibility problem in their adaptation process. However, they have only addressed a limited number of disabilities.

SUPPLE [6] have proposed an automatic personalization of UIs suitable for people with motor and vision impairments. They have adapted the UIs to person's abilities, devices, preferences, and tasks.

EGOKI [1] is an automatic generator of accessible UIs allowing people with disabilities to access supportive ubiquitous services. EGOKI follows a model-based approach and selects suitable interaction resources and modalities depending on users? capabilities. The major limitation of these automated approaches is that they have applied the personalisation of UIs on specific prototypes. However, in our approach we adapt any kind of UI to any kind of user disability considering the execution platform modalities.

3   The Adaptation Approach of UIs to the Accessibility Context

We propose a *Generic Model-Driven Adaptation Approach based on the Context of Accessibility*. Hence, we adapt any kind of UI to the developed context of accessibility based on a series of parameterized meta-model transformations. The approach focuses on the use of *modality-transformation* as a key solution to suit the capacities of users with special needs. In fact, the employability of the multi-modality facilitates, firstly, the interaction of the disabled user with the UI and secondly with the platform capacities considering the accessibility context. Furthermore, we have fixed adaptation strategies for each type of disability in order to develop the target meta-models. In this paper, we will be limited only to the case of *blindness disability* which will be presented afterwards.

The proposed approach includes four principals phases:

Abstract modelling of the non adapted-UI using a Reverse Engineering technique
In this phase, we abstract the executed non-adapted UI from the implementation and the modality details by providing tan abstract UI non adapted model. This model (PIM-model) represents different abstract and structural elements composing the UI and their relationships.

This phase is based on two steps:

- **Step 1** is the extraction of the different elements and their relationships from the executable non adapted UI to build a *UI-tree* using YED tool [21]. The *UI-tree* is a graph of the structured *UI-elements* which facilitates the development of the *non adapted PIM-model*.
- **Step 2** is the development of the abstract UI model from the *UI-tree*. It transforms the *UI-tree* to an *UML class diagram model*. Each class of this model represents a *tree-node* which is an *UI-element*. The associations of the class diagram model describe the relationships existing between UI-elements represented as edges in the *UI-tree*. The resulted model is conformed to the non adapted UI meta-model.

This metamodel has to describe any type of UIs. It includes the information about the employed modalities (input, output) defined at the high level of abstraction.

Development of an ontology describing the context of accessibility
We have developed an ontology representing knowledge about all accessibility concepts such as the user disability profile, the user situations, the user profile, the technical context and the environment context. This ontology will serves as input for the adaptation process and the specific transformation of the approach. The ontology instances represent the captured real values of the current accessibility context.

Adaptation process of the non adapted-UI according to an instance of the accessibility context ontology
It represents the kernel of the approach. It ensures the adaptation of any type of UIs to any accessibility context. The adaptation process transforms the *Non Adapted UI Meta-model* to an *UI-Disability-meta-model* using a given accessibility context ontology instance. It provides an adapted UI model. It is a parametrized transformation.

Specific transformation of the *adapted UI-PIM* to a specific platform of execution
In this phase, we transforms the *adapted UI-PIM* provided from the adaptation process to a *PSM model* (*Modality-PSM*) depending on the modalities of the execution platforms.
    This phase includes two steps:

- **Step 1** is an exogenous transformation which represents the *PIM to PSM* transformation depending on the modality
- **Step 2** is an endogenous transformation which is the *PSM to PSM* transformation depending on the target platform web, desktop or mobile.

    Table 1 recapitulates different intervening source and target meta-models during the *PIM to PIM* and *PIM to PSM* transformations represented in Fig. 1. In this figure, we have only focused on the *PSM to PSM* transformation for the web platform.
    In this paper, we have considered only sensory impairments. We have been limited to blindness, low vision and deafness impairments. For each category, we have defined the corresponding target metamodel namely, *BlindnessAdaptedPIM*, *LowVisionAdaptedPIM*, *DeafnessAdaptedPIM* and *HardDeafnessAdaptedPIM* (Cf. Table 1).

4   The Metamodel Transformation

The meta-model transformation is based on a set of rules according to the set of the given disability values. These rules are divided into two types:

Table 1. Source and target Meta-models intervening during the PIM2PIM and PIM2PSM transformation

Transformation type	Source metamodel	Target metamodel
Transformation PIM2PIM	Non-AdaptedPIM-Metamodel	BlindnessAdaptedMetamodel DeafnessAdaptedMetamodel LowVisionAdaptedMetamodel HardDeafnessAdaptedMetamodel
Transformation PIM2PSM	BlindnessAdaptedMetamodel DeafnessAdaptedMetamodel LowVisionAdaptedMetamodel HardDeafnessAdaptedMetamodel	VocalPSM-Metamodel GraphicalPSM-Metamodel MultimodalPSM-Metamodel

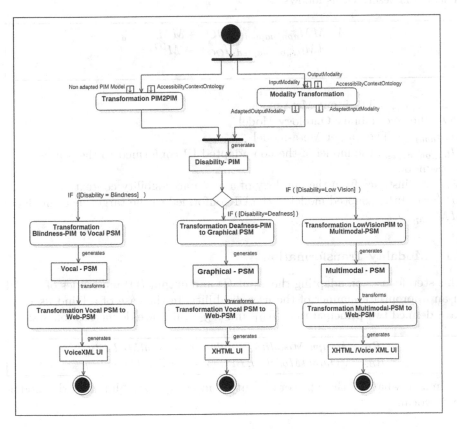

Fig. 1. Diagram of activity of the whole approach process from the adaptation process to the specific transformation cibling the web platform

- *Mapping rules*: are used to match an element from the source meta-model to its correspondent of the target meta-model.
- *Adaptation rules*: are used to structure the adapted UI model. In fact, during the adaptation process, these rules provide the UI framework of the correspondent element provided by the mapping rule. The UI framework is defined accordingly to the user disability context.

The specification of transformation rules is defined as follow:

> *For each Element E of* Source Metamodel, *match an element E′ from* Target Metamodel *based on an instance of the ontology representing a given accessibility context Instance(OO).*

To introduce the syntax of mapping rules, we defined the adaptation function A which is described as follows:

$$A : MM_{non_a dapted} \times OO \to MM_{adapted}$$
$$(M_{UI_n on_a dapted}, I_{OO}) \mapsto M^{UI_{adapted}}$$

$MM_{non_a dapted}$ The input Meta-model
OO: The Accessibility Ontology Model
$MM_{adapted}$: The Target Meta-model
$M_{UI_n on_a dapted}$: the model of the non adapted UI conformed to the source meta-model
I_{OO}: the instance from the ontology of a given accessibility context.
$M^{UI_{adapted}}$:the adapted model of the UI conformed to the target meta-model
$MM_{adapted}$

4.1 Modality Transformation

This step focuses on adapting the input (I) and output (O) modalities of the UI in an appropriate manner of the user disability. In the case of a blind user, we have defined two principal rules R_{B1} and R_{B2} which are defined as follows:

$$R_{B1} : A(InputModality, Blindness) = VocalModality$$
$$R_{B2} : A(OutputModality, Blindness) = VocalModality$$

In fact, whatever the input or the output modality, for a blindness, the modality is vocal.

4.2 Transformation PIM2PIM: Case of Blindness Disability

In this transformation, we use three strategies:

– **Strategy 1:** Since the problem of blind users is related to graphical elements of the UI and in order to offer perceptible elements for the her/him, we will adopt the vocal mode to represent the different type of elements of the adapted UI. Hence, each graphical element will be transformed to a vocal one. This will be done through mapping rules.

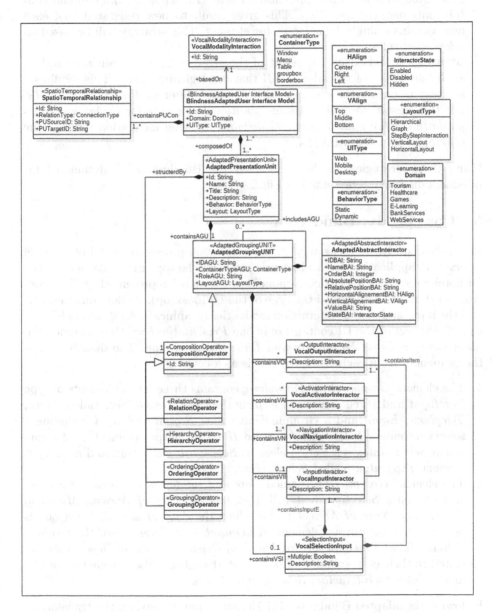

Fig. 2. Blindness-PIM-Metamodel specific to blindness disability

- **Strategy 2:** The use of vocal modality into a UI causes a disruption of the user's concentration and his attention. This problem occurs when the user is faced to fill out a form. For this purpose, we will minimize the number of input elements (*InputInteractor*)per grouping unit (*GroupingUnit*). Therefore, we propose to put only one *InputInteractor* in each grouping unit of type *GroupingUnit*. Each presentation unit (*PresentationUnit*) should contain only one *GroupingUnit*. This gives result to new generated UIs, each one contains a single *InputInteractor* element. This strategy will be based on *adaptation rules*.
- **Strategy 3:** Based on the result of the strategy 2, we obtain several *PresentationUNIT*s of the adapted UI that are logically linked. This requires a strategy to ensure the dialogue between these different *PresentationUNIT*s. For this reason, we will add some additional elements for navigation *NavigationInteractor* named *next* and *previous* allowing navigation between the different *PresentationUNIT*s.

Using these strategies, we have obtained the Blindness-PIM-Metamodel for blindness disability represented in Fig. 2.

5 Case Study: Blind User

In this case study, we focus only on the adaptation process of an UI of an hotel reservation application for a blind user using his laptop. Figure 3a depicts the UI hotel reservation and its corresponding PIM model represented by the Ecore [16]. To start, we determined the type of the UI (desktop), its domain (tourism) and the input and output interaction modalities (graphical). As shown in Fig. 3a, the PIM model of the UI contains only one *PresentationUnit* that includes two main *GroupingUnit*s *Formulaire* and *Date and validation*. The distribution of the elements within each *GroupingUnit* is as follows:

1. The element *GroupingUnit Formulaire* contains three input elements of type *TextInput* and three associated elements of type *TextOutput*: called *Name*, *Telephone*, *Email* and a GroupingUnit called *Region and hotel* including a selection element *SelectionInput* called *Hotel*, an output element *TextOutput* called *Select Hotel*, a selection element *SelectionInput region* and an output element *TextOutput* called *Select region*.
2. The element *GroupingUnit* named *Date and validation* contains three selection elements *SelectionInput* called as follows: *Day of Arrival, Month of Arrival* and *Year of Arrival* to introduce the date of arrival. Each one is associated to an output element *TextOutput*. It includes, also, three others *SelectionInput Day of departure, Month of Departure, Year of Departure* associated to their correspondent *TextOutput*. It contains also, two activator elements *ActivatorInteractor*: *Reserve* and *Cancel*.

Following the adapted Blindness PIM Metamodel and based on the transformation rules, the obtained result is the generation of adapted UIs represented into Fig. 3b, c, d. The result is generated by Kermeta language [14].

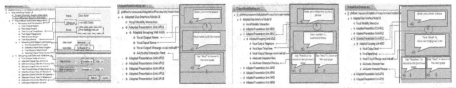

(a) Reservation hotel Non(b) UI-1: PresentationUNIT(c) UI-2: PresentationUNIT(d) UI-3: PresentationUNIT
adapted UI   1   2   3

Fig. 3. The adaptation of a partial from the Reservation Hotel UI (a) based on the metamodel transformation for blind users for generating several Presentation UNIT (b) UI-1, (c) UI-2, (d) UI-3, and others.

6   Evaluation, Results and Interpretation

To asses the results produced by our methodology, we have conducted an empirical study to improve the satisfaction of users with disabilities towards the proposed strategies and the interaction modalities. Users must express their real feeling and their comfort when interacting with adapted UIs. For that end, we have based on the interface UI-1 (see Fig. 3a). As apparatus, we have used a PC model $ASUSN56$ with a screen size $15,4$" set to 1920 by 1080 pixels resolution, with a $64bit$ color palette. The apparatus is equipped with a loud speaker that will be used for voice output and a microphone for voice input. To evaluate the usability of the approach, 42 participants are selected carefully to achieve the desired results where 12 participants are blind, 14 are visually impaired and 16 are deaf. The picked subjects have different skills (low, medium, high) on using computing platforms.

Two instrument were the basis of this empirical study:

- **System Usability Scale (SUS):** we have based on the standardized SUS questionnaire [11,19] to be filled by subjects. SUS is a reliable low cost usability scale used for global assessment of system's usability aiming to determine the level of user's satisfaction of the given system. It consists of 10 items [19] measuring two factors: the *usability* and the *learnability* [11]. The usability is described through 8 items which are $Q1$, $Q2$, $Q3$, $Q5$, $Q6$, $Q7$, $Q8$ and $Q9$. While the *learnability* is defined by the 2 items $Q4$ and $Q10$. Participants are asked to provide a $5-point$ scales numbered from 1 anchored with *"Strongly Disagree"* to 5 anchored with *"Strongly Agree"*.
- **Test Level Satisfaction:** This metric measures the relative satisfaction and preference among the *adapted UI-1* and the adapted interaction modalities that match better each disability. Each participant is asked to evaluate its satisfaction by providing a $7-point$ scales numbered from 1 anchored with *"Very Bad"* to 7 anchored with *"Excellent"*.

To estimate the reliability of the SUS questionnaire, we have used the coefficient **Cronbach's Alpha** [5] where the threshold of acceptability is 0.7. The results recapitulated in Table 2 show that the $SUS\ score = 73.92$ which represents a

Table 2. Reliability statistics

	N of items	Alpha's cronbach	SUS score	Std.dev
Usability	8	0.781	64.78	7.79
Learnability	2	0.592	9.14	4.14
Total	10	0.839	73.92	

good SUS score result. On the other hand, the value of the Alpha $\alpha = 0.839$ > 0.8 which represents good internal consistency among the items. Besides, considering the two factors usability and learnability, it represents a reasonable and acceptable reability in term of usability factor ($\alpha = 0.781$) however, it is considered a questionable scale for learnability factor ($\alpha = 0.592$).

Figure 4 represents the result of test level satisfaction performed by all participant considering their experience with computing platforms.

These results indicate that all users find that it is usable to use the system but it is difficult to learn rapidly how to interact with the UIs using the different interaction modalities. It should be noted that this problem is remarkable for blind users using vocal modality whereas those who are deaf and visually impaired encounter fewer difficulties using the graphic modality. The rate of satisfaction is high when users are experienced with the use of computing platform specifically deaf and visually impaired users.

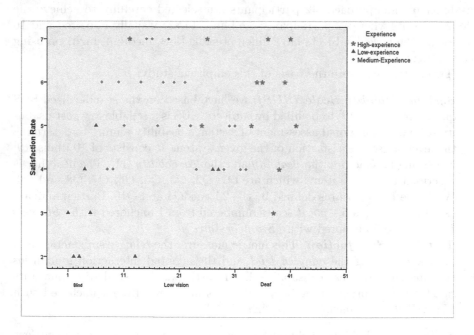

Fig. 4. Test level satisfaction

7   Conclusion

In this paper, we have presented an MDE approach for the generation of adaptable UIs considering the context of accessibility. The approach is based on meta-model transformations. Thus, we have defined a set of transformation rules (mapping and adaptation rules) for the different transformations. One case study has been described showing how this approach can support the adaptation process in the case of blind users. An empirical study has been conducted to evaluate the usability of the approach and the efficiency of the different developed meta-model transformations and their associated transformation rules. As future work, we would like to develop a graphical tool using the Eclipse Graphical Modeling Framework (GMF) [8] in order to easily draw UI models conforming to the proposed meta-models. We aims to make an automatic process of the whole approach.

References

1. Abascal, J., Aizpurua, A., Cearreta, I., Gamecho, B., Garay, N., Miñón, R.: A modular approach to user interface adaptation for people with disabilities in ubiquitous environments, in Internal Technical report No. EHU-KAT-IK-01-11 (2011)
2. Benaboud, R., Sahnoun, Z., Maamri, R.: User's preferences and experiences based web services discovery using ontologies. In: RCIS, pp. 121–126 (2010)
3. Brossard, A., Abed, M., Kolski, C.: Taking context into account in conceptual models using a Model Driven Engineering approach. Inf. Softw. Technol. **53**(12), 1349–1369 (2011)
4. Bouchelligua, W., Mahfoudhi, A., Benammar, L., Rebai, S., Abed, M.: An MDE approach for user interface adaptation to the context of use. In: Bernhaupt, R., Forbrig, P., Gulliksen, J., Lárusdóttir, M. (eds.) HCSE 2010. LNCS, vol. 6409, pp. 62–78. Springer, Heidelberg (2010). doi:10.1007/978-3-642-16488-0_6
5. Carricano, M., Poujol, F.: Analyse de données avec SPSS. Pearson Education France, Paris (2008)
6. Gajos, Z., Weld, D.S., Wobbrock, J.O.: Automatically generating personalized user interfaces with supple. Artif. Intell. **174**, 910–950 (2010)
7. Henry, S.H.: Web Content Accessibility Guidelines (WCAG) Overview (2012). http://www.w3.org/WAI
8. IBM, Eclipse Graphical Modeling Framework (GMF). http://www.eclipse.org/modeling/gmf
9. ISO: ISO 9241-171, Ergonomics of human-system interaction, Part 171: Guidance on software accessibility (2008)
10. ISO: ISO/IEC DIS 40500 Information technology, W3C Web Content Accessibility Guidelines (WCAG) 2.0 (TC/SC: JTC 1) (2012)
11. Lewis, J.R., Sauro, J.: The factor structure of the system usability scale. In: Kurosu, M. (ed.) HCD 2009. LNCS, vol. 5619, pp. 94–103. Springer, Heidelberg (2009). doi:10.1007/978-3-642-02806-9_12
12. Minon, R., Paterno, F., Arrue, M., Abascal, J.: Integrating adaptation rules for people with special needs in model-based UI development process. J. Univ. Access Inf. Soc. **15**, 153–168 (2015). Springer Verlag

13. Mitrovic, N., Bobed, C., Mena, E.: A review of user interface description languages for mobile applications. In: The Tenth International Conference on Mobile Ubiquitous Computing, Systems, Services and Technologies UBICOMM (2016)

14. Muller, P.-A., Fleurey, F., Jézéquel, J.-M.: Weaving executability into object-oriented meta-languages. In: Briand, L., Williams, C. (eds.) MODELS 2005. LNCS, vol. 3713, pp. 264–278. Springer, Heidelberg (2005). doi:10.1007/11557432_19

15. OMG, Model Driven Architecture (MDA), document number ormsc/2001-07-01 (2001)

16. OMG, EcoreTools - Graphical Modeling for Ecore. http://www.eclipse.org/ecoretools/

17. Oliveira, K., Bacha, F., Mnasser, H., Abed, M.: Transportation ontology definition and application for the content personalization of user interfaces. J. Expert Syst. Appl. **40**, 3145–3159 (2013)

18. Paternò, F., Santoro, C., Spano, L.D.: Model-based design of multi-device interactive applications based on web services. In: Gross, T., Gulliksen, J., Kotzé, P., Oestreicher, L., Palanque, P., Prates, R.O., Winckler, M. (eds.) INTERACT 2009. LNCS, vol. 5726, pp. 892–905. Springer, Heidelberg (2009). doi:10.1007/978-3-642-03655-2_98

19. Sauro, J.: Measuring usability with the System Usability Scale (SUS). https://measuringu.com/sus/(2011)

20. Thevenin, D.: Adaptation en interaction homme-machine: Le cas de la plasticité, Ph.D. thesis. Université Joseph Fourier, Grenoble, France (2001)

21. yEd Graph Editor.: (2016). https://www.yworks.com/products/yed

22. Zouhaier, L., Hlaoui Bendaly, Y., Jemni Ben Ayed, L.: Automatic generation of UIs for disabled users using context-aware techniques and reasoning. In: Proceedings of the 5th the International Conference on Knowledge Engineering and Ontology Development KEOD (2013)

23. Zouhaier, L., Hlaoui Bendaly, Y., Jemni Ben Ayed, L.: A global approach of accessible context-sensitive user interface. J. Data Process. **3**(1), 34–44 (2013)

24. Zouhaier, L., Hlaoui Bendaly, Y., Jemni Ben Ayed, L.: A model driven approach for improving the generation of accessible user interfaces. In: ICSOFT-PT (2015)

25. Zouhaier, L., Hlaoui Bendaly, Y., Jemni Ben Ayed, L.: Generating accessible multimodal user interfaces using MDA-based adaptation approach. In: COMPSAC (2014)

26. Zouhaier, L., Hlaoui Bendaly, Y., Jemni Ben Ayed, L.: A MDA-based approach for enabling accessibility adaptation of user interface for disabled people, In: Proceedings of the 16th International Conference on Enterprise Information Systems, ICEIS, pp. 120–127 (2014)

Biometrics and Pattern Recognition Applications

SVM Kernel Configuration and Optimization for the Handwritten Digit Recognition

Monika Drewnik[✉] and Zbigniew Pasternak-Winiarski

Faculty of Mathematics and Information Science, Warsaw University of Technology,
Koszykowa 75, 00-662 Warsaw, Poland
{m.drewnik,z.pasternak-winiarski}@mini.pw.edu.pl
http://www.mini.pw.edu.pl

Abstract. The paper presents optimization of kernel methods in the task of handwritten digits identification. Because such digits can be written in various ways (depending on the person's individual characteristics), the task is difficult (subsequent categories often overlap). Therefore, the application of kernel methods, such as SVM (Support Vector Machines), is justified. Experiments consist in implementing multiple kernels and optimizing their parameters. The Monte Carlo method was used to optimize kernel parameters. It turned out to be a simple and fast method, compared to other optimization algorithms. Presented results cover the dependency between the classification accuracy and the type and parameters of selected kernel.

Keywords: Support Vector Machines · Classification · Optical character recognition · Reproducing kernel

1 Introduction

The automated character recognition is the important part of the content extraction from handwritten documents. Multiple approaches were applied to this task so far. Many of them belong to the Artificial Intelligence (AI) domain. Advancement in computer technologies allows for introducing more computationally demanding approaches to the problem, being the sub domain of the pattern recognition methodology. Methods applied there include statistical approaches and Artificial Neural Networks (ANN) (see Ref. [19]). Because the particular characters are written differently by various people, any AI method should consider the uncertainty (various handwriting characteristics, noise, etc.). This way Support Vector Machines (SVM) (see Ref. [1]) or Fuzzy Logic (FL) (see Ref. [9]) gain importance. Both are considered as theoretically optimal classifiers in the uncertainty conditions. However, only the former approach is able to automatically learn from the available data sets. Therefore, it is often applied to the image and speech recognition (see Ref. [10]), or in the diagnostics of analog systems (see Ref. [5]).

The paper presents kernel-based learning methods used to the handwritten digits recognition. As the classifier, SVM were applied. The presented problem

© IFIP International Federation for Information Processing 2017
Published by Springer International Publishing AG 2017. All Rights Reserved
K. Saeed et al. (Eds.): CISIM 2017, LNCS 10244, pp. 87–98, 2017.
DOI: 10.1007/978-3-319-59105-6_8

is the classical pattern recognition task, aiming at categorizing objects of different types. In the presented research handwritten digits are analyzed and identified. As the same digit is written differently by various people (may be bolder or thicker, askew, etc.), the task requires sophisticated approaches for data processing. To correctly apply SVM to the task, the proper kernel with adjusted parameters must be used. Despite numerous approaches, this problem still is challenging for researchers. In this paper the systematic overview of kernel functions implementation (with optimized parameters) for the SVM classifier is performed.

The structure of the paper is as follows. Section 2 contains the problem statement and related work. Application of SVM to the classification of digits is described in Sect. 3. Section 4 contains experimental results, in which comparison of SVM kernels for classification is demonstrated, and where influence of the regularization coefficient on the classification accuracy are verified. Conclusions and directions for further research are presented in Sect. 5.

2   Problem Statement and Related Work

The handwritten digit recognition (Fig. 1) is a difficult task and attempts to solve it have been made since the seventies of the last century. The importance of the task is related with the writer identification, automated extraction of information from scanned papers and other applications.

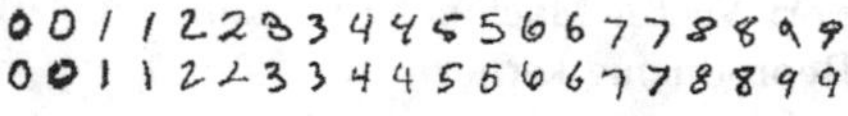

Fig. 1. Digits to recognize (see Ref. [10]).

Details of the considered problem are as follows:

In the text present on the scanned sheet of paper, analyzed characters are located. The task is to distinguish digits from all other symbols (including noisy components) and subsequently identify particular digits with the minimum sample error, defined as the percentage of incorrectly classified objects. In the numerical approach, the identification task requires introducing the separating hyperplane with the minimal error. As the subsequent digits may be similar to each other, their categories overlap, making flawless separation impossible. Formally, the following target function is to be minimized:

$$f(\varepsilon, w) = \frac{1}{2} \|w\|^2 + C \sum_{i=1}^{n} \varepsilon_i,$$

where:

ε_i- elements on the incorrect half of the separating hyperplane,

C- regularization coefficient,

w- the SVM weights vector. They must be adjusted so the error is minimal.

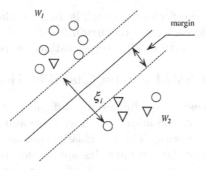

Fig. 2. Feature space with the margin of error (see Ref. [10]).

In such a case approaches considering the separation margin (with two weights of support vectors w_1 and w_2 in Fig. 2) are preferred.

The problem of the handwritten digits recognition has been extensively studied during the last few years, leading to more or less successful solutions. Methods used for this purpose belong to both image recognition and artificial intelligence domains (see Ref. [7]). To solve the task, three steps must be performed, all influencing the classification accuracy. These are selection of features, selection of the classifier and its optimization. The first problem leads to multiple sets of characteristic values describing the image, starting from pixel maps (see Ref. [20]) through the block wise histograms of local digit orientations (see Ref. [17]) and histogram-oriented gradients (see Ref. [8]), up to Freeman codes (see Ref. [3]), Zernike moments, Fourier descriptors or Karhunen-Loeve features (see Ref. [6]). The classifiers applied involve in most cases various types of Artificial Neural Networks (ANN), such as Multilayered Perceptron (MLP) (see Ref. [18]). Other approaches include the Random Forest (RF) (see Ref. [4]) or linear classifiers (see Ref. [16]).

Because of popularity and confirmed efficiency of SVM, they were used in the presented work. The main challenges involving their exploitation to the presented task are the classifier's optimization and its adjustment to available data to maximize the accuracy. To solve the problem, the proper kernel must be selected and its parameters adjusted. Presented works are usually based on the typical SVM kernels: Radial Basis Function (RBF), polynomial, linear and sigmoidal (see Ref. [8]). Additionally, minimum kernel was used (see Ref. [17]). In (Ref. [15]) the intersection kernel was introduced. Selection of kernel parameters often involves the designer's experience. Alternatively, optimization methods are used, such as simulated annealing (see Ref. [5]), Genetic Algorithm (GA) (see Ref. [11]) or Particle Swarm Optimization (PSO) (see Ref. [2]). Although ready-made solutions for particular problems are available, the procedures have to be repeated for every new analyzed object. This justifies searching for novel algorithms and their configuration. In the following work the original approach to the classifier optimization is presented. First, the wide set of kernels is applied, including multiple functions ensuring the potentially high accuracy of SVM.

Secondly, the Monte Carlo stochastic search is used to select kernel parameters. This approach is simple compared to currently applied algorithms, hopefully giving comparable results with smaller computational effort.

3   Application of SVM to the Classification of Digits

The SVM classifier is a useful tool for solving difficult real-world problems, performing well in uncertainty conditions (such as noise and inseparable examples belonging to different categories). This is a classical extension of neural networks, robust to noise and uncertainty in data. Its application requires solving multiple configuration problems, such as selection of the proper kernel and setting its parameters (depending on the particular kernel type). Although in the literature this problem was widely considered, there was no thorough investigation conducted for the handwritten digit recognition. This section contains information about SVM details required for the optimization of the identification process.

3.1   Description of Applied Kernels

In most computing environments (such as Matlab) and programming languages (such as Java), the SVM toolbox or library is present. It usually contains a couple of the most popular kernels (such as linear, RBF and polynomial), which proven their usefulness in multiple applications. Because many other functions can be used for this purpose, it is reasonable to apply them as well, in hope of increasing the classification accuracy. This section introduces all implemented functions with their parameters.

The introduced kernels (see Ref. [12]) were tested on both synthetic and real-world data sets. The first one is related with the binary XOR problem, while the second one consists of features extracted from optically scanned digits. This way it is twice verified if selected functions are capable of solving the linearly non-separable problem.

The exploited real-world set contains ten thousand examples, each with 76 attributes. Original data vectors contained 171 attributes, extracted from the black-and-white picture. They were first preprocessed to eliminate quasi-stationary features (i.e. the ones with the smallest variance). Then, 50 percent of remaining attributes were eliminated, giving 76 attributes processed by classifiers.

Mathematical description of kernels uses the following notation:
$\langle x, y \rangle = x^T y$ - scalar product,
$|x - y| = \sum_{i=1}^{n} |x_i - y_i|$ - the first norm,
$\|x - y\|^2 = \sum_{i=1}^{n} |x_i - y_i|^2$ - the second norm squared,
$\|x - y\|^d = \sum_{i=1}^{n} |x_i - y_i|^d$ - d norm to the power d.
The standard kernels widely used were tested:

– Linear - the simplest one with small computational requirements, not ensuring linear separability of objects in the original feature space. It is not parametrized.

$$K(x, y) = \langle x, y \rangle + c \tag{1}$$

- Radial basis function (RBF), being the fundamental positive-valued kernel, used because of usually high classification scores. Its parameter is the width of the Gaussian curve γ.

$$K(x, y) = exp\left(-\gamma \left\| x - y \right\|^2\right) \tag{2}$$

- Polynomial kernel is preferred for problems with normalized data. Its parameter is the polynomial degree d.

$$K(x, y) = (\gamma \left\langle x, y \right\rangle + c)^d \tag{3}$$

- The hyperbolic tangent (sigmoid) is applied as the activation function of ANN. The SVM with such a function is expected to have at least comparable (if not better) classification accuracy. Its parameter is the steepness of the curve γ.

$$K(x, y) = tanh\left(\gamma \left\langle x, y \right\rangle + c\right) \tag{4}$$

The calibration coefficient c determines the position of the kernel function in the feature space. It is initially set to 0.

Additional kernels were considered in experiments. Although they are well-known, their usefulness for the handwritten digit recognition was not verified so far. They are the following:

- The Laplacian kernel

$$K(x, y) = exp\left(-\gamma \left| x - y \right|\right) \tag{5}$$

is equivalent to the exponential one $K(x, y) = exp\left(-\frac{|x-y|}{2\gamma^2}\right)$, but is less susceptible to changes of the γ parameter.
- The sinc wave kernel (sinc) is symmetric and non-negative.

$$K(x, y) = sinc\left| x - y \right| = \frac{sin\left| x - y \right|}{\left| x - y \right|} \tag{6}$$

- The sinc2 kernel has characteristics similar to sinc.

$$K(x, y) = sinc\left\| x - y \right\|^2 = \frac{sin\left\| x - y \right\|^2}{\left\| x - y \right\|^2} \tag{7}$$

- The quadratic kernel is less computationally costly than the Gaussian one and should be applied when the training time is significant.

$$K(x, y) = 1 - \frac{\left\| x - y \right\|^2}{\left\| x - y \right\|^2 + c} \tag{8}$$

- The non-positive and definite multiquadratic kernel is applied in the same fields as the quadratic one.

$$K(x, y) = -\sqrt{\left\| x - y \right\|^2 + c^2} \tag{9}$$

– The inverse multiquadric kernel.

$$K(x,y) = \frac{1}{\sqrt{\|x-y\|^2 + c^2}} \tag{10}$$

– The log kernel is conditionally positive definite.

$$K(x,y) = -log\left(\|x-y\|^d + 1\right) \tag{11}$$

– The Cauchy kernel comes from the Cauchy distribution. It can be used in the analysis of multidimensional spaces.

$$K(x,y) = \frac{1}{1 + \frac{\|x-y\|^2}{c^2}} \tag{12}$$

– The generalized T-Student kernel has a positive semi-definite kernel matrix.

$$K(x,y) = \frac{1}{1 + \|x-y\|^d} \tag{13}$$

4   Experimental Results

The experiments consisted in training and testing the SVM with the selected kernel on the synthetic and real-world data. Parameters of each kernel were optimized to maximize the object classification accuracy. In the handwritten digit recognition task experiments were divided into two steps: optimization of kernel parameter with the constant regularization coefficient and optimization of the regularization coefficient for the optimal (previously determined) value parameter. Also, the real-world data (further called original set) was disturbed randomly to obtain object more difficult to identify (further called modified set). The data set was divided into the training L and testing T one in the 7:3 ratio. The division process was repeated ten times to ensure objectivity of the obtained results.

Processing of the XOR problem set was successful for most kernels. However, the 'minimum' $K(x,y) = \sum_{i=1}^{n} min(x_i, y_i)$ and the 'power' $K(x,y) = -\|x-y\|^d$ kernels failed to satisfactorily learn on this set. Below experimental results are presented.

4.1   Digit Identification

In Table 1, optimal results of the original data identification for the applied kernels are shown. All experiments were conducted for the constant regularization coefficient ($C = 16$). The column v represents the number of generated support vectors, a_L is the classification accuracy for the training set, while a_T is the accuracy on the testing set.

Table 1. Classification efficiency comparison between optimal kernel parameters.

No	Kernel	v	a_L	a_T
1	'laplacian' $\gamma = 0.01$	2649	1.0	**0.9647**
2	'minimum'	2078	1.0	**0.9607**
2	'power' $d = 1$	2078	1.0	**0.9607**
4	'quadratic' $c = 100$	2389	0.9994	**0.9580**
5	'cauchy' $c = 10$	2389	0.9994	**0.9580**
6	'multiquadric' $c = 5$	2026	1.0	**0.9573**
7	'rbf', $\gamma = 1/n$	2349	0.9997	**0.9557**
8	'log' $d = 1$	4415	1.0	0.9553
9	'inversemultiquadric' $c = 5$	3016	0.9963	0.9550
10	'poly', $d = 1$	1355	0.9777	0.9490
11	'linear'	1066	0.9946	0.9400
12	'tstudent' $d = 1$	6830	1.0	0.9064
13	'sinc2'	6998	1.0	0.2063
14	'sinc'	6998	1.0	0.1793
15	'sigmoid'	6926	0.1136	0.1133

Rows in bold refer to kernel configurations giving better classification results than the reference RBF kernel. Large number of support vectors suggests over-learning, which is confirmed by the low classification score for the testing set T. In such a situation the SVM efficiency for the training set is high (usually close to 100 percents), but performance on the testing set is much lower. The Gaussian function with the $\gamma = \frac{1}{n}$ is the best of all standard function. However, the Laplacian kernel with the $\gamma = 0.01$ coefficient outperforms it, which justifies its usage. In general, smaller values of kernel parameters usually give better classification results. This is because the separating hyperplane is relatively simple and has better generalization abilities.

Random modification of the original data set consisted in disturbing the selected number of features. Each one was changed by adding the value up to ± 10 percent of the original value. The process was repeated for three, ten, twenty and all 76 features, obtaining four versions of the modified set, respectively T_3, T_{10}, T_{20} and T_{76}. In Table 2 results of classification for different kernels (with optimized parameters) on the modified set are presented.

Change in three randomly selected attributes in general does not influence the classification accuracy. The SVM is able to select other features, for which distinguishing between digits is still possible. Classification results are then identical as for original sets. Again, the Laplacian kernel (with $\gamma = 0.01$) is globally the best for modified data sets. On the other hand, the sigmoidal kernel has the lowest accuracy. Results for the minimum and power kernels are identical,

Table 2. Comparison of optimal kernel configurations efficiency to modified data sets.

No	Kernel	a_{T_3}	$a_{T_{10}}$	$a_{T_{20}}$	$a_{T_{76}}$
1	'laplacian'	0.9647	0.9627	0.9540	0.0893
2	'minimum'	0.9607	0.9587	0.9394	0.0893
2	'power'	0.9607	0.9587	0.9394	0.0893
4	'quadratic'	0.9580	0.9547	0.9160	0.0893
4	'cauchy'	0.9580	0.9547	0.9160	0.0893
6	'multiquadric'	0.9573	0.9510	0.9104	0.0893
7	'rbf'	0.9557	0.9527	0.9150	0.0893
8	'log'	0.9553	0.9540	0.9494	0.0893
9	'inversemultiquadric'	0.9550	0.9553	0.9254	0.0893
10	'poly'	0.9490	0.9414	0.8767	0.0899
11	'linear'	0.9400	0.9254	0.8311	0.1006
12	'tstudent'	0.9064	0.9057	0.8950	0.0893
13	'sinc2'	0.2063	0.2146	0.2079	0.1099
14	'sinc'	0.1793	0.1846	0.1603	0.1173
15	'sigmoid'	0.1133	0.1133	0.1133	0.1133

regardless of the applied data sets. The same is for the quadratic (with $c = 100$) and Cauchy (with $c = 10$) kernels.

In most of kernel functions, disturbance in the attributes' values decreases the classification accuracy. On the other hand, in some cases (like sinc and sinc2 kernels) the operation slightly increases the classification accuracy. For the sigmoidal function, the classification accuracy remains unchanged (and still too low to be considered in practice).

4.2 Influence of the Regularization Coefficient on the Classification Accuracy

In this experiment, we checked the relation between the penalty parameter C and the error term, and how the regularization coefficient influences results. The selected values were used to measure the influence of C on the digit classification accuracy. Measurements were conducted for $C = 5, 10, 15, 16, 17, 20, 30$. In Table 3 results of the classification for different kernels (with optimized parameters) for the regularization coefficient $C = 10$ are presented.

For the majority of kernels (without linear and inversemultiquadric kernels) the regularization coefficient $C = 10$ leads to the best results of classification. However, the original value (i.e. $C = 16$) gives the multiquadratic kernel advantage over the RBF. Again, results for the minimum and power kernels are identical, regardless the regularization coefficient. The same is for the quadratic and Cauchy kernels. For all cases, the regularization coefficient C, the Laplacian

Table 3. Classification efficiency comparison for parameters C.

No	Kernel	C	v	a_L	a_T
1	'laplacian' $\gamma = 0.01$	$C = 10$	2644	1.0	**0.9647**
2	'minimum'	$C = all$	2078	1.0	**0.9607**
2	'power' d = 1	$C = all$	2078	1.0	**0.9607**
4	'quadratic' c = 100	$C = 10$	2383	0.9989	**0.9587**
4	'cauchy' c = 10	$C = 10$	2383	0.9989	**0.9587**
6	'rbf', $\gamma = 1/n$	$C = 10$	2349	0.9989	**0.9580**
7	'multiquadric' c = 5	$C > 9$	2026	1.0	0.9573
8	'inversemultiquadric' c = 5	$C = 30$	3038	0.9994	0.9567
9	'log' d = 1	$C = all$	4415	1.0	0.9553
10	'poly', d = 1	$C = 10$	1419	0.9731	0.9500
11	'linear'	$C = 5$	1088	0.9924	0.9414
12	'tstudent' d = 1	$C = all$	6830	1.0	0.9064
13	'sinc2'	$C = all$	6998	1.0	0.2063
14	'sinc'	$C = all$	6998	1.0	0.1793
15	'sigmoid'	$C = all$	6926	0.1136	0.1133

kernel (with $\gamma = 0.01$) is globally the best. It is the most likely related with dimensions of feature space after the kernel transformation. In the case when the same results were obtained by two different kernels (for instance, minimum and power with d = 1, or quadratic with c = 100 and Cauchy for c = 10), the transformation is virtually identical. For some kernels (sigmoidal, sinc, sinc2, log, tstudent, power, minimum) the regularization coefficient C did not influence results of classification (for all values of C, identical outcomes were obtained).

4.3   Optimization of Kernels' Parameters

The standard operation during the classifier configuration is the kernel parameters' configuration. Multiple heuristic algorithms exist, useful for this purpose (see Refs. [13,14]).

Firstly, we chose parameters of all kernels intuitively. The obtained results are in Tables 4 and 5.

Secondly, in the presented research the relatively simple Monte Carlo approach was exploited. It consists in the repeated random selection of values from the predefined range according to the selected probability distribution. This approach is effective for optimization of the single parameter, faster than, for instance, simulated annealing of the evolutionary algorithm. Kernel parameters were selected according to the uniform distribution and the range of values adjusted for each kernel individually. The optimization was implemented with the constant value of the regularization coefficient ($C = 16$). The obtained results

Table 4. Results of the SVM classification for various configurations of the rbf kernel.

No	Parameter γ	v	a_L	a_T
1	$\gamma = 1/n$	2349	0.9997	**0.9557**
2	$\gamma = 0.001$	1880	0.9681	0.9497
3	$\gamma = 0.01$	2143	0.9990	0.9553
4	$\gamma = 0.25$	6819	1.0	0.5875
5	$\gamma = 0.5$	6994	1.0	0.3442
6	$\gamma = 1$	6998	1.0	0.1160
7	$\gamma = 2(= 10, 100)$	6998	1.0	0.1133

Table 5. Results of the SVM classification for various configurations of the Laplacian kernel.

No	Parameter γ	v	a_L	a_T
1	$\gamma = 0$	6926	0.1136	0.1133
2	$\gamma = 0.0001$	3903	0.9464	0.9330
3	$\gamma = 0.001$	2279	0.9860	0.9590
4	$\gamma = 0.005$	2366	1.0	0.9637
5	$\gamma = 0.01$	2649	1.0	**0.9647**
6	$\gamma = 0.1$	5823	1.0	0.9190
7	$\gamma = 0.25$	6995	1.0	0.5388
8	$\gamma = 0.5(= 1)$	6998	1.0	0.1133

for kernels with similar ranges of the parameter (i.e. RBF and Laplacian) are presented in Fig. 3. In both cases, similar behavior of the function for changed values can be observed. The Laplacian kernel is better in the whole range, its maximal classification outcome was obtained for the $\gamma = 0.01$ coefficient.

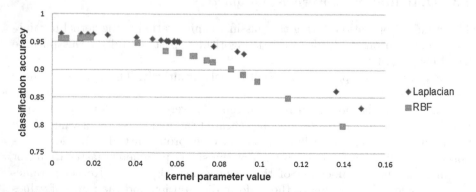

Fig. 3. Results of the SVM classification for various configurations of the Laplacian kernel and the RBF kernel.

5   Conclusions

The paper presented application of the SVM classifier tree to the identification of the handwritten digits in the presence of noise. The standard configuration of the multi-class SVM classifier was used for the task of the digit identification. Experiments with multiple kernels showed that although the most popular Gaussian function performs properly, other choices, such as the Laplacian kernel may perform even better. The processed data sets are easy to classify, as the performance of SVM for most kernels is above 90 percent. The best outcomes were obtained for kernel parameters selected according to the Monte Carlo approach. It gives comparable results to other methods, such as the simulated annealing (see Ref. [5]) or the evolutionary approach), presenting greater simplicity. The disadvantage of the presented approach is overlearning, observed for most kernels. This is the effect of excessive adjusting the classifier to the training data, leading to the low generalization ability. Future research require introducing more real-world data to verify the SVM performance against samples of digits produced by various groups of people (children, disabled, etc.). The amount of available data for the classifier training influences its efficiency. The open question is, what is the minimal amount of training samples, ensuring the maximum classification accuracy. Also, implementation of additional kernels for the symbol classification would be advisable.

References

1. Abbas, N., Chibani, Y., Nemmour, H.: Handwritten digit recognition based on a DSmT-SVM parallel combination. In: International Conference on Frontiers in Handwriting Recognition (ICFHR), Bari, 18–20 September, pp. 241–246 (2012)
2. Ardjani, F., Sadouni, K.: Optimization of SVM multiclass by particle swarm (PSO-SVM). I.J. Modern Educ. Comput. Sci. **2**, 32–38 (2010)
3. Bernard, M., Fromont, E., Habbard, A., Sebban, M.: Handwritten digit recognition using edit distance-based KNN. In: Teaching Machine Learning Workshop, Edinburgh, Scotland, United Kingdom (2012)
4. Bernard, S., Heutte, L., Adam, S.: Using random forests for handwritten digit recognition. In: Proceedings of the 9th IAPR/IEEE International Conference on Document Analysis and Recognition ICDAR 2007, Curitiba, Brazil, pp. 1043–1047, September 2007
5. Bilski, P.: Automated selection of kernel parameters in diagnostics of analog systems. Przegląd Elektrotechniczny **87**(5), 9–13 (2011)
6. Van Breukelen, M., Duin, R., Tax, D., Den Hartog, J.E.: Handwritten digit recognition by combined classifiers. Kybernetika **34**(4), 381–386 (1998)
7. Liu, C.L., Nakashima, K., Sako, H., Fujisawa, H.: Handwritten digit recognition: benchmarking of state-of-the-art techniques. Pattern Recogn. **36**(10), 2271–2285 (2003)
8. Ebrahimzadeh, R., Jampour, M.: Efficient handwritten digit recognition based on histogram of oriented gradients and SVM. Int. J. Comput. Appl. (0975-8887) **104**(9), 10–13 (2014)

9. Hanmandlu, M., Chakraborty, S.: Fuzzy logic based handwritten character recognition. In: International Conference on Image Processing, vol. 3, Thessaloniki, Greece, pp. 42–45 (2001)

10. Homenda, W., Jastrzębska, A., Pedrycz, W.: Rejecting foreign elements in pattern recognition problem: reinforced training of rejection level. In: Proceedings of the ICAART 2015, 7th International Conference on Agents and Artificial Intelligence, Lisbon, Portugal, 10-12 January, pp. 90–99. SciTePress - Science and Technology Publications (2015). ISBN: 978-989-758-073-4

11. Huang, C.L., Wang, C.J.: A GA-based feature selection and parameters optimization for support vector machines. Expert Syst. Appl. **31**, 231–240 (2006)

12. Kernel Functions for Machine Learning Applications. http://crsouza.blogspot.com/2010/03/kernel-functions-for-machine-learning.html

13. LeCun, Y., Jackel, L., Bottou, L., Brunot, A., Cortes, C., Denker, J., Drucker, H., Guyon, I., Müller, U., Säckinger, E., Simard, P., Vapnik, V.: A comparison of learning algorithms for handwritten digit recognition. In Fogelman, F., Gallinari, P. (eds.) Proceedings of the 1995 International Conference on Artificial Neural Networks (ICANN 1995), Paris, pp. 53–60 (1995)

14. LeCun, Y., Jackel, L., Bottou, L., Brunot, A., Cortes, C., Denker, J., Drucker, H., Guyon, I., Müller, U., Säckinger, E., Simard, P., Vapnik, V.: Comparison of classifier methods: a case study in handwritten digit recognition. In: Proceedings of the 12th International Conference on Pattern Recognition and Neural Networks, Jerusalem (1994)

15. Maji, S., Berg, A.C., Malik, J.: Classification using intersection kernel support vector machines is efficient. In: IEEE Conference on Computer Vision and Pattern Recognition, CVPR 2008, pp. 1–8, June 2008

16. Maji, S., Berg, A.C.: Max margin additive classifiers for detection. In: Proceedings of International Conference on Computer Vision (2009)

17. Maji, S., Malik, J.: Fast and accurate digit classification. Technical report No. UCB/EECS-2009-159, 25 November 2009

18. Shah, F.T., Yousaf, K.: Handwritten digit recognition using image processing and neural networks. In: Proceedings of the World Congress on Engineering, WCE 2007, vol. I, London, U.K., 2–4 July 2007

19. Shah, P., Karamchandani, S., Nadkar, T., Gulechha, N.: OCR-based chassis-number recognition using artificial neural networks. In: IEEE International Conference on Vehicular Electronics and Safety (ICVES), Pune, 11–12 November, pp. 31–34 (2009)

20. Wilder, K.: http://oldmill.uchicago.edu/~wilder/Mnist/

Object Classification Using Sequences of Zernike Moments

Aneta Górniak[(✉)] [iD] and Ewa Skubalska-Rafajłowicz[(✉)] [iD]

Wrocław University of Science and Technology, Wrocław, Poland
{aneta.gorniak,ewa.skubalska-rafajlowicz}@pwr.edu.pl

Abstract. In this paper we propose a method of object classification based on the sequences of Zernike moments. The method makes use of the pattern recognition properties of Zernike moments and expands it to the problem of classification. Since the distinctive features of the classified objects are carried over to the Zernike moments, the proposed method allows for a robust, rotation and translation invariant classification of complex objects in grayscale images. In this approach, each object class has defined a reference Zernike moment sequence that is used as the prototype of the class. The object's affiliation to the class is decided with the MSE criterion calculated for the object's Zernike moments sequence and the reference Zernike moments sequence of the class. The method is tested using grayscale images of handwritten digits and microscopic sections.

Keywords: Image processing · Microscopic image · Object matching · Classification · Zernike moments

1 Introduction

Image recognition is considered one of the main branches of image processing. It may pertain to such fields as pattern recognition and analysis or image description and finds application in many fields of study including medicine, astronomy, digital communication technologies, military industry and many more [11].

The core problem of image recognition lies within recognition of objects and characters regardless of their position, size and orientation in the image. Through the space of time many methods of image recognition were proposed. One of the approaches dedicated to solving this problem, and which is the focus of this paper, revolves around the application of geometrical moments and orthogonal polynomials [11]. Moments have a history of being used in image matching, recognition and classification [5,8,13]. They serve such purposes as feature detection, feature description or feature extraction [2]. One of the more explored variants of this approach involves the use of Zernike polynomials as the basis function in these moments [2,7,9,10].

Zernike moments were originally introduced in the 1930s by physicist and Noble prize winner Fritz Zernike to describe optical aberrations.

© IFIP International Federation for Information Processing 2017
Published by Springer International Publishing AG 2017. All Rights Reserved
K. Saeed et al. (Eds.): CISIM 2017, LNCS 10244, pp. 99–109, 2017.
DOI: 10.1007/978-3-319-59105-6_9

Because of the orthogonal radial polynomials used as the basis of Zernike moments, the moments do not contain redundant information [10]. Zernike moments are known to be translation, rotation and scale invariant [3,6,7,12]. It is possible to reconstruct an image from the set of Zernike moments [11]. The number of details in the reconstructed image and the resemblance to the original image depend on the level of the order used in the reconstruction process. For the low-order Zernike moments describe the general shape of the image, while the high-order Zernike moments cover more detailed aspects of the image [10].

Nowadays, Zernike moments are used in image shape feature extraction and description or content-based image retrieval [10], the region-based matching [2]. The more specific cases cover matching and recognition of characters and objects [7] or human faces [1], emblem detection and retrieval [4].

In this paper we propose a method of object classification based on the sequence of Zernike moments. Since it has been shown that Zernike moments can be successfully applied to pattern recognition, we chose to expand that property and apply it in the field of classification. The proposed method is based on the notion that the absolute value of Zernike moments of a given order will have an approximate value for similar-looking objects. Having the value of a Zernike moment at the span of a certain number of order levels allows for the construction of a Zernike moment sequence with a distinguished value pattern shared between objects of a similar shape.

The paper is organized as follows. Section 2 contains the necessary definitions of complex Zernike moments and Zernike polynomials. Section 3 shows Zernike moments as image descriptors and how they are applied in the construction of a Zernike moment sequence. Section 4 provides the description to the proposed method of classification using the sequences of Zernike moments. Section 5 describes the applied classification experiments and the data used in those experiments. Finally, in Sect. 6, we present a brief conclusion to the paper.

2   Zernike Moments

The basis of a complex Zernike moment is a set of Zernike complete orthogonal polynomials defined over the interior of the unit disc in the polar coordinate space, i.e., $x^2 + y^2 = 1$ [11]. Let us denote the set of Zernike polynomials as $V_{nm}(x,y)$ and defined with

$$V_{nm}(x,y) = V_{nm}(\rho,\theta) = R_{nm}(\rho)\exp(jm\theta). \qquad (1)$$

The Zernike polynomial is split into the real part R_{nm} (the radial polynomial) and the complex part $\exp(jm\theta)$. In this equation n is a positive integer and m is a positive (and negative) integer subjected to constraints

$$m \in \{0, \pm 1, \ldots, \pm |n| \quad | \quad n - |m| \quad \text{even}\}, \qquad (2)$$

ρ is the length of vector from origin to (x,y) pixel, θ is an angle between vector ρ and x-axis in a counter-clockwise direction. The radial polynomial R_{nm} is defined as

$$R_{nm}(\rho) = \sum_{s=0}^{(n-|m|)/2} (-1)^s \frac{(n-s)!}{s!(\frac{n+|m|}{2}-s)!(\frac{n-|m|}{2}-s)!}\rho^{n-2s}, \qquad (3)$$

where $R_{nm}(\rho) = R_{n(-m)}(\rho)$.

Let $f(x,y)$ be the continuous image intensity function. The two-dimensional complex Zernike moment of order n and repetition m is defined as

$$A_{nm} = \frac{n+1}{\pi} \int_x \int_y f(x,y)[V_{nm}(x,y)]^* dx dy \qquad (4)$$

where $[V_{nm}(x,y)]^*$ is the complex conjugate of Zernike polynomial $V_{nm}(x,y)$ that follows $[V_{nm}(x,y)]^* = V_{n(-m)}(x,y)$.

For the computer digital image, let us denote the intensity of the image pixel as $I(x,y)$, so the Eq. (4) can be represented as

$$A_{nm} = \frac{n+1}{\pi} \sum_x \sum_y I(x,y)[V_{nm}(x,y)]^* \qquad (5)$$

Having all moments A_{nm} of the image function $f(x,y)$ up to the given order of n_{max} it is possible to reconstruct a discrete function $\hat{f}(x,y)$ with matching moments A_{nm} [7]

$$\hat{f}(x,y) \approx \sum_{n=0}^{n_{max}} \sum_m A_{nm} V_{nm}(\rho,\theta) \qquad (6)$$

where m is the subject to the same constraints as in Eq. (2).

3   Image Description with the Use of Zernike Moments

Each image can be represented with a sequence of Zernike moments A_{nm}

$$\{A_{0,0}, A_{1,1}, A_{2,0}, A_{2,2}, \ldots, A_{n_{max},m}\}, \qquad (7)$$

where $n = 0, \ldots n_{max}$ and m is subject to usual constraints (2).

Each moment carries a different piece of information pertaining to the image. A fair number of Zernike moments allows for a detailed image characteristic and the focus on some moments allows for the characteristic of a singular image feature. It is important to note that the number of Zernike moments affects the quality of image reconstruction and shows the way the number of moments may influence the general image characteristics [10].

We used the respective moments A_{nm} for $n = 0, \ldots, n_{max}$ to construct the image characteristic. Since moments A_{nm} are dependent on the values of n and m, thus they cannot be unequivocally ordered in a linear manner. Therefore to simplify the image description the moments were grouped by ascending order n following

$$A_n = \sum_m A_{nm}. \qquad (8)$$

where m is (2). Since our goal is to have a descriptor that is rotation and translation invariant we used the absolute values of subsequent moments A_n, thus the final sequence is of the form

$$\{|A_1|, |A_2|, \ldots, |A_{n_{max}}|\}. \tag{9}$$

In the final image description we skipped the value of A_0.

4   Applying Zernike Moments to Image Classification

We assume that the images belonging to the same group of objects will share similar features (Eq. 9). The notion allows for the construction of a referential Zernike moment sequence for a class of images and may allow for image classification based on this sequence (prototype of the class).

The referential sequence (class prototype - cp) constructed for the class k of images was obtained as a mean value of all Zernike moment sequences for a given class k

$$cp_k = \{\frac{1}{N} \sum_{i=1}^{N} |A_1^i|, \frac{1}{N} \sum_{i=1}^{N} |A_2^i|, \ldots, \frac{1}{N} \sum_{i=1}^{N} |A_{n_{max}}^i|\} \tag{10}$$

where k is the index of the class, N is the number of images used in building of the reference and A_n^i is the value of the Zernike moment of order n of the image i in the series where $i = 1, \ldots, N$ and $n = 1, \ldots, n_{max}$.

In order to use a reference Zernike moment sequence effectively, there is a need to assign a certain margin of error for any classification attempt. Therefore for every point in the reference we calculated an acceptable deviation value from the point for the image being classified

$$d_k = \{d_1^k, d_2^k, \ldots, d_{n_{max}}^k\} \tag{11}$$

The deviation for the point of reference n in the class prototype k is as follows

$$d_k(n) = 3 \cdot \sigma = 3 \cdot \sqrt{\frac{1}{N} \sum_{i=1}^{N} (A_n^i - cp_k(n))^2}, \quad i = 1, \ldots, N, \tag{12}$$

where $cp_k(n)$ is the value of A_n from the class prototype cp_k in (10). It is the assumed maximal possible deviation for the reference point $n = 1, \ldots, n_{max}$ in the complete image set of sample size N.

The image falls into a class when the absolute difference between the absolute value of its Zernike moments and the value of the reference point falls into the ascribed deviation margin

$$|cp_k(n) - A_n| \leq d_k(n). \tag{13}$$

The need for a different deviation value for every point stems from the Zernike moment's property where the low-order moments respond to a general image feature (like its general shape or size) and go into more detail with the high-order moments (small distortions in the object's general shape). Therefore it is prudent to leave a wider deviation margin for the high-order reference points, where we expect greater differences between images. If the end goal is to classify images only on the basis of the general shape it may be beneficial to cut off the high-order moments completely from calculations. The purpose of the inclusion of this condition is to accept into the class only sequences that follow its Zernike moment pattern. Otherwise, the criterion of the match remains vague and does not discourage the mismatch on the basis of the minor deviations from the reference.

As mentioned earlier we assume that images of the same object will share a similar Zernike moments sequence, therefore the difference between the reference sequence and the image sequence should fall within the permitted deviation margin. As a criterion of classification we used the standard mean square error (MSE) in the form

$$\min_k Err(k) = MSE(k) = \frac{1}{n_{max}} \sum_{n=1}^{n_{max}} (cp_k(n) - A_n)^2. \tag{14}$$

For an object to belong to the class its Zernike moment sequence has to fulfil the MSE criterion from (14) and the deviation condition from (13), otherwise the image remains unclassified.

5   Experiments and Discussion

The experiment data sets consist of images in grayscale. Image pixels are encoded in the range of 0 to 1, where the value of 0 corresponds to black and 1 to white. The data sets vary based on the subject they represent and the size of the images. The first experiment is performed on the series of microscopic images divided into five classes of objects. The size of the image in this group is 256×256 pixels. There are 41 images in this data set (I - 5, II - 10, III - 9, IV - 9, V - 8). The second experiment is run on the set of digital scans of handwritten digits from number 1 to 9 and the image size of 28×28 pixels. There is a total of 900 images in this data set divided into subsets of 100 images for every digit. The data set comes from the MNIST dataset of handwritten digits (http://yann.lecun.com/exdb/ mnist/). In the third experiment we used the MPEG-7 Core Experiment CE-Shape-1 Test Set from http://www.dabi.temple.edu/~shape/MPEG7/dataset. html that consists of binary images of object and animal shapes. We chose 5 groups of different animal shapes labelled from A to E and of 20 images each (100 images in the total). The standard image size in this group is 256×256 pixels. The fourth experiment was performed on the data set of various object images shown in different stages of 3D rotation. We used 8 complete groups of object sets numbered from o1 to o8, each set containing 72 images of the object. The final data set consisted of 572 object images of the size 128×128 pixels. This data comes from the Columbia University Image Library (COIL-20) (http://www1. cs.columbia.edu/CAVE/software/softlib/coil-20.php). Figures 1, 2, 3 and 4 show sample images from data sets we have used in our experiments.

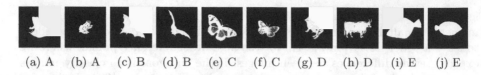

(a) A   (b) A   (c) B   (d) B   (e) C   (f) C   (g) D   (h) D   (i) E   (j) E

Fig. 1. Sample images from classes A to E containing animal shapes. The MPEG-7 Core Experiment CE-Shape-1 Test Set

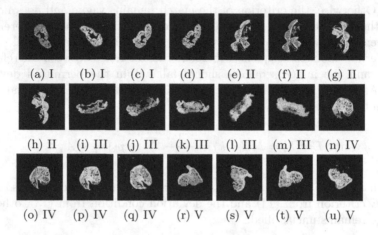

(a) I   (b) I   (c) I   (d) I   (e) II   (f) II   (g) II

(h) II   (i) III   (j) III   (k) III   (l) III   (m) III   (n) IV

(o) IV   (p) IV   (q) IV   (r) V   (s) V   (t) V   (u) V

Fig. 2. Sample images from classes I to V containing microscopic images.

The goal of this experiment is to determine when the Zernike moment descriptor can be used to classify object images and when to refrain from using it. The experiment consists of three stages:

1. Calculation of Zernike moment sequence for every image in the data set.
2. Construction of the class prototype using Zernike moment sequence.
3. Testing of image classification on the data set using the reference sequence.

In the beginning, we calculated the Zernike moment sequence for every image in the data set according to (Eq. 9). Next, we divided every image set into a learning and a testing set. The learning set is used to create the prototype of the class (Eq. 10). The remaining images are put into the testing set. Depending on the sample size, we used either half (the digit and the 3D object data sets) or all the images from the class (the microscopic image and the animal shapes data sets) to obtain the class prototype Zernike sequence. When constructing the sequence it is advisable to use a diversified learning set so that the deviation margin of the reference sequence includes a wide array of class objects. The purpose of dividing the data set into two subsets was to have a reference sequence that is based on actual images from the class and an unbiased testing set to test the classification method.

The prototype Zernike moment sequence for a class was constructed as presented in Eqs. (10) and (12). We constructed 5 prototype Zernike moment

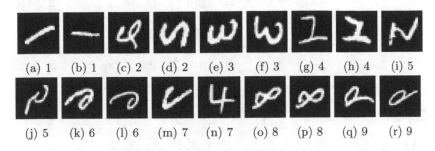

Fig. 3. Sample images from classes 1 to 9 containing handwritten digits images. MNIST dataset of handwritten digits.

Fig. 4. Sample images from classes o1 to o8 containing 3D object images. Columbia University Image Library (COIL-20).

sequences for microscopic images classes (denoted from I to V), 9 prototype sequences for digit classes (denoted from 1 to 9 respectively), 5 prototype sequences for animal shape classes (denoted from A to E) and 8 prototype sequences for object images (denoted from o1 to o8). The obtained prototype sequences are presented in Fig. 5. Due to the numerical calculation constraint we calculated the Zernike moments up to $n_{max} = 40$. It was noted during the testing that the longer Zernike moment sequences generated more accurate classification. Therefore, it is advisable to use the sequence of the highest order n possible.

We tested the proposed method of classification on the sample and the testing set combined. Due to the restriction caused by the differences in the size of the images we ran four testing experiments: one for each image data set.

We ascertained the accuracy of the classification by the percentage of the images classified correctly as belonging to their class of origin:

$$p = \frac{\# \text{ of images classified correctly}}{\text{initial} \# \text{ of the images in the class}}. \tag{15}$$

Results of the classification are shown in Table 1. The first noticeable finding is the discrepancy of results for the handwritten digit data set from other data

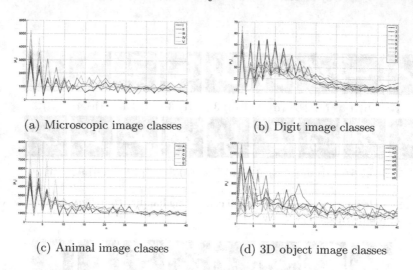

(a) Microscopic image classes   (b) Digit image classes

(c) Animal image classes   (d) 3D object image classes

Fig. 5. Presentation of the Zernike moment sequences for all class prototypes within the four image groups.

sets. The accuracy of that classification in every case is below 0.5. The results for the macroscopic image classification (bar sample III) falls into the range of 0.8–1.0 accuracy and for the 3D object image classification it is the 0.7–1.0 range (bar sample o4). The animal shape image classification is the most mixed group as some of the results fall within the 0.85–1.00 accuracy range (samples A and E) and some into the 0.5–0.6 accuracy range (samples B–D). Studying the graphic presentation of the reference Zernike moment sequence of the classes in Fig. 5 there is a noticeable correlation between the Zernike moment values and the classification results. When the characteristics share too many similar features there is difficulty with differentiation between classes as is noticeable in the case

Table 1. Results of classification for all classes.

class	I	II	III	IV	V
p(%)	1.00	0.80	0.44	0.89	0.88

class	1	2	3	4	5	6	7	8	9
p(%)	0.42	0.26	0.46	0.11	0.44	0.35	0.26	0.44	0.20

class	A	B	C	D	E
p(%)	0.85	0.60	0.50	0.50	1.00

class	o1	o2	o3	o4	o5	o6	o7	o8
p(%)	0.69	0.75	0.79	0.59	0.73	1.00	0.79	1.00

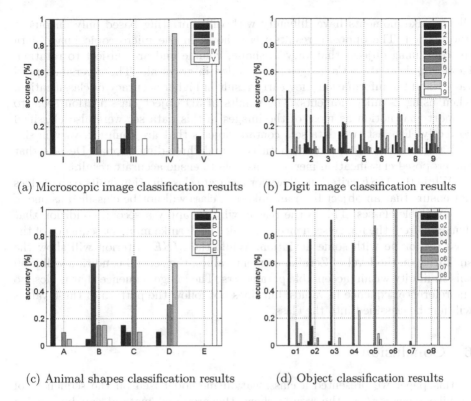

(a) Microscopic image classification results   (b) Digit image classification results

(c) Animal shapes classification results   (d) Object classification results

Fig. 6. Presentation of the classification results. The graph shows how the images from the class were distributed by the proposed method of classification.

of the handwritten digit data set and some of the classes in the animal shape data set. The distribution of misclassified objects is shown in Fig. 6.

We can differentiate classes using their Zernike moment sequence. In cases of microscopic image series and the 3D object image series the differences between classes of objects is easily noticeable. Therefore, the classification results tend to have a higher level of accuracy. The classes of handwritten digits aren't that distinct and some of the numbers' reference Zernike moment sequences share a similar shape. The type of the object used has an influence on the shape of the characteristic based on the Zernike moment sequence. The handwritten digit image series contains very little distinctive information as most of the analysed objects are composed only of basic curves and lines. Since the module of a Zernike moment is rotation invariant there is little chance to differentiate a six from a nine. That lack of distinctive information is a cause of a common misclassification of images in this data set. A similar case is present in the animal shape classification. The images in this data set, while containing a very diverse representation of shapes within the class, carry only black and white pixel values, which translates into less diverse information to be processed. Both of those properties seem to heavily influence the results of classification and show that the Zernike moments have difficulty with differentiating based only on binary information. The opposite results were shown in the microscopic image data set containing objects that vary in shape, volume and are subject to rotation. However, this data set's images are encoded in grayscale. The diversified pixel values and the information they carry result in higher accuracy of classification, when using Zernike moments. The results of 3D object classification seem to support that notion as most of the images in this data set were also classified correctly. The last two data sets contain objects that are complex, vary in size and are subjected to rotation, both two- and three-dimensional. Despite that the proposed classification method was able to ensue accurate results.

While the MSE criterion allows for accurate classification on its own, it does not ensure that an object from an unknown class will not be classified as one of the available classes. This is the reason why we apply a second condition that demands from the image sequence to mimic the Zernike moment sequence of the class prototype with some deviation. While the MSE criterion will show the similarity on the level of Zernike moment values, the second condition will keep this similarity within acceptable parameters. The image sequence that is close to the reference sequence in values, but does not follow the pattern of these values will not be classified into the class.

6   Conclusion

In this paper we presented a classification method based on the sequences of Zernike moments. As the results show, the proposed method can be applied to classification of images that contain a substantial amount of information to process like images in grayscale. The approach makes use of the distinctive shape and volume of the object that get translated into calculated Zernike moments. The sequence constructed with the Zernike moments carrying such information, allows for a unique image description that is shared between similar-looking objects. The other advantage of using Zernike moments is their scale, translation and rotation invariance property that allows for omitting some of the preprocessing stages of image processing.

The proposed method of classification is shown to be a useful tool that is simple in application and allows for a robust, scale, rotation and translation invariant classification of complex objects in grayscale images.

Acknowledgements. The authors express their special thanks to Dr. Agnieszka Malińska and to professor Maciej Zabel from the University School of Medicine, Poznan, Poland for the microscopy section images. This research was supported by 0401/0114/16 grant at the Faculty of Electronics, Wrocław University of Science and Technology.

References

1. Alirezaee, S., Ahmadi, M., Aghaeinia, H., Faez, K.: A weighted Pseudo-Zernike feature extractor for face recognition. In: IEEE International Conference on Systems, Man and Cybernetics, vol. 3, pp. 2128–2132 (2005). doi:10.1109/ICSMC. 2005.1571463
2. Chen, Z., Sun, S.K.: A Zernike moment phase-based descriptor for local image representation and matching. IEEE Trans. Image Process. **19**(1), 205–219 (2010). doi:10.1109/TIP.2009.2032890
3. Chong, C.W., Raveendran, P., Mukundan, R.: Translation invariants of Zernike moments. Pattern Recogn. **36**(8), 1765–1773 (2003). doi:10.1016/S0031-3203(02)00353-9
4. Cura, E., Tepper, M., Mejail, M.: Content-based emblem retrieval using Zernike moments. In: Bloch, I., Cesar, R.M. (eds.) CIARP 2010. LNCS, vol. 6419, pp. 79–86. Springer, Heidelberg (2010). doi:10.1007/978-3-642-16687-7_15
5. Hu, M.K.: Visual pattern recognition by moment invariants. IRE Trans. Inf. Theor. **8**(2), 179–187 (1962). doi:10.1109/TIT.1962.1057692
6. Kamila, N.K., Mahapatra, S., Nanda, S.: Invariance image analysis using modified Zernike moments. Pattern Recogn. Lett. **26**(6), 747–753 (2005). doi:10.1016/j.patrec.2004.09.026
7. Khotanzad, A., Hong, Y.H.: Invariant image recognition by Zernike moments. IEEE Trans. Pattern Anal. Mach. Intell. **12**(5), 489–497 (1990). doi:10.1109/34. 55109
8. Liao, S.X., Pawlak, M.: On image analysis by moments. IEEE Trans. Pattern Anal. Mach. Intell. **18**(3), 254–266 (1996). doi:10.1109/34.485554
9. Liao, S.X., Pawlak, M.: On the accuracy of Zernike moments for image analysis. IEEE Trans. Pattern Anal. Mach. Intell. **20**(12), 1358–1364 (1998). doi:10.1109/34.735809
10. Liu, M., He, Y., Ye, B.: Image Zernike moments shape feature evaluation based on image reconstruction. Geo-Spatial Inf. Sci. **10**(3), 191–195 (2007). doi:10.1007/s11806-007-0060-x
11. Pawlak, M.: Image Analysis by Moments: Reconstruction and Computational Aspects. Oficyna Wydawnicza Politechniki Wrocławskiej, Wrocław (2006)
12. Suk, T., Flusser, J., Zitova, B.: Moments and Moment Invariants in Pattern Recognition. John Wiley and Sons Ltd., Chichester (2009)
13. Teague, M.R.: Image analysis via the general theory of moments. Opt. Soc. Am. **70**(8), 920–930 (1979). doi:10.1364/JOSA.70.000920

New Year's Day Speeches of Czech Presidents: Phonetic Analysis and Text Analysis

Milan Jičínský$^{(\boxtimes)}$ and Jaroslav Marek

Fakulta elektrotechniky a informatiky, Univerzita Pardubice,
Studentská 95, 530 02 Pardubice I, Czech Republic
milan.jicinsky@student.upce.cz,
Jaroslav.Marek@upce.cz

Abstract. The aim of our study is verification of programmed algorithms of phonetic analysis using concrete data, and reassurance that it works as also sought after. For our testing, the appropriate recordings of New Year's Day speeches of Czech and Czechoslovak presidents are available. The very first available recording of presidential speech comes from 1935. All transcripts and recordings of the last 87 speeches are located on the web page www.rozhlas.cz. The primary goal of this paper is to analyze voice characteristics of the speaker (log energy, speech velocity and Zero crossing rate). Especially words "with greatest energy" will be found. There will be a list of words having the highest energy values. The most interesting results will be presented by graphical tools. Using a software, capable of text analysis, transcript characteristics such as most frequent words, length of words, total number of words and different words will be computed. The most frequent words will be presented. Political speeches often become the subject of various analyses. Our calculation allows a new perspective on speeches. It is interesting to compare the most frequent semantic words and words with the greatest energy. The results can be historically important. It allows an extraction of new information from available data and scientifically different approach.

Keywords: New Year's Day speeches of Czech presidents · Intensity of speech · Vocabulary richness · Speech velocity · Zero crossing rate · Length of words

1 Introduction

Nowadays analysis of speech is very popular. It started in the second half of 20th century when basic signal characteristics were discovered. Fundamentals are well described in [1–3]. This field of study evolved very quickly so there are many applications from key word detection [4] across transcription of fluent speech [5] to recognition of speaker [6]. This article is reserved for those who want to study phonetic analysis and its fundamentals. Even historians whose field of study is 20th century in the Czech Republic can appreciate the most frequented words and words with the highest energy. Linguists can be satisfied with changes in individual speeches whether it's written or spoken.

Many authors aim their work on linguistic analysis of political speeches. For example, articles End-of-year speeches of Italian presidents or inaugural speeches of

K. Saeed et al. (Eds.): CISIM 2017, LNCS 10244, pp. 110–121, 2017.
DOI: 10.1007/978-3-319-59105-6_10

US presidents were researched in [7, 8]. Relationship between ideology and language and thematic concentration of Czechoslovak New Year's Day speeches is analyzed in article [9]. Of course, it is very interesting to study influences of ideology, originality of author and his abilities to differ from uniformity. The most frequent words can provide an information about recent years because they react on the most important events. Some of those words will be listed.

Main goal of this publication is to present words that were said with the greatest energy. Words with the greatest energy allows to track what president emphasized on during a reading. Emphasis of the speaker will be probably on positive words. The only exception could be the time of war. Ideological words may be emphasized in some speeches. There will be one more characteristic calculated for each speech – speech velocity.

2   Voice Characteristics

Analysis of recordings of New Year's Day speeches will be introduced in this chapter. The intensity of voice (energy) and speech velocity will represent voice characteristic of speaker. Energy tells something about how much emphasis speaker uses and speech velocity shows how fast speaker speaks. These variables can be influenced e.g. by age or by sickness. Then the words having the greatest energy can be found. It could be interesting to compare these words with most frequent thematic words. President didn't have to be an author of written text. But he could highlight any words he wanted to (Fig. 1). It depended on what he considered to be important. This is the example of individuality. Then ZCR (zero crossing rate) characteristics will be shown.

Fig. 1. "Dear fellow citizens" – Václav Havel (1998). Source: own.

2.1   Obtaining Data and Its Processing

Source data have been obtained from website www.rozhlas.cz. Speeches are recorded with useful software Audacity. Sampling rate of each speech is 8 kHz. Each recording is modified because the original ones contain a music before the speech starts. Calculations of voice parameters are realized in MATLAB (Fig. 2). Scheme of processing can be simplified as on Fig. 3.

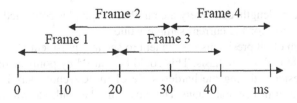

Fig. 2. Segmentation of recording into frames. Source: own.

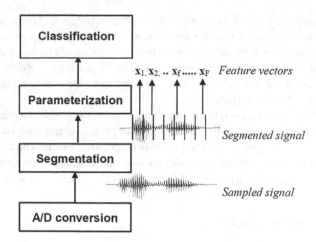

Fig. 3. Audio processing. Source: own.

Segmentation means that the record is divided into frames of the same length (typically 20 ms long). Frames are overlapping each other right in the half (in this case). Overlapping is recommended to the fact that parameters can be changed in jumps. So this enhancement improves the dramatic changes and it can describe even changes near an edge of frame without loss of useful data. After the segmentation follows a parameterization. Feature vector values of each frame is computed during the parameterization. Features can be divided into: basic, spectral, cepstral and dynamic. ZCR and energy ranks among the basic features. Feature extraction and segmentation is also discussed in [2].

2.2   Intensity of Voice

The intensity of voice is characterized by energy. So the energy is a key parameter which defines the intensity of voice. Energy is defined as the sum of squared values of samples within one frame. Logarithm function is used for better range of energy values. In this case Log energy of ordinary noise is around 5. Whenever speech is contained in recording, values of energy are greater for those frames. Typically, the energy of speaking person can reach even value of 15. It depends on how loud speaker speaks. Log energy is defined as

$$E = \log\left(\sum_{n=0}^{L-1} x^2(n)\right),\tag{1}$$

where L is the frame length, concretely the number of samples contained in the frame. x (n) is the designation for the current sample value.

In comparison of all presidents it's evident to see that president Hácha spoke not as loud as others. He had no emphasis. This could be caused by political situation. Hácha used to be a president during the hardest time of the Czechoslovak history. He was helpless president of protectorate state. The only thing he could do was to make people

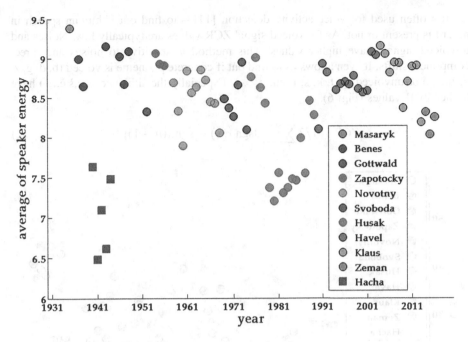

Fig. 4. Log energy: mean value. Source: own.

feel calm and safe, even if it wasn't possible. As for president Husák, very significant decrease of energy was observed between years 1978 and 1979 (Fig. 4).

2.3 ZCR

Zero crossing rate is a parameter that characterizes changing of sign from negative to positive or back. Zero crossing rate is related to the frequency. There is one value of ZCR for each frame (the same as for the energy). The principle of ZCR can be easily explained with Fig. 5. ZCR value is equal to the count of all dots. The dots are placed to the points where signal intersects x axis and changes the sign.

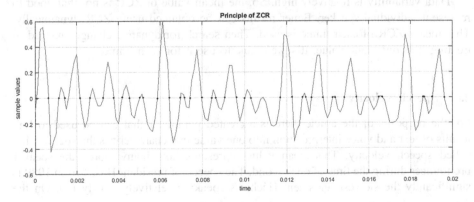

Fig. 5. Explanation of ZCR - 20 ms frame containing of phoneme "a". Source: own.

It's often used for voice activity detection [11] – to find out if human speech in record is present or not. As for voiced signal ZCR values are typically low. Noises and unvoiced signals have higher values. This method is sensitive to noises and direct component shifts. It even allows us to find out if concrete phoneme is voiced (b, d, g, z, v, h, ...) or unvoiced (p, t, k, s, f, ch, c, ...). Especially the sibilance (s,c,š,č,...) have higher ZCR values (Fig. 6).

$$ZCR = 1/2 \sum_{n=1}^{L-1} |\mathrm{sgn}\, x(n) - \mathrm{sgn}\, x(n-1)|. \tag{2}$$

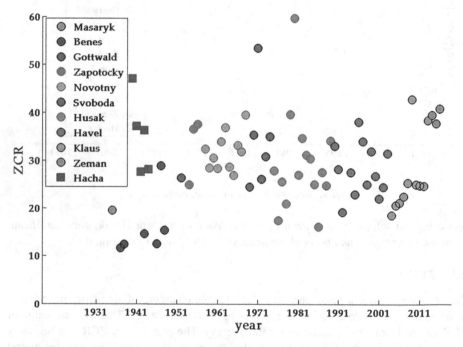

Fig. 6. Zero crossing rate: mean value. Source: own.

Data variability is relatively high. So, the mean value of ZCR is not that good to represent individual speaker. Better results can be obtained using ZCR dynamically. That means ZCR of each frame is used. Then search for dynamic changes instead of treating it as one static value. It's preferable to use it for each frame.

2.4   Speech Velocity

For the purposes of the article there is a created parameter that can be used to link results of text and voice interpretation into one value that characterizes the speaker. It's called speech velocity. This mean value represents how many words the speaker pronounces during the time of one second. The speech of president Husák from 1989 is significantly the slowest. President Hácha is speaking relatively slowly too. On the

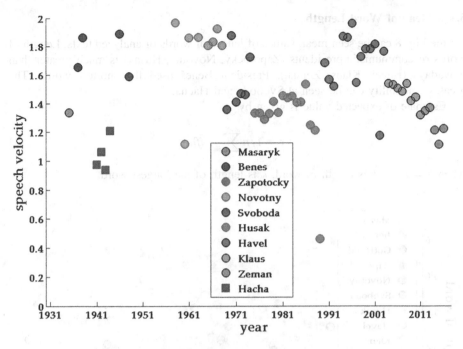

Fig. 7. Speech velocity: mean value. Source: own.

other hand, the fastest tempo of speaking can be recognized in speeches from 1938, 1943 (Beneš), 1959 (Novotný) and 1996 (Havel) (Fig. 7).

3   Characteristics of Written Text

All studies are realized for 87 speeches of Czechoslovak presidents, Czech presidents or Czechoslovak prime ministers. The unique situation happened due to the World War II. The Czechoslovak Republic had two presidents. President Beneš left his country and exiled to the Great Britain. But he was still very politically active. Then Hácha was chosen to be a president of protectorate. So, both groups of speeches were analyzed between 1940 and 1945. On the other hand, president in exile is considered to be more important subject of our analysis.

We can expect changes in using of different length words during a long history of New Year's Day speeches. Therefore, the first aim of our calculation is to determine average of word length. Calculations of text parameters are made using software based on Java [10] called "Statistika v lexikální analýze". This GUI (Graphical User Interface) has been created during diploma thesis. It makes easier the whole text processing. The software allows to analyze frequent letters and words, length of words, aggregation and alliteration and some other features. The original purpose of existence of software is analysis of poems and its translations as in [12].

3.1   Mean of Word Length

On the Fig. 8 can be seen mean values of length of words of analyzed texts. Length of words of communistic presidents (Zápotocký, Novotný, Husák) is much greater than nowadays (Havel, Klaus, Zeman). President Beneš used the shortest words. The greatest variability can be seen at Svoboda and Hácha.

Estimate of expected value is given by

$$\bar{x} = 1/n \sum\nolimits_{i=1}^{k} if_i, \tag{3}$$

where $i = 1, ..., k$ is length of word, k is length of the longest word.

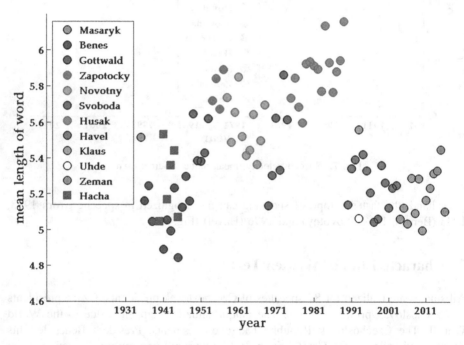

Fig. 8. Length of words: mean value. Source: own.

3.2   The Most Frequent Words

Conjunctions and prepositions of course ranks among the most frequent words. Conjunction "a" is the most frequent in all speeches except Novotný (1964) – "v", Svoboda (1973) – "v" and Hácha (1944) – "se". Figure 10 is the list of sorted conjunctions and prepositions used from first to fourth position. The common words can be seen. The most frequent words with meaning will be presented in Fig. 10 too. These words differ much more than prepositions. Presidents react on current political events such as crisis, protectorate, war or return of democracy. Meaning words can provide a quick preview of content. Comparison with inaugural speeches of US presidents can be interesting. As for words with meaning, for example Roosevelt (1933) said words: HAVE, NATIONAL

Tomáš Garrique Masaryk (1850-1937)

1935: a, se, na, v	národů	států	pokoj	V HOSPODÁŘSKÉM i politickém

Edvard Beneš (1884-1948)

1936: a, aby, v, i	národ	prezident	stát	-
1937: a, v, se, že	demokracie	evropě	dnešní	BUDEME
1938: a, v, je, co	rok	státu	dobré	NA POLI politickém
1941: a, v, se, na	bude	zase	vánoce	-
1942: a, se, to, že	války	vítězství	dnes	-
1943: a, že, v, se	bude	německo	dnes	KDYBY SNAD tak zvaná slovenská vláda
1944: a, v, to, se	naší	svazu	sovětského	-
1945: a, v, na, že	bude	dnes	roku	-
1946: a, v, se, to	nové	dnes	války	po utrpeních VÁLEČNÝCH z rukou nepřátel
1947: a, v, na, o	zjevy	bude	dnešní	o zrození ČLOVĚKA nového
1948: a, i, na, se	život	člověk	roku	I TO bude našemu životu prospěšné

Emil Hácha (1872-1945)

1939: -				NEMŮŽE
1940: a, z, i, v	srdce	dětem	večer	V PLNÉM kruhu svých nejbližších
1941: a, v, se, na	národní	doba	národa	SVĚTOVÝ přerod
1942: a, na, v, jím	vánoce	radosti	dnes	vedle ZÁŘÍCÍHO vánočního stromku
1943: se, v, a, všech	říše	vánoce	děj	NEVÁHEJTE
1944: a, na, že, v	říše	národu	spoluobčané	-
1945: a, se, že, v	válka	vánoce	radosti	-

Klement Gottwald (1896-1953)

1949: a, v, k, na	našeho	plánu	roku	-
1950: a, o, v, že	procent	roku	více	-
1951: a, v, na, o	roce	naše	minulém	-
1952: a, v, na, se	roce	více	průmyslu	UBRÁNILI mír
1953: a, v, že, na	míru	sovětského	války	-

Antonín Zápotocký (1884-1957)

1954: a, v, i, na	hospodářství	mzdno	mír	KULTURNÍ úrovně našeho lidu
1955: a, i, v, se	míru	národní	republiky	naše mírumilovné BUDOVÁNÍ
1956: a, i, v, se	budování	míru	republiky	zaměstnancům V LIDOVÉ i státní správě
1957: a, i, v, na	lidu	roku	uhlí	-

Antonín Novotný (1904-1975)

1958: a, v, se, na	strany	lidu	komunistické	PŘILOŽÍME-LI všichni ruku
1959: a, v, na, o	výsledky	práce	dnes	cílem je BUDOVAT socialistický řád
1960: a, v, se, na	zemědělství	roce	československa	jaké JSOU dosavadní výsledky
1961: a, v, se, na	socialistické	práce	společnosti	UPEVŇOVAT naši československou
1962: a, v, na, se	hospodářství	roku	rok	OBRAZ růstu životní úrovně
1963: a, na, v, se	sjezdu	usnesení	socialistické	JEJICH cílem je vytvořit
1964: v, a, na, i	hospodářství	roku	národní	CO DNES můžeme říci
1965: a, v, i, na	hospodářství	společnosti	roce	VYBUDOVALI jsme socialismus
1966: a, v, na, se	společnosti	hospodářství	vývoj	BUDOU-LI chtít národní výbory
1967: a, v, na, že	hospodářství	životní	roce	UVOLNÍM mezinárodního napětí
1968: a, v, i, na	republiky	socialismu	roku	PUJDE-LI i letos hospodářský vývoj

Ludvík Svoboda (1895-1979)

1969: a, v, i, na	rok	práce	lidu	která přes všechna DRAMATA
1970: a, v, i, to	země	rozvoje	roce	ZABEZPEČUJÍCÍ všestranný rozvoj
1971: a, i, v, se	socialistické	práce	rozvoje	KAŽDÉHO z nás
1972: a, v, vám, i	rok	program	komunistické	PŘEJI Vám všem
1973: v, a, se, i	roce	úspěchů	mezinárodní	USILUJEME o rozvoj
1974: a, se, v, pro	komunistické	rozvoj	roku	díky UVĚDOMĚLÉMU pochopení

Gustáv Husák (1913-1991)

1975: a, v, i, se	lidu	roce	hospodářství	všech MÍROVÝCH sil ve světě
1976: a, v, i, na	lidu	československa	národní	přičiňme se všichni
1977: a, v, i, na	roku	práci	lidu	S VĚDOMÍM odpovědných hospodářů
1978: a, v, i, se	lidu	rok	státu	PŮSOBÍ vnější dopady na naši ekonomiku
1979: a, v, se, i	lidu	roku	socialistické	V SOULADU se záměry plánu
1980: a, v, se, na	lidu	roku	socialistického	SOUČASNĚ jsou u zdrojem jistoty
1981: a, v, i, se	lidu	práce	roce	ve ZKUŠENOSTI s budováním
1982: a, v, se, s	socialistického	lidu	práce	ÚROVEŇ a řízení a kvalitu veškeré práce
1983: a, v, na, i	lidu	státy	roku	K CÍLI však může vést
1984: a, v, pro, se	lidu	světě	přátelé	PŘIJAI.I jsme nezbytné závěry
1985: a, v, na, se	roku	národní	vlasti	ŠIROKÁ společenská a pracovní aktivita
1986: a, v, se, na	práce	lidu	roku	VYKONANOU práci přitom hodnotíme
1987: a, v, se, i	roku	národní	socialistické	hodnotíme VŠAK realisticky
1988: a, v, je, na	práci	roku	národní	uvítali jsme UPŘÍMNĚ výsledky
1989: a, v, na, k	společnosti	zasedání	práci	VYUŽÍVÁME to, co je možné uplatnit

Václav Havel (1936-2011)

1990: a, se, že, v	republice	země	národy	BYLO by velmi nerozumné
1991: a, v, se, že	rok	věřím	systém	MILI spoluobčané
1992: a, se, v, že	rokem	státní	hledáme	TO všechno je samozřejmě dobré

předseda vlády Václav Klaus (1941)

1993: a, se, v, na	české	republiky	stát	-

předseda parlamentu Milan Uhde (1936)

1993: a, se, je, že	domov	stát	života	-

Václav Havel (1936-2011)

1994: a, se, v, na	stát	občanské	společnosti	než ÚCTU ke všemu nestandardnímu
1995: a, se, v, je	stát	politiky	naděje	I NADĚJE je práce, práce možná obtížná
1996: a, se, že, v	zemi	státu	společností	MYSLÍM, že i soudobý vývoj
1997: a, k, se, je	znamení	člověk	věci	což NENÍ zároveň bytostí
1998: a, se, to, v	politika	znamená	věci	MILI spoluobčané
1999: a, se, v, i	zdí	evropy	lety	MÍRA našeho zápalu pro vizi
2000: a, se, i, že	života	světa	lidí	VÍM, jak to zní nepopulárně
2001: a, v, je, se	zájmu	lidí	společnosti	VŠICHNI přece víme
2002: a, se, o, že	státem	evropské	země	POMOHLO by nám, uvědomit si
2003: a, se, v, na	státu	rok	soužití	MILI spoluobčané

Václav Klaus (1941)

2004: a, se, v, i	rok	zemi	české	že TÍMTO okamžikem
2005: a, se, v, na	rok	stát	země	UČÍME se rozlišovat
2006: a, v, se, že	evropské	život	roku	po ODMÍTNUTÍ EVROPSKÉ ústavy
2007: a, se, v, že	roku	evropské	nic	NESMÍ nám být lhostejné
2008: a, se, v, i	rok	země	přicházejí	chtěl bych V ás UBEZPEČIT
2009: a, v, se, k	rok	unie	evropské	URČITĚ tímto kouzelným proutkem
2010: a, se, v, to	rok	pokles	občanům	URČITĚ lépe než bylo
2011: a, se, v, to	rok	vláda	hlasům	UVNITŘ společnosti
2012: a, se, v, že	rok	zemi	evropě	NA ROKY bývají posilovány
2013: a, v, je, se	den	zemi	rok	UVNITŘ obcí

Miloš Zeman (1944)

2014: a, se, že, jsem	roku	poděkovat	život	NEMLUVÍM teď o rozdělené společnosti
2015: se, že, jsem	státní	nikdy	rok	MÁM-LI hodnotit vládu
2016: a, že, je, se	země	roce	republiky	DRUHOU dobrou zprávou

Fig. 9. The most frequent words (Czech version). Source: own.

Tomáš Garrique Masaryk (1850-1937)				
1935: and, with, or, in	nations	states	serenity	ECONOMIC and political
Edvard Beneš (1884-1948)				
1936: and, that, in, even	nation	president	state	-
1937: and, in, with, that	democracy	Europe	today	we WILL
1938: and, in, is, what	year	state	good	political ARENA
1941: and, in, with, on	will	again	Christmas	-
1942: and, with, to, that	war	victory	today	-
1943: and, that, in, with	will	Germany	today	MAYBE IF so-called Slovak Government
1944: and, in, to, with	our	union	soviet	-
1945: and, in, on, that	will	today	year	-
1946: and, in, with, it	new	today	war	after WAR suffering at the hands of enemies
1947: and, in, on, about	apparitions	will	today	the birth of a new MAN
1948: and, even, on, with	live	human	year	AND IT will be beneficial to our lives
Emil Hácha (1872-1945)				
1939: -	-	-	-	CAN NOT
1940: and, from, even, in	heart	child	night	FULL family circle
1941: and, in, with, on	national	period	nations	WORLD rebirth
1942: and, on, in, them	Christmas	pleasures	today	beside the GLOWING Christmas tree
1943: with, in, and, all	empire	Christmas	plot	DO NOT HESITATE
1944: and, on, that, in	empire	nation	pleasures	-
1945: and, with, that, in	war	Christmas	joy	-
Klement Gottwald (1896-1953)				
1949: and, in, to, on	our	plan	year	-
1950: and, about, in, that	percent	year	more	-
1951: and, in, on, about	year	our	last	-
1952: and, in, on, with	year	more	industry	WITHSTOOD peace
1953: and, in, that, on	peace	soviet	war	-
Antonín Zápotocký (1884-1957)				
1954: and, in, even, on	economy	necessary	peace	CULTURAL level of our people
1955: and, even, in, with	peace	nation	republic	our peaceful BUILDING
1956: and, even, in, with	building	peace	republic	employees IN FOLK and state
1957: and, even, in, on	people	year	coal	-
Antonín Novotný (1904-1975)				
1958: and, in, with, on	party	people	communistic	If we ENCLOSE hand
1959: and, in, on, about	results	work	today	the aim is to BUILD a socialist order
1960: and, in, with, on	agriculture	year	czechoslovakia	What ARE the existing results
1961: and, in, with, on	socialistic	year	society	STRENGTHEN our czechoslovac
1962: and, in, on, with	economy	year	year	IMAGE of linving standards growth
1963: and, on, in, with	congress	decree	socialistic	THEIR goal is to create
1964: in, and, on, even	economy	year	nation	WHAT TODAY can we say
1965: and, in, even, on	economy	society	year	We have BUILT socialism
1966: and, in, on, with	society	economy	progression	IF THEY WANT national committees
1967: and, in, on, that	economy	vital	year	THAW of international tensions
1968: and, in, even, on	republic	socialismus	national	IF IT GOES this year economic development
Ludvík Svoboda (1895-1979)				
1969: and, in, even, on	year	work	people	that despite all the DRAMA
1970: and, in, even, it	country	advancement	year	ENSURING all-round development
1971: and, even, in, with	socialistic	work	advancement	EACH of us
1972: and, in, You, even	year	program	communistic	I WISH you all
1973: in, and, with, even	year	achievements	international	We SEEK to develop
1974: and, with, in, for	comunistic	advancement	year	thanks CONSCIOUS understanding
Gustav Husák (1913-1991)				
1975: and, in, even, with	people	year	economy	All PEACEKEEPING force in the world
1976: and, in, even, on	people	czechoslovac	national	LET US ALL
1977: and, in, even, on	year	work	people	AWARE responsible landlords
1978: and, in, even, with	people	year	public	OPERATES external impacts on our economy
1979: and, in, with, even	people	year	socialistic	in ACCORDANCE with the intent Plan
1980: and, in, with, on	people	year	socialistic	CURRENT are a source of security
1981: and, in, with, on	people	work	year	in-building EXPERIENCE
1982: and, in, with, with	socialistic	people	work	LEVEL, quality, management of all labor
1983: and, in, on, even	people	states	year	however, it lead to the DESTINATION
1984: and, in, for, with	people	world	friends	we ADOPTED the necessary conclusions
1985: and, in, on, with	year	nation	motherland	BROAD social and work-related activity
1986: and, in, with, on	work	people	year	work DONE we simultaneously evaluate
1987: and, in, with, even	year	nation	socialistic	HOWEVER realistically evaluate
1988: and, in, is, on	work	year	national	We SINCERELY welcome the results
1989: and, in, on, about	society	meeting	work	We UTILIZE what may be exercised
Václav Havel (1936-2011)				
1990: and, with, that, in	republic	country	nations	It WOULD be very unwise
1991: and, in, with, that	year	believe	system	DEAR fellows
1992: and, with, in, that	year	state	search	THIS is all good, of course,
Prime minister Václav Klaus (1941)				
1993: and, with, in, on	czech	republic	state	-
Chair of parliament Milan Uhde (1936)				
1993: and, with, je, that	home	state	life	-
Václav Havel (1936-2011)				
1994: and, with, in, on	polity	civil	society	than RESPECT for all nonstandard
1995: and, with, in, is	polity	politics	hope	even HOPE is work, maybe difficult
1996: and, with, that, in	country	state	society	I THINK that contemporary developments
1997: and, to, with, is	sign	human	things	This is NOT the same time being
1998: and, with, to, in	policy	means	things	DEAR fellows
1999: and, with, in, even	wall	Europe	years	RATE our passion for vision
2000: and, with, even, that	life	world	peoples	I KNOW how unpopular it sounds
2001: and, in, is, with	interest	people	society	We ALL know yet
2002: and, with, about, that	polity	European	country	It would help us realize
2003: and, in, in, is	polity	year	cohabitation	DEAR fellows
Václav Klaus (1941)				
2004: and, with, in, even	year	country	czech	that THIS moment
2005: and, with, in, on	year	state	country	are LEARNING to distinguish
2006: and, in, with, that	European	life	year	after the rejection of the European Constitution
2007: and, in, with, that	year	European	nothing	MUST NOT be indifferent to us
2008: and, in, with, even	year	country	coming	I would like to ASSURE you
2009: and, in, with, to	year	Union	european	CERTAINLY this magic wand
2010: and, with, in, it	year	decrease	citizen	CERTAINLY better than
2011: and, with, in, it	year	government	voices	INSIDE society
2012: and, with, in, that	year	country	Europe	CLAIMS are strengthening
2013: and, in, is, am	year	country	year	INSIDE municipalities
Miloš Zeman (1944)				
2014: and, with, that, am	year	thank	life	I AM NOT TALKING about the division of society
2015: and, with, that, with	public	never	year	If I HAVE TO evaluate government
2016: and, that, is, with	country	year	republic	SECOND good news

Fig. 10. The most frequent words and words with the highest energy. Source: own.

and Truman (1949) used the words: WORD, HAVE, NATIONS, PEACE, FREEDOM, PEOPLE, FREE, UNITED, MORE, SECURITY, DEMOCRACY [7]. See Fig. 9 or 10.

Figures are divided into some subsections. As mentioned before, the Czechoslovak Republic had two presidents between 1940 and 1945. In 1993 the second anomaly appeared. The Czechoslovak republic ceased to exist. Since 1993 the country was divided into two smaller autonomous countries: The Czech Republic and the Slovak Republic. So, the president Václav Havel had no speech in 1993. Prime ministers were speaking to their nations instead of president.

Rows are sorted by years. Each row has its color depending on president or prime minister. Colors were chosen according to all figures. The first column contains first four most frequent conjunctions and prepositions. Then there are three columns containing the most frequent words sorted by order. The last column shows the word with the highest energy. Those words are written by uppercase.

3.3 Number of Words

Scatter chart will be used to demonstrate a vocabulary richness. Coordinates on axis x means total number of words in speech and coordinates on axis y means total number of different words. Functional dependency can be modeled by Gompertz curve. Presidents with values above the curve have greater ratio of words than other presidents. Language richness of speeches under the curve can be considered lesser. In article [9] author mentioned that thematic concentration of president Havel is surprisingly low. But this claim doesn't seem to correspond with language richness. According to the Fig. 10, ratio of number of different words and total number of words is greater as for Havel. This could be caused by choosing different methods of evaluating language richness (Fig. 11).

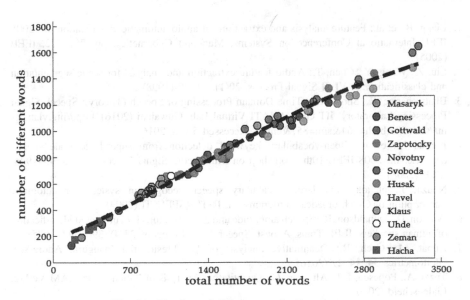

Fig. 11. Number of different words. Source: own.

4 Conclusions

This article's goal is to present results of our research and show that data we already had can be processed in different way. The extraction of information is much discussed nowadays. Main purpose of research is finding the words with the greatest energy. Because they have historical importance, they can be used as keywords and they even characterize the speaker.

Scale of publication doesn't allow to detail comment and the description of used algorithms. Many hours of machine time have been needed during the calculations of phonetic parameters of speeches. Archive [13] contains 74 speeches. So, this is more than 19 h of recordings to be analyzed. Before calculation of mean values of ZCR and Log energy, there was an extensive table for each speech. Presented parameters were created by reducing the table containing millions of values (each frame parameter values) into one mean value. Unreduced data may be used for further analysis.

Comparing the table of most frequent thematic words with table containing the words pronounced with the greatest energy brings almost no match. The speaker didn't emphasize the most frequent words. But he chose to highlight other words. For example, Masaryk talked about economy. Beneš emphasized the war and human kind. Novotný insisted on hard work and improving the communistic country. Havel emphasized the very first words: "Dear fellow citizens." It can provide some information without listening to the whole speech. It even characterizes the president himself and an era of each president (the most important events, standard of living, relationship between president and citizens).

References

1. Liang, B., et al.: Feature analysis and extraction for audio automatic classification. In: 2005 IEEE International Conference on Systems, Man and Cybernetics, pp. 767–772. IEEE (2005)
2. Liu, Z., Wang, Y., Chen, T.: Audio feature extraction and analysis for scene segmentation and classification. J. VLSI Signal Process. **20**(1), 61–79 (1998)
3. Bhattacharjee, R.: Short Term Time Domain Processing of Speech (Theory): Speech Signal Processing Laboratory. IIT GUWAHATI Virtual Lab, Guwahati (2016). http://iitg.vlab.co.in/?sub=59&brch=164&sim=857&cnt=1. Accessed 5 Dec 2016
4. Kanda, N., et al.: Open-vocabulary keyword detection from super-large scale speech database. In: 2008 IEEE 10th Workshop on Multimedia Signal Processing, pp. 939–944. IEEE (2008)
5. Nouza, J., et al.: Very large vocabulary speech recognition system for automatic transcription of Czech broadcast programs. In: INTERSPEECH (2004)
6. Wasson, D., Donaldson, R.: Speech amplitude and zero crossings for automated identification of human speakers. IEEE Trans. Acoust. Speech Signal Process. **23**(4), 390–392 (1975)
7. Kubát, M., Čech, R.: Quantitative analysis of US Presidential Inaugural Addresses. Glottometrics **34**, 14–27 (2016)
8. Tuzzi, A., Popescu, I.-I., Altmann, G.: Quantitative Analysis of Italian Texts. RAM-Verlag, Lüdenscheid (2010)

9. Čech, R.: Language and ideology: quantitative thematic analysis of New Year speeches given by Czechoslovak and Czech presidents (1949–2011). Qual. Quant. **48**, 899–910 (2014)
10. Šlahora, J.: Matematická lingvistika a překlady básně E.A. Poea Havran. Master thesis. University Pardubice, Faculty of electrical engineering and informatics, Pardubice (2015). https://dk.upce.cz/bitstream/handle/10195/60403/SlahoraJ_MatematickaLingvistika_JM_2015.zip?sequence=1&isAllowed=y. Accessed 5 Dec 2016
11. Bachu, R., Kopparthi, S., Adapa, B., Barkana, B.: Separation of voiced and unvoiced using zero crossing rate and energy of the speech signal. In: American Society for Engineering Education (ASEE) Zone Conference Proceedings, pp. 1–7 (2008)
12. Marek, J., Šlahora, J.: Měření podobnosti překladů básně Havran. Forum Statisticum Slovacum, vol. X(5), pp. 90–95 (2013). ISSN: 1336-7420
13. URL: http://www.rozhlas.cz/zpravy/data/_zprava/od-tgm-k-zemanovi-poslechnete-si-vanocni-a-novorocni-projevy-vsech-prezidentu–1436738. Accessed 17 Dec 2016

Classifier Selection for Motor Imagery Brain Computer Interface

Izabela Rejer[1(✉)] and Robert Burduk[2]

[1] Faculty of Computer Science and Information Technology,
West Pomeranian University of Technology, Żołnierska Street 52,
71–210 Szczecin, Poland
irejer@wi.zut.edu.pl
[2] Department of Systems and Computer Networks,
Wroclaw University of Science and Technology,
Wybrzeże Wyspiańskiego 27, 50–370 Wrocław, Poland
robert.burduk@pwr.edu.pl

Abstract. The classification process in the domain of brain computer interfaces (BCI) is usually carried out with simple linear classifiers, like LDA or SVM. Non-linear classifiers rarely provide a sufficient increase in the classification accuracy to use them in BCI. However, there is one more type of classifiers that could be taken into consideration when looking for a way to increase the accuracy - boosting classifiers. These classification algorithms are not common in BCI practice, but they proved to be very efficient in other applications.

Keywords: Imagery brain computer interface · Classification · Boosting

1 Introduction

A brain-computer interface (BCI) is a control and communication system in which the control commands and messages are not transmitted via the standard outputs of a central nervous system, but are read directly from the user's brain. Nowadays there are a lot of different devices for recording the brain activity, however, due to relatively low costs, high mobility, and non-invasiveness, EEG devices are usually used for outside-lab BCIs. There are three main types of EEG-BCIs: SSVEP-BCI, P300-BCI, and MI-BCI. In each of them, different brain potentials are used to control the interface.

SSVEP-BCI is controlled by steady state visually evoked potentials (SSVEPs). These potentials are recorded from the occipital cortex when a user is exposed to a visual stimulus flickering with a steady frequency. Since the stimulus fundamental frequency (and also the harmonics) can be observed in EEG recording, different control commands are encoded with stimuli of different frequency, each delivered by different stimuli providers (usually LEDs).

K. Saeed et al. (Eds.): CISIM 2017, LNCS 10244, pp. 122–130, 2017.
DOI: 10.1007/978-3-319-59105-6_11

The control signals in P300-BCI are positive potentials that appear over the parietal cortex when a user perceives a rare and significant stimulus. The P300 potential can be detected in the brain activity approximately 300 ms after the stimulus is presented. The control process in P300-BCI is based on picking out the objects from a set of objects displayed on the screen [3]. The user's task is to focus the attention on one of the objects. The objects are highlighted randomly - each time the object chosen by the user is highlighted, P300 potential appears over the parietal cortex.

While the brain potentials used in SSVEP-BCI and P300-BCI are evoked potentials (both need external stimulation to be evoked in the user's brain), MI-BCI is based on spontaneous potentials, evoked by the user. The potentials used for controlling MI-BCI, called motor rhythms, can be detected over the motor cortex when the user performs real or imagery movements.

Out of these three types of BCI, MI-BCI is the most natural and so the most welcome in practical applications. Its main benefit is that it does not require any external stimulation - the mental states needed to perform the actions are evoked only at the user's will. This means that the user can use the interface at any time while performing other actions (e.g. reading a text). Hence, the interface can be always in the stand-by state waiting for a user's command. In theory P300-BCI or SSVEP-BCI could be also constantly on, but in practice flickering light or highlighting objects constantly present at the user's field of view would be extremely tiring. However, there is no free lunch, MI-BCI is the most convenient for the user, but it provides the smallest number of control states. Usually only 2–4 direct commands can be obtained with this type of interface (corresponding to the motor imagery of: left and right hand, feet, and tongue). Moreover, the potentials related to motor imagery are difficult to extract from a scalp EEG, especially in the case of a beginner user.

In fact, MI-BCI can be successfully used in practice, but the user has to learn first how to perform the motor imagery at all, and then how to perform it effectively. As Pfurtscheller et al. and Guger et al. report in [7,8,15] even 80–97% of classification accuracy can be obtained after 6–10 twenty-minute sessions. If the training is shorter, the results are not so impressive. In [5] Gauger et al. report that only in 20% of 99 subjects the brain patterns related to left-right hand motor imagery were possible to be distinguished with an accuracy greater than 80% after 20–30 min of training. For 70% of 99 subjects the classification accuracy was about 60–80%. In the case of remaining subjects, the classification accuracy of motor imagery of left and right hand was below 60%.

In MI-BCI and other biometric systems, simple individual classifiers are usually used in the classification process, e.g. linear discriminant analysis (LDA) [6], Fisher linear discriminant analysis (FDA) [13], k-NN classifier [16,17], distinction sensitive learning vector quantization classifier (DSLVQ) [15] or minimum Mahalanobis distance (MDA) classifier [14]. The boosting algorithms are also an effective method of producing a very accurate classification rule [9], however, they are rarely used in BCI domain [12]. In general, they are a combination of so-called weak classifiers. A weak classifier learns on various training examples sampled from the original learning set. The sampling procedure is based on the weight of each example. In each iteration, the weights of examples are changed. The final decision of the boosting algorithm is determined on the ensemble of classifiers derived from each iteration of the algorithm.

The aim of this paper is to compare the performance of four boosting classifiers (AdaBoost, RealAdaBoost, GentleAdaBoost, and our modification of AdaBoost formulated in Sect. 2) and three classic classification algorithms: LDA, SVM, and k-NN. We would like to find out whether the boosting scheme, where the weak classifiers are joined to create a strong one, will provide at least similar results as the methods that proved to be very successful in BCI field. We perform our analysis over EEG data that were acquired during a MI-BCI session.

The rest of this paper is organized as follows. In Sect. 2 our modification of AdaBoost algorithm is presented. The experimental evaluation, discussion and conclusions from the experiments are presented in Sect. 3. Finally, some conclusions are given.

2   AdaBoost Algorithm

In recent years many modifications of algorithms based on the boosting idea appeared. For example, AdaBoost.OC algorithm [20] is a combination of AdaBoost method and ECOC model, LogitBoost algorithm [5] utilizes the model of logistic regression, FloatBoost algorithm [11] removes those classifiers in subsequent iterations which do not fulfill the quality condition assumed and in [2] the methods of modifying weights of the examples are described.

It is worth mentioning that in the work [1] a common name for boosting type algorithms was proposed, the acronym ARCing for Adaptive Resampling and Combining was created, and also a new algorithm named ARC-x4 was presented. In this work we use the three well-known boosting algorithms (AdaBoost, RealAdaBoost and GentleAdaBoost), together with our modification of the classic AdaBoost algorithm.

One of the main factors that have an effect on the action of AdaBoost algorithm is the selection of weights assigned to individual elements of the learning set. Let's propose then a modification of AdaBoost algorithm which will represent imprecision in values of weights obtained in subsequent iterations of the algorithm. Such imprecision will be defined by parameters k and λ. The second parameter defines certain linear combination of the upper and lower value of weights obtained after modification by k. The algorithm steps are presented in Table 1.

If the values of functions $\overline{e_b} = e_b + k$, $\underline{e_b} = e_b - k$ obtained in point 4c are outside the range of values $[0, 1]$, then the values of these functions should be modified (point 4d). This procedure seems to be used extremely rarely due to the possible values of the error e_b and the assumed values of the k parameter. In the earlier work [2] the changes in weights values depended on the iteration of the algorithm. In this work the changes in weights do not depend on the iteration of the algorithm.

Table 1. Algorithm B1M-AdaBoost

---

1. Initialize λ and k.
2. Initialize the weight vector $w_{1,1} = ... = w_{1,n} = 1/n$.
3. Assign weights to the learning sample LS_n.
4. For $b = 1, 2, ..., B$:
    a. At the base of LS_n learn the classifier Ψ_b,
    b. Calculate the classification error $e_b = \sum_{i=1}^{n} w_{b,i} * I(\Psi_b(x_i) \neq j_i)$,
    c. Calculate $\overline{e_b} = e_b + k$, $\underline{e_b} = e_b - k$
    d. If $\overline{e_b} > 1$ then $\overline{e_b} = 1$, If $\underline{e_b} < 0$ then $\underline{e_b} = 0$
    e. Calculate $\overline{c_b} = \frac{\ln(1-\overline{e_b})}{\overline{e_b}}$, $\underline{c_b} = \frac{\ln(1-\underline{e_b})}{\underline{e_b}}$
    f. Update weights:
    $$\overline{w_i}(b+1) = \frac{w_{b,i} \exp(\overline{c_b}*I(\Psi_b(x_i)\neq j_i))}{\sum_{j=1}^{n}(w_{b,j} \exp(\overline{c_b}*I(\Psi_b(x_i)\neq j_i)))}, \quad i = 1,..n,$$
    $$\underline{w_i}(b+1) = \frac{w_{b,i}) \exp(\underline{c_b}*I(\Psi_b(x_i)\neq j_i))}{\sum_{j=1}^{n}(w_{b,j} \exp(\underline{c_b}*I(\Psi_b(x_i)\neq j_i)))}, \quad i = 1,..n,$$
    g. Calculate $c_b = \lambda * \overline{c_b} + (1 - \lambda)\underline{c_b}$,
    h. Calculate $w_{b+1,i} = \lambda * \overline{w_i}(b+1) + (1 - \lambda) * \underline{w_i}(b+1)$,
    i. Assign updated weights to the learning sample LS_n.
5. Classify observation x according to the rule:
    $$\Psi_{IFw-AdaBoost}(x) = sign\left(\sum_{b=1}^{B} c_b \Psi_b(x)\right).$$

---

3 Experimental Studies

The experiment was performed with a male subject, aged 32. The subject was right-handed, had normal vision and did not report any mental disorders. The experiment was conducted according to the Helsinki declaration on proper treatment of human subjects. Written consent was obtained from the subject.

The subject was placed in a comfortable chair and EEG electrodes were applied on his head. In order to limit the number of artifacts, the participant was instructed to stay relaxed and not move. The start of the experiment was announced by a short sound signal. 200 trials were recorded during the experiment. Each trial started with a picture of an arrow pointing to the left or right displayed on a computer screen. The screen was located about 70 cm from the subject's eyes. The task of the subject was to imagine the wrist rotation of the hand indicated by the arrow (arrow to the left - left hand; arrow to the right - right hand). The arrow directions for the succeeding trials were chosen randomly. There were no breaks between trials. The experiment was divided into 4 sessions, 50 trials each. The trial length was fixed and was equal to 10 s. There were 3-minute breaks between sessions.

EEG data was recorded from two monopolar channels at a sampling frequency of 256 Hz. Four passive electrodes were used in the experiments. Two of them were attached to the subject's scalp at C3 and C4 positions according to the International 10–20 system [10]. The reference and ground electrodes were located at Fpz and the right mastoid, respectively. The impedance of the electrodes was kept below $5\,k\Omega$. The EEG signal was acquired with Discovery 20 amplifier (BrainMaster) and recorded with OpenVibe Software [19].

During the data recording stage some restrictions to the experiment protocol were introduced in order to preliminarily limit the number of artifacts in the recording. These restrictions, however, could not eliminate the artifacts fully. Therefore, in order to enhance the signal-to-noise ratio (SNR), the recorded EEG signal had to be subjected to some preprocessing. Since the most artifacts are outside the frequency band where motor potentials are searched for (alpha and beta frequency band), simple band-pass filtering in the 6–30 Hz frequency range was used in the reported survey. According to Fatourechi et al. low-pass filtering should remove most of EMG artifacts and high-pass filtering should remove EOG artifacts [4]. Moreover, the low-pass filtering allows also eliminating the artifacts caused by power lines that are in the 50 Hz range (in Poland). A Butterworth band-pass filter of the 4th order was used to filter the EEG data.

The classification of the motor imagery EEG data was performed with power band features. Twelve frequency bands were used to extract the features: alpha band (8–13 Hz), beta band (13–30 Hz), five sub-bands of alpha band (8–9 Hz; 9–10 Hz; 10–11 Hz; 11–12 Hz; 12–13 Hz), five sub-bands of beta band (13–17 Hz; 17–20 Hz; 20–23 Hz; 23–26 Hz; 26–30 Hz). The features were calculated separately per each second of the recording, hence there were 240 features. Due to a high number of features, the feature selection process was performed with LASSO algorithm [10]. Taking into account a small number of samples (200 samples), the number of classes (2 classes), and the possibility of using non-linear classifiers, we decided that no more than 8 features should be used in the classification process [18].

In the classification process four different classifier types were tested: boosting classifiers, LDA, SVM, and k-NN. First, we compared four boosting algorithms described in detail in Sect. 3. Then, we moved to SVM classifiers. Here we compared SVMs with different kernel functions: linear, quadratic, polynomial, and rbf. Finally, we tested k-NN classifiers with different values of k parameter (k was set to 1, 3, 5, and 7). The performance of each classifier, regardless of its type, was evaluated with 10-fold cross-validation scheme.

4   Results

Figure 1 presents the results of the experiments, in which Boosting algorithms were used. The experiments were performed for 200 iterations for both learning Fig. 1(a) and testing Fig. 1(b) process. Three versions of Boosting algorithms (AdaBoost – B1, RealAdaBoost – B2, GentleAdaBoost – B3) were used in research as well as the modification of AdaBoost algorithm presented in this work (B1M) with $\lambda = 0$ and $k = 0.025$. The classification accuracy presented in Fig. 1(a) indicate unequivocally that the classifiers were overtrained. Such classifiers behavior might be a result of small learning sets - each of them contained only 191 elements. The testing error was in the range of 37–32%, which was

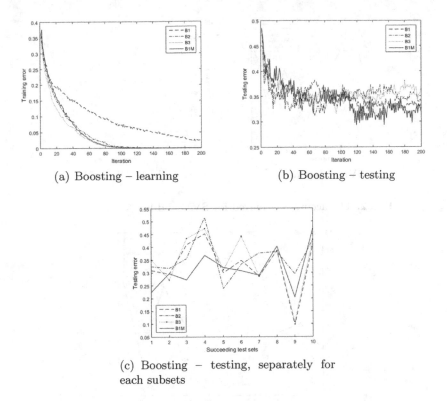

(a) Boosting – learning

(b) Boosting – testing

(c) Boosting – testing, separately for each subsets

Fig. 1. The accuracy achieved for boosting classifiers

an average of 10 repetitions. The best results were obtained for the proposed modification of the AdaBoost algorithm. The average results from the iterations from 120 to 130 were used in the analysis. They are presented in Fig. 1(c). The X axis indicates the index of the testing subset.

Figure 2 presents the classification results for the algorithms from k-NN and SVM group. The algorithms that were characterized by stable classification for different testing subsets were selected for the final analysis. These were SVM with the linear kernel and k-NN with 3 neighbors.

The classification error obtained with the use of the selected algorithms is shown in Fig. 3 and in Table 2.

Three from the selected algorithms (B1M, linear SVM, LDA) were characterized by similar average errors. The difference (for both the average and the median) was no higher than 2%. The proposed boosting algorithm was the most stable due to the fact that the spread of results for the individual learning subsets was no higher than 23%, while for the two other algorithms it was 38% and 33% respectively. 3-NN algorithm had the same dispersion of results (23%), however the correctness of the classification was inferior by 5% when compared with the results obtained for the boosting algorithm.

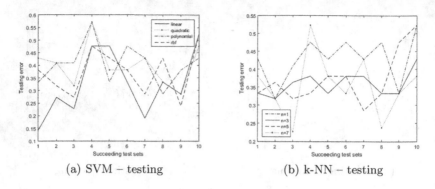

(a) SVM – testing   (b) k-NN – testing

Fig. 2. The accuracy achieved for SVM and k-NN classifiers

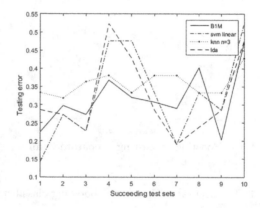

Fig. 3. The comparison of the accuracy achieved for four selected classifiers

Table 2. The error (in %) obtained for four selected classifiers for 10 testing subsets

Algorithm	Testing subsets										Mean	Median
	1	2	3	4	5	6	7	8	9	10		
B1M	23	30	27	37	32	31	29	40	20	47	32	30
SVM linear	14	27	23	48	48	33	19	33	29	52	33	31
3-NN	33	36	32	33	38	38	29	33	48	52	37	35
LDA	29	27	23	52	43	29	19	24	29	48	32	29

5   Conclusion

In the paper we compared the performance of four boosting classifiers
(AdaBoost, RealAdaBoost, GentleAdaBoost, and our modification of AdaBoost
- B1M) and three classic classification algorithms: LDA, SVM, and k-NN. After
the comparison, performed over the EEG data acquired during a MI-BCI session, we found out that our modification of AdaBoost provided the best results

among the four boosting algorithms and almost all other classifiers tested. Two exceptions were LDA and SVM with linear kernel, the performance of which was on the same level as in the case of B1M.

The analysis, the outcome of which was presented in the paper, was meant as a preliminarily study on the application of boosting algorithms in BCI domain. Because our results were on the same level as the results of two classifiers leading in BCI research, we plan to extend our analysis to more subjects. Moreover, since the results obtained with the use of the boosting algorithm proposed in this paper were the most stable, we believe that it can bring real benefits when used not in an off-line but in an on-line BCI mode.

Acknowledgments. This work was supported in part by the statutory funds of the Department of Systems and Computer Networks, Wroclaw University of Science and Technology.

References

1. Breiman, L., et al.: Arcing classifier. Ann. Stat. **26**(3), 801–849 (1998)
2. Burduk, R.: The AdaBoost algorithm with the imprecision determine the weights of the observations. In: Nguyen, N.T., Attachoo, B., Trawiński, B., Somboonviwat, K. (eds.) ACIIDS 2014. LNCS, vol. 8398, pp. 110–116. Springer, Cham (2014). doi:10.1007/978-3-319-05458-2_12
3. Donnerer, M., Steed, A.: Using a p300 brain-computer interface in an immersive virtual environment. Presence Teleoperators Virtual Environ. **19**(1), 12–24 (2010)
4. Fatourechi, M., Bashashati, A., Ward, R.K., Birch, G.E.: Emg and eog artifacts in brain computer interface systems: a survey. Clin. Neurophysiol. **118**(3), 480–494 (2007)
5. Friedman, J., Hastie, T., Tibshirani, R., et al.: Additive logistic regression: a statistical view of boosting. Ann. Stat. **28**(2), 337–407 (2000)
6. Guger, C., Edlinger, G., Harkam, W., Niedermayer, I., Pfurtscheller, G.: How many people are able to operate an EEG-based brain-computer interface (BCI)? IEEE Trans. Neural Syst. Rehabil. Eng. **11**(2), 145–147 (2003)
7. Guger, C., Schlogl, A., Neuper, C., Walterspacher, D., Strein, T., Pfurtscheller, G.: Rapid prototyping of an EEG-based brain-computer interface (BCI). IEEE Trans. Neural Syst. Rehabil. Eng. **9**(1), 49–58 (2001)
8. Guger, C., Schlogl, A., Walterspacher, D., Pfurtscheller, G.: Design of an EEG-based brain-computer interface (BCI) from standard components running in real-time under windows-entwurf eines eeg-basierten brain-computer interfaces (bci) mit standardkomponenten, das unter windows in echtzeit arbeitet. Biomedizinische Technik/Biomed. Eng. **44**(1–2), 12–16 (1999)
9. Hayashi, I., Tsuruse, S., Suzuki, J., Kozma,R.T.: A proposal for applying PDI-boosting to brain-computer interfaces. In: 2012 IEEE International Conference on Fuzzy Systems (FUZZ-IEEE), pp. 1–6. IEEE (2012)
10. Jasper, H.H.: The ten twenty electrode system of the international federation. Electroencephalogr. Clin. Neurophysiol. **10**, 371–375 (1958)
11. Li, S.Z., Zhang, Z.: Floatboost learning and statistical face detection. IEEE Trans. Pattern Anal. Mach. Intell. **26**(9), 1112–1123 (2004)

12. Liu, Y., Zhang, H., Zhao, Q., Zhang, L.: Common spatial-spectral boosting pattern for brain-computer interface. In: Proceedings of the Twenty-First European Conference on Artificial Intelligence, pp. 537–542. IOS Press (2014)

13. Müller-Putz, G.R., Kaiser, V., Solis-Escalante, T., Pfurtscheller, G.: Fast set-up asynchronous brain-switch based on detection of foot motor imagery in 1-channel EEG. Med. Biol. Eng. Comput. **48**(3), 229–233 (2010)

14. Pfurtscheller, G., Brunner, C., Schlögl, A., Da Silva, F.L.: Mu rhythm (de) synchronization and EEG single-trial classification of different motor imagery tasks. NeuroImage **31**(1), 153–159 (2006)

15. Pfurtscheller, G., Neuper, C., Schlogl, A., Lugger, K.: Separability of EEG signals recorded during right and left motor imagery using adaptive autoregressive parameters. IEEE Trans. Rehabil. Eng. **6**(3), 316–325 (1998)

16. Porwik, P., Doroz, R., Orczyk, T.: The k-NN classifier and self-adaptive hotelling data reduction technique in handwritten signatures recognition. Pattern Anal. Appl. **18**(4), 983–1001 (2015)

17. Porwik, P., Orczyk, T., Lewandowski, M., Cholewa, M.: Feature projection k-NN classifier model for imbalanced and incomplete medical data. Biocybern. Biomed. Eng. **36**(4), 644–656 (2016)

18. Raudys, S.J., Jain, A.K., et al.: Small sample size effects in statistical pattern recognition: recommendations for practitioners. IEEE Trans. Pattern Anal. Mach. Intell. **13**(3), 252–264 (1991)

19. Renard, Y., Lotte, F., Gibert, G., Congedo, M., Maby, E., Delannoy, V., Bertrand, O., Lécuyer, A.: OpenViBE: an open-source software platform to design, test, and use brain-computer interfaces in real and virtual environments. Presence Teleoperators Virtual Environ. **19**(1), 35–53 (2010)

20. Schapire, R.E.: Using output codes to boost multiclass learning problems. ICML **97**, 313–321 (1997)

A Multimodal Face and Fingerprint Recognition Biometrics System

Maciej Szymkowski[(✉)] and Khalid Saeed

Faculty of Computer Science,
Bialystok University of Technology, Bialystok, Poland
szymkowskimack@gmail.com, k.saeed@pb.edu.pl

Abstract. Biometrics helps protect users' data against hackers. There are two groups of biometrics features, the first contains physiological features and the second consists of behavioral traits. In the case of biometrics safety procedure the user does not need to remember his/her password because they always have them. It is proved that physiological biometrics can grant higher accuracy than systems that base on behavioral traits. One of the most popular physiological features are fingerprints and face. In the work presented in this paper, these two features are taken into consideration at the same time in a multimodal system. The accuracy of user identification is calculated for each of the two features individually and also for them when combined together.

Keywords: Face · Fingerprint · Biometrics · Physiological biometrics · Identification · Security systems · Multimodal systems · Fusion

1 Introduction

Recent research is showing that most of security systems are at the risk of breaking their hedges. To protect users' data, biometrics safety procedures introduce the possibility of increasing the system protection level. The main reason of using this kind of safety procedure is that the user does not need to carry the tokens or remember the password. People are simply recognized by the features showing 'what they are' - they are authenticated by their physiological or behavioral characteristics. In biometrics safety systems, simply, the user himself is the key. Fingerprints, retina, face or other measurable traits could play the role of the password, a key that is not as easy to break as the traditional one because human traits are not easy to imitate.

There are two groups of biometrics features. The first is a group that contains representatives of physiological traits. For instance, face, fingerprint, retina or hand geometry are classified as participants of this group. It means that these features are connected with how human organism is built. In the case of behavioral biometrics features, keystroke dynamics, voice or signature are connected with this group.

In the system described in this work, only physiological features are taken into consideration. It is connected with the fact that they are not easy to imitate and that each man have these features unique. On the other hand one can claim that behavioral traits are easier to implement because they, in the most of the cases, do not need any specialized hardware and could be collected without notifying the user. This statement

K. Saeed et al. (Eds.): CISIM 2017, LNCS 10244, pp. 131–140, 2017.
DOI: 10.1007/978-3-319-59105-6_12

is true but samples of behavioral traits differ from each other even within the same user and hence the repeatability is very low because it is hard to repeat proper activity each time in exactly the same manner. Moreover, physiological traits grant higher level of identification accuracy because of their uniqueness.

The system presented in this paper is multimodal. It means that at least two features are combined in order to check whether this combination gives higher accuracy than the data obtained from each of the selected traits separately. Another goal of the presented approach is to check whether more data to analyze can lead to more accurate classification. In the authors' approach fingerprint and face were chosen. Each of them can easily be collected because most of personal computers contain cameras whilst the fingerprint scanners are available and built-in scanners in the laptops and mobile phones are becoming more popular.

2 Known Approaches

Lately more interest in the case of face and fingerprint recognition has been observed. To present the current state of the knowledge, the authors of this work selected a few different approaches that can be compared with the idea presented in this paper.

In [1] an idea that uses eigenvectors to identify user by his face is described. In 1987 the originators of this approach were Sirovich and Kirby although eigenvectors as a significant part of human recognition algorithm were firstly used by Matthew Turk and Alex Paul Pentland. Their algorithm mainly bases on principal component analysis (PCA), in which one of the most essential steps is the image conversion to vertical vector to be a part of the analyzed matrix. Then the mean value of each horizontal vector is calculated and finally the mean vertical vector is obtained to subtract from each of the matrix vertical vectors. The matrix values normalization is done to change all matrix values into 0–255 interval. Then main principal values of matrix and each of vertical vectors are calculated. Authors of this algorithm, have only described the processing method, they do not present or compare results.

Authors of [2] mostly based on the idea that was presented by Turk and Pentland in [1]. In the case of Eigenface technique one can easily observe that variation was maximized, while in Fisherface method, the main aim is to maximize mean distance between classes and to minimize variance within each class. Authors of this approach prepared an algorithm in which the Modified Fisher Linear Discriminant Model (MFLD) is used. This model consist of decomposition of Fisher Linear Discriminant into simultaneous diagonalization of the two within- and between-class scatter matrices. As the second part of the work Fuzzy Fisher Linear Discriminant (FFLD) was mentioned. One of the main goals of authors approach was dimensionality reduction of analyzed matrix by which algorithm could be more efficient. To measure distance between two samples, Euclidean metric was used. Authors claimed that by usage of MFLD, accuracy of user identification was 91.4% and for FFLD it equals 94.8%.

Completely different approach, one could observe in the method called Local binary pattern histograms (LBPH). In [1, 2] whole image was taken into consideration in contrary to Eigenface and Fisherface techniques, in method that is presented in [3], image local features are taken into account. For each pixel, binary string is determined.

It is created by comparison between analyzed pixel value and values of all his neighbors. Therefore each pixel is described by p-value binary string, where p is a number of neighbors that were taken into consideration in the comparison process. This string is called local binary pattern (LBP). The main idea of this algorithm is connected with dividing an input image into m different parts and calculating function LBP for each, previously separated part. Then for each region histogram that is created on the basis of calculated LBP and specific vector basing on histograms are prepared. For new sample that was not stored in the database, histogram vector is calculated and it is compared with all vectors that are in the database. Authors of this approach have only described the processing method, they do not present or compare results.

In the solution that was originally published in [4], one can observe that authors mainly focused on interesting processing algorithm for fingerprint feature extraction. In the case of this algorithm ridge bifurcations, ridge endings, core and deltas, as a kind of minutiae, are detected. Moreover authors presented their own idea by which all minutiae could be easily described. Feature vector of the whole fingerprint is prepared with usage of minutiae-type, their location and orientation. Authors of [4] claim that there is no such a need to begin fingerprint analysis with image preprocessing (for instance improving contrast or histogram alignment). The authors' algorithm starts with image analysis methods such as initial segmentation, orientation computation and ridge frequency computation. As the main purpose of this stage, localization of a fingerprint area on the image, orientation of each pixel and calculation frequency of ridges are mentioned. On the basis of [4] one could get into know that these steps are enough to prepare fingerprint image to filtration process. Moreover, in this paper authors presented an interesting idea by which spurious minutiae could be easily removed. As it was in the case of [1, 3] in this paper only processing method is described, authors do not present or compare obtained results.

Another solution that was originally published in [5], presents the processing algorithm that could be used to prepare two fingerprints to comparison procedure. One can easily observe that unlike algorithm presented in [4], this one is taking into account only two types of minutiae that are ridge ending and ridge bifurcation. This approach is using CN algorithm to detect different types of minutiae and different image analysis operations that have to prepare an image to minutiae classification. Feature vector consists of minutiae type and localization. Authors of this approach also described comparison method between two different fingerprints. They take into account number of minutiae in two compared images and by its usage determine matching score of analyzed fingerprints. Despite the fact that the whole comparison procedure was described, no information about accuracy of proposed approach were attached in this work.

The algorithm that is presented in [6], as the one described in [5], deals with two types of minutiae – ridge ending and ridge bifurcation but it also takes into consideration Core in fingerprint. Moreover in this solution is not described any specific identification algorithm. On the other hand on the basis of this algorithm, one can easily prepare feature vector by which comparison between two fingerprint images will be done. In the case of this approach, additional image analysis operations are done on an image. These steps are used to obtain image from which minutiae could be extract.

Due to the fact that in this work authors deal with the problem of multimodal biometrics system, a few works about this kind of systems were also analyzed.

In [7] authors presented a system that bases on two behavioral features that are keystroke dynamics and mouse movement. The dynamics of moving and mouse button dwell times were taken into consideration. Authors prepared simple comparison method by which interesting results were obtained. As a classifier k-Nearest Neighbor was used. Authors measured the accuracy for different number of nearest neighbors and for each of the analyzed features separately and also for combination of keystroke dynamics and mouse movement. The best results were obtained in the case of combination of two features and accuracy was 68.8%. All accuracies for other traits were lower than in the case of fusion system.

In the literature there are several examples of multimodal biometrics systems. There are a few different ideas of how these solutions should work [8–10]. In the papers [8, 9], no specific solution was presented. Only the main aim and the idea of multimodal biometrics systems were described.

Multimodal biometrics systems that combine face and fingerprint were presented in [11, 12]. In [11] authors used face and fingerprint as the primary characteristics and gender, ethnicity, height as soft characteristics. Experiments were done on a database that consists of 263 users. Results show that the recognition accuracy of the primary characteristics can be improved by additional step that basis on soft characteristics.

Authors of [12] also presented the work about multimodal face and fingerprint biometrics system. Face verification module incorporates Gabor Wavelet texture features and face edges. For the fingerprint classification, authors prepared an algorithm that basis on minutiae detection and builds feature vector for each fingerprint from the database and for a new sample. Authors claimed that their system could be effectively used for people identification at airports.

3 Proposed Approach

In order to measure accuracy of each of the proposed ways of user identification, an algorithm with its computer implementation in Java are presented. Two algorithms were implemented – one for face recognition and one for fingerprint classification. In the case of face recognition problem, Eigenface method [1] was used. This idea was selected due to the high accuracy level, effectiveness of processing process and simplicity of implementation. It was implemented with the usage of Java CV, which also provides methods by which programmer could easily grab current image from the camera connected to the computer.

Each of users in our database is described by three images of his fingerprint and by three images of his face. In the case of fingerprint classification, authors prepared their own approach that provides a procedure for fingerprint image processing. After image processing, feature vector is generated. Manhattan distance is then followed with classic k-Nearest Neighbor algorithm. All steps of this approach are presented in the form of block diagram in Fig. 1.

At the beginning of fingerprint image processing the image is binarized. Different strategies of binarization were described in [13]. Authors decided to implement manual binarization with threshold set at 215. Pixel value is set to black if condition presented in (1) is satisfied, where x and y are the position of the X and Y axis respectively and R

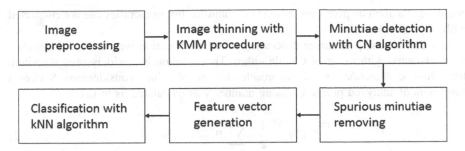

Fig. 1. Block diagram of fingerprint algorithm that was implemented in the application

is red channel pixel value at the given location. Accordingly G is for green channel value and B is for blue. The results of this procedure and the original image are presented respectively in Fig. 2a and b.

$$\frac{R_{x,y} + G_{x,y} + B_{x,y}}{3} > threshold \tag{1}$$

(a)   (b)   (c)

Fig. 2. Original image (a) image after binarization procedure (b) and image after thinning procedure (c).

As the second step of image preprocessing morphological closing is proposed. This step is connected with the quality of captured images. Due to the fact that these images are not in the best quality, small spaces in fingerprint are visible. Authors implemented this kind of morphological operation because it consists of image erosion preceded by image dilation. It causes that small spacing are filled with black pixels that represents elements belonging to fingerprint and then additional, redundant black pixels are removed. By this operation the fingerprint image quality is a little bit raised.

In Fig. 2c. fingerprint image after thinning procedure is presented. By this step all fingerprint lines are reduced to 1-pixel width. It was done due to the fact that redundant pixels could make significant impact on minutiae detection method. Additional pixels could be classified as pixels that belongs to minutiae but in fact they are not connected with the real one.

As the third step of image processing minutiae detection was done. All minutiae were extracted with usage of CN algorithm. This solution is a widely-used algorithm for minutiae detection. In this approach authors take into consideration 8 closest neighbors of analyzed pixels. Crossing number was calculated as in (2).

$$CN = \frac{1}{2} \cdot \sum_{i=1}^{8} |P_i - P_{i-1}| \tag{2}$$

By calculation of this number analyzed pixel could be properly classified. When $CN = 0$ it means that this pixel belongs to background, $CN = 1$ – means that analyzed pixel is ridge terminal, $CN = 2$ – points at ridge continuation and $CN = 3$ – return information that pixel is ridge bifurcation.

Due to the low quality of processed image, as another step spurious minutiae removing was presented. This step was done in the same way as it was described in [4]. It means that distance between minutiae and all of its neighbors is calculated. If this distance is too low, minutiae is classified as spurious and is removed. After removing all redundant minutiae, feature vector is generated. In the case of this approach it consists only of two simple information – number of ridge endings and number of ridge bifurcations. All steps of the processing algorithm are presented in Table 1.

Table 1. Fingerprint processing algorithm

Input: Image that is provided by the user.
Output: Feature vector that describes fingerprint.
1.   Binarize input image with manual thresholding binarization method. Set binarization_threshold = 215.
2.   Do morphological closing with 3x3 mask on the image obtained after step 1.
3.   Do thinning with usage of KMM algorithm.
4.   Detect all minutiae likely structures on the fingerprint image with usage of CN algorithm.

5.   Remove spurious minutiae
      a.   Set minutiae_threshold = 60.
      b.   For each detected minutiae:
          i. Measure distance to all other minutiae
         ii. If at least one distance is lower than minutiae_threshold remove minutiae that is too close to analyzed one.

6.   Count number of ridge bifurcations and ridge endings.
7.   Create feature vector that consists of numbers established in step number 6.

In the case of classification, distances between new samples feature vector and all feature vectors of all samples that are stored in the database are measured. Then classification is done with classic *k*-NN algorithm. Classification procedure is presented in Table 2. In Table 3 description of multimodal system is provided.

Table 2. Fingerprint classification procedure

Input: Fingerprint image sample that is not stored in the database.
Output: Classification decision.
1.   Create feature vector for the new sample with usage of fingerprint processing algorithm described in Table 1.

2.   For each image in the database:
       a.   Create feature vector for currently analyzed image.
       b.   Measure distance between feature vectors of currently analyzed image and the new samples one.
       c.   Add calculated value to the list with the information about image class.

3.   Calculate with k-Nearest Neighbor algorithm the most probable class for the new sample.

Table 3. Multimodal system description

Input: Face and fingerprint images that are not stored in the database.
Output: Classification decision
1.   Create feature vector for fingerprint image and classify it with usage of classification procedure described in Table 2.
2.   Classify face image with usage of Eigenface algorithm.

3.   Compare classification decisions:
       a.   If both algorithms return the same user class then user is recognized as the one pointed by both procedures.
       b.   If classes returned by both algorithms are different then user is not recognized.

4.   Return classification decision.

4 Results of the Experiment

Authors' database consists of 50 users that are described by 3 fingerprint samples and 3 face samples each. Experiments were based on dividing the database into two 75-samples sets that were: test and learning set. Also different number of input samples modifications were taken into consideration. Accuracy was also measured for 5, 10, 20, 30, 40 and 45 users. Fingerprint images were obtained with Futronic® FS80 fingerprint scanner, face photos were done with Tracer® PC Prospecto Cam.

In Fig. 3 results of two implemented algorithms were presented. As one can observe better results were obtained with usage of face identification algorithm. Results of this way of identification was nearby 100% mostly for each of number of users. In the case of proposed fingerprint classification algorithm with increasing number of users, classification accuracy decreases. Probably it was connected with the fact that simple feature vector was used to describe each of sample. One can observe that by usage of more complex descriptor accuracy level could be higher.

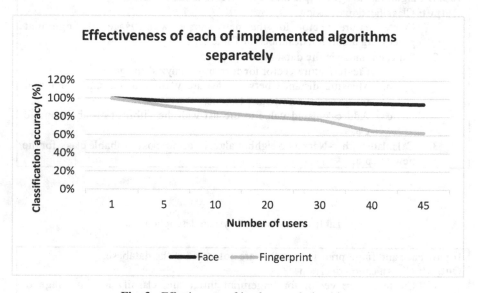

Fig. 3. Effectiveness of implemented algorithms

In Fig. 4. the accuracy results of each of identification methods are presented in comparison with the approach when those two features are analyzed simultaneously. One can easily observe that combination of these two algorithms gives quite good results.

On the basis of the results that are presented in Fig. 4, one can observe that the best implemented algorithm was Eigenface that was used to recognize user by his face. On the other hand, the worst was fingerprint algorithm. As it was mentioned before, this results is caused by simple feature vector. It is observable that two fingerprints that have similar numbers of ridge bifurcations and ridge endings could be classified as fingerprints that belongs to one man. Results that were obtained with combination of these two features are quite good. These results present that user could be recognized on the basis of his face and fingerprint with the accuracy ratio that is nearby 81%.

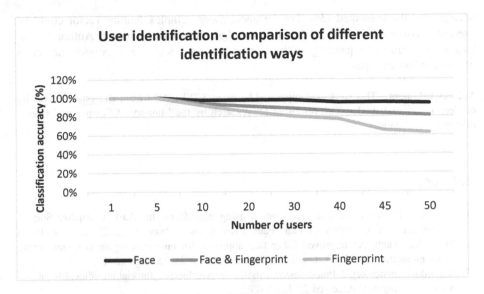

Fig. 4. Comparison of different identification ways

5 Conclusions and Future Work

Biometrics security procedures provide new high standard of security methods that can be used in different programs or devices. One can observe that even if user knows how fingerprint or the face of other user looks like, it is really hard for him to imitate these features. What is more, recent cameras or fingerprint scanners take into consideration not only the form of analyzed feature but also its life span. For instance in the case of cameras, user have to move his head in the left and in the right side. By this step false faces, prepared by photos could be detected. Other solution is connected with finger-prints. Fingerprint scanners could also detect temperature of finger and its structure. By these ideas, false fingerprints created with the usage of different materials can also be tracked down.

As expected, combining of two human, physiological features allowed to obtain quite good recognition ratio in the case of user identification. It is easily observable that the accuracy of user identification for both of analyzed features was 81%. This result provides that proposed solution could be implemented in real circumstances. What is more combination of two features can assure better recognition ratio than relying on only one human trait. Proposed fingerprint algorithm accuracy ratio was 62.5%. It is easily observable that combination of face and fingerprint provided better recognition ratio than the approach based only on fingerprint.

The approach presented in this work, can be used in the case of user verification problem. Moreover, one can easily observe that biometrics safety procedure that were implemented in this program, assure satisfying verification accuracy level.

As future work the authors would work under more detailed fingerprint processing algorithm and more effective face identification model. These steps aim to increase accuracy of the presented idea. For instance, more complex feature vector could be used. Moreover different face identification algorithms will be tested. Authors' database is continuously expanding. In the near feature authors would work under detection of more minutiae types.

Acknowledgment. This work was supported by grant S/WI/1/2013 from Białystok University of Technology and funded with resources for research by the Ministry of Science and Higher Education in Poland.

References

1. Turk, M., Pentland, A.: Face recognition using eigenfaces. In: IEEE Computer Society Conference on Computer Vision and Pattern Recognition, Proceedings CVPR 1991 (1991)
2. More, V., Wagh, A.: Improved fisher face approach for human recognition system using facial biometrics. Int. J. Inf. Commun. Technol. Res. 2(2), 135–139 (2012)
3. http://docs.opencv.org/2.4/modules/contrib/doc/facerec/facerec_tutorial.html#local-binary-patterns-histograms. Accessed 20 Jan 2017
4. Surmacz, K., Saeed, K., Rapta, P.: An improved algorithm for feature extraction from a fingerprint fuzzy image. Optica Applicata 43(3), 515–527 (2013)
5. Ravi, J., Raja, K.B., Venugopal, K.R.: Fingerprint recognition using minutia score matching. Int. J. Eng. Sci. Technol. 1, 35–42 (2009)
6. Gnanasivam, P., Muttan, S.: An efficient algorithm for fingerprint preprocessing and feature extraction. Procedia Comput. Sci. 2, 133–142 (2010)
7. Panasiuk, P., Szymkowski, M., Dąbrowski, M., Saeed, K.: A multimodal biometric user identification system based on keystroke dynamics and mouse movements. In: Saeed, K., Homenda, W. (eds.) CISIM 2016. LNCS, vol. 9842, pp. 672–681. Springer, Cham (2016). doi:10.1007/978-3-319-45378-1_58
8. Panchal, T., Singh, A.: Multimodal biometric system. Int. J. Adv. Res. Comput. Sci. Softw. Eng. 3, 1360–1363 (2013)
9. Ross, A., Jain, A.: Multimodal biometrics: an overview. In: Proceedings of 12th European Signal Processing Conference (EUSIPCO), Vienna, Austria, pp. 1221–1224, September 2004
10. Gavrilova, M., Monwar, M.: Multimodal biometrics and intelligent image processing for security systems. United States of America, ISBN: 978-1-4666-3646-0 (2013)
11. Jain, A.K., Nandakumar, K., Lu, X., Park, U.: Integrating faces, fingerprints, and soft biometric traits for user recognition. In: Maltoni, D., Jain, A.K. (eds.) BioAW 2004. LNCS, vol. 3087, pp. 259–269. Springer, Heidelberg (2004). doi:10.1007/978-3-540-25976-3_24
12. Seralkhatem Osman Ali, A., Sagayan, V., Saeed Malik, A., Rasheed, W.: A combined face, fingerprint authentication system. In: Proceedings of the 18th IEEE International Symposium on Consumer Electronics (ISCE 2014), pp. 127–129 (2014)
13. Chaki, N., Shaikh, S.H., Saeed, K.: Exploring Image Binarization Techniques. SCI, vol. 560. Springer, New Delhi (2014). doi:10.1007/978-81-322-1907-1

Keystroke Dynamics and Finger Knuckle Imaging Fusion for Continuous User Verification

Tomasz Emanuel Wesołowski, Rafal Doroz(✉), Krzysztof Wrobel, and Hossein Safaverdi

Institute of Computer Science, University of Silesia, Katowice, Poland
{tomasz.wesolowski,rafal.doroz,krzysztof.wrobel,
hossein.safaverdi}@us.edu.pl

Abstract. The paper presents a novel user identity verification method based on fusion of keystroke dynamics and knuckle images analysis. In our solution the verification is performed by an ensemble of classifiers used to verify the identity of an active user. A proposed verification module works on a database which comprises of data representing keystroke dynamics and knuckle images. The usability of the introduced approach was tested experimentally. The obtained results confirm that the proposed fusion method gives better results than the use of a single biometric feature only. For this reason our method can be used for increasing a protection level of computer resources against impostors. The paper presents preliminary research conducted to assess the potential of biometric methods fusion.

Keywords: Biometrics · Keystroke dynamics · Finger knuckle · User verification

1 Introduction

Increasing computer systems security is a crucial task in the world dominated by electronically stored personal data and sensitive information. The number of attacks is increasing year by year. Only within the years 2014 and 2015 the amount of individuals affected by security breaches, where sensitive personal data such as electronic health records were stolen, increased hundred times [17]. The attacks themselves are becoming more and more sophisticated. There is various kinds of cyber attacks therefore different cyber attack detection strategies have to be developed [11]. Attacks can come from outside of the computer system but a big part of intrusions consists of insider attacks [13]. Hence the requirement for novel security measures is very high. As the main goal of biometrics is the automatic recognition of individuals based on the knowledge of their physical or behavioral characteristics, biometric methods are commonly used in IT security systems because of their high effectiveness.

Behavioral biometric methods use, among other things, an analysis of the movements of various manipulators (eg. a computer mouse [16]) or the dynamics

© IFIP International Federation for Information Processing 2017
Published by Springer International Publishing AG 2017. All Rights Reserved
K. Saeed et al. (Eds.): CISIM 2017, LNCS 10244, pp. 141–152, 2017.
DOI: 10.1007/978-3-319-59105-6_13

of typing on a computer keyboard (keystroke dynamics) [1,2,12,15]. An analysis of keystroke dynamics involves detection of a rhythm and habits of a computer user while typing on a keyboard [18]. As the result of such an analysis, a user profile is obtained that can then be used in the access authorization systems. In our approach the registration of the user activity while working with a keyboard is performed automatically and continuously in the background, without additionally involving a user. The data are captured on the fly and saved in text files on the ongoing basis. Based on these text logs keystroke dynamics analysis is performed in order to verify an active user's access permissions. The big advantage of the proposed method is that user verification can be performed continuously on the fly. To increase a protection level the proposed in this paper approach combines the keystroke dynamics with another biometric method based on finger knuckle pattern recognition. Image acquisition is performed using a dedicated device especially designed for this purpose [3].

An intrusion detection can be performed in various ways. Literature sources indicate among others methods based on a fuzzy approach [7]. However more frequently proposed solutions are based on classifiers. The in this paper proposed approach is based on classification. Ensembles of classifiers are used to classify features derived from keystroke dynamics analysis and a single classifier approach is used with knuckle patterns.

The goal of the described research is to develop a real time user verification system based on fusion of keystroke dynamics and finger knuckle images analysis. However a method of analyzing the finger knuckle on the fly not been developed yet as it needs a lot of resources to analyze the images in a real time. Before the decision was made it was necessary to verify, if it is worth investing time and resources in developing such a method and, if the fusion of keystroke dynamics and finger knuckle analysis is potentially interesting. Therefore the preliminary research was conducted to assess the potential of the above mentioned biometric methods fusion. This paper presents the preliminary results of an intruder detection system based on the introduced novel approach.

2   Proposed Biometric User Verification System

The proposed computer security approach involves two phases: legitimate user profiling and active user verification. In the first stage user profiling is performed that consists of recording a legitimate user activity while working with a keyboard and acquiring this user's finger knuckle images. Based on the acquired data user's profile is being established according to the procedures described in the following sections of this paper.

After establishing user's profile in the first stage the profile can be used for verification of an active user in the second stage. The proposed user verification model shown in Fig. 1 connects two methods of user verification. The introduced approach is based on the fusion of keystroke dynamics and knuckle analysis. For the purpose of the fusion the biometric user verification methods were chosen that according to the [17] for keystroke based approach and [3] for finger knuckle pattern analysis perform better than other methods described in literature.

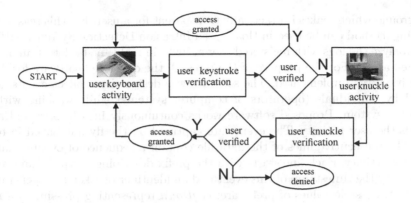

Fig. 1. The proposed biometric user verification algorithm

User activity should be verified continuously, in the background, while a user is performing his everyday tasks. To allow this, all keyboard events generated by the user are recorded and time dependencies between them are analyzed. The keystroke verification unit basing on the profiles of legitimate users and recorded activity of an at the moment active user establishes a decision if the activity belongs to a legitimate user. If the user has been successfully verified an access is granted and the verification procedure continues. In case the verification was not successful there is a suspicion that an active user is an intruder. Therefore an additional verification is made by means of knuckle pattern recognition unit after taking a picture of the user's finger knuckles. If the user has been successfully verified an access is granted and the verification procedure continues with the keystroke based verification. If, again, the verification has not been successful an access to resources is denied and the security breach alert is generated.

2.1 Keystroke Based Subsystem

Keystroke dynamics refers to a typing pattern of an individual which in practice constitutes a so called profile. In the proposed method a profile of a user contains information on a sequence of key events and time dependencies that occur between the key events. The advantage of the proposed profiling method is that activity data collecting and analyzing is performed continuously in the

```
keyDown, 1396968151226, ID15
keyUp,    1396968151376, ID15
keyDown, 1396968152306, L3
keyDown, 1396968153376, ID34
keyUp,    1396968152446, L3
keyUp,    1396968153576, ID34
```

Fig. 2. A fragment of an input dataset with recorded keyboard events

background which makes it practically transparent for a user. For this reason the profiling method can be used in Host-based Intrusion Detection Systems (HIDS) that analyze the logs with registered user activity in real time to detect an unauthorized access. For the purpose of the research the dedicated software for data acquisition was implemented. The software was designed to collect events generated by individuals (operators of computer systems) while working with a protected system. Proposed software works continuously in a background and records the user activity. The events are captured on the fly and saved in text files. The consecutive lines of the data file contain a sequence of events related to a user activity. Each line starts with the prefix describing a type of an event, followed by the timestamp of this event and an identifier of a key that generated the event. Possible values of prefix are: *keyDown* representing pressing of a key and *keyUp* for key release event. An example of a raw input data is presented in Fig. 2. Such a recorded raw data can be presented in a data vector form (1). Data of a single j-th keyboard event for a given user constitute a vector $\mathbf{e}_j$:

$$\mathbf{e}_j = [type_j, t_j, \omega_j], \tag{1}$$

where $type \in \{keyDown, keyUp\}$ describes a type of a j-th event; t_j is a timestamp of a given event; ω_j is an identifier of a used key.

Activity data analysis is carried out separately for each user identified in the system by user identifier uid. All vectors $\mathbf{e}_j$ of the same user constitute this user activity dataset E^{uid}. In practice a number of vectors $\mathbf{e}_j$ is limited by period of time when the user activity was recorded.

Data in this form are difficult to interpret because they do not provide directly in-formation on how a user interacts with a computer system. Therefore it is necessary to process the data to obtain characteristics of a user by extracting time dependencies between keyboard events generated while the user was working. It should be noted that during the user activity analysis not only single characters are taken into account but pairs of keys are analyzed as well (for example when writing capital letters). In the proposed method there are 113 separate keys and key pairs considered.

Time dependencies were depicted as a difference of time between two keyboard events and were calculated according to the following rules. Time dependencies for single keys are represented by dwell times (time when a key stays pressed) and for pairs of keys by a delay time between two consecutive key down events of the overlapping keys (as shown in Fig. 3). In the next step time dependencies representing a use of the same key or key pair are grouped together. As, in total, there are 113 different keys and key pairs, there are also 113 separate time dependency groups G^k, $k = 1, \ldots, 113$ considered. The allowed number of time dependencies stored in a single group is limited by the parameter g. Each time a number of time dependencies in any of the groups G^k reaches g a feature vector $\mathbf{F}$ is created and this group that reached the limit is cleared. The value of parameter $g = 15$ has been determined experimentally.

Based on time dependencies stored in all previously formed groups G^k a feature vector $\mathbf{F} = [f_1, \ldots, f_{113}]$ is constructed as follows. The k-th element

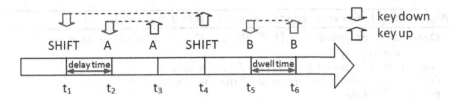

Fig. 3. Time dependencies between keyboard events

f_k of the vector $\mathbf{F}$ is calculated as the standard deviation of time dependencies stored in a k-th group G^k. For a given user identified by uid (based on this user's input data set) more feature vectors $\mathbf{F}$ are created and a profile $\Phi^{uid} = \{\mathbf{F}_1^{uid}, \mathbf{F}_2^{uid}, \dots, \mathbf{F}_z^{uid}\}$ describing the activity of a user in a computer system is constituted. The value of the parameter $z = 100$ has been determined experimentally. User's profile Φ^{uid} is stored in the database to be used by a classification based intrusion detection module. User profiling method based on keystroke analysis used in this proposed approach is described in details in [17].

The keystroke verification system is based on three ensembles of classifiers EC_a, $a = 1, \dots, 3$. Each of them consists of four heterogeneous classifiers: $\Psi^{(1)}$, $\Psi^{(2)}$, $\Psi^{(3)}$ and $\Psi^{(4)}$. The ensembles of classifiers EC_a work simultaneously and each one of them is trained using a separate training set TS_a (see Fig. 4) established by means of the Algorithm 1. The general structure of the proposed classification module is presented in Fig. 4.

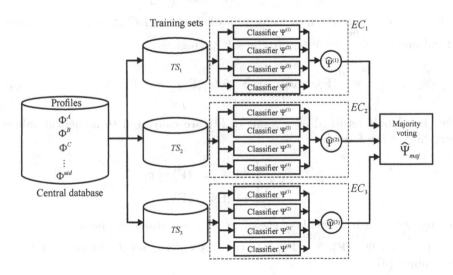

Fig. 4. The general scheme of the proposed classification module

User verification consists in assigning a user to one of two possible classes: legitimate user or an intruder. A classifier Ψ maps the vector $\mathbf{F}$ of a given user

---

Algorithm 1. Creating the training data sets TS_a, $a = 1, ..., 3$

Data: users' profiles $\Phi^{uid} = \{\mathbf{F}_1^{uid}, \mathbf{F}_2^{uid}, ..., \mathbf{F}_z^{uid}\}$ comprising feature vectors
    $\mathbf{F} = [f_1, f_2, ..., f_{113}]$
Result: training sets TS_1, TS_2 and TS_3 of a user uid

1   $O^{uid} := n$ randomly chosen vectors $\mathbf{F}$ from user's profile Φ^{uid} and $n \leq z$;
2   **for** $a = 1$ **to** 3 **do**
3      $O^a := n$ randomly chosen vectors $\mathbf{F}$ from another (randomly chosen) user's
       profile, and $n \leq z$;
4      $TS_a := O^{uid} \cup O^a$;
5 **return** TS_1, TS_2, TS_3;

---

to a class label c_j, where $j \in \{1, 2\}$:

$$\Psi(\mathbf{F}) \rightarrow c_j \in C. \tag{2}$$

In the proposed approach, the classifiers $\Psi^{(i)}$ return a probability $\hat{p}_i(c_j|\mathbf{F})$, $j \in \{1, 2\}$ that a given object $\mathbf{F}$ belongs to a class c_j. At the input of the node $\widehat{\Psi}^{(a)}$ (Fig. 4) the following data matrix is introduced:

$$I^{(a)}(\mathbf{F}) = \begin{bmatrix} \hat{p}_1(c_1|\mathbf{F}) & \hat{p}_1(c_2|\mathbf{F}) \\ \hat{p}_2(c_1|\mathbf{F}) & \hat{p}_2(c_2|\mathbf{F}) \\ \hat{p}_3(c_1|\mathbf{F}) & \hat{p}_3(c_2|\mathbf{F}) \\ \hat{p}_4(c_1|\mathbf{F}) & \hat{p}_4(c_2|\mathbf{F}) \end{bmatrix}. \tag{3}$$

Following the classification, each ensemble of classifiers EC_a, $a = 1, .., 3$ generates a local decision $\widehat{\Psi}^{(a)}$ according to the soft voting:

$$\widehat{\Psi}^{(a)}(\mathbf{F}) = \arg\max_{c_j \in C} \sum_{i=1}^{4} \hat{p}_i(c_j|\mathbf{F}), \quad a = 1, .., 3. \tag{4}$$

The class labels returned as a result of (4) are converted to numerical values according to the formula:

$$\widehat{\Psi}^{(a)}(\mathbf{F}) = \begin{cases} -1 \text{ if } \widehat{\Psi}^{(a)}(\mathbf{F}) = c_1 \\ +1 \text{ if } \widehat{\Psi}^{(a)}(\mathbf{F}) = c_2 \end{cases} \tag{5}$$

The results of each ensemble of classifiers EC_a are stored in the set $L = \{\widehat{\Psi}^{(1)}(\mathbf{F}), \widehat{\Psi}^{(2)}(\mathbf{F}), \widehat{\Psi}^{(3)}(\mathbf{F})\}$. On the basis of the set L the value of LS is determined (6).

$$LS(\mathbf{F}) = \sum_{a=1}^{3} \widehat{\Psi}^{(a)}(\mathbf{F}) \in L, a = 1, .., 3. \tag{6}$$

If the value of $LS(\mathbf{F})$ is greater than a threshold τ than the user is allowed to keep working, and the process of keystroke verification is repeated continuously.

Otherwise the user must proceed to knuckle verification stage. The influence of the threshold τ value on the keystroke verification accuracy is presented in the section concerning experiments.

2.2   Knuckle Analysis Subsystem

The aim of knuckle image analysis is to compare and find the similarity between the knuckle image of a person being verified and the reference knuckle images. The reference knuckle images are the images that have been acquired from a user and stored in the database during the profiling phase. In our method a special device was used for knuckle image acquisition. This device consists of a box that has a camera and three built in, white LED-lights. The purpose of the LED-lights is to illuminate the fingers equally from different directions. When taking a picture the camera is focused on the index finger. The example of finger knuckle image acquisition is shown in Fig. 5.

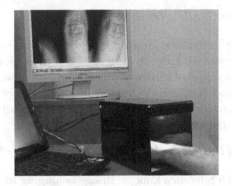

Fig. 5. Finger knuckle image acquisition

After a knuckle image acquisition an analysis is carried out which consists in extracting finger ridges. At first, the Hessian filtering was applied. The reason to choose this filtering method is, that it can detect the local strength of lines, ridges and direction of edges [4,5,9]. In the next step to the analyzed image a binarization is applied using the Otsu method - a well known binarization technique. This method assumes that there are two different classes in the image, foreground (object) and background. Classes are separated from each other by an intensity factor. The Otsu method automatically seeks for the optimum threshold that can maximize the distance between these two classes [10]. On the binarized image a skeletonization is performed which allows to reduce the thickness of lines in the image to one pixel. In the presented method the Pavlidis thinning algorithm was applied. In Fig. 6 all stages of line extraction are shown. The detailed description of the acquisition procedure is presented in [3].

Upon completion of image analysis, for a verified person (let it be denoted as A), two sets X and Y are formed. The set X contains values of similarity

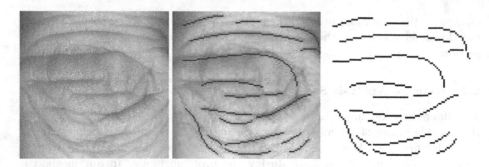

Fig. 6. Stages of finger knuckle image analysis

coefficients calculated between all possible pairs of images taken from the person A. All elements of the set X are assigned to the class c_1. The construction of the set X is shown below:

$$X = \{sim(ImR_i^A, ImR_j^A)\}, \quad i, j = 1, \ldots, r, \quad i \neq j, \tag{7}$$

where ImR_i^A is an i-th reference knuckle image of the person A being verified, r is a number of all reference knuckle images of the person A.

The set Y contains values of similarity coefficients calculated between knuckle images of person A and the knuckle images of another user B, where $B \neq A$, randomly selected from a database. The elements of the set Y are assigned to the class c_2. The construction of the set Y is shown below:

$$Y = \{sim(ImR_i^A, ImR_j^B)\}, \quad i = 1, \ldots, r, \quad j = 1, \ldots, s, \tag{8}$$

where ImR_i^A is the i-th reference knuckle image belonging to the person A being verified, r is the number of all reference knuckle images of person A, ImR_j^B is the j-th reference knuckle image of the person B, s is the number of analyzed reference knuckle images of person B.

To avoid imbalanced data [6] the number of elements in the set X should be close to the number of elements in set Y. This assumption is fulfilled if the number of knuckle images used for creating the set Y is equal to $s = r - 1$.

In the presented method, the similarity between any two knuckle images is estimated based on the shape and localization of the knuckle ridges. The comparison of images is carried out by means of the Normal Cross Correlation (NCC) technique. The NCC has been widely used as a metric to evaluate the degree of a similarity (or dissimilarity) between two compared images [8]. In our method all images must have the same size and the shape of a square.

To find the similarity $sim(Im1, Im2)$ between two images denoted as $Im1$ and $Im2$ the image $Im1$ is divided into the square shaped sub-images. A length of a side of these sub-images is a parameter of the method. Each k-th sub-image in $Im1$ is treated as a template and is noted as T_k. The task is to find a fragment in the tested image $Im2$ which has the most similarity to the template T_k. An example of searching for the sub-image T_1 in the image $Im2$ is shown in Fig. 7.

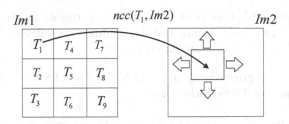

Fig. 7. Searching for the template T_1 within the image $Im2$.

By means of the following formula the similarity between a template T_k and tested image $Im2$ is calculated:

$$ncc(T_k, Im2) = \max \left(\frac{\sum_{(i,j)\in T_k} Im2(x+i, y+j) \cdot T_k(i,j)}{\sqrt{\sum_{(i,j)\in T_k} Im2^2(x+i, y+j)} \cdot \sqrt{\sum_{(i,j)\in T_k} T_k^2(i,j)}} \right).$$
(9)

The final similarity between the images $Im1$ and $Im2$ is calculated using (10).

$$sim(Im1,\ Im2) = mean\{ncc(T_1,\ Im2), ncc(T_2,\ Im2), \ldots, ncc(T_b,\ Im2)\},$$
(10)

where b is the number of all sub-images T_k created in the image $Im1$.

After the creation the sets X and Y the tested knuckle image Im^* is compared with a random image in the database taken from the person who claimed the identity (let it be A). The result of comparison is an object d^*:

$$d^* = sim(Im^*,\ Im_i^A),$$
(11)

where, Im^* is the knuckle image to be verified and Im_i^A is a randomly selected original knuckle image of the person A.

Next, the verified knuckle image Im^* is used in the classification stage, where the k-NN classifier is applied [14]. In this approach for k-NN classifier the commonly used Euclidean distance metric is used. In the classification stage first, the distances between classified object d^* and objects from X and Y sets are determined. The selection of the value of parameter k for the k-NN classifier is presented in section concerning experiments. Based on majority, the k-NN gives a decision to which class (c_1 or c_2) the classified object d^* belongs to.

$$\widehat{\Psi}^{knu}(d^*) \to c_j, j \in \{1, 2\}.$$
(12)

If the object d^* belongs to the class c_1 it means that the verified knuckle image Im^* comes from the legitimate user.

2.3   Fusion of the Methods

The proposed system is based on fusion of two verification methods. The ultimate decision of the user verification depends on both: keystroke and knuckle image verification results. This task is done by analyzing the value of τ, which is the result of the keystroke verification, and the parameter k value in k-NN method. The rules of fusion system are presented below:

$$\text{decision} = \begin{cases} \text{access granted} & if \quad (LS > \tau') \ or \ (LS > \tau'' \ and \ k > k^*) \\ \text{access denied} & otherwise \end{cases}$$

(13)

Values of parameters τ', τ'' and k^* have been described in experiments section.

3   Experimental Results

The efficiency of the proposed method has been investigated experimentally. The researches have been conducted on a database which consists of 4000 vectors **F** and 150 knuckle images acquired from 30 persons. All experiments were repeated 10 times to provide better statistical accuracy and then the average values of evaluation metrics for all trials were calculated.

The proposed architecture of the classification module for keystroke dynamics based verification assumes the use of four single classifiers in an ensemble: C4.5, Bayesian Network, Support Vector Machine, Random Forest. Those classifiers were chosen because of their high accuracy confirmed in [17]. The aim of the first stage of this research was to determine an optimal values of parameters τ', τ'' and k^*. The values of mentioned parameters were determined by use of grid search procedure from the following sets $\tau', \tau'' \in \{1, 2, 3\}$, $k^* \in \{1, 3, 5, 7\}$.

The experiments were conducted several times. Each time we used different numbers of knuckle images n and r to determine the sets X and Y. Table 1 shows the best obtained results and the values of the parameters τ', τ'' and k^* for which these results were obtained.

Table 1. The best results and the values of parameters used in experiments.

Number of elements in sets X & Y	FAR [%]	FRR [%]	AER [%]	ACC [%]	τ'	τ''	k^*
4 and 4	7.72 ± 1.36	19.38 ± 2.32	13.55 ± 1.73	93.36 ± 1.89	3	2	5
6 and 6	6.38 ± 0.51	12.56 ± 1.45	9.47 ± 2.12	95.17 ± 2.54	3	2	5
8 and 8	1.07 ± 1.47	3.35 ± 2.04	2.21 ± 1.76	98.50 ± 1.33	3	2	5
10 and 10	1.11 ± 1.13	3.33 ± 2.26	2.22 ± 1.64	98.49 ± 1.22	3	2	7
12 and 12	1.09 ± 1.45	3.36 ± 2.35	2.22 ± 1.32	98.51 ± 1.53	3	2	5

Based on the obtained results we can state that the optimal values of the parameters for the proposed method are $\tau' = 3$, $\tau'' = 2$ and $k^* = 5$. When we analyze the influence of a number of knuckle images on the results of an investigation, we can observe that the efficiency of the classification is the best when we analyze only 8 knuckle images from each person.

In order to fully assess the effectiveness of the proposed fusion-based approach, its efficiency has been compared with the efficiencies obtained by each of the biometrical verification methods separately. For this purpose the optimal values of parameters τ and k have been selected once again but this time the efficiency of each verification method (keystroke verification and knuckle verification) has been assessed independently. The comparison of efficiency obtained by the fusion-based method and each individual verification method is presented in Table 2.

Table 2. The comparison of the performance of various verification methods.

Method	FAR [%]	FRR [%]	AER [%]	ACC [%]
Keystroke	5.59 ± 1.16	7.94 ± 1.46	5.41 ± 1.72	97.83 ± 3.28
Knuckle	4.30 ± 0.23	8.19 ± 1.05	6.24 ± 1.09	95.96 ± 7.53
Keystroke + Knuckle	1.07 ± 1.47	3.35 ± 2.04	2.21 ± 1.76	98.50 ± 1.33

By analyzing Table 2, we can notice that the fusion of two methods allows to obtain better efficiency in classification than using only one of these methods separately.

4 Conclusions

This paper presents the preliminary results for the biometric user verification system based on the fusion of keystroke and knuckle analysis. The experiments were conducted to assess the potential of the mentioned biometric methods fusion. The obtained results show that the fusion of the two methods performs better than the keystroke and knuckle analysis separate. Therefore, there is a motivation to continue this research and to develop a real time knuckle analysis method allowing o verify finger knuckles of a computer user while typing on the keyboard. This seems to be a complex task due to the constant movement of fingers over the keyboard. Preliminary research and experiments show that basing on images of the user's knuckles taken in various hand positions it is difficult to verify an identity of a user.

What more, all the image processing has to be performed in the background of the computer system while users are performing everyday tasks. Depending on the frequency of taking a picture this can cause some computer system efficiency issues. Solving the issues mentioned above is the next step of our research on developing fusion-based computer user continuous verification method.

References

1. Alsultan, A., Warwick, K.: Keystroke dynamics authentication: a survey of free-text methods. Int. J. Comput. Sci. Issues **10**, 1–10 (2013)
2. Banerjee, S.P., Woodard, D.L.: Biometric authentication and identification using keystroke dynamics: a survey. J. Pattern Recogn. Res. **7**, 116–139 (2012)
3. Doroz, R., Wrobel, K., Porwik, P., Safaverdi, H., Senejko, M., Jezewski, J., Popielski, P., Wilczynski, S., Koprowski, R., Wrobel, Z.: A new personal verification technique using Finger-Knuckle imaging. In: Nguyen, N.-T., Manolopoulos, Y., Iliadis, L., Trawiński, B. (eds.) ICCCI 2016. LNCS, vol. 9876, pp. 515–524. Springer, Cham (2016). doi:10.1007/978-3-319-45246-3_49
4. Iwahori, Y., Hattori, A., Adachi, Y., et al.: Automatic detection of Polyp using Hessian Filter and HOG features. Procedia Comput. Sci. **60**(1), 730–739 (2015)
5. Jin, J., Yang, L., Zhang, X., et al.: Vascular tree segmentation in medical images using Hessian-based multiscale filtering and level set method. Comput. Math. Meth. Med. (2013)
6. Krawczyk, B., Wozniak, M., Schaefer, G.: Cost-sensitive decision tree ensembles for effective imbalanced classification. Appl. Soft Comput. **14**, 554–562 (2014)
7. Kudlacik, P., Porwik, P., Wesolowski, T.: Fuzzy approach for intrusion detection based on user's commands. Soft Comput. **20**, 2705–2719 (2016)
8. Nakhmani, A., Tannenbaum, A.: A new distance measure based on generalized image normalized cross-correlation for robust video tracking and image recognition. Pattern Recogn. Lett. **34**(3), 315–321 (2013)
9. Nitsch, J., Klein, J., Miller, D., Sure, U., Hahn, H.K.: Automatic segmentation of the Cerebral Falx and adjacent Gyri in 2D ultrasound images. In: Handels, H., Deserno, T.M., Meinzer, H.-P., Tolxdorff, T. (eds.) Bildverarbeitung für die Medizin 2015. I, pp. 287–292. Springer, Heidelberg (2015). doi:10.1007/978-3-662-46224-9_50
10. Otsu, N.: A threshold selection method from gray-level histograms. IEEE Trans. Syst. Man Cybern. **9**, 62–66 (1979)
11. Raiyn, J.: A survey of cyber attack detection strategies. Int. J. Secur. Appl. **8**(1), 247–256 (2014)
12. Rybnik, M., Tabedzki, M., Adamski, M., Saeed, K.: An exploration of keystroke dynamics authentication using non-fixed text of various length. In: Proceedings of International Conference on Biometrics and Kansei Engineering (ICBAKE), pp. 245–250 (2013)
13. Salem, M.B., Hershkop, S., Stolfo, S.J.: A survey of insider attack detection research. Adv. Inf. Secur. **39**, 69–90 (2008)
14. Shakhnarovich, G., Darrell, T., Indyk, P.: Nearest-Neighbor Methods in Learning and Vision: Theory and Practice. Neural Information Processing. MIT Press, Cambridge (2006)
15. Teh, P.S., Teoh, A.B.J., Yue, S.: A survey of keystroke dynamics biometrics. Sci. World J. **2013**, 24 (2013)
16. Wesolowski, T., Palys, M., Kudlacik, P.: Computer user verification based on mouse activity analysis. Stud. Comput. Intell. **598**, 61–70 (2015)
17. Wesolowski, T.E., Porwik, P., Doroz, R.: Electronic health record security based on ensemble classification of keystroke dynamics. Appl. Artif. Intell. **30**, 521–540 (2016)
18. Zhong, Y., Deng, Y., Jain, A.K.: Keystroke dynamics for user authentication. In: IEEE Computer Society Conference on Computer Vision and Pattern Recognition Workshops, pp. 117–123 (2012)

Data Analysis and Information Retrieval

NMF in Screening Some Spirometric Data, an Insight into 12-Dimensional Data Space

Anna M. Bartkowiak[1]([✉]) and Jerzy Liebhart[2]

[1] Institute of Computer Science, Wroclaw University, 50-383 Wroclaw, Poland
aba@cs.uni.edu.pl
[2] Department and Clinic of Internal Diseases and Allergology,
Wroclaw Medical University, Wroclaw, Poland

Abstract. We present the usage of the Non-negative Matrix Factorization (NMF), an unsupervised machine learning method, which learns normal and abnormal state of patient's ventilatory systems. This is done using samples of patients having defects of obturative and restrictive kind and a control group.

We show that the NMF method can identify patients being in the normal state and screen them off from the remaining patients; however the kind of the ventilatory disorder for the remaining patients is not recognized. This is confronted with clustering provided by the k-means method and visualization of the 12-dimensional data using heatmaps and Kohonen's self-organizing maps.

The data set can be reconstructed with a 0.9746 accuracy (fraction of explained variance) from 6 base vectors provided by the NMF and using appropriate encoders provided also by the NMF; while 3 factors yield an 0.8573 fraction of explained variance.

Keywords: Healthy state · Abnormal state · Non-negative matrix factorization (NMF) · Heatmap · Self-organizing map (SOM) · Inner factors · Reconstruction of data

1 Introduction

Non-linear Matrix Factorization launched in [9] is a method for *approximating* a given real data matrix by derived factor matrices of lower rank. It may by aligned with two others methods serving for this purpose for a centenary of years: Principal Components (PCA) and Singular Value Decomposition (SVD) [6] based on spectral decomposition of a (preprocessed) data matrix. There are essential differences in the criteria of optimality of these methods, which lead to different factorization of the given data matrix. Generally speaking, NMF works on the assumption that both the analyzed data matrix and the derived factor matrices should be non-negative, that is to mean, their elements are allowed to show only non-negative values. It appears that this leads to better interpretability of

© IFIP International Federation for Information Processing 2017
Published by Springer International Publishing AG 2017. All Rights Reserved
K. Saeed et al. (Eds.): CISIM 2017, LNCS 10244, pp. 155–166, 2017.
DOI: 10.1007/978-3-319-59105-6_14

the derived factors. The NMF method gains more and more popularity, especially that feasible algorithms working under the constraints of non-negativity of all the derived elements have been elaborated (see, e.g., [4]). There are also algorithms for big data and data streams [14].

All the three mentioned data analysis methods (PCA, SVD and NMF) are frequently viewed also as dimensionality reducing methods. A satisfactory ('good') reduction to dimensionality equal 2 or 3 makes, that the data may be visualized in a 2D or 3D space, and usually we have some additional information on the fidelity of this visualization. By looking at the 2D or 3D representation, we may get insight into the multivariate data space. Such a visualization may also be the basis for finding some structure in the data, e.g. some clusters. This is difficult to achieve when working with PCA or SVD. However NMF, thanks to the non-negative constraints, may provide directly some information on the group membership of the data vectors contained in the analyzed data set. In the following we will consider *data vectors* that denote some *subjects* (e.g. patients), each of them characterized by a number of attributes, called in statistical data analysis *variables*. The clustering information is not always meaningful, and for some data sets we may get the clustering of the subjects, and for other not [1,15]. Moreover, sometimes we may get even a *bi-clustering*, that is a simultaneous clustering both of subjects and of variables [7,10]. Of course, the NMF – as *a priori* un-supervised machine learning method – gets only the data for analysis, however it gets no *a priori* information on the putative groups contained in the analyzed data.

The main goal of this paper is to explore the clustering ability of NMF when applied to a real medical data set concerned with diagnosing normal and abnormal state of a sample of patients, part of them suffering from pulmonary diseases, and the other part being in normal state. The data set is not big; it contains 77 patients, each characterized by 12 variables. We will show in detail that NMF is able to screen off the normal state patients, and even find some outliers in the data. We will confirm our results by using alternate visualization methods dealing with multivariate data. This statement ends the first Section of the paper.

In next Sect. 2, we will show in more detail the pulmonary data used in our elaboration. They will be visualized by a heatmap. Then, Sect. 3 shows the details of the NMF model and its work when reducing the dimensions of the data to rank 2 and rank 3. The indication of the clusters will be discussed. Section 4 shows analogous results obtained by the k-means method, when splitting directly the data into $k = 2$ and $k = 3$ clusters. Section 5 shows an alternate multivariate visualization of the of the data using Kohonen's self-organizing maps. Also the placement of the true group structure obtained from an independent medical diagnosis is depicted. Finally, Sect. 6 contains a global summary and final conclusions.

2 The Analyzed Data Set

The data were gathered in the Department and Clinic of Internal Medicine and Allergology, Wroclaw Medical University. We consider a multivariate data sample containing patients being either in the normal or the abnormal state of their ventilatory system. The abnormal state was diagnosed as *obturation* or *restriction* in ventilatory disorders. In the elaborated sample counting $n = 77$ patients we have:

- Group 1, $n_1 = 28$ patients with obturative disorders,
- Group 2, $n_2 = 21$ patients with restrictive disorders,
- Group 3, $n_2 = 28$ patients with normal functioning, serving as control.

Each patient has its record (data vector) composed of 15 values: Patient's ID no., residual value (RV), total lung capacity (TLC), weight, height and 10 various spirometric variables derived from the patient's spirogram. The data were gathered with the aim to predict the RV and TLC variables (they need measurements using a different device) just from the spirometric variables considered as predictors [3, 11]. In the following we will use from the these records only 12 variables defined in Table 1.

The twelve variables displayed in Table 1 will be hereafter called 'spirometric variables'. The first two of them are weight and height, the remaining ten – as obtained from a spirogram – are *sensu stricto* spirometric variables.

The recorded data are memorized as the $n \times m$ matrix $\mathbf{X}$ (with $n = 77$ and $m = 12$) containing in its rows the patients and in its columns the values of the variables characterizing the patients. The rows of $\mathbf{X}$ contain firstly the $n_1 = 28$ patients of group 1 (obturation), next the $n_2 = 21$ patients from group 2 (restriction), and finally the $n_3 = 28$ patients from group 3 (normal, control).

Table 1. Labels and definitions of the variables used in our analysis

X1:	Age [years],
X2:	Height [cm],
X3:	FVC, Forced Vital Capacity $[cm^3]$,
X4:	$FVC\%$ evaluated as $FVC/FVC_{predicted} \times 100$ [%],
X5:	FEV_1, Forced Expiratory Volume in one second $[cm^3]$,
X6:	Ratio $FEV_1/FVC \times 100$ [%],
X7:	$FEF_{0.2-1.2}$, Forced Expiratory Flow at the level of $0.2 - 1.2\,dm^3$ of FVC $[dm^3/min]$,
X8:	$MMFR$, Maximal Mid–expiratory Flow Rate $[dm^3/min]$,
X9:	$MMFT$, Maximal Mid–expiratory Flow Time [sec],
X10:	Ratio $MMFR/MMFT$ $[dm^3/min^2]$,
X11:	Ratio $FEF_{0.2-1.2}/FVC$ calculated as $1000\times$ X7/X3 $[min^{-1}]$,
X12:	Ratio $FVC/MMFT$ $[cm^3/sec]$

All elements of the data matrix **X** were strictly positive, however its columns were expressed in different scales. To annihilate the effects of largely differentiated scales of variables, the columns of the data matrix were standardized by 'range' to take values from the [0,1] interval. The data matrix with standardized elements will be referred to as **Xs**.

A holistic view of a not very big data matrix with non-negative elements may be obtained by displaying its values in the form of a heatmap. As such, the data matrix is considered as an image in the scale of an assumed color palette defined in computer graphics as colormap. Figure 1 shows such a heatmap of the transposed matrix $(\mathbf{Xs})^T$ of our data, when using the colormap *JET* (the default in Matlab).

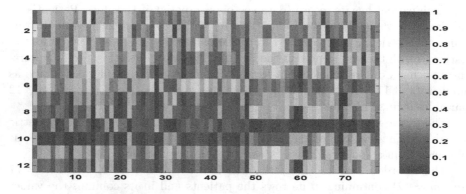

Fig. 1. Heatmap for $(\mathbf{Xs})^T$, the transposed standardized data matrix

The vertical constituents (columns) of the image are 77 columns numbered $1, 2, \ldots, 77$. They correspond to the subsequent patients constituting our data set. The no.s in the x-axis denote patients. Each column j visualizes the 12-dimensional data vector recorded for the j-th patient. In particular, no.s 1–28 indicate patients from group 1 (obturation), no.s 29–49 from group 2 (restriction), and no.s 50–77 from group 3 (normal, control)

Looking at Fig. 1 one may state that the patient group 3 (no.s 50–77) is clearly different as the groups 1 and 2 with no.s 1–49. The conclusion is: the group 3 of patients differs much in its inner structure from the the remaining two groups which look rather similar. Therefore, the 'normal' group should be rather easily identifiable in the data, while for the disease groups (obturation and restriction) this is doubtful.

3   The NMF Method

The NMF (non-negative matrix approximation) method was launched in [9] with the idea to find inner (hidden, unobservable) structure of the data which could be parameterized by lower rank factor matrices permitting to reconstruct the observed data matrix $\mathbf{V}$. It was assumed that the approximation (*alias* reconstruction) will be of the form $\mathbf{V} \approx \mathbf{WH}$, with $\mathbf{W}$ and $\mathbf{H}$ denoting the inner structure factors found using an appropriate goodness of fit criterion. The methodology proved to yield very interesting applications and was subsequently developed using other variants of approach (see, e.g., [4,14–17]) and exploiting its properties (see, e.g., [1,2,10,12]). In the following we use matrix denotation $\mathbf{V}, \mathbf{W}, \mathbf{H}$ introduced in [9].

Suppose, we have data observed for n subjects characterized by m variables denoting attributes of the subjects. If we are more interested in the subjects (in their relationship, clustering) then we should put them in the columns of the matrix $\mathbf{V}$ to be dealt with by NMF. In such a case the model NMF is given as

$$\mathbf{V}_{m \times n} \approx \mathbf{W}_{m \times r} \mathbf{H}_{r \times n}, \tag{1}$$

where r is usually much smaller as $min(n, m)$ and is called *rank* of approximation.

The column vectors in $\mathbf{W}$ are called *base vectors*, they play the role of a kind of prototypes (representatives) of the subjects included into the data. If the data set contains r groups (clusters), then the derived base vectors are expected to be representatives of these groups [5].

The column vectors in $\mathbf{H} = [\mathbf{h}_1, \ldots, \mathbf{h}_n]$ are called *encoders* or *coefficient vectors*, they play a crucial role in reconstructing the matrix $\mathbf{V}$ from the base vectors $\mathbf{W} = [\mathbf{w}_1, \ldots, \mathbf{w}_r]$.

We will carry out the NMF approximation of the observed (visible) data matrix $\mathbf{V}_{12 \times 77}$ by rank $r = 2$ and $r = 3$ factors. Computations will be done using the Matlab function snmf available at http://mikkelschmidt.dk/code.html. The criterium of goodness of fit of the model is the *explained variance* defined as follows

$$explained\ variance = (sst - sse)/sst, \tag{2}$$

where sst denotes the total sum of squares of deviations of elements v_{ij} from their overall mean, and sse is the sum of squared terms of errors $e_{ij} = v_{ij} - (\mathbf{WH})_{ij}$.

We start computing the NMF factorization for rank $r = 2$, obtaining the approximation $\mathbf{V}_{12 \times 77} \approx \mathbf{W}_{12 \times 2} \mathbf{H}_{2 \times 77}$. In such a case there are only two base vectors $\mathbf{w}_1, \mathbf{w}_2$. Simple linear algebra shows, that these two vectors, combined in various proportions (each proportions taken as one column vector from the set $\mathbf{H} = [\mathbf{h}_1, \ldots, \mathbf{h}_n]$), permit to reconstruct in sequence the subjects vectors $\mathbf{v}_1, \ldots, \mathbf{v}_n$ contained in $\mathbf{V}$. For example, the 1st and 2nd subjects from $\mathbf{V}$, that is the subject vectors $\mathbf{v}_1$ and $\mathbf{v}_2$ are reconstructed as

$$\mathbf{v}_1 = \mathbf{w}_1 h_{11} + \mathbf{w}_2 h_{21}, \quad \mathbf{v}_2 = \mathbf{w}_1 h_{12} + \mathbf{w}_2 h_{22}, \quad \ldots \tag{3}$$

and so on. The elements of the coefficient vector $\mathbf{h}_j$ say how important are subsequent base vectors $w_1, \ldots, w_r$ in reproducing just the j-th subject vector. This may be seen globally when inspecting the row profiles of $\mathbf{H}$ depicted in Fig. 2 (for $r = 2$) and in Fig. 3 (for $r = 2$).

We formulate the following *Principle of group assignment in NMF*:
Find for given j, $(j = 1, 2, \ldots n)$, which of the coefficients h_{ij}, $(i = 1, \ldots, r)$ is

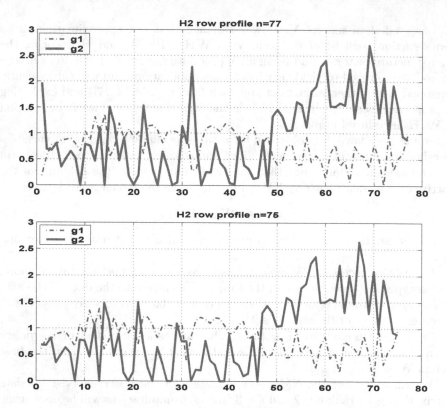

Fig. 2. NMF for $r = 2$. Top: Profiles of the coefficient matrix $H_{2 \times 77}$ obtained when using the entire data matrix **V**. Notice the outstanding green pics for $no.\,1$ and $no.\,32$. Bottom: Profiles of the coefficient matrix $H_{2 \times 75}$ obtained when using the data matrix **V** from which the outlying vectors $no.\,1$ and $no.\,32$ were removed. Notice in both exhibits the discrepancy of the green and blue curves for the last 28 indices in the x-axis indicating patients from the control group. (Color figure online)

the largest. Say this is the i_{max} coefficient. Then assign the j-th data vector to the group no. i_{max}.

Figure 2, top exhibit, shows the row profiles plot of the coefficient matrix **H** obtained for $r = 2$. We see the values h_{1j} and h_{2j}, for the indices $j = 1, 2, \ldots, 77$, connected into two curves colored in blue and green respectively. The blue and green curves show - for the index j - the prevalence of the subject coefficient $\mathbf{h}_j$ to the first or second basic vector. This prevalence means that the respective base vector has a larger contribution in reconstructing the object no. j. In such a way the subjects are assigned to one of the two groups represented by the two base vectors.

Looking at the top exhibit in Fig. 2 we see there a particular intertwining of the two curves. For $j = 1$ to 49 (patients with obturation or restriction) the two curves are intermingled with a slight prevalence of the blue curve. Moreover, for $j = 1$ and $j = 32$ there are two big eruptions of the green curve. For $j = 50$ to

77 (patients from the normal group) the green curve connected with the base vector $\mathbf{w}_2$ is decidedly dominating.

The analysis was repeated with the data set reduced to 75 patients (patients *no.* 1 and *no.* 32 notified as outliers were removed). Results of the new analysis, without the two outliers, are shown in bottom exhibit of Fig. 2 and look more consistent. The essential pattern noticed in the top panel is present also here: the control group is decidedly connected with the base vector $\mathbf{w}_2$; the obturation and restriction groups show the same intermingled pattern with a mild preference of the base vector $\mathbf{w}_1$.

When looking at Fig. 2 one may come to the following conclusion: Similarly as in the heatmap, one sees here clearly a subdivision of the entire data into two

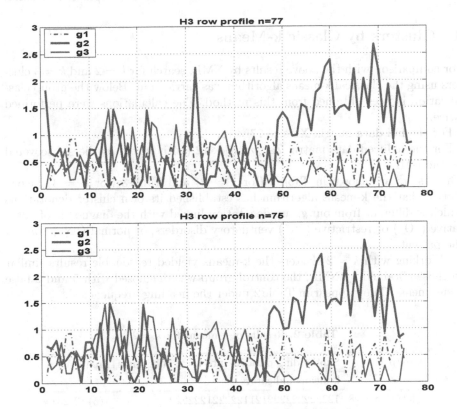

Fig. 3. NMF for rank $r = 3$. Top: Profiles of the coefficient matrix $\mathbf{H}_{3 \times 77}$ obtained when using the entire data matrix $\mathbf{V}$. Bottom: Profiles of the coefficient matrix $\mathbf{H}_{3 \times 75}$ obtained when using the data matrix $\mathbf{V}$ from which the subjects *no.* 1 and *no.* 32 were removed. Notice the big discrepancy of the red curve from both the green and the blue curve when observed for the last 28 indices in the x-axis – the red curve indicating the control group - is for no.s starting from *no.* 49 decidedly dominating. Notice also the appearance of two new pics of the red curve for no.s covering the first group (obturation). (Color figure online)

groups: the 'normal' state group (no.s 50 through 77) and the abnormal group designated by no.s 1–49. The group assignment for the normal group is good: 26 out from 28 patients are correctly located. Thus the first kind error is small. However the second kind error is considerable: several patients from the disease group are assigned to the normal, i.e. healthy group. Removing some putative outliers reduces the erroneous assignments in the disease group.

The analysis of the results obtained when assuming 3 groups of data (see Fig. 3) shows clearly that the assumption on 3 groups of data cannot be sustained.

Concerning the efficacy of the approximation measured by the fraction of explained variance (2): The models using $r = 2$ and $r = 3$ explain 79.18% and 87.43% of total variance. Model with $r = 6$ yields 97.46% of explained variance.

4   Clusters by Classic k-Means

For comparison with the above results by NMF, search for $k = 2$ and $k = 3$ clusters using the classical k-means algorithm was carried out. Below the group classification indices obtained from this method. The calculations were performed twice:

• For the full data matrix **Xs** size 77×12,
• For the reduced data matrix **Zs** size 77×12 (without two outliers discovered by the NMF).

The results are shown in Table 2 (for $k = 2$) and Table 3 (for $k = 3$) below. Notice that the k-means algorithm has established its own cluster denotations which is different from our group denotation linked with the diagnostic of obturative ("O") or restrictive ("R") ventilatory disorders, or normal ("N") state of the patient.

Working with $k = 2$ clusters the k-means yielded reasonable results similar to those obtained by NMF: the control group was diagnosed with 5 and 2 false assignments. They appear in Table 2 under the heading 'frequencies'.

Table 2. Results of k-means for $k = 2$

Group ↓	Subdividing data Xs into k = 2 subgroups	Frequencies
	k-means indicators	
g1 "O" n = 28	1222222222221211222221222222	1(5), 2(23)
g2 "R" n = 21	212122222222222222221	1(3), 2(18)
g3 "N" n = 28	1122111111111111111111121122	1(23), 2(5)
	Zs, i.e. Xs with two outliers removed	
g1 "O" n = 27	222222222221211222221222222	1(4), 2(23)
g2 "R" n = 20	21222222222222222221	1(2), 2(18)
g3 "N" n = 28	1111111111111111111111111122	1(26), 2(2)

Table 3. Results of k-means for $k = 3$

Group ↓	Subdividing data Xs into $k = 3$ subgroups k-means indicators	Frequencies
g1 "O" n = 28	12223222322222312223331233233	1(3), 2(15) 3(10)
g2 "R" n = 21	322123332333323333232	1(1), 2(7) 3(13)
g3 "N" n = 28	1222112111111111211112121122	1(19), 2(9) 3(0)
	Zs, i.e. Xs with two outliers removed	
g1 "O" n = 27	333233323333213332221322322	1(2) 2(10) 3(15)
g2 "R" n = 20	23332223222232222323	1(0) 2(13) 3(7)
g3 "N" n = 28	1333113111111111311113131133	1(19) 2(0) 3(9)

For $k = 3$ clusters the results from k-means were much worse as those by NMF: the control group was diagnosed with 9 false assignments both in **Xs** and **Zs**. The assignment to groups 2 and 3 was a mess of '2' and '3' assignments.

5   Visualization of the Data Using Kohonen's SOM

Now we visualize the data matrix **Xs** using Kohonen's SOMs. The SOM (self-organizing map) is *de facto* a neural network which reflects specifically the positions of data points in the multi-dimensional data space with preserving the data neighborhood topology. The principles of the method and the tricky algorithm are described in [8]. Maps obtained for our data - obtained using the free Matlab SOM toolbox [13] - are shown in Fig. 4. One may notice there that the maps have rectangular shape and are composed from $M = 11 \times 4 = 44$ equal size hexagons.

The SOM methodology performs a *vector quantization* and subdivides the data space into M so called Voronoi regions. The regions contain all the data points and reflect their density in the data space; some regions may be empty. There is a strict correspondence between the hexagons in the map and the Voronoi regions in the multivariate data space. We can find which data points are very near each other, and which are distant. Each Voronoi region has a representative data point (called codebook vector), which is in one-to-one correspondence to the center of hexagon associated with the respective Voronoi Region. There are two fitness indices: the quantization error vqe (means the average distance of data points in one Voronoi region to their representative codebook vector located in that region; for our data $vqe = 0.304$) and the topological error tpe (says, how many hexagons being neighboring hexagons in the map are not neighboring Voronoi regions in the data space; for our map we got $tpe = 0.0000$).

Now, where are our patient vectors from the categories "O", "R", and "N"? We found and identified all of them using the hit utility of the toolbox. The respective information (how many items from each group are represented by

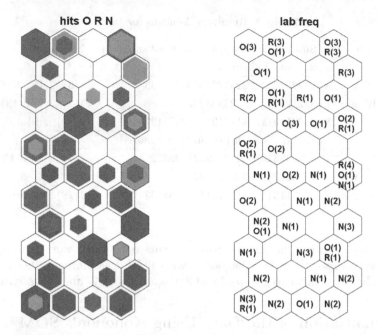

SOM 11x4   X 77x12

Fig. 4. Data groups assignment in Kohonen SOM. Letters O, R, N denote data points identified with patients belonging to the Obturation, Restriction or Normal group according the definition in Sect. 2. Colors red, green, blue are linked with groups "O", "R", "N" appropriately. Notice, that the "N"s appear in the southern part of the maps, while the "O"s and the "R"s reside in the northern part of the maps. (Color figure online)

each hexagon) is inscribed as ordinary text onto the map located in the right exhibit of Fig. 4. E.g., one may notice in the displayed map, that the utmost south-west hexagon (coordinates 11,1) contains three "Ns" and one "R" items (this "R" item happens to be the outlier no. 32 found by NMF and visible in Fig. 2, top exhibit).

Having the allocation of each data vector, one may display them group-wise, assigning to them specific colors and drawing in each map hexagon a smaller colored one, with radius proportional to the square root frequency of items linked to the given hexagon. The result is shown in the map appearing in Fig. 4, left exhibit. Looking at that exhibit, it is interesting to find that items of the 3 groups of our data are spread out over the entire map. Blue color (denoting "N" items) concentrates rather in the south of the map, however the region is not pure. In particular, there are two outliers at the south edge (no.s 1 and 32 notified previously and removed from part of our analyzes shown in Sect. 3). There is also one other "O" and one other "R" outlier located at the south-west edge. The 'disease' items (linked with red and green) appear intermixed in the upper

part of the same map, however some of them invade the blue territory of the
"N" items. This observation is in agreement with the former comment on the
results of NMF, that the results displayed in Figs. 2 and 3 are supporting the
assumption on only $r = 2$ discernible clusters in the analyzed data.

6   General Summary and Concluding Remarks

The aim of the investigation was to explore the role of the NMF (non-negative
matrix factorization) method when applied to real medical data. We have considered for this purpose a medical data set obtained from spirographic investigation
of 3 groups of patients diagnosed as having two kinds of ventilatory disorders
(g1, obturation, n = 28, and g2, restriction, n = 21) and additionally a control
group (g3, normal, n = 28). Each patient was characterized by 12 variables, 10
of them being spirogram characteristics.

The NMF is a model based approach which can find in data some hidden
factors (unobservable inner structure) permitting to reconstruct the entire data
set with a hopefully small error. It was reported, that this inner structure might
be connected with some groups into which the investigated data samples can
be subdivided. In medical context this might mean subdivision into subgroups
of various subtypes, e.g. various types of a disease. Our question was: Can the
various types (groups of patients appearing in our data) be recognized – in a
unsupervised way – by the NMF algorithm?

Our results. We have applied the NMF method seeking for k = 2 and k = 3
inner factors. The results from NMF were confronted with the *classic k-means*
and two graphical methods: *Kohonen SOM* and *heatmaps* permitting to get
a holistic vision of the 12-dimensional data vectors contained in the analyzed
data set.

Conclusions from the investigation:

1. The NMF is able to recognize the normal group (92.86 % accuracy), however
   it can not recognize properly the abnormal state groups.
2. The NMF has an ability to recognize outliers hidden in the data.
3. Comparing to clustering abilities of the classic k-means, the NMF is superior.
4. The overall inspection of the results leads to the conclusion that the NMF
   has some abilities to recognize the group structure and can be considered as
   a 'weak learner', that - along with others weak learners - might be useful in
   ensemble learning.

References

1. Bartkowiak, A.M.: Classic and convex non-negative matrix visualization in clustering two benchmark data. Przeglad Elektrotechniczny **R93**(1), 53–59 (2017)
2. Bartkowiak, A.M., Zimroz, R.: NMF and PCA as applied to gearbox fault data.
   In: Jackowski, K., Burduk, R., Walkowiak, K., Woźniak, M., Yin, H. (eds.)
   IDEAL 2015. LNCS, vol. 9375, pp. 199–206. Springer, Cham (2015). doi:10.1007/
   978-3-319-24834-9_24

3. Bartkowiak, A., Liebhart, E.: Estimation of the spirometric residual volume (RV) by a regression built from Gower distances. Biometrical J. **37**(2), 131–149 (1995)
4. Cichocki, A., Zdunek, R., Phan, A.H., Amari, S.: Nonnegative Matrix and Tensor Factorizations. Applications to Exploratory Multi-way Data Analysis and Blind Source Separation. Wiley, Chichester (2009)
5. Ding, C., Li, T., Jordan, M.: Convex and semi-nonnegative matrix factorizations. IEEE Trans. Pattern Anal. Mach. Intell. (TPAMI) **32**, 45–55 (2010)
6. Jolliffe, I.T.: Principal Component Analysis, 2nd edn. Springer, New York (2002)
7. Kasim, A., Shkedy, Z., Kaiser, S., Hochreiter, S., Talloen, S. (eds.): Applied Biclustering Methods for Big and High-Dimensional Data Using R. CRC Press, Taylor & Francis Group, A Chapman & Hall Book, Boca Raton (2017)
8. Kohonen, T.: Self-Organizing Maps, Third Extended Edition. Springer, Heidelberg (2001)
9. Lee, D.D., Seung, H.S.: Learning the parts of objects by nonnegative matrix factorization. Nature **401**, 788–791 (1999)
10. Li, Y., Ngom, A.: The non-negative matrix factorization toolbox for biological data mining. BMC Source Code Biol. Med. **8**(10), 1–15 (2013)
11. Liebhart, J., Bartkowiak, A., Liebhart, E.: The impact of outliers in in the regression estimating TLC from age and some spirometric observations. Model. Simul. Control C **15**, 1–19 (1989). AMSE Press
12. Schmidt, M.N., Larsen, J., Hsiao, F.-T.: Wind noise reduction using non-negative sparse coding. In: IEEE International Workshop on Machine Learning for Signal Processing, (MLSP), pp. 431–436, August 2007
13. Vesanto, J., et al.: SOM Toolbox for Matlab 5, Som Toolbox Team, HUT, Finland. Libella Oy, Espoo, Version 0beta 2.0, pp. 1–54, November 2001
14. Zdunek, R.: Extraction of nonnegative features from multidimensional nonstationary signals. In: Tan, Y., Shi, Y. (eds.) DMBD 2016. LNCS, pp. 557–566. Springer, Heidelberg (2016)
15. Zdunek, R.: Convex nonnegative matrix factorization with Rank-1 update for clustering. In: Rutkowski, L., Korytkowski, M., Scherer, R., Tadeusiewicz, R., Zadeh, L.A., Zurada, J.M. (eds.) ICAISC 2015. LNCS, vol. 9120, pp. 59–68. Springer, Cham (2015). doi:10.1007/978-3-319-19369-4_6
16. Zdunek, R.: Data clustering with semi-binary nonnegative matrix factorization. In: Rutkowski, L., Tadeusiewicz, R., Zadeh, L.A., Zurada, J.M. (eds.) ICAISC 2008. LNCS, vol. 5097, pp. 705–716. Springer, Heidelberg (2008). doi:10.1007/978-3-540-69731-2_68
17. Zurada, J.M., Ensari, T., Asi, E.H., Chorowski, J.: Nonnegative matrix factorization and its application to pattern recognition and text mining. In: Proceedings of the 13th Federated Conference on Computer Science and Information Systems, Cracow, pp. 11–16 (2013)

Gesture Recognition in 3D Space Using Dimensionally Reduced Set of Features

Łukasz Gadomer[(⊠)] and Marcin Skoczylas

Faculty of Computer Science, Bialystok University of Technology,
Wiejska 45A, 15-351 Bialystok, Poland
{l.gadomer,m.skoczylas}@pb.edu.pl
http://www.wi.pb.edu.pl

Abstract. In this study authors present a solution to track and recognize arbitrary gestures of hands in three dimensional space and review the recognition accuracy. The idea of this novel gesture recognition system is described and results of research made on a recorded gesture data set are presented. Gesture instances were defined by user standing in different distances from the controller, in different placements of their field of vision and with different speeds, making recognition velocity and position invariant. Authors' goal was to find the minimal number of features that give satisfying gesture classification result in order to achieve a compromise between accuracy and computation time. In this publication progress of the research on gesture recognition problem is described and a comparative study is presented.

Keywords: Gesture recognition · Features · Dimensionality reduction · Singular value decomposition

1 Introduction

This paper presents a solution which allows tracking hand gestures in three dimensional space that can be inserted into a CAVE3D (Automatic Virtual Environment, see Fig. 1).

System consists of two main parts: a gesture recognition tool and a graphical environment. The gesture recognition tool allows user to create gestures database, learn it using one of selected classifiers and then recognize gestures performed by the user in real time. Implemented solution allows recognition of gestures recorded with varied velocity and with different user placement relating to the controller, so it is velocity and position invariant. It also contains build–in features that test recognition accuracy which are helpful during research and tests of the quality of this solution.

The whole system allows real–time position and velocity invariant gesture recognition: preparation of user's own set of gestures, classifiers learning, and then recognition of gestures in real–time using selected classifiers, it is a novel and innovative solution.

© IFIP International Federation for Information Processing 2017
Published by Springer International Publishing AG 2017. All Rights Reserved
K. Saeed et al. (Eds.): CISIM 2017, LNCS 10244, pp. 167–179, 2017.
DOI: 10.1007/978-3-319-59105-6_15

Fig. 1. Cave3D experimental setup consists of 3 screens with 3D projectors that are surrounding the user.

The main purpose of the work described in this paper is to reduce size of the data set and computation time of gesture recognition while maintaining the highest possible classification accuracy. To achieve this, number of attributes was reduced by extracting features from a prepared data set, performing dimensionality reduction and checking what is the minimal number of features needed to achieve satisfying accuracy. This goal was achieved, and the important issues concerning this work are described in the following paragraphs.

This work is the continuation of researches presented in [4,6].

2   Related Work

The problem of gesture recognition is a challenging and popular issue. Many researchers tried to resolve it in their own way. Diversity of approaches is, inter alia, a consequence of different possible ways of gesture representation. Very often gesture is represented as a movement of single body's part, usually a hand. This approach is the same that was described in the following gesture definition: *gestures are* "movements of the arms and hands which are closely synchronized with the flow of speech" [3].

In [7] authors studied possibility of gesture recognition using accelerometer MEMS (Microelectromechanical System). This device was controlled by user's hand and its movement in three dimensions was observed. Authors performed their research on seven simple gestures. The same device was used in [1] to resolve similar problem. In that work, the gesture classification was realized using Dynamic Time Warping (DTW) algorithm. A database consisting of 3780 instances of gestures, grouped into 18 different decision classes was used. Another solution which is based on the accelerometer device and the same classification algorithm is described in [8]. In this publication authors tested classification accuracy in two cases: user-relevant and user-irrelevant. Their research database contained 3200 instances, each of them represented one of eight different gestures. In this case every single instance of gesture took the same time (3,40 s). In all these solutions gestures were treated the same way as presented in following paragraphs – as a movement of one single point, which represents user's palm in three dimensional space.

Another example of tracking hand's movement was described in [9]. In this case to track gestures authors used a finger–worn device which was similar to a ring – it was called Magic Ring (MR). They presented personalized gesture recognition using a method of adaptive template adjustment. Another exemplary gesture recognition solution is called 1$ [5]. This name was given to symbolize algorithm's low cost and simplicity – it's implementation took only about a hundred lines of code. According to authors' description it works satisfyingly even there is only one training instance of each gesture. This work was an inspiration for the authors of [2]. They designed a solution based on the algorithm described in [5] which used Sparse Representation (SR) and Compressed Sensing (CS) methods.

3   Gesture Data Collecting and Processing

In this section authors describe issues connected with gesture data collection and processing. That was described in details in [4,6], however let's outline briefly here: first, user has to prepare his own data set. He stands before the controller and performs gestures, signaling beginning and end of the gesture[1] Then he can save created data set and use it for two purposes:

1. Learn selected classifier and use it to perform gesture recognition in real time,
2. Use selected data set for classifier's parameters optimization and measure the recognition accuracy to evaluate solution quality.

The first issue was described widely in [6]. In this publication authors would like to concentrate on the progress which concerns the second one.

The issues connected with position and speed invariance was widely described in [4,6]. For this reason, we do not concentrate about them in this paper.

3.1   Gesture Dataset

Gesture database included 12 different gestures shown in Table 1, recorded as values in relative data format. Each gesture type (a decision class) was recorded 80 times which in total sums up to a gesture database consisting of 960 gestures. All of gestures were performed by four different users – each user recorded 20 gestures. What is more, they were asked to perform gestures in a different way and change their positions a bit between every gesture. As a result, every

---

[1] It can be done by clicking "start recognition" and "end recognition" in our software. It can be done, for example, with a help of the operator, who can decide when are start and finish moments and that method was used in the data collecting process.

recorded instance was a bit different than others. Gestures were recorded with different velocities, users were standing in different distances to the controller and they were placed in a different parts of detecting range. Such way of performing gestures provided research data that allows test of position and velocity invariance in a real scenario. In addition, recordings that were not perfect were also included into the dataset (but recordings were not repeated), making the data set even more difficult to analyze. The only limitation in recording instances was assumption that every gesture should be performed in the same direction. It means that, for instance, every horizontal line is performed from left side to right side.

As it is shown in Table 1, all gestures are two–dimensional by their definition (for example, brackets are designed to be two–dimensional, etc.). However they are captured in three–dimensional space. Device captured depth, that was recorded and written to the dataset the same way as width and height. It means that it was also important if the data collecting participants were performing movements in depth dimension. We have chosen such gestures, but there would be no problem to choose, for examples, "push" and "pull" ones – whichever selected gestures would be, the algorithm should work the same way.

All of recorded gestures were shuffled and written into a single dataset. The information about gesture performer was not saved. It means that gesture recognition is fully user–independent.

Table 1. Gestures dataset

Gesture shape	Starting point
(	Top
)	Top
<	Top
>	Top
∧	Left
\	Top
/	Top
|	Top
—	Right
~	Left
O	Top
8	Top

3.2   Feature Data Representation

Number of attributes in a data set depends on the length of gesture. Authors assumed that all gestures have 40 samples, three dimensions each, which makes 120 attributes. Recording 40 samples using Kinect controller takes a bit more than one second. It does not mean that user has to perform the gesture in exactly one second – it can take any amount of time. This assumed number is just a final length of the gesture after scaling.

To resolve this problem authors decided to extract features from the gesture instances. The advantage of this solution is the fact that it is possible to extract a given number of features independently from the gesture length. It means, no matter how long the gesture is, the number of features is always the same. This allows reduction or extension of dimension to the same number of dimensions, allowing to have unlimited length of gestures.

To extract data features authors decided to transform the prepared data set following way: from a relative hand position absolute values were computed, but always starting from point (0, 0, 0). That means gesture's samples values were translated to the beginning of the coordinate system. Authors performed this operation to express real movements of the hand – representation used in [6] was a proper one for direct recognition, but in authors' opinion it needs above transformation to achieve features that express the given problem best way.

Table 2 shows features extracted from the prepared dataset. Popular statistical and signal features were selected. As it is presented, most of these features were computed independently for each axis and for all of the axes together. Axis to axis features were computed between the cartesian of axes. In total 49 features were extracted. In the Table 2 n is the number of samples k and l are the sample pair of axes and a is the sample.

4   Dimensionality Reduction

One of the main objective in this publication is to check whether the minimal number of features exists that allows to achieve rewarding gesture classification accuracy. As it was mentioned in Sect. 3.2, 49 features were extracted. This is the maximal number of dimensions proposed in our computations. The next step is the dimensionality reduction, which objective is to reduce number of features. To achieve this a Singular Value Decomposition (SVD) algorithm was used, but considering only real numbers (which is a right assumption for the purposes of our gesture recognition problems, where numbers cannot be complex).

The singular value decomposition of $m \times n$ matrix M is a $M = U\Sigma V^*$ factorization, where:

- U is a $m \times m$ unitary matrix,
- Σ is a $m \times n$ rectangular diagonal matrix with non-negative real numbers on the diagonal,
- V^* is a $n \times n$ unitary matrix, which is a transposition of V.

Values that are placed on the diagonal of Σ are called singular values of matrix M. The m columns of U are known as left–singular vectors of M and the n columns of V are called right–singular vectors of M.

First, the SVD algorithm is performed on all set of n features. Then, to reduce this data set to k dimensions, all elements of $k + 1$ to n columns of Σ

Table 2. Extracted features

Feature	Description	Equation	Computed for
Average	Sum of samples divided by number of samples	$\dfrac{1}{n}\sum_{i=1}^{n} a_i$	Each axis, all of the axes
Standard deviation	Measure that is used to quantify amount of dispersion of a set of samples	$\sqrt{\dfrac{1}{n}\sum_{i=1}^{n}(a_i - \bar{a})^2}$	Each axis, all of the axes
Variance	Measure that expresses how far a set of samples is spread out	$\dfrac{1}{n}\sum_{i=1}^{n}(a_i - \bar{a})^2$	Each axis, all of the axes
Ratio	Relationship between range of two sets of samples	$\dfrac{\max(k_i) - \min(k_i)}{\max(l_i) - \min(l_i)}$	Each pair of axes
Covariance	Measure that expresses how much two sets of samples are related	$\dfrac{1}{n}\sum_{i=1}^{n} kl - \bar{k}\bar{l}$	Each pair of axes
Correlation	Measure that expresses how much two sets of samples are related	$\dfrac{\sum_{i=1}^{n} kl - \bar{k}\bar{l}}{\sqrt{\sum_{i=1}^{n}(k_i - \bar{k})^2 \sum_{i=1}^{n}(l_i - \bar{l})^2}}$	Each pair of axes
Skewness	Measure of asymmetry of set of samples	$\dfrac{\sqrt{n}\sum_{i=1}^{n}(a_i - \bar{a})^3}{\sqrt{\sum_{i=1}^{n}(a_i - \bar{a})^2}^{\,3}}$	Each axis, all of the axes
Kurtosis	Measure of tailedness of set of samples	$\dfrac{n\sum_{i=1}^{n}(a_i - \bar{a})^4}{\sqrt{\sum_{i=1}^{n}(a_i - \bar{a})^2}^{\,4}}$	Each axis, all of the axes
Signal magnitude area	Measure of magnitude of set of samples	$\sum_{i=1}^{n} x_i$	Each axis, all of the axes
Signal magnitude vector	Measure of degree of movement intensity	$\sum_{i=1}^{n}\sqrt{x_i^2 + y_i^2 + z_i^2}$	All of the axes
Root mean square	Measure defined as a square root of mean of squares of a sample	$\sqrt{\dfrac{1}{n}\sum_{i=1}^{n} a_i^2}$	Each axis, all of the axes
Mean deviation	Average of absolute deviations from a central point of set of samples	$\dfrac{1}{n}\sum_{i=1}^{n}|a_i - \bar{a}_i|$	Each axis, all of the axes
Interquartile range	Difference between the upper and lower quartiles of set of samples	$Q_3 - Q_1$	Each axis
Energy	Energy of set of samples	$\sum_{i=1}^{n}|a_i|^2$	Each axis, all of the axes

and V matrices and rows of U matrices are set to zeroes. Then a new M' matrix is computed according to the procedure presented before. As a result, its first k columns are different from 0 — these columns form a new, dimensionally reduced set of features.

5 Research Description

For accuracy testing purposes and to achieve best results in gestures recognition problem, authors performed several experiments with collected gesture data. Aim of this study was to check the classifiers, primarily to identify accuracy in different gestures recognition, as well as speed of calculations.

5.1 Parameters Optimization

The basic issue connected with classification using many classifiers, especially SVM, is a parameter optimization. This process is essential due to the fact that classification accuracy highly depends on parameters of the classifier. Parameters have to fit the character of data. It is a serious problem because there is no simple way of selecting proper parameters. A popular method to obtain kernel parameters is a grid search. Note, that it is also possible that selected parameters do not fit to the testing set. All these facts mean that parameter optimization does not have a perfect solution – choosing good parameters is rather a compromise than a sure answer.

To minimize risk of data fitting authors decided to perform parameter optimization, use a single random data set division (but the same each time) and the 5–fold cross-validation. This division assumes that in every one of the five parts there are the same number of each gesture class instances. For each parameter combination the dataset was randomly divided into five parts, but taking into account that described assumption. Classifier is then learned using four of these parts and tested using the fifth, out–of–bag (OOB) part. This process is repeated five times (each time the other part is OOB part) and then the result is averaged. The same actions are performed for each of parameters combination and the best one is selected.

Because of long time of computations, the parameter optimization procedure was performed in a parallel way. The parallelisation ratio was computed on a single personal computer with Intel i7 processor (8 cores, 16 threads).

5.2 Classification

After selection of best classifiers' parameters (and kernel function parameters for the SVM classifier) authors performed data classification using the obtained parameters set. Similarly to parameter optimization, 5–fold cross validation was used, but the classification with 100 different random divisions was performed, not only the single one. The whole classification process was the same that it was in the case of parameters optimization – the difference is that research results were averaged over all these 100 divisions, and that value was recorded as a final classification accuracy.

5.3   Research Parts – Two Experiments

Authors performed two main parts of the research and recognition accuracy evaluation.

The first experiment concerns analysis how tested classifiers deal with gesture classification problem. Evaluation of all four classifiers in two cases was performed: with and without the normalization. Additionally, for SVM classifier, five kernel functions were tested independently. Such research gave a large number of results, and they are summarized and presented in Sect. 6.

For the latter, a Singular Value Decomposition was used to find the minimal number of features that give satisfying gesture classification results in order to obtain a compromise between the accuracy and computation time. To achieve this, gesture classification accuracy with the increase of number of dimensions was compared. In addition, best results using full data representation to feature data representation were compared, in order to check if new way of expressing data does not cause the severe drop of the classification accuracy.

One of the main purpose of second experiment was to check how many features are enough to achieve satisfactory classification accuracy. To accomplish this, dimensionality of data set was reduced, so that each example with 49 features was reduced iteratively into 48 new data sets that consisted from 1 to 48 features. Each of these data sets was tested using method described above. This allowed us to judge how an addition of a single dimension to a data set affects the classification accuracy.

All the results obtained are presented and discussed in Sect. 6.

6   Results and Discussion

6.1   First Experiment

First experiment was performed using relative data representation. For each classifier one configuration was selected that achieved best results based on recognition accuracy comparison, and then these were compared with other classifiers' best configurations. Summarized results are presented in Table 3.

On the basis of these observations, authors conclude that for the given problem of classification of gestures the best results are obtained using the SVM classifier. SVM performed best in the shortest possible time and was characterized by a low diversity of the results achieved in subsequent repetitions.

Table 3. Results of measurements obtained using selected classifiers

Classifier	SVM	NN	RBF	LMT
Average classification accuracy	95.85	92.74	92.16	90.04
Mean standard deviation of the accuracy	3.74	5.60	6.00	6.11
Calculations time	207.41	21819.19	201.23	5630.90

The results of SVM kernels comparison are shown in Table 4. As we can see, in all the cases accuracy obtained using normalization is better than without using it. The best result was produced using wavelet kernel, but the difference between this kernel and the others was not large. It is important to note that without normalization Wavelet kernel generally gives much worse results. Authors have chosen best possible parameters and final results were good, but without cross validation it would be really hard to choose because most of parameters without normalization yielded bad results with the Wavelet kernel.

Table 4. Results of measurements obtained using selected SVM kernels

Kernel	Lienar	Polynomial	Radial	Sigmoid	Wavelet
Without normalization	94.30	94.46	95.50	95.00	95.62
With normalization	95.01	95.36	95.46	95.69	95.85

Considering results of presented research it is also worth to note what are the reasons of recognition mistakes. Figure 2 shows classification errors for opening bracket gesture. The most problematic were gestures similar to less–than sign and often they were incorrectly recognized as a vertical line. It is vital to note visual similarity between these gestures. When the user marks the curve too sharply while performing opening bracket gesture, it makes similar to less–than sign. When user marks this curve not sharply enough, gesture starts to look like a vertical line gesture. This explains reasons of classification errors. Analysis of incorrectly classified instances of other gestures confirmed that observation.

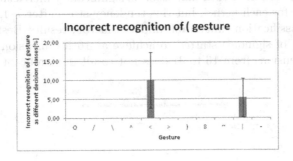

Fig. 2. Incorrect recognition of opening bracket gesture as different decision classes

6.2   Second Experiment

The first tested approach was a check difference between classification accuracy using relative data representation, achieved in the first experiment, and the proposed feature representation using 49 or less proposed features. This was

Table 5. Comparison of relative data representation and feature data representation classification accuracy

Kernel function	Relative data [%]	Features [%]
Linear	95.01	94.15
Polynomial	95.36	94.15
Sigmoid	95.46	77.90
RBF	95.69	92.85
Wavelet	95.85	93.11

checked for each of five proposed kernel functions. The results are presented in Table 5.

As it is shown in Sect. 5, for four of five kernels the difference was about 1.5%–3% (it was bigger for sigmoid kernel). It is a noticeable drop of classification accuracy, which confirms that feature extraction causes loss of some information. The other reason can be not perfect choice of features that were extracted – this can be checked in further research. On the other hand, by performing feature extraction we reduced the number of dimensions more than twice (from 120 to 49), as a result we also reduced the classification time. We judge the 1.5%–3% difference is a price worth to pay for more than twice reduction of computation time.

The main part of our research dealt with classification accuracy using data sets that consisted of different number of dimensions. Authors checked 49 data sets having number of dimensions from 1 to 49 (with a step of 1). The results are presented in Fig. 3.

First of all, addition of each dimension is significantly increasing the classification accuracy for each kernel, but this tendency stops after 7–12 dimensions. At this point classification gains stable and satisfactory results. Best results most kernels (instead of sigmoid) started to achieve at 16th dimension. The further increase of dimensions from 16 to 31 does not result in significant classification

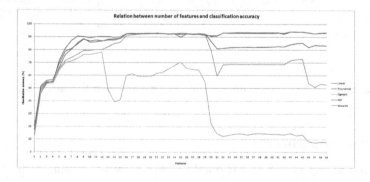

Fig. 3. Classification accuracy referring to the number of dimensions

accuracy growth, which means next features do not provide any more important information about data. After 31th dimension in three of five kernels classification accuracy drops, that means some information is excessive and is bringing unnecessary noise to the data set for these kernel functions.

The best results in 16–31 dimensions were comparable for each kernel function, but not sigmoid. Slightly better in this range is a wavelet function. In the larger number of dimensions the best classification accuracy was achieved by linear and polynomial kernel functions, and they achieved best results in the whole research. Sigmoid functions, comparing to the other ones, gave unsatisfactional results. We were unable to select a correct set of parameters for this function to achieve results comparable to other ones.

In Fig. 4 the best results achieved during the parameters optimization process are shown. Figure 5 shows differences between classification accuracy achieved during optimization of parameters.

In almost all of the cases results achieved using parameters optimization were better than during the research. Differences are the result of data overfitting. For four of five kernels (instead of the wavelet one) the differences were oscilating about 0%–3% all the time. For wavelet kernel the differences were much larger.

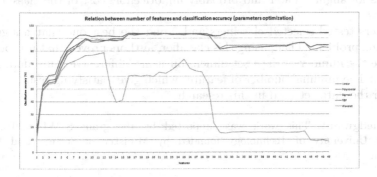

Fig. 4. Classification accuracy referring to the number of dimensions — parameter optimization

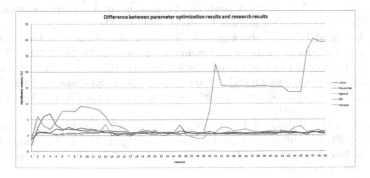

Fig. 5. Differences between parameter optimization accuracy and research accuracy

For 0 to 30 dimensions they did not exceed 10%. For the larger number of dimensions (above 30) it was oscilating between 15% and 30%. It means this kernel function is the most sensitive to selection of parameters.

7   Conclusion

The method and algorithm of real-time gestures recognition described in this paper can be inserted into the CAVE3D system. Gestures can be successfully recognized using classifiers. Selection of appropriate classifier to solve the problem of gestures recognition is crucial. Based on studies presented in this paper it can be concluded that the decision should fall on the SVM classifier. It should be emphasized however, that results could be slightly different for different sets of gestures or other selected classifiers parameters, but taking into account specific nature of the problem and carefully conducted study by authors, the result of them can be considered as representative for a given research problem.

Also, according to the research presented in this paper, only 16 features are enough to achieve results that are about 1.5%–3% worse than using full data representation. This means that it is possible to reduce data set size about 7–8 times for slightly lower and probably unnoticeable cost of the classification accuracy.

Authors tested selected classifiers and found the best one that fits gesture recognition problem. Then, using this classifier, authors proved that it is possible to reduce the number of data set dimension using different feature data representation. The minimal number of features which gives satisfying result was also found for the data set used in this research.

Acknowledgment. This work was supported by the grant S/WI/1/2013 from Bialystok University of Technology founded by Ministry of Science and Higher Education.

References

1. Akl, A., Feng, C., Valaee, S.: A novel accelerometer-based gesture recognition system. IEEE Trans. Sig. Process. **59**(12), 6197–6205 (2011)
2. Boyali, A., Kavakli, M.: A robust gesture recognition algorithm based on sparse representation, random projections and compressed sensing. In: 2012 7th IEEE Conference on Industrial Electronics and Applications (ICIEA), pp. 243–249, July 2012
3. McNeill, D.: Gesture and Thought. University of Chichago Press, Chicago (2007)
4. Gadomer, Ł.: Towards gesture recognition in three-dimensional space. Adv. Comput. Sci. Res. **12**, 5–20 (2015)
5. Wobbrock, J.O., Wilson, A.D., Li, Y.: Gestures without libraries, toolkits or training: a $1 recognizer for user interface prototypes. In: ACM Symposium on User Interface Software and Technology (UIST 2007), Newport, Rhode Island, pp. 159–168, July 2007
6. Gadomer, Ł., Skoczylas, M.: Real time gesture recognition using selected classifiers. Architecturae et Atribus **6**(1), 14–18 (2014)

7. Xu, R., Zhou, S., Li, W.J.: Mems accelerometer based nonspecific-user hand gesture recognition. IEEE Sens. J. **12**(5), 1166–1173 (2012)
8. Hussain, S.M.A., Rashid, A.B.M.H.: User independent hand gesture recognition by accelerated DTW. In: 2012 International Conference on Informatics, Electronics Vision (ICIEV), pp. 1033–1037, May 2012
9. Zhou, Y., Saito, D., Jing, L.: Adaptive template adjustment for personalized gesture recognition based on a finger-worn device. In: 2013 International Joint Conference on Awareness Science and Technology and UBI-Media Computing (iCAST-UMEDIA), pp. 610–614, November 2013

Using Cluster–Context Fuzzy Decision Trees in Fuzzy Random Forest

Łukasz Gadomer[(⊠)] and Zenon A. Sosnowski

Faculty of Computer Science, Bialystok University of Technology,
Wiejska 45A, 15-351 Bialystok, Poland
{l.gadomer,z.sosnowski}@pb.edu.pl
http://www.wi.pb.edu.pl

Abstract. Cluster–Context Fuzzy Decision Tree is the classifier which joins C–Fuzzy Decision Tree with Context–Based Fuzzy Clustering method. The idea of using this kind of tree in the Fuzzy Random Forest is presented in this paper. The created ensemble classifier has similar assumptions to the Fuzzy Random Forest, but differs in the kind of used trees and all aspects connected with this difference. The quality of the created classifier was evaluated by several experiments performed on different datasets. There were tested both datasets with discrete and continuous attributes and decision classes. The aspect of using a randomness in the created classifier was also evaluated.

Keywords: Context–Cluster Fuzzy Decision Tree · C–Fuzzy Decision Tree · Context–Based Fuzzy Clustering · Fuzzy Random Forest

1 Introduction

The classification and regression are popular problems in data science. There were created many solutions in order to deal with these issues. In this paper authors present their innovative ensemble classifier which was designed in order to meet both these problems. The idea of this solution is creating a classifier which works with the similar assumptions to Fuzzy Random Forest [1] but instead of Janikow Fuzzy Trees [2] it uses Cluster–Context Fuzzy Decision Trees [3]. This kind of tree connects the Context–Based Fuzzy Clustering [4,5] with C–Fuzzy Decision Tree [6]. The objective of this paper was to prove that the created classifier can successfully deal with both regression and classification problems.

The first part of this paper treats about theoretical aspects of the created classifier. The theory about Context–Based Fuzzy Clustering [4,5], C–Fuzzy Decision Trees [6], Context–Cluster Fuzzy Decision Trees [3] and C–Fuzzy Random Forest [1] is described there. After that, the idea of using Cluster–Context Fuzzy Decision Trees in Fuzzy Random Forest is presented. Then, the performed experiments with the achieved results are shown. The results achieved by created trees

© IFIP International Federation for Information Processing 2017
Published by Springer International Publishing AG 2017. All Rights Reserved
K. Saeed et al. (Eds.): CISIM 2017, LNCS 10244, pp. 180–192, 2017.
DOI: 10.1007/978-3-319-59105-6_16

grouped into the forest were compared with the ones obtained with the trees working singly. The influence of using randomness during the tree construction process on the achieved results is also tested. The quality of the created solution is evaluated on the different datasets, containing continuous and discrete attributes, both for classification and regression problems.

2 Notation

In this paper we used the following notations (based on [1,6]):

- K is the number of contexts,
- k is a particular context
- T is the number of tree groups in the ensemble; in each tree group there are K trees connected with the contextes,
- t is the particular tree group,
- t_k is a particular tree in t group
- N_t is the number of nodes in the tree group t_k,
- n is a particular leaf reached in a tree group t_k,
- I is the number of classes,
- i is a particular class,
- C is the number of clusters,
- c is a particular cluster,
- E is a training dataset,
- e is a data instance,
- $V_k = [V_{1k}, V_{2k}, ..., V_{bk}]$ is the variability vector for k context,
- $U_k = [U_{1k}, U_{2k}, ..., U_{|E|k}]$ is the tree's partition matrix of the training objects for k context,
- $U_{ik} = [u_{1k}, u_{2k}, ..., u_{Ck}]$ are memberships of the ith object to the c cluster for k context,
- $B = \{B_1, B_2, ..., B_b\}$ are the unsplitted nodes,
- S is the number of objects from the dataset for which the membership function value is greater than 0 for t_k tree in k context,
- s is the particular object,
- $X = [X_1, X_2, ..., X_K]$ is the vector of objects from the dataset for which the membership function value is greater than 0 for whole tree t,
- $X_k = [X_{1k}, X_{2k}, ..., X_{Ck}]$ is the vector of objects from the dataset for which the membership function value is greater than 0 for c cluster,
- $X_{ck} = [x_1, x_2, ..., x_S, y_k]$ is the vector of objects from the dataset for which the membership function value is greater than 0 for c cluster for k context.

3 Related Work

3.1 C–Fuzzy Decision Trees

C–Fuzzy Decision Trees are the kind of trees proposed by W. Pedrycz and Z.A. Sosnowski in [6]. The main motivation to create these trees was the awareness of problems and limits of traditional decision trees, which usually operate on a relatively small set of discrete attributes, choose the single attribute which brings the most information gain to split the node during the tree construction process and are designed to operate on discrete class problems (in their traditional form – the continuous problems are handled by regression trees). The creating of C–Fuzzy Decision Trees was intended to be a solution of these problems. According to their assumptions, C–Fuzzy Decision Trees treat data as collection of information granules, analogous to fuzzy clusters. These granules are generic building blocks of the tree – the data is grouped in such multivariable granules characterized by high homogenity (low variablity).

The first step of C–Fuzzy Decision Tree construction process is grouping the data set into c clusters. It is performed in the way that the similar objects are placed in the same cluster. Each cluster is characterized by its centroid, called prototype, which is randomly selected first and then improved iteratively. After the grouping objects into clusters is finished, the given heterogenity criterion is used to compute the diversity of the each of these clusters. This value decides if the node is selected to split or not. From all of the nodes the one with the lowest diversity value is chosen to split. This node is divided into c clusters using fuzzy clustering method [7]. After that, for each node created that way, the diversity is computed and the selection to split is performed. These steps are repeated until the algorithm achieves the given stop criterion. Each node of the tree has 0 or c children. The growth of the tree can be breadth or deep intensive.

The tree growth stop criterion could be, for example, defined in the following way: [6]

- All nodes achieve higher heterogenity than assumed boundary value,
- There aren't enough elements in any node to perform the split. The minimal number of elements in the node which allows for the split is c,
- The structurability index achieves the lower value than assumed boundary value,
- The number of iterations (splits) achieved the boundary value.

After the tree is constructed it can be used in classification mode. Each object which has to be classified starts from the root node. The membership degrees (numbers between 0 and 1 which sums to 1 for the node's children) of this object to the children of the given node are computed. The object gets to the node where he belongs with the highest membership among the computed ones. The same operation is repeated until the object achieves to the node which has no children. The classification result is the class assigned to this node.

3.2   Context–Based Fuzzy Clustering

Clustering is a tool used for data analysis which purpose is to find structures (groups) in multivariable datasets. The idea of context–based clustering [4] is to search such groups of data with applying the context. The context is a kind of information granule, defined in a decision attribute, using which the search for structure in the data is focused. The general task of clustering, formulated as *reveal a structure in data* X, with context–based clustering is reformulated as *reveal a structure in data* X *in context* A, where A is the information granule of interest (context of clustering).

The conditioning aspect (context sensitivity) of the clustering mechanism is used in the algorithm by taking into consideration the conditioning variable (context) assuming the values $f_1, f_2, ..., f_N$ on the corresponding patterns. In other words, f_k is the level of involvement of x_k in the considered context, $f_k = A(x_k)$. f_k can be connected with computed membership values of x_k, say $u_{1k}, u_{2k}, ..., u_{Ck}$ the way expressed in the following formula:

$$\sum_{i=1}^{c} u_{ik} = f_k, k = 1, 2, ..., N \tag{1}$$

It is important that the selected context directly impacts the resulting data to be considered. The finite support of context A does not take into consideration these data points which the membership values are equal to zero. It means only a certain subset of the original data to be used for further clustering. Considering this fact, the partition matrix U, previously defined as

$$U = \left\{ u_{ik} \in [0,1] \middle| \sum_{i=1}^{c} u_{ik} = 1 \text{ and } 0 < \sum_{k=1}^{N} u_{ik} < N \text{ for all } i = 1, 2, ..., c \right\} \tag{2}$$

can be modified into the family

$$U(A) = \left\{ u_{ik} \in [0,1] \middle| \sum_{i=1}^{c} u_{ik} = f_k \forall k \text{ and } 0 < \sum_{k=1}^{N} u_{ik} < N \forall i \right\} \tag{3}$$

The overall Context–Based Fuzzy Clustering algorithm can be summarized as the following sequence of steps (the number of clusters c is given):

1. Select the termination criterion ε ($\varepsilon > 0$), distance function $||\cdot||$, fuzzification parameter m (by default $m = 2.0$), then initialize the partition matrix $U \in U$.
2. Calculate prototypes (centers) of the clusters the same way as in standard FCM algorithm [7]:

$$v_i = \frac{\sum_{k=1}^{N} u_{ik}^m x_k}{\sum_{k=1}^{N} u_{ik}^m}, i = 1, 2, ..., c \tag{4}$$

3. Update partition matrix

$$u_{ik} = \frac{f_k}{\sum_{j=1}^{c} \left(\frac{||x_k - v_i||}{||x_k - v_j||} \right)^{\frac{2}{m-1}}}, i = 1, 2, ..., c, j = 1, 2, ..., N \tag{5}$$

4. Compare U' to U. If $||U' - U|| < \varepsilon$, then stop, else return to step (2) and proceed with computing by setting up U equal to U'

Used distance function is the weighted Euclidean distance function, defined as follows:

$$\|a - b\| = \sum_{i=1}^{n} \frac{(a_i - b_i)^2}{\sigma_i^2} \tag{6}$$

where σ_i are standard deviations of the corresponding attributes.

3.3   Cluster–Context Fuzzy Decision Trees

The main idea of Cluster–Context Fuzzy Decision Trees is joining Context–Based Clustering, presented in Sect. 3.2 and C–Fuzzy Decision Trees, described in Sect. 3.1. This kind of trees were presented in [3]. Author predicted that joining these two algorithms allows to achieve better results than C–Fuzzy Decision Trees, especially for regression problem.

It is important to notice that notation presented in Sect. 2 each Cluster–Context Fuzzy Decision Tree t consists of k C–Fuzzy Decision Trees t_k. It means that the structure called "tree" t when writing about Cluster–Context Fuzzy Decision Trees refers to the group of C–Fuzzy Decision Trees t_k, not a single tree. As it can be confusing, it is worth to remember about it.

The first thing which should be done before starting construction of Cluster–Context Fuzzy Decision Tree is dividing decision attribute into contexts. The number of contexts is the algorithm parameter which should be adjusted according to the dataset. In the theoretically perfect situation the number of contexts should respond the number of object groups in the dataset. The division can be performed using any membership function. In this research three membership functions were chosen: gaussian, trapezoidal and triangular. The example division result using these functions into five contexts is presented in Fig. 1.

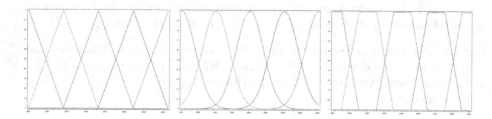

Fig. 1. Example division of decision attribute into five contexts using (from left) triangular, gaussian and trapezoidal membership functions.

In order to fit the division to the given problem in the best possible way it is also possible to configure the shape of membership function. In the created solution authors allowed to do this using "context configuration" parameter – its default value is 1, lower numbers makes contexts wider, higher numbers – shorter. Figure 1 showed divisions for default context configuration value, on Fig. 2 the example divisions using values 0.6 and 1.6 are presented.

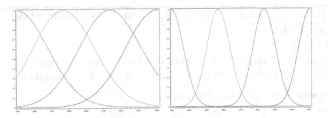

Fig. 2. Example division of decision attribute into four contexts using gaussian function with context configuration value (from left) 0.6 and 1.6.

Algorithm 1. Cluster–Context Fuzzy Decision Tree learning

1: **procedure** CC–FDTLEARNING
2:    **for** 1 to K **do**
3:        1. Start with the examples in X_k
4:        2. Create C–Fuzzy Decision Tree for context k using Algorithm 2
5:    **end for**
6: **end procedure**

When contexts are prepared, it is possible to create and learn Cluster–Context Fuzzy Decision Trees according to the Algorithm 1.

Each C–Fuzzy Decision Tree in Cluster–Context Fuzzy Decision Tree is created using Algorithm 2.

Algorithm 2. C–Fuzzy Decision Tree learning

1: **procedure** C–FDTLEARNING
2:    1. Start with the examples in X_k for k context,
3:    2. Create the partition matrix U_k randomly
4:    3. Perform FCM
5:    **while** Stop criterion is not satisfied **do**
6:        4. Divide the samples belonging to the splitted node into its children
7:        5. Make a random selection of nodes from the set of unsplitted nodes B
8:        6. Compute the variability matrix V_k
9:        7. Choose the node with maximum variability to split nodes
10:        8. Perform FCM
11:    **end while**
12: **end procedure**

Created Cluster–Context Fuzzy Decision Tree can be used in classification and regression process. It is performed according to the Algorithm 3.

3.4 Fuzzy Random Forests

The Fuzzy Random Forest classifier was first presented in [8] and then widely described in [1,9]. The mentioned classifier was based on two papers cited

---
Algorithm 3. Cluster–Context Fuzzy Decision Trees classification
---
1: **procedure** CC–FDTCLASSIFICATION
2:     **for** 1 to K **do**
3:         1. Run the example x_k to obtain the tree's partition matrix U_{ik}
4:         2. Choose the class c where $c = arg \max\limits_{i,i=1,2,...,I} U_{ik}$ (classification) or choose the node n where $n = \max U_{ik}$ (regression)
5:     **end for**
6:     Assign to class with the higher U_{ik} value from k achieved values (classification) or compute the distance between the y_k and the decision value in the chosen node n (regression)
7: **end procedure**
---

before: [2, 10]. Fuzzy random forest, according to its assumptions, combines the robustness of ensemble classifiers, the power of the randomness to decrease the correlation between the trees and increase the diversity of them and the flexibility of fuzzy logic for dealing with imperfect data [1].

Fuzzy random forest construction process is similar to Forest–RI, described in [10]. After the forest is constructed, the algorithm begins its working from the root of each tree. First, a random set of attributes is chosen (it has the same size for each node). For each of these attributes information gain is computed, using all of the objects from training set. Attribute with the highest information gain is chosen to node split. When the node is splitted, selected attribute is removed from the set of attributes possible to select in order to divide the following nodes. Then, for all of the following tree nodes, this operation is repeated using a new set of randomly selected attributes (attributes which were used before are excluded from the selection) and the same training set.

According to described algorithm trees are constructed. Each tree is created using randomly selected set of attributes, different for each tree, which ensures diversity of trees in the forest.

4   Using Cluster–Context Fuzzy Decision Trees in Fuzzy Random Forest

The classifier which uses Cluster–Context Fuzzy Decision Trees in Fuzzy Random Forest is proposed in this section. This ensemble classifier bases on the idea of Fuzzy Random Forest and uses Cluster–Context Fuzzy Decision Trees as constituent classifiers. The idea of Fuzzy Random Forest with C–Fuzzy Decision Trees was presented in [11]. It is expected that introducing the contexts with their advantages into the forest will increase the classification accuracy, especially in the area of continuous decision class problems.

The randomness in the created classifier is ensured by two main aspects. The first of them refers to the assumptions of Random Forest. When the tree is being constructed, the node to split is selected randomly. It can be full randomness (selecting the random node to split instead of the most heterogenous) or limited (selecting the set of nodes with the highest diversity, then randomly selecting one of them to perform the split). The second aspect refers to the C–Fuzzy Decision Trees, which take part in Cluster–Context Fuzzy Decision Trees, and it concerns partition matrix creation process. The first coordinates of centroids (prototypes) of each clusters are selected randomly. Objects which belong to the parent node are divided into clusters grouped around these prototypes using the shortest distance criterion. After that the prototypes and the partition matrix are being corrected iteratively until they achieve the stop criterion. What is more, each tree in the forest can be selected from the set of created trees. Each tree from such set is tested and the best of them is being chosen as the part of forest. The size of this set is given and the same for the each tree in the forest.

The split selection idea is similar to the one used in Fuzzy Random Forest, but it refers to nodes instead of attributes. In Fuzzy Random Forest, the random attribute was being chosen to split during the Fuzzy Trees construction process. In Fuzzy Random Forest with Cluster–Context Decision Trees the choice concerns the node to split selection. Some nodes does not have to be splitted (it can happen when the stop criterion is achieved). Each Cluster–Context Fuzzy Decision Tree in the forest can be similar or different – it depends on the chosen algorithm parameters. It allows to adjust the classifier to the given problem in a flexible way.

The Fuzzy Random Forest with Cluster–Context Fuzzy Decision Trees is created using Algorithm 4.

Algorithm 4. Fuzzy Random Forest with Cluster–Context Fuzzy Decision Trees learning

---

1: **procedure** FRFwCC–FDTLEARNING
2:     **for** 1 to T **do**
3:         1. Take a random sample of $|E|$ examples with replacement from the dataset E
4:         2. Apply Algorithm 1 to the subset of examples obtained in the previous step to construct C–Fuzzy Decision Tree
5:     **end for**
6: **end procedure**

The constructed forest can be used for classification and regression problems. For the classification issue, the decision–making strategy assumpts making the final decision by forest after individual decisions of trees are made. This process is performed according to the Algorithm 5.

The weighted averaging is performed to let the best trees in the forest (the ones which during the learning process achieved the lowest prediction error) have the biggest influence on the final prediction. It is performed according to the following formula:

Algorithm 5. Fuzzy Random Forest with Cluster–Context Fuzzy Decision Trees classification

---
1: **procedure** FRFwCC–FDTCLASSIFICATION
2:     Perform tree's individual decisions according to Algorithm 3
3:     Assign to class according to the simple majority vote of trees decisions (classification) or perform weighted averaging the final prediction (regression)
4: **end procedure**

$$\text{result} = \frac{\sum\limits_{i=1}^{T} \text{result}_i \times \text{result}_{T-i}}{\frac{n(n+1)}{2}}, \forall i \ \text{result}_i < \text{result}_{i+1} \tag{7}$$

5   Experimental Studies

The main objectives of performed experiments were to test the quality of created classifier on classification and regression process and to check the influence of the randomness on the results. To check the classification process, experiments were performed on four popular datasets from UCI Machine Learning Repository [12]: Ionosphere, Dermatology, Pima–Diabetes and Hepatitis. To check the regression process another two datasets from this repository were used: Automobile Data and Housing.

Each dataset was randomly divided into five equal parts (or as close to the equal as it's possible). For classification problems, each of these parts had the same proportions of objects with each decision class (or as close to the same as it's possible). This random and proportional division was saved and used for each experiment.

Each experiment was performed with 5–fold crossvalidation. Four of five parts were used to train the forest, one to test it. This operation was repeated five times, each time the other part was excluded from the training process and used for evaluation. At the end all classification accuracies of the out of bag parts were averaged.

Classification parameters were chosen individually for each dataset with parameter optimization process. There were tested multiple combinations of parameters for forests which consist of five trees. According to these results the classification parameter combinations for the final classifier were chosen. Each forest in the experiment consist of fifty trees.

Achieved results were compared with Fuzzy Random Forest with C–Fuzzy Decision Trees and Fuzzy Random Forest C–Fuzzy Decision Trees. Some of the results which serve as a base to compare were presented in our previous work: [11].

All of the results are presented in Sect. 6.

6   Results and Discussion

The classifiers' parameters chosen for each dataset are presented in Table 1.

Table 1. Classifier parameters for datasets

Dataset	Hepatitis	Dermatology	Pima Indians Diabetes	Ionosphere	Auto data	Housing
Number of clusters	2	2	2	2	2	3
Number of contexts	3	2	3	2	9	2
Membership function	Gaussian	Triangular	Gaussian	Gaussian	Gaussian	Gaussian
Context configuration	0.6	1.6	0.6	0.6	0.6	0.6

6.1   Datasets with Continuous Decision Attribute

The results achieved for datasets with continuous decision attribute are presented in Table 2. Numbers in the table are the average distances between the predicted value and the original value.

As it was expected, ensemble classifiers which use Cluster–Context Fuzzy Decision Trees allowed to achieve better results that forests with C–Fuzzy Decision Trees. The differences were more significant for Auto Data dataset. For housing dataset all results achieved using ensembles with Cluster–Context Fuzzy Decision Trees were also better that using forests with C–Fuzzy Decision Trees, but the differences were smaller.

For each of created ensemble classifiers: Fuzzy Forest with C–Fuzzy Decision Trees, Fuzzy Random Forest with C–Fuzzy Decision Trees, Fuzzy Forest with Cluster–Context Fuzzy Decision Trees and Fuzzy Random Forest with Cluster–Context Fuzzy Decision Trees results achieved using weights were better that without using them. It clearly means that it is worth to use weighted average instead of arithmetic average. The arithmetic average of the results achieved by trees which are part of the forest does not allow to use the full strength of the ensemble. The weighted average allows forest to work the way it was designed for.

For the ensemble which use C–Fuzzy Decision Trees in most cases using randomness increased the quality of the classifier. The difference was more significant for Auto Data dataset. For Housing dataset the differences between using randomness and not were slight. It means that using randomness can improve the classification accuracy, but it depends on the dataset and the classifier's configuration.

Table 2. Results for datasets with continuous class attribute

Dataset	Auto data	Housing
Fuzzy Forest with C–Fuzzy Decision Trees without weights	3277.55	3.98
Fuzzy Forest with C–Fuzzy Decision Trees with weights	3244	3.92
Fuzzy Random Forest with C–Fuzzy Decision Trees without weights	3192.9	3.97
Fuzzy Random Forest with C–Fuzzy Decision Trees with weights	3178.26	3.94
Fuzzy Forest with Cluster–Context Fuzzy Decision Trees without weights	3064.58	3.91
Fuzzy Forest with Cluster–Context Fuzzy Decision Trees with weights	3025.41	3.86
Fuzzy Random Forest with Cluster–Context Fuzzy Decision Trees without weights	3023.92	3.87
Fuzzy Random Forest with Cluster–Context Fuzzy Decision Trees with weights	3015.59	3.85

6.2 Datasets with Discrete Decision Class

The results achieved for datasets with discrete decision class are presented in Table 3.

In most cases using forest with Cluster–Context Fuzzy Decision Trees allowed to achieve better results that with ensemble using C–Fuzzy Decision Trees. Using randomness in Fuzzy Random Forest with Cluster–Context Fuzzy Decision Trees in most cases also allowed to improve classification accuracy (for Dermatology dataset it was the same, for the other ones it was better). All of these improvements were small but noticeable.

It is worth to notice the reason classification of the accuracy improvement in the given classifier configuration. On the sample visualization of contexts presented in Fig. 2 it is showed that for the context configuration parameter equal to 0.6 all of the contexts are relative wide. For the decision attribute division into two or three contexts all of these contexts, for all of the decision attribute's values, has a value greater than zero. It means for each context no objects from the dataset are excluded from the C–Fuzzy Decision Trees which are part of Cluster–Context Decision Tree. In this case the ensemble classifier with Cluster–Context Fuzzy Decision Tree works the similar way to the forest with C–Fuzzy Decision Trees, but each tree is chosen from the best of K. In this special case choosing the best trees allowed to slightly improve classification accuracies. It is also worth to notice that during the parameters optimization the other (typical) cases produced a little worse results that the given one.

Table 3. Classification errors for datasets with discrete class attribute

Dataset	Hepatitis	Dermatology	Pima Indians Diabetes	Ionosphere
Fuzzy Forest with C–Fuzzy Decision Trees	34.19	2.99	26.31	13.39
Fuzzy Random Forest with C–Fuzzy Decision Trees	34.19	2.18	26.56	12.24
Fuzzy Forest with Cluster–Context Fuzzy Decision Trees	34.84	2.73	26.05	12.25
Fuzzy Random Forest with Cluster–Context Fuzzy Decision Trees	34.19	2.73	25.92	11.68

7 Conclusion

The Fuzzy Random Forest with Cluster–Context Decision Trees classifier was presented in this paper. The created solution was tested using datasets both with continuous and discrete decision attribute. The classification accuracy was compared with the results achieved with the Fuzzy Random Forest with C–Fuzzy Decision Trees. The experiments showed that in most cases Fuzzy Random Forest with Cluster–Context Decision Trees gives better results that Fuzzy Random Forest with C–Fuzzy Decision Trees, especially for datasets with continuous decision attribute. It was also showed that using weights are really important for datasets with continuous decision attribute. All these results showed that the Fuzzy Random Forest with Cluster–Context Decision Trees is the valuable ensemble classifier which can allow to achieve good results in many classification or regression problems.

Acknowledgment. This work was supported by the grant S/WI/1/2013 from Bialystok University of Technology founded by Ministry of Science and Higher Education.

References

1. Bonissone, P.P., Cadenas, J.M., Garrido, M.C., Di'az-Valladares, R.A.: A fuzzy random forest. Int. J. Approximate Reasoning **51**(7), 729–747 (2010)
2. Janikow, C.Z.: Fuzzy decision trees: issues and methods. IEEE Trans. Syst. Man Cybern. Part B (Cybern.) **28**(1), 1–14 (1998)
3. Sosnowski, Z.A.: Decision rules with fuzzy granulation of knowledge. Symulacja w Badaniach i Rozwoju **3**(4), 225–232 (2012). (in Polish)
4. Pedrycz, W.: Conditional fuzzy C-means. Pattern Recogn. Lett. **17**(6), 625–631 (1996)
5. Pedrycz, W., Sosnowski, Z.A.: Designing decision trees with the use of fuzzy granulation. IEEE Trans. Syst. Man Cybern. Part A Syst. Hum. **30**(2), 151–159 (2000)

6. Pedrycz, W., Sosnowski, Z.A.: C-fuzzy decision trees. IEEE Trans. Syst. Man Cybern. Part C (Appl. Rev.) **35**(4), 498–511 (2005)
7. Bezdek, J.C.: Pattern Recognition with Fuzzy Objective Function Algorithms. Kluwer Academic Publishers, Norwell (1981)
8. Bonissone, P.P., Cadenas, J.M., Garrido, M.C., Di'az-valladares, R.A.: A fuzzy random forest: fundamental for design and construction. In: Proceedings of the 12th International Conference on Information Processing and Management of Uncertainty in Knowledge-Based Systems (IPMU 2008), pp. 1231–1238 (2008)
9. Bonissone, P.P., Cadenas, J.M., Garrido, M.C., Di'az-Valladares, R.A.: Combination methods in a Fuzzy random forest. In: IEEE International Conference on Systems, Man and Cybernetics, SMC 2008, pp. 1794–1799, October 2008
10. Breiman, L.: Random forests. Mach. Learn. **45**(1), 5–32 (2001)
11. Gadomer, Ł., Sosnowski, Z.A.: Fuzzy random forest with C–fuzzy decision trees. In: Saeed, K., Homenda, W. (eds.) CISIM 2016. LNCS, vol. 9842, pp. 481–492. Springer, Cham (2016). doi:10.1007/978-3-319-45378-1_43
12. Lichman, M.: UCI machine learning repository (2013)

Split-and-merge Tweak in Cross Entropy Clustering

Krzysztof Hajto, Konrad Kamieniecki, Krzysztof Misztal$^{(\boxtimes)}$,
and Przemysław Spurek

Faculty of Mathematics and Computer Science, Jagiellonian University,
Łojasiewicza 6, 30-348 Kraków, Poland
{krzysztof.hajto,krzysztof.misztal,przemyslaw.spurek}@ii.uj.edu.pl,
konrad.kamieniecki@alumni.uj.edu.pl

Abstract. In order to solve the local convergence problem of the Cross Entropy Clustering algorithm, a split-and-merge operation is introduced to escape from local minima and reach a better solution. We describe the theoretical aspects of the method in a limited space, present a few strategies of tweaking the clustering algorithm and compare them with existing solutions. The experiments show that the presented approach increases flexibility and effectiveness of the whole algorithm.

Keywords: Cross entropy clustering · Clusters splitting · Clusters merging

1 Introduction

Clustering plays a basic role in many parts of data engineering, pattern recognition, data mining, data quantization and image analysis [5,6,15]. Some of the most important clustering algorithms are based on density estimation.

In the probabilistic model construction for univariate and multivariate data, finite mixture models have been widely used. The capability of representing arbitrary complex probability density functions (pdfs) enables it to have many applications not only in unsupervised learning [8], but also in (Bayesian) supervised learning or in parameter estimation of class-conditional pdfs [4].

One of the most important clustering method is based on GMM (Gaussian Mixture Models), which uses the Expectation maximization (EM) algorithm. Unfortunately, GMM has strong limitations related to its optimization procedure, which has to be applied in each iteration of the EM algorithm. While the expectation step is relatively simple, the maximization step usually needs complicated numerical optimization [2,9]. Because of its greedy nature, the EM algorithm is sensitive to the initial configuration and usually gets stuck at local maxima. Moreover, there is a problem with choosing the correct number of clusters.

© IFIP International Federation for Information Processing 2017
Published by Springer International Publishing AG 2017. All Rights Reserved
K. Saeed et al. (Eds.): CISIM 2017, LNCS 10244, pp. 193–204, 2017.
DOI: 10.1007/978-3-319-59105-6_17

A feasible way for solving this problem is to choose several sets of initial values, then proceed respectively with the EM algorithms, and finally choose the best outcome set as the estimation. In most cases, the Bayesian information criterion (BIC) is used to establish the best result and final number of clusters. However, this will certainly increase computational complexity, since we have to apply a method many times with different initial parameters.

In order to solve this problem, many various methods were introduced. In [14] the authors proposed a split-and-merge EM (SMEM) algorithm in which they applied a split-and-merge operation to the EM algorithm. The basic idea of the SMEM algorithm is: after the convergence of the usual EM algorithm, we first use the split-and-merge operation to update the values of some parameters among all the parameters, then we perform the next round of the usual EM algorithm, and alternatively iterate the split-and-merge operation and the EM algorithm until some criterion is met. However, the split or merge method is a linear heuristic procedure without theoretical support. Moreover, the split or merge of the mean vector is independent of the covariance matrix, and vice versa.

In [17] authors propose two split methods based on SVD and the Cholesky decomposition of the covariance matrices. Shoham presented a robust cluster-ing algorithm by creating a deterministic agglomeration EM (DAGEM) with multivariate t-distributions [11]. It was derived from the DAEM algorithm and achieved encouraging performance. Because the initial component number is much larger than the true number, the computation load is one to two orders of magnitude heavier than EM [11]. In [16] authors present Competitive EM (CEM) which uses an information theory based criterion for split and merge operations. The initial component number and model parameters can be set arbitrarily and the split and merge operation can be selected efficiently. In [7] the authors present a method that uses two different split and merge criteria. Homogeneity criterion decides whether two clusters should be merged or not (clusters which touch each other or slightly overlap can be merged, if they fulfill the homogeneity criterion). The split criterion is based on a penalized Bayesian information criterion (BIC), evaluated for the actual clusters and hypothetically split clusters, updated in the previous incremental learning step.

In all of the methods the basic idea is to construct a split merge strategy by analyzing cluster shapes. The idea is to avoid a local minima by applying some unconventional operation. The main problem is that such an operation does not depend on the cost function, that is minimized by the EM algorithms. Moreover, after the split or merge operation it is non trivial how to update the parameters of the components, since each point belongs to all cluster with different probability.

In this paper we present a split and merge strategy which solves these two basic problems. First of all, a simpler optimization procedure Cross Entropy Clustering (CEC) [13] is used instead of EM. The goal of CEC is to optimally approximate the scatter of a data set $X \subset \mathbb{R}^d$ by a function which is a small modification of EM (for more information see Sect. 2). It occurs that at the small cost of having a minimally worse density approximation [13], we gain an efficient method which can be easily adapted for more complicated density models. Moreover, we can treat clusters separately which allows us to update the parameters of clusters more easily (each point belongs to only one group).

Furthermore, we can treat each cluster as a new dataset, that is separated from other data, and apply the CEC algorithm in that single cluster. The new division of the cluster is accepted if the global value of the cost function is lower. Similarly, we can verify if the merge of two clusters decreases the cost function.

Let us discuss the contents of the paper. In the first part of our work we briefly describe the CEC algorithm together with the basic structures which we can use in model construction. Then we describe the split-and-merge tweak in detail. At the end of this paper we present results of numerical experiments and conclusions.

2   Split-and-merge Cross Entropy Clustering

In this section the Split-and-merge Cross Entropy Clustering method will be presented. Our method is based on the CEC approach. Therefore, we start with a short introduction to the method. Since CEC is similar to EM in many aspects, let us first recall that, in general, EM aims to find $p_1, \ldots, p_k \geq 0$ ($\sum_{i=1}^{k} p_i = 1$) and $f_1, \ldots, f_k$ Gaussian densities (where k is given beforehand and denotes the number of densities for which the convex combination builds the desired density model) such that the convex combination $f = p_1 f_1 + \ldots + p_k f_k$ optimally approximates the scatter of our data X with respect to the MLE cost function

$$\mathrm{MLE}(f, X) = - \sum_{x \in X} \ln(p_1 f_1(x) + \ldots + p_k f_k(x)). \qquad (1)$$

A goal of CEC is to minimize the cost function, which is a minor modification of the one given in (1) by substituting the sum with the maximum:

$$\mathrm{CEC}(f, X) = - \sum_{x \in X} \ln(\max(p_1 f_1(x), \ldots, p_k f_k(x))). \qquad (2)$$

Instead of focusing on the density estimation as its main task, CEC aims at solving the clustering problem directly. As it turns out, at the small cost of having a minimally worse density approximation [13], we gain speed in implementation[1] and the ease of using less complicated density models. This is an advantage, roughly speaking, because the models do not mix with each other since we take the maximum instead of the sum.

To explain cross entropy clustering (CEC), we need to first introduce an energy function for the purpose of minimizing, which uses cross entropy. But let's start with the definition of cross entropy itself.

---

[1] We can often use the Hartigan approach to clustering, which is faster and typically finds better minimas.

By the cross-entropy of the dataset $X \subset \mathbb{R}^d$ with respect to density f we understand

$$H^\times(X \| f) = -\frac{1}{|X|} \sum_{x \in X} \ln f(x).$$

Cross entropy corresponds to the theoretical code-length of compression. Let us consider the case of partitioning $X \subset \mathbb{R}^N$ into pairwise disjoint sets $X_1, \ldots, X_k$, such that elements of X_i are encoded by the optimal density from family $\mathcal{F}$. In this case, the cross-entropy with respect to a family of coding densities $\mathcal{F}$ is given by $H^\times(X \| \mathcal{F}) = \inf_{f \in \mathcal{F}} H^\times(X \| f)$. Thus, the mean code-length of a randomly chosen element x equals

$$E(X_1, \ldots; X_k, \mathcal{F}) := \sum_{i=1}^{k} p_i \cdot (-\ln(p_i) + H^\times(X_i \| \mathcal{F}_i)), \tag{3}$$

where $p_i = \frac{|X_i|}{|X|}$.

The aim of CEC is to find a partitioning of $X \subset \mathbb{R}^N$ into pairwise disjoint sets X_i, $i = 1, \ldots, k$ which minimizes the function given by (3). The minimization of (3) is equivalent to optimization of (2). In our case we consider as a $\mathcal{F}$ a family of all Gaussian distributions[2] $\mathcal{G}$. According to [13], for single piece $X_i \subset \mathbb{R}^N$ considered with respect to $\mathcal{N}(\mu, \Sigma) \in \mathcal{G}$ we can get that

$$H^\times(X_i \| \mathcal{N}(\mu, \Sigma)) = \frac{N}{2} \ln(2\pi) + \frac{1}{2} \mathrm{tr}(\Sigma^{-1} \Sigma_{X_i}) + \frac{1}{2} \ln \det(\Sigma), \tag{4}$$

where Σ_{X_i} is a covariance matrix of X_i, which allows as to easily calculate the cost function (3).

Let us now briefly introduce the algorithm step by step. The CEC clustering method starts from an initial clustering, which can be obtained randomly or by the use of the k-means++ [1] approach. Then the following two simple steps are applied simultaneously. First, we estimate the parameters of the optimal Gaussian function in each cluster. In the second step, we construct a new division of X by adding points to the closest cluster, or rather, to the closest Gaussian density. Specifically, we assign a point $x \in X$ to the cluster $i \in \{1, \ldots, k\}$ such that

$$-\ln(p_i) - \ln\left(\mathcal{N}(x; \mu_i, \Sigma_i)\right)$$

is minimal.

We apply the above steps simultaneously until the change of the cost function is smaller than a predefined threshold or if the clusters did not change at all.

This approach causes a problem with local minima. Therefore, we apply a two point strategy for increasing the performance of the algorithm. More precisely, we apply a split and merge strategy.

---

[2] We can also consider same Gaussians subfamilies [10, 12, 13].

2.1   Merge Strategies

Let us consider Gaussian densities $\mathcal{G}$. For two disjoint sets X and Y ($X, Y \subset \mathbb{R}^N$), we want to develop a condition under which we should combine them into one cluster, rather then consider them separately – namely, energy/cost of $X \cup Y$ is less then sum of energy of X and Y. This condition is given by

$$E(X \cup Y, \mathcal{G}) \leq E(X, \mathcal{G}) + E(Y, \mathcal{G}). \tag{5}$$

For the general case, it is very difficult to solve the above inequality and give an analytical solution. Thus, for simplicity of the problem, it is necessary to put some restrictions on the sets X and Y. In this section we solve this in a one dimensional real space under same constraint about sets X and Y. But before that, let us now recall the following important remark which simplifies our situation.

Remark 1. Let X, Y be given as finite subsets of $\mathbb{R}^N$. Assume additionally that $X \cap Y = \emptyset$. Then

$$m_{X \cup Y} = p_X m_X + p_Y m_Y$$
$$\Sigma_{X \cup Y} = p_X \Sigma_X + p_Y \Sigma_Y + p_X p_Y (m_X - m_Y)(m_X - m_Y)^T$$

where $p_X = \frac{|X|}{|X|+|Y|}, p_Y = \frac{|Y|}{|X|+|Y|}$.

Theorem 1. *Let X, Y be given as finite subsets of $\mathbb{R}$. Assume additionally that*

- $X \cap Y = \emptyset$,
- $|X| = |Y|$,
- $\Sigma_X = \Sigma_Y = \Sigma = (\sigma^2)$ *for an arbitrary $\sigma > 0$.*

Then the distributions $\mathcal{N}(m_X, \Sigma)$ and $\mathcal{N}(m_Y, \Sigma)$ should be combined into one Gaussian distribution $\mathcal{N}(\frac{1}{2}(m_X + m_Y), (\sigma^2 + \frac{1}{4}(m_X - m_Y)^2))$ with respect to condition (5) iff

$$|m_X - m_Y| < 2\sqrt{3}\sigma,$$

where m_X, m_Y denote the mean values of sets X, Y.

Proof. Let us consider Eq. (5) under the terms of our theorem. This leds us to

$$-\ln(1) + H^\times(X \cup Y \| \mathcal{G}) \leq \frac{1}{2} \cdot \left(-\ln(\frac{1}{2}) + H^\times(X \| \mathcal{G})\right) + \frac{1}{2} \cdot \left(-\ln(\frac{1}{2}) + H^\times(Y \| \mathcal{G})\right).$$

By Eq. (4) we get

$$\frac{N}{2} \ln(2\pi e) + \frac{1}{2} \ln \det(\Sigma_{X \cup Y}) \leq \frac{1}{2}\left(\ln 2 + \frac{N}{2} \ln(2\pi e) + \frac{1}{2} \ln \det(\Sigma) \right)$$
$$+ \frac{1}{2}\left(\ln 2 + \frac{N}{2} \ln(2\pi e) + \frac{1}{2} \ln \det(\Sigma) \right),$$

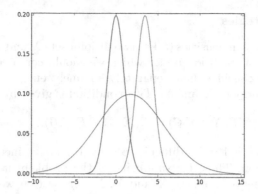

Fig. 1. Comparison of density descriptions of two sets. First, the sum of two densities $\mathcal{N}(0,1)$ (the blue one) and $\mathcal{N}(2\sqrt{3},1)$ (the green one) describe separated clusters, while the density $\mathcal{N}(\sqrt{3},4)$ (the red one) presents the best description of their set combination. (Color figure online)

and consequently $\ln\det(\Sigma_{X\cup Y}) \leq \ln(4\det(\Sigma))$. Finally, by Remark 1 we obtain

$$\det(\Sigma_{X\cup Y}) \leq 4\det(\Sigma), \tag{6}$$

where $\Sigma_{X\cup Y} = \Sigma + \frac{1}{4}(\mathrm{m}_X - \mathrm{m}_Y)(\mathrm{m}_X - \mathrm{m}_Y)^T$.

In the case of one dimensional space the Eq. (6) simplifies to

$$\sigma^2 + \frac{1}{4}(\mathrm{m}_X - \mathrm{m}_Y)^2 \leq 4\sigma^2$$

which ends the proof.

Figure 1 presents a simple illustration of the above theorem in the case of $\sigma = 1$.

It needs to be highlighted that even in one dimensional space our considerations were limited to strong constraints, which shows how it is a very hard task in the general case.

In the approach proposed by the authors for the merge problem we will always check the condition (5) directly. However, we will use Remark 1, according to which we do not need to recalculate the covariance matrix for a cluster combination, which simplifies and speeds up the calculations.

2.2   Split Strategies

The decision about splitting a given cluster $X \subset \mathbb{R}^N$ into two parts X_1, X_2 ($X_1 \cup X_2 = X$, $X_1 \cap X_2 = \emptyset$) for CEC clustering in our case is given by the following

- run CEC clustering with two clusters for set X,
- for obtained clusters X_1 and X_2, if $E(X,\mathcal{G}) \geq E(X_1,\mathcal{G}) + E(X_2,\mathcal{G})$ then replace cluster X by X_1 and X_2.

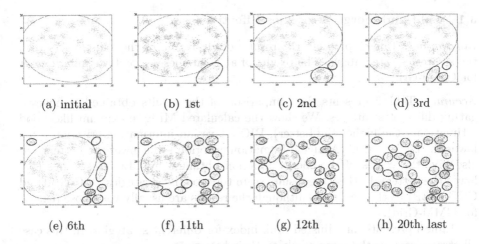

(a) initial   (b) 1st   (c) 2nd   (d) 3rd

(e) 6th   (f) 11th   (g) 12th   (h) 20th, last

Fig. 2. Split strategy. An initial clustering (with one cluster) is divided into as many clusters as needed using the split strategy. The numbers below the images present the numbers of waves of divisions. Those do not correspond to the number of clusters since multiple divisions can happen simultaneously.

The approach, in this case, is similar to the merge strategy, since we also want to decrease energy. Figure 2 presents division steps for a sample set from CEC clustering.

3   Proposed Strategies and Experiments

We develop a few strategies to check when split and merge steps should be applied during CEC clustering. We denote them as follows:

– CEC-FAF – the merge and split are performed when a CEC iteration did not reduce energy, the merge step is performed as many times as possible;
– CEC-FSF – the merge and split are performed when a CEC iteration did not reduce energy, the merge is performed only once at a time;
– CEC-P3AF – the merge is performed every third iteration as many times as possible, the split is performed if a CEC iteration(including the merge) did not reduce energy,
– CEC-P1SP1 – the merge and split are performed in every iteration, the merge is performed once at most in each iteration.

We compare them with

– CEC-Grid – we apply CEC clustering with a starting number of clusters from 2 to 70 and then we choose the best result according to the lowest Bayesian information criterion (BIC);
– GMM-Grid – we used the Project R package mclust [3] which performs a grid search for finding the optimal numbers of mixture components (clusters) according to the BIC criterion. The considered range of the number of clusters was the same as in CEC-Grid.

3.1   Split-and-merge Strategies Effectiveness

Illustrations: Table 1 presents the results of clustering of the sample sets with the strategies listed above. The results of all strategies are pretty similar except for GMM-Grid.

Accuracy: Table 2 presents the comparison of the results obtained by investigating different strategies. We show the calculated MLE (maximum likelihood estimation – the higher the better), BIC (Bayesian information criterion – the lower the better), AIC (Akaike information criterion – the lower the better) and also give the values of the energy function obtained by CEC clusterings (the lower the better). In this case results seem to favor the strategies CEC-Grid and CEC-P1SP1 as the best ones, although the results are usually very close (except for GMM-Grid).

Table 3 presents an adjusted rank index for different strategies. In this case all strategies gave the same result on their best runs.

Energy: Figure 3 presents the comparison of the energy function during clustering under different strategies. The results show that CEC-Grid and CEC-P1SP1 reach minimum in the smallest number of steps.

Table 1. Comparison of different CEC split and merge strategies with GMM clustering.

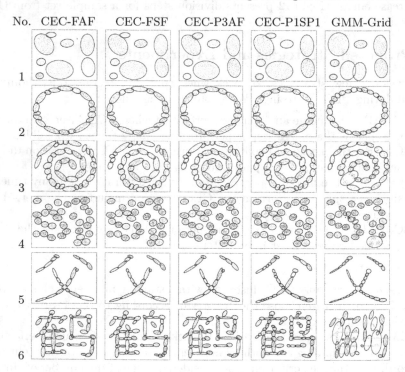

Table 2. Effectiveness of clustering for datasets from Fig. 1. Table presents a comparison of results for various criteria with the best strategies selected (the marked ones).

Set	Method	MLE	AIC	BIC	cost	No. clust
1	CEC-Grid	-5028.89	10135.77	10317.88	6.387748	7
	CEC-FAF	-4971.75	10090.16	10274.28	6.372357	8
	CEC-FSF	-4972.59	10092.01	10274.28	6.368866	8
	CEC-P3AF	-4985.80	10088.99	10274.28	6.375692	8
	CEC-P1SP1	-4973.65	10092.16	10274.27	6.369666	8
	GMM-Grid	-5052.78	10171.55	10325.65		8
2	CEC-Grid	-4772.61	9828.48	10164.06	4.820493	12
	CEC-FAF	-4910.83	9840.92	10190.31	5.086688	18
	CEC-FSF	-4826.43	9840.41	10181.07	5.086773	18
	CEC-P3AF	-4831.82	9841.64	10183.92	5.086012	17
	CEC-P1SP1	-4827.30	9840.52	10181.90	5.088752	18
	GMM-Grid	-4844.54	9923.09	10497.30		29
3	CEC-Grid	-5302.07	10933.03	11523.40	5.337437	24
	CEC-FAF	-5296.87	10949.07	11511.24	5.545499	35
	CEC-FSF	-5297.57	10954.84	11516.37	5.544520	38
	CEC-P3AF	-5295.65	10953.27	11503.95	5.546854	36
	CEC-P1SP1	-5293.99	10943.12	11494.34	5.546223	38
	GMM-Grid	-5476.76	11275.40	12065.55		40
4	CEC-Grid	-17345.28	35275.38	36420.90	5.626151	28
	CEC-FAF	-17469.87	35247.75	36177.78	5.791727	31
	CEC-FSF	-17469.87	35247.75	36177.78	5.791727	31
	CEC-P3AF	-17469.87	35247.75	36177.78	5.791727	31
	CEC-P1SP1	-17469.87	35247.75	36177.78	5.791727	31
	GMM-Grid	-17857.81	35933.63	36591.90		27
5	CEC-Grid	1169.98	-2142.05	-1908.32	-1.55705	7
	CEC-FAF	1260.44	-2259.60	-1780.56	-2.23154	20
	CEC-FSF	1261.10	-2252.04	-1765.01	-2.39991	20
	CEC-P3AF	1259.68	-2260.20	-1781.17	-2.47543	19
	CEC-P1SP1	1279.09	-2227.21	-1613.51	-1.76784	29
	GMM-Grid	1048.00	-1854.02	-1312.30		30
6	CEC-Grid	1585.14	-2822.28	-2088.01	-1.00290	25
	CEC-FAF	1762.23	-2876.52	-1554.79	-1.09039	46
	CEC-FSF	1738.68	-2876.18	-1566.58	-0.96549	54
	CEC-P3AF	1758.68	-2893.73	-1658.30	-1.19903	42
	CEC-P1SP1	1790.03	-2855.14	-1260.18	-0.85854	63
	GMM-Grid	815.81	-1413.62	-834.12		27

Table 3. Adjusted rank index (the higher the better) for datasets 1 and 4 from Fig. 1 under different strategies.

Set	CEC-P1SP1	GMM-Grid	CEC-Grid
1	0.9687795	0.801032	0.997804
4	0.9471447	0.847442	0.877827

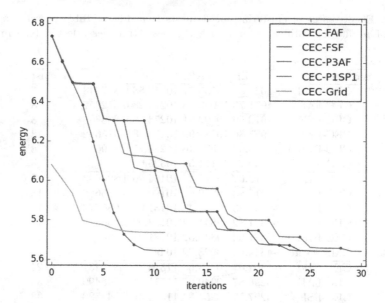

Fig. 3. Energy during clustering iterations under different strategies. The split and merge strategies were all started with a single cluster.

Table 4. The results of algorithms in the case of data from UCI repository.

Set	Method	MLE	AIC	BIC	cost	No. clust
cancer	CEC-Grid	-5397.75	12541.50	14248.87	12.6645	26
	CEC-FAF	-5724.97	12311.94	14124.35	11.3153	8
	CEC-FSF	-5276.11	11738.21	13842.75	11.1355	11
	CEC-P3AF	-5383.41	12222.18	13691.71	10.5129	15
	CEC-P1SP1	-4399.87	12037.74	15161.96	11.4671	30
	GMM-Grid	-5556.90	11551.97	12548.34		16
iris	CEC-Grid	-147.29	537.78	619.07	0.7153	11
	CEC-FAF	-166.91	529.32	619.07	0.7874	66
	CEC-FSF	-206.48	522.96	619.07	1.2747	53
	CEC-P3AF	-203.29	516.58	653.35	1.3382	49
	CEC-P1SP1	-205.56	541.42	658.23	1.2750	56
	GMM-Grid	-221.20	506.40	602.74		4
seeds	CEC-Grid	2751.91	-5291.82	-4937.03	-2.4818	6
	CEC-FAF	2088.59	-3897.19	-3428.59	-2.3327	5
	CEC-FSF	2082.18	-3880.36	-3405.07	-2.5921	6
	CEC-P3AF	2302.52	-4463.04	-4225.39	-2.1047	4
	CEC-P1SP1	2868.88	-5056.88	-4581.59	-2.4040	13
	GMM-Grid	1157.24	-2064.48	-1646.09		11
wine	CEC-Grid	-2455.36	6452.88	7984.43	11.17177	14
	CEC-FAF	-2306.49	6674.17	7190.19	11.64549	12
	CEC-FSF	-2604.09	6667.63	7562.31	16.40669	10
	CEC-P3AF	-2805.89	6738.39	7403.39	13.86455	8
	CEC-P1SP1	-2378.48	6873.21	8524.56	11.52989	11
	GMM-Grid	-2966.22	6320.44	6937.71		7

Speed: While the above could suggest the CEC-P1SP1 strategy was the fastest, take note that because it performs both split and merge operations at each iteration, the iterations themself are more expensive computational-wise. A direct time measurement of the strategies revealed CEC-FSF to be the fastest, followed closely by CEC-P3AF.

3.2 Split-and-merge CEC in Higher Dimensions

Table 4 presents the results obtained with the same strategies and algorithms on higher dimensional data. In this experiment there was much more variation both between the strategies and between different runs of the same strategy. It appears that the algorithm suffers from the curse of dimensionality and has trouble finding the right number of clusters in higher dimensional data. This is most evident in the iris dataset, where it overshots that number tenfold.

4 Conclusions and Future Work

We have proposed an approach for the split and merge problem in CEC clustering. It was shown that even in a one dimensional space the condition is not so easy to assess. Thus, in the proposed approach, we implicitly use the formula to decide if two clusters should be combined. Our experiments present that the strategy when the merge and split are performed in every iteration and the merge is performed once at most in each iteration can be competitive to classical CEC or even CEC-Grid.

Our future work will focus on developing new measures which will allow us to solve the split problem using information theory.

Acknowledgement. The research of Krzysztof Misztal is supported by the National Science Centre (Poland) [grant no. 2012/07/N/ST6/02192]. The research of Przemysław Spurek by the National Science Centre (Poland) [Grant No. 2015/19/D/ST6/01472].

References

1. Arthur, D., Vassilvitskii, S.: K-means++: the advantages of careful seeding. In: Proceedings of the Eighteenth Annual ACM-SIAM Symposium on Discrete Algorithms, pp. 1027–1035. Society for Industrial and Applied Mathematics (2007)
2. Celeux, G., Govaert, G.: Gaussian parsimonious clustering models. Pattern Recognit. **28**(5), 781–793 (1995)
3. Fraley, C., Raftery, A.E.: MCLUST: software for model-based cluster analysis. J. Classif. **16**(2), 297–306 (1999)
4. Hinton, G.E., Dayan, P., Revow, M.: Modeling the manifolds of images of handwritten digits. IEEE Trans. Neural Networks **8**(1), 65–74 (1997)
5. Jain, A.K.: Data clustering: 50 years beyond k-means. Pattern Recogn. Lett. **31**(8), 651–666 (2010)

6. Jain, A.K., Murty, M.N., Flynn, P.J.: Data clustering: a review. ACM Comput. Surv. (CSUR) **31**(3), 264–323 (1999)
7. Lughofer, E.: A dynamic split-and-merge approach for evolving cluster models. Evolving Syst. **3**(3), 135–151 (2012)
8. Maulik, U., Bandyopadhyay, S.: Genetic algorithm-based clustering technique. Pattern Recogn. **33**(9), 1455–1465 (2000)
9. McLachlan, G., Krishnan, T.: The EM Algorithm and Extensions, vol. 382. Wiley (2007)
10. Misztal, K., Spurek, P., Saeed, E., Saeed, K., Tabor, J.: Cross entropy clustering approach to iris segmentation for biometrics purpose. Schedae Informaticae **24**, 31–40 (2015)
11. Shoham, S.: Robust clustering by deterministic agglomeration EM of mixtures of multivariate t-distributions. Pattern Recogn. **35**(5), 1127–1142 (2002)
12. Tabor, J., Misztal, K.: Detection of elliptical shapes via cross-entropy clustering. In: Sanches, J.M., Micó, L., Cardoso, J.S. (eds.) IbPRIA 2013. LNCS, vol. 7887, pp. 656–663. Springer, Heidelberg (2013). doi:10.1007/978-3-642-38628-2_78
13. Tabor, J., Spurek, P.: Cross-entropy clustering. Pattern Recogn. **47**(9), 3046–3059 (2014)
14. Ueda, N., Nakano, R., Ghahramani, Z., Hinton, G.E.: SMEM algorithm for mixture models. Neural Comput. **12**(9), 2109–2128 (2000)
15. Xu, R., Wunsch, D.: Clustering. Wiley-IEEE Press (2009)
16. Zhang, B., Zhang, C., Yi, X.: Competitive EM algorithm for finite mixture models. Pattern Recogn. **37**(1), 131–144 (2004)
17. Zhang, Z., Chen, C., Sun, J., Chan, K.L.: Em algorithms for gaussian mixtures with split-and-merge operation. Pattern Recogn. **36**(9), 1973–1983 (2003)

Evaluation of Chord and Chroma Features and Dynamic Time Warping Scores on Cover Song Identification Task

Ladislav Maršík[3]([⊠]), Martin Rusek[1], Kateřina Slaninová[1,2], Jan Martinovič[1,2], and Jaroslav Pokorný[3]

[1] IT4Innovations, VŠB - Technical University of Ostrava,
17. listopadu 15/2172, 708 33 Ostrava, Czech Republic
{martin.rusek,katerina.slaninova,jan.martinovic}@vsb.cz
[2] Department of Computer Science, FEECS, VŠB - Technical University of Ostrava,
17. listopadu 15/2172, 708 33 Ostrava-Poruba, Czech Republic
[3] Department of Software Engineering, Faculty of Mathematics and Physics,
Charles University, Malostranské nám. 25, Prague, Czech Republic
{marsik,pokorny}@ksi.mff.cuni.cz

Abstract. Cover song identification has been a popular task within music information retrieval in the 20th century. The task is to identify a different version or performance of a previously recorded song. Unlike audio search for an exact matching song, this task has not yet been popularized among users, due to an ambiguous definition of a cover song and the complexity of the problem. With a great variety of methods proposed on the benchmarking challenges, it is increasingly difficult to compare advantages and disadvantages of the features and algorithms. We provide a comparison of three levels of feature extraction (chroma features, chroma vector distances, chord distances) and show how each level affects the results. We further distinguish five scores for dynamic time warping method, to find the best performance in conjunction with the features. Results were evaluated on covers80 and SecondHandSongs datasets and compared to the state-of-the-art.

Keywords: Music information retrieval · Chroma features · Chord distance · Chroma vector distance · Cover song identification · Dynamic time warping

1 Introduction

A cover song is an alternative version, performance, or recording of a previously published musical piece. The author of a cover song may choose to differ from the original piece in several musical aspects: instrumentation and arrangement, tonality and harmony, song structure, melody, tempo, lyrics, or language. Thus, Cover Song Identification (CSI) task is a difficult challenge in choosing the

K. Saeed et al. (Eds.): CISIM 2017, LNCS 10244, pp. 205–217, 2017.
DOI: 10.1007/978-3-319-59105-6_18

best techniques, features and algorithms, and has been a vivid field of research within music information retrieval in the last decade. The state-of-the-art methods are evaluated annually on the benchmarking challenge MIREX (Music Information Retrieval Evaluation Exchange)[1] with up to 8 algorithms posted every year since 2006.

Musicians often use *chord progressions* (a sequence of chord labels) when replicating a musical piece originating from another author. Chord progressions and other harmony features contain deeper underlying music information, which is typically retained in cover songs, while tempo, style or instrumentation changes [7]. The common technique to obtain these features is to use the Discrete-Time Fourier transform (DFT), resulting in so-called *chroma features* [1], from which chords are derived by further processing. Both chroma features and chord progressions are commonly used for CSI [3,13,22].

The recent CSI studies focus on finding a proper harmony fingerprint of the song, to be able to work with large music databases [4,13,19]. Such fingerprint should reduce the complex information from the audio, keeping only the relevant harmony movements. In the light of the recent proposals [6,21], *chord distances* can be used in addition to the chord labels, to extract meaningful harmony features. If used properly, chord distances can help with the problem of a *key transposition* [12], when the cover song is played in a different key from the original.

To understand the concept of a chord distance, we can imagine chords as points in space, with assigned distances (forming a chord distance model). One of the straightforward applications of this model could be to treat the music as a path in this space. In our work we test this idea: we derive a chord distance from every pair of successive chords to obtain a time series descriptor, which we then use for CSI. Furthermore, we apply the same idea also for chroma features, by defining *chroma vector distances* as another time series for comparison. Lastly, we are aware of the danger of losing relevant information by extracting these features. Our study therefore compares the fingerprints with the lower-level *"raw"* *chroma vectors*, from which the fingerprints were extracted.

To determine a similarity between the time series, it is convenient to use Dynamic Time Warping (DTW), which has long been used in signal processing [18,22]. In our work we are interested not only in the different levels of feature extraction, but also in the comparison of five different DTW scores. As such, our task is to provide leads for the best feature-score combination for CSI.

We continue in Sect. 2 with the survey of CSI works most related to us. Then in Sect. 3 we provide the insight into the music harmony features that we use. In Sect. 4 we overview the DTW algorithm and the different DTW scores. In Sect. 5 we show our results on covers80[2] and SecondHandSongs[3] datasets and compare with the state-of-the-art results. We wrap up in Sect. 6 with the conclusion and our future work.

---

[1] http://www.music-ir.org/mirex/wiki/MIREX_HOME.

[2] https://labrosa.ee.columbia.edu/projects/coversongs/covers80.

[3] https://labrosa.ee.columbia.edu/millionsong/secondhand.

2   Related Work

CSI task has been added to MIREX benchmarking in 2006, which was the first time that the task was given an academic attention. Now it is one of over fifteen annually evaluated tasks, including Audio Melody Extraction, Audio Chord Estimation, and others. The LabROSA system achieved the best results in the first year of the CSI benchmarking, with beat-synchronous chroma features [7]. Chroma vectors were calculated for beat-length segments of the songs, where beats were extracted by preprocessing. The result of 34 correctly identified covers from covers80 dataset was a promising start, proving that harmony features such as chroma vectors are meaningful for CSI task.

The winning submission in the 2007 benchmarking was a system developed by Serra et al. [22]. Based on an extensive series of experiments, the authors have proposed improvements, notably: the use of improved chroma features (HPCP [12], with an improved resolution of 36 bins), tackling the key transposition problem using a shift based on the global song profile, binary similarity matrix, dynamic programming and a local alignment (Smith-Waterman algorithm). DTW with various constrains was used for the similarity measures.

The best results in MIREX at the time of writing this paper were achieved in 2009 by an improved version of [22] (Serra et al. [23]). The system correctly identified 2426 out of 3300 cover songs (73.5%). The most important improvements were: using a cross-recurrence plot instead of the binary similarity matrix, and reasoning that a maximal length of diagonal lines (L_{max}) experimentally proved to have the highest discriminative power. The final measure (Q_{max}) was a slight modification of L_{max}, accounting for the tempo changes (the curvature of the line) and gaps.

The idea that the harmonic content should be invariant over the cover songs is a centerpiece of most of the CSI works. While some authors used chroma vectors (or their variants) to capture the harmonic content, other experimented with using chord sequences. Lee [15] used Hidden Markov Models to extract chords from chroma vectors and then compared the chord sequences using DTW. Bello [2] and Robine et al. [20] have studied string alignment methods. The chord-based algorithms were outperformed by the above mentioned chroma-based systems on MIREX, however, a full potential of chords has not been explored yet, especially with the possibility of evaluating chord distances for the progression.

The most recent trend in CSI is to pioneer new ways of feature extraction (2D Fourier Transform Magnitude [4], usage of MFCC [24]), new similarity measures (Shannon information [10]), or database pruning and combining various features based on machine learning [19]. The focus is shifting to the large-scale methods rather than outperforming the results on the smaller benchmarking datasets.

3   Chord and Chroma Features

3.1   Chroma Features

Chroma features are commonly referring to a series of 12-dimensional vectors of floating-point numbers, capturing the presence of each tone in a short music moment [12]. The concept has been proposed and studied at the beginning of 21st century by multiple authors; we first became aware of it in the work of Bartsch and Wakefield [1] and Fujishima [11]. Chroma features are obtained directly from DFT output by grouping frequencies that belong together in one frequency bin, where the bins are set by the tempered tuning of the piano scale. The resulting vector has the form:

$$< c_A, c_{A\#}, c_B, c_C, c_{C\#}, c_D, c_{D\#}, c_E, c_F, c_{F\#}, c_G, c_{G\#} >$$

where $c_A \in \mathbb{R}$ represents the presence of the A tone, $c_{A\#} \in \mathbb{R}$ represents the presence of the $A\#$ tone, etc. The value distribution of $c_A, c_{A\#}, \ldots$ depends on the algorithm used, but it is a common practice to normalize to $[0, 1]$ interval, where the loudness ratio is preserved in between the tones. For more information on chroma features, we refer the reader to Bartsch and Wakefield [1].

Since chroma features have long been used for CSI, we choose them as our first (and reference) feature for comparison. To achieve a proper search for a cover song transposed to a different key, we perform a circular shift to all 12 possible transpositions of the song before the comparison, as was done in [8] or [13].

3.2   Chord Distances

The use of chord distances for CSI is our first innovation: we form a time series of chord distances as a reasonably small fingerprint for the work with large music datasets. Chord distances are a subject of the recent research in music information retrieval, but the concept of a chord distance still remains ambiguous, as there are many definitions to choose from [21]. As a result, further study on how all of these distances may be used for CSI, has not been executed, to the best of our knowledge.

Thanks to Rocher et al., we have a thorough review available of the common chord distances, including musicology, geometric or computational approaches [21]. Nine chord distances are compared, and tested on the chord estimation task, with Tonal Pitch Space (TPS) distance [6] performing the best for the root and mode estimation.

In this paper our goal is not to compare the various chord distances available, but rather to choose a representative distance, that can best suite the CSI task. From the recent studies, TPS [6] and Chord Complexity Distance [16] are suitable candidates. If the distance is evaluated simply for each pair of successive chords, the resulting series can represent the characteristic curvature of the song, as seen on Fig. 1.

Chord Complexity Distance. We proceed by employing Chord Complexity Distance (ChordCD) of the two chords, since it is a simple, yet discriminative alternative to the more complex TPS distance.

Based on the same principles as TPS, ChordCD also takes into account the key for the transition, and the exact construction of the two chords. Our simplification lies in weighting the presence of non-chord and non-key tones, achieving

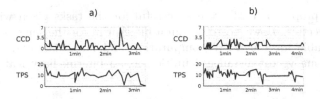

Fig. 1. Analysis of songs: (a) Hallelujah by Bastian Baker and (b) Wonderwall by Oasis, for both Tonal Pitch Space distance (TPS) and Chord Complexity Distance (CCD). Peaks on (a) represent a complex chord progression before the chorus in 0:35, 1:15, or 2:30. Peaks on (b) around 0:40, 1:30 and 2:30 correspond to the A5 chord followed by B7sus4 chord.

a complexity distance (as opposed to the use of Circle of Fifths in TPS). The system for deriving ChordCD can be considered as a grammar-like system. The chord consists of multiple tones, forming a sentential form in the music grammar. Chord distance is a number of steps of the derivation from one sentential form to another (see Fig. 2). We define *add* and *remove* derivations for adding/removing a tone from the same key. If the tone has to be moved outside the key, the derivation *alter* can perform alteration, with the inverse derivation *alter-back*. ChordCD is therefore a variation of an edit distance, while the constrains for adding/altering the tones are making it relevant in the tonal space.

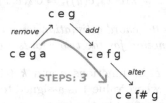

Fig. 2. ChordCD model for chord distances based on adding tones from the same key, and altering the tones outside the key. The key is evaluated for each chord tuple. Separate rules apply for changes between Tonic, Subdominant and Dominant [16].

The transitions between Tonic, Subdominant and Dominant triads are considered non-complex and yield 0 complexity of the transition. On the other hand, transitions in between chords with added dissonances yield higher complexity measures, as seen on Fig. 2. For more information and implementation details, we refer the reader to the complexity model explanation in [16].

3.3   Chroma Vector Distances

To the best of our knowledge, there have been no recent efforts in deriving distances in between the chroma vectors. We attribute this to the fact that the methods proposed [7,23] were successful for the tasks given with the 12-dimensional vectors. However, to obtain a fingerprint for the song, which would be more suitable for the DTW computation and large datasets, we proceed with the chroma vector distance definition as an intermediary feature for our comparison.

Chroma Complexity Distance. We propose a Chroma Complexity Distance (ChromaCD) definition based on a simple vector difference of the chroma vectors. We propose to improve this difference by weighting each bin according to the tone it represents. The details are in the following definition:

Definition 1. *For chroma vectors x and y, chroma complexity distance $\delta(x,y)$ is defined as:*

$$\delta(x,y) = \sum_{i=1}^{12} |w(x)_i x_i - w(y)_i y_i|$$

where $w(x)$ and $w(y)$ are 12-dimensional weight vectors similar to chroma vectors, having their 12 weight values dependent on the context for the transition from x to y, by the following rules:

$$w(x)_i = 0 \Leftrightarrow c(x)_i = 1$$
$$w(x)_i = 1 \Leftrightarrow k(c(x), c(y))_i = 1 \wedge c(x)_i = 0$$
$$w(x)_i = 2 \Leftrightarrow k(c(x), c(y))_i = 0 \wedge c(x)_i = 0$$

where function $c(x)$ returns the chord estimation for the chroma x, and function $k(c,d)$ returns the key estimation for the two chords c and d.

Remark 1. Return values of the functions c and k (chords and keys) are 12-dimensional binary vectors, where value 1 is assigned to the tones present in the chord (key), and value 0 is assigned to the tones not present in the chord (key).

Functions for chord and key estimation can be chosen independently from the definition. We have employed a simple chord estimation, where $c(x)$, is the closest chord (by Euclidean distance) to the chroma vector x. The key estimation can be accomplished by a ranked list of chord usage for a given key (more used chords have higher ranks in the list). Function k then simply chooses a key for which the sum of ranks of the two chords is minimal. We employ the tonal harmony ranking described in [16] (chord complexity), but any valid ranking can be used, e.g. based on statistics or perception.

In a simple example, chroma vectors x and y may both be estimated to A *major* chord ($c(x) = c(y) = <1,0,0,0,1,0,0,1,0,0,0,0>$), with A *major* being the common key ($k(c(x), c(y)) = <1,0,1,0,1,1,0,1,0,1,0,1>$). The weight vectors represent the context of this transition: $w(x) = w(y) = <0,2,1,2,0,1,2,0,2,1,2,1>$ (notice the chord tones having $w(x)_i = 0$, scale tones having $w(x)_i = 1$ and non-chord, non-scale tones having $w(x)_i = 2$). We treat chord tones in the chroma vectors as non-complex, therefore we do not weight the changes among the chord tones (e.g. simple music accompaniment); we assign weights to the more dissonant changes.

The proposed definition is very close to the ChordCD defined earlier for chords: adding a non-key tone is twice as complex as adding a non-chord tone from the key. Both distances are robust to the key transposition of the cover song, but it comes with a common disadvantage - dependency on chord and key estimation techniques.

4   Dynamic Time Warping

Dynamic Time Warping [18] is a method used for determining an optimal alignment between two time series. Based on this, an alignment score (distance) is calculated. Main advantages of DTW are the ability to compare sequences which differ in length and its generality. When introduced, DTW was used mainly for speech recognition, but thanks to the benefits mentioned, it quickly spread into other areas such as robotics, medicine, video games, music processing and many more. Importantly for our work, DTW is a straightforward technique to identify a cover song played in a different tempo.

4.1   Principles of DTW

Let us consider time series S and T. The basic idea behind DTW is to compare every data point from time series S with every data point in time series T. By this the distance matrix is built in which minimal warping path is found.

Definition 2. *Warping path in the distance matrix M is a sequence $W = (w_1, ..., w_l)$, where $w_l = M(i, j)$ and $l \in [1, |W|]$ that satisfies the following conditions.*

1. Condition of boundaries: $w_1 = (1, 1)$ and $w_l = (|S|, |T|)$
2. Condition of a step size: $w_{l+1} - w_l \in \{(1, 0), (0, 1), (1, 1)\}$ for $l \in [1, |W| - 1]$

In the end DTW distance is calculated using Eqs. (4.1) or (4.2)[17].

$$DTW(S, T) = \min \left\{ \sqrt{\sum_{l=1}^{L} w_l} \right. \tag{4.1}$$

$$DTW(S, T) = \min \left\{ \frac{1}{L} \sqrt{\sum_{l=1}^{L} w_l} \right. \tag{4.2}$$

Where L is the length of warping path W. Equation (4.2) for calculating the score is divided by the length of the warping path to account for the situations when compared sequences have different lengths. *Identity* occurs when $DTW = 0$.

4.2   Similarity in DTW

Standard Eqs. (4.1) and (4.2) have unfortunately one main problem when we use them for calculating DTW score. The score is not normalized in the interval $[0, 1]$, which means that it is difficult to compare DTW results across different datasets. For that reason we are testing three equations for calculating similarity by using the information from building the distance matrix and the warping path.

$$DTW_{sim}(S, T) = \frac{|S| + |T|}{|S| + l + |T| + u} \qquad (4.3)$$

The first similarity score (4.3) [25] which we use is simply obtained by dividing the original length of the sequences by the length of the sequences containing the edit information. Compared to other methods which deal with the alignment of sequences, for example the Needleman-Wunsch algorithm (used for alignment of DNA sequences), DTW edits do not prolong the sequences in the resulting alignment. Edits in the DTW method occur in the situation when a continuous sequence of elements from one time series is collapsing into one point of another time series and vice versa (see Fig. 3). In Eq. (4.3) l and u are the values of horizontal and vertical movements in the warping path, where every l or u movement means an insertion of edit information into the sequence.

735163904359361672803187743642088405827481111813597826625128290003

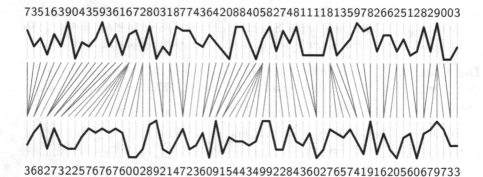

36827322576767600289214723609154434992284360276574191620560679733

Fig. 3. Example of DTW alignment between two time series. Directions of collapsing points are depicted by blue and red colors. The green lines connect elements mapped in one to one relationship.

This score is in the interval $[0, 1]$, where *identity* $= 1$. One disadvantage of this score is that when $DTW_{sim} = 1$ it doesn't necessarily mean that the compared sequences are identical. It only means that the compared time series are aligned to each other by one point to one point relationship. In the classic DTW this score would never be 1 if the lengths of the compared sequences are different.

The second similarity score that we test in this paper is the following equation [14].

$$DTW_{sim}(S,T) = 1 - \frac{\sqrt{DTW(S,T)}}{\sqrt{DTW_{max}(S,T)}} \tag{4.4}$$

We calculate the similarity by dividing the score from $DTW(S,T)$ by maximal value DTW_{max} which can theoretically occur. Let us consider time series $S \in O^{|S|}$ and $T \in O^{|T|}$, where O is the domain of the analyzed sequences. Maximal DTW score can be obtained by calculating DTW for sequences S', T', where $S' \in \{s'_1, ..., s'_i\}, \forall n \in \{1, ..., i\}(s'_n = min(O))$ and $T' \in \{t'_1, ..., t'_j\}, \forall n \in \{1, ..., j\}(t'_n = max(O))$. The result is subtracted from 1 so that *identity* occurs when $DTW_{max} = 1$ and difference when $DTW_{max} = 0$.

Our third similarity score for the comparison (4.5) [14] is a slightly adjusted version of the Eq. (4.4).

$$DTW_{sim}(S,T) = \left(1 - \frac{\sqrt{DTW(S,T)}}{\sqrt{DTW_{max}(S,T)}}\right) \cdot \frac{min(|S|, |T|)}{max(|S|, |T|)} \tag{4.5}$$

The Eq. (4.4) is multiplied by a coefficient calculated from differences in lengths of the compared sequences. By this we penalize the comparison of time series with the different lengths.

Obviously, it would be extremely inefficient to calculate DTW two times, one for standard DTW and one for DTW_{max}. Fortunately, the calculation of DTW_{max} can be simplified as seen in the Eq. (4.6).

$$DTW_{max}(S,T) = \sqrt{(max(O) - min(O))^2 \cdot max(|S|, |T|)} \tag{4.6}$$

5   Experiments

We have performed a series of experiments on two commonly used music datasets: covers80 [9] and SecondHandSongs [5]. For feature extraction, we have used a combination of Vamp Plugins[4] (NNLS Chroma, Chordino and Key Detector). We have further processed the resulting features with our Harmony Analyser software[5] to obtain the chord and chroma vector distances. All experiments were run on the Anselm[6] supercomputer in IT4Innovations National Supercomputing Center, where we used one computational node (Two Intel Sandy Bridge E5-2665 processors, each having 8 cores, 2.4 GHz and 32 GB RAM).

The covers80 dataset consists of 160 songs organized as 80 musical works, each in two versions. The first versions of the songs are used as queries for the search in the whole set of the second versions of the songs.

---

[4] http://www.vamp-plugins.org.
[5] http://www.harmony-analyser.org.
[6] https://docs.it4i.cz/anselm/hardware-overview.

SecondHandSongs is a set of 18,196 tracks with 5,854 cover song clusters (average cluster size is 3.11). For our comparison, we have taken a chunk of 999 songs (295 clusters) from SecondHandSongs train set - the first 999 songs listed in the official dataset information file.

5.1 Comparison of Features and DTW Scores

Our first results are the comparison in between the feature-score combinations within the same dataset. A standard evaluation metric for MIREX is the use of Mean arithmetic of Average Precision (MAP). MAP score takes into account the ranking of each cover song, and assigns the weights according to the rank. The result is in the interval $[0, 1]$, higher values mean that the cover songs ranked high and close together. For datasets of thousands of songs and small cover song clusters, MAP values are likely to be ~ 0.1 [4].

We can see the comparison in the Tables 1 and 2. Raw chroma vectors have outperformed chord and chroma vector distances. We attribute this to the fact that 12-dimensional chroma vectors contain much more information than the one-dimensional ChromaCD. The information is reduced even more with the chord distances (ChordCD). The execution time to obtain similarity matrices was: $\simeq 56$ s for raw chroma vectors, $\simeq 51$ s for ChromaCD and 25 ms for ChordCD time series for covers80 dataset. We can see a marginally better performance for ChromaCD. However, the performance difference is reduced on the larger dataset: on SecondHandSongs dataset the execution time is $\simeq 550$ s for raw chroma vectors and $\simeq 100$ s for ChordCD time series.

Comparison of all results over all data formats shows, that the best results are provided by DTW scores (4.1), (4.3) and (4.4) in this order. Scores (4.2) and (4.5) provide very poor results and we deem them as not suited for CSI task.

5.2 Comparison to the State-of-the-art

Besides MAP results we have examined Mean Average Rank (MAR) of the covers and the number of correctly identified covers (for covers80 dataset), to be able to compare our results with the state-of-the-art methods. MAR values are between $[1, N]$ where N is the number of songs, and we aim to achieve the lowest value possible.

Table 1. MAP results for each DTW score and feature for covers80 dataset.

Score	Raw chroma vectors	ChromaCD	ChordCD
Score (4.1)	**0.482**	0.094	0.142
Score (4.2)	0.103	0.070	0.071
Score (4.3)	0.417	0.174	0.156
Score (4.4)	0.454	0.061	0.114
Score (4.5)	0.082	0.041	0.034

Table 2. MAP results for each DTW score and feature for SecondHandSongs dataset.

Score	Raw chroma vectors	ChromaCD	ChordCD
Score (4.1)	**0.107**	0.031	0.019
Score (4.2)	0.021	0.014	0.014
Score (4.3)	0.029	0.035	0.021
Score (4.4)	0.043	0.015	0.012
Score (4.5)	0.008	0.008	0.009

An overview of MAR results can be seen in the Tables 3 and 4. For the SecondHandSongs dataset, the MAR metrics were evaluated before us by Bertin-Mahieux and Ellis [3,4]. They achieved average rank of 2,939 for over 12,960 songs [4], and 308,369 for 1 million songs [3]. In our experiments, Raw chroma vectors have the average rank **321 out of 999** songs, closely followed by ChromaCD (average rank 341). That is a worse result than the state-of-the-art, but a promising result for ChromaCD. For covers80 dataset, the results were similar, raw chroma vectors outperforming the simple distances (best average rank **14 out of 80** songs). The number of correctly identified covers was **33**, which was in fact achieved by the score (4.1) with a slightly worse average rank. This is similar to the first LabROSA system results [7]. On the other hand, ChromaCD achieved only 6 identified covers, despite the promising average rank. This shows that ChromaCD keep the relevant tonal information, but are not self-contained (too much extraction, and the differences between the songs are getting lost).

We have also gathered the first experimental results with TPS chord distance [6] for CSI task. TPS has outperformed the more simple ChordCD, with the best result **0.198** MAP and **27.575** MAR for covers80 dataset. Note that these results are better in MAP than ChromaCD. These first experiments are promising for a further study of TPS.

Table 3. Comparison of mean average rank score on covers80 dataset.

Score	Raw chroma vectors	ChromaCD	ChordCD
Score (4.1)	15.688	30.450	32.825
Score (4.3)	15.025	21.538	26.688
Score (4.4)	**13.963**	36.587	35.688

Table 4. Comparison of mean average rank score on SecondHandSongs dataset.

Score	Raw chroma vectors	ChromaCD	ChordCD
Score (4.1)	**321.033**	382.686	402.829
Score (4.3)	362.050	341.092	407.792
Score (4.4)	374.675	414.561	426.181

6   Conclusion and Future Work

We have tested and compared three levels of feature extraction and five different scores for DTW method on covers80 and SecondHandSongs datasets. From experimental results we have found out the best DTW score, and obtained a competitive result for chroma vector distances and TPS distance. Overall, we conclude that simplifying the chroma information in the way that a distance is evaluated from consecutive chords or chroma vectors is (by itself) not a good approach for the CSI task, despite the interesting visualizations of the time series. But it can be helpful as one of the features used in a more complex system. Possibilities for the future study are: experimenting with TPS distance, comparison of all possible chord or chroma vector distances, but more importantly, finding other ways of employing these distance measures (e.g. using the distances as a similarity measure in DTW, rather than a feature). We think that for such difficult tasks as CSI, a good selection and combination of features is the way to obtain the best results.

Acknowledgments. This work has been partially funded by the Charles University, project GA UK No. 1580317, project SVV 260451, by grant of SGS No. SP2017/177 "Optimization of machine learning algorithms for the HPC platform", VŠB - Technical University of Ostrava, Czech Republic, by The Ministry of Education, Youth and Sports of the Czech Republic from the National Programme of Sustainability (NPU II) project "IT4Innovations excellence in science - LQ1602" and by the IT4Innovations infrastructure which is supported from the Large Infrastructures for Research, Experimental Development and Innovations project "IT4Innovations National Supercomputing Center - LM2015070".

References

1. Bartsch, M.A., Wakefield, G.H.: To catch a chorus: using chroma-based representations for audio thumbnailing. In: IEEE Workshop on Applications of Signal Processing to Audio and Acoustics, WASPAA 2001 (2001)
2. Bello, J.P.: Audio-based cover song retrieval using approximate chord sequences: testing shifts, gaps, swaps and beats. In: Music Information Retrieval Evaluation eXchange, MIREX 2007 (2007)
3. Bertin-Mahieux, T., Ellis, D.P.W.: Large-scale cover song recognition using hashed chroma landmarks. In: IEEE Workshop on the Applications of Signal Processing to Audio and Acoustics, WASPAA 2011. IEEE (2011)
4. Bertin-Mahieux, T., Ellis, D.P.: Large-scale cover song recognition using the 2D fourier transform magnitude. In: Proceedings of the 13th International Society for Music Information Retrieval Conference, ISMIR 2012 (2012)
5. Bertin-Mahieux, T., Ellis, D.P., Whitman, B., Lamere, P.: The million song dataset. In: Proceedings of the 12th International Society for Music Information Retrieval Conference, ISMIR 2011 (2011)
6. De Haas, W.B., Veltkamp, R., Wiering, F.: Tonal pitch step distance: a similarity measure for chord progressions. In: Proceedings of the 9th International Conference on Music Information Retrieval, ISMIR 2008 (2008)

7. Ellis, D.P.W., Poliner, G.E.: Identifying 'Cover Songs' with chroma features and dynamic programming beat tracking. In: Proceedings of the IEEE International Conference on Acoustics, Speech and Signal Processing, ICASSP 2007 (2007)
8. Ellis, D.P.W.: Identifying 'Cover Songs' with beat-synchronous chroma features. In: Music Information Retrieval Evaluation eXchange, MIREX 2006 (2006)
9. Ellis, D.P.W., Cotton, C.V.: The 2007 LabROSA Cover Song Detection System. In: Music Information Retrieval Evaluation eXchange, MIREX 2007 (2007)
10. Foster, P., Dixon, S., Klapuri, A.: Identifying cover songs using information-theoretic measures of similarity. IEEE/ACM Trans. Audio Speech Lang. Process. **23**(6), 993–1005 (2015)
11. Fujishima, T.: Realtime chord recognition of musical sound: a system using common lisp music. In: Proceedings of the International Computer Music Conference, ICMC 1999 (1999)
12. Gómez, E.: Tonal description of music audio signals, Ph.D. thesis, Universitat Pompeu Fabra (2006)
13. Khadkevich, M., Omologo, M.: Large-scale cover song identification using chord profiles. In: Proceedings of the 14th International Society for Music Information Retrieval Conference, ISMIR 2013 (2013)
14. Kocyan, T.: Adapting case-based reasoning for processing natural phenomena data, Ph.D. thesis, VŠB Technical University of Ostrava (2015)
15. Lee, K.: Identifying cover songs from audio using harmonic representation. In: Music Information Retrieval Evaluation eXchange, MIREX 2006 (2006)
16. Marsik, L., Pokorny, J., Ilcik, M.: Towards a harmonic complexity of musical pieces. In: Proceedings of the 14th Annual International Workshop on Databases, Texts, Specifications and Objects (DATESO 2014), CEUR Workshop Proceedings, vol. 1139 (2014). CEUR-WS.org
17. Mueen, A., Keogh, E.J.: Extracting optimal performance from dynamic time warping, KDD 2016 (2016)
18. Müller, M.: Information Retrieval for Music and Motion. Springer, Heidelberg (2007)
19. Osmalskyj, J., Piérard, S., Van Droogenbroeck, M., Embrechts, J.J.: Efficient database pruning for large-scale cover song recognition. In: International Conference on Acoustics, Speech, and Signal Processing, ICASSP 2013 (2013)
20. Robine, M., Hanna, P., Ferraro, P., Allali, J.: Adaptation of string matching algorithms for identification of near-duplicate music documents. In: Proceedings of the International SIGIR Workshop on Plagiarism Analysis, Authorship Identification, and Near-Duplicate Detection, SIGIR-PAN 2007 (2007)
21. Rocher, T., Robine, M., Hanna, P., Desainte-Catherine, M.: A survey of chord distances with comparison for chord analysis. In: Proceedings of the International Computer Music Conference, ICMC 2010 (2010)
22. Serrà, J., Gómez, E., Herrera, P., Serra, X.: Chroma binary similarity and local alignment applied to cover song identification. IEEE Trans. Audio Speech Lang. Process. **16**, 1138–1152 (2008)
23. Serrà, J., Serra, X., Andrzejak, R.G.: Cross recurrence quantification for cover song identification. New J. Phys. **11**(9), 093017 (2009)
24. Tralie, C.J., Bendich, P.: Cover song identification with timbral shape sequences. In: Music Information Retrieval Evaluation eXchange, MIREX 2015 (2015)
25. Vlachos, M., Hadjieleftheriou, M., Gunopulos, D., Keogh, E.: Indexing multidimensional time-series. VLDB J. **15**(1), 1–20 (2006)

Algorithms for Automatic Selection
of Allophones to the Acoustic Units Database

Janusz Rafałko[✉]

Faculty of Mathematics and Information Science,
Warsaw University of Technology, Warsaw, Poland
j.rafalko@mini.pw.edu.pl

Abstract. The paper presents algorithms and coefficients developed in order to select specific acoustic units to the base used in concatenative speech synthesis. The approach is based on the assumption that the database is created automatically. In the natural speech signal, which is a sample of the voice of a particular person, the acoustic unit must be marked and then cut out. This generates often very large, redundant collection of units from which the best units should be selected to the final base. Described coefficients refer to allophones databases in TTS synthesis.

Keywords: TTS · Speech synthesis · Phoneme · Allophone · Selection of acoustic units

1 Introduction

In concatenative speech synthesis one of the very important elements is a database of speech units containing natural acoustic unit of speech. The units may be allophones, diphones, syllables or others. Nowadays in current synthesis systems, such bases are created manually or by using algorithms that automate part of the process. When using automated algorithms, the first step is to obtain a set of units, which is a redundant set. It contains many of the same elements, but from different words. The boundaries of such allophones can be marked in various ways and could be marked incorrectly. In the concatenative approach only one copy of each unit is needed in the final database. Therefore, an appropriate selection should be done.

The article presents developed coefficients which allow us to make a units selection and select the appropriate allophones into the database. The units, which are evaluated, are the acoustic allophones. This database is intended to be used directly in the TTS synthesizer based precisely on these units. It is possible, however, to extend this to databases created with other units.

2 The Set of Acoustic Units

Different approaches to speech synthesis on the basis of the text are described quite detailed in [1, 2]. In the synthesizer, signal compiled from natural speech segments is subjected to a modification in which the prosodic signal parameters are changed.

© IFIP International Federation for Information Processing 2017
Published by Springer International Publishing AG 2017. All Rights Reserved
K. Saeed et al. (Eds.): CISIM 2017, LNCS 10244, pp. 218–226, 2017.
DOI: 10.1007/978-3-319-59105-6_19

In [3] there are basic assumptions of concatenated TTS system for Polish language, based on allophones in the context of the synthesis of Slavic languages. This paper refers to the acoustic units, which include several context groups of a tested phoneme, which can be identified with acoustic allophone presented in [4] by W. Jassem.

The advantages of the choice of allophones as basic units [5, 6] are based on the fact that speech units retain the synergistic effects between sounds. The difficulty with this approach is the need for precise marking of allophones' borders in the segmentation of a natural speech signal.

The set of acoustic units may be created manually, or by using suitable algorithms. In this case, it is used modified DTW (Dynamic Time Wrapping) algorithm to create this set, which automatically marked the boundaries of all allophones in natural speech signal [7]. As the result, created collection contains many of the same units. It happens so, because the corpus of the speech on the basis of which the set is created is redundant, it contains the whole words, sentences and texts in which the unit occurs multiple times.

3   The Acoustic Units Selection

In order to create the base of acoustic units it is necessary to analyse in detail all the received units. First it is necessary to remove the units which are not suitable to the final allophone base. After rejecting the worst, however, we are still left with redundant units from which we should select the best ones. Selection is performed using a reference base realized manually. This is the allophone base units of professional voice actor working as a radio presenter.

3.1   Rejection of the Worst

The main reasons for the use of this operation is the phenomena of reduction and simplification of phonemes in natural speech leading to almost complete disappearance of phonemes, with the result that the phonetic content of the synthesized speech does not coincide with natural speech, e.g. wiśniewski → viɕɲɛsci (alphabet IPA – International Phonetic Alphabet). Another reason is the inaccurate markings of the natural signal in the process of boundaries setting, with the result that a segment whose acoustic content does not correspond to the phonetic content is cut out from the natural speech.

Figure 1 shows an allophone o0022 cut out from natural signal in the automatic segmentation. This presents the situation of inadequate marking of the borders in the unit cut out automatically (b), in comparison with that of the reference (a). As it can be seen, the phonetic contents of unit is different from the pattern. Similarly, the duration differs significantly from the duration of reference one. The time scale on both figures is the same. The duration of the reference unit is about 0.11 s, while the tested unit is 0.08 s.

Rejection operation is achieved by testing the time parameters, i.e. the duration of the allophone, and parameters of acoustically - phonetical, i.e. the cost of matching in segmentation algorithm with units of the reference base. The duration of the test units T_T obtained in the segmentation process is compared with the duration of reference

a)

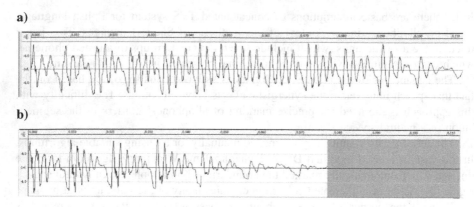

b)

Fig. 1. Inaccuracy in the marking of the allophone border.

units T_R used in the synthesis module. Duration of units from reference base of professional voice actor is in the range from 35 ms to 0.52 s. Length of automatically cut units is in the range from about 0.05 ms to 1.6 s.

Figures 2 and 3 show histograms of units duration, the first of reference base and the second of units cut automatically. The reference base contains about 2,000 units, while a collection of units cut automatically contains more than 11,000 items.

Such a large number of received units is related precisely to the redundancy of the acoustic corpus, where one element is presented in more than a hundred copies. As it can be seen on the graphs, units durations of the reference base and the set cut automatically have similar distributions. There are about 40 units which are too short, of duration less than 20 ms in this collection and about 70 units which are too long with the duration of more than 0.7 s. This is less than 1% of all units cut automatically. Of course, this does not mean that only those units should be rejected. There may be more units cut automatically which are too short or too long in relation to its pattern. In this criterion, the difference in durations of the reference unit and units obtained

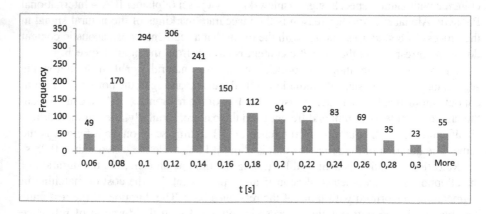

Fig. 2. Histogram of duration of allophones in the reference base.

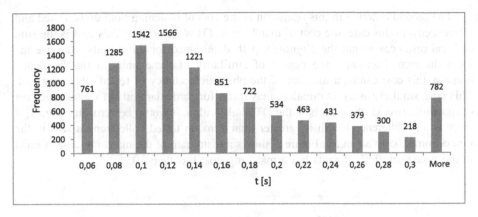

Fig. 3. Histogram of duration of allophones cut automatically.

automatically is important. Because the allophones units have different lengths, they cannot be taken as a measure of absolute error but a relative error, according to the formula (1).

$$\delta_t = \frac{|T_T - T_R|}{T_R} > \alpha \tag{1}$$

If the relative error of the units duration is greater than the threshold, the element is rejected. Figure 4 shows the relative error of the units duration of exemplary set. About 80% of cut allophones have a duration error less than 50%. Experimentally, for different collections it has been determined that if the error exceeds 80%, then such allophone is not suitable for the final base. There are about 1,000 of such allophones in the sample set, which is less than 9% of their total number. This means that the parameter α should be 0.8.

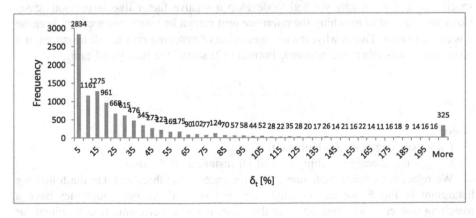

Fig. 4. Histogram of duration relative error of allophones.

The second criterion in this operation is the cost of matching both units, tested and referenced - in this case, the cost of matching in DTW algorithm. This cost is the sum of local distances within the alignment path determined for those units. Because the local distance determines the degree of similarity of these units in the frequency domain, this cost can be a measure of the phonetic accuracy of tested allophone unit. This cost, similarly as a unit duration, may differ for particular units. If we take the cost of matching two identical units in the DTW algorithm, it would be zero. In contrast, if there is any difference it will be greater than zero. In tested collections it was in the range from 0.05 to about 50. Figure 5 shows a histogram of the matching cost of units in the tested set. 90% of units has a matching cost less than 10.

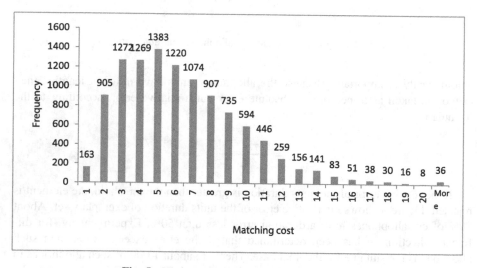

Fig. 5. Histogram of allophones matching cost.

In case of this parameter, similarly to the previous case, it largely depends on the specific unit. That is why we had to develop a relative factor like in previous case. However, the cost of matching the reference unit cannot be taken into account, because it is equal to zero. That is why, the average value of matching cost for all instances of a given entity was taken into account. Formula (2) shows the developed ratio:

$$\delta_C = \frac{|C_P - C_{Pave}|}{C_{Pave}} > \beta \tag{2}$$

where:

C_P – matching cost of allophone unit

C_{Pave} – the average matching cost of all instances of the unit

We reject units where matching cost error exceeds the threshold. On the following histogram in Fig. 6, we can conclude that the 90% of cut out allophones have a matching cost error less than 35%. In this case, it was experimentally determined for

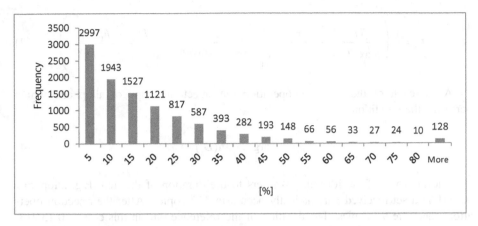

Fig. 6. Histogram of relative matching cost error of allophones.

varied sets that an error greater than 50% disqualifies such cut unit from the use in output base. This is about 3.5% of the total number of units.

As a result of the rejection process all the copies for which $\delta_t > \alpha$ or $\delta_C > \beta$ are excluded from further processing. As the experiments show, the best results of this operations are obtained at $\alpha = 0.8$ and $\beta = 0.5$.

3.2   The Selection of Acoustic Units

Number of copies of the allophone units which have undergone rejection operation, depends on the number of such units in the acoustic corpus, the quality of the voice actor's speech and the accuracy of the marking of unit boundaries. For the pieces that remain in the set after rejection the selection operation is applied, which produces one and the best representative of any unit.

The acoustically - phonetical characteristics of each copy of allophone which past rejection should already be good enough to be put it in the created base. Taking into account that the resulting elements will be modified in the process of prosodic modi-fication in speech synthesis, the most typical item by the value of prosodic charac-teristics should be selected: the basic tone frequency F_0, amplitude A and duration T. As such an item in the operation selection is selected, it has been chosen the entity which has the characteristics closest to the average values of these parameters. If after the rejection operation number of copies of the unit is n, then for each such unit the duration T_i, the average amplitude A_i^{ave}, and the average value of frequency of the basic tone F_{0i}^{ave} is evaluated. Then we calculate the average values for the entire set of units of one type: T^{AVE}, A^{AVE} and F_0^{AVE}. Normalized in scale [0...1] similarity coefficient of unit prosodic characteristics, which could be called the selection coefficient, is calcu-lated as:

$$D_i = \frac{1}{3} \left(\frac{|T_i - T^{AVE}|}{\max\limits_{j=1}^{n} |T_j - T^{AVE}|} + \frac{|A_i^{ave} - A^{AVE}|}{\max\limits_{j=1}^{n} |A_j^{ave} - A^{AVE}|} + \frac{F_{0i}^{ave} - F_0^{AVE}|}{\max\limits_{j=1}^{n} |F_{0j}^{ave} - F_0^{AVE}|} \right) \qquad (3)$$

As a result of the selection operation we select the copy of allophone which performs the condition:

$$k = \arg \min\limits_{i=1}^{n}(D_i) \qquad (4)$$

The first part of the formula (3) refers to the duration of the unit. E.g. allophone A1001 in a set received automatically occurs in 117 copies. After the rejection operation, there are 96 copies. The duration of the reference unit in this case is 0.1359 s, and the average duration of the set of units is 0.1534 s. The selected unit is the one with a duration of 0.1592 s. This is shown in the Fig. 7.

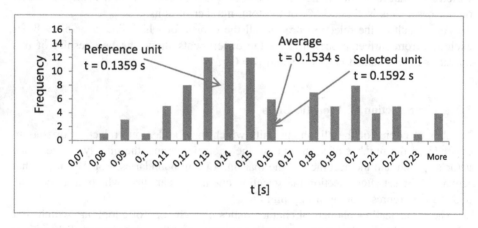

Fig. 7. Histogram of duration of a set A1001 units in selection operation.

A second part of selection coefficient refers to the amplitude of the allophones units therefore it is associated with the volume of the signal. Before the segmentation, the speech signal has been normalized, so it is possible to compare amplitude of the same units cut out from different words.

For an exemplary set of A1001 units in the Fig. 8 we showed the amplitude histogram and selected unit which goes to the final base.

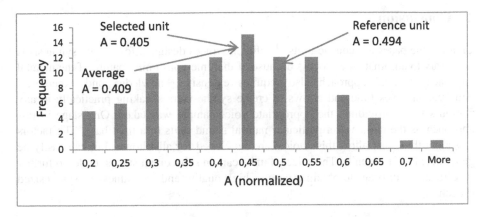

Fig. 8. Histogram of amplitude of a set A1001 units in selection operation.

The last part of the selection coefficient refers to the frequency of the basic tone. This value must also be selected as close to the average as possible. As the Fig. 9 shows, the average F_0 of this set differs from F_0 of reference unit. This is due to the fact that the reference base it is the voice of a different person than the voice of person who recorded the acoustic corpus. The unit chosen into the base has a higher frequency of the basic tone than average. This is due to the fact that, according to the formula (3), simultaneously the three parameters must be selected to be as close as possible to the average. This is provided by the selection coefficient developed by the author and described above.

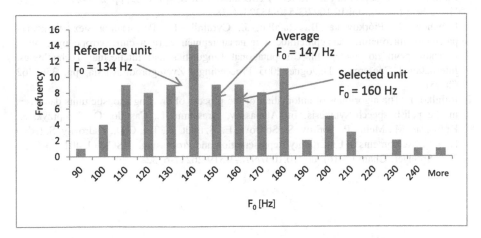

Fig. 9. Histogram of basic tone frequency of a set A1001 units in selection operation.

As a result of these algorithms we create a set of units which will be placed in an allophone base.

4   Conclusion

Creating the bases of acoustic units of different voices designed for speech synthesis is necessary to automate the process because of the time-consuming nature of the manual approach. Manual approach also requires extensive knowledge and experience. Automation saves time and allows to create synthesizers speaking practically in any person's voice providing, the appropriate voice sample was taken. One stage in this approach, is the choice of a particular natural sound units to a final base. The factors and algorithms that allow this choice, are developed for allophones, but can easily be generalized to other units. The selected units can, in subsequent stages, undergo further modifications in order to obtain a base of high quality and naturalness of synthesized speech.

Bibliography

1. Taylor P.: Text-to-Speech Synthesis. Cambridge University Press, Cambridge (2009)
2. Van Santen, J., Sproat, R., Olive, J., Hirshberg, J.: Progress in Speech Synthesis. Springer, New York (1997)
3. Szpilewski, E., Piórkowska, B., Rafałko, J., Lobanov, B., Kiselov, V., Tsirulnik, L.: Polish TTS in multi-voice slavonic languages speech synthesis system. In: SPECOM 2004 Proceedings, 9th International Conference Speech and Computer, Saint-Petersburg, Russia, pp. 565–570 (2004)
4. Jassem, W.: Podstawy fonetyki akustycznej, wyd. PWN, Warszawa (1973)
5. Matoušek, J.: Building a new Czech text-to-speech system using triphone-based speech units. In: Sojka, P., Kopeček, I., Pala, K. (eds.) TSD 2000. LNCS, vol. 1902, pp. 223–228. Springer, Heidelberg (2000). doi:10.1007/3-540-45323-7_38
6. Lobanov, B., Piórkowska, B., Rafałko, J., Cyrulnik, L.: Реализация межъязыковых различий интонации завиершённости и незавиершённости в синтезаторе русской и полской речи по тексту. In: Computational Linguistics and Intellectual Technologies, International Conference Dialogue 2005 Proceedings, Zvenigorod, Russia, pp. 356–362 (2005)
7. Rafałko, J.: The algorithms of automation of the process of creating acoustic units databases in the polish speech synthesis. In: Atanassov, Krassimir T., Castillo, O., Kacprzyk, J., Krawczak, M., Melin, P., Sotirov, S., Sotirova, E., Szmidt, E., Tré, G.D., Zadrożny, S. (eds.) Novel Developments in Uncertainty Representation and Processing. AISC, vol. 401, pp. 373–383. Springer, Cham (2016). doi:10.1007/978-3-319-26211-6_32

Engineering of Enterprise Software Products

Blockchain Transaction Analysis
Using Dominant Sets

Malik Khurram Awan and Agostino Cortesi[✉]

DAIS - Ca' Foscari University, Venice, Italy
cortesi@unive.it

Abstract. Blockchain is an emerging backbone technology behind different crypto-currencies. It can also be used for other purposes and areas. There are different scalability issues associated with blockchain. It is important to know the in depth structure of blockchain by identifying common behaviors of the transactions and the effect of these behaviors on the nodes of the network. Dominant set approach can categorize the blockchain transactions into different clusters without mentioning number of clusters in advance. The experimental evaluation of blockchain transactions shows better clustering accuracy of dominant set approach than existing method of central clustering approach.

Keywords: Transaction behavior analysis · Blockchain technology · Clustering

1 Introduction

Blockchain is a technology that is working behind bitcoin. The rising adoption and promising security of blockchain technology has the potential to reshape the current infrastructure of different business areas. In bitcoin, blockchain is a decentralized ledger containing the complete transaction history which is public at each node. All transactions are locked with the information of time, date, nodes and the amount. Nodes generate transactions and broadcast them to the network. Miners generate new blocks by solving proof-of-work and broadcast them to the network.

Blockchain analysis under different clustering heuristics can help to study its in-depth structure and to know the behavior of nodes and associated transactions. The clustering results obtained from these heuristics can also be useful for backend designers of the blockchain technology. These days achieving scalability in blockchain is a heated topic. Many researchers have presented different approaches and ideas for the scalability of blockchain to get better throughput in minimum latency. The recent research work [3,5,7,10,12,15,20,24] of past two years about scalability issues of blockchain model it is shown that blockchain incur storage, latency, security, processing and bandwidth problems [5,12,15,20,24]. Different researchers have carried out research activities

© IFIP International Federation for Information Processing 2017
Published by Springer International Publishing AG 2017. All Rights Reserved
K. Saeed et al. (Eds.): CISIM 2017, LNCS 10244, pp. 229–239, 2017.
DOI: 10.1007/978-3-319-59105-6_20

by introducing some new proposals and improving the existing mechanism of blockchain in different crypto-curriencies [1,4,8,9,11,13,14,16,19,25]. In [18] the authors discovered that by making the clustering of non-real account names of users according to their shared ownership and associated real names can give the clearer picture of the cryptocurrency. In [17] transaction volume per node is presented with clustering coefficients per node in the bitcoin network.

Inside blockchain network, there are thousands of transactions which are increasing over time. To manage and organize this increasing number of transactions it is important to study their common behavior. Clustering these increasing number of transactions can help to find out the transactions with common behavior and to identify and trace anomalous transactions.

This paper is a step towards it by using the dominant set approach for blockchain transactions that automatically categorize the blockchain transactions into different clusters without specifying number of clusters in advance. The percentage accuracy of experimental results show better performance of dominant set approach than existing method of central clustering approach.

In next Sect. 2 we highlight the basic terminologies and algorithmic structure of dominant set approach. Section 3 shows experimental results, evaluation measures and the results summary. Conclusion is discussed in Sect. 4.

2   Background

Generally clustering can be categorized into two types: central and pairwise. Central clustering is a feature based clustering. K-means algorithm is a type of feature based clustering. Pairwise clustering is a graph based clustering and a more general approach and adaptable in the sense that the algorithm works fine with wider range of input forms.

Dominant set clustering framework has been defined and introduced in [22,23]. The clustering method of choice is dominant sets, a pairwise clustering method that generalizes the idea of maximal clique to weighted graphs. It works with pairwise similarities i.e. metric embedding is not needed. For an undirected unweighted graph $G = (V, E)$, *clique* can be defined as a subset of mutually adjacent nodes where $V = \{1, 2 \ldots, n\}$ denotes vertex set and $E \subseteq V \times V$ represents the edge set. The key notions and definitions of the dominant set approach are discussed below:

For a non-empty set of vertices $S \subseteq V$ and $i \in V$. The average weighted degree of node i w.r.t set S is defined as:

$$AWDeg_S(i) = \frac{1}{|S|} \sum_{j \in S} w_{i,j} \tag{1}$$

In case of relative similarity $\phi_S(i, j)$, when node j does not belong to set S as shown in Fig. 1. We can measure the similarity between nodes i and j w.r.t the average similarity between node i and its neighbors in S which is expressed as:

$$\phi_S(i, j) = w_{i,j} - AWDeg_S(i) \tag{2}$$

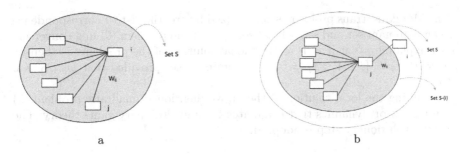

Fig. 1. (a) Average weighted degree of node i (b) Relative similarity between two nodes

For set $S \subseteq V$ and $i \in S$ we can compute the weight of node i w.r.t S:

$$W_S(i) = \begin{cases} 1 & if\ |S| = 1 \\ \sum_{j \in S \setminus \{i\}} \phi_{S \setminus \{i\}}(j, i) W_{S \setminus \{i\}}(j) & otherwise \end{cases} \qquad (3)$$

Total weight of the set S can be calculated by adding up all weights of $W_S(i)$ of the above mentioned recursive function.

$$W(S) = \sum_{i \in S} W_S(i) \qquad (4)$$

Further in [22,23] set S is specified as dominant set by defining the internal and external criteria of clustering as:

I. $W_S(i) > 0$ for all $i \in S$

II. $W_{S \cup \{i\}}(i) < 0$ for all $i \notin S$

The authors in [22,23] transformed the combinatorial problem of identifying dominant set in graph into quadratic optimization problem and the use of dynamic system of evolutionary game theory to solve it. Which is a general-form of a problem in graph theory known as Motzkin-Straus problem [21]. The findings in [22,23] reveal that there is a one-to-one correspondence between dominant sets and the strict local maximizer of the problem.

$$max\ \ x^T W x \ \ \ \ subject.to\ \ x \in \Delta \qquad (5)$$

where $\Delta_n = \{\bar{x} \in R_+^n : \bar{x} \geq \bar{0}, \bar{e}^T \bar{x} = 1\}$ is the standard simplex. The weighted characteristic vector of a dominant set S, which is a strict local solution of the problem (5) is defined as:

$$x^S = \begin{cases} \frac{W_S(i)}{W(S)} & if\ i \in S; \\ 0 & otherwise. \end{cases}$$

The Motzkin-Straus problem is generalized by creating 1-to-1 correspondence between dominant set and strict local solution of the problem (5) in a conversely way by explaining that if x^* is a strict local solution of the problem (5) then its support $\sigma(x^*) = \{i \in V : x_i^* \neq 0\}$ is a dominant set provided that $w_{\sigma \cup \{i\}} \neq 0$ $\forall i \neq \sigma$.

For finding the local solution of the above mentioned quadratic problem (5) we use replicator dynamics that originates from evolutionary game theory. The following evolutionary step is adopted.

$$x_i(t+1) = x_i(t)\frac{(AX)_i}{X(t)^T AX(t)} \tag{6}$$

For $i = 1 \ldots n$, all trajectories that start within standard simplex $\triangle$ will remain in the simplex $\triangle$ for any number or iterations of (6). Let A be a non-negative symmetric matrix so the objective function will strictly increase along any non-constant trajectory of (6). The asymptotically stable points correspond to dominant set for the similarity matrix A. With an affinity matrix A of graph G the abstract algorithmic structure of dominant set clustering approach is:

```
Partition_into_dominant_sets(G,A)
begin
    repeat
       extract dominant_set
       remove extracted dominant_set from graph G
    until all vertices are clustered
end
Extract_transaction_dominant_set_edges(G,Dominant_sets,K)
begin
  index←1
    repeat
       if(Dominant_sets==index)
         Show it in graph G}
         index←index+1
    until (index <= K)
end
```

3   Results and Evaluation

This section highlights the detail description about performed experiments mentioned in Sect. 3.1 and the results comparison with different evaluation measures in Sect. 3.3. The experimental evaluation summary is mentioned in Sect. 3.4.

3.1   Experimental Settings

We have selected a sample of 2,048 vectors of blockchain transaction data. The pairwise distance between two set of observations has been computed by using standardized euclidean distance similarity function. The transaction data has

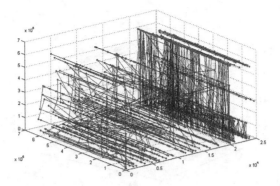

Fig. 2. Sample output of blockchain transaction edges (Color figure online)

been experimented in matlab with different parameters and settings. Some graph structures have been studied with gephi graph visualization tool. The machine used to perform experiments and compute the clustering results is a standard computer with 2.3 GHz Intel Dual-core with 3GB RAM.

3.2 Experimental Results

Dominant set approach and central clustering approach has been applied on standard blockchain transactions data. With K as number of clusters, the sample output of first 2,048 vectors of transaction edges are shown in Fig. 2. With dominant set approach, only 2 required clusters of transaction edges are extracted out of the whole graph. Transactions edges that show 'similar behavior' are in one cluster(blue) and the transaction edges that show 'different behavior' are in another cluster(green) as shown in Fig. 3. With K-means approach, we have extracted 2 clusters(red and blue) from the whole transaction graph which is actually a partitioning of the whole graph as shown in Fig. 4.

3.3 Evaluation Measures and Comparison

There are different measures for comparing clustering results. Clustering results of blockchain transactions are evaluated by computing silhouette value and rand index value. Silhouette values of results are computed to know about well-separatedness of clusters and their average is calculated to get better quantitative analysis view. Silhouette value plots are shown in Figs. 5 and 6.

Table 1 shows average silhouette value computed for range of values of K for both approaches as shown in Fig. 7

Rand index is usually used to see the accuracy or measure of similarity between two clusterings. Mathematically rand index is defined as:

$$R = \frac{2(a+b)}{n(n+1)}$$

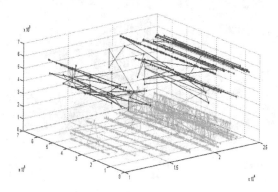

Fig. 3. Sample result of transaction clustered edges after dominant set approach with K = 2 (Color figure online)

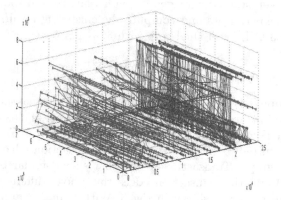

Fig. 4. Sample result of transaction clustered edges after K-means with K = 2 (Color figure online)

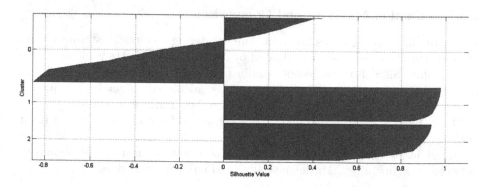

Fig. 5. Dominant Set silhouette value plot of sample with K = 2

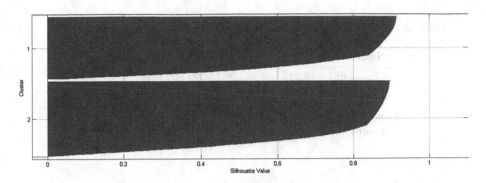

Fig. 6. K-means silhouette value plot of sample with K = 2

Table 1. Average silhouette values for dominant set and K-means clustering from 3 to 7

Clusters	3	4	5	6	7
Dominantset average Silhouette value	0.5001	0.5627	0.5566	0.5566	0.5566
K-means average Silhouette value	0.6678	0.6073	0.6972	0.6632	0.6437

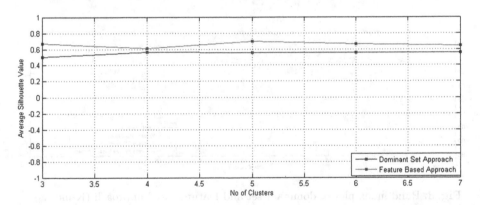

Fig. 7. Average silhouette value plot for dominant set and feature based approach(K-means)

For analysis and evaluation 6 clusters have been selected for the calculation of percentage accuracy and rand index for both approaches as shown in Tables 2 and 3. The plotted results are shown in Figs. 8 and 9.

From Fig. 8 rand index plot shows that at around cluster 3 the slope is getting lower in dominant set approach. The result accuracy plot as shown in Fig. 9 shows that the percentage result accuracy of clustering results of dominant set is better than K-means approach that shows less spike at around cluster 4.

Table 2. Rand index and accuracy for dominant set clustering from 1 to 6

Clusters	1	2	3	4	5	6
%Rand index	62.16	88.25	98.55	99.80	100	100
%Accuracy	24.70	51.70	84.13	91.35	98.63	100
Rand index	0.62	0.88	0.98	0.99	1.0	1.0
Accuracy	0.24	0.51	0.84	0.91	0.98	1.0

Table 3. Rand index and accuracy for K-means clustering from 1 to 6

Clusters	1	2	3	4	5	6
%Rand index	17.96	64.00	70.78	82.08	86.60	99.53
%Accuracy	20.31	38.37	44.62	61.86	71.38	99.36
Rand index	0.17	0.64	0.70	0.82	0.86	0.99
Accuracy	0.20	0.38	0.44	0.61	0.71	0.99

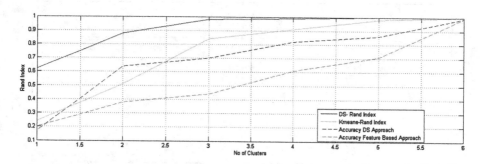

Fig. 8. Rand index plot of dominant set and feature based approach (K-means)

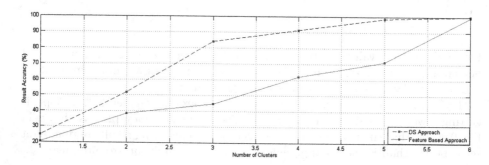

Fig. 9. Result accuracy plot of dominant set and feature based approach (K-means)

3.4 Summary of the Results

The experimental evaluation explains that: (1) dominant set method performs well for 2,048 vectors of blockchain transaction data (2) transactions with 'similar behavior' are clustered without specifying number of clusters in advance (3) with dominant set approach transactions subgraph with 'similar behavior' is extracted out of the main graph, and (4) percentage result accuracy shows better clustering results in dominant set method than feature based approach when number of clusters increases.

3.5 Constraints and Complexity

Some constraints related to experimental results are: (1) smooth running of experiments mainly depend on size of the blockchain transactions selected, and (2) hardware specification. The standard approach used here to find dominant set is replicator dynamics. From theoretical point of view, replicator dynamics has quadratic $O(n^2)$ computational complexity in every step of the dynamics for a dataset with n points.

4 Conclusion

We analyzed blockchain transaction data with pairwise dominant set and central clustering approaches by testing and evaluating it with different measures and settings. The experimental and evaluation results show better clustering accuracy of dominant set approach than existing method of central clustering approach. The in-depth information coming out of the dominant set clustering analysis can be useful for blockchain maintainers and to accurately identify anomalous transactions in the blockchain.

From scalability point of view, further study is needed for the concept of centralized blockchain with distributed chain of dominant set labels of the transactions.

Finally, in would be interesting to investigate the impact of alternative approaches to the analysis of blockchain systems, like for instance semantics-based static analysis techniques, that already provided interesting results in security analysis of software systems [2,6,26].

References

1. Back, A., Corallo, M., Dashjr, L., Friedenbach, M., Maxwell, G., Miller, A., Poelstra, A., Timon, J., Wuille, P.: Enabling Blockchain Innovations with Pegged Sidechains (2014)
2. Barbon, G., Cortesi, A., Ferrara, P., Pistoia, M., Tripp, O.: Privacy analysis of android apps: implicit flows and quantitative analysis. In: Saeed, K., Homenda, W. (eds.) CISIM 2015. LNCS, vol. 9339, pp. 3–23. Springer, Cham (2015). doi:10.1007/978-3-319-24369-6_1

3. Beck, R., Czepluch, J.S., Lollike, N., Malone, S.: Blockchain-The Gateway to Trust-Free Cryptographic Transactions. In: ECIS, Turkey (2016)
4. Bamert, T., Decker, C., Elsen, L., Wattenhofer, R., Welten, S.: Have a snack, pay with bitcoins. In: IEEE 13th International Conference on Peer-to-Peer Computing, Italy, pp. 1–5 (2013)
5. Bonneau, J., Miller, A., Clark, J., Narayanan, A., Kroll, J.A., Felten, E.W.: SoK: research perspectives and challenges for bitcoin and cryptocurriencies. In: IEEE Symposium on Security and Privacy (2015)
6. Cortesi, A., Ferrara, P., Pistoia, M., Tripp, O.: Datacentric Semantics for Verification of Privacy Policy Compliance by Mobile Applications. In: D'Souza, D., Lal, A., Larsen, K.G. (eds.) VMCAI 2015. LNCS, vol. 8931, pp. 61–79. Springer, Heidelberg (2015). doi:10.1007/978-3-662-46081-8_4
7. Croman, K., Decker, C., Eyal, I., Gencer, A.E., Juel, A., Koshba, A., Miller, A., Saxena, P., Shi, E., Sirer, E.G., Song, D., Wattenhofer, R.: On Scaling Decentralized Blockchains (2016)
8. Decker, C., Wattenhofer, R.: Information Propagation in the Bitcoin Networks. In: IEEE Thirteenth International Conference on Peer-to-Peer Computing, Italy (2013)
9. Decker, C., Wattenhofer, R.: Bitcoin transaction Malleability and MtGox. In: Kutyłowski, M., Vaidya, J. (eds.) ESORICS 2014. LNCS, vol. 8713, pp. 313–326. Springer, Cham (2014). doi:10.1007/978-3-319-11212-1_18
10. Decker, C., Wattenhofer, R.: A Fast and Scalable Payment Network with Bitcoin Duplex Micropayment Channels. In: 17th International Symposium, Canada, pp. 3–18 (2015)
11. Doll, A., Chagani, S., Kranch, M., Murti, V.: Btctrackr: finding and displaying clusters in bitcoin. Princeton University, USA (2014)
12. Eyal, I., Gencer, A.E., Sirer, E.G., Renesse, R.V.: Bitcoin-NG: a scalable blockchain protocol. In: 13th USENIX Symposium on Networked Systems Design and Implementation, USA (2016)
13. Eyal, I., Sirer, E.G.: Majority is not Enough: Bitcoin Mining is Vulnerable. Cornell University, USA (2014)
14. King, S., Nadal, S.: PPCoin: Peer-to-peer Crypto-Currency with Proof-of-Stake (2012)
15. Kosba, A., Miller, A., Shi, E., Wen, Z.: Hawk: The Blockchain Model of Cryptography and Privacy-Preserving Smart Contracts. In: Cryptology ePrint Archive (2015)
16. Kroll, J.A., Davey, I.C., Felten, E.W.: The economics of bitcoin minning or, bitcoin in the presence of adversaries. In: 12th Workshop on the Economics of Information Security (2013)
17. Lischke, M., Fabians, B.: Analyzing the Bitcoin Network: The First Four Years (2016)
18. Meiklejohn, S., Pomarole, M., Jordan, G., Levchenko, K., McCoy, D., Voelker, G.M., Savage, S.: A fistful of bitcoins: characterizing payments among men with no names. In: Proceedings of Internet Measurement Conference, Spain, pp. 127–140 (2013)
19. Miers, I., Garman, C., Green, M., Rubin, A.D.: Zerocoin: Anonymous Distributed e-Cash from Bitcoin. In: IEEE Symposium on Security and Privacy (2013)
20. Miller, A., Jansen, R.: Shadow-bitcoin: scalable simulation via direct execution of multi-threaded applications. In: IARC Cryptology ePrint Archive (2015)
21. Motzkin, T.S., Straus, E.G.: Maxima for Graphs and a new Proof of a Theorem of Turan (1965)

22. Pavan, M., Pelillo, M.: A New Graph-theoretic Approach to Clustering and Segmentation. In: CVPR (2003)
23. Pavan, M., Pelillo, M.: Dominant Sets and Pairwise Clustering. In: IEEE Transactions on Pattern Analysis and Machine Intelligence, pp. 167–172 (2007)
24. Pazmino, J.E., Rodrigues, S.: Simply dividing a bitcoin network node may reduce
transaction verification time. In: SIJ Transactions on Computer Networks and
Communication Engineering, pp. 17–21 (2015)
25. Ried, F., Harrigan, M.: An Analysis of Anonymity in the Bitcoin System. In:
Security and Privacy in Social Networks, pp. 197–223 (2013)
26. Zanioli, M., Ferrara, P., Cortesi, A.: SAILS: static analysis of information leakage
with sample. In: Proceedings of the ACM Symposium on Applied Computing, SAC
2012, pp. 1308–1313 (2012)

Ontology Driven Conceptualization of Context-Dependent Data Streams and Streaming Databases

Shreya Banerjee[(⊠)] and Anirban Sarkar

Department of Computer Applications, National Institute of Technology,
Durgapur, India
shreya.banerjee85@gmail.com, sarkar.anirban@gmail.com

Abstract. Heterogeneous stream formats, related contexts, vocabularies and schema structures are key difficulties to facilitate sharing and extracting knowledge from stream databases. To resolve these heterogeneities, the key challenge is how to provide common semantic representation for context-dependent data stream formats along with streaming databases. To address such issues, this paper proposes an ontology driven formal semantics of context-dependent data streams together with a universal conceptualization of streaming databases. The novelty of this work is to handle heterogeneity, large volume and availability of streaming data, such as web content, commercial broadcasting data etc. It also facilitates to recognize evolving information from semantic representation of data streams at conceptual modelling level. Besides, the proposed conceptual model is flexible to represent finite partition of stream and thus help in data stream storing and further querying. The conceptualization is implemented using an ontology editorial tool Protégé for the initial validation of proposed set of formal semantics. Several crucial properties of the proposed conceptualization are specified in order to exhibit the benefits of the proposed work. The expressiveness of proposed model is illustrated using a suitable case study.

Keywords: Data stream · Conceptual model · Context modelling · Streaming databases · Ontology

1 Introduction

In recent years, with the advancement of information and web technology, several applications need to work with continuous data generating processes. Those data are dynamic, time sensitive and continuous in nature. Data generated from Web-clicks, network monitoring, commercial broadcasting, sensor nets and stock quotes are few examples of such data [7]. These types of data are considered as a stream (data stream) rather than static snapshots [6]. Distinct *Data Stream Management Systems (DSMS)* are developed for processing and analysis of these data streams. Those DSMS are built due to limitations of traditional data management systems towards managing distinct data streams [2]. Hence, a well-organized model of data streams is the key requirement for proficient management of those data streams by DSMS. However, data streams have several exceptional characteristics, which make them difficult to model. *Firstly*, a data

© IFIP International Federation for Information Processing 2017
Published by Springer International Publishing AG 2017. All Rights Reserved
K. Saeed et al. (Eds.): CISIM 2017, LNCS 10244, pp. 240–252, 2017.
DOI: 10.1007/978-3-319-59105-6_21

stream is usually defined as "an unbounded sequence of values continuously appended, each of which carries a time stamp that typically indicates when it has been produced" [6]. *Secondly*, in different applications these continuous data are represented in different ways such as a discrete signal, an event log or a combination of trained series [15]. *Thirdly*, rapid changing of underlying contextual information of data streams generated in diverse domains has serious consequences in deriving useful decisions from complex real time applications [4]. *Fourthly*, distinct back-end databases ranging from strict schema-based (for example Relational Databases) to flexible schema based (for example NoSQL Databases) are used to store theses data streams in structured, semi-structured or unstructured way. *Finally*, a fixed or flexible finite partition, called *window*, are made from this continuous unbounded sequence while streams have to be stored or retrieved from databases [11]. Hence, several challenges exists in efficient modelling of data streams in order to facilitate sharing of information related to data streams across different applications and DSMS. *Starting with*, how to represent common description of heterogeneous data streams semantically and syntactically. *Secondly*, how different surrounding contexts (contextual information) of data streams are represented in a uniform way. *Thirdly*, how evolving contexts of data streams can be recognized so that realization of dynamically added contextual information towards data streams is achieved efficiently. To handle these issues, ontology will be beneficial. The key reason for applying ontology is that it can establish consensus on unifying conceptualization of heterogeneous data stream formats and related contexts. Ontology is defined as a formal, explicit specification of shared conceptualization in terms of concepts, relationships present between those concepts and related axioms [8].

Existing research works, primarily, focus on semantic representations of resources and devices producing data streams. However, less attention is paid towards uniform semantic representation of distinct context dependent data streams and further heterogeneous streaming databases. In [1, 3, 7, 15], authors have described abstract semantics of streams. Authors in [7] have described an extensible framework that facilitates experimenting with different algorithms related with data stream mining tasks. In [2, 11], authors have described powerful operator algebra for data streams. Both of these approaches have facilitated in supporting multiple query languages and data models. Semantic Sensor Network (SSN) ontology [5] represents a high-level general schema of sensor systems. IoT-A and IoT.est [12] provide architectural base for utilization and representation of domain knowledge in sensor networks with some services and test concepts. The Observation & Measurement (O&M) description of sensory Data are described as a part of Sensor Web Enablement (SWE) standards from the Open Geospatial Consortium (OGC) [9]. However, this description is based on XML (Extensible Markup Language) which has weak semantic structure for expressing and describing stream data ontology in more detail. Through approaches regarding Semantic Sensor Web (SSW), context information such as time, space is added with sensors. However, these approaches are mostly specific to certain domain and thus are not in high-level abstraction [13]. Besides, none of these approaches has explored the representation of contextual information related to data streams and streaming databases.

To address aforementioned challenges regarding modelling of data streams, an effort has been made in this paper to provide precise semantics towards data streams, related contexts and streaming databases. For this purpose, an ontology driven conceptualization of data streams along with its related context is devised. The novelties of the proposed ontology driven conceptual model are many-folds. The proposed conceptualization efficiently deals with generic semantics towards modelling of variety of data streams, resources producing those data streams and streaming databases. It further facilitates in sharing and preserving strong interoperability in heterogeneous applications and DSMS. Next, the proposed conceptualization aids in recognizing static and evolving contextual information related to data streams along with a set of distinct relationships. This essence of context sensitivity approach helps in reducing search spaces during the time of querying on data streams. Besides, the proposed conceptual model may assist in future in the extraction of new knowledge from data streams since it is ontology driven and hence based on Open World Assumption (OWA) [8]. Moreover, it has also provided discreetness in continuous streaming by representing finite, indefinite, fixed and flexible partition of data streams.

2 Proposed Ontology Driven Conceptual Model for Context-Dependent Data Streams

The proposed conceptual model formalizes a common set of constructs and relation-ships for conceptualization of context-dependent data streams and streaming databases. The proposed model comprises of three interrelated layers (*Collection*, *Family* and *Stream*) and their identifiable construct types. Besides, the constructs are related with each other using different relationships. The proposed model is specified axiomatically using both first order and higher order logic to represent semantics of data-stream constructs and their interrelationships. The key constructs and distinct relationships of the proposed model are specified in Fig. 1. In this figure, *Collection*, *Family* and *Stream* layers are represented using shapes of rectangle, rounded rectangle and oval respectively. Details of the proposed model are specified in following sections.

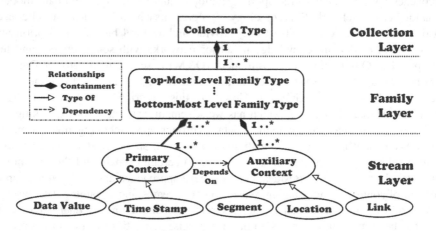

Fig. 1. Proposed conceptual model for data-streams

2.1 Constructs in Proposed Conceptual Model

Proposed model consists of three main layers, namely, *Collection*, *Family* and *Stream*. These three layers have their respective construct types *Collection (Col)*, *Family (FA)* and *Stream_Context (Str)*. Formal axioms of these constructs are specified below and different interrelationship among those constructs are described in Sect. 2.3.

(a) *Collection Layer*: It is the upper-most layer of the data model. *Collections(Col)* are main identifiable constructs of this layer. Semantically related *Families(FA)* (Intermediate layer of the proposed model) are grouped together to form a *Collection(Col)*.

$F1$: $\forall x \exists l \exists c \exists v (Col(x) \leftrightarrow (HT(c) \wedge FA(l) \wedge Cnt_{col}(v)))$

Explanation: Here, *HT* is *Has Time* relationship and Cnt_{col} is *Containment relationship*. F14 and F19 formalizes *Containment* and *Has Time* relationship. Further, *x, l, c, v* are instances of *Collections, Family, Has Time* and *Containment* relationship.

(b) *Family Layer*: It is the intermediate layer of the conceptual model. *Families* are main identifiable constructs of this layer. This layer may be composed of number of levels to reflect the fact of continuous encapsulation of data. Further, the lowest level of *Family* layer may be combined of semantically related data streams and its contexts.

$\forall x \exists u \exists a \exists r \exists m \exists d \exists l \exists c \exists v \exists n (FA(x) \leftrightarrow (FA_{llev}(u) \vee FA_{ulev}(a) \vee FA_{lev}(r)$

$F2$: $\quad \vee Icnt_{FA}(m) \vee Col(d)) \wedge HT(l) \wedge Cnt_{FA}(c) \wedge primary\_context(v)$

$\quad \wedge auxiliary\_context(n)))$

Explanation: Here, FA_{llev}, FA_{ulev} and FA_{lev} are denoted as *Families* in the bottom-most level, in the top-most level and in any level respectively. *IcntFA* is *Inverse Containmnet* and *CntFA* is *Containment relationship*. Later, in Sect. 2.3 axiom *F17* formalizes *Inverse Containment* relationship. Further, *primary_context()* and *auxiliary_context()* are predicates representing *Primary Contexts* and *Auxiliary Contexts* of Stream. Related axioms are specified in axioms *F3, F4, F5* and *F6*.

(c) *Stream_Context Layer*: This is the lower-most layer of the proposed conceptual model. Data-Streams may be represented in this layer formally. Data stream is an indefinite ordered sequence of data points, each of which carry a time stamp. These data points can be ranged from structured to unstructured type. Besides this, these data points may be related with precise contextual information that are useful to characterize the features of streams which are necessary in order to interact between users and applications. Detailed formalizations of *Stream_Context* are specified in Sect. 2.2.

2.2 Conceptualization of Stream Context

Stream Context is precise information useful to describe data stream, and its surrounding concepts. Two types of contexts are used to represent data streams in *Stream_Context* layer. One is *Primary Context (PC)* and another is *Auxiliary Context (AC)* that may provide useful information towards *Primary Contexts*. Hence, a data-stream may be defined as an ordered indefinite sequence of *Primary Contexts* and its related *Auxiliary Contexts*. Related axiom is

$\forall x \exists y \exists z \exists t1 \exists t2 (stream(x) \leftrightarrow ((Union\_of((\square PC(data\_value(y))$

$F3$: $\quad \wedge time\_stamp(t1)) \wedge AC(z)), (\square PC(data\_value(y) \wedge time\_stamp(t2))$

$\quad \wedge AC(z)))) \wedge (t1 < t2) \wedge (number\_of\_data\_value(\infty))))$

Explanation: Here, *number_of_data_value()* is a predicate implying that a data-stream may be infinite; *data_value()* and *time_stamp()* are predicates implying data values and their corresponding time stamps respectively; $\Box$ operator implies mandatory participation of the argument and *Union_of()* is a predicate implying the union of arguments. Axioms F4 and F6 formalize the *Primary* and *Auxiliary Context* respectively.

(*a*) *Primary Context*: This represents basic information about data stream. Basic information of data stream mandatorily includes the data value at a specific time. The data value and its related specific time collectively can be called as a *Frame*.

$$\forall x \exists v \exists t1 \exists t2 \exists t (PC(x) \leftrightarrow (\Box(data\_value(x,v) \wedge starting\_time(t1)$$

F4: $\wedge\ ending\_time(t2) \wedge (existence(x) \leftrightarrow (t1 \wedge t2 \wedge duration(t1,t2)))$

$$\wedge\ ((\neg existence(x) \wedge time(t)) \leftrightarrow (t \wedge (t<t1) \wedge (t>t2))))))$$

F5: $\forall x \exists v \exists t (Frame(x) \leftrightarrow (\Box PC(data\_value(y) \wedge time\_stamp(t1))))$

Explanation: Here, *starting_time()* and *ending_time()* are predicates implying start time and end time of respective arguments. Further, predicate *existence()* implies the existence time duration of the argument.

(*b*) *Auxiliary Context*: This context provides additional information relevant for *Primary Context*. For example, let assume humidity sensor generates data stream of humidity values. Then location may be an auxiliary context related to the primary context humidity. *Auxiliary Context* can be of several types as specified below.

F6:
$$\forall x \exists a1 \exists a2 \exists a3 ((PC(x) \wedge AC(a1) \wedge AC(a2) \wedge AC(a3))$$
$$\leftrightarrow ((pair(a1,a2,a3)) \rightarrow x))$$

Explanation: Here, *pair()* is a predicate implying the pairing of the respective *Auxiliary Contexts*.

(*i*) *Segment Context*: *Segment* represents a finite partition of the data-stream containing ordered sequences of *Primary Contexts* when the stream is to be going to store in a database. This size of partition may be fixed or flexible depending on the number of instances of a *Frame*. Axiom *F5* formally represent *Frame*. Axioms related to *Segment Context* are specified below.

$$\forall x \exists y \exists z \exists m (Segment(x) \leftrightarrow (stream\_store((Union\_of((\Box Frame(y)$$

F7: $\wedge\ Other\_AC(z)) \wedge (\Box Frame(m) \wedge Other\_AC(z)))) \wedge (t1<t2)$

$$\wedge\ number\_of\_data\_value(finite))))$$

F8: $\forall x ((segment(x) \wedge size(x)) \leftrightarrow (number\_of\_instance(Frame))$

F9: $\forall x \exists y \exists l ((PC(x) \wedge segment(y) \wedge has\_auxiliary\_context(l)) \leftrightarrow l(x,y))$

Explanation: Here, *has_auxiliary_context()* has created a relationship instance *l* that has attached *Primary Context* with *Auxiliary_Context*. Details of this relationship are stated in Sect. 2.3. Besides, *size()* is a predicate implying the length of the *Segment*.

(*ii*) *Location Context*: This represents the current location/resources those holding the *Primary Context* with a specific time stamp. Assume, *L* is the set of locations. Related axioms are specified below.

F10: $\forall l ((l \in Location) \leftrightarrow Q(L(Location)))$

Explanation: Here, *Q* is a predicate and *L* (*Location*) is a function returning locations of a *Primary Context*.

$F11$: $\forall x \exists y \exists t ((PC(x) \wedge location(y) \wedge has\_auxiliary\_context(l)) \leftrightarrow l(x,y))$

(*iii*) *Link Context*: This represents how the *Primary Contexts* are communicated over communication channel in terms of simplex, duplex etc. Besides, multiple segments of similar or multiple data streams may be available in communication channel following some sequences. Hence, segment wise communications may be present within both of single stream and multiple data streams.

$F12$:
$$\forall x \exists y \exists z \exists l \exists k \exists m \exists n ((Link(x) \wedge stream(l) \wedge stream(k)$$
$$\wedge\, l(segment(PC(y) \wedge PC(z))) \wedge k(segment(PC(m) \wedge PC(n))))$$
$$\leftrightarrow ((Communication\_type\_between(((PC(y) \wedge PC(z)) \vee ((PC(m) \wedge PC(n))))$$
$$\vee (communication\_type\_between((PC(y) \vee PC(z)) \wedge (PC(m) \vee PC(n)))))))$$

$F13$: $\forall x \exists y ((PC(x) \wedge Link(y) \wedge has\_auxiliary\_context(l)) \leftrightarrow l(x,y))$

Explanation: Here, *Communication_type_between()* is a predicate implying the type of communication between *Segments* of single or multiple *Primary Contexts*.

These proposed *Auxiliary Contexts* are of minimal set. More distinct *Auxiliary Contexts* may be appended towards *Primary Contexts* based on design demand. Hence, proposed conceptualization realizes both static and evolving contextual information.

(*c*) *Finite Partition of Data Stream*: *Segment* has represented the finite partition of infinite data-streams for storing data-streams in database. Similarly, for the retrieval purpose another finite partition of data-streams can be defined as a *Window*. The size of *Window* may be fixed or flexible depending on numbers of instances of time stamps. Later, different data-stream query operators can be defined on this *Window*. The axiom of *Window* is as follows.

$F14$:
$$\forall x \exists y \exists z \exists m (Window(x)$$
$$\leftrightarrow (stream\_retrieve((Union\_of(((\Box Frame(y) \wedge Other\_AC(z)) \wedge (\Box Frame(m)$$
$$\wedge\, Other\_AC(z)))) \wedge (t1 < t2) \wedge number\_of\_data\_value(finite))))$$

$F15$: $\forall x ((window(x) \wedge size(x)) \leftrightarrow (number\_of\_instance(Frame)))$

2.3 Relationships in Proposed Conceptual Model

Distinct constructs of proposed conceptual model are interrelated. These relationships can be of two types – *Inter layer* and *Intra layer* [14]. *Inter-layer relationships* can be between dissimilar construct types of three different layers. *Intra-layer relationships* can be between similar construct types of identical layer. Different relationships may be present within a data stream, data stream and its related contextual information, and in the layer hierarchy of streaming databases. These relationships may be *Containment*, *Inverse Containment*, *Has_auxiliary_Context*, *Reverse_has_auxiliary_context*, *Sequence*, and *HasTime*. Former two are of *Inter-layer* and *Intra-layer* kind of relationship and the rest all are of *Intra-layer* kind of relationship.

(*a*) *Containment* (*Cnt*): *Containment* relationships can be present between two construct types when one encapsulates similar or different types of constructs.

$F16$:
$$\forall x (Cnt(x) \leftrightarrow \exists y \exists^n z (Cmp(y) \wedge Cmp(z) \wedge ((sl(y,z) \wedge lev(y)$$
$$\wedge\, lev_{Next}(z)) \vee (dl(y,z) \wedge layer(y) \wedge layer_{Next}(z))) \wedge x(y,z) \wedge \neg(y = z)$$
$$\wedge (k(range(x) = z)) \wedge (m(domain(x) = y)) \wedge ((p(value(k) = 1)$$
$$\vee greaterthan(value(k), 1)))))$$

Explanation: Let, *sl()* is a predicate. Arguments of *sl()* are construct types (*Cmp*) and express the fact that they are of similar type. In contrast, *dl()* is a predicate that takes *Cmp* (construct types) as arguments and articulates that its arguments are in different layers and are of dissimilar types. Besides, *range()* and *domain()* are functions returning target and source domain of relationships respectively; k and m are predicates specifying those functions; *value()* is a function returning number of instances encapsulated; *greaterthan()* is a predicate implying whether the first argument is greater than second argument; *lev()* and $lev_{Next}()$ are predicates implying whether arguments of these belongs to a level and its next lower level respectively; *layer()* and $layer_{Next}()$ are predicates implying whether arguments of these belongs to a layer or its next lower layer respectively; and p is a predicate.

(*b*) *Inverse Containment (Icnt)*: This relationship enables one construct type to de-encapsulate itself in order to encapsulate *Families* towards *Collections* dynamically.

$$F17: \begin{aligned} &\forall x(Icnt(x) \leftrightarrow \exists y \exists^n z(Cmp(y) \wedge Cmp(z) \wedge ((FA(y,z) \wedge lev(y) \\ &\wedge lev_{Next}(z)) \vee (Col(y) \wedge FA(z) \wedge layer(y) \wedge layer_{Next}(z))) \wedge x(z,y) \wedge \neg(y=z) \\ &\wedge (k(range(x)=y)) \wedge (m(domain(x)=z)) \wedge ((p(value(k)=1) \\ &\vee greaterthan(value(k),1))))) \end{aligned}$$

(*c*) *Has_auxiliary_Context (HAC)*: This relationship connects *Primary Context* with *Auxiliary Context*.

$F18$: $\forall x \exists y \exists l((PC(x) \wedge AC(y) \wedge HAC(l)) \leftrightarrow l(x,y))$

(*d*) *Reverse_has_auxiliary_context (RHAC)*: This relationship may connect *Auxiliary Contexts* with *Primary Contexts* dynamically. This relationship is in reverse order of *Has_auxiliary_Context*.

$F19$: $\forall x \exists y \exists l((PC(x) \wedge AC(y) \wedge RHAC(l)) \leftrightarrow l(x,y))$

(*e*) *Sequence (Seq)*: This is the relationship between two or more *Primary Contexts* when the data value of a particular time stamp is connected with the data value of the successive time stamp.

$$F20: \begin{aligned} &\forall x \exists f1 \exists f2 \exists f3 \exists y1 \exists y2 \exists y3 \exists l \exists t1 \exists t2((Frame(f1,f2,f3) \\ &\wedge data\_value(y1,y2,y3) \wedge time(t1,t2,t3) \wedge f1(y1 \wedge t1) \wedge f2(y2 \wedge t2) \wedge f3(y3 \wedge t3) \\ &\wedge Seq(l) \wedge (t1 < t2 < t3)) \leftrightarrow (l(y1,y2,y3) \wedge \neg(y1=y2=y3) \\ &\wedge (((succecive\_order(y1,y2) \wedge succecive\_order(y2,y3)) \\ &\rightarrow succecive\_order(y1,y3))) \wedge ((succecive\_order(y1,y2)) \\ &\rightarrow \neg(succecive\_order(y2,y1)))))) \end{aligned}$$

Explanation: Here, *succecive_order()* is a predicate implying that the second argument is coming in next sequence of the first argument. Contrary, by reversing the order of arguments of the predicate *succecive_order()*, flow of the data stream can be realized in the reverse direction. In this way, dynamically appended data values towards data streams can be recognized.

(f) Has Time (HT): This relationship represents the connection between data value and its existence time stamps. The axiom of this relationship is

$F21$: $\exists i \exists j [HT(i) \leftrightarrow \exists t \exists x [(t \in Tm) \land data\_value(x) \land i(x,t)]$

Explanation: Here, *Tm* is a set of timestamps.

The proposed conceptual model thus represents formal and universal vocabularies of context-dependent data streams and streaming databases. Using the axioms of stream layer, semantics of data stream and its associated heterogeneous context is specified. Likewise, through the entire layer hierarchy the proposed model is capable to represent common conceptualization of different streaming databases ranging from strict to flexible schema based. Thus, the proposed conceptualization deals with heterogeneity issue of data streams. Further, the proposed conceptual model is in high level abstraction. Hence, representation of large volume of data streams can be managed using this proposed conceptualization efficiently in conceptual level. Besides, using *Has_auxiliary_Context* and *Inverse Containment* relationships dynamically added contextual information towards the domain have been recognized. In this way, the proposed conceptualization may facilitate in future in deriving new knowledge from data streams. Further, using *Sequence* relationship the rapid availability of data points towards data stream is realized. Furthermore, *Segment* and *Window* partition has facilitated in realizing discreteness among continuous stream. Moreover, the proposed conceptualization model is flexible as it provides flexible finite size towards data-streams using *Segment* and *Window*. It has also recognized the communication and available sequences between *Segments* or *Windows* of similar or multiple data-streams. Several other related crucial features are described in Sect. 5.

3 Protégé Implementation of the Proposed Model

The proposed meta-model has been implemented in this section using OWL (Web Ontology Language) based ontology editorial tool Protégé [10]. Protégé facilitates representation of formally expressed axiom set of this proposed conceptualization towards OWL logic. It is composed of a number of reasoners for automated inference on ontological theory expressed in OWL logic. OWL is based on Description Logic.

Three layers and their construct types have been mapped towards Protégé Classes. Besides, six key relationships of the proposed conceptualization are specified as Object Properties in Protégé. The mapping from the proposed conceptualization towards Protégé is specified in Table 1. Further, several Object Properties in the proposed conceptualization may have multiple sub object properties. Such as INTER_CONTAINMENT has sub property called INTER_CONTAINMENT_COLLECTION_FAMILY. Figure 2 describes the graph obtained through OntoGraf plug-in in Protégé.

Table 1. Mapping from proposed conceptual model towards Protégé

Constructs in proposed conceptualization	Corresponding constructs in Protégé
Collection	COLLECTION
Family	FAMILY
Stream context	STREAM_CONTEXT
Primary context	PRIMARY_CONTEXT
Auxiliary context	AUXILIARY_CONTEXT
Segment context	SEGMENT_CONTEXT
Link	LINK_CONTEXT
Location context	LOCATION_CONTEXT
data_value	DATA_VALUE
time_stamp	TIME_STAMP
Containment	INTER_CONTAINMENT
	INTRA_CONTAINMENT
Inverse containment	INTRA_INVERSE_CONTAINMET
	INTER_INVERSE_CONTAINMENT
Has_auxiliary_context	HAS_AUXILIARY_CONTEXT
Reverse_has_auxiliary_context	REVERSE_HAS_AUXILIARY_CONTEXT
Sequence	SEQUENCE
Has time	HAS TIME

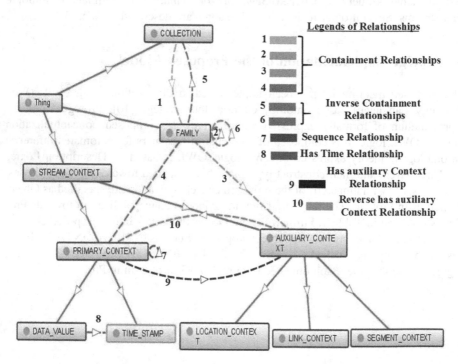

Fig. 2. Ontological graph of the proposed conceptual model using OntoGraf plug-in in Protégé

4   Illustration of the Proposed Conceptual Model

Let, an application is aimed to determine whether a car-driver is relaxed or stressed when the driver has to drive in a predefined route from one starting point to a specific destination and return to the starting point within predefined time duration. Besides, drivers are warned about the remaining time to reach the destination. Five sensor signals - Heart Rate (HR), Finger Temperature (FT), Respiration Rate (RR), Carbon-di-oxide (CO_2) and Oxygen Saturation ($SpO2$) have been recorded. This case study has been adopted from [4].

In this case study, all five sensor signals are of stream data Heart Rate (HR) sensor's primary context is recorded heartbeat. Heartbeats have specific values in a specific time. Besides, Heart Rate is dependent on particular location of the driver. Similarly, other sensors' recorded data have specific values in specific time. Further, all of them have auxiliary contexts. Such as Heart Rate has auxiliary contexts location, age, weight etc. According to this case study, the driver's recorded sensor data will be a *Collection*. Driver will be a *Family*. Further, driver has five *Primary Contexts – Heartbeat, Finger Temperature, Respiration Rate, Carbon di oxide* and *Oxygen Saturation*. Each *Primary Context* has values and related time stamps. Besides, all are related to *Auxiliary Context* such as location, body size. Key elements of this case study have been listed below.

Drivers' recorded Data (*Driver*)

Driver (*Heart Rate, Finger Temperature, Respiration Rate, Carbon di Oxide, Oxygen Saturation*);

Heart Rate ({heartbeat, time stamp}, {BODY_WEIGHT, AGE, BODY_-POSITION, GENDER, MEDICAL_HISTORY, DRIVER'S LOCATION});

Finger Temperature ({temperature, time stamp}, {AGE, GENDER, MEDI-CAL_HISTORY, DRIVER'S LOCATION});

Respiration Rate ({respiration_rate, time stamp}, {GENDER, MUSCLE TYPE, DRIVER'S LOCATION});

CO2 ({amount of CO2, time stamp}, {DRIVER'S LOCATION});

SpO2 ({amount of SpO2, time stamp}, {DRIVER'S LOCATION})

Nomenclatures of key elements in the case study are represented as, (i) Collections are in **bold** letters; (ii) Families are in *italics* letters; (iii) Primary Stream Contexts are in "small" letter cases; and (iv) Auxiliary Stream Contexts are in "CAPITAL" letter.

In this section, the case study has been implemented using the ontology editorial tool Protégé. Key constructs of the case study have been mapped towards Protégé as specified in Sect. 2. Figure 3 is displaying the partial ontology graph of this case study showing only heart rate stream along with its auxiliary contexts. The graph is obtained through OntoGraf plug-in of Protégé.

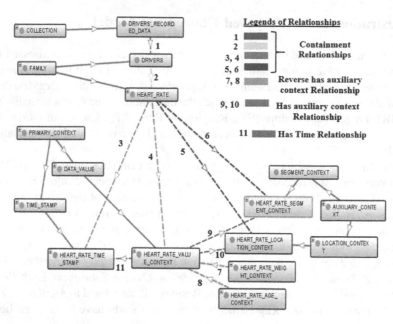

Fig. 3. The partial ontological graph displaying primary context of heart rate using auxiliary context and obtained through OntoGraf plug-in in Protégé

5 Features of Proposed Conceptualization

Proposed conceptualization possess several crucial features. Those features are *Abstraction* and *Reusability*, *Adaptability*, *Flexibility*, *Interoperability*, *Productivity* and *Context Sensitivity*.

(i)   *Abstraction* and *Reusability*: Proposed conceptualization is in high-level abstraction due to representation of data streams independent of any domain. Hence, it is reused in large numbers of domain.

(ii) *Adaptability*: Proposed conceptualization is able to recognize evolving contextual information using *Reverse_has_auxiliary_context*. Thus, it is adaptable towards changing surrounding environment.

(iii) *Flexibility*: Using this proposed conceptualization bounded, unbounded, fixed and flexible partition of bounded sequence of data streams are represented through Frame, Segment and Window. In this way, the proposed conceptualization is flexible.

(iv) *Interoperability*: With the aid of generic formal semantics, proposed conceptualization provides interoperable uniform representation towards heterogeneous data streams and streaming databases.

(v)   *Productivity*: The proposed conceptualization is productive as through this specification compatibility among different heterogeneous data streams, streaming databases and applications can be maximized.

(vi) *Context Sensitivity*: The proposed conceptualization is able to recognize related contextual information of both data streams and resources. Thus, the proposed model is context sensitive. This further facilitates validation and analysis of data streams.

6 Conclusion and Future Work

The paper has proposed an ontology driven common semantics towards context-dependent data streams and heterogeneous streaming databases. The objective of the proposed work is to model data streams and related contexts in a uniform way so that strong interoperability can be sustained among heterogeneous applications utilizing data streams. The novelty of the proposed ontology driven conceptualization is to support in realization of continuous temporal nature, static and evolving contexts related to data streams, homogeneity in heterogeneity formats, and rapid availability of data streams. The proposed conceptualization is capable to provide generic semantics towards contents of data streams and resources producing those data streams. Further, the proposed conceptualization is flexible enough to represent discreteness within infinite data streams and provide choices of fixed or variable partitions of data streams for storing and retrieval purpose. In this way, the proposed conceptualization may facilitate in future in deriving knowledge and decisions from data streams.

Future work will include semantical validation of the proposed ontology driven conceptualization of stream data. Further, ontology driven formal specification of a query language for retrieval of data streams is another important future work.

References

1. Abadi, D.J., Carney, D., Çetintemel, U., Cherniack, M., Convey, C., Lee, S., Stonebraker, M., Tatbul, N., Zdonik, S.: Aurora: a new model and architecture for data stream manage-ment. VLDB J. Int. J. Very Large Data Bases **12**(2), 120–139 (2003)
2. Appelrath, H., Geesen, D., Grawunder, M., Michelsen, T., Nicklas D.: Odysseus: a highly customizable framework for creating efficient event stream management systems. In: 6th ACM International Conference on Distributed Event-Based Systems, pp. 367–368. ACM, New York (2012)
3. Arasu, A., Babcock, B., Babu, S., Cieslewicz, J., Datar, M., Ito, K., Motwani, R., Srivasta-va, U., Widom, J.: Stream: the stanford data stream management system. Technical report 641, Stanford InfoLab (2004)
4. Begum, S., Barua, S., Filla, R., Ahmed, M.U.: Physiological sensor signals classification for healthcare using sensor data fusion and case-based reasoning. Expert Syst. Appl. **41**(2), 295–305 (2014)
5. Compton, M., Barnaghi, P., Bermudez, L., Castro, R.G., Corcho, O., Cox, S., Graybeal, J., Hauswirth, M., Henson, C., Herzog, A., Huang, V., Janowicz, K., Kelsey, W.D., Phuoc, D. L., Lefort, L., Leggieri, M., Neuhaus, H., Nikilov, A., Page, K., Passant, A., Sheth, A., Taylor, K.: The SSN ontology of the W3C semantic sensor network incubator group. Web Semant.: Sci. Serv. Agents World Wide Web **17**, 25–32 (2012)

6. Ediger, D., Jiang, K., Riedy, J., Bader, D. A.: Massive streaming data analytics: a case study with clustering coefficients. In: 2010 IEEE International Symposium on Parallel and Distributed Processing, Workshops and PhD Forum (IPDPSW, 2010), pp. 1–8 (2010)

7. Forrest, J.: stream: a framework for data stream modeling in R. B.S. Thesis, Southern Methodist University, Dallas, TX, United States (2011)

8. Guarino, N., Oberle, D., Staab, S.: What is an ontology? In: Staab, S., Studer, R. (eds.) Handbook on Ontologies. International Handbooks on Information Systems, 2nd edn., pp. 1–7. Springer, Heidelberg (2009)

9. Henson, C.A., Neuhaus, H., Sheth, A.P., Thirunarayan, K., Buyya, R.: An ontological representation of time series observations on the semantic sensor web. In: 1st International Workshop on the Semantic Sensor Web (SemSensWeb 2009), pp. 79–94 (2009)

10. Horridge, M.: A practical guide to building owl ontologies using Protégé 4 and COODETools, Edition 1.3. The University of Manchester (2011). https://mariaiulianadascalu.files.wordpress.com/2014/02/owl-cs-manchester-ac-uk_-eowltutorialp4_v1_3.pdf

11. Kramer, J., Seeger, B.: Semantics and implementation of continuous sliding window queries over data streams. ACM Trans. Database Syst. (TODS) 34(1), 4:1–4:49 (2009)

12. Wang, W., De, S., Toenjes, R., Reetz, E., Moessner, K.: A comprehensive ontology for knowledge representation in the internet of things. In: 11th International Conference on Trust, Security and Privacy in Computing and Communications (IEEE TRUSTCOM), pp. 1793–1798. IEEE Computer Society (2012)

13. Wang, X., Zhang, X., Li, M.: A survey on semantic sensor web: sensor ontology, map-ping and query. Int. J. u- e- Serv. Sci. Technol. 8(10), 325–342 (2015)

14. Banerjee, S., Sarkar, A.: Ontology driven meta-modeling for NoSQL databases: a con-ceptual perspective. Int. J. Softw. Engg. Appl. Sci. Eng. Res. Support Soc. (SERSC) 10(12), 41–64 (2016)

15. Zaniolo, C.: Logical foundations of continuous query languages for data streams. In: Barceló, P., Pichler, R. (eds.) Datalog 2.0 2012. LNCS, vol. 7494, pp. 177–189. Springer, Heidelberg (2012). doi:10.1007/978-3-642-32925-8_18

Towards the Exploitation of Statistical Language Models for Sentiment Analysis of Twitter Posts

Sukriti Bhattacharya[1]([⊠]) and Prasun Banerjee[2]

[1] University College London, London, UK
s.bhattacharya@cs.ucl.ac.uk
[2] University of Calcutta, Kolkata, India
banerjee.prasun@gmail.com

Abstract. In this paper, we investigate the utility of linguistic features for detecting the sentiment of twitter messages. The sentiment is defined to be a personal positive or negative feelings. We built n-gram language models over zoos of positive and negative tweets. We assert the polarity of a given tweet by observing the perplexity with the positive or negative language model. The given tweet is considered to be close to the language model that assigns lower perplexity.

Keywords: Sentiment analysis · N-gram Language Model · Perplexity

1 Introduction

Sentiment Analysis is one of the interesting applications of text analytics. Although the term is often associated with sentiment classification of documents, broadly speaking it refers to the use of text analytics approaches applied to the set of problems related to identifying and extracting subjective material in text sources. In the past few years, Online Social Networks (OSNs) have been around for helping people to have virtual communities and communications without time and geographical restrictions. The data in OSN contains opinions, emotions and views of people from all corners of the globe. The exponential growth of data in social networks has resulted in a goldmine in form of wealth of data which can be subjected to mining for extracting business intelligence. Sentiment analysis is one of the open research avenues that have high-utility to exploit social media for the growth of real world enterprises. For instance Twitter tweets, when carefully analysed, can provide valuable insights that can pave way for contextual advertising. Spurred by that growth, companies and media organisations are increasingly seeking ways to mine Twitter for information about what people think and feel about their products and services. tweetfeel[1], and Social Mention[2] are just a few who advertise Twitter sentiment analysis as one of their services.

---

[1] http://twitdom.com/tweetfeel/.
[2] http://www.socialmention.com/.

© IFIP International Federation for Information Processing 2017
Published by Springer International Publishing AG 2017. All Rights Reserved
K. Saeed et al. (Eds.): CISIM 2017, LNCS 10244, pp. 253–263, 2017.
DOI: 10.1007/978-3-319-59105-6_22

In this paper, we describe a language model based approach for classifying tweets into positive and negative sentiment. To overcome the 140-character text limitation, most of the useful information is obfuscated by abbreviations and embedded in unstructured tweet text. Therefore, we choose *n-gram* language model as it takes no advantage of the fact that what is being modelled is language, it may be a sequence of arbitrary symbols, with no deep structure, intention or thought behind them. Our method is a fairly simple variant of scoring by perplexity according to an in-domain language model. The perplexity of a language model with respect to a sample of text, t, is the reciprocal of the geometric average of the probabilities of the predictions in t. The language model with the smaller perplexity will be the one that assigns the larger probability to t. Based on this hypothesis we built two language models on positive and negative tweet samples using KenLM[3] [24] natural language toolkit. We are interested in the fact how well a language model predicts the unseen tweet by calculating the perplexity. Perplexity is subject to sampling error. To make fine distinctions between language models the perplexity should be measured with respect to a large sample. The preliminary experiments, carried out on tweets from Stanford University twitter corpus [27] (containing 800,000 positive and 605,087 negative tweets, respectively), show that the perplexity of a tweet, given two Language Models calculated over positive and negative sentiment of tweets, respectively could efficiently capture the sentiment of that tweet with relatively good accuracy (78%) and low false positive rate (0.19).

The paper is organised as follows, in Sect. 2 we give a brief overview of statistical language modeling focusing on n-gram language model. In the next section we list some related work. We introduce the proposed methodology in Sect. 4. Section 5 describes the evaluation of our proposed methodology by providing the experimental set up and results. We conclude with future work in Sect. 6.

2   Statistical Language Model

Language modeling is the attempt to characterize, capture and exploit regularities in natural language. Natural language is an immensely complicated phenomenon. In addition, any medium for natural language is subject to noise, distortion and loss. The need to model language arises out of this uncertainty. Natural language can be viewed as a stochastic process. Every sentence, document, or other contextual unit of text is treated as a random variable with some probability distribution. Let $\mathcal{L} = w_1^n \stackrel{def}{=} w_1, w_2, \ldots, w_n$, where w_i's are the words that make up the hypothesis. This may be decomposed into a series of multiplications of conditional probabilities (chain rule), as follows:

$$P(\mathcal{L}) = \prod_{i=1}^{n} P(w_i \mid w_1^{i-1}) \tag{1}$$

---

[3] http://kheafield.com/code/kenlm/.

$P(w_i \mid w_1^{i-1})$ is often written as $P(w \mid h)$, where $h \overset{def}{=} w_1^{i-1}$ is called the history. The event space (h, w) is very large, and no reasonable amount of data would be sufficient to span it. It is therefore useful to introduce a mapping, $\phi(.)$ that divides the set of possible histories into K *equivalence classes*. Different language modelling techniques arise from applying different equivalence mappings.

From the information theoretic point of view, language is considered as an information source, a high-order Markov chain $\mathcal{L}$ [1], which emits a sequence of symbols w_i from a finite alphabet often called the vocabulary $\mathcal{V}$. The distribution of the next symbol is highly dependent on the identity of the previous ones. $\mathcal{L}$ has a certain inherent entropy $\mathcal{H}$, the amount of non-redundant information conveyed per word, on average, by $\mathcal{L}$. Language modelling in its modern incarnation has its roots in the pioneering work of Claude Shannon. According to Shannon's theorem [2], any encoding of $\mathcal{L}$ must use at least $\mathcal{H}$ bits per word, on average. Under this view, the goal of statistical language modeling is to identify and exploit sources of information in the language stream, so as to bring the perceived entropy down, as close as possible to its true value.

2.1   N-gram Approach

As described in Sect. 2, when estimating the probability of the occurrence of a word, w_i, given a history, h_i, it is helpful to define a mapping $\phi(\cdot)$ that divides the set of possible histories into K equivalence classes. The most frequently used approach is to distinguish equivalence classes by the most recent $N - 1$ words in the history. This implies that each word depends not on the entire history of words that come before it, but on the previous $N - 1$ words only. Therefore, the probability of a word occurring is estimated according to the following conditional distribution:

$$P(w_i \mid h_i) \simeq P(w_i \mid \phi(h_i)) = P(w_i \mid w_{i-N+1}^{i-1}) \tag{2}$$

This is known as an N-gram model. By combining the N-gram probabilities of each word in the sentence, using the product rule of conditional probabilities, we can estimate the probability of the sentence:

$$P(w_1^n) \simeq \prod_{i=1}^{n} P(w_i \mid w_{i-N+1}^{i-1}) \tag{3}$$

The choice of N is based on a trade-off between detail and reliability, and will be dependent on the quantity of training data available. A bigram $(N = 2)$ language model will have larger equivalence classes, and hence fewer parameters than a trigram $(N = 3)$ model. Parameters in bigram model will therefore be more reliably estimated, while a trigram model will be more precise, and will therefore be a more accurate model, provided there is sufficient training data. For the quantities of language model training data typically available at present, trigram models strike the best balance between precision and robustness, although interest is growing in moving to 4-gram models and beyond [3].

2.2   Smoothing

The key difficulty with using n-gram language models is that of data sparsity. Data sparsity makes the model inaccurate for sequences of words that appear rarely. One can never have enough training data to estimate all of the model's parameters reliably. The parameters of this model, i.e. the conditional probabilities, are estimated using the maximum likelihood criterion on a collection of training text data. The maximum likelihood estimate (MLE) for an N-gram is calculated as the count (i.e. number of times a certain N-gram was encountered in the training corpus) of a current N-gram normalised by the number of all N-grams, sharing the same N-1 history. As the sum of all n-grams sharing the same N-1 history is actually a count of the history itself, the likelihood estimation finally gets the realisation as shown in Eq. 4, where $C(\cdot)$ is an N-gram count and n is the order of an N-gram.

$$P(w_i \mid w_{i-N+1}^{i-1}) = \frac{C(w_{i-N+1}^i)}{\sum_j C(w_{i-N+1}^j)} = \frac{C(w_{i-N+1}^i)}{\sum_j C(w_{i-N+1}^{i-1})} \tag{4}$$

The maximum likelihood solution is problematic as it assigns unseen N-grams a probability of 0 and does not generalize well. The problem of unseen n-grams becomes more severe when moving towards higher order n-gram models. While these models enable us to capture more context, their estimated conditional probabilities becomes more sparse and less robust. To address this problem, smoothing is used, where the probabilities of observed n-grams are discounted and the discounted probability mass is re-distributed to assign non-zero probabilities to unseen N-grams. The most widely-used smoothing algorithms for such models are, Good-Turing smoothing [4], interpolation smoothing [5,6], Katz smoothing [7] and Kneser-Ney [8] smoothing. An extensive survey of different smoothing techniques are given by Goodman [9].

2.3   Performance Measure for Language Models

When a language model is viewed as an information source, the entropy defines the best level a perfect language model which takes account of all possible linguistic information can reach. Entropy of a discrete distribution P over the event space X is defined as:

$$\mathcal{H}[P] = - \sum_{x \in X} P(x) \, log_2 \, P(x) \tag{5}$$

The entropy of a distribution P measures how many bits you need on average to encode data from P with the code that is optimal for P. Entropy is the average number of 0/1 questions needed to describe an outcome from $P(x)$. If we are interested in the fact how well a language model predicts the unseen data, this should be measured by calculating cross-entropy [25] of the distribution function of $P_T(x)$ of the text, with regard of the probability function $P_M(x)$ of the model.

That is, cross-entropy is the entropy of some data T as estimated by a model M is defined as:

$$\times \mathcal{H}[T \parallel M] = - \sum_{x \in X} P_T(x) \; log_2 \; P_M(x) \qquad (6)$$

Intuitively speaking, cross entropy is the entropy of T as "perceived" by the model M. Therefore, a good model is one which has a low entropy, and hence assigns a high probability to the test text. Often, the *perplexity* [26] of the text with regard to the model is reported. It is defined as:

$$\mathsf{PP}_M(T) = 2^{\mathcal{H}(T \parallel M)} = P(w_1^n)^{-1/n} \qquad (7)$$

There is no clear justification in the literature for the use of perplexity over cross-entropy, however perplexity has the appealing quality of describing intuitively how good a language model. Intuitively, perplexity can be roughly interpreted as the "branching factor", or the geometric average number of choices the language model has when predicting the next word. Hence, low perplexity is desirable.

3   Related Work

Wilson et al. [10] focused on phrase-level sentiment analysis to know whether a given expression is polar or neutral. The approach was to find contextual polarity for neutral, positive and negative values. Esuli and Sebastiani [11] exploited the SentiWordNet which is an existing lexical resource available for opinion mining (OM). A synset in this dictionary is associated with three numerical scores namely Pos(s), Neg(s) and Obj(s). Narayanan et al. [12] used conditional sentences, for instance "if your Nokia phone is not good, buy Samsung phone" for sentiment analysis. Authors in [16] explored contextual advertising based on the results of sentiment analysis. They used sentiment detection for identifying contexts and do advertising in a web based applications. This is known as Sentiment-Oriented Contextual Advertising (SOCA). This framework combines both contextual advertising and sentiment analysis in order to achieve best way of using advertisements in web based applications. In [13] authors focused on classification of sentimental polarities. They compared both blog and review data for empirical study. They performed Information Retrieval (IR) based topic analysis. Polarity classification is used for sentiment analysis. A lexicon-based method is proposed for sentiment analysis in [14]. They used a calculator known as Semantic Orientation CALculator (SO-CAL) by using a dictionary of words. The dictionary contains words and corresponding SO values. Wu and Ren [15] state that social networking web sites are producing huge amount of data that can provide a wealth of information pertaining to user behaviour. They designed models for sentimental analysis of Twitter posts. Especially they focused on users influenced and influencing probabilities. They classified the probabilities into negative and positive influencing probabilities. Zhang et al. [17] focused on sentiment analysis for stock trend forecasting. Bayesian model is used for classification. Authors in [18] proposed construction of dictionary for sentiment analysis using semi-supervised learning approach. Stock market news dataset is used for sentiment analysis. Guptha and Shalini [19] used blogs and forums in order to identify Indian railway performance and perform sentiment analysis on it for improving the performance of Indian railways. A polarity dictionary is produced in order to have classification of tweets in order to find whether a sentiment is positive or negative or neutral. Kontopoulos et al. [20] used Onto-Gen for visualising ontology for sentiment analysis based on the tweets collected from Twitter. They stated that ontology is machine-readable conceptualisation of shared content. [21] explored real time event detection by analysing Twitter posts. Especially their methodology throws light into real-time event detection pertaining to earth-quake reporting. Authors in [22] employed machine learning techniques for sentiment classification. They used Naive Bayes and Support Vector Machine (SVM) for the classification. Both are the supervised learning methods. [23] proposed a methodology based on ontology. It is named as Ontology-based Sentiment Analysis Process for Social Media Context (OSAPS).

4   Methodology

The proposed framework shown in Fig. 1 mainly consists of 3 phases,

1. Preprocessing.
2. Training.
3. Classification.

4.1   Preprocessing

Tweets contain colloquial dialect, or informal languages. In this phase the system executes a series of commands to clean text, removes punctuation, special characters, embedded HTTP links, extra spaces, digits, tag Patterns, '@' patterns (A de facto standard to include the @ symbol before the username) and the emoji patterns. It also converts the upper case letters to lower case.

4.2   Training

The cleaned tweets are then divided into two separate zoos based on their polarity - positive and negative feelings, respectively. The KenLM language modeling toolkit was applied to train and binarise the clean tweets. We have used KenLM to model two different language models based on the sentiment polarity (positive and negative, respectively) using a preferably large set of training tweets comprised of different values of n-grams (n = 2 to 6).

KenLM [24] developed by Kenneth Heafield, implements two data structures that allow very efficient language queries, a fast probing hash table, and a more compact but slower trie. The KenLM library packs use the Kneser-Ney smoothing method. Knesser-Ney Smoothing is helpful for generalisation and for testing when the test data has words not already present in the vocabulary.

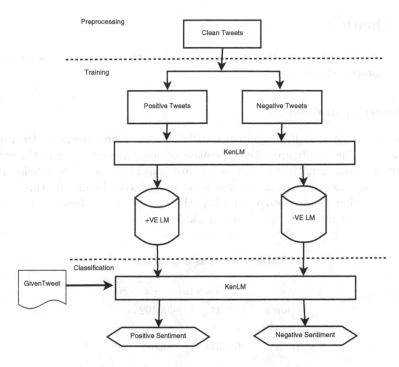

Fig. 1. Sentiment analysis framework

4.3 Classification

Given the parameters in Table 1, the system asks the question *"In which zoo is t more likely to belong?"*. Using perplexity measure the classifier answers the natural question *"Considering our language models as tweet sentiment analyser, which is more likely to generate our suspect tweet t?"*.

Table 1. Parameters of our classifier

t	given tweet to classify
q_p	n-gram model built from zoo of positive tweets
q_n	n-gram model built from zoo of negative tweets

Therefore, the sentiment of a given tweet t will be determined as positive (or negative) by the perplexity measure (Eq. 7) based classifier, $PP(t, q_p, q_n)$ defined as follows:

$$PP(t, q_p, q_n) = \begin{cases} \text{Positive} & \text{if } PP_{q_p}(t) < PP_{q_n}(t) \\ \text{Negative} & \text{if } PP_{q_n}(t) < PP_{q_p}(t) \end{cases} \tag{8}$$

5   Evaluation

In this section we provide the detailed results of the experiments carried out using the proposed framework.

5.1   Experimental Setup

We evaluated our classifier against 1405087 tweets from Stanford University Corpus[4] [27]. The tweets are labeled positive or negative according to the emoticon. For example, emoticons such as ':)' are considered positive labels of the tweets and emoticons such as ':(' are used as negative labels. In this experiment we considered only positive and negative tweets and we ignored all neutral tweets, the exact numbers are shown in Table 2.

Table 2. Corpus description

	+ve Tweets	−ve Tweets
Train set	533334	403392
Test set	266666	201695
Total	800,000	605087

In this experiment we used two-third of the original dataset to train the language model and the remaining one-third to test (Table 2). We train two different language models for both the positive and negative training corpus. The only parameter is the size of the n-gram, i.e. the value of n. We chose $n = 2$ to 6 for each corpus to strike a balance between memory use and providing sufficient information to produce good results.

KenLM tool was used to generate the language models. KenLM uses a smoothing method called modified Kneser-Ney. It is a very memory and time efficient implementation of Kneaser-Ney smoothing and officially distributed with

Table 3. Time and memory consumption for +ve language model construction

n	Size (MB)	Time ($\approx$ mins)
2	83.5	2
3	282.4	3.5
4	583.8	8
5	947.7	12.5
6	1325.0	20

---

[4] http://cs.stanford.edu/people/alecmgo/trainingandtestdata.zip.

Table 4. Classifier accuracy and false positive

n	Accuracy	False positive
2	0.7808	0.195
3	0.7739	0.202
4	0.7718	0.203
5	0.7713	0.204
6	0.7711	0.204

Moses[5]. For ARPA file format the size of the languages models and the computation time is shown in Table 3. The time consumption depends on two factors,
the order of n-gram language model and the size of the corpus in terms of individual file size. On the other hand the memory consumption does not depend of
the corpus size or individual file size in the corpus. It only depends on the order
of the language model.

5.2   Results and Discussion

In a pilot experiment with gram size varies from 2 to 6 and on the dataset
presented in Table 2, we obtained results shown in Table 4. The highest accuracy
of 78% is reached for bi-gram language model. It is interesting to see that the
accuracies calculated with rest of the gram values (n = 3 to 6) are almost similar
to each other, as shown in Fig. 2(a). The false positive rates shown in Fig. 2(b)
is not satisfactory either.

Although, we achieved the best false positive rate (0.19) for bi-gram language
model but it does not show any significant improvement comparing to other
gram values. We assume that this is due to the fact that during preprocessing

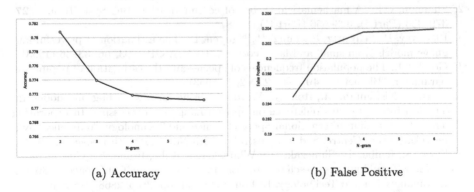

(a) Accuracy   (b) False Positive

Fig. 2. Classifier accuracy and false positive

---

[5] http://www.statmt.org/moses/?n=FactoredTraining.BuildingLanguageModel.

of tweets (Sect. 4.1) we removed some important emojis and special characters. We believe, both the accuracy and false positive would be far better if we were to carry out different information theoretic measures to clean the tweets during preprocessing phase.

6   Conclusion

In this paper we have explored the utility of language models and perplexity, a measure to determine the coverage of a language model given a text, for analysing the sentiment of a tweet with a reference corpus. The current finding shows the sentiment analysis can be achieved with the use of language models, especially in the field of social customer relationship managements (CRM) where customer feedbacks on several aspects can be categorised as positive and negative sentiments. We have provided empirical evidence that the training set i.e., the positive and negative tweet samples used to construct a language model has a large influence on the resulting accuracy. Sentiment analysis over twitter data faces several new challenges due to typical short length and irregular structure. Although, finding new methods for such analysis is the main challenge, but the performance of such analysis depends on identifying new sets of features to add to the trained model for sentiment identification, that includes hashtags, emoticons and the presence of intensifiers such as all-capital letters and character repetitions etc. A major determinant of the future direction of this research may lie with a clear definition of such feature identification, at the same time we will explore even richer linguistic analysis, for example, parsing, semantic analysis and topic modeling. Finally, we hope that the methodology and the results presented in this paper will provide a benchmark for future proposals and research efforts.

References

1. Abramson, N.: Information Theory and Coding. McGraw-Hill, New York (1963)
2. Shannon, C.E.: A mathematical theory of communication. Bell Syst. Tech. J. **27**, 379–423 (Part I), 623–656 (Part II) (1948)
3. Placeway, P., Schwartz, R., Fung, P., Nguyen, L.: The estimation of powerful language models from small and large corpora. In: ICASSP 1993, pp. 33–36 (1993)
4. Good, I.J.: The population frequencies of species and the estimation of population parameters. Biometrika **40**(3–4), 237–264 (1953)
5. Mori, S., Nishimura, M., Itoh, N.: Word clustering for a word bi-gram model. In: The 5th International Conference on Spoken Language Processing, Incorporating The 7th Australian International Speech Science and Technology Conference, Sydney Convention Centre, Sydney, Australia, 30th November–4th December 1998
6. Furui, S., Ichiba, T., Shinozaki, T., Whittaker, E.W.D., Iwano, K.: Cluster-based modeling for ubiquitous speech recognition. In: 9th European Conference on Speech Communication and Technology, Lisbon, Portugal, pp. 2865–2868, 4–8 September 2005
7. Katz, S.: Estimation of probabilities from sparse data for the language model component of a speech recognizer. IEEE Trans. Acoust. Speech Signal Process. **35**(3), 400–401 (1987)

8. Kneser, R., Ney, H.: Improved backing-off for M-gram language modeling. In: 1995 International Conference on Acoustics, Speech, and Signal Processing, Detroit, Michigan, USA, pp. 181–184, 8–12 May 1995

9. Chen, S.F., Goodman, J.: An empirical study of smoothing techniques for language modeling. Comput. Speech Lang. **13**(4), 359–393 (1999)

10. Wilson, T., Wiebe, J., Hoffmann, P.: Recognizing contextual polarity in phrase-level sentiment analysis, pp. 347–354. Association for Computational Linguistics (2005)

11. Esuli, A., Sebastiani, F.: SENTIWORDNET: a publicly available lexical resource for opinion mining, pp. 1–6. ACM (2005)

12. Narayanan, R., Liu, B., Choudhary, A.: Sentiment analysis of conditional sentences. In: Conference on Empirical Methods in Natural Language Processing, pp. 180–189 (2009)

13. Liu, F., Wang, D., Li, B., Liu, B.: Improving blog polarity classification via topic analysis and adaptive methods. In: The 2010 Annual Conference of the North American Chapter of the ACL, pp. 1–4 (2010)

14. Taboada, M., Brooke, J., Tofiloski, M., Voll, K., Stede, M.: Lexicon-based methods for sentiment analysis, vol. 37, pp. 1–42. Association for Computational Linguistics (2011)

15. Wu, Y., Ren, F.: Learning sentimental influence in twitter. In: International Conference on Future Computer Sciences and Application, pp. 1–4 (2011)

16. Fan, T.K., Chang, C.H.: Sentiment-oriented contextual advertising. Knowl. Inf. Syst. **23**, 321–344 (2010)

17. Zhang, K., Li, L., Li, P., Teng, W.: Stock trend forecasting method based on sentiment analysis and system similarity model. In: The 6th International Forum on Strategic Technology, pp. 1–5 (2011)

18. Mizumoto, K., Yanagimoto, H., Yoshioka, M.: Sentiment analysis of stock market news with semi-supervised learning. In: IEEE/ACIS 11th International Conference on Computer and Information Science, pp. 1–4 (2012)

19. Gupta, A.R., Shalini, L.: Improvisation of experience of Indian railways using sentimental analysis. Int. J. Comput. Appl. **66**, 16–18 (2013)

20. Kontopoulos, E., Berberidis, C., Dergiades, T., Bassiliades, N.: Ontology-based sentiment analysis of twitter posts. Expert Syst. Appl. **40**(10), 4065–4074 (2013). Elsevier

21. Sakaki, T., Okazaki, M., Matsuo, Y.: Tweet analysis for real-time event detection and earthquake reporting system development. IEEE Trans. Knowl. Data Eng. **25**(4), 1–13 (2013)

22. Wawre, S.V., Deshmukh, S.N.: Sentiment classification using machine learning techniques. Int. J. Sci. Res. **5**(4), 1–3 (2016)

23. Thakor, P., Sasi, S.: Ontology-based sentiment analysis process for social media content. Procedia Comput. Sci. **53**, 199–207 (2015). Elsevier

24. Heafield, K.: KenLM: Faster and smaller language model queries. In: Sixth Workshop on Statistical Machine Translation (2011)

25. Rosenfeld, R.: A maximum entropy approach to adaptive statistical language modeling. Comput. Speech Lang. **10**, 187–228 (1996)

26. Jelinek, F., Mercer, R.L., Bahl, L.R., Baker, J.K.: Perplexity-a measure of the difficulty of speech recognition tasks. J. Acoust. Soc. Am. **62**, S63 (1977)

27. Go, A., Bhayani, R., Huang, L.: Twitter sentiment classification using distant supervision. In Final Projects from CS224N for Spring 2008/2009 at the Stanford Natural Language Processing Group (2009)

POMSec: Pseudo-Opportunistic, Multipath Secured Routing Protocol for Communications in Smart Grid

Manali Chakraborty[✉], Novarun Deb, and Nabendu Chaki

University of Calcutta, Kolkata, India
manali4mkolkata@gmail.com

Abstract. Traffic engineering governs the operational performance of a network and its optimization. Splitting the network traffic using multipath routing is one of the standard techniques of traffic engineering. Multipath routing maximizes network resource utilization and throughput by giving nodes a choice of next hops for the same destination along with minimizing the delay. On the other hand, Opportunistic routing minimizes operational cost and the burden of redundant route maintenance by using a constrained redundancy in route selection. POMSec: Pseudo Opportunistic, Multipath Secure routing is one such algorithm that combines the advantages of both the routing methods and additionally implements an underlying trust model to secure the communication in Smart Grid.

Keywords: Opportunistic routing · Multipath routing · Wireless sensor network · Security · Energy efficiency · Smart Grid

1 Introduction

Wireless sensor networks are burdened with the task of transferring data from one node to another via wireless links and multiple hops, considering all the adversaries in the network. Each of the factors like unpredictable environmental behavior, dynamic network topologies, unreliable nature of communication or a combination of these may further contribute to failure of network services. Due to its dynamic nature, WSN is suitable for various types of applications [18]. However, security is one of the most important aspect of every application with different QoS requirements, such as, throughput, energy efficiency, delay, etc. Security of any application is generally determined by its attributes [21]. However, security solutions for sensor networks are different from ordinary networks having infrastructure. Besides, every application domain has its own unique characteristics and QoS parameters. Thus, it requires a secure and reliable routing protocol which will comply with application specific QoS parameters as well [5].

In traditional routing the route between a pair of nodes is always static and data packets are transmitted through intermediate nodes over that pre determined route. Whereas, multipath routing adds desired level of redundancy to

© IFIP International Federation for Information Processing 2017
Published by Springer International Publishing AG 2017. All Rights Reserved
K. Saeed et al. (Eds.): CISIM 2017, LNCS 10244, pp. 264–276, 2017.
DOI: 10.1007/978-3-319-59105-6_23

overcome link failures utilizing alternative routes [7]. Besides, in multipath routing environment, link failures do not always result in the initiation of route discovery. This is because the network is k - fault tolerant, for small values of k and hence link failures do not bring network services to a halt [6]. Besides, multipath routing provides better load balancing and bandwidth aggregation [8].

There exist several works, [11–15] which propose to utilize multiple routes in order to provide stability and reliability in the network. However, in spite of all these benefits, multipath routing has several disadvantages: (1) Using multiple routes can increase significant energy cost, which is one of the most important QoS metric in WSNs; (2) Multiple route discovery and maintenance at every hop induces the operational cost of the network; and (3) Besides, multiple routes can introduce channel contentions and interference in the network, which result in the increment of delivery delay as well as cause transmission failures [12].

Opportunistic routing (OR) [17], or anypath routing, is another routing protocol which takes advantage of the broadcasting ability of nodes in wireless medium. It does not use multiple routes, but selects best possible relay nodes among a set of candidate nodes to improve reliability, efficiency and fault tolerance. In OR, first, a source node broadcasts a packet among its neighbors. Then these candidate nodes select a best relay node among itself using some coordination algorithm and forward the data packet through that node. The same process continues until the transmission is successful, i.e., the specified packet reaches its destination.

We have considered Smart Grid as an application domain of our proposed routing protocol. Now, due to specific demands of Smart Grid, the associated communication system should have these following characteristics [19,20]:

- It should consider different type of traffic patterns in the network, e.g., unicast, multicast and broadcast.
- It need to be scalable and flexible to incorporate new renewable sources and distributed energy resources in the network.
- Due to the large and evolving architecture of smart Grid, distributed or cluster based networks will be more suitable for it.
- The communication system should monitor the network devices and perform fault detection, isolation, and recovery.
- Every device should get uniquely identified and addressed.
- It should support different QoS parameters for a variety of applications and functions which have different latency and loss requirements, different bandwidth, different security requirements, different real time and non real time data constraints etc.
- Besides, the communication system should be interoperable, dynamic, cost effective, open to active standards and public interfaces, backward compatible and most importantly secure to all the vulnerabilities from inside and outside of the network.

Now, multipath routing and OR, both have their advantages and disadvantages. Multipath routing provides better reliability and fault tolerance, whereas

OR improves network performances and also supports different traffic patterns. However, multipath routing suffers from operational overhead of discovering and maintaining routes in every hop, which inturn increase the contention in the network. OR also suffers from duplicate reception problem at the destination and single path breakdown problem. Thus, it will be more effective to integrate the positive sides of both these paradigms in a single routing protocol.

The proposed work is a secure and pseudo opportunistic, multipath routing scheme that offers efficient load balancing. Like traditional OR methods, our protocol dynamically selects a set of forwarding nodes for packet transmission. However, the number of routes for packet transmission is not static, and the number of routes varies with the status of each intermediate node, at every hop along the path. The degree of routes at each hop depends heavily on the trust worthiness of neighbouring nodes. As an example, it may act like single-path routing, if the nodes are trustworthy and the communication is reliable and meets network requirements. Otherwise, the number of paths increased. The selection process is run-time and dynamic.

The idea of using selective multipath routing is first proposed in ETSeM [1]. In ETSeM each node is equipped to choose a set of forwarding nodes among its neighbours to transmit data. Route selection depends on the energy of nodes and number of paths set up through the nodes. However, the proposed routing protocol in [1] has not been associated with any security measures to detect threats and this inspires us to propose a new secure routing algorithm where an additional trust model [3] is combined with routing mechanism. In the proposed work, every node evaluate the trust value of its next hop neighbour and the routes are selected based on these trust values. The proposed protocol offers the flexibility that it may use multiple paths with high degree of multiplicity when the intermediate destinations are not that trusted. On the contrary, the protocol save resources, and checks congestion by choosing a single path or lesser number of alternate paths for the next hop according to the health value of its neighbour nodes. Because of these characteristics, our proposed algorithm has been referred as Pseudo Opportunistic, Multipath Secure (POMSec) routing protocol. We have simulated our protocol using QualNet 5.2 and also compares the results with [1] and another trust model proposed in [2].

The organization of this paper is described as follows: Sect. 2 gives the state of the art review on related works and Sect. 3 describes the proposed process in brief. The simulation results are presented in Sect. 4. Finally Sect. 5 concludes the paper.

2   State-of-the-Art Review

In this section, we discuss some of the significant works on multi-path as well as opportunistic routing for wireless networks. Besides, Sect. 2.3 discusses some of the existing trust models.

2.1   Multi-path Routing Protocols

Effectiveness of multipath routing protocols primarily rely on two aspects: route discovery and route selection process [4]. The multipath routing algorithm proposed in [9], has two different protocols: one for searching different multiple and node disjoint paths and another is for allocating the traffic optimally through those disjoint paths. Authors claimed that the algorithm works distributively and optimally balances the load in the network. In [12], each node first built a set of partially disjoint paths to destination among its neighbours.

REER [13] considers remaining energy level and available buffer size of a node, and Signal-to-Noise ratio to determine next hop forwarding node in the route. This algorithm has two methods of traffic allocation. First method selects a group of candidate nodes between every hop, and then the best route is chosen for data transmission. The second method breaks the transmitted message into several equal sized segments and then adds a XOR based error correction code with them and transmits them through different paths. Thus guarantees the arrival of the packet to the destination without any delay.

RELAX [14] effectively utilizes the relaxation technique of batteries to improve network lifetime. It also uses some metrics like remaining energy, Signal-to-Noise ratio, and other variables to predict the best next hop node. RELAX splits the transmitted message into several equal sized segments, and then add XOR based FEC with them and transmit them through different paths. Thus, the protocol does not require flooding when there is a link failure and hence the lifetime of the network is increased.

SEEMPr [15], tries to balance both the reliability and lifetime of a network, by providing the concept of criticality factor. The criticality factor determines the urgency of delivering a data packet. All packets do not have the same urgency. Thus, high priority packets follow optimal path, while other packets are sent through sub-optimal routes. Thus the energy consumption is distributed over the network.

The review above reflects that there already exist a good number of papers on multipath routing protocols. However, the trust worthiness of participating nodes is often not considered by the above protocols. In [6], a secret-sharing algorithm has been used to secure the network. However, the degree of multiple path selection on a hop to hop basis depending on the trust-value of the next hop destination has not really been considered in the existing approaches.

2.2   Opportunistic Routing Protocols

Several works have been proposed in the field of OR. [18] presents a survey of existing OR protocols in wireless network. Although OR is gaining a lot of attention due to its improved performance over other routing protocols in wireless environment, there is not much work present in Smart Grid area.

PLC-OR [22] is a power line communication based opportunistic routing in Smart Grid. Authors in this paper, uses static topological information of nodes to construct a routing table. It always selects a single path to the destination to avoid duplicate packet reception problem at the final destination. They used Dijkstra's algorithm for shortest path selection at each hop. Authors claim to reduce the transmission cost by using a static PLC-AN.

Authors of [23] proposed another OR for Smart Grid. However, this algorithm differs from the previous one in terms of its ability to handle varying topology in a network. They also introduced a new parameter depending on the transmission time for existing routes to calculate the best forwarding node among a set of forward nodes. The estimation method of transmission time is based on the outage probability of the PLC channel. Using simulation and theoretical methods, authors claimed to prove that the throughput of the network can be maximized if remaining transmission time is used to select and identify the forwarding nodes.

Analysing the existing works on opportunistic routing protocol reflects that it performs better in a static network, otherwise the operational cost exceeds the performance gain of the network. Thus, the tradeoff between progressing gain and processing delay and cost will be one of the main important concern for OR. OR does not come with any inherent security model. Thus, providing a secure transmission will be another important aspect while implementing OR in Smart Grid. Furthermore, duplicate packet delivery is another problem for OR. It generally causes due to broadcasting nature of wireless media and the use of isometric antennas. Authors of [22] claim to solve this problem by not allowing multipath routing, which restricted the selection of forwarding nodes within same transmission domain for a particular sender node. However, this inturn defeats the main purpose of OR, which exploits the broadcasting nature of wireless networks.

2.3   Trust Models

Authors in [2] proposed an honesty based intrusion detection system for MANETs. In HIDS, each node is tagged with an unique identifier and an honesty metric. This honesty metric of each node gets updated periodically based on the packet forwarding information provided by one-hop neighbours.

TIDS [3] is a another intrusion detection system for Wireless Ad-Hoc Networks that uses the trust evolution process to mitigate threats. Each node in the network is assigned a predetermined and fixed trust value. As the node spends time within the network, its trust value gets updated. Trust value of nodes get updated based on direct references and indirect recommendations. Trust values of one - hop neighbours are evaluated as part of two different processes.

In [10], another trust based model is proposed. The trust value of each node is calculated as a function of three different QoS parameters. A peer node will get rewarded every time it behaves properly with its neighbours. Thus the trustworthiness of each node depends on how it interacts and whether its neighbours are satisfied with its quality of service.

After reviewing several routing protocols and trust models we can conclude that neither multipath routing nor OR is perfectly tailor made for Smart Grid. In order to maximize the performance of Smart Grid, a combination of both the paradigms is necessary. Besides, there rarely exist some works, where trust models have been used in route discovery. This inspires us to propose an intelligent, selective and secure routing protocol which can use the perks of both opportunistic and multipath routing protocols with additional security mechanisms.

3   Description of the Process

This section briefly describes our proposed protocol for secure communication in Smart grid. Route selection in POMSec is dependent on energy depletion rate of the nodes, existing paths through the nodes and the trustworthiness of the nodes and their neighbours.

These following set of principles govern the proper execution of the proposed algorithm:

- Every node maintains two arrays – *Health* and *Trust*, of all its neighbour nodes.
- Every node has to store two variables – *Remaining Energy* and *Path*.
- Packet Receive (*PR*) and Packet Send (*PS*) counters are stored in nodes, along with the addresses of the nodes from which it receive the packets and to which it forward those packets. After a certain time frame (decided by the system operator), these counter values are sent to the node's one-hop neighbours.
- The health of each node N depends on trust-worthiness of the nodes, the remaining energy of it and on the number of paths through N.

3.1   The Trust Model

In order to secure our protocol we evaluated the trust of each node. The evaluation process is done by a node for its one hop neighbours and vice versa. The trust model has two main underlying concepts: *Direct Valuation* and *Indirect Reference* [3].

Direct Valuation refers to the trust value evaluated by a node. It is calculated using two different parameters: *Risk* and *Reputation.Risk* measures a node's behavior in recent past and *Reputation* assess a node's long term behavior. These two parameters helps to achieve an optimality by balancing the most recent behavior of a node in contrast to its long term behavior. On the other hand, *Indirect Reference* are considered from those entire one-hop neighbors that are common to both the evaluator node and the target node.

At time t, an evaluator node calculates the *Risk* and *Reputation* of its neighbour node i as,

$$Risk = \sum_t |PR_i - PS_i| \tag{1}$$

$$Reputation = \sum_t^{t-n} |PR_i - PS_i| \tag{2}$$

The *Indirect Reference* for m number of common neighbour Nodes (ND) between evaluator and target node, can be evaluated as,

$$Indirect\ Reference = \sum_{ND=1}^{m} \sum_{t}^{t-n} |PR_i - PS_i| \tag{3}$$

The reward for a node for the last time slice, is calculated using these three metrics as follows [3]:

$$\text{"}Reward = (\alpha * Risk) + (\beta * Reputation) + (\gamma * Indirect\ Reference)\text{"} \tag{4}$$

---

1. For EVERY node Broadcasts a HELLO message.

2. If a node receives a HELLO message, it replies with a REPLY HELLO message containing four variables – PR, PS, REMAINING ENERGY and PATH.

3. If a node receives a REPLY HELLO message –
   (a) Extracts the value of the Variables – PR, PS, REMAINING ENERGY and PATH, and calculate the HEALTH, for each of its Neighbour nodes.
   (b) Every node stores the address of each neighbour node with the value of their corresponding HEALTH, in an array.

4. If a node is a SOURCE node OR receives a ROUTE REQUEST message, Checks its array for the HEALTHIEST node in its Neighbour.

   If the value of the HEALTHIEST node is > 90%
       Send a ROUTE REQUEST message to the HEALTHIEST node.

   Else if the value of the HEALTHIEST node is > 75%
       Send a ROUTE REQUEST message to the HEALTHIEST and second HEALTHIEST node.

   Else if the value of the HEALTHIEST node is > 60%
       Send a ROUTE REQUEST message to the HEALTHIEST, second HEALTHIEST and third HEALTHIEST node.

   Else if the value of the HEALTHIEST node is > 45%
       Send a ROUTE REQUEST message to the HEALTHIEST, second HEALTHIEST, third HEALTHIEST and fourth HEALTHIEST node.

   Else
       Flood the ROUTE REQUEST message.

5. If a node receives a ROUTE REQUEST message it will RELAY the ROUTE REQUEST message as in STEP 4.

6. If a node is a DESTINATION node OR receives a ROUTE REPLY message, it will initiate a ROUTE REPLY message to the nodes, from which it gets the ROUTE REQUEST message.

Fig. 1. Working principle of POMSec.

The above formula generates reward points for each nodes by assigning weights to α, β and γ. Also, these coefficients are normalized so that $\alpha+\beta+\gamma = 1$. Now, we can calculate the trust value as:

$$\text{``}Trust(t) = Trust(t-1) + Reward\text{''} \tag{5}$$

If the value for the variable *Trust* of a node, crosses the threshold value, then it considered as an attacker. The trust value of a node may vary according to Eq. (5).

3.2 Proposed Algorithm

An outline of our proposed algorithm using the above mentioned trust model is given in Fig. 1. The value of the metric *PATH* is increased by one, whenever a node receives a ROUTE_REPLY packet. A source node can transmits data using the path that's derived this way. The load to the destination node is distributed proportionally through the routes according to the health of each node.

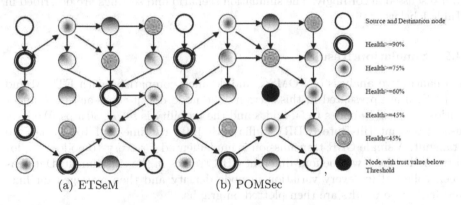

(a) ETSeM   (b) POMSec

Fig. 2. Data communication between Source and Destination using ETSeM and POMSec.

Figure 2(a) illustrates the route selection process of the ETSeM algorithm given in [1]. The significance of the algorithm after incorporating the trust model along the route selection process is depicted in Fig. 2(b). Figures 2(a) and (b) has the same set of nodes. The black node in Fig. 2(b) is detected as malicious in spite of its health more than or equal to 90%. This is because the trust value of the node is less than the threshold. POMSec can avoid all such malicious nodes in the route selection process with the help of the underlying trust model.

4   Experiments and Results

4.1   Simulation Settings

We have compared and analyzed the performance of POMSec with two different algorithms. First, another trust model, proposed in [2] is used with the ETSeM

Table 1. Parameter settings for simulation environment

Parameter	Value
Experimental area	$1500 * 1500 \, \text{m}^2$
Running time for each simulation	$100 \, \text{s}$
Mac Layer protocol	DCF of IEEE 802.11b standard
Traffic Model	CBR
Number of CBR traffics	10% of the total number of nodes
Mobility	Random Waypoint
Initial Energy level for each node	5000

algorithm. Let's refer this change in the rest of this paper as H-ETSeM. Thereafter, extensive simulations of POMSec, ETSeM [1] and H-ETSeM have been successfully performed in QualNet and the results have been plotted as graphs and discussed accordingly. The simulation scenario and settings are described in Table 1 below:

4.2 Simulation Results

A quantitative analysis of POMSec and detailed comparison with ETSeM and H-ETSeM are presented in this section. The node density for each experiment varies between 10 nodes to 50 nodes and the mobility is set at 30 mps. We have used Constant Bit-Rate (CBR) traffic with 100 s runtime and 100 packets to transmit. A single CBR transmission is implemented for every 10 nodes, i.e., for forty nodes there will be four different CBR traffics in the experiment. Data has been collected for every variation in node density and then averaged for final results. These results are then plotted on graphs.

Packet Delivery Ratio. The first simulation checks the Packet Delivery Ratio (PDR) of POMSec and also compares it with others. PDR is an important parameter in routing and quite standard too. PDR represents the ratio of successfully receiving packets at destination over the packets sent by the sender through CBR traffic. Figure 3(a) shows the PDR for original ETSeM, H-ETSeM and POMSec. POMSec demonstrates more stable and higher PDR than the other two algorithms, inspite of having a trust based evaluation method in route selection.

Throughput. Throughput is a measurement of how much data passed through a network in unit amount of time. In this simulation we measured it in Kilobits/sec by observing CBR Server stats. The results in Fig. 3(b) shows that the throughput for POMSec is better comparing to the other two algorithms. POMSec obviously looks promising in terms of efficient path selection and decision-making and better throughput values.

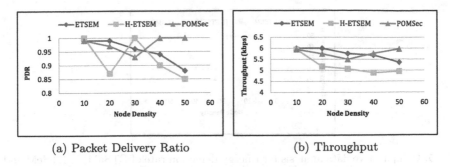

(a) Packet Delivery Ratio   (b) Throughput

Fig. 3. Comparative data analysis for PDR and throughput of ETSeM, H-ETSeM and POMSec.

End to End Delay. It represents the total time required by every CBR packet to reach its destination. Figure 4(a) depicts that POMSec offers much smaller delay than both the algorithms, which in turn proves the effectiveness of our trust model. H-ETSeM brings in more instability with increasing node density as compared to ETSeM. This actually confirms that the overhead for trust value updation increases with higher number of nodes.

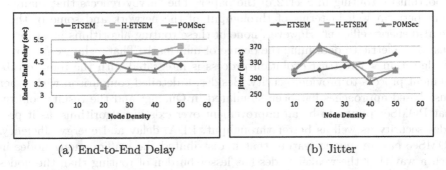

(a) End-to-End Delay   (b) Jitter

Fig. 4. Comparative data analysis for End-to-end delay and Jitter of ETSeM, H-ETSeM and POMSec.

Jitter. In networking, the word jitter represents the average of the deviation of a packet against the mean latency of the network [16]. Figure 4(b) shows that the Jitter of H-ETSeM and POMSec are quite identical, and as the degree of nodes increase in the network, it appears to decrease and become stable after sometime.

Energy Depletion Rate. Energy efficiency is one of the most critical QoS metric for various Wireless environments. The calculations for energy depletion of each node according to their expenses for packet transmission, neighbourhood discovery, trust evolution and route maintenance, along with the updation rule

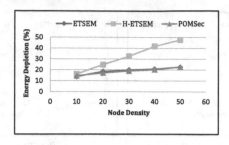

Fig. 5. Comparative data analysis for Energy depletion rate of ETSeM, H-ETSeM and POMSec.

has been additionally coded in simulation environment. The results in Fig. 5 are very interesting and informative. Inspite of additional trust evaluation overhead POMSec has almost similar trend as ETSeM. This confirms that our trust model is much light weight and it does not add extra burdens in the routing.

5   Conclusion

We have done a detailed study of the existing works in multipath routing and opportunistic routing in Sect. 2 of the paper. The survey reflects that many of them perform well in terms of throughput of the network and some of them are also energy efficient. However, none of these routing algorithms incorporate trust as a metric to determine the degree of multipath. Thats why we proposed an algorithm where trust evolution process is integrated with the route establishment process to provide security. Besides, a detailed comparison with other trust based approaches has been simulated in Qualnet and the results confirm that POMSec proves to be an improvement over existing algorithms, as it provides security as well as better throughput, PDA, delay and energy efficiency. POMSec has an unique feature that it distributed the traffic among nodes in such a way that the weaker nodes has lesser burden of routing than the nodes with more resources.

Acknowledgments. We would like to thank the Centre of Excellence in System Biology and Biomedical Engineering (TEQIP II), University of Calcutta for infrastructural and financial support towards publishing the results of our research work. This work is a part of the Ph.D. work of Manali Chakraborty, a Senior Research Fellow of Council of Scientific & Industrial Research (CSIR), Government of India. We would like to acknowledge CSIR, for providing the support required for carrying out the research work.

References

1. Chakraborty, M., Chaki, N.: ETSeM: a energy-aware, trust-based, selective multipath routing protocol. In: Cortesi, A., Chaki, N., Saeed, K., Wierzchoń, S. (eds.) CISIM 2012. LNCS, vol. 7564, pp. 351–360. Springer, Heidelberg (2012). doi:10. 1007/978-3-642-33260-9_30

2. Sen, P., Chaki, N., Chaki, R.: HIDS: honesty-rate based collaborative intrusion detection system for mobile ad-hoc networks. In: Computer Information Systems and Industrial Management, pp. 121–126 (2008)

3. Deb, N., Chaki, N.: TIDS: trust-based intrusion detection system for wireless ad-hoc networks. In: Cortesi, A., Chaki, N., Saeed, K., Wierzchoń, S. (eds.) CISIM 2012. LNCS, vol. 7564, pp. 80–91. Springer, Heidelberg (2012). doi:10.1007/978-3-642-33260-9_6

4. Deb, N., Chakraborty, M., Chaki, N.: Honesty and trust bases IDS solutions. In: Chaki, N., Chaki, R. (eds.) Intrusion Detection in Wireless Ad Hoc Networks, pp. 111–145. CRC Press, Taylor & Francis Group (2014)

5. Lee, S.-W., Choi, J.Y., Lim, K.W., Ko, Y.-B., Roh, B.-H.: A reliable and hybrid multipath routing protocol for multi-interface tactical ad hoc networks. In: The Military Communication Conference, pp. 1531–1536 (2010)

6. Mueller, S., Tsang, R.P., Ghosal, D.: Multipath routing in mobile ad hoc networks: issues and challenges. In: Calzarossa, M.C., Gelenbe, E. (eds.) MASCOTS 2003. LNCS, vol. 2965, pp. 209–234. Springer, Heidelberg (2004). doi:10.1007/978-3-540-24663-3_10

7. Marina, M.K., Das, S.R.: Ad hoc on-demand multipath distance vector routing, Computer Science Department, Stony Brook University (2003)

8. Ganjali, Y., Keshavarzian, A.: Load balancing in ad hoc networks: single-path routing vs. multi-path routing. In: IEEE International Advance Computing Conference, IACC 2009, pp. 32–34 (2009)

9. Lu, Y.M., Wong, V.W.S.: An energy-efficient multipath routing protocol for wireless sensor networks. Int. J. Commun. Syst. 20, 747–766 (2007)

10. Xiong, L., Liu, L.: Building trust in decentralized peer-to-peer electronic communities. In: Proceedings of the 5th International Conference on Electronic Commerce Research (ICECR-5) (2002)

11. Zhang, J., Jeong, C.K., Lee, G.Y., Kim, H.J.: Cluster-based multi-path routing algorithm for multi-hop wireless network. Int. J. Future Gener. Commun. Netw. (2009)

12. Agrakhed, J., Biradar, G.S., Mytri, V.D.: Energy efficient interference aware Multipath Routing protocol in WMSN. In: 2011 Annual IEEE India Conference (INDICON), pp. 1–4 (2011)

13. Yahya, B., Ben-Othman, J.: REER: robust and energy efficient multipath routing protocol for wireless sensor networks. In: Global Telecommunications Conference, GLOBECOM, pp. 1–7. IEEE (2009)

14. Yahya, B., Ben-Othman, J.: RELAX: an energy efficient multipath routing protocol for wireless sensor networks. In: Proceedings of IEEE International Conference on Communications (ICC), pp. 1–6 (2010)

15. Varma, S., Tiwary, U.S., Jain, A., Sharma, T.: Statistical energy efficient multipath routing protocol. In: International Conference on Information Networking (ICOIN), pp. 1–5 (2008)

16. Comer, D.E.: Computer Networks and Internets, p. 476. Prentice Hall, Upper Saddle River (2008)

17. Hsu, C.-J., Liu, H.-I., Seah, W.K.G.: Opportunistic routing - a review and the challenges ahead. Comput. Netw. 55, 3592–3603 (2011)

18. Boa, W., Chuanhea, H., Layuanb, L., Wenzhonga, Y.: Trust-based minimum cost opportunistic routing for Ad hoc networks. J. Syst. Softw. 84, 2107–2122 (2011)

19. NIST Special Publication 1108, NIST Framework and Roadmap for Smart Grid Interoperability Standards, Release 1.0, U.S. Department of Commerce, January 2010

20. Cagri Gungor, V., Lambert, F.C.: A survey on communication networks for electric system automation. Comput. Netw. **50**, 877–897 (2006). Elsevier
21. Cheng, L., Niu, J., Cao, J.: QoS aware geographic opportunistic routing in wireless sensor networks. IEEE Trans. Parallel Distrib. Syst. **25**(7), 1864–1875 (2014)
22. Yoon, S.-G., Jang, S., Kim, Y.-H., Bahk, S.: Opportunistic routing for smart grid with power line communication access networks. IEEE Trans. Smart Grid **5**(1), 303–311 (2014)
23. Qian, Y., Zhang, C., Xu, Z., Shu, F., Dong, L., Li, J.: A reliable opportunistic routing for smart grid with in-home power line communication networks. Inf. Sci. **59**, 1–13 (2016). Science China Press and Springer-Verlag Berlin Heidelberg

Context Driven Approach for Enterprise Architecture Framework

Priyanka Chakraborty[(✉)] and Anirban Sarkar

Department of Computer Applications, National Institute of Technology,
Durgapur, India
priyankalnitdgp@gmail.com, sarkar.anirban@gmail.com

Abstract. Decision making process within the enterprise is complex due to unavailability of widely accepted, flexible and dynamic Enterprise Architecture Framework (EAF) that comprises of service-based applications and has strong dependency on Service Oriented Architecture (SOA). Rapidly changing business scenarios have become normal characteristics of SOA based applications and Enterprise Information System. Existing non-SOA based EAFs are lacking of flexibility, scalability, context sensitivity, re-configurability and agility. On the other hand, existing SOA-based EAFs are merely capable to handle context sensitivity, reusability and agility of Enterprise Information System. To address such issues, this paper proposes a novel SOA-based EAF, called SCORE architecture, comprised of five loosely coupled layers namely, Subject layer, Context layer, Object layer, Role layer and Essence layer. Moreover, a set of relationships are proposed for SCORE architecture to exhibits the intra-layer and inter-layer associations among the constructs of different layers. Further, the inter-layer interactions and message flows in SCORE framework are analyzed using UML notations. The proposed enterprise architecture is illustrated using a suitable case study. Finally, a comparative study is performed with the Zachman Framework [1], to exhibit the benefits of the proposed EAF in the context of Enterprise Information system.

Keywords: Enterprise architecture framework · Service oriented architecture · Context driven · Re-configurability · Agility

1 Introduction

Enterprise Architecture (EA) [2] is defined as it provides a "knowledge base and support for decision making within the enterprise and it serves as the blueprint of current situation and strategy for future directions of the enterprise". Enterprise Architecture Framework (EAF) defines logical structure and systematic approach to create and maintain the Enterprise. An Ideal EA Framework should include-Business Value Measurement Metrics, EA Initiative Model, EA Maturity Model, Enterprise Communication Model.

Zachman Framework [3] is considered as the pioneer in the field of EAF. It introduces the concept of 5W1H (What, How, Where, Who When and Why) for five different Stakeholders (Planner, Owner, Designer, Builder, Integrator and User) in an

K. Saeed et al. (Eds.): CISIM 2017, LNCS 10244, pp. 277–289, 2017.
DOI: 10.1007/978-3-319-59105-6_24

Enterprise. Based on Zachman Framework approach, several Architecture Frameworks have been proposed such as, *TOGAF* Framework (The Open Group Architecture Framework) [4], *MODAF* (British Ministry of Defense Architecture Framework) [5], *FEAF* (Federal Enterprise Architecture Framework) [6], *DODAF* (Department of Defense Architecture Framework) [7], Treasury Enterprise Architecture Framework (*TEAF*) [8], NATO Architecture Framework (*NAF*) [9], 4+1 View Model of Architecture [10], and *GERAM* (Generalized Enterprise Reference Architecture and Methodology) [11]. These non-SOA based EAF suffers from absence of (i) scalability, (ii) inflexibility to address the continuously changing business requirements of the Enterprise, (iii) re-configurability, (iv) context sensitivity, (v) well-defined model and (vi) traceability. Integration of SOA with existing Enterprise Frameworks resolves many of issues such as scalability, flexibility. Further, SOA based EAFs [12–15] provides loosely coupled and reusable frameworks. But, still many serious challenges exist which require complex engineering tasks. Existing SOA based enterprise architectures are lacking of emphasizing proper subject orientation, context sensitivity and re-configurability property of Enterprise Architecture. Thus, there exist several research questions like, (i) How to make the Enterprise Architecture Framework components re-configurable and adaptive to changes? (ii) How to achieve context sensitivity in Enterprise Architecture Framework? (iii) How to increase the usability of EAF for all major stakeholders?

To address the above issues, a new enterprise architectural framework, called SCORE framework has been proposed in this paper. This framework focuses on the context sensitivity, subject orientation concept, re-usable and re-configurable capability and flexibility of EAF. SCORE framework contains five layers such as Subject layer, Context Layer, Object layer, Role layer and Essence layer. *Subject layer* defines the interested business topics and related set of goals in enterprise information system. *Context* defines all type of valid and required information that is needed to characterize the situation and surroundings of an entity [16]. Entities may be person, business elements, data set or any kind of resources related to the Enterprise. Context also describes how the entities are related to each other. Thus, context of an entity gives more clear, accurate and useful information about the current situation (like its location, situatedness, interaction with the applications, dependencies on other entities) of an entity. Context of an entity frequently changes with the changing situation and surroundings of that entity, because new attributes are required to characterize the new situation of the entity. Adoption the concept of context makes EAF more expressive, more effective and more flexible. As result, EAF can be easily adaptable of changes in enterprise like, changing business requirements, changing market situation. Integration of service concepts in *object layer*, make SCORE architecture loosely coupled, platform independent, scalable and reconfigurable framework. These mechanisms help SCORE framework to deal with the changing environment of Enterprise. Subject and context orientation in SCORE framework will give privilege to stakeholders (defined by *Role*) to realize and describe business topics, related goals, activities and business entities more clearly and conveniently.

2 Related Work

Several non-SOA based EAFs are described in recent literatures like, Zachman Framework [2, 3], *TOGAF* Framework [4], *MODAF* [5], *FEAF* [6], *DODAF* [7], *TEAF* [8], *NAF* [9], 4+1 View Model of Architecture [10] and *GERAM* [11] Enterprise Architecture Framework. Zachman Framework, MODAF, DoDAF, TOGAF, NAF and FEAF support SOA implementation to some extent while, GERAM, TEAF and 4+1 view model do not support SOA implementation.

There are many approaches regarding the integration of SOA with the Zachman framework [12]. *Approach one*: Adding Service Column as the seventh Column. *Approach two*: SOA on Nine Square: In this approach, the logical position of SOA is at the intersection of "System Model" (Designer perspective) and "Function" column. However, SOA does not only consider the applications and functions of the system, rather it affects information sharing and the network interaction with applications. Therefore, SOA affects all the neighboring eight cells of Zachman Framework. Thus SOA is integrated in the first three columns (What, How, Where) and three perspectives (Owner, Designer, Builder). *Approach three*: This approach integrates SOA in the third (Network) column because SOA concentrates on the connection among all its elements. In this column, different stakeholders view SOA from different perspectives. SOA has been integrated in MODAF [13, 14], DoDAF [13, 14], TOGAF [13, 14], NAF [15] and FEAF [13, 14] frameworks. All the SOA based frameworks are suffering from lack of subject orientation, re-configurability and context sensitivity property. Therefore, a new architecture framework is required that will support re-configurability, reusability and context sensitivity property of EAF.

3 SCORE: The Proposed Architecture

Majority of existing frameworks suffer from several drawbacks such as, handling scalability, context sensitivity, re-configurability, reusability and agility. These deficiencies can be overcome in the proposed architecture named as SCORE architecture, which is a context sensitive, re-configurable, reusable and agile Enterprise Architectural Framework. It comprises of five layers namely, Subject Layer, Context Layer, Object Layer, Role Layer and Essence Layer. These layers are loosely coupled, so any lower level layer can be changed according to business requirements, without making any change in upper level layers. It also increases reusability- any other applications can use the functionalities exposed by the layers. In object layer, different relationships exist among three kinds of objects (structural element objects, activity objects and event objects). Similar goal can be achieved by different interaction paths existing among the objects. Reconfigurable services have been incorporated as a part of the activity objects. Thus, object layer is capable to handle any type of changes in internal and external business environment.

3.1   SCORE Architecture Layers and Components

Proposed SCORE architecture uses the top down approach. Here, business topic and corresponding related set of goals have been decided first. Depending on the goal, context, object, role and essence are to be determined. If any goal is changed according to the changing needs of organization, then context, object, role and essence are also to be changed. Five layers of SCORE architecture are shown in Fig. 1 and all notations, used in Fig. 1, are listed in Table 1.

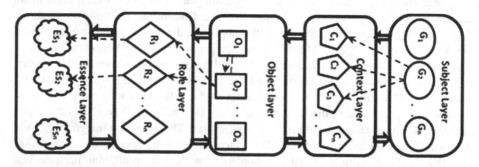

Fig. 1. SCORE architecture for enterprise architecture

Table 1. Summary of notations used in SCORE architecture

SCORE architecture Constructs	Notations	Interpretations
Business Topic	BT	Interested business subject of the enterprise.
Goal	G	Set of goals to be achieved in specific business topic
Sub goal	SG	A goal is comprised of a set of sub goals.
Context	C	Related information required to describe the background information of enterprise entities.
Object	O	Any type of structural entity, activity or event, related to the enterprise.
Activity Object	A	All kinds of activities, initiated by any entity or any event.
Structural Object	S	Any kind of data objects, actor object and interface objects.
Event Object	E	All types of events those results in an activity.
Role	R	Role separates whole object set into different regions.
Essence	Es	Ensure that set of quality metrics are being achieved during accessing of specific set of services

(a) Subject Layer: Subject Layer is the outermost layer that concerns about the business topics, related set of goals and sub goals hierarchies of the enterprise.

Management authority decides business topics depending on the area of interest. Business topics may have a set of Goals. Each goal again can be divided into several sub goals. This layer answers the questions like, what are the business topics and goals related to the specific enterprise. Why those particular business objectives are selected? What is the motivation behind it?

Formally, in Enterprise architecture, a Business topic (*BT*) can be expressed using a set of goals (*G*). Further each goal is comprised of a set of sub-goals (*SG*).

$$BT = \{BT_1, BT_2, BT_3, \ldots, BT_n\}$$

$$BT_i \rightarrow (G_{i1} \cup G_{i2} \cup \ldots \cup G_{ij})$$

Where, S_i is an interested Business Topic, G_{ij} is related goal of S_i

$$G_{ij} \rightarrow (SG_{ij1} \cup SG_{ij2} \cup SG_{ij3} \cup \ldots SG_{ijk}),$$

Where, SG_{ijk} is a sub goal of G_{ij}.

(b) Context Layer: This layer focuses on context that is any kind of related information about the entities to characterize the present situation and surroundings of entities related to the Enterprise. Context can be of two types, (i) primary context and (ii) secondary or auxiliary context. All contexts those are compulsory to describe the situation of a particular entity uniquely are referred as primary context. Secondary context is required to describe the particular entity in more detail. It adds extra information about the situation of entity.

Depending on what questions of the Subject layer, what contexts are to be taken are decided in this layer. So, this layer answers what context is needed to describe the situation and surroundings of a specific entity type? What kind of dependencies and relationships exist among all the entities?

Each goal (*G*) or sub-goal (*SG*) of Subject Layer is realized by certain set of contexts (*C*). So, Goal is any unordered combination of certain set of contexts. These can be expressed as,

$$G = C_1 \times C_2 \times \ldots \times C_n \text{ where } G \neq \Phi$$

Goal can also be expressed as the function of a set of contexts.

$$f(C_1, C_2, C_3, \ldots \ldots, C_n) = G$$

Primary context (*PC*) cannot be empty set. Existence of secondary context depends on the presence of primary context. Set of primary context (*PC*) and set of secondary context (*SC*) are disjoint sets. Formal description of the above discussion is as follows

$$PC = \{PC_1, PC_2, \ldots \ldots, PC_m\}, SC = \{SC_1, SC_2, \ldots \ldots, SC_r\},$$
$$PC \rightarrow SC, PC \neq \Phi, PC \cap SC = \Phi$$

(c) Object Layer: Object can be of three different categories like: (i) structural element objects *(SEO)* to represent the actors, any documents containing dataset and any interface, (ii) activity objects *(AO)* or functional object to represent functional unit and (iii) Event objects *(EO)* to denote events those initiates an activity. These three object types are dependent on each other. A structural element object *(SEO)* initiates an activity object *(AO)* as the result of occurrence of an event object *(EO)*. This can be formally described as, $EO \rightarrow AO$, $EO \rightarrow AO$. Activity objects or Functional objects are further divided in two groups like (i) Business Process Objects and (ii) Service Objects. If process (P) exists, then only services (S) exist. So, $P \rightarrow S$. In this layer, any functional unit or any business activity can be represented as services. Service is platform independent that is it does not bother about the underlying technology, enterprise environment. Implementation of service in this layer makes object reconfigurable, so that they can be easily changeable to support the internal and external changing environment of organization.

(d) Role Layer: This layer is all about the Role in the Enterprise. Role includes all the actors related to the enterprise like, owner, designer, planer, developer, customer, and database. Role makes separation of the entire object set depending on different activities. Same structural element object may play different roles depending on what kind of activities they performed. Different roles may collaborate among them. This layer contains who questions. Formal representation is as follows

$$R = \{R_1, R_2, \ldots, R_n\}$$

One role can be assigned for any combination of objects. So maximum value of R can be $R_{max} = [P(SEO \cup AO \cup EO) - \Phi]$.

(e) Essence Layer: This layer takes care of quality of service (QoS) and it describes how effectively enterprise services are integrated and composed based on stakeholders' requirements. An EAF is said to be of good quality if it satisfies the quality factors like understandability, completeness, conciseness, portability, consistency, maintainability, testability, usability, reliability and security. Quality factors help to check the efficiency of the proposed EAF on, (i) whether all defined GOALs of the enterprise are achieved; (ii) whether the proposed EAF is scalable and platform independent, (iii) whether the EAF works properly for a certain time period when there is no changes occurred in system, (iv) which structural element object *(SEO)* plays specific role by performing different activities, for a certain time period, (v) whether the services are available to the stakeholders in given time.

A structural element object *(SEO)* may perform different roles *(R)* by executing distinct set of services $\bar{S}'$, in different time periods. Essence is defined as whether quality metrics are being achieved during accessing of the set of services. Essence varies with time (t) and role(R), and it can be denoted by $Es(R, t)$.

Formal representation of above description of essence *(Es)* is as follows,

$$Es_{t2}^{t1} \rightarrow (R_i, \bar{S}')$$

Where, Es_{t2}^{t1} denotes Essence from time period from t_1 to t_2, R_i is a certain role and $\bar{S}' \subseteq S$, S is set of services.

$$\exists i \{ (R_i \rightarrow \bar{S}') \wedge \left(R_i \rightarrow Es_{t2}^{t1} \right) \}$$

The detail example of the Essence concept has been described in the case study and its diagram (Sect. 5).

3.2 Relationships in SCORE Architecture

In the above diagram, various intra-layer and inter-layer relationships exist among different constructs of five layers. Inter-layer relationships exist among different types of constructs from different layers and Intra-layer relationships exist among same type of constructs within the same layer. Realized By relationship can be both Inter-layer and Intra-layer relationship, while, containment, association and collaboration relation-ships are Intra-layer relationships. All notations, used to represent the relationships, are given in Table 2.

Table 2. Summary of notations of relationships used in SCORE architecture

SCORE architecture Relationships	Notations	Description
Containment/Inclusion	**<P,Or>**	Intra-layer relationship where, P denotes participation and O_r denotes order of occurrence.
Association	<0..*> <0..*>	Intra-layer relationship with cardinality
Realized By	--------→	Both Inter-layer and Intra-layer Relationship.
Collaboration	-------	Intra-layer relationship.
Data/Message flow	⟹	Inter-layer Relationship.

(a) *Containment / Inclusion Relationship:* It exists when one construct encapsulates other similar type of constructs. P is the participation pattern that is denoted by integer *1* for total participation and integer *0* for optional participation. Order *(Or)*, denoted by an integer, represents the sequence of occurrences of the relationships. Zero *(0)* denotes the sequence of that relationship is not important. Same order of two relationships represents simultaneous occurrences of those two relationships.

(b) *Association Relationship:* It depicts logical or physical connection between two similar types of constructs, by which those constructs can be aggregated to perform any task. Cardinality of this relationship shows number of occurrences in one constructs are connected with the number of occurrences in other type of constructs.

(c) *Realized By Relationship:* It describes how functionality of one type of construct can be realized by other type of constructs.

(d) *Collaboration Relationship:* It represents interactions between two roles.

(e) *Data/Message Flow:* It depicts direction of data or message flow between five layers of SCORE architecture (Fig. 2).

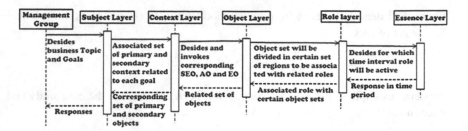

Fig. 2. Sequence Diagram for inter layer interaction in SCORE

4 Analysis of SCORE Architecture Using UML Notation

In this section, various inter-layer interactions among all five layers of SCORE architecture are represented and analyzed using UML notations. It demonstrates the behavioral aspects of SCORE framework. Management group interacts with subject layer. In subject layer, set of sub goals are introduced related to each goal. Primary and secondary contexts related to each goal are invoked in context layer. Then, corresponding structural, activity and event objects are to be decided and invoked in object layer. All the roles who handle related objects are invoked in role layer. Essence layer takes care of quality of services. It also describes for what time a specific role is to be active.

5 Illustration of SCORE Architecture Using a Case Study

To illustrate the proposed architecture, a case study has been performed on Care management system provided by Electronic Health Record (EHR) System. In this system, patients are benefited by the medical guideline and health care plan, after the consultation with specialist doctors. Figure 3 has been illustrated using this case study.

According to SCORE architecture, the Subject layer is all about the business topic and related set of Goal of the organization. Here, business topic (BT) is giving Clinical Care of patient. It comprises of certain set of goals like (i) Patient Registration and collection of patient case history (G_1) and (ii) Medication and Giving care plan and guidelines (G_2). Goal G_1 has set of sub goals like, (i) Collection of patient information and collection of previous documents and reports (SG_1) and (ii) Listing out all present problems (SG_2). Goal G_2 has sub goals like (i) proper diagnosis from all symptoms and medication (SG_3), (iii) giving care plan and guidelines (SG_4).

Second layer contains context. Patient entity possesses the following attributes as context like patient id (C_1), age (C_2), address (C_3), phone number (C_4), gender (C_5), weight (C_6), Blood Pressure (C_7) and Present Symptoms (C_8). Patient id (C_1) is primary context and all other contexts are secondary contexts. Any previous report has report id (C_9), type of report (blood report, X ray report, E.C.G Report, Other Report) (C_{10}). Prescribed Medicine has primary context, medicine name (C_{11}). Generated Health Report has context Report ID (C_{12}), Care plan and guideline also have an ID (C_{13}) as its primary context.

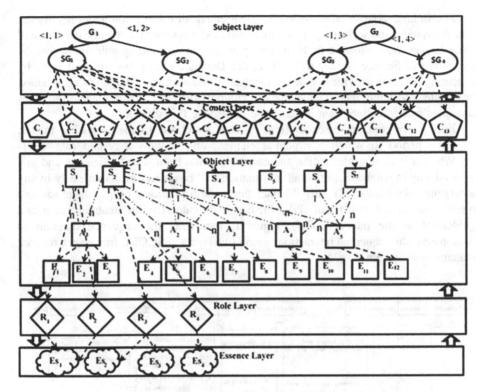

Fig. 3. Five Layers of SCORE in care management system

Third layer contains objects. Here, one type of structural objects is all actors like patients (S_1) and the database (S_2) where all patient records are stored. Data objects are all information about a patient (S_3) that will be stored in database, previous reports (S_4) and generated health report (S_5) and guidelines and care plan (S_6). Interface object is the object where output of any activity object will be reflected. Here electronic gazettes, used for producing output (S_7) are used as interface objects. Here, activity objects are activities and functional units like, patient registration (A_1), taking patient information and case history and storing all information in database (A_2), diagnosis of diseases (A_3), prescribing proper medicine (A_4) and providing treatment plan and guidelines (A_5). All events those are required to perform a specific action are also shown in the following diagram. Activity Object A_1 will be performed with help of a set of events like, logging in to the system (E_1), entering patient details (E_2) and pressing save/submit button (E_3). A_2 activity can be realized of certain set of events like; entering patient case history (E_4), Uploading previous reports (E_5) and clicking of save button (E_6). A_3 activity can be realized by following set of events like, considering all symptoms and performing analysis (E_7) and producing result on screen (E_8). A_4 comprises of events like, searching for effective medicine for that particular diagnosis (E_9) and generating health report containing those medicines (E_{10}). A_5 will be accomplished by realization of events like generating care plan (E_{11}) and displaying the plan on output interface (E_{12}).

Fourth layer contains role. When a patient enters all information about his disease into the system, and seeks proper diagnosis and medicines for him, then he plays role of Drug Seeker (*R1*), when he finds for care plan and corresponding guidelines, then he plays role of Service Seeker (*R2*). Here, the Database (*S2*) plays different roles by executing different activities. When, a database provides proper diagnosis information and related medicines then it plays role of Drug provider (*R3*). When, database supplies care plan and guidelines then it plays role of Service Provider (*R4*).

Fifth layer contains essence. Here essence is related to the following matter: (i) Time period in which a structural element object plays a certain role. (*Es1*) (ii) Whether Patient's information and case history has been stored efficiently and in a secured way in database, so that all information will be always available easily in any emergency situation (*Es2*). (iii) Whether this system provides, proper diagnosis and medication service (*Es3*) and (iv) Whether it provides fruitful treatment plan and guidelines to the patients (*Es4*). Figure 4, represents the sequence diagram to demonstrate the sequential interaction among five layers of SCORE framework for care management System (Fig. 5).

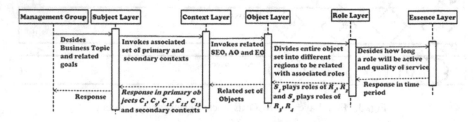

Fig. 4. Sequence diagram for care management system

	What/Data	How/Function	Where/Network	Who/People	When/Time	Why/Motivation
Planner's View	List of things important to the business	List of processes that the business perform	List of locations in which the business operates	List of organizations important to the business	List of events/cycles important to the business	List of business goals/strategies
Owner View	e.g. Semantic model	e.g. Business Process Model	e.g. Logistics Network	e.g. Work Flow Model	e.g. Master Schedule	e.g. Business Plan
Designer's View	e.g. Logical data Model	e.g. Application Architecture	e.g. Distributed System architecture	e.g. Human Interface Architecture	e.g. Processing Structure	e.g. Business Rule Model
Builder's View	e.g. Physical data Model	e.g. System Design	e.g. Technical Architecture	e.g. Presentation Architecture	e.g. Control Structure	e.g. Rule Design
Integrator's View	e.g. data Definition	e.g. Program	e.g. Network Architecture	e.g. Security Architecture	e.g. Timing definition	e.g. Rule Specification
User's View	Data Implementation	Function Implementation	Network Implementation	Organization Implementation	Schedule Implementation	Strategy Implementation

Subject Layer — Context Layer — Object Layer — Role Layer — Essence Layer

Fig. 5. Mapping of different columns of Zachman framework to SCORE architecture

6 SCORE Framework in the Context of Zachman Framework

The proposed SCORE framework for enterprise architecture is comprised of five loosely coupled layers in contrary to the Zachman framework, which is represented in matrix form. Five layers of SCORE are Subject layer, Context layer, Object layer, Role layer and Essence layer. Subject Layer of SCORE deals with the Business Objective and corresponding set of goals and sub goals hierarchies and it realize the concepts of "Why/Motivation" facets (sixth column) in Zachman framework. However, subject layer of proposed framework is comparatively better capable to provide more detail representation of business objectives. Context Layer of SCORE comprises of all constructs of "Where/Network" column (first Column) and "When/Time" col umn (fifth column) of Zachman framework. In addition, context layer of SCORE includes the facets and related concepts corresponding to the background information related to situatedness and location of different enterprise entities. Third layer in SCORE enterprise architecture, namely object layer, deals with various structural, activity and event objects of an enterprise. Structural objects including various data set, devices can realize the concepts of "What/Data" column in Zachman framework. On the other hand, activity objects along with functional units realize the facets of "How/Function" column in Zachman framework. However, Zachman framework does not give the concept related to events and reconfigurable services in compare to the SCORE architecture. Fourth layer of SCORE containing the concept of roles that can be mapped to "Who/People" (fourth column) concept of Zachman framework. Further, Zachman framework has not considered can artifacts related to the quality requirements including essential non-functional characteristics of enterprise system architecture. However, SCORE has considered such concepts in fifth layer, called Essence Layer. Thus, SCORE provides more broader views and benefits than Zachman framework. Besides, the proposed SCORE framework comprised of different types of relationships (both intra-layer and inter-layer) to exhibit the associativity among the concepts and constructs of enterprise architecture distributed over different layers. Moreover, layered architecture with loosely coupled layers makes SCORE framework more flexible and scalable, as reconfiguration of any components of lower-level layers will hardly affect the upper level layers.

7 Conclusion and Future Work

This paper proposes a new enterprise architecture framework, called, SCORE architecture, which is comprised of five loosely coupled layers namely, subject layer, context layer, object layer, role layer and essence layer. Subject layer considers about Business topic, related goal and sub goals hierarchies and motivation of an enterprise. Context layer provides related knowledge about surrounding environment, location, situatedness and time of business entities. Object layer handles various types of objects like, structural element objects, activity objects and event objects of enterprise. The benefits of SOA features are considered inherent of object layer. Role layer contains all type of roles those will be played by different types of structural elements depending upon what kind of activities they performed. Essence layer concentrates on the quality metrics and security metrics of systems. The proposed framework supports several crucial properties like, subject orientation, re-usability, context sensitivity, re-configurability and agility. The SCORE architecture includes the notion of quality of services and nonfunctional properties of EAFs. Proposed EAF is comprised of different relationships those show the interaction and association among various constructs of different layer. The flow of enterprise information through the layers of SCORE architecture is analyzed in using UML notations. A detailed illustration also has been discussed using the case study based on Clinical Care management.

A comparative study also has been performed between the proposed SCORE framework and Zachman framework. It shows that SCORE framework includes several advantages over the Zachman framework in terms of representation of business topics and related goals, enhancement of the facets of "Where" and "When" concepts of Zachman. Further, the proposed EAF provides relevant knowledge about the situatedness and location of business entities. Object layer of SCORE framework integrates SOA properties and notion of event objects makes the framework loosely coupled and adaptive towards business changes. In contrary to the existing SOA-based EAFs, SCORE framework facilitates Subject orientation, Context Sensitivity and Essence features. Moreover, layered architecture of SCORE framework makes it more flexible and scalable in comparison with existing EAFs proposals.

Future work will concentrates on the extension of the proposed SCORE architecture with the detailed formal representation of business subjects, their goals and information flow and interaction mechanism within the different layers. Enhancement of the reconfigurable capability in different layers of SCORE architecture is also a prime objective as future research.

References

1. Zachman, J.A.: A framework for information systems architecture. IBM systems J. **26**(3), 276–292 (1987)
2. Armour, F.J., Kaisler, S.H., Liu, S.Y.: A big-picture look at enterprise architectures. IT Prof. **1**(1), 35–42 (1999)
3. Radwan, A., Aarabi, M.: Study of implementing Zachman framework for modeling information systems for manufacturing enterprises aggregate planning. In: International Conference on Industrial Engineering and Operations Management, Kuala Lumpur, Malaysia, pp. 9–14 (2011)
4. Edward, I.Y.M., Shalannanda, W., Lestariningati, S.I., Agusdian, A.: E-Government Master plan design with TOGAF framework. In: 8th International Conference on Telecommunication Systems Services and Applications (TSSA), pp. 1–6. IEEE, Kuta (2014)
5. Bailey, I.: Brief Introduction to MODAF with v1.2 Updates. In: IET Seminar on Enterprise Architecture Frameworks, pp. 1–18. IET, London (2008)
6. Wang, W., Gao, C.H., Lin, S.F., Yin, G.F.: Modeling technologies of FEA grid services and grid information management structure for FEA grid portal. In: WRI World Congress on Software Engineering (WCSE 2009), pp. 108–113. IEEE, Xiamen (2009)

7. The DoDAF Architecture Framework Version 2.02. http://dodcio.defense.gov/Portals/0/Documents/DODAF/DoDAF_v2-02_web.pdf
8. Treasury Enterprise Architecture Framework. https://www.scribd.com/document/63363136/Treasury-Enterprise-Architecture-Framework-TEAF
9. Ota, D., Gerz, M.: Benefits and challenges of architecture frameworks. In: Sixteenth International Command and Control Research and Technology Symposium (16TH ICCRTS), Qu'ebec City, Qu'ebec Canada (2011)
10. Kruchten, P.B.: The 4+1 view model of architecture. IEEE Softw. **12**(6), 42–50 (1995)
11. Bernus, P., Noran, O., Molina, A.: Enterprise architecture: twenty years of the GERAM framework. Ann. Rev. Control **39**(2015), 83–93 (2015)
12. Alwadain, A., Korthaus, A., Fielt, E., Rosemann, M.: Integrating SOA into an enterprise architecture- a comparative analysis of alternative approaches. In: 5th IFIP International Conference on Research and Practical Issues of Enterprise Information Systems (CONFENIS), Natal, Brazil (2010)
13. Alwadain, A., Fielt, E., Korthaus, A., Rosenmann, M.: Where do we find services in enterprise architectures? a comparative approach. In: 22nd Australasian Conference on Information Systems (ACIS 2011), Sydney, Australia (2011)
14. Jamjoom, M.M., Alghamdi, A.S., Ahmed, I.: Service oriented architecture support in various architecture frameworks: a brief review. In: Ao, S.I., Douglas, C., Grundfest, W.S., Burgstone, J. (eds.) Proceedings of the World Congress on Engineering and Computer Science, vol. 2, pp. 1338–1343. Newswood Limited, San Francisco, USA (2012)
15. Wang, L., Luo, A.M.: Service view description of a service oriented C4ISR architecture framework. In: IITA International Conference on Services Science, Management and Engineering (SSME 2009), pp. 237–241. IEEE, Zhangjiajie (2009)
16. Abowd, Gregory D., Dey, Anind K., Brown, Peter J., Davies, Nigel, Smith, Mark, Steggles, Pete: Towards a Better Understanding of Context and Context-Awareness. In: Gellersen, Hans-W. (ed.) HUC 1999. LNCS, vol. 1707, pp. 304–307. Springer, Heidelberg (1999). doi:10.1007/3-540-48157-5_29

Localization based Anti-Void Clustering Approach (LAVCA) for Energy Efficient Routing in Wireless Sensor Network

Ayan Kumar Das[1]([✉]) and Rituparna Chaki[2]

[1] Birla Institute of Technology, Mesra, Patna Campus, Patna, India
das.ayan777@gmail.com
[2] University of Calcutta, Calcutta, India
rituchaki@gmail.com

Abstract. Energy efficient routing is the main challenge of the researchers in the field of wireless sensor network for a long decade. Resource constrained sensor nodes demand energy consumption as less as possible. Energy efficiency can be achieved by localization and clustering technique. Localization is used to find out the location of sensor nodes without the help of GPS and avoids broadcasting of too many messages to save energy. Event based clustering approach can reduce data redundancy in order to avoid wastage of energy. The proposed approach LAVCA has used both of the techniques in order to diminish energy consumption and increase network lifetime up to a great extent. Packet loss has also been reduced by involving an anti-void approach, called rolling ball technique. Simulation results show that the energy efficiency has been enhanced with compare to CASER, EEHC and DEEC.

Keywords: DVHop · Rolling ball · Anti-void · WSN · Localization

1 Introduction

A wireless sensor network (WSN) is a wireless network consists of interconnected set of sensor nodes. Each sensor node consists of a trans-receiver, battery, a memory of small size and a low capacity processor. The low cost sensor nodes and easy deployment techniques of sensor networks have led to the use of wireless sensor network in various applications like military activities, health care, disaster management, traffic analysis and many more. In such remote monitoring system, a large number of sensor nodes are randomly deployed within the remote places. This results in more than one node sensing the same event. All these nodes try to send redundant data to the server using multiple paths leading to a huge amount of energy drainage. Energy preservation is the high requirement of mobile nodes in this system. Thus it is obvious that the flat routing schemes have the tendency to have excessive data redundancy and hence leads to poor network lifetime. Hierarchical cluster based approach is taken into consideration to enhance the network performance and save battery power of sensor nodes. In a cluster, node whose priority is higher than other nodes in the network is called dominating node or cluster head. The responsibility of a cluster head is to gather the data from other member nodes of the cluster, reduce the redundant data and send the aggregated data to the sink node. Locations of the nodes need to be calculated in order to make the cluster. Global Positioning System (GPS) can be used to find the position of the nodes. The high deployment cost of GPS and high consumption of energy to find the location have forced the researchers to design other localization algorithms. DVHop [24] is an example of such a localization algorithm. This can be used to find location of the sensor nodes and thus create the clusters according to those locations. Cluster head has to forward the aggregated data to the sink node to inform about some specific event. Greedy forwarding [12] is a technique by which aggregated data can be forwarded from cluster head to sink node.

In greedy forwarding technique, the next hop will be selected by a locally optimal greedy choice of the forwarding cluster head. The locally optimal choice means the neighbour node, which is geographically closest to the packet destination will be the next hop node. Figure 1 describes an example of greedy next hop choice.

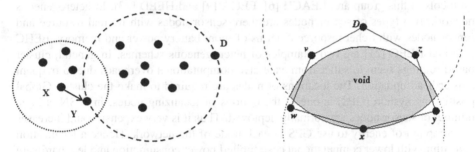

Fig. 1. Greedy forwarding example   **Fig. 2.** Void problem

In Fig. 1, node X and node D are cluster head and sink node respectively. Let it consider that the distance between Y and D is least among the neighbors of X. Thus the packet is forwarded from X to Y and the process repeats until it reaches to D.

In Fig. 2, we observe the problems arising due to greedy forwarding algorithm. It is obvious, that node x is closer to D than its two neighbors w and y. Hence x will not be able to choose any of the paths (x→y→z→D) or (x→w→v→D) and unable to send the packet directly to D as it is out of the radio range of x. No neighbors are there in the intersection area of x's circular radio range and the circle about D of radius |xD|. This shaded region (in Fig. 2) can be termed as void and the problem of packet drop from node x is known as void problem.

In this paper the proposed Localization based Anti-Void Clustering Approach (LAVCA) for Energy Efficient Routing in WSN has used DVHop technique to find the location of the nodes, minimize the error of that calculated location, form cluster with the help of those calculated locations. The entire process saves a lot of energy consumption. The data is being sent to the sink node by using greedy forwarding technique. The void problem is being reduced by using rolling ball technique to reduce the data loss and increase the delivery rate.

The rest of the paper is organized as follows: Sect. 2 describes some of the related works, Sect. 3 includes the proposed methodology, Sect. 4 shows the simulation result, Sect. 5 is the concluding part and references are included in Section (References).

2 Related Work

WSNs have been deployed in remote areas for many of the applications. In remote areas recharge of battery is almost impossible and thus energy saving is the major concern for the researchers in this field. The other issues related to WSN are—security [3, 18], sensor localization [4], network lifetime [5], and sink mobility [7].

The grouping of nodes is very important to reduce data redundancy and thus to avoid wastage of energy. Hierarchical or cluster-based routing [8, 10, 14, 15] are well-known techniques to group the nodes into multiple clusters. Based on the nature of sensors constituting the network, hierarchical clustering may be homogenous or heterogeneous. The homogeneous network is consists of same type of sensor nodes. Some of routing protocols in this group are: LEACH [6], EECA [9] and HEED [23]. In heterogeneous network, two types of sensor nodes are there-sensor nodes with normal resource and sensor nodes with richer resource in terms of more battery power and memory. EEHC [13] and DEEC [21] are two examples of heterogeneous schemes. In general, cluster based routings seem to suffer from excessive computational overheads due to frequent cluster head updation. The locations of nodes are required to make the cluster. Global positioning system (GPS) is one of the options of localizing nodes. In WSN, a huge number of sensor nodes are normally deployed. Thus it is very expensive and increases consumption of energy to use GPS in each node of the network. Hence a localization algorithm with lower computational cost, limited power consumption and less hardware requirement is a challenging task for WSN [16]. Two types of localization algorithms have been proposed–range based and range free algorithms.

Range based algorithms [11] have used the distance estimation information for the purpose of localization. The accuracy of localization is higher in these algorithms. The deployment cost is increased for the use of additional hardware in order to measure the distance for large scale networks. However, the orientation information or distance between nodes is not required in range free algorithms. Many range free algorithms like Centroid, Amorphous, Approximate Point-In Triangle test, distance vector hop (DV-Hop) [24], have been designed for cost effectiveness and simplicity. The good coverage quality and feasibility makes DV-Hop most popular among other mentioned algorithms.

Once the locations of the nodes are calculated and clusters are being formed, the aggregated data should be sent to the sink node. Greedy forwarding (GF) algorithm [12] is one of the well known algorithms to send the data from cluster head to sink node. This algorithm states that the forwarding node will forward the packet via one hop neighbor [2]. The process will be repeated until the destination is reached. This technique does not incur additional overhead cost and is proven as efficient to reduce energy consumption. In this approach local minima or void problem [12] may arise. The void problem refers to the situation where one node will not be able to forward the data packet to the next hop as no other node exists that has shorter distance to destination node than itself. This problem may create black hole within the network and cause packet drops and huge amount of energy drainage.

Routing algorithms designed to resolve the void problem are categorized in two groups- non graph based scheme [17] and graph based scheme [12, 19, 22]. The authors of [20] introduces BOUNDHOLE algorithm to detect the holes and find an alternative route to the destination. This algorithm is used to separate the boundary of the holes and routes the packets according to greedy forwarding method [12]. The major problem of this algorithm is the false boundary detection, which increases the probability of falling into a loop. This may take a longer routing delay and wastage of great amount of energy causing degradation of the performance. The false boundary detection problem of BOUNDHOLE approach has been reduced by the author of Greedy anti-void routing (GAR) [12] protocol. It introduces a rolling ball method. The rolling ball is hinged at the node affected by the void problem and rotates anti-clock wise with R/2 radius. The node that is closer to the destination node and intersects with the rolling ball first, will be the next hop node. The process repeats until the data packet reaches to the destination node. GAR performs better than BOUNDHOLE, still due to the visit of unnecessary nodes, GAR causes higher energy consumption.

It is clear from the state of the art study that many algorithms have been designed to implement energy efficient routing protocol with the help of cluster based approach. In WSN, the dense deployment of sensor nodes increases data redundancy, which causes a great amount of energy wastage. Thus grouping of the nodes of a particular region into a cluster, send all the sensed data through the cluster head to the sink node is better option for energy efficiency. The positions of the nodes are required to know in order to make the cluster. Though, GPS can help to find the position, it is economically difficult to attach a GPS with all the sensor nodes. The GPS based positioning system is also infeasible in remote places with coverage problem. Thus some localization technique is required to know the positions of the sensor nodes. The novelty of this paper is, the location of the nodes have been calculated in order to make the cluster without using GPS, thus reducing the deployment as well as overhead cost. Instead of making cluster throughout the network, use of event based clustering helps to save from a great amount of energy wastage.

3 Proposed Work

The proposed approach has used DVHop based localization technique [24] to know the positions of the sensor nodes, followed by creation of cluster with the help of those positions and choose the cluster head. Greedy forwarding method is used to forward the aggregated data to the sink node. Rolling ball technique is used to avoid Anti-void problem. The module wise description is given in the following sub sections.

3.1 Location Discovery of Individual Nodes

The deployment of sensor nodes should be done in such a way that a fewer number of nodes will have the Global Positioning System (GPS) and the rest of the nodes do not have that system. The nodes enabled with GPS are aware of their location and are called anchor nodes. The nodes without a GPS system use DVHop [24] technique to find their location with the help of anchor nodes. It is economically difficult to attach

GPS system in all the sensor nodes. The broadcasting of position information from all the nodes also leads to a great amount of energy depletion. Thus to minimize energy consumption during location discovery, the DVHop technique is used for most of the nodes. The proposed logic involves three steps to calculate the location of a node.

In the first step, as in DVHop location information of hop count and anchor nodes are broadcasted by the beacon packets. Each node maintains a table (xi, y_i, hop_i) for every anchor node located in the position (x_i, y_i) and the minimum number of hops from that i^{th} anchor node is hop_i. In case of multiple received packets, the least hop count value to a particular anchor node will be settled as the hop count value of the table. This mechanism helps to all the nodes in the network to obtain minimum hop count value from every anchor node.

In the second step, average size for one hop ($E_{HopSize_i}$) is calculated for an anchor node, with respect to other anchor nodes as in Eq. (1).

$$E_{HopSize_i} = \left(\sum_{i \neq j} \sqrt{(x_i - x_j)^2 + (y_i - y_j)^2} \right) / \left(\sum_{i \neq j} h_{min_{ij}} \right) \qquad (1)$$

Where, (x_i, y_i) and (x_j, y_j) are the coordinates of anchor node i and j, h_{ij} is the minimum number of hops between nodes i and j. Once hop size is calculated, anchor nodes broadcast its hop size in the network by the use of flooding. The unknown node 'u' (the location information of which is unknown) saves the first arrived message (hop-size) after receiving the hop-size information and then transmits to neighbors. In this way, most nodes receive hop size of the nearest anchor node. The distance ($dist_{ua}$) between an unknown node 'u' and anchor node 'a' is calculated as in Eq. (2).

$$dist_{ua} = E_{HopSize_i} \times hop_{ua} \qquad (2)$$

Where, $HopSize_i$ is the hopsize between the unknown node 'u' and its nearest anchor node i, hop_{ua} is the minimum number of hops between anchor node 'a' and unknown node 'u'.

In the final step, polygon method is used to estimate the location of unknown nodes. Let us assume that, (x, y) is the location of unknown node u, (x_i, y_i) is the location of ith anchor node, and d_i is the distance between the unknown node u and anchor node i. Therefore, distance of unknown node u from n number of anchor nodes is given by Eq. (3).

$$\begin{cases} (x - x_1)^2 + (y - y_1)^2 = d_1^2 \\ (x - x_2)^2 + (y - y_2)^2 = d_2^2 \\ \quad \cdot \\ \quad \cdot \\ \quad \cdot \\ (x - x_n)^2 + (y - y_n)^2 = d_n^2 \end{cases} \qquad (3)$$

Subtraction of first equation from the last will generate the following equation-

$$\left\{ (x - x_1)^2 - (x - x_n)^2 \right\} - \left\{ (y - y_1)^2 - (y - y_n)^2 \right\} = d_1^2 - d_n^2 \qquad (4)$$

Equation 4 can be simplified as follows-

$$2x(x_1 - x_n) + 2y(y_1 - y_n) = x_1^2 + y_1^2 - x_n^2 - y_n^2 + d_n^2 - d_1^2 \tag{5}$$

Equation 5 can be represented in matrix form as in Eq. 6.

$$AX = B \tag{6}$$

Where, A, X and B are given as:

$$A = \begin{bmatrix} 2(x_1 - x_n) & 2(y_1 - y_n) \\ 2(x_2 - x_n) & 2(y_2 - y_n) \\ \vdots & \vdots \\ 2(x_{n-1} - x_n) & 2(y_{n-1} - y_n) \end{bmatrix} \quad B = \begin{bmatrix} x_1^2 + y_1^2 - x_n^2 - y_n^2 + d_n^2 - d_1^2 \\ x_2^2 + y_2^2 - x_n^2 - y_n^2 + d_n^2 - d_1^2 \\ \vdots \\ x_{n-1}^2 + y_{n-1}^2 - x_n^2 - y_n^2 + d_n^2 - d_{n-1}^2 \end{bmatrix}$$

and, $X = \begin{bmatrix} x \\ y \end{bmatrix}$.

Thus, Location of unknown node u can be calculated by using the lst square method as in Eq. 7.

$$X = (A'A)^{-1}A'B. \tag{7}$$

where, A'. represents the transpose of matrix A.

3.2   Cluster Formation and Cluster Head Selection

All the nodes calculate their locations by the technique discussed in the previous section. The locations are used to form the cluster and select the cluster head. In this protocol, the nodes will not be involved in cluster formation process in order to save energy. Only the nodes involved in sensing an event are used to form the cluster. These nodes are known as active nodes. All the active nodes send their location to other active nodes. Let the locations of the active nodes are (x_i, y_i), where $i = 1, 2,..., n$. The location of the centroid (x_c, y_c) of these active nodes can be calculated as—

$$x_c = \frac{\sum_{i=1}^{n} x_i}{n} \tag{8}$$

$$y_c = \frac{\sum_{i=1}^{n} y_i}{n} \tag{9}$$

The cluster is formed as a circle, the radius of which is the distance between the centroid (x_c, y_c) and the farthest active node as this circle includes all the active nodes. The cluster head should the node, the location of which is nearer to the centroid and the remaining energy is higher than other members of the cluster. In this regard every member node calculates their competition bid value (CV) to compete as a candidate for cluster head selection process as in Eq. (9).

$$CV = k \times \frac{E_{Ri}}{d_{ci}}, \forall i = 1, 2, \ldots, n \qquad (10)$$

Where, n number of member nodes are there in the cluster, E_{Ri} is the remaining energy of the ith node and d_{ci} is the distance of node i from the centroid. Each node sends their CV value to other member nodes of the cluster. The node with highest CV value declares itself as a cluster head.

3.3   Greedy Forwarding of Aggregated Data to the Sink Node

Here we are trying to forward the aggregated data to the sink node, reducing the void problem in an energy efficient way. This is achieved by using greedy forwarding technique. In this forwarding technique the network is represented by a set of sensor nodes $N = \{N_i \mid \forall i\}$. The locations pertaining to nodes of set N can be represented by the set $P = \{P_{Ni} \mid P_{Ni} = (x_{Ni}, y_{Ni}), \forall i\}$. $D = \{D(P_{Ni}, R) \mid \forall i\}$ is the set of closed disks defining the transmission ranges of N, where $D(P_{Ni}, R) = \{x \mid \|x\text{-}P_{Ni}\| \leq R, \forall x \in R^2\}$. The center of the closed disk is $P_{Ni}$and R represents the radius of the transmission range for each node N_i. Hence the network model can be represented by a unit disk graph

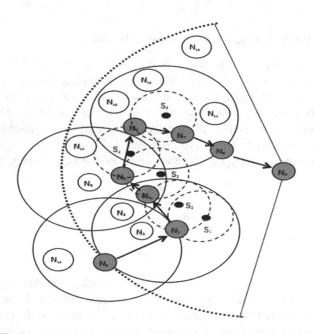

Fig. 3. Construction of routing path with resolving void problem

(UDG) as G(P, E), where the edge set $E = \{E_{ij} \mid E_{ij} = (P_{Ni}, P_{Nj}), P_{Ni} \in D(P_{Nj}, R), \forall i \neq j\}$. The neighbor table for each N_i is defined as–

$$T_{Ni} = \{[ID_{Nk}, P_{Nk}] \mid P_{Nk} \in D(P_{Ni}, R), \forall k \neq i\}$$

where, ID_{Nk} is the designated identification number for the node N_k. In greedy forwarding algorithm it is assumed that the source node N_S is aware of the location of the destination node N_D. The next hop is selected to forward the data packet from T_{NS}. Two conditions have to be satisfied for the next hop selection as- (1) which has the shortest distance from the destination node N_D among the nodes in T_{NS}, and (2) is located closer to N_D, compared to the distance from N_S and N_D. The process continued until the destination is reached. In this technique void problem may arise when a forwarding node will not have any suitable neighbor to forward the data packet. Then all the incoming packets will be dropped at that node.

The proposed LAVCA protocol is designed in such a way that void problem can be resolved. The rolling ball concept is used to perform the task. The technique is depicted in Fig. 3, where, the source node N_S wants to send the packet to destination node N_D. N_S chooses the next hop node to N_1 as per greedy forwarding algorithm. The void problem occurs at node N_1. To solve the problem a circle is formed, the center point of which is S_1 and the radius is R/2 where the transmission range is R. The circle is hinged at N_1 and starts anti clockwise rolling until a node has been encountered by the boundary of the circle (N_4 in the example of Fig. 3). Thus the data packet is moved from N_1 to N_4, where a new circle will be formed of equal size, which is centered at s_2 and hinged at node N_4. The counterclockwise rolling procedure finds node N_5 as next hop node. The process repeats until the node N_7 is reached, which is considered to have a smaller distance to the destination node N_D than that of N_1 to N_D. At node N_7, the conventional greedy forwarding scheme is resumed. Thus the resulting path becomes N_S, N_1, N_4, N_5, N_6, N_7, N_8, and N_D. The algorithm of this forwarding technique is as follows—

Function forward_to_ SinkNode
Begin
1. Read the location of N_S and N_D.
2. N_S initiates transmission using greedy forwarding algorithm.
3. If $d(N_j, N_D) < d(N_i, N_D)$ then execute step 3.
4.   Set N_j as the next hop.
5.   If node is in void location then
6.   Call the function Rolling_Ball
7.   Else
8.   Perform the greedy forwarding algorithm
9.   End If
10. End If
End

Function Rolling_Ball
Begin
1.   Read location of N_{local} and radius R.
2.   If $d(N_{local}, N_D) < (N_i, N_D)$ then
3.   Assign a rolling ball RB_{Ni} $(S_i, R/2)$ at the center of N_{local}
4.   Rotate the ball in anti-clock wise direction
5.   If a ball hits any node then
6.   The node is assigned as the new hop N_i
7. N_{local} will pass the packet to N_i
8.   End If
9.   Else
10.   Route the packets using greedy forwarding algorithm
11.   End If
End

4   Simulation Result

The performance of LAVCA protocol is simulated by the tool NS2. The performance of LAVCA is compared with CASER [1], EEHC [13] and DEEC [21]. The simulation parameters are mentioned in Table 1.

Table 1. List of parameters

Parameters	Description
Network size	100 nodes
Initial energy	50 J per node
Sensor node	Imote2
Radio frequency	13 MHz
Number of rounds	At least 20

The process of data collection from member nodes of a cluster by the cluster head, aggregate and encrypt that and forward that to the sink node is known as a round. The nodes with energy value which is below a threshold value, is known as dead node. The number of dead nodes is obtained after completion of each round. Figure 4 traces the rate of increase in the number of dead nodes for six rounds. The existing routing logics CASER, EEHC, and DEEC are also simulated to obtain the number of dead nodes. CASER uses a grid based routing protocol where the next adjacent grid will be selected based on probability value. This probability value is calculated based on average residual energy of the grid. DEEC uses a probability value based on the ratio of residual energy of a node to that of the total network for selection of a node as cluster head. It also predicts that equal amount of energy will be lost at each round. The algorithm EEHC has also considered the residual energy of each node as the only parameter for selecting the cluster head. Proposed protocol LAVCA makes the cluster in circle form and chooses the cluster head nearer by the centroid position of that cluster. Additionally the remaining energies of the member nodes, which are nearby to centroid position are also considered. Thus the selected cluster head will be having more residual energy and also located in a well-connected position. LAVCA finds the location of the node by DVHop method instead of get it from GPS system. Thus it decreases the depletion of energy at the time of cluster formation. Hence the graph of Fig. 4 shows better result in case of LAVCA, as more nodes die in CASER, EEHC, and DEECover the same number of rounds.

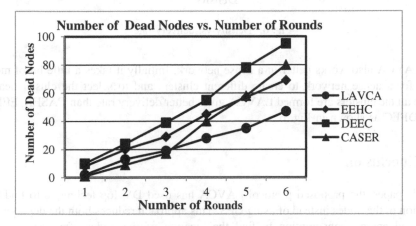

Fig. 4. Number of dead nodes vs. number of rounds

The number of packets successfully delivered to the base station is known as throughput. As the load increases with time, the throughput is also increasing. The network will be congested after a certain amount of time, which leads to decrease the throughput. Figure 5 shows that LAVCA is controlling the congestion more efficiently and the decrease in throughput is less than the algorithms CASER, EEHC, and DEEC.

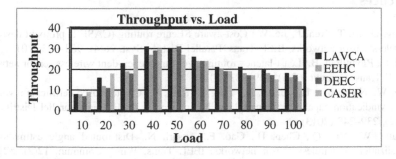

Fig. 5. Throughput vs. load

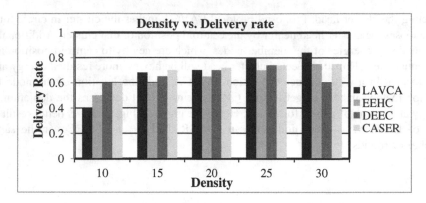

Fig. 6. Density vs. delivery rate

LAVCA also works better in a dense network. Initially it takes a little bit of more time for a dense network to create different clusters and to select the cluster heads. Once all the clusters are formed LAVCA gives better delivery rate than CASER, EEHC and DEEC as shown in Fig. 6.

5   Conclusion

In this paper, the proposed protocol LAVCA has used DVHop technique to find the location of the nodes instead of using GPS. This approach reduces both the deployment cost and energy consumption to find the location of the nodes after deployment. In LAVCA, event based cluster formation reduces data redundancy and improves the performance in terms of energy efficiency. Greedy forwarding technique is used to forward the aggregated data from cluster head to sink node. Void problem is minimized by using rolling ball technique to increase the delivery rate. The simulation results show that LAVCA performs better in terms of number of dead nodes, throughput and delivery rate with compare to CASER, EEHC and DEEC.

References

1. Tang, D., Li, T., Ren, J., Jie, W.: Cost-aware SEcure routing (CASER) protocol design for wireless sensor networks. IEEE Trans. Parallel Distrib. Syst. **26**(4), 960–973 (2015)
2. Lai, S., Ravindran, B.: Least-latency routing over time-depen-dent wireless sensor networks. IEEE Trans. Comput. **62**(5), 969–983 (2013)
3. Liu, W., Nishiyama, H., Ansari, N., Yang, J., Kato, N.: Cluster-based certificate revocation with vindication capability for mobile ad hoc networks. IEEE Trans. Parallel Distrib. Syst. **24**(2), 239–249 (2013)
4. Zhang, W., Yin, Q., Chen, H., Gao, F., Ansari, N.: Distributed angle estimation for localization in wireless sensor networks. IEEE Trans. Wirel. Commun. **12**(2), 527–537 (2013)

5. Abdulla, A., Nishiyama, H., Yang, J., Ansari, N., Kato, N.: HYMN: a novel hybrid multi-hop routing algorithm to improve the longevity of WSNs. IEEE Trans. Wirel. Commun. 11(7), 2531–2541 (2012)
6. Geetha, V.A, Kallapurb, P.V., Tellajeerac, S.: Clustering in wireless sensor networks: performance comparison of LEACH & LEACH-C protocols using NS2. In: Proceedings of 2nd International Conference on Computer Communication, Control and Information Technology (C3IT-2012), vol. 4, pp. 163–170. Elsevier (2012)
7. Nakayama, H., Fadlullah, Z., Ansari, N., Kato, N.: A novel scheme for WSAN sink mobility based on clustering and set packing techniques. IEEE Trans. Autom. Control 56(10), 2381–2389 (2011)
8. Venu Madhav, T., Sarma, N.V.S.N.: Maximizing network lifetime through varying transmission radii with energy efficient cluster routing algorithm in wireless sensor networks. In: Proceedings of International Conference on Network Communication and Computer (ICNCC 2011), pp. 576–580 (2011)
9. Chao, S., Wang, R.-C., Huang, H.-P., Sun, L.-J.: Energy efficient clustering algorithm for data aggregation in WSN. J. China Univ. Posts Telecommun. 17, 104–109 (2010). Elsevier
10. Sara, G.S., Kalaiarasi, R., Neelavathy Pari, S., Sridharan, D.: Energy efficient clustering and routing in mobile wireless sensor network. Int. J. Wirel. Mob. Netw. (IJWMN) 2(4), 106–114 (2010)
11. Gao, G.Q., Lei, L.: An improved node localization algorithm based on DV-Hop in WSN. In: 2nd International Conference on Advanced Computer Control (ICACC), vol. 4, pp. 321–324 (2010)
12. Wen-Jiunn Liu, K.-T.F.: Greedy routing with anti-void traversal for wireless sensor networks. IEEE Trans. Mob. Comput. 8(7), 910–922 (2009)
13. Kumar, D., Aseri, T.C., Patel, R.B.: Energy efficient heterogeneous clustered scheme for wireless sensor network. J. Comput. Commun. 32(4), 662–667 (2009). Elsevier
14. Chamam, A., Pierre, S.: On planning of WSNs: energy efficient clustering under the joint routing and coverage constraint. IEEE Trans. Mob. Comput. 8(8), 1077–1086 (2009)
15. Hong-bing, C., Geng, Y., Hu, S.-J.: NHRPA: a novel hierarchical routing protocol algorithm for wireless sensor networks. J. China Univ. Posts Telecommun. 15(3), 75–81 (2008). Elsevier
16. Lee, H., Wicke, M., Kusy, B., Guibas, L.: Localization of mobile users using trajectory matching. In: MELT 2008 Proceedings of the First ACM International Workshop on Mobile Entity Localization and Tracking in GPS-less Environments, New York, USA, pp. 123–128 (2008)
17. Chen, D., Varshney, P.K.: On-demand geographic forwarding for data delivery in wireless sensor networks. Elsevier Comput. Comm. 30(14–15), 2954–2967 (2007)
18. Sakarindr, P., Ansari, N.: Security services in group communications over wireless infrastructure, mobile ad hoc, and wireless sensor networks. IEEE Wirel. Commun. 14(5), 8–20 (2007)
19. Frey, H., Stojmenovic, I.: On delivery guarantees of face and combined greedy face routing in ad hoc and sensor net-works. In: Proceedings of the ACM MobiCom 2006, pp. 390–401 (2006)
20. Fang, Q., Gao, J., Guibas, L.: Locating and bypassing holes in sensor networks. Mobile Netw. Appl. 11(2), 187–200 (2006)
21. Qing, L., Zhu, Q., Wang, M.: Design of a distributed energy-efficient clustering algorithm for heterogeneous wireless sensor networks. J. Comput. Commun. 29(12), 2230–2237 (2006). doi:10.1016/j.comcom.2006.02.017. Elsevier

22. Leong, B., Mitra, S., Liskov, B.: Path vector face routing: geographic routing with local face information. In: Proceedings of the IEEE International Conference Network Protocols (ICNP 2005), pp. 147–158 (2005)

23. Younis, O., Fahmy, S.: HEED: a hybrid, energy-efficient, distributed clustering approach for ad hoc sensor networks. Mob. Comput. IEEE Trans. 3(4), 366–379 (2004). ISSN: 1536-1233

24. Niculescu, D., Nath, B.: DV based positioning in ad hoc networks. Telecommun. Syst. 22(1–4), 267–280 (2003)

Expressing and Applying C++ Code Transformations for the HDF5 API Through a DSL

Martin Golasowski[1]([✉]), João Bispo[2], Jan Martinovič[1], Kateřina Slaninová[1], and João M.P. Cardoso[2]([✉])

[1] IT4Innovations, VŠB - Technical University of Ostrava,
17. listopadu 15/2172, 708 33 Ostrava, Czech Republic
{martin.golasowski,jan.martinovic,katerina.slaninova}@vsb.cz
[2] Faculdade de Engenharia da Universidade do Porto,
Rua Dr. Roberto Frias, s/n, 4200-465 Porto, Portugal
jbispo@fe.up.pt, jmpc@acm.org

Abstract. Hierarchical Data Format (HDF5) is a popular binary storage solution in high performance computing (HPC) and other scientific fields. It has bindings for many popular programming languages, including C++, which is widely used in the HPC field. Its C++ API requires mapping of the native C++ data types to types native to the HDF5 API. This task can be error prone, especially when working with complex data structures, which are usually stored using HDF5 compound data types. Due to the lack of a comprehensive reflection mechanism in C++, the mapping code for data manipulation has to be hand-written for each compound type separately. This approach is vulnerable to bugs and mistakes, which can be eliminated by using an automated code generation phase. In this paper we present an approach implemented in the LARA language and supported by the tool Clava, which allows us to automate the generation of the HDF5 data access code for complex data structures in C++.

Keywords: HDF5 · Domain specific language · LARA · Source-to-source · Aspect oriented · Clava · Code generation

1 Introduction

Source-to-source transformation is a process during which a program source code is automatically created or updated according to a given set of inputs. It can be used for various tasks, such as low-level optimization for a given target platform, templating, integration and more. In this paper, we demonstrate how we can overcome the lack of compile-time reflection in C++, by applying user-defined transformations written in an aspect-oriented domain-specific language.

Reflection is the ability of a computer program to examine and/or modify its own structure. It usually provides information about the type of a given

© IFIP International Federation for Information Processing 2017
Published by Springer International Publishing AG 2017. All Rights Reserved
K. Saeed et al. (Eds.): CISIM 2017, LNCS 10244, pp. 303–314, 2017.
DOI: 10.1007/978-3-319-59105-6_26

object, its inheritance hierarchy, its attributes and more, and can even be used to manipulate the code itself during run-time. This ability is available in many interpreted languages, such as Python, Ruby, Lua, Java or C#, usually thanks to the underlying virtual machine or interpreter.

The current version of the C++ language is C++17. Its features have been recently added into commonly used compilers such as the GNU GCC or Intel C++ Compiler. However, reflection is not among these features yet, though several proposals has been recently published [8]. Based on the speed of implementation of the new standards in mainline compilers and their adoption by programmers, it can be said that C++ does not have comprehensive support for compile-time reflection yet. We briefly mention several alternative tools and approaches to this problem in Sect. 2.

One of the common use cases for reflection is mapping an object to a persistent data structure, where individual attributes of the object are examined and stored in a proper way. In the use case presented in this paper, we are storing a complex data structure representing a traffic navigation routing index in a HDF5 based binary file. Without proper reflection, we have to manually create the code that maps the C++ structures to the objects in the HDF5 file. This code implements several time-consuming data processing tasks that are executed on an HPC cluster, which places severe constraints on the robustness of the code and the entire process.

In this paper we present a method, based on the LARA language, for automatic generation of the mapping code. Section 3 explains the routing index and its HDF5-based storage. Section 4 presents the LARA language and its toolset, which can be used to define the desired code transformations in a robust and flexible way. Section 5 shows a concrete application of the approach on our data processing code and its integration in our build process.

2 Related Work

There are several approaches to reflection in the C++ language. One of them is through extensive use of macros to annotate individual classes and attributes, a solution that is popular for example among game engines [2]. Its pitfalls are the inability to use reflection on non-modifiable code (e.g., third-party libraries) and its reliance on uncommon language constructs. A similar approach can be implemented using templates, at the cost of an increase in complexity of the code, compilation times and requirements for its maintenance.

Another approach is based on external tools which parse source code and have a certain knowledge of the code structure, such as the Meta object compiler, which is part of the Qt GUI framework. This tool produces source code for annotated C++ classes extended with support for accessing run-time information and a dynamic property system [5,13]. This tool, however, provides only a fixed feature set intended for development in the Qt framework.

Domain-specific languages (DSLs) such as LARA can provide the desired level of flexibility and robustness for our purposes. The LARA language has been inspired by AOP approaches, including AspectJ and AspectC++. AspectJ [10] extends Java in order to provide better modularity for Java programs, and has a very mature tool support. AspectJ join points are limited to object-oriented concepts, such as classes, method calls and fields, and several works try to complement AspectJ. AspectC++ [14] is an AOP extension to the C++ programming language inspired by AspectJ and uses similar concepts, adapted to C++.

In traditional AOP approaches, aspects usually define behavior which is executed during runtime, at the specified join points. LARA differs from traditional AOP in that it uses aspects to describe source code analysis and transformations, which currently are executed statically, at compile time. Due to this difference in approach, tools like AspectJ and AspectC++ usually do not consider join points which are common in LARA, such as local variables, statements, loops, and conditional constructs.

There are several term rewriting-inspired approaches for code analysis and transformation, such as Stratego/XT [6] and Rascal [11], which require the user to provide a complete grammar for the target language. On the other hand, LARA promotes the usage of existing compiler frameworks (e.g. Clang [1] in the case of this work) for parsing, analysis and transformations. Another distinct feature of LARA is that *weavers* can be built in an incremental fashion, adding *join points*, *attributes* and *actions* as needed (see Sect. 4).

3 Hierarchical Data Format for Routing Index

Binary formats offer efficient and fast data storage. However, custom implementations can be cumbersome and fragile, especially in multi-platform environment. The Hierarchical Data Format [9] (HDF) provides a binary storage format implementation for storing large volumes of complex data. It has been developed mainly for storing scientific data, however, since then it has been adopted by many other industries. The HDF allows easy and consistent sharing of binary data across various platforms and environments, which is one of its main advantages. There are two main versions of the HDF format. In this paper, we exclusively refer to the HDF5 version [9]. HDF5 implements a storage model which resembles a standard file system hierarchy, with a tree of folders and files. The basic HDF5 file objects are *Groups*, *Datasets* and *Attributes*. Groups can hold one or more datasets; both groups and datasets can have attributes associated. Each HDF file has one root group. The datasets are used for the actual storage of multi-dimensional data of a given type.

3.1 Routing Use Case

The HDF5 provides APIs for a large number of major programming languages such as Python, C/C++, Java or even CLI .NET. Our codebase is written mainly in C++, hence we refer to the native HDF5 C++ API in this paper. In our approach for graph data for traffic navigation routing index, individual road segments, junctions and other elements of a road network are represented by a set of vertices and oriented edges. The edges have associated a number of parameters such as length, max. allowed speed or category. Graph representation of a road network of single country such as the Czech Republic can have millions of vertices and edges. The vertices and edges in the HDF5 file are divided in subsets (graph parts) which reside in their corresponding groups. Mapping of the graph parts to the individual vertices is stored in the NodeMap dataset located in the root group of the file. The parts can be determined either by geography or other topological properties of the graph. Each graph part group then contains the Edges, EdgeData and Nodes datasets. All datasets in our case are two-dimensional, where rows hold individual records and columns hold their attributes. References to records in other datasets in our case are represented by storing an index of the referenced record rather than using the native HDF5 reference mechanism.

The edges reference their metadata stored in the EdgeData dataset. There is only a limited number of unique values of the edge metadata, hence it is efficient to store them in a separate dataset. Relationship between nodes and edges is represented by the edgesIndex column in the Nodes dataset which references rows in the Edges dataset. The Edges then hold reference to the Nodes via their ID. Graphical visualisation of the routing index structure is in Fig. 1.

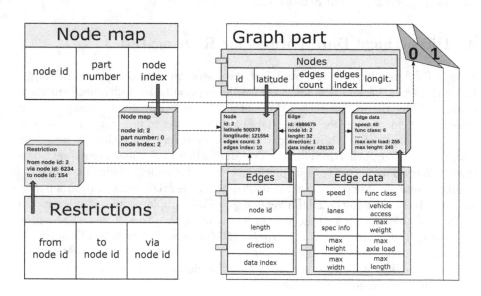

Fig. 1. Routing index layout in a HDF5 file

4   C++ Code Manipulation

LARA [4, 7] is a Domain-Specific Language (DSL) for source-code manipulation and analysis, inspired by Aspect-Oriented programming (AOP). It has specific keywords and semantics to query and modify points of interest (i.e., *join points*) in the source code, and provides general-purpose computation by supporting arbitrary JavaScript code. Join points provide *attributes*, for querying information about that point in the code, and *actions*, which apply transformations to that point.

Figure 2 presents LARA code which adds `include` directives to a file, using a join point action. Line 1 declares an *aspect*, the top-level unit in LARA (which is similar to a function). Line 2 declares the inputs of the aspect, which in this case is a `file` join point. By convention, names of variables that represent join points are prefixed with a dollar-sign ($) in LARA. Line 4 uses a `select` to capture all the classes definitions that appear in the current program. Lines 5–8 represent an `apply` block that performs some work over the join points captured in the previous `select`. In this case, it executes a file *action* (`$targetFile.exec`) that adds an include directive to the file, corresponding to the file that belongs to the given join point (`addIncludeJp($class)`). This example shows a common pattern in LARA, which is to select some points in the source code and then act over them, possibly modifying the source code.

4.1 Clava

Unlike most source-to-source approaches, LARA was designed to be independent on the target language, which allows the LARA framework to be reused for several languages [12]. This was achieved by decoupling the specification of the points of interest from the LARA language. To use LARA code to transform a specific language (e.g., C++ in this case), we need to build a tool (called *weaver*) which connects the language specification to the target code representation, e.g., an Abstract Syntax Tree (AST).

```
1  aspectdef AddClassInclude
2    input $targetFile end
3
4    select class end
5    apply
6      // Add an include to $targetFile for the file where class is declarated
7      $targetFile.exec addIncludeJp($class);
8    end
9
10 end
```

Fig. 2. A simple LARA aspect that inserts, in a given file, an include directive for every class that appears in the source code.

Figure 3 shows Clava [3], a C/C++ weaver we developed that uses the LARA framework to enable C++ code manipulation[1]. Clava is mostly implemented in Java, and internally uses a binary based on Clang [1] to dump information about C/C++ programs. This information is then parsed and used to build a custom

---

[1] An online demo version is available at http://specs.fe.up.pt/tools/clava.

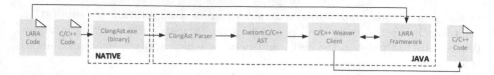

Fig. 3. Block diagram of the tool Clava.

AST, which the weaver client uses in the queries, modifications and source-code generation specified in LARA code (which is interpreted by the LARA framework).

5 Use Case

In this section we present and explain the LARA code developed to automatically generate type mapping functions from classes and structs (henceforth referred to as *records*) present in the source code. The presented version generates a new class for each record found in the code, and this class has a single static method that returns a *CompType* object, which can then be passed to the HDF5 API calls when that particular record is accessed. In the example in Fig. 4, for demonstration purposes, we include the code in the same file as the original record. However, in the code presented in this section we create new files for the generated code, to avoid adding a dependency to HDF5 in every source-file that wants to use the record (note that both cases can be expressed in LARA). Currently, the type-mapping code is generated for all classes and structures in the given source files, but the code can be easily adapted to filter unwanted records (e.g., by providing a list of class/struct names, or files).

```
1  #include <H5Cpp.h>
2
3  struct NodePosition {
4      int nodeId;
5      int partNumber;
6      int nodeIndex;
7  };
8
9  class NodePositionType {
10  public:
11    static H5::CompType GetCompType() {
12    H5::CompType itype(sizeof(Routing::NodePosition));
13    itype.insertMember("nodeId",
14      offsetof(Routing::NodePosition, nodeId), H5::PredType::NATIVE_INT32);
15    itype.insertMember("partNumber",
16      offsetof(Routing::NodePosition, partNumber), H5::PredType::NATIVE_INT32);
17    itype.insertMember("nodeIndex",
18      offsetof(Routing::NodePosition, nodeIndex), H5::PredType::NATIVE_INT32);
19    return itype;
20    }
21  };
```

Fig. 4. Generated compound type code for the `NodePosition` structure

5.1   LARA for HDF5

Figure 5 presents the *use* relationships for the aspect Hdf5Types, which generates
HDF5 interface code for C++ records. It uses a LARA aspect, RecordToHdf5,
which generates the implementation code for a single record, and two *code definitions*, a LARA mechanism for writing parameterizable escaped code (see Fig. 7).
The aspect RecordToHdf5 uses a JavaScript function, toHdf5.

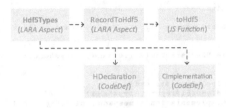

Fig. 5. *use* relationships for the aspect Hdf5Types.

Figure 6 shows the code for a working version of the Hdf5Types aspect. As
input, it receives a path to the base destination folder of the generated code,
and a namespace for the generated functions, with optional default values for
the inputs (line 2).

Lines 5–6 use a Factory provided by Clava (i.e., AstFactory) that allows
the creation of new AST nodes, that can then be inserted in the code tree. The
AstFactory always returns join points, which can be handled the same way as
the join points created by select statements. In this case, two join points of
type file are created, one for the header file (*CompType.h*) and another for the
implementation file (*CompType.cpp*).

Lines 8–11 select the program join point and add the newly created files
with the action addFile. Line 15 selects all the records in the source code that
are either of kind class or of kind struct, which are then iterated over in the
apply block in lines 16–27. This block creates the declarations for the header
and the implementation file using the code definitions in Fig. 7 (lines 20 and 25,
respectively). It also adds to the implementation file an include directive for
the current record (line 23), creates the code for the body of the implementation
function by calling the aspect RecordToHdf5 (line 24) and inserts the code of
the function in the implementation file (line 26).

Lines 30–32 finish the header file by adding an include to the HDF5 CPP
library, creating the namespace and inserting the code created in the apply block
into the file. Lines 35–36 finish the implementation file by adding two necessary
includes.

Figure 8 shows the code for the LARA aspect RecordToHdf5, called in the
previous aspect. RecordToHdf5 iterates over all the fields in the record given
as input (line 7), ignores all fields that are constant (line 9) or not public (line
10) and creates the code for the specific type of the field using the JavaScript
function toHdf5, ignoring cases that are not supported (lines 13–14). Features

```
 1 aspectdef Hdf5Types
 2  input srcFolder = "./", namespace = "HDF5Types" end
 3
 4  var filepath = srcFolder + "/lara-generated"; // Folder for the generated files
 5  var $compTypeC = AstFactory.file("CompType.cpp", filepath); // Create files for
 6  var $compTypeH = AstFactory.file("CompType.h", filepath); // the generated code
 7
 8  select program end  // Add files to the program.
 9  apply
10   $program.exec addFile($compTypeC); $program.exec addFile($compTypeH);
11  end
12
13  var hDeclarationsCode = "";
14
15  select file.record{kind === "class", kind === "struct"} end // Iterate over records
16  apply
17   var className = $record.name + "Type"; var typeName = "itype";
18
19   /* CompType.h file */
20   hDeclarationsCode += HDeclaration($file.name, className);
21
22   /* CompType.cpp file */
23   $compTypeC.exec addIncludeJp($record); // Add include to the record file
24   call result : RecordToHdf5($record, typeName); // C/C++ type to HDF5 type
25   var cxxFunction = CImplementation(namespace, className, code);
26   $compTypeC.exec insertAfter(AstFactory.declLiteral(cxxFunction));
27  end
28
29  /* CompType.h file */
30  $compTypeH.exec addInclude("H5Cpp.h", true); // Add include to HDF5 CPP library
31  hDeclarationsCode = 'namespace '+namespace +' {' + hDeclarationsCode + "}";
32  $compTypeH.exec insertAfter(AstFactory.declLiteral(hDeclarationsCode));
33
34  /* CompType.cpp file */
35  $compTypeC.exec addInclude("CompType.h", false); // Add includes for
36  $compTypeC.exec addInclude("H5CompType.h", true); // for CompTypes
37
38 end
```

Fig. 6. LARA code for the aspect Hdf5Types.

```
 1 codedef HDeclaration(filename, className) %{
 2 //   [[filename]]
 3 class [[className]] {
 4  public:
 5   static H5::CompType GetCompType();
 6 };
 7 }% end
 8
 9 codedef CImplementation(namespace, className, body) %{
10 H5::CompType [[namespace]]::[[className]]::GetCompType() {
11 [[body]]
12
13     return itype;
14 }
15 }% end
```

Fig. 7. Code definitions HDeclaration and CImplementation, used in aspect Hdf5Types.

that appear for the first time in this example are the use of the attribute type (lines 5, 9 and 13), an attribute common to all join points in Clava and that returns a special kind of join point that represents a C/C++ type; and the use of inlined escaped code in the lines 15–17 (i.e., %{...}%).

```
1  aspectdef RecordToHdf5
2   input $record, typeName end
3   output code end
4
5   var recordType = $record.type.code;
6   code = "H5::CompType "+ typeName +"(sizeof("+recordType+"));\n";
7   select $record.field end
8   apply
9    if($field.type.constant) continue; // Ignore constant fields
10    if(!$field.isPublic) continue; // Ignore private and protected fields
11
12    fieldName = $field.name;
13    var HDF5Type = toHdf5($field.type);
14    if(HDF5Type === undefined) continue; // Warning message omitted
15    var offset = %{offsetof([[recordType]], [[fieldName]])}%;
16    var params = %{"[[fieldName]]",[[offset]], [[HDF5Type]]}%;
17    code += %{[[typeName]].insertMember([[params]]);}% + "\n";
18   end
19  end
```

Fig. 8. LARA code for the aspect `RecordToHdf5`.

The Clang compiler has a very rich AST with detailed information, not only about the source code itself, but also about the types used in the code, which are also represented as an AST. Clava takes advantage of this information and gives access to this AST for types by providing a join point `type`, which can be accessed from any join point using the attribute `type`.

The JavaScript function `toHdf5` (Fig. 9) uses the attributes of the join point `type` extensively to generate the code for the HDF5 interface. The function starts by *desugaring* the type (line 8). Clang supports type *sugaring*, which means that if, for instance, we define in C/C++ a custom type `typedef int foo` and declare a variable `foo a`, a will appear in the AST as having the type `foo`, and not `int`. The attribute `desugar` returns the desugared version of the corresponding type (or the type itself, if it is already desugared).

Next, there are several special cases which need to be handled. For instance, C++ enumerations can customize the underlying integer type. If the type is an enumeration, the function is called recursively for the integer type of the enumeration (lines 10–12). Other example is the case of `vector` types, which appear in the AST as a `TemplateSpecializationType` (i.e., any type template that has been specialized, such has `vector<int>`). In this case, the function is also called recursively, this time for the specialization type.

After handling the special cases, the function uses the attribute `code` to obtain the code representation of the type and consult the table `HDF5Types`, which maps C/C++ types to the corresponding HDF5 types.

Table 1 shows several code metrics[2]. The code for the aspect totals 84 lines of code (LoC), including LARA code, Javascript code and code definitions, and generated around 100 lines of code for this use case (note that the aspect code is generic, and can be used for other use cases). If the generated code had to be written by hand, it would represent about 24% of the LoC of this use case.

---

[2] LoC for LARA aspects were counted by hand. LoC for C++ code uses the L-SLOC value provided by LocMetrics (http://www.locmetrics.com/).

```
 1  var HDF5Types = {}; // Table with mapping between C/C++ and HDF5 types
 2  HDF5Types["int"] = "NATIVE_INT";
 3  HDF5Types["float"] = "NATIVE_FLOAT";
 4  HDF5Types["uint16_t"] = "NATIVE_UINT16";
 5  ... // Other mappings
 6
 7  function toHdf5($type) {
 8    $type = $type.desugar; // Desugar type
 9
10    if($type.kind === "EnumType") { // Special case: enum
11      return toHdf5($type.integerType);
12    }
13
14    if($type.kind === "TemplateSpecializationType" && // Special case: vector
15      $type.templateName === "vector") {
16
17      var templateType = '&' + toHdf5($type.firstArgType);
18      return 'H5::VarLenType('+templateType+')';
19    }
20
21    ... // Other special cases
22
23    var HDF5Type = HDF5Types[$type.code];
24    if(HDF5Type === undefined) return undefined; // Warning message omitted
25
26    return 'H5::PredType::' + HDF5Type; // Base HDF5Type
27  }
```

Fig. 9. JavaScript code for the function `toHdf5`.

5.2 CMake Integration

Since Clava is a Java program, a Java runtime is the only system dependency required to execute the LARA aspect. Clava uses Clang underneath, and packages custom pre-compiled binaries for Windows, Ubuntu and CentOS platforms. The integration is done by defining a custom build step via *add_custom_command()* which produces the generated files and adds them as dependencies to the executable targets defined in CMakeLists. This integration allows a seamless use of this LARA toolset within a single build process.

Table 1. Code metrics for the use case.

Use case			LARA		
#files	#records	#fields	LoC	Aspects LoC	Generated LoC
15	10	47	308	84	98

6 Conclusion

In this paper, we presented a possible solution to missing support for compile-time reflection in C++. Our solution is based on the domain-specific language LARA, which is used to write source-to-source transformations, and the tool Clava, which executes the LARA code over C/C++ programs. We have demonstrated its usage by generating a native C++ API for the HDF5 library, without modifications in the original source code. The generated code is used to store a traffic navigation routing index for processing on HPC infrastructure. Our use case is complex both in terms of structural complexity and data volume, and we needed to implement a robust and flexible approach to generate the data access code and integrate it into our build process. In Sect. 5.2 we introduced a basic approach for integration of the code generation process in CMake, by using custom build commands. The Clava tool is called during the build configuration to produce the type mapping code between C++ and HDF5 API.

Ongoing work includes adding support for custom compound types (e.g., fields that are user-defined classes/structs) and LARA and Clava support for custom #pragma constructs in the code, that can be used to mark arbitrary blocks of code to be processed by the LARA aspects. This approach can be used to apply a large number of custom optimizations (e.g., in the context of HPC systems) or to generate a concrete implementation of the data access layer on top of an existing abstract data storage library.

Acknowledgment. This work has been partially funded by ANTAREX, a project supported by the EU H2020 FET-HPC program under grant 671623, by The Ministry of Education, Youth and Sports of the Czech Republic from the National Programme of Sustainability (NPU II) project "IT4Innovations excellence in science - LQ1602" and by grant of SGS No. SP2017/177 "Optimization of machine learning algorithms for the HPC platform", VŠB-Technical University of Ostrava, Czech Republic.

References

1. Clang. clang.llvm.org. Accessed 28 Feb 2017
2. Unreal engine documentation. https://docs.unrealengine.com/latest/INT/Programming/UnrealArchitecture/Reference/index.html
3. Bispo, J.: Clava: C++ language + lara weaver and code transformer - antarex technical report v0.1. (2017)
4. Bispo, J., Cardoso, J.M.: A matlab subset to c compiler targeting embedded systems. Soft. Pract. Exp. **47**(2), 249–272 (2017)
5. Blanchette, J., Summerfield, M.: C++ GUI Programming with Qt 4. Prentice Hall Professional, Upper Saddle River (2006)
6. Bravenboer, M., Kalleberg, K.T., Vermaas, R., Visser, E.: Stratego/xt 0.17. a language and toolset for program transformation. Sci. Comput. Program. **72**(1–2), 52–70 (2008)
7. Cardoso, J.M.P., Carvalho, T., Coutinho, J.G.F., Luk, W., Nobre, R., Diniz, P., Petrov, Z.: Lara: an aspect-oriented programming language for embedded systems. In: Proceedings of the 11th Annual International Conference on AOP Software Development, pp. 179–190. ACM (2012)
8. Chochlık, M.: Implementing the factory pattern with the help of reflection. Comput. Inf. **35**(3), 653–686 (2016)
9. Folk, M., Heber, G., Koziol, Q., Pourmal, E., Robinson, D.: An overview of the hdf5 technology suite and its applications. In: Proceedings of the EDBT/ICDT 2011 Workshop on Array Databases, pp. 36–47. ACM (2011)
10. Gradecki, J.D., Lesiecki, N.: Mastering AspectJ: Aspect-Oriented Programming in Java. Wiley, New York (2003)

11. Klint, P., Van Der Storm, T., Vinju, J.: Rascal: a domain specific language for source code analysis and manipulation. In: Source Code Analysis and Manipulation 2009, SCAM 2009, pp. 168–177. IEEE (2009)
12. Pinto, P., Carvalho, T., Bispo, J., Cardoso, J.M.: Lara as a language-independent aspect-oriented programming approach. In: Proceedings of the 32th Annual ACM Symposium on Applied Computing. ACM (2017, to appear)
13. Qt: Qt documentation. http://doc.qt.io/qt-5/why-moc.html. Accessed Feb 2017
14. Spinczyk, O., Gal, A., Schröder-Preikschat, W.: Aspectc++: an aspect-oriented extension to the c++ programming language. In: Proceedings of the 14th International Conference on Tools Pacific, CRPIT 2002, Darlinghurst, Australia, pp. 53–60 (2002)

Clustering of Mobile Subscriber's Location Statistics for Travel Demand Zones Diversity

Marcin Luckner[1(✉)], Aneta Rosłan[1], Izabela Krzemińska[2], Jarosław Legierski[1,2], and Robert Kunicki[3]

[1] Faculty of Mathematics and Information Science,
Warsaw University of Technology, ul. Koszykowa 75, 00-662 Warsaw, Poland
mluckner@mini.pw.edu.pl, aneta.roslan@gmail.com
[2] Orange Labs Poland, Orange Polska S.A., ul. Obrzeżna 7, 02-691 Warsaw, Poland
{izabela.krzeminska,jaroslaw.legierski}@orange.com
[3] Department of Computer Science and Information Processing,
The City of Warsaw, pl. Bankowy 2, 00-095 Warsaw, Poland
rkunicki@um.warszawa.pl

Abstract. Current knowledge on travel demand is necessary to keep a travel demand model up to date. However, the data gathering is a laborious and costly task. One of the approaches to this issues can be the utilisation of mobile data. In this work, we used mobile subscriber's location statistics to define a daily characteristic of mobile events occurrences registered by Base Transceiver Stations (BTS). For types of preprocessed data were tested to create stable clusters of BTS according to registered routines. The obtained results were used to find similar travel demand zones from the Warsaw public transport demand model according to a daily activity of the citizens. The obtained results can be used to update the model or to plan a cohesive strategy of public transport development.

1 Introduction

Knowledge on travel demand is a key aspect of a transport development. It can be gathered using a detailed survey and passenger counting and used to build up detailed travel demand models.

However, the model may be very fast out of date in dynamically growing metropolises. It is not possible to repeat wide passengers research very often. We need a method to update the travel demand model continuously.

Mobile subscriber's location statistics is a data source that can be used to update the model. A daily distribution of events registered in a Base Transceiver Station (BTS) creates a characteristic of the area covered by BTS's signal. Next, similar characteristics can be grouped to create an area of common daily characteristic. The areas represent a different daily distribution of the citizens and can be used to characterise travel demand zones.

In this work, we used the Self-Organizing Map (SOM) to cluster similar mobile subscriber's location daily statistics. Four types of preprocessed input

© IFIP International Federation for Information Processing 2017
Published by Springer International Publishing AG 2017. All Rights Reserved
K. Saeed et al. (Eds.): CISIM 2017, LNCS 10244, pp. 315–326, 2017.
DOI: 10.1007/978-3-319-59105-6_27

data were discussed. The data were used to create clusters of the same characteristic. The clusters with the most appropriate properties were merged with the existing travel demand zones in the City of Warsaw. As the result, we obtained the travel demand zones divided into clusters of the same daily citizens' activity.

The rest of this work is structured as follows. Section 2 briefly describes related works. Section 3 presents used data: Mobile subscriber's location statistics and the travel demand zones. Section 4 describes the used clustering model and a data preparation. Section 5 discuss the obtained results. Finally, Sect. 6 presents conclusions and future works.

2   Related Work

In our model, we try to update a travel demand models using mobile data. Work [2] presented an alternative solution of counting and surveying to clarify the demand data. The paper dealt with the issue of needed sample size to produce reliable results. The same authors proposed in Work [1] a theory of iterative estimation method of reliable passenger data. Work [4] presented the system based on transportation software-VISUM. The system integrated real–time data with static planning model. A similar solution is applied in our work, where the static travel demand zones are merged with the dynamic mobile subscriber's location statistics. Work [8] presented an alternative calibration of a Dynamic Traffic Assignment (DTA) model. Demand matrices were estimated by a bi–level optimisation problem and manually adjusted supply parameters.

In literature can be found mobile phone data analysis based on Call Detail Record (CDR) exploration [5,7]. Using CDR data we can recognise and analyse trajectories for each user separately. The trajectories are built on the base of the user activity in the mobile network when each event – originating and answering the call or sending/receiving xMS message – can be correlated with its location. Therefore, CDR data are easier to analyse and bring more information like additional information about the direction and speed of movement. Also, the level of analysing is different because a single mobile terminal is an observable marker of the users. However, these analyses are not legally permitted – according to EU law directives – without the consent of the user in most European Union countries. That moves the scope of the analysis, rather in the area of theoretical possibilities with no chance for practical use. The existing number of mobile devices tracked with the users' consents is insufficient for big studies. Another problem is the unknown bias of the consents on the collected data.

3   Data

3.1   Mobile Subscriber's Location Statistics

Mobile subscriber's location statistics contains information on the number of terminals communicated with given cells of the Public Land Mobile Network (PLMN) of Orange telecommunication provider in Warsaw municipal area.

Based on that, the assumption is made, that at least given number of terminals, in given period of time was in the area covered by given cell. Cellular systems are separate for each telecommunication technology (2G/3G/LTE). The number of cells in given area is derivative of technology and capacity of BTS.

The coverage of single Cell can be different depending on area topology (up to 1 km in urban area, 20 km in rural) so the accuracy of this location is not as well as e.g. for GPS based solutions. When adding to it information that every cell has different area coverage in each technology (2G/3G/LTE) it brings complexity to the analysis.

Another problem which requires a separate solution is the rule of network paging. A network paging contains a current location status and it is always done together with users actions like calls or SMS exchange and it brings the localisation note (cellid). But inactive terminals logged in the network but without any action of the user are periodically updated accordingly to network and terminal settings. Usually, it is done every 1–2 h after the last event with location status.

The terminal location is detected on the basis of network events (13 different events are taken into account) that are triggered together with voice and xMS communication.

For statistics collection dedicated system on telecommunication provider presented in Fig. 1 was used.

Statistics were collected in a quarter long, a hour long, and daily intervals. Statistics were also collected in a division into events generated by active subscribers and a periodic location update for terminals. Additionally, the overall statistics were created.

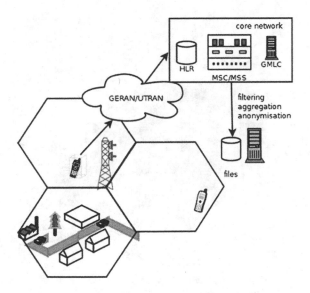

Fig. 1. Mobile subscriber's location statistics collection system

In our work, we possessed samples of data from the urban area from selected cells located in Warsaw and also from selected cells from the Warsaw suburban area. The raw stream of data from the mobile cells in Warsaw was between 300 and 400 events per second. The average file size with the raw data from 24 h for Warsaw area is about 100 MB. However, based on legal regulation in Polish Telecommunication Law, analysing this data in the raw state is not allowed without consent of the users. Therefore, the internal mechanism was implemented, and the data were collected from the early beginning as total sums in flat files containing the following columns: a latitude and longitude (in the WGS84 coordinate system) of the centre of the cell, the radius of the cell, the number of terminals in period for the defined cell, and the time stamp.

What is important, this method protects the privacy of the network users in the best possible manner. The data are collected only in the form of statistics which means: total sum of detections for a cell and there is no possibility of reversing this process. The processed data never originate from individual terminals. Statistics describe rather the load of the BTS than any characteristic of the individual users.

3.2   Travel Demand Zones

The travel demand zones for Warsaw are presented in Fig. 2. The zones were created during the Warsaw Research Movement project in 2015 [3]. The project

Fig. 2. Travel demand zones for Warsaw and neighbourhood communes [3]

developed the traffic model by a consortium composed of PBS Sp. o.o. (leader), Cracow University of Technology, and Warsaw University of Technology, on a request of the Capital City Warsaw.

Warsaw was divided into 896 interior areas, where 801 are municipal and 25 are from suburban ones. The centre of every region is considered as the start and end points of every travel area. During the determination of the regions, there were many factors taken into account, like the type and its function. Occurring communication barriers, like railway lines, were marked as the boundaries between the areas.

For each interior area, for the existing condition and forecasting periods, were assigned 186 variables. The variables include, among others, the number of inhabitants, workplaces, places in schools, the surfaces of objects selected category (residential, services, offices). These data may be used to estimate how many people start or finish trips in each region. Details are given in [3].

In our project, we used spatial characteristics of the zones – delivered as SHP files – to localise BTSs on their area. The geometry of the zones was transferred from the EPSG: 5300 coordinate system to the WGS84 (EPSG:4326) coordinate system used to describe BTSs localisations. Next, the geometry was validated to remove self–intersections from the zones.

4   Clusterisation

4.1   Self-Organizing Map

Collected data were clustered using the Self-Organizing Map (SOM) [6]. SOM is a fully connected single-layer linear network, where the output is organized in a two–dimensional matrix of nodes. The fundamental of the SOM is the soft competition between the nodes in the output layer. The winner shares the success with the neighbour nodes.

The SOM maps from the input data space $\mathbb{R}^n$ onto a two–dimensional matrix of modes called a map grid. A parametric reference vector $y_i \in \mathbb{R}^n$ is associated with i-th node on the map.

An input vector $x \in \mathbb{R}^n$ is compared with the y_i. The SOM can use any metric. In our model the winning node is calculated by

$$y = \arg\min_{y_i} \left(\sum_{i=1}^{n} (|x_i - y_i|)^2 \right) \tag{1}$$

and x is mapped onto y according to the parameter values y_i.

The distance is a commonly used modified Euclidean distance because we are not concerned with the actual numerical distance from the input. The computed value is some sort of uniform scale in order to compare each node to the input vector. This equation provides that, eliminating the need for a computationally expensive square root operation for every node in the network.

The map is being updated by an iterative presentation of learning data.

$$y_i(t+1) = y_i(y) + n_i(t, x(t) - y_i(t)). \tag{2}$$

The function n_i defines a neighbourhood and may vary in time according to the learning rate.

The SOM was implemented in R using the kohonen package [9]. During our tests the implementation was started with default parameters. Data were presented to the network 100 times. At the same time, the learning rate declined linearly from 0.05 to 0.01. The radius of the neighbourhood started with a value that covers 2/3 of all unit-to-unit distances. The initial weight given to the $X \subset \mathbb{R}^n$ map in the calculation of distances for updating $Y = \uplus_i^n y_i$, and to the Y map for updating X was going linearly from 0.75 to 0.5 during the training. The initial values of y_i were selected randomly.

4.2   Preparation of Input Data

Each BTS_i is characterised by a radius BTS_i^r, a latitude BTS_i^{lat}, and a longitude BTS_i^{long}. The number of events depends on a discrete time and is defined as $BTS_i^e(t)$. The vector of $BTS_i^e(t)$ for $t \in [1, \ldots, 24]$ defines a daily distribution of events registered on BTS_i.

A BTS radius BTS_i^r can vary from 1 to 3933 m. Raw data $BTS_i^e(t)$ – calculated per hour – are subscribers' logins amount and does not consider BTS range and area. During one day, 24 values of subscribers amount per hour gives subscriber's distribution. Distribution range is then arbitrarily large.

For analysis we used both the raw and normalised data. The normalisation considered two differences in area and time distribution. Four data sets were created: *abs_inf*, *per_inf*, *abs_nrm*, and *per_nrm*.

The sets with the *abs* prefix contained absolute values of events $BTS_i^e(t)$ not normalised according to BTS_i range. The sets with the *per* prefix contained values calculated per area

$$|BTS_i^e(t)| = \frac{BTS_i^e(t)}{\pi (BTS_i^r)^2} \tag{3}$$

The next step was a normalisation according to daily distribution. The sets with the *inf* suffix contained values of the events not normalised according to the daily distribution.

The sets with the *nrm* suffix contained values normalised to the range $[0, 1]$. According to the previous normalisation the sets consist of values

$$\overline{BTS_i^e(t)} = \frac{BTS_i^e(t)}{\max_{t=1}^{24} (BTS_i^e(t))}$$

$$\overline{|BTS_i^e(t)|} = \frac{|BTS_i^e(t)|}{\max_{t=1}^{24} (|BTS_i^e(t)|)} \tag{4}$$

For clusterisation based on BTSs the SOM uses vectors from R^{24} of values $BTS_i^e(t)$, $|BTS_i^e(t)|$, $\overline{BTS_i^e(t)}$, or $\overline{|BTS_i^e(t)|}$. Let us define $\boldsymbol{BTS_i}$ as a vector of daily events for BTS_i without deciding what kind of normalisation was used to calculate the vector. The vectors were used directly to train a SOM using BTSs.

To train a SOM using the zones a conversion of a set of vectors BTS connected with BTSs into vectors connected with the zones is required. The simplest method is to assign whole BTS and all its measurements to the zone which contains BTS's coordinates (geometry centre). Zones are distinct and so each BTS is contained by no more than one zone. It is the simplest and the least expensive assignment. The method has some disadvantages. The actual range of BTS and zone are ignored, it behaves as all subscribers were in the BTS centre.

Let us define a membership function of zone Z_i connected with a polygon Z_i^P. For a BTS with the coordinates $(BTS_j^{lat}, BTS_j^{long})$ the membership function is

$$\mu(i,j) = \begin{cases} 1 & \text{if } (BTS_j^{lat}, BTS_j^{long}) \in Z_i^P \\ 0 & \text{otherwise} \end{cases}. \tag{5}$$

Using (5), we can define the vector of daily events for the zone Z_i as

$$Z_i = \sum_{j=1}^{|BTS|} \mu(i,j) BTS_j. \tag{6}$$

5   Tests

The aim of the test was to find BTSs with common events distribution during the day. A 5×5 SOM network model was created and trained with data from working days. The given data were from 16.05.2016 (16th May) to 26.06.2016 (26th June). From this range, all weekend were removed as well as 26.05.2016, which was a Holiday (Corpus Christi). As a testing day 17.05.2016 (Tuesday) was used. The data were clustered into 5 groups. The number of groups was a balance between a disparity of classes and a diversity of classes. The increase of the number of classes created small clusters. The reduction of the number of classes gave an extensive cluster that contained various types of the characteristics.

Table 1. Clusters for raw data

Id	Count		Percentage	
	BTS	Nodes	BTS	Nodes
1	13	1	0.32	4.00
2	118	4	2.94	16.00
3	322	7	8.02	28.00
4	3528	12	87.83	48.00
5	36	1	0.9	4.00

Tests on Raw Data. For the first test the raw data were used. Data were collected in the *abs_inf* dataset. Table 1 contains information on the created clusters. A single cluster covered a majority of BTS and almost half of all SOM's nodes.

The results were not helpful to analyse the events distribution. Most of the BTS were in nodes with a flat similar daily characteristic.

Tests on Data Normalised by Area. In the second test, data from the *abs_inf* set were normalised per area using normalisation formula (4). As the result the *per_inf* dataset was created.

Data normalised per area did not improved the obtained results. Table 2 shows that nearly all BTSs were grouped in a single cluster. Increasing of the number of the iterations in the learning process did not change the results. Every but 5 BTSs are in the single cluster.

Table 2. Clusters for area normalised data

Id	Count		Percentage	
	BTS	Nodes	BTS	Nodes
1	1	1	0.02	4.00
2	4012	21	99.88	84.00
3	1	1	0.02	4.00
4	2	1	0.05	4.00
5	1	1	0.02	4.00

The area normalisation flats characteristics of the BTSs so much they cannot be distinguished any more. Figure 3 compares characteristics of three BTSs. Figure 3a shows the daily characteristics calculated on raw data when Fig. 3b shows the characteristics for the same BTSs but on data normalised by area.

The comparison shows that two characteristics were flatten by the normalisation. The example conveys a reason of the reduction of data to a single cluster.

Tests on Daily Normalised Data. In the next tests, data from the *abs_inf* and *per_inf* were daily normalised using formulas (3). As the result the *abs_nrm* and *per_nrm* datasets were created.

Both datasets gave the same result. The previous normalisation did not influence on the normalisation process where input data are scaled to $[0; 1]$ range.

Table 3 shows the obtained results. The results are more balanced than before. There still exists a domination of one cluster over the rest in sense of grouped BTSs but each of groups contain at least hundreds of BTSs. Additionally, in all cluster except one the number of used nodes is very balanced.

Figure 4 shows codes that are values associated with SOM nodes. The codes show a variety of characteristics in the clusters. Thanks to the normalization

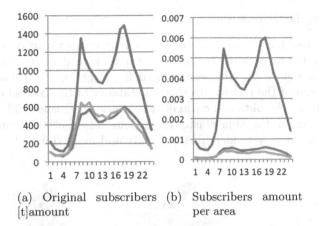

(a) Original subscribers [t]amount

(b) Subscribers amount per area

Fig. 3. Three sample BTS characteristics before and after recalculate per area

Table 3. Clusters for daily normalised data

Id	Count		Percentage	
	BTS	Nodes	BTS	Nodes
1	938	5	23.35	20.00
2	480	4	11.95	16.00
3	429	4	10.68	16.00
4	1926	9	47.95	36.00
5	244	3	6.07	12.00

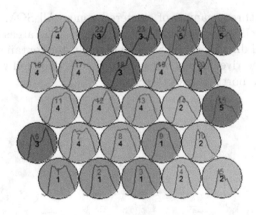

Fig. 4. Distribution of clusters among SOM nodes

and vertical alignment of characteristics the groups can be interpreted. The SOM identified forms with two clear peaks. Some of them have an equal height and some have one higher peak. There are also forms with the mild wide top.

5.1 Clusters Distributions

For the future test have been done on the *per_nrm* dataset that contained daily normalised data. The SOM algorithm was started with default parameters but with three different seeds. The seed value defined random initialisation of the clusters. The aim of the test was to check a stability of the created clusters.

Figure 5 shows the obtained clusters. The obtained clusters differ but there are areas that stay in the same cluster for various initialisation parameters. The examples of the areas were identified manually and marked in red.

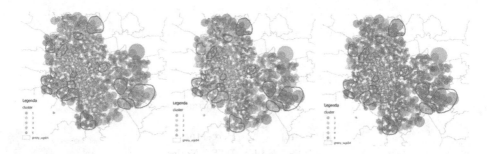

Fig. 5. BTS clusters (Color figure online)

The last test was an aggregation of BTS data with the zones. The greedy method was used to group BTS data in the zones according to formula (6). A BTS was assigned to the zone that contained its centre. The BTS data were a daily normalised data.

Figure 6 shows three example of clustered zones. All SOM parameters were default only the seed was changing. We can show static areas as in the case of the clusters created directly on BTSs. The blue cluster contains zones placed on the east bank of the river in a south part and goes diagonally from south-west to north-east in the north part of the city.

Fig. 6. Demanding zones clusters

The obtained results from both approaches cover each other at least partially. And in both cases, stable clusters can be defined. These results are most promising. Even the initial segmentation on all distributions already shows differentiation on the map where you can classify urban areas as a typical night or day. One can see large "day" clusters in the form of shopping centres and offices and "night" clusters of sleeping quarters.

For example office zones Służewiec Przemyslowy (Industrial Sluzewiec) in the south of Warsaw and Al Jerozolimskie in the west are visible. The major shopping centres in Warsaw such as Galeria Mokotów, Złote Tarasy and Arkadia can be also identified. The sleeping quarters Tarchomin in the north of Warsaw, Ursus on the west side and Wawer in the east are marked.

At this moment all zones of the same type – residential, services, offices – are detected manually using visualisations of several iterations of the clustering algorithm. An automation of the process is planned in the future.

6   Conclusions

In this work, we proposed how to convert the mobile subscriber's location statistics into a diversity of the transport demand zones according to a daily activity of the citizens.

Presented analysis shows that even aggregates in units of time can provide useful information after the use of appropriate methods of statistical processing. Topic requires further research, but even those so far are very promising and brings a lot of valuable information.

The obtained results are not as valuable as tracking the mobile device can be. But it is a good trade off to have less amount of information from big and reliable data rather than to have a big amount of information from a small not representative probe. Presented analysis shows that even aggregates in units of time can provide useful information after the use of appropriate methods of statistical processing. Topic requires further research, but even those so far are very promising and brings a lot of valuable information. The obtained diversity may be used to detect starting areas of travels for the given time of a day. Similarly, possible aims of travels can be detected.

The definition of the similar transport demand zones can be also useful in anomaly detection when an observed schema in the given zone does not fulfil the expected pattern for a type of the zone. However, in this case, the resolution of the measures should be higher than one hour.

Finally, the results may be concluded with strategy decisions of a public transport development. One of the applications of our work can be the demarcation of the paying parking zone. The longer observation of daily routines should tell us which zones should be included. Similarly, in work [10] toll on a regional expressway were estimated.

Acknowledgements. This research has been supported by the European Union's Horizon 2020 research and innovation programme under grant agreement No. 688380 *VaVeL: Variety, Veracity, VaLue: Handling the Multiplicity of Urban Sensors.*

References

1. Horváth, B., Horváth, R.: Real network test of an iterative origin-destination matrix estimator in urban public transport. In: 2014 18th International Conference on System Theory, Control and Computing (ICSTCC), pp. 715–719, October 2014
2. Horváth, B., Horváth, R.: Estimation of sample size to forecast travel demand in urban public transport. In: 2015 International Conference on Models and Technologies for Intelligent Transportation Systems (MT-ITS), pp. 300–303, June 2015
3. Kostelecka, A., Szarata, A., Jacyna, M.: Warsaw' traffic measurement 2015. Technical report, PBS Sp. z o.o, Cracow University of Technology, Warsaw University of Technology (2015). http://transport.um.warszawa.pl/warszawskie-badanie-ruchu-2015/model-ruchu
4. Liu, H., Sun, J., Zhu, Z.: Study on processes reengineering of transportation planning. In: 2008 International Conference on Intelligent Computation Technology and Automation (ICICTA), vol. 2, pp. 494–497, October 2008
5. Lorenzo, G.D., Sbodio, M., Calabrese, F., Berlingerio, M., Pinelli, F., Nair, R.: Allaboard: visual exploration of cellphone mobility data to optimise public transport. IEEE Trans. Vis. Comput. Graph. **22**(2), 1036–1050 (2016)
6. Murtagh, F., Hernández-Pajares, M.: The kohonen self-organizing map method: an assessment. J. Classif. **12**(2), 165–190 (1995). http://dx.doi.org/10.1007/BF03040854
7. Pinelli, F., Nair, R., Calabrese, F., Berlingerio, M., Lorenzo, G.D., Sbodio, M.L.: Data-driven transit network design from mobile phone trajectories. IEEE Trans. Intell. Transp. Syst. **17**(6), 1724–1733 (2016)
8. Seyedabrishami, S., Nazemi, M., Shafiei, M.: Off-line calibration of a macroscopic dynamic traffic assignment model: iterative demand-supply parameters estimation. In: 17th International IEEE Conference on Intelligent Transportation Systems (ITSC), pp. 2035–2040, October 2014
9. Wehrens, R., Buydens, L.: Self- and super-organising maps in r: the kohonen package. J. Stat. Softw. **21**(5), 1–19 (2007). http://www.jstatsoft.org/v21/i05
10. Zhang, M.M., Wei, J.: Optimization for urban traffic assignment by congestion toll levied on regional expressway. In: 2008 Workshop on Power Electronics and Intelligent Transportation System, pp. 472–475, August 2008

Share Market Sectoral Indices Movement Forecast with Lagged Correlation and Association Rule Mining

Giridhar Maji[1], Soumya Sen[2(✉)], and Amitrajit Sarkar[3]

[1] Department of Electrical Engineering, Asansol Polytechnic, Asansol, India
Giridhar.Maji@gmail.com
[2] AK Choudhury School of Information Technology,
University of Calcutta, Kolkata, India
iamsoumyasen@gmail.com
[3] Ara Institute of Canterbury, Christchurch, New Zealand
Amitrajit.Sarkar@ara.ac.nz

Abstract. This paper analyses the correlation between two different sectoral indices (e.g. between Automobile sector index and between Metal sector index, between Bank sector index and IT sectoral index etc.) in a time lagged manner. Lagging period is varied from 1 day to 5 days to investigate if any selected sector has lagged influence over any other sectoral index movement. If any upward/downward movement of a sectoral index (sector A) is correlated with similar upward/downward movement of another sectoral index (Sector B) with a time lag of 'd' days, then with association rule mining support and confidence is calculated for the combination. If d is the lag for which support and confidence is maximum then depending on the higher correlation as well as higher support and confidence value it is possible to forecast future (d days ahead of current day) movement of sector B based on present day movement of sector A. This model first uses correlational analysis to identify the level of dependence among two different sectors, then considers only those sectors having higher value of correlation for association rule mining. Those sector are not considered for which combination correlation is very low or 0.

This model has been tested with Indian share market data (NSE sectoral index data of 6 sectors) of 2015. Result shows it is possible to predict in short term (1 to 5 days in future) price movement of sectoral indices using other lagged correlated sector price index movement.

Keywords: Stock indices prediction · Lagged correlation · Association rule mining

1 Introduction

Predicting the future stock prices are the most important queries for the investors in share market. Many different techniques, mathematical formulation, genetic algorithm (GA) based models, neural network models, machine learning based techniques etc. have been proposed and tested with mixed success [1–3, 15]. Predicting the future price

© IFIP International Federation for Information Processing 2017
Published by Springer International Publishing AG 2017. All Rights Reserved
K. Saeed et al. (Eds.): CISIM 2017, LNCS 10244, pp. 327–340, 2017.
DOI: 10.1007/978-3-319-59105-6_28

of some stock is inherently difficult as the price movement depends on large number of issues–greatly of macro-economic, micro-economic, technical parameters as well as a lot of unknown parameters which come in to the context all of a sudden. Future stock price of a company becomes stochastic due to difference in perception about the future of the company among investors. A group of investor foresees a future uptrend or good earnings for the company and they expect its stock price to go up in near future. Therefore they buy at current price to sell at some higher price in future and earn profit. At the same time some other groups of investors with a perception that the company's future outlook is not so good and stock prices may fall in future, they sell with current price with a view to latter buy the same or more quantity of shares with lower price in future to earn profit. The basic idea behind technical analysis is that current stock price of a company incorporates impacts and effects of economic, financial, political and psychological factors. It studies the historical stock prices and assumes that the future trend will follow the past behavior. The technical analysis offers information about the possible future evolution of the stock market. Technical analysis is done based on a lot of different technical indicator parameters such as 'n-days moving average' (where 'n' can be 5/10/20/50 etc. days), 'n-days weighted average', MACD, relative strength index, momentum etc. along with price-to-earnings ratio, dividend yield, profit margin, return on investment etc. [2, 3, 12, 15]. But investor's perception also depends on rumors & market speculation and some unforeseen sudden big events and their unknown reaction towards stock prices of different companies. This later part makes the "sell" or "buy" decision of an investor a stochastic random event but due to the technical parameters it is also not totally unpredictable.

In any Stock market listed companies are categorized into different sectors depending on the business domain the company belongs to. We have considered the following six sectors for our study: Banks, Automobiles, IT & Software, Metals, Pharmaceuticals and FMCG (Fast Moving Consumer Goods). These different sectors have sectoral index to represent their aggregated trends in a stock exchange. It is similar to the stock exchange index (for example SENSEX, NIFTY in BSE and NSE). These sectoral indices react with different external and internal events differently and hence their movement. Same external event may affect different industry sector differently. Depending on a many different factors some sectoral index moves in positive direction while in the same time some other sector moves into the negative zone (or may remain neutral). As an example when dollar value increases with respect to Indian Rupee (INR) almost all export companies of India gains and IT sectors majorly get most of the benefits as they earn in dollar and spend in INR. At the same time importers incur losses.

This is a very complex relationship to measure. In this research work we aim to focus on this in terms of following issues:

1. If these reactions with the external factors are correlated between the sectors.
2. Identifying how different sectors are related? They may be highly correlated, neutral or not co-related at all.
3. Among the highly correlated sector pairs which are positively correlated and which are negatively correlated.
4. Is there any correlation among the highly correlated sector pairs with some days lag, i.e. if today's sectoral index movement of sector-A is correlated with sectoral index

movement of sector-B on d days in future. If we find a high correlation among two different sectors with a time lag of d days then we can forecast sectoral index movement of Sector-B, 'd' days ahead.

In the next sub section we briefly discuss about Indian share market as well as sectoral indices that are considered in this case study. Then we will discuss about Association rule mining techniques along with support and confidence that will be used in our analysis.

An Overview of Indian Share Market

Two most important stock exchanges in India are BSE and NSE. The Bombay Stock Exchange (BSE) is one of the oldest stock exchanges in India and one of the top stock exchanges globally with respect to number of listed companies and market capitalization. The 30 company index from BSE is known as SENSEX or BSE30 is a stock market index of 30 well established and financially sound companies listed on BSE. These are some of the largest and most actively traded stocks, hence it is considered as representative of various industrial sectors of the Indian economy. It is published since 1st January 1986 and regarded as the pulse of the domestic stock markets in India [9]. The NIFTY 50 index is national stock exchange of India's benchmark stock market index for Indian equity market [10]. It covers 22 sectors of Indian economy. As SENSEX and NIFTY is used to understand average trend and movement of BSE and NSE for almost all financial purposes, each stock exchange has industry sectors and each sector has many sectoral index(s) that reflect the behavior and performance of the concerned sector. In this study following 6 sectors are considered: Auto, Bank, Pharma, FMCG, IT and Metal. All index values are taken from NIFTY industrial sectors. Different sectoral index(s) consists of different number of representative company stocks. For example NSE Auto Index consists of 15 stocks and NIFTY bank index comprises of 12 banking sector stocks.

Statistical Correlation

Let Xt and Yt are two given time series closing prices for N days. If we consider a lag of d days between them then **co-variance** between the two series is defined as-

$$\sigma XY(d) = \frac{1}{N-1} \sum_{t=1}^{N} (Xt\text{-}d - \mu X)(Yt - \mu Y) \tag{1}$$

Where μ_X and μ_Y are the sample means of the time series X and Y.

Cross correlation between them is defined as-

$$rxy(d) = \frac{\sigma XY}{\sigma X \sigma Y} \tag{2}$$

where $\sigma X = \sqrt{(Sx)}$, and $\sigma Y = \sqrt{(Sy)}$;

Sx, Sy being the sample standard deviations of series X and Y.

The value of r varies between +1 to −1. Depending on the sign of r following can be inferred:

- Positive correlation: r value closer to +1 signifies strong positive correlation between the variables. An r value of exact +1 indicates a perfect positive fit. Any positive r values between 0 and +1 indicates that the relationship between x and y variables are such that with increase in values of X, Y value also increases.
- Negative correlation: If x and y have a strong negative linear correlation, r is close to an r value of exactly −1 indicates a perfect negative fit. Negative values indicate a relationship between x and y such that as values for x increase, values for y decrease.
- No correlation: r value closer to 0 signifies that there is no linear correlation or a very weak correlation. In other words x and y values are completely un-correlated and there is a random, relationship between the two variables x, y.

A perfect correlation of ±1 means that all the data points are lying on a straight line. Correlation coefficient 'r' does not have a dimension; hence it does not depend on the units used. Generally an 'r' value of greater than 0.8 is considered as highly correlated and less than 0.5 is considered weakly correlated. A point to remember is that above threshold values vary with the 'type' of data used. Generally with noisy data less threshold values are considered.

Association Rule Mining

Data mining, an important part of knowledge discovery in databases (KDD) process employs many different techniques for knowledge discovery and prediction such as classification, clustering, sequential pattern mining, association rule mining and analysis. Nowadays it is used in almost all the data driven decision models such as business analysis, strategic decision making, financial forecasting, future sales prediction etc. Agrawal [13] first introduced association rules for frequent pattern mining among items in large transaction dataset. They introduced the *Apriori* principle which says: Any subset of a frequent itemset must be frequent. Hence it can also be said in another term as: No superset of any infrequent itemset should be calculated for further processing. From the frequent item-sets a set of strong rules are calculated. Strength of a rule is measured based on support and confidence values. Not all frequent item-sets are considered as strong, only those with a minimum support and confidence are considered for the next step. This *Aprori* principle eliminates the 'curse of dimensionality' and makes computations feasible. Let us consider an association rule:{bread, sugar} => {butter} It indicates if people are buying bread and sugar then they may also buy butter. Association rule mining (ARM) is used here to show the relationship between different item-sets. It is also known as market basket analysis. An association rule is expressed in the form of an implication as:

$$X \rightarrow Y, \text{ where X and Y are disjoint item-sets, i.e. } X \cap Y = \emptyset.$$

Support and confidence measures the strength of an association rule. Support is used to find how frequently a rule is applicable, whereas confidence finds how frequently items in itemset Y also appear in transactions containing itemset X. The formal definitions of these metrics are:

Support is the fraction of the total transactions that matches the rule. It is defined for rule R as the ratio of the number of occurrence of R, given all occurrences of all rules [3].

$$\text{Support } (X \rightarrow Y) = P(X \cup Y) = \frac{\#\text{ of Transactions containing both X and Y}}{Total \ \# \ of \ Transactions} \quad (3)$$

Support of the rule {tire, auto accessories} → {Automotive Service} is 0.98 signifies that 98% of people who purchase tires and auto accessories also get automotive services done.

Confidence signifies the strength of the rule. The confidence of a rule X -> Y, is the ratio of the number of occurrences of Y given X, among all other occurrences given X [3].

$$\text{Confidence } (X \rightarrow Y) = P(Y|X), \text{ the probability of Y given X}$$
$$= \frac{\#\text{of Transactions containing both X and Y}}{\#of \ Transactions \ containing \ X} \quad (4)$$

A minimum support threshold value (min_sup) is generally defined to select the point of interest. It is used to discard those itemsets with support less than min_sup as that may not be interesting from business perspective. Confidence gives an idea of the conditional probability of Y given X. It is a measure of reliability of the inference made by a rule. Higher value of confidence implies that it is more likely for Y to be present in transactions that contain X.

One important point to consider is that not all strong rules (based on support and confidence values) are necessarily interesting. As we can see support-confidence framework can be misleading; it can identify a rule (A =>B) as interesting (strong) when, in fact the occurrence of A might not imply the occurrence of B. Correlation Analysis provides an alternative framework for finding interesting relationships and allows to improve understanding of meaning of some association rules. **Measure of interest or Lift** is one of such correlational measure of association rules. Lift is defined as [19]:

$$\text{Lift } (A, B) = \frac{P(A \cup B)}{P(A) \ P(B)} \quad (5)$$

If lift = 1 i.e. $P(A \cup B) = P(A) \ P(B)$, then the occurrence of itemset A is independent of the occurrence of B; or else both the item-sets are dependent and correlated. If lift value is less than 1 then A and B are negatively correlated i.e. occurrence of one likely implies the absence of the other. A lift value of more than 1 implies positive correlation between A and B.

2 Related Study

Several researches have been done over the period on predicting future stock price or price movement direction (upward or downward) along with trend analysis based on mainly different statistical modeling [3, 4, 6–8, 14, 15]. Rusu et al. discussed stock forecasting [14] methods used by classical approaches such as fundamentalists and chartists and at the same time discussed various recent stochastic methods like white noise, random walk, auto-regressive models etc. In another research work [4] various models used for stock price prediction using SAS© System tools. Models like Time Series analysis, Auto Regression (AR), Exponential Smoothening, Moving Average (MA) etc. has been discussed along with illustrated procedure for FORECAST and ARIMA (Autoregressive Integrated Moving Average) models. Dutta et al. [15] used logistic regression methods with various financial ratios as independent variables to cluster selected 30 stocks into good and bad performing groups based on rate of return. Another model CARIMA [5] (Cross Correlation Autoregressive Integrated Moving Average) was proposed to predict short term stock price. Main idea of CARIMA is to find the most highly correlated stock to predict the target price. Stock prices of SET50 from Stock Exchange of Thailand has been used to test the effectiveness of the model with better price trend prediction with similar % MAE (Mean Absolute Error) than ARIMA model. In another study work authors investigated stock index co-movement between two different countries namely Taiwan and Hong Kong using association rules and cluster analysis [6]. They have used 30 categories of stock indices as decision variables to observe the behavior of stock index association. This study tried to identify the correlation between the similar category sectoral index movements between two different countries and that also used to recommend investment portfolio as a follow up reference. Forecasting horizon is the time lag between the price movement of independent stock price and correlated stock price. If two stocks are highly correlated with a delay of d days then following the trend of former stock, latter one's trend can be predicted d days ahead. The above method is proposed with suitable generic algorithm for automated data preprocessing and analysis using correlation [8]. This model has predicted with 67% accuracy while tested with real stock market data. Authors in [16] has analyzed correlation between stock price fluctuation, gold price and US dollar price along with association rule induction methods amongst different stocks of same sector. A rigorous mathematical discussion on ten different data mining techniques such as Support vector machine (SVM), Least squares support vector machine (LS-SVM), Linear discriminant analysis (LDA), Quadratic discriminant analysis (QDA), Logit model, neural network, Bayesian models etc. has been discussed in [17]. In another work authors proposed and evaluated a stock price prediction based recommender system [18] that used historical stock prices as input to the system and applied regression trees for dimensionality reduction and Self Organizing Maps (SOM) for clustering. The proposed system helped investors with possible profit-making opportunities with buy or sell recommendations.

The main objective of this research work is to measure the association between sectors pair-wise instead of specific stock. These would provide an integrated view of stock market including several business sectors. Here we study time lagged prediction model for the analysis on the well-established, industry defined sectors or domains of businesses like automobile, banking, reality, metal etc. As we identify the sectors instead of specific stock we able to consider number of stocks at a time and could choose the top performing stocks of the sector as required. The sectoral index of each sector has been used to find the correlation in our study. This way total number of possible sector pair reduces drastically and at the same time individual investors can gain an idea to which sectoral stocks are going to give good earning in short-term. Similarly mutual fund managers can also use it to diversify their sectoral portfolio as the movement trend of sectors is going to be identified.

3   Methodology

Research Framework
The research framework of this study is shown in Fig. 1. It involves collecting index values of 6 industrial sectors from NSE. Each trading days closing prices are used as the raw input data for our analysis. Initial time series plotting of sectoral indices of selected sectors gives a basic graphical visualization of the raw data about their co-movement pattern. Figure 2 shows the time series plot of the selected sectors. Raw dataset is then processed into proper format to be used in association rule mining and for correlation analysis.

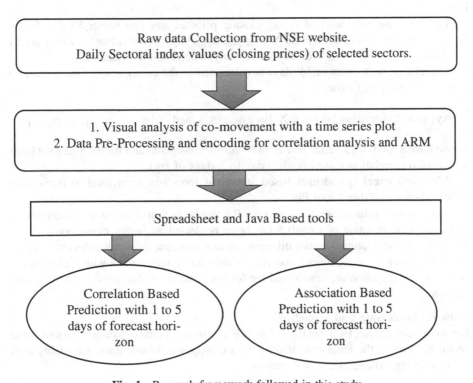

Fig. 1. Research framework followed in this study

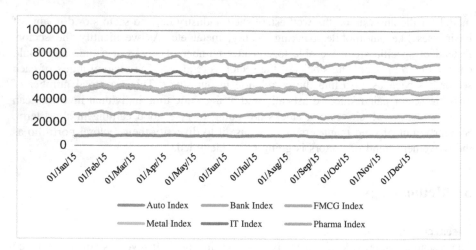

Fig. 2. Movement of six sectoral indices (Closing price index) during Jan to Dec 2015

Correlation Analysis

Our data set consists of day wise closing prices of 6 different sectoral indices of 2015. We then calculated pairwise correlation for all the possible pair of sectors with a lag of 0 day to 5 days. A delay of 0 day means same day correlation between the two sectoral indices.

Let's say we have total of N day closing price of any two sector S1 and S2 as $X = \{p_1, p_2...p_n\}$ for sector S1 and $Y = \{p_{1+d}, p_{2+d},... p_{n+d}\}$ for sector S2 where prices are from $(1 + d)$ day to $(n + d)$ day i.e. 'd' days ahead of the prices in X.

Correlation with delay of 'd' days is calculated as the correlation between the two data arrays X, Y as below:

$$rxy(d) = \text{Correlation between X } \{p_1,\ p_2...p_n\} \text{ and } Y\{p_{1+d},\ p_{2+d}, \cdots p_{n+d}\}$$

So we have a total of 15 sector pair from 6 sectors considered and for each pair we have a total of 6 correlation values (with 0 day to 5 days of lag).

Microsoft excel spreadsheet based statistical tools has been used to derive the results shown in Table 1 and Fig. 3.

In this study a correlation value of r >= 0.8 has been considered as good correlation and a correlation value of r <= 0.5 has been neglected as 'weak or no correlation'. Based on the correlation between different sectoral movements sector pairs are selected for further analysis using association rule mining. Only sector pairs with high positive or negative correlation are considered for further analysis as discussed in the next sub section.

Data Preprocessing and Encoding

Let's consider dataset $Ps = \{pi\}$; $i = 1$ to N is the sectoral index closing values of some sector S; N being the number of trading days considered. Whole dataset contains such sectoral index closing prices of 6 sectors.

Table 1. Correlation values (r) among different sector pairs with different day lag.

Day Lag->	0	1	2	3	4	5
Auto-Bank	0.9638	0.9633	0.9625	0.9618	0.9611	0.9604
Auto- FMCG	0.8827	0.8821	0.8813	0.8805	0.8796	0.8787
Auto-Metal	−0.4220	−0.4228	−0.4238	−0.4248	−0.4257	−0.4266
Auto- IT	0.9491	0.9491	0.9489	0.9488	0.9485	0.9482
Auto-Pharma	0.9723	0.9725	0.9725	0.9725	0.9725	0.9725
Bank-FMCG	0.8094	0.8089	0.8083	0.8076	0.8067	0.8058
Bank-Metal	−0.2981	−0.2997	−0.3018	−0.3039	−0.3059	−0.3078
Bank-IT	0.8779	0.8772	0.8764	0.8757	0.8748	0.8741
Bank-Pharma	0.9226	0.9227	0.9226	0.9224	0.9223	0.9222
FMCG-Metal	−0.6889	−0.6891	−0.6892	−0.6893	−0.6894	−0.6894
FMCG-IT	0.8508	0.8515	0.8523	0.8531	0.8538	0.8546
FMCG-Pharma	0.9027	0.9028	0.9028	0.9029	0.9031	0.9032
Metal-IT	−0.4010	−0.4014	−0.4018	−0.4023	−0.4028	−0.4032
Metal-Pharma	−0.5442	−0.5432	−0.5423	−0.5415	−0.5405	−0.5395
IT-Pharma	0.9492	0.9491	0.9489	0.9487	0.9485	0.9484

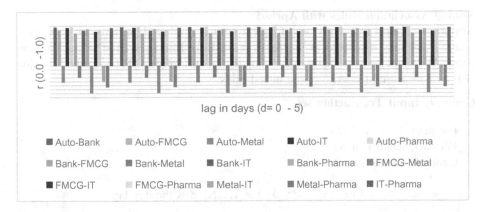

Fig. 3. Correlations among six sectoral indices with a day lag of 0 day to 5 days.

Let's also define tolerance Δt as the percentage of value up to which we ignore price changes i.e. we take consider it as no-change if percentage price change is less than equals to Δt. For our experiments we have considered $\Delta t = 0.2$ as it gives good results. We have varied it from 0 to 1 and selected 0.2.

Step 1:   change in index values are calculated for each sector as follows:

$$\Delta pi = \ pi+1 - pi$$

Step 2:   Different sectoral index values has different base and movement amount in absolute values so to normalize all sectors we consider percentage change. It is calculated as below:

$$Ci = (\Delta pi/pj)$$

Ci value may be positive or negative depending on the price movement of the sectoral index

Step 3:   Sectoral index price percentage change is encoded as follows:

$$vi = \begin{cases} +1 & if\ Ci > +\Delta t \\ 0 & if - \Delta t \le Ci \le +\Delta t \\ -1 & if\ Ci < -\Delta t \end{cases} \qquad (6)$$

Here v_i becomes +1 if change is in positive direction i.e. sectoral index moves upwards. It becomes −1 if change is in negative direction i.e. sectoral index moves downward. A value of 0 is assigned if the change in percentage value is below considered tolerance limit. We consider it as 'no-change' or 'no-movement'.

Mining Association Rules with Apriori

Apriori is the most frequently used frequent itemset mining algorithm with good time bound as already discussed in the Association Rule Mining section in Introduction above. We adapt the association rule mining using Apriori from [11] and used lift value [19] as a measure of interest of the mined rules.

Generate Input Transaction set

For days d = 0 to 5 Do
For each sector pair S1, S2
Generate transactions T as:

$$T_d = \left\{ v_i^{s1},\ v_{i+d}^{s2} \right\};\ i = 1\ldots N;\ d\ is\ the\ day\ lag.$$

T_d is a set of 2 item itemsets with possible items as '+1', '−1' and '0'. For example if sector S1 has positive upward movement from i^{th} day to $(i + d)^{th}$ day and sector S2 has a negative movement between i^{th} day to $(i + d)^{th}$ day then i^{th} itemset in Td becomes (+1, −1), similarly for $(i + 1)^{th}$ day's itemset will be (+1, +1) if both the sector shows an upward movement from $(i + 1)^{th}$ day to $(i + 1 + d)^{th}$ day.

Apriori algorithm is now suitably modified to be used on above generated transactions T = {Td}; d = 0 to 5, to find the association between any two sectors movement trend. Here we restrict our analysis in finding association between any two sectors, where index movement direction of one sectoral index is used to find the probability of movement direction of another sectoral index. It is possible to use the same algorithm to find association rules where multiple sectoral index movements will be used to predict the movement of some another sectoral index.

Let min_s = minimum threshold support for an itemset to be considered. It is used only to retain healthy rules.

In a similar way min_c = minimum threshold for confidence measure.

L_k is the k-element itemset generated from $(k - 1)$ element item-sets using Apriori principle.

Deriving the Association rules with Apriori

1. Find all individual elements (1 element itemset, L1) from Transactions dataset Td with support more than min_s. L1 consists of only '+1', or '−1' or '0'.
2. DO
   a. Use previously found j element itemset (Lj) to find all (j + 1) element itemsets with a minimum support of min_s.
   b. This becomes the set of all frequent (j + 1) itemsets that are interesting
   c. Divide each frequent itemset X into two parts antecedent (LHS) and consequent (RHS). The Association rule becomes of the form R: LHS-> RHS.
   d. The confidence of such a rule is calculated as:

$$\text{Confidence } (R) := \text{support}(X)/\text{support}(LHS)$$

   e. Discard all rules whose confidence is less than min_c.
3. WHILE itemset size less than k.

Rank the Generated Association Rules

Rank all the derived association rules as per there support and confidence value. Top K rules are of importance. Value of K depends on the investors risk profile and preferences.

4 Results and Analysis

We have used open source java based frequent pattern mining library SPMF [7] for deriving association rules with apriori and suitably modified to incorporate other required changes. For our experiments we have considered minimum support as 0.2, minimum confidence value as 0.4 and minimum lift as 0.1 with acceptable results. Fig. 2 shows the initial time series plotting of different sectors where co-movement patterns can be visually seen. One important point to consider regarding Fig. 2 is that it shows same day co-movement pattern, hence it cannot be used for prediction analysis. So next logical step is to introduce some days lag between any two sectoral index movements and find if there is any correlation. Then correlation coefficient among different sector pairs with different delay period from 0 day to 5 days has been calculated as shown in Table 1. Different correlation values are plotted against delay in Fig. 3 to show the positive, negative as well as no-correlation between different sectors with varying delays. It is observed that a day lag of 0 denotes same day index movement correlation. Hence high same day correlation does not help in forecasting as that cannot be used to gain profit. Finally Table 2 shows the top 15 association rules that are mined using the above mentioned method and ranked as per rules' support and confidence measure. As a measure of interest of the rules lift values are also calculated

Table 2. Top 15 Association rules generated

Rule#	Sector pair	Delay (days)	Association rule	Supp	Conf	Lift
R0	Metal-Pharma	5	$-1 \Longrightarrow 1$	0.4198	0.4951	0.562
R1	FMCG-Metal	2	$-1 \Longrightarrow 1$	0.4106	0.4856	0.556
R2	Auto-Bank	5	$1 \Longrightarrow -1$	0.4033	0.4851	0.572
R2	IT-Pharma	5	$-1 \Longrightarrow 1$	0.3951	0.5161	0.562
R3	FMCG-Pharma	3	$-1 \Longrightarrow 1$	0.3918	0.4120	0.558
R4	Metal-Pharma	2	$-1 \Longrightarrow 1$	0.3902	0.4550	0.521
R5	Bank-FMCG	5	$-1 \Longrightarrow 1$	0.3827	0.4721	0.539
R6	Auto-Bank	1	$1 \Longrightarrow -1$	0.3806	0.4476	0.537
R7	FMCG-Metal	1	$-1 \Longrightarrow 1$	0.3765	0.4471	0.5111
R8	FMCG-Pharma	2	$-1 \Longrightarrow 1$	0.3699	0.4973	0.525
R9	Bank-IT	5	$-1 \Longrightarrow 1$	0.3663	0.4406	0.5228
R10	IT-Pharma	2	$-1 \Longrightarrow 1$	0.3659	0.4762	0.5223
R11	Bank-FMCG	4	$-1 \Longrightarrow 1$	0.3607	0.4444	0.5091
R12	Metal-Pharma	4	$-1 \Longrightarrow 1$	0.3607	0.4251	0.4825
R13	FMCG-Pharma	4	$-1 \Longrightarrow 1$	0.3566	0.4833	0.50833
R14	FMCG-Metal	4	$-1 \Longrightarrow 1$	0.3566	0.4244	0.4838

and shown. From the results we see that amongst considered 6 sectors metal and FMCG go hand in hand where as auto index has very low co movement with other sectors considered. IT and pharma index also shows similar pattern. From pure economic point of view both IT and pharma sector greatly dependent on dollar exchange value and with the changes in dollar price both the sector reacts similarly. Auto index movements were very low during the year 2015 than all other sectors and it again can be attributed to non-reduction of car loan interest rates during the year. So this gives out some interesting correlation between different sectors. Rule R0 is interpreted as if metal index goes down then after 5 days pharma sector may be up with a support of 42% and confidence of 49.5%. Similarly rule R2 indicates if auto index moves up then with a forecasting horizon of 5 days metal index may move downwards. Corresponding lift values also support our prediction as lift values are less than 1 so it implies negative correlation.

5   Conclusion and Future Work

Association rule mining along with statistical correlation analysis has been applied on sectoral index dataset to investigate co-movement patterns among them. Aprori algorithm, a well-known frequent itemset mining tool has been modified and applied for the present analysis. This study finds that different sectoral indices are correlated among themselves. One more interesting finding is that there exists a time delayed lagged correlation between different sectoral indices. This correlation can be exploited to predict the future index movement direction with a forecast horizon of d days where d is the number of day lag considered. Hence this model can be used by different investors in balancing their portfolio to minimize risk as well as in deciding which sector to invest next. This model can be considered for short term investment as only prediction of next few days is possible using current day's sectoral index movements. Results shows that some sectors are completely un-correlated but some are highly correlated (positively or negatively) with correlation coefficient values more than 0.8.

Future work will include analysis considering all sectors at a time instead of only a single sector predicts another. For example in this study association rules of the form, R: S1 -> S2 is used for simplicity, but in future all possible rules of the form R: (S1... Sj) -> Sk, where all other sectors jointly predicts some another sector's movement can be studied. Artificial neural network models can also be considered in combination with association rules to predict the sectoral index movement. In this study only historical closing values of indices are considered but there are many other factors and features like trading volume, market capitalization, debt ratio etc. that can be considered for prediction.

References

1. Liu, C., Malik, H.: A new investment strategy based on data mining and neural networks. In: 2014 International Joint Conference on Neural Networks (IJCNN), pp. 3094–3099. IEEE, July 2014
2. Inthachot, M., Boonjing, V., Intakosum, S.: Artificial neural network and genetic algorithm hybrid intelligence for predicting thai stock price index trend. Comput. Intell. Neurosci. **2016**, 1–8 (2016). Article ID: 3045254
3. de Oliveira, F.A., Nobre, C.N., Zárate, L.E.: Applying artificial neural networks to prediction of stock price and improvement of the directional prediction index–Case study of PETR4, petrobras, Brazil. Expert Syst. Appl. **40**(18), 7596–7606 (2013)
4. Reddy, B.S.: Prediction of stock market indices—using SAS. In: 2010 2nd IEEE International Conference on Information and Financial Engineering (ICIFE), pp. 112–116. IEEE, September 2010
5. Wichaidit, S., Kittitornkun, S.: Predicting SET50 stock prices using CARIMA (cross correlation ARIMA). In: 2015 International Conference on Computer Science and Engineering Conference (ICSEC), pp. 1–4. IEEE, November 2015
6. Liao, S.H., Chou, S.Y.: Data mining investigation of co-movements on the Taiwan and China stock markets for future investment portfolio. Expert Syst. Appl. **40**(5), 1542–1554 (2013)
7. Fournier-Viger, P., Gomariz, A., Soltani, A., Gueniche, T.: SPMF: open-source data mining platform (2013). http://www.philippe-fournier-viger.com/spmf/
8. Fonseka, C., Liyanage, L.: A data mining algorithm to analyse stock market data using lagged correlation. In: 2008 4th International Conference on Information and Automation for Sustainability, ICIAFS 2008, pp. 163–166. IEEE, December 2008
9. BSE India. http://www.bseindia.com. Accessed 26 Jan 2017
10. NSE India. http://www.nseindia.com. Accessed 26 Jan 2017
11. Dongre, J., Prajapati, G.L., Tokekar, S.V.: The role of Apriori algorithm for finding the association rules in data mining. In: 2014 International Conference on Issues and Challenges in Intelligent Computing Techniques (ICICT), pp. 657–660. IEEE (2014)

12. Imandoust, S.B., Bolandraftar, M.: Forecasting the direction of stock market index movement using three data mining techniques: the case of Tehran Stock Exchange. Int. J. Eng. Res. Appl (2014). ISSN 2248-9622
13. Agrawal, R., Imieliński, T., Swami, A.: Mining association rules between sets of items in large databases. ACM Sigmod Rec. 22(2), 207–216 (1993). ACM
14. Rusu, V., Rusu, C.: Forecasting methods and stock market analysis. Creative Math. 12, 103–110 (2003)
15. Dutta, A., Bandopadhyay, G., Sengupta, S.: Prediction of stock performance in indian stock market using logistic regression. Int. J. Bus. Inf. 7(1), 105 (2015)
16. Mahajan, K.S., Kulkarni, R.V.: Application of data mining tools for selected scripts of stock market. Int. J. Data Min. Knowl. Manage. Proc. 4(4), 55 (2014)
17. Ou, P., Wang, H.: Prediction of stock market index movement by ten data mining techniques. Mod. Appl. Sci. 3(12), 28 (2009)
18. Nair, B.B., Kumar, P.S., Sakthivel, N.R., Vipin, U.: Clustering stock price time series data to generate stock trading recommendations: An empirical study. Expert Syst. Appl. 70, 20–36 (2017)
19. Brin, S., Motwani, R., Ullman, J.D., Tsur, S.: Dynamic itemset counting and implication rules for market basket data. ACM Sigmod Rec. 26(2), 255–264 (1997). ACM

Task Allocation Strategies for FPGA Based Heterogeneous System on Chip

Atanu Majumder, Sangeet Saha$^{(\boxtimes)}$, and Amlan Chakrabarti

A.K. Choudhury School of IT, University of Calcutta, Kolkata, India
a.majumder007@gmail.com, sangeet.saha87@gmail.com, amlanc@ieee.org

Abstract. FPGA based heterogeneous System On Chips (SOCs) have become a prospective processing platform for modern performance-sensitive systems, like automotive, avionics, chemical reactor etc. In such system, *"makespan"* time minimization plays a crucial role to achieve higher throughput as well as performance efficiency and thus, efficient task allocation schemes are indeed essential. This paper presents two task allocation algorithms for such FPGA based heterogeneous SOCs. The first allocation strategy is based on well known "Branch and Bound" optimization technique. Secondly, we proposed a novel heuristic based allocation mechanism, *TAMF (Task Allocation Mechanism for FPGA based heterogeneous SOC)*. The simulation based experimental results reveal that both the strategies are able to provide lower *makespan* time over various simulation scenarios with acceptable runtime overheads. Achieved simulation results are further tested through a validation, carried out on practical ZYNQ SOC platform using standard benchmark task sets.

Keywords: Tasks allocation · FPGA · Branch and bound · *makespan* time

1 Introduction

Embedded systems are now-a-days employing FPGAs as a prospecting computing platform in various fields, ranging from avionic and automotive systems, nuclear reactors [1] to synthetic vision, object tracking [2] etc. These FPGAs provide the performance efficiency of a dedicated hardware as well as flexibility of a general purpose processor. Recently, FPGAs are also being integrated in *System on Chip (SOC)* along with pre-fabricated Hard-core processors and Soft-core processors (Constructed using FPGA logic) [3]. Such "Heterogeneous" systems contain different Processing Elements (PEs) with certain performance characteristic and can execute a set of tasks by assigning them on suitable PEs.

As an interesting example, such heterogeneous SOCs may be used as a performance efficient processing platform for automotive systems. In automotive systems [4], an ample amount of routine tasks need to be executed at system instantiation before its full phase functioning begins. Suppose, this SOC will perform the parallel execution of those initial set of tasks by appropriately assigning

© IFIP International Federation for Information Processing 2017
Published by Springer International Publishing AG 2017. All Rights Reserved
K. Saeed et al. (Eds.): CISIM 2017, LNCS 10244, pp. 341–353, 2017.
DOI: 10.1007/978-3-319-59105-6_29

them on individual PEs, such that the completion time of all tasks are minimized and the system can quickly start functioning, after its instantiation. Therefore, it is essential to have well defined tasks allocation strategy, feasibility criteria for achieving high resource utilization with performance efficiency.

In this paper, we propose two novel static tasks allocation strategies for FPGA based heterogeneous SOCs. The first strategy is optimal "Branch and Bound" [5] based task allocation technique and the second one, is based on heuristic approach, coined as *TAMF* allocation strategy. The contributions of this work can be summarized as follows:

- ILP based problem formulation for tasks assignments on FPGA based heterogeneous SOCs.
- Employing the optimal "Branch and Bound" strategy for tasks assignments.
- Proposal of a new *TAMF* heuristic for faster tasks allotments.
- The experimental results reveal the efficacy of the proposed approaches in various simulation scenarios and also showed that the performance of *TAMF* is comparable to optimal Branch and Bound technique in most of the cases.
- Validation of the proposed tasks allocation strategies on actual FPGA based heterogeneous SOC named ZYNQ [3], using benchmark task sets.

The rest of the paper is organized as follows. The next section provides a brief discussion on important related works conducted. This is followed by a discussion on the system model adopted in this work in Sect. 3. In Sect. 4, we present the formulation of the tasks allocation problem. The proposed Branch and Bound based strategy and TAMF with illustrating examples, are discussed in Sects. 5 and 6, respectively. Section 7 presents simulation based experimental results along with analysis and discussion on the same. The validation of the approaches on ZYNQ platform is discussed in Sect. 8. The paper finally concludes in Sect. 9.

2   Related Work

The generic problem of efficient task allocation on heterogeneous multiprocessor systems (with CPUs and GPUs or Processors having different instruction sets) have drawn considerable research interest in last few years [6,7]. One stream of researchers [8,9] have delved towards finding out the efficient allocation schemes for *dependent* task sets. On the other hand, a plethora of research works [10,11] are available which dealt with *independent* tasks sets. Authors in [10], present an Integer Linear Programming (ILP) based tasks allotment scheme which guarantees the execution speedup upto a certain bound. In [11], authors proposed two tasks assignment algorithms and discussed about the performance between migrative allocation approach which allows tasks migration among different types of processors and the non-migrative approach. Further, the problem of tasks handling in heterogeneous multiprocessor systems has spun-off in another direction where tasks could be *static* or *dynamic* in nature. In [12], authors considered static allocation where the tasks remain quantitatively constant through out the schedule. Similarly in [13], authors proposed a dynamic allocation technique for heterogeneous multiprocessor system where tasks arrive in arbitrary instances.

Minimization of the *makespan*[1] time remains one of the principal research focus for researchers during allocation of tasks on heterogeneous multiprocessors. Thus, the researchers reported both fast heuristic based algorithms as well as optimal algorithms. Heuristics based independent task allocation strategies such as greedy approach, ant colony optimization techniques can be found in [14]. In [15], authors proposed "Branch and Bound" based optimization strategy to achieve optimal solution. However, literatures about tasks allocation on FPGA based heterogeneous SOCs with proper optimization technique is merely a handful. The existing research works [16,17] mainly employed hardware and software tasks partitioning as a tasks allocation strategy. The computation intensive tasks are being executed using FPGA fabric as a hardware task whereas tasks having less computation requirements are assigned to CPUs for execution as a software task. However, such allotments are often plagued with some limitations.

3   System Model and Assumptions

The system model, considered in this work is a FPGA based heterogeneous SOC. Our heterogeneous SOC contains an FPGA logic area and pre-fabricated Hard Cores (HCs). Further, the FPGA logic consists of Reconfigurable Regions or tiles (RRs) to execute hardware tasks and Soft Cores (SCs) (which constructed using FPGA logic) for software tasks execution. Hence, the system model under consideration contains three distinct types of PEs that is RR, SC, HC which completely resembles with modern ZYNQ [3] architecture. Depending upon the SOC architecture, a particular type of PE could exist in multiple units.

Being an embedded system, the initial distributions of tasks are known at design time and each task is capable of running on each type of PEs. The proposed system model is further characterized by the following assumptions:

- A task cannot execute simultaneously on two distinct PEs at same instant and will be strictly executed on a single PE (till it execution requirements fulfills), which implies that tasks are non-migrative in nature.
- Tasks are independent and thus, each PEs can operate in parallel to execute an individual task.
- The cost of execution of each task over each distinct type of PEs is calculated through profiling and stored in offline.
- PEs are capable to suffice the memory and I/O requirements of any task.

At system instantiation (time, $t = 0$), a fixed number of tasks will arrive for possible allotment on SOC and will be stored in a queue. Our strategy will attempt to allocate tasks, such that the makespan time gets minimized. Algorithms will operate through a dedicated HC (termed as *allocator*) and will allocate tasks on

---

[1] It is the total length of the schedule i.e. when all the tasks have finished their execution.

respective PEs, as per the outcome. The pictorial representation of the proposed system model is shown in Fig. 1. A practical validation of the proposed system model on physical ZYNQ platform is illustrated in Sect. 8.

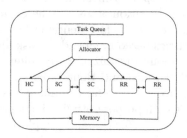

Fig. 1. System model

4   Problem Formulation

Let us assume a task set $\tau = \{T_1, T_2, ..., T_N\}$, arrives for possible allotment over $\mathcal{M}$ distinct types of PEs where each jth type of PE is comprised of k^j units. Such multiple units of a particular type of PE is individually referred as *"core"*. It may be noted that the cost of execution of a task, will be same for all the cores which belong to a particular type of PE.

At a particular instant t, we can allocate atmost $(\sum_{j=1}^{\mathcal{M}} k^j)$ tasks for parallel execution over all resources. Let, $C_{i,j}$ denotes the cost of execution incurred by T_i when assigned to j^{th} type of PE. Let us define a binary variable t_{ikj} as follows:

$$t_{ikj} = \begin{cases} 1, & \text{When } T_i \text{ is assigned to any one of the } k^j \text{ cores of } j^{th} \text{ type PE} \\ 0, & \text{otherwise} \end{cases}$$

Hence, we can illustrate the makespan time mk as:

$$mk = Max\{\sum_{i=1}^{\eta} \sum_{i'=1}^{k^j} C_{ij} * t_{ikj}\}, \quad \forall j \in \mathcal{M} \tag{1}$$

where, η denotes the number of tasks assigned to j^{th} type of PE.

In order to achieve lower mk, the objective function can be defined as:

$$\text{Minimize} \quad mk \tag{2}$$

Subject to the following constraints:

- The maximum number of tasks that can operate in parallel at a particular instant, can be atmost equal to the total number of available resources.
- No task can simultaneously execute on different resources. Thus, at a particular instant, following equation has to be satisfied.

$$\sum_{j=1}^{M} \sum_{i'=1}^{k^j} t_{ikj} \leq \sum_{j=1}^{M} k^j \tag{3}$$

5   Branch and Bound Based Allocation Strategy

The above problem formulation clearly depicts that the proposed task allotment phenomena turns into an ILP based optimization problem and hence, NP-complete in nature [18]. Once a problem enrolls into the NP-complete category, it is very unlikely that an algorithm with polynomial time complexity can be designed in order to solve that one. The optimal Branch and Bound [5], implicitly enumerates all of the feasible solutions by forming and traversing a *"state space tree."*[2] The tree is constructed using *DFS* [19] algorithm. At each node of the *state space tree*, the *Lower Bound (LB)* has to be calculated such that, search effort for probing the solution space can be reduced.

The cost incurred by the allocated tasks and the probable (underestimate) cost that will be incurred by the remaining unallocated tasks, will reflect as a sum in *LB*. Similarly, *Upper Bound (UB)*, is calculated by considering the worst case cost (instead of minimum cost) of the unallocated tasks.

At a particular node (N_T), if the calculated *LB* appears to be larger or equal to the best solution result found so far, then the enumeration of the subtree rooted at N_T can be skipped. It definitely implies that some nodes and subtrees will be *"pruned-off"* but it will obviously not jeopardize the optimality.

The pseudo-code for the proposed Branch and Bound strategy is shown in Algorithm 1. In the following section, we will illustrate an example which will depicts our proposed Branch and Bound allocation strategy through a test case.

Algorithm 1. Branch and Bound Based Allocation Strategy

Input: Task set τ, $\mathcal{M}$ types of PEs (including k^j units)
Output: Allocation of tasks which provide minimum mk.

1 For each PE, calculate the minimum task execution costs;
2 Sum up those minimum execution costs and assign to *Start_Value*;
3 **while** τ *is not empty* **do**
4   **for** *each task* $T_i \in \tau$ **do**
5   Find the *LB* for each type of PEs;
6   Find task T_β which provides *min-LB* (minimum *LB*) for say, j^{th} PE;
7   {In case of multiple existence of *min-LB*, choose any arbitary T_β};
8   Calculate *UB* of T_β for that j^{th} PE;
9   *Allocated_Value* = Summation of the costs of already allocated task/tasks;
10   **if** *(min-LB + Allocated_Value)* $\geq$ *Start_Value* **AND** *min-LB* $<$ *UB* **then**
11   Assign T_β to j^{th} PE;
12   Remove T_β from the τ;
13   **else**
14   Choose the next *min-LB*;
15   Go to step 10;

16 Find mk using Eq. 1.

---

[2] A tree constructed in the solution space.

5.1   An Example of Branch and Bound (BnB) Based Strategy

Let us consider six tasks, $\tau = \{T_1, T_2, ..., T_6\}$ that appear for the possible allotment (such that *makespan* time get minimized) in our proposed FPGA based heterogeneous SOC. Let us assume that system under consideration contains, one unit of RR ($k^1 = 1$), two units of SC (hence, $k^2 = 2$; $core_1$ and $core_2$ of SC) and two cores of HC ($k^3 = 2$), one of which is dedicatedly acting as *allocator*. The performance of each task over these three ($\mathcal{M} = 3$) distinct types of PEs is measured through profiling and displayed in Table 1.[3] It may be noted that the execution performance for both the cores of SC will be same and hence, not explicitly shown in the Table 1.

Table 1. Tasks parameters

PEs	Tasks					
	T_1	T_2	T_3	T_4	T_5	T_6
HC	4	5	1	14	5	5
SC	3	7	3	11	4	3
RR	7	9	5	9	9	5

Table 2. Tasks LBs

PEs	Tasks					
	T_1	T_2	T_3	T_4	T_5	T_6
HC	15	16	12	25	16	14
SC	12	16	15	20	13	**12**
RR	14	16	15	16	16	12

The minimum execution cost demanded by HC is one time-unit for executing T_3. Similarly, SC demands minimum three time-units for both the cores and RR demands minimum five time-units while executing the tasks T_6 and T_3, respectively. Hence, $Start\_Value = 1 + 3 + 3 + 5 = 12$.

A particular LB value can be calculated as follows: let us consider, T_6 is allocated in SC and thus, the incurred cost of T_6 will be **3** time-units. This allocation implies that, SC ($core_1$) and T_6 will be out of consideration for the next course of calculation. The minimum cost that will be incurred by *remaining unallocated tasks* can be found as: "minimum execution cost demand by HC": 1 + "minimum execution cost demand by SC ($core_2$)": 3 + "minimum execution cost demand by RR": 5. Hence, the corresponding LB becomes: $3 + (1 + 3 + 5) = 12$. Similarly, by considering each individual allotment possibilities, LBs for each task corresponding to each type of processing resource is calculated and shown in tabular form in the Table 2.

Following the steps 6–8 of Algorithm 1, min-LB can be found as 12 of T_6 for SC ($core_1$). Hence, UB of T_6 for SC can be calculated as follows: "maximum execution cost for HC": (**14**) + "maximum execution cost for SC ($core_2$)": (**11**)+ "maximum execution cost for RR": (**9**) + cost of T_6 for SC ($core_1$) (**3**). Hence, UB of task T_6 for SC becomes: 37. Before the task allocation procedure begins, $Allocated\_Value$ is initialized as zero. Thus, it may be observed that T_6

---

[3] The values corresponding to tasks are depicting the execution cost in terms of time-units.

is satisfying the conditions stated in step 10 of the Algorithm 1. Hence, T_6 successfully assigned to SC ($core_1$) and removed from the task set τ. In the same way, following the steps of Algorithm 1, the allocation procedure will continue until τ becomes empty. The final task allocation scenario and corresponding mk is shown in Table 3.

6   TAMF-Working Principle

It is worth mentioning that Branch and Bound strategy demands higher degree of computations and may become computationally intensive when the number of task increases. Hence, we propose a novel heuristic based tasks allocation strategy called TAMF. TAMF will be executed once at system instantiation and tasks will be allocated as per the achieved task-to-PE mapping information.

At the beginning of TAMF, the task set τ gets ready with sorted execution cost of each task (in non-decreasing order) for different types of PEs. We assume that each type of PE provides minimum execution cost for atleast one task. Hence, TAMF will choose the element of the sorted sequence for allocation. It ensures that the task will be allocated to that particular PE for which it has the minimum execution cost. Now as soon as core/cores of a PE, finishes its pre-assigned execution, it will look for the next most eligible candidate task T_α. T_α can only be allocated to a "free"[4] PE, if and only if the following two conditions hold alternatively:

i. The execution cost of the T_α is minimum for the free PE (among all PEs).
ii. The execution cost of the T_α for the free PE $\leq$ average execution cost of T_α.

Here, both the conditions attempt to ensure that T_α should completes with its lower execution requirement and thus, maximizing the probability of having minimum mk. Moreover, the allocation of T_α to any other PE might not be able to provide better mk. TAMF will continue its own operation till any unallocated task remains. The pseudo-code for TAMF is depicted in Algorithm 2.

Table 3. Tasks allotment and mk: BnB Based

PEs	Allocated task(s)	Consumed cost	mk
HC	T_2, T_3	$5+1=6$	9
SC	$Core_1 <= T_1, T_5$	$3+4=7$	
	$Core_2 <= T_6$	3	
RR	T_4	9	

Table 4. Tasks allotment by TAMF

PEs	Time								
	1	2	3	4	5	6	7	8	9
HC	T_2					T_3			
SC ($core_1$)	T_1		T_6						
SC ($core_2$)	T_5								
RR									T_4

---

[4] The PE finished its earlier execution and currently not executing any task.

Algorithm 2. TAMF

Input: Task set τ, $\mathcal{M}$ types of PEs

Output: Allocation of tasks for achieveing minimum mk.

1 $\{T_\alpha$: next candidate task; $C_{\alpha j}$: execution cost of T_α in j^{th} PE; $C_{\alpha j}^{min} = \min\{C_{\alpha j}\}$, $\forall j \in \mathcal{M}$: minimum execution cost of T_α in j^{th} PE; $C_\alpha^{avg} = \sum_{j=1}^{M} C_{\alpha j}/\mathcal{M}$: average execution cost of T_α over all PEs$\}$;

2 **while** τ *is not empty* **do**

3   **for** *each* j^{th} *free PE*, $j \in \mathcal{M}$ **do**

4   **if** $C_{\alpha j} == C_{\alpha j}^{min}$ **OR** $C_{\alpha j} \leq C_\alpha^{avg}$ **then**

5   Assign T_α to the jth PE;

6   Remove T_α from τ;

7   j^{th} PE become *free* when $C_{\alpha j}$ completes.;

8 Find mk using Eq. 1;

6.1 TAMF in Work: An Example

Let us consider, the same set of tasks τ as shown in Table 1. As stated earlier, in this case τ contains all the parameters in a sorted fashion. Let us consider T_1 as a first candidate for allocation. It may be noted that the execution cost of T_1, related to each PEs is already being stored in a sorted sequence. T_1 consumes minimum execution cost 3 time units while executes in SC. On the other hand, the average execution cost of T_1 over all PEs becomes: $\{(3+4+7)/3\}$. It may be observed that T_1 satisfies the condition, stated in step 4 of the algorithm 2. Hence, T_1 is allocated on SC (arbitrarily, $core_1$) and removed from τ.

By following the same way, T_2 gets allocated in HC but T_3 could get allocated in HC when T_2 finishes. Similarly, other tasks will be allocated by the following algorithm 2. The respective allocation and execution sequence of each task is shown in Table 4. It is very much evident that all the tasks complete their execution requirements within 9 time units and thus, $mk = 9$.

7 Experiments and Results

The performance of the Branch and Bound based strategy and TAMF have been evaluated by conducting simulation based experiments using randomly generated task sets whose execution cost corresponding to a PE have been taken from normal distribution. The performance metrics used for evaluation are *makespan* time as defined in Eq. 1 and the Computational Overheads, CO (measured in terms of consumed clock cycles/CPU ticks). Data sets for various values of N (10 to 30)[5], have been generated on systems containing total 2 to 8 cores of three types of PEs. Each result is generated by executing 50 different instances of each data set type and then taking the average over these 50 runs.

---

[5] Routine tasks within an embedded system typically lies within this range [20].

Table 5 shows the performance variation of Branch and Bound (BnB) based strategy and TAMF over different number of processing resources. It may be observed from the third and fourth column of the table, that BnB based technique can effectively eliminate the possible numbers of solution (by traversing less number of nodes) through an intelligent pruning technique. Moreover, as N increases, the computation overhead related to the LB estimation also increases (lines 4–5, Algorithm 1) and thus, the CO_{BnB} of overall strategy increases. Another notable observation reveals that when the number of processing resources increases by keeping N fixed, the number of traversed node (AF prun) as well as CO_{BnB} also increases, this is mainly because the additional overheads incurred in LB calculation for the increment in processing resources. This observations is also supported by Fig. 2(a).

Table 5 also establishes the fact that TAMF demands less computational overhead than Branch and Bound based strategy. This observation may be attributed to the fact that being a heuristic based policy, TAMF does not implicitly enumerate all possible solutions instead, employs task selection mechanism with linear overhead and thus, costs less CO_{TAMF}. Moreover, like BnB based strategy, increase in N also endorses increment in TAMF's overheads. However, if BnB based strategy and TAMF runs on an *allocator* whose frequency is 1.5 GHz then CO_{BnB} and CO_{TAMF} for $N = 10$ (with six processing resources) becomes 0.72 and 0.16 in milliseconds, respectively. Figure 2(b), depicts bar chart showing *makespan* time (mk) produced by Branch and Bound based strategy and TAMF for number of tasks (N) varying from 10 to 30 with constant number of processing resources as 8. From the respective figure, it is very much evident that in most

Table 5. Performance of Branch and Bound (BnB) based strategy and TAMF

PEs[a]	N	BF Prun	AF Prun	CO_{BnB}	CO_{TAMF}
HC - 2	10	> 100^2	330	1080551	243112
	15	> 100^2	720	2775883	384098
SC - 2	20	> 100^2	1260	5490998	535518
	25	> 100^2	1950	9675934	679567
RR - 2	30	> 100^2	2790	15481722	832551
HC - 3	10	> 100^2	440	1755676	252107
	15	> 100^2	960	4621855	391578
SC - 3	20	> 100^2	1680	10279888	552077
	25	> 100^2	2600	17389423	724583
RR - 2	30	> 100^2	3720	28938997	877661

N: Number of tasks, **BF Prun**; **AF Prun**: Numbers of expected and actual nodes traveled respectively, CO_{BnB}: Computational overheads in terms of Clock ticks for Branch and Bound based strategy, CO_{TAMF}: Computational Overheads for TAMF
[a] PEs with individual number of cores

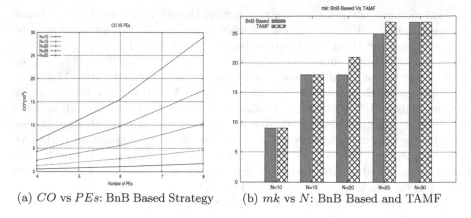

(a) CO vs PEs: BnB Based Strategy   (b) mk vs N: BnB Based and TAMF

Fig. 2. Performance of BnB based strategy and TAMF

of the cases, the efficiency of Branch and Bound based strategy and TAMF (in terms of mk) is comparable. Through a deeper observation, it can be observed that for $N = 20$ tasks, BnB based strategy provides $mk = 18$ (slightly lower) while TAMF produces $mk = 21$. However, TAMF will cost $CO_{TAMF}=552112$ clock cycle which is 18.6% lower than the BnB based strategy (refer, Table 5).

8   Validation in Physical ZYNQ Platform

Besides of the thorough theoretical and simulation studies, we have also validated the proposed strategies in actual FPGA based heterogeneous SOC (ZYNQ:ZC702) with synthetic task sets. The platform contains three distinct types of PEs that is the FPGA chip, dual core ARM Cortex-A9 processor and MicroBlaze (MB) processor. In the ZYNQ board, these ARMs are located in PS (Processing System) region and FPGA logics are separate as PL (Programmable logic) region [3]. In PL, the Reconfigurable Regions (RRs) are done to carry out the hardware task execution and Soft Core (SC) MB executes software tasks. In PS, ARMs are pre-fabricated and hence, termed as Hard Core (HC). It may be observed that the ZYNQ architecture resembles our adopted system model. Xilinx PlanAhead 14.4 and XPS, EDK, SDK 14.4 [3] tools are have been used for this validations.

8.1   Customization of the Platform

For the purpose of the meaningful validation, the ZYNQ platform needs to be architecturally customized.

- In the PL, RR was properly marked and the execution of each task on that RR is ensured by properly maintaining the UCF [3] constraints.

- Two MBs are added in the PL using XPS IP-core. RR and MB are connected through inter PL bus architecture.
- The RR, MB both are operated with PLs clock (FCCLK) of 50 MHz frequency.
- One ARM core (*core*-0) is kept for possible task allotment and another ARM (*core*-1) works as *allocator*. These ARMs are operating using 667 MHz frequency.
- Both the PS and PL are communicating through GP0 and GP1 port. PS and PL are also connected with OCM (On-Chip Memory) using AXI bus.

8.2   Synthetic Task Set Creation

To cope-up with the customized platform, it is essential to have proper set of tasks. In our validation, we have constructed and profiled the sets of task. These task sets are taken from well known Benchmark task set named ITC'99 benchmarks [21]. This Benchmark consists of numerous task such as *"Adder"*, *"Decoder"*, *"Integer to Float conversion"* etc.

- Synthetic hardware tasks are created using VHDL code and performance of each such tasks is measured forming proper test-bench.
- Software tasks are written in system-c code. The execution performance of those tasks are measured for both MB and ARM. The execution cost of sample tasks is shown in Table 6.
- At design time, each hardware task is stored in its executable format (as *.bit*) in external memory. In ZYNQ, such *.bit* files are stored in *SD* card.
- Software tasks are stored in executable (*.elf*) format in the external *SD* card.
- This external memory is present in PS region and linked with the *allocator*.

8.3   Implementation and Outcomes

Both the strategies (Branch and Bound based and TAMF) are coded in system-c, compiled and stored (as respective executable format) in the *SD* card. At the system instantiation, ZYNQ starts booting from *SD* card and *core*-1 of ARM (*allocator*), initiates the execution of the respective strategy. After completion, the tasks allocation information are stored in a log file, in the external memory. Now *core*-1, will start allocation by transferring the respective *.bit* file to the PL (if a task is assigned to PL region) and *.elf* to MB, *core*-0 of ARM respectively. In the similar way, the *allocator* further reads the task assignment information from the stored log file and allocates tasks (in their respective executable format) from external memory to appropriate PEs.

Table 7 shows the performance of BnB based allocation strategy and TAMF over different number of processing resources, on the ZYNQ platform. From the table, it can be concluded that the trends of results in the actual platform concur with the outcomes obtained through simulation studies.

Table 6. Benchmark tasks execution overhead (clock ticks unit) on ZYNQ

PEs	Dec	Add	I2F	Lg2
HC	460158	455920	464819	451817
RR	750	35112	70089	465335
SC	41312	42736	87733	581298

Table 7. Performance on ZYNQ

PEs	N	BF Prun	AF Prun	CO_{BnB}	CO_{TAMF}
HC - 1	10	$> 100^2$	330	1268233	483468
SC - 2	-	-	-	-	-
RR - 2	20	$> 100^2$	1260	1988597	791436

9   Conclusion

In this paper, we presented methodologies for allocating task sets on FPGA based heterogeneous SOC such that *makespan* is minimized. An optimal strategy and heuristic based technique is discussed. We designed, implemented and evaluated the algorithms using simulation based experiments and the simulation results were further validated through real implementation on ZYNQ platform.

Acknowledgments. This work was supported in part by the TCS Research Fellowship Award, granted to Sangeet Saha and TEQIP Phase-II project of University of Calcutta, India.

References

1. Hayashi, T., Kojima, A., Miyazaki, T., Oda, N., Wakita, K., Furusawa, T.: Application of FPGA to nuclear power plant I&C systems. In: Yoshikawa, H., Zhang, Z. (eds.) Progress of Nuclear Safety for Symbiosis and Sustainability, pp. 41–47. Springer, Tokyo (2014). doi:10.1007/978-4-431-54610-8_5
2. Jin, J., Lee, S., Jeon, B., Nguyen, T.T., Jeon, J.W.: Real-time multiple object centroid tracking for gesture recognition based on FPGA. In: Proceedings of the 7th International Conference on Ubiquitous Information, Management and Communication, p. 80. ACM (2013)
3. Crockett, L.H., Elliot, R.A., Enderwitz, M.A., Stewart, R.W.: The Zynq Book: Embedded Processing with the Arm Cortex-A9 on the Xilinx Zynq-7000 All Programmable Soc. Strathclyde Academic Media (2014)
4. Fürst, S., Mössinger, J., Bunzel, S., Weber, T., Kirschke-Biller, F., Heitkämper, P., Kinkelin, G., Nishikawa, K., Lange, K.: Autosar-a worldwide standard is on the road. In: International VDI Congress Electronic Systems for Vehicles, vol. 62 (2009)
5. Corrêa, R., Ferreira, A.: Branch and bound. Parallel Algorithms for Irregular Problems: State of the Art, pp. 157–176 (2013)
6. Moreira, O., Valente, F., Bekooij, M.: Scheduling multiple independent hard-real-time jobs on a heterogeneous multiprocessor. In: Proceedings of the 7th ACM & IEEE International Conference on Embedded Software, pp. 57–66. ACM (2007)
7. Satish, N.R., Ravindran, K., Keutzer, K.: Scheduling task dependence graphs with variable task execution times onto heterogeneous multiprocessors. In: Proceedings of the 8th ACM International Conference on Embedded Software, pp. 149–158. ACM (2008)

8. Dhingra, S., Gupta, S.B., Biswas, R.: Hybrid gasa for bi-criteria multiprocessor task scheduling with precedence constraints. Comput. Appl. Int. J. **1**(1), 11–21 (2014)

9. Biswas, S.K., Rauniyar, A., Muhuri, P.K.: Multi-objective bayesian optimization algorithm for real-time task scheduling on heterogeneous multiprocessors. In: 2016 IEEE Congress on Evolutionary Computation (CEC), pp. 2844–2851. IEEE (2016)

10. Baruah, S.K., Bonifaci, V., Bruni, R., Marchetti-Spaccamela, A.: ILP-based approaches to partitioning recurrent workloads upon heterogeneous multiprocessors. In: ECRTS, pp. 215–225 (2016)

11. Raravi, G., Andersson, B., Nélis, V., Bletsas, K.: Task assignment algorithms for two-type heterogeneous multiprocessors. Real-Time Syst. **50**(1), 87–141 (2014)

12. Kofler, K., Grasso, I., Cosenza, B., Fahringer, T.: An automatic input-sensitive approach for heterogeneous task partitioning. In: Proceedings of the 27th International ACM Conference on International Conference on Supercomputing, pp. 149–160 (2013)

13. Tabatabaee, H., Akbarzadeh-T, M.R., Pariz, N.: Dynamic task scheduling modeling in unstructured heterogeneous multiprocessor systems. J. Zhejiang Univ. Sci. C **15**(6), 423–434 (2014)

14. Luo, P., Lü, K., Shi, Z.: A revisit of fast greedy heuristics for mapping a class of independent tasks onto heterogeneous computing systems. J. Parallel Distrib. Comput. **67**(6), 695–714 (2007)

15. Chow, K.W., Liu, B.: On mapping signal processing algorithms to a heterogeneous multiprocessor system. In: 1991 International Conference on Acoustics, Speech, and Signal Processing, ICASSP 1991, pp. 1585–1588. IEEE (1991)

16. Pagani, M., Marinoni, M., Biondi, A., Balsini, A., Buttazzo, G.: Towards real-time operating systems for heterogeneous reconfigurable platforms. In: OSPERT 2016, pp. 49–54 (2016)

17. Li, L., Sun, J., Li, W., Lv, Z., Guan, F.: Hardware/software partitioning based on hybrid genetic and tabu search in the dynamically reconfigurable system. Int. J. Control Autom. **8**(1), 29–36 (2015)

18. Papadimitriou, C.H.: Computational Complexity. Wiley, Chichester (2003)

19. Everitt, T., Hutter, M.: Analytical results on the BFS vs. DFS algorithm selection problem. Part I: tree search. In: Pfahringer, B., Renz, J. (eds.) AI 2015. LNCS, vol. 9457, pp. 157–165. Springer, Cham (2015). doi:10.1007/978-3-319-26350-2_14

20. Chattopadhyay, S.: Embedded System Design. PHI Learning Pvt. Ltd., Delhi (2013)

21. Davidson, S.: Itc'99 benchmark circuits-preliminary results. In: Proceedings of International Test Conference 1999, pp. 1125–1125. IEEE (1999)

Productivity Oriented Cooperative Approach to Scheduling IT Project Tasks

Tadeusz Nowicki[✉] and Robert Waszkowski

Military University of Technology, Warsaw, Poland
{tadeusz.nowicki, robert.waszkowski}@wat.edu.pl

Abstract. Task execution duration depends on the employee who performs the task. Specifically in IT projects, an experienced employee can perform assigned tasks several times faster than a novice worker can. Preparing the schedule, project manager should take into account individuals' productivity determined by analyzing historical data of tasks implementation. Consequently, measured productivity is used in preparing the schedule in an optimal manner (minimizing the time needed to complete project tasks by a team of workers with different skills). As an extension of previous studies the authors formulate a linear programming problem including the possible cooperation of employees with tasks execution. The result of the conducted research is a complete package supporting project managers in determining productivity and scheduling.

Keywords: IT project management · Scheduling · Linear programming

1 Introduction

One of the most important task for project managers is to prepare the schedule. To arrange an optimal schedule the manager must have knowledge of tasks structure and their workload. Tasks structure is based on the execution order, determining predecessors and successors of each task. Workload is defined as the standard time needed to complete each task [1, 5, 6, 9–14]. In many works the authors consider the situation where co-operators are allowed [2–4]. However, it is not assumed that co-operation is not additive. In addition, co-operation does not reduce the costs, but shorten the execution time of a set of tasks. In this paper is considered exactly such a problem.

In fact, duration of the task execution depends on the employee who performs the task. In many situations, experience and skills of workers can result in significant differences in the execution time of tasks. According to the conducted research, an experienced employee can perform assigned tasks several times faster than a novice worker.

The manager usually has a team composed of both experienced and novice staff. Therefore, it is crucial which worker will perform a given task. The correct assignment of the task performers can result in a significant shortening duration of the overall project.

In practice, the knowledge about the productivity of each team member increases with the development time. If the manager is able to measure productivity, he can reschedule next stages of the project in a way to achieve optimal results. Therefore, the

© IFIP International Federation for Information Processing 2017
Published by Springer International Publishing AG 2017. All Rights Reserved
K. Saeed et al. (Eds.): CISIM 2017, LNCS 10244, pp. 354–365, 2017.
DOI: 10.1007/978-3-319-59105-6_30

toolkit of a project manager must be equipped with computer-aided tools, allowing him/her to prepare the schedule as a result of a defined optimization problem. Preparing the schedule project manager should take into account individuals' productivity determined by analyzing historical data of tasks implementation. Consequently, measured productivity is used in preparing the schedule in an optimal manner (minimizing the time needed to complete project tasks by a team of workers with different skills).

In the article we assume scheduling of the project on the understanding that employees can cooperate and divide daily working time between tasks. It means that a task can be performed by more than one worker at the same time and a worker can perform more than one task at a time.

2   Mathematicl Model

2.1   The Problem Formulation

We assume that:
$R = \{1, 2, 3, \ldots, r, \ldots, R\}$ - is a set of numbers of the project task types
$Z = \{1, 2, 3, \ldots, z, \ldots, Z\}$ - is a set of numbers of project tasks

The types of project tasks, that have to be performed, can be described by the vector:

$$R^Z = (r_1, r_2, \ldots, r_z, \ldots, r_Z)$$

where r_z - is the number of the type of the z-th task, $r_z \in R, z \in Z$.

The task performance time is defined as an average time needed to perform the task by a worker without special skills. This time is called the reference time. The reference time is used to determine the task performance time of more qualified worker. The reference times for project tasks can be described by the vector:

$$C^w = \left(c_1^w, c_2^w, \ldots, c_z^w, \ldots, c_Z^w\right), z \in Z$$

The project tasks can include information about the need to perform other tasks before you started current task. Predecessors can be described by a matrix

$$D = \left[d_{ij}\right]_{z \times z}$$

where

$$d_{z_1 z_2} = \begin{cases} 1 - \text{if the execution of task } z_2 \text{ have to precede} \\ \quad\quad \text{the execution of task } z_1 \\ 0 - \text{otherwise} \end{cases}$$
$$z_1, z_1 \in Z$$

For the description of workers we assume that
$P = \{1,2,3,\ldots,p,\ldots,P\}$ – set of number of employees, to be taken into account in the tasks execution.

The suitability for performance of specific types of tasks can be defined for each employee. Let it be described by following matrix

$$U = [u_{pr}]_{P \times R}$$

where

$$u_{pr} = \begin{cases} 1 - \text{when the p}^{th} \text{ employee is able to accomplish the task of type r} \\ 0 - \text{otherwise} \end{cases}$$
$$p \in P, r \in R$$

The productivity of individual employees is different during the performance of different types of tasks. The difference in productivity of a given employee at a particular type of task is defined by a coefficient β, that represents how many standard time units assigned to perform a particular task the worker performs in one unit of his working time. Thus, the effectiveness of workers in the tasks of different types is defined by vector

$$\beta_p = (\beta_{p1}, \beta_{p2}, \ldots, \beta_{pr}, \ldots, \beta_{pR}), p \in P$$

Of course, if the p-th employee is not suitable for the task of r-type, which is defined in the matrix U: $u_{pr} = 0$, then there is also equality $\beta_{pr} = 0$.

Taking into account the productivity of the employee, the time for the task by the p-th worker (provided that the employee p suited to this type of task, namely $\beta_{pr} > 0$, $u_{pr} = 1$) is:

$$c_{pz} = \frac{c_z^w}{\beta_{pr_z}}$$

where

$$p \in P, z \in Z, r_z \in R^z, c_z^w \in C^w$$

2.2   Decision Variables

The decision relating to the project schedule is described by matrix-vector:

$$(X, T, X')$$

where:

$$X = [x_{pz}]_{P \times Z}$$

and

$$x_{pz} = \begin{cases} 1 - \text{if the p} - th \text{ worker will perform z} - th \text{ task} \\ 0 - \text{otherwise} \end{cases}$$
$$p \in P, z \in Z,$$

$$T = (\tau_1, \tau_2, \ldots, \tau_z, \ldots, \tau_Z),$$

$$\tau_z - \text{start time(number of an hour)of the z} - th \text{ task,}$$

and

$$X' = \left[x'_{pz}\right]_{PxZ}$$

$$x'_{pz} = \begin{cases} t'_{pz} - \text{if } x_{pz} = 1 \quad \text{than } t'_{pz} \in \{1, 2, \ldots, l_p\} \text{means amount of hours during a day,} \\ \qquad\qquad\quad \text{when p - th worker perfoms z - th task} \\ 0 - \text{if } x_{pz} = 0 \end{cases}$$

x'_{pz} can also be represented using binary variables x'_{pzl}, and then becomes:

$$x'_{pz} = \sum_{l=1}^{l_p} x'_{pz'l}$$

2.3   Problem Constraints

CA: each task must be completed by exactly one worker

$$\sum_{p=1}^{P} u_{pr_z} x_{pz} = 1, z \in Z \quad (CA)$$

CB: each worker has to perform at least one task

$$\sum_{z=1}^{Z} u_{pr_z} x_{pz} \geq 1, p \in P \quad (CB)$$

CC: task precedence must be taken into account
  The condition that the task z'' must precede task z' can be written as follows:

$$\tau_{z'} \geq d_{z'z''} \cdot \left(\tau_{z''} + \sum_{\substack{p = 1 \\ u_{pr_{z''}} \neq 0}}^{P} x_{pz''} \cdot \frac{c_{z''}^w}{\beta_{pr_{z''}}} \right) \quad (CC)$$

for $z', z'' \in Z, z' \neq z''$

CD: the worker cannot work more than l_p (i.e. 8) hours per day

To check the condition that the employee does not work more than eight hours a day, for each of the individual tasks, check for all tasks occurring at the time of its initiation, if the amount of time spent per day on their implementation does not exceed eight hours.

To select tasks that are performed at the start time of another task it should be noted that the task z' continues at the start time of the task z'' if each of the following inequalities is true:

$$\begin{cases} \tau_{z'} \leq \tau_{z''} \\ \tau_{z'} + c_{z'} \geq \tau_{z''} \end{cases}, z', z'' \in Z \qquad \begin{matrix} (CDA) \\ (CDB) \end{matrix}$$

Where inequality (CDA) means that the task z' begins earlier than the task z'' and inequality (CDB) means that the task z'' begins at the time the task z' lasts.

The way to check if the inequality $\sum_j a_j x_j \leq b$ is satisfied in [15].

Inequality $\tau_{z'} \leq \tau_{z''}$ is equal to $\tau_{z'} - \tau_{z''} \leq 0$, and the inequality (CDA) becomes:

$$\begin{cases} \tau_{z'} - \tau_{z''} + M \cdot e^1_{z'z''} \leq M + 0 \\ \tau_{z'} - \tau_{z''} - (m - \varepsilon) \cdot e^1_{z'z''} \geq 0 + \varepsilon \end{cases}, z', z'' \in Z \qquad \begin{matrix} (CDA1) \\ (CDA2) \end{matrix}$$

where m and M are, respectively, the lower and upper bound of the expression $(\tau_{z'} - \tau_{z''})$ and ε is a small number that causes the failure of inequality.

If the set of all possible occurrences of the expression $(\tau_{z'} - \tau_{z''})$ is defined as:

$$W = \{(\tau_{z'} - \tau_{z''}) : z', z'' \in Z\}$$

then the lower and upper bound should be considered as such values of m and M, that satisfy the inequalities:

$$\begin{cases} m \leq y \\ M \geq y \end{cases}, y \in W$$

After applying these transformations indicator variable $e^1_{z'z''} = 1$, when the inequality. (CDA) is satisfied.

The way to check if the inequality $\sum_j a_j x_j \geq b$ is satisfied in [15].

Inequality $\tau_{z'} + c_{z'} \geq \tau_{z''}$ can also be written as $\tau_{z'} - \tau_{z''} + c_{z'} \geq 0$.

In addition, substituting $c_{z'} = \sum_{p=1}^P \frac{c^w_{z'}}{\beta_{pr_{z'}}} \cdot x_{pz'}$ inequality can be written as

$$\tau_{z'} - \tau_{z''} + \sum_{p=1}^P \frac{c^w_{z'}}{\beta_{pr_{z'}}} \cdot x_{pz'} \geq 0$$

and then we have constraints in the form of:

$$
\begin{cases}
\tau_{z'} - \tau_{z''} + \displaystyle\sum_{\substack{p=1 \\ \beta_{pr_z} \neq 0}}^{P} \frac{c_{z'}^{w}}{\beta_{pr_z}} \cdot x_{pz'} + m \cdot e_{z'z''}^{2} \geq m+b \quad (CDB1) \\[4mm]
\tau_{z'} - \tau_{z''} + \displaystyle\sum_{\substack{p=1 \\ \beta_{pr_z} \neq 0}}^{P} \frac{c_{z'}^{w}}{\beta_{pr_z}} \cdot x_{pz'} - (M+\varepsilon)e_{z'z''}^{2} \leq b-\varepsilon \quad (CDB2) \\[4mm]
\hspace{4cm} , z', z'' \in Z
\end{cases}
$$

That means that $e_{z'z''}^{2} = 1$, when the inequality (CDB) is satisfied.

If l_p is the number of allowable hours of work per day for a p-th worker, then:

$$
\sum_{z'=1}^{Z} \left(e_{z'z''}^{1} \cdot e_{z'z''}^{2} \cdot x_{pz'}' \right) \leq l_p, p \in P, z'' \in Z
$$

In the further considerations it is necessary to use binary variables. Thus x_{pz}' can be written as:

$$
x_{pz}' = \sum_{l=1}^{l_p} x_{pz'l}'
$$

and after substitution:

$$
\sum_{z'=1}^{Z} \left(e_{z'z''}^{1} \cdot e_{z'z''}^{2} \cdot \sum_{l=1}^{l_p} x_{pz'l}' \right) \leq l_p, p \in P, z'' \in Z \; (*)
$$

It should be noted that the sum is over all z, also for the case where $z' = z''$.

It is a non-linear inequality. Linearization method for such inequalities is described in [15]. Let $y_{pz'z''l}' = e_{z'z''}^{1} \cdot e_{z'z''}^{2} \cdot x_{pz'l}'$. We then have:

$$
\sum_{z'=1}^{Z} \sum_{l=1}^{l_p} y_{pz'z''l}' \leq l_p, p \in P, z'' \in Z \quad (CDC)
$$

With additional constraints defined as:

$$
\begin{cases}
e_{z'z''}^{1} + e_{z'z''}^{2} + x_{pz'l}' - y_{pz'z''l}' \leq 2 \quad (CDD1) \\[2mm]
e_{z'z''}^{1} + e_{z'z''}^{2} + x_{pz'l}' - 3y_{pz'z''l}' \geq 0 \quad (CDD2) \\[2mm]
\hspace{1.5cm} p \in P, z'z'', \in Z, l \in L
\end{cases}
$$

After this transformation, we obtain the linear inequalities.

2.4   Objective Function

We have the objective function:

$$F(X,T,X') = \max_{z \in Z} \{\tau_Z + c_Z\}$$

and optimization problem:

$$\min_{X,T,X'} F(X,T,X')$$

So we have:

$$\min_{X,T,X'} \max_{z \in Z} \{\tau_Z + c_Z\}$$

what can be replaced with a linear optimization problem:

$\min_{X,T,X'} g$ - new linear objective function

$g \geq \tau_Z + c_Z, z \in Z$ - additional constraint

or, considering that:

$$c_z = \frac{c_z^w}{\sum_{p=1}^{P} \beta_{pr_z} \cdot x_{pz} \cdot \frac{\bar{x}_{pz}}{l_p}}$$
$$\beta_{pr_z} \neq 0$$

we have additional constraint as follow:

$$g \geq \tau_z + \frac{c_z^w}{\sum_{p=1}^{P} \beta_{pr_z} \cdot x_{pz} \cdot \frac{\bar{x}_{pz}}{l_p}}, z \in Z \quad (CX)$$
$$\beta_{pr_z} \neq 0$$

2.5   Optimization Problem

Accordingly, the full optimization problem is as follows:

$$\min_{X,T,X'} g$$

subject to

$$\sum_{p=1}^{P} u_{pr_z} x_{pz} = 1, z \in Z \quad (CA)$$

$$\sum_{z=1}^{Z} u_{pr_z} x_{pz} \geq 1, p \in P \quad \text{(CB)}$$

$$\tau_{z'} \geq d_{z'z''} \cdot \left(\tau_{z''} + \sum_{\substack{p=1 \\ u_{pr_{z'}} \neq 0}}^{P} x_{pz''} \cdot \frac{c_{z''}^{w}}{\beta_{pr_{z''}}} \right) \quad \text{(CC)}, z', z'' \in Z, z' \neq z''$$

$$\begin{cases} \tau_{z'} - \tau_{z''} + M \cdot e_{z'z''}^{1} \leq M + 0 & (CDA1) \\ \tau_{z'} - \tau_{z''} - (m - \varepsilon) \cdot e_{z'z''}^{1} \geq 0 + \varepsilon & (CDA2) \end{cases}, z', z'' \in Z$$

$$\begin{cases} \tau_{z'} - \tau_{z''} + \sum_{\substack{p=1 \\ \beta_{pr_z} \neq 0}}^{P} \frac{c_{z'}^{w}}{\beta_{pr_z}} \cdot x_{pz'} + m \cdot e_{z'z''}^{2} \geq m + b & (CDB1) \\ \tau_{z'} - \tau_{z''} + \sum_{\substack{p=1 \\ \beta_{pr_z} \neq 0}}^{P} \frac{c_{z'}^{w}}{\beta_{pr_z}} \cdot x_{pz'} - (M + \varepsilon) e_{z'z''}^{2} \leq b - \varepsilon & (CDB2) \end{cases}, z', z'' \in Z$$

$$\sum_{z'=1}^{Z} \sum_{l=1}^{l_p} y'_{pz'z''l} \leq l_p, p \in P, z'' \in Z \quad \text{(CDC)}$$

$$\begin{cases} e_{z'z''}^{1} + e_{z'z''}^{2} + x'_{pz'l} - y'_{pz'z''l} \leq 2 & (CDD1) \\ e_{z'z''}^{1} + e_{z'z''}^{2} + x'_{pz'l} - 3y'_{pz'z''zl} \geq 0 & (CDD2) \end{cases}, p \in P, z', z'' \in Z, l \in L$$

$$g \geq \tau_z + \frac{c_z^{w}}{\sum_{\substack{p=1 \\ \beta_{pr_z} \neq 0}}^{P} \beta_{pr_z} \cdot x_{pz} \cdot \frac{\bar{x}_{pz}}{l_p}}, z \in Z \quad \text{(CX)}$$

3 Comparison of Scheduling and Without Scheduling Cooperation

Below provides results of sample solutions of the task of determining the schedule for versions with and without the cooperation of employees [1, 5, 6, 9–14]. The solution of the same problem in two versions gives you the opportunity to direct comparison of results.

The problem with no cooperation is described in detail in [7]. Let us compare the scheduling results concerning cooperation possibility described in the current article with the results based on the scheduling model described in [7].

For evaluation of the method for determining the optimal allocation of workers to the tasks let us consider the following case.

Let 3 equally complex design tasks will be performed by 2 employees of equal productivity. Individual tasks do not depend on each other, and so they can be performed at the same time and in any order. The workload for each task is 8 h, and the productivity of each worker is 1.

3.1   Case #1. Scheduling with no Cooperation

Let us consider the case where the cooperation of employees in carrying out the task is not allowed. The results of the calculations for such case is shown in the following table and is described in the Gantt chart and resource load chart. (Table 1, Figs. 1 and 2)

Table 1. Results for case #1 – no cooperation

Task	Workload [h]	Predecessor	Employee assigned	Productivity	Start time	Duration [h]	End time
1	8		1	1	0	8	8
2	8		2	1	0	8	8
3	8		1	1	8	8	16

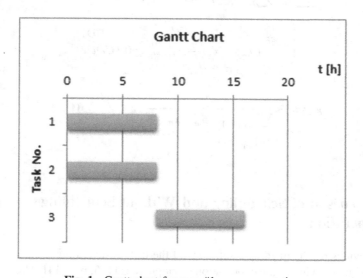

Fig. 1. Gantt chart for case #1 – no cooperation

On the resource load chart, it is shown the usage of the two employees labeled with different colors. The upper course of the graph for the selected worker means that the worker is working on a task, the lower - means that an employee at a given time is not used for the implementation of any task.

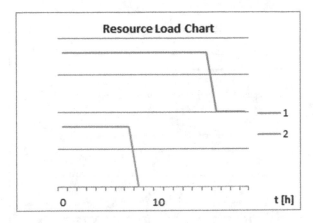

Fig. 2. Resource load chart for case #1 – no cooperation

3.2   Case #2. Scheduling with Cooperation

Let us consider the case where the cooperation of employees in carrying out the task is allowed.

Table 2. Results for case #2 – cooperation

Task	Workload [h]	Predecessor	Employee assigned	Productivity	Start time	Duration [h]	End time
1	8		1	1	0	8	8
2	8		2	1	0	8	8
3	8		1, 2	1, 1	8	4	12

The results of the calculations for such case is shown in the following table and is described in the Gantt chart and resource load chart. (Table 2, Figs. 3 and 4)

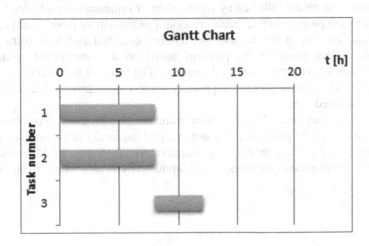

Fig. 3. Gantt chart for case #2 – cooperation

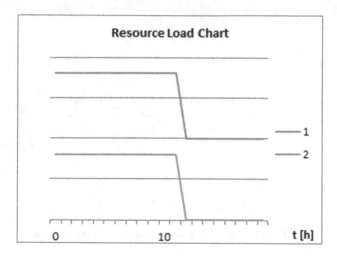

Fig. 4. Resource load chart for case #2 – cooperation

Just like before, on the resource load chart, it is shown the usage of the two employees labeled with different colors. The upper course of the graph for the selected worker means that the worker is working on a task, the lower - means that an employee at a given time is not used for the implementation of any task.

Assuming the cooperation opportunities of workers in the implementation of the design tasks, significant reduction of the overall duration time and a better use of resources is achieved. Employees are equally loaded throughout the duration of the project.

4   Conclusion

The mathematical model followed by formulation of optimization problems has been developed for the purpose of a schedule creation. Productivity of project team members is taken into account in the model. The authors designed and built software that formulates a linear programming problem based on a mathematical model. The problem is then solved using numerical methods. The result of the conducted research is a complete IT solution package supporting project managers in determining pro-ductivity and scheduling.

As for the further research it is worth to examine the possibility to prepare models for other variants of the problem, as far as to rebuild the model in a way that could use the estimation of the future productivity. Furthermore, the impact of differentiation of the software development processes on the productivity is also worth researching.

References

1. Brucker, P.: Scheduling Algorithms. Springer, Heidelberg (2007)
2. Chen, Z.L., Hall, N.G.: Supply chain scheduling: conflict and cooperation in assembly systems. Oper. Res. **55**(6), 1072–1089 (2007)
3. Calleja, P., Estévez-Fernández, A., Borm, P., Hamers, H.: Job scheduling, cooperation, and control. Oper. Res. Lett. **34**(1), 22–28 (2006)
4. Chryssis, G., Russell, A., Shvartsman, A.A.: Work-competitive scheduling for cooperative computing with dynamic groups. SIAM J. Comput. **34**(4), 848–862 (2005)
5. El-Rewini, H., Lewis, T.G., Ali, H.H.: Task Scheduling in Parallel and Distributed Systems. Prentice Hall Series in Innovative Technology, Upper Saddle River (1994)
6. Janiak, A.: Scheduling in Computer and Manufacturing Systems. WKŁ Publisher, Warsaw (2006)
7. Nowicki, T., Waszkowski, R.: The method for solving productivity oriented scheduling problem. Research in Logistics and Production, Poznan University of Technology (2013)
8. Nowicki, T.: Linear Mixed Equivalent of a Stochastic Scheduling Problem with Different Processors. Biul. WAT/4/1994 (1994)
9. Nowicki, T.: Stochastic bi-objective scheduling problem in a multiprocessor computer system. In: The 5'th International Workshop on Project Management and Scheduling. 11–13 April 1996, Poznań (1996)
10. Pinedo, M.L.: Scheduling. Theory, Algorithms and Systems. Springer, New York (2008)
11. Pinedo, M.L.: Scheduling. Planning and Scheduling in Manufacturing and Services. Springer, New York (2005)
12. Pochet, Y., Wolsey, L.A.: Production Planning by Mixed Integer Programming. Springer, New York (2005)
13. Simchi-Levi, D., Chen, X., Bramel, J.: The Logic of Logistics. Springer, New York (1997)
14. Sinnen, O.: Task Scheduling for Parallel Systems. Willey, Hoboken (2006)
15. Waszkowski, R.: Methods and Tools for Productivity Evaluation in IT Projects. Doctoral Disertation, WAT, Warszawa (2012)

Sequential Purchase Recommendation System for E-Commerce Sites

Shivani Saini[(✉)], Sunil Saumya[(✉)], and Jyoti Prakash Singh[(✉)]

National Institute of Technology Patna, Bihar, India
{shivani.cspg15,sunils.cse15,jps}@nitp.ac.in

Abstract. To find out which product should be recommended to the customer and when to recommend is done by the recommender system. Different approaches by using customer profile and product description are used to build recommender system. Although these information are not enough to recommend, sometimes buying of some products occurs in a stepwise manner, where buying of one product follows the buying of other products. The purpose of this research is to find the sequences followed by customers while purchasing products to improve the efficiency of recommender system. Sequence pattern mining is used to find out the order of purchasing products. The duration we find tells the time gap between the purchased product and recommendation of next sequential products.

Keywords: Data mining · Sequential pattern · Recommendation system · E-commerce

1 Introduction

Recommendation of products to attract their customers have become norm of every e-commerce website. A good recommendation system surely increases business of these sites as users may find their choice without too much searching. The analysis of popular e-commerce website, such as *flipkart.com, amazon.in* and *snapdeal.com* etc. reveals that recommendations to the users are made based on their browsing history or user's previous purchase pattern. Most of these recommendation system is applied to new products or services. But there are several merchandise which is regularly used by the users and brought in by the user at regular interval. An example of such products and recommendation is recently started by Amazon, which they have termed *subscribe and save* option. With *subscribe and save* option, Amazon offers some extra discounts on some selected products. On careful and detailed analysis, it was found that most of these items belong to grocery and packaged food items such as *Coffee, Tea* etc. Further analysis shows that not all grocery items are put under this option. For example, Amazon has given *subscribe and save* option for the product "Bru instant coffee 100g" but not for "Nescafe instant coffee 100g". This was the main motivation behind this work as why and how Amazon has decided some products to

K. Saeed et al. (Eds.): CISIM 2017, LNCS 10244, pp. 366–375, 2017.
DOI: 10.1007/978-3-319-59105-6_31

put them under *subscribe and save* option. Another interesting thing is that in Amazon *subscribe and save* option only same items are offered for discount. In this article, we are trying to find the sequence of all items which are brought regularity. We are not only finding the same product purchased every month, but, also the different products purchased one after another in a sequence. This type of mining generally used for sequential data, such as Books (divided into parts or the story in a sequence), TV serials, Movies (divided into parts or the story in a sequence). But, we believe this type of sequences can also exist between one or more products. User buy some products in a sequence, for example, most of the user buy mobile phone and mobile cover in a sequence. So, we are trying to find out such kind of sequences, in online shopping as shown in Table 1.

Table 1. Products purchased by the users

User	Month	Items purchased
User1	January	Soap, Coffee, Mobile phone
User1	February	Book, Coffee
User1	March	Mobile cover, Coffee
User2	January	Coffee,Tea
User2	February	Coffee, Book
User2	March	Coffee
User3	January	Mobile phone
User3	March	Mobile cover

From the Table 1, it is clear that the purchasing nature of the different user may not be similar. User1 and User3 have the similar purchasing patterns. They first purchase mobile phone, then purchased the mobile cover. Similarly, User1 and User3 has the similar purchasing patterns, as they have repeatedly purchased coffee every month. In this article, we are trying to find out the common purchase sequences among all the users. The sequences may consist the same items or different ones. Our main objective of this article is to find out the sequences in the online product purchasing system, i.e., the sequences frequent among all users and Intra-duration in the sequence.

The rest of the article is organized as follows: Sect. 2 is the literature review. In Sect. 3 we discuss the methodology by which we are finding the frequent purchase pattern sequences. The results are explained in Sect. 4, in Sect. 5 we discuss our findings and Sect. 6 is concluding our work.

2 Literature Review

In this section, a brief introduction about the recommendation system is presented. Recommender systems are software tools and techniques that give the suggestion to users to see or buy the items based on their browsing history, previous purchase history or by using their pattern of purchase history [3,10]. A recommendation system is widely used in almost every field such as movie recommendation, music, book, news, television shows, community question answer website, product recommendation, and many others. Since, taste of persons is not similar so, the recommendation is also not similar for all users.

A recommendation system is basically divided into three types: (a) Content based filtering [6], (b) Collaborative filtering [2] and (c) Hybrid approaches [4].

(a) Content-based filtering: This works with data that are provided by the users either explicitly (ratings) or implicitly (clicking on a link). Based on these data a user profile is generated to perform the recommendation to the similar user. The more participation of a user leads more accurate recommendation. Recommendation using the content is performed using the similarity score between the user profile and item profile, and finally, the top score item is recommended to the user. Since, the recommendation is performed based on user previous purchase history so, the most difficult problem of this approach is recommendation for new users, as there is no purchase history availability of new users.

(b) Collaborative filtering: It is a technique of making an automatic prediction system about the user with the help of other similar user's choice or information. Assumption used in collaborative filtering is to select and aggregate other user's opinion to provide a better recommendation of the active user's preferences. Probably, they assume that, if users agree about the quality or relevance of any items, then they may agree about other items. For example, if a group of user like the same product as *user x*, then *user x* is likely to like the product they like which he hasn't yet seen.

(c) Hybrid filtering: The concept of content based filtering and collaborative filtering is combined, to predict the next item more accurately. A work introduced by Liu et al. [8] used hybrid recommendation method that combines the segmentation-based sequential rule method with the segmentation-based KNN-CF method. The proposed method is based on user's RFM values. Where RFM (R = Recency, F = Frequency, and M = Monetary) is indicating the user activeness on the e-commerce website. The RFM value will be used to group the user in various clusters. Choi et al. [5] proposed a work which is the hybrid of implicit rating and explicit rating. They integrate collaborative filtering approach with a sequence pattern algorithm for improving the recommendation quality.

Mcauley et al. [12] built the recommendation system on the basis of product image and its matching accessories. Another work proposed by Mcauley et al. [11] built a network of substitutable and complementary products.

None of the above talked recommendation system focused on the sequences occur in the user's previous purchase history in the online purchase system. The problem of sequential pattern mining (SPM) was first introduced by Agrawal and Srikant [1]. In [1], the SPM was defined as follows: From a given database of sequences, where each sequence consists of a list of different transactions ordered by transaction time and a set of items, sequential pattern mining basically mines all such kinds of sequential patterns with a user specified minimum support value. Minimum support of a pattern is defined as the number of data sequences that contains such patterns. The discovery of such sequence required for various types of algorithms [1]. Many approaches are used to find out what would be the next product purchased by the user. Haiyun Lu [9] proposed an idea for recommendation of items which is based on sequential pattern mining. They used the users previous purchase history data to analyze the user purchase behavior at a particular location. The patterns are used to recommend the next category purchase item to a user in a particular location. Huang et al. [6] proposed a system based on sequential pattern which predicts the customer's time-invariant purchase behavior for food items in a supermarket. Khandaga et al. [7] proposed a mechanism which focused food recommendation system. As, today it is the biggest question "WHAT TO EAT". People always getting confused with their food choice. If a system recommends a right food items, then the user may like the system.

3   Methodology

It may be possible that a user purchase more than one item together but not always. There is a high possibility that if item1 is purchased today, then after a few days item2 would be purchased. Which item would be purchased together have well explained by Agrawal and Srikant [1]. They introduced Apriori algorithm in which, the whole dataset is scan number of times and with the help of user input minimum support and confidence value, the frequent purchase item set was extracted. For example, if item A and B are frequent pattern, then the association rule might be either $A \rightarrow B$ *or* $B \rightarrow A$ or it may be possible that item A and B purchased together. But, Aprioi is not able to find out the exact order in which the product might be purchased by the user. To resolve this issue, Sequential Pattern Discovery using Equivalence classes (SPADE) algorithm was introduced by Zaki et al. [13].

In this article, we are working with amazon dataset. With the help of SPADE algorithm we are trying to find out Frequent Sequential Purchase Pattern. The flow chart of our proposed work is shown in Fig. 1. In Fig. 1, U1, U2, U3 are users and A, B, C, D are products. Since, the structure of the dataset is not formatted as we required, so we have done some pre-processing steps to convert the dataset in our required format. In the next step, we apply sequence mining algorithm [13] to find out the sequences available in the dataset. Next we find out the time gap between the purchase of first product and next sequential product.

3.1   Dataset

To perform our analysis, we download the amazon dataset, which is available online[1]. It contains 82,677,139 (approx. 82 million) ratings of 9,874,213 products

---

[1] http://jmcauley.ucsd.edu/data/amazon/.

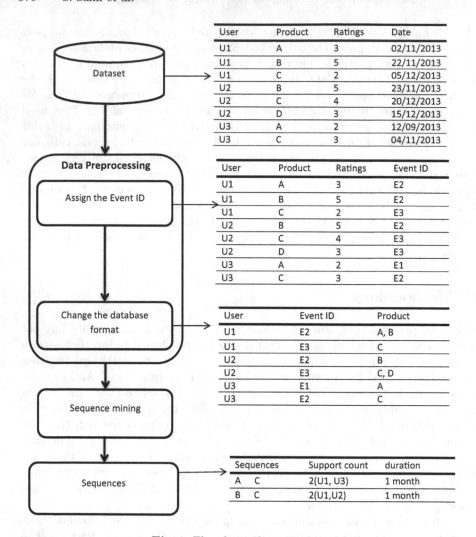

Fig. 1. Flowchart of proposed work

given by 21,176,523 users. Ratings are given by the user, since the year 1997 to 2014. Our proposal consists some assumption that is listed below:

Assumptions

- The transaction data is not available due to security and privacy concern. So, we are assuming that the user has given the review after purchasing the item.
- We are not concerned about the rating given by the user.

The Amazon dataset format is shown in Table 2. Here Product ID is *asin* (Amazon Standard Identification Number) number of the product which is used by Amazon to uniquely identify the products.

Table 2. Snapshot of dataset

USER ID	PRODUCT ID	Ratings	DATE
A1CCQTW8Q1XJ6E	B0002QB9NE	3	15-12-2013
A14R9XMZVJ6INB	B00EM5POSW	5	21-12-2013
A14RFF9JUIM34U	B00004Z1SX	2	02-12-2013
A14RFF9JUIM34U	B0002L5R78	1	14-10-2013
A14S2P9NK1V9VW	B000GQVVU6	3	26-01-2013

3.2 Data Preprocessing

In this section, we discuss about the data preprocessing steps. An example of the data preprocessing steps is shown in Table 3, in which the Table 3(a) is the same dataset format that we downloaded from amazon website and the Table 3(b) is coming after the preprocessing step.

Table 3. Change the database format (a) Before preprocessing step (b) After preprocessing step

USER	DATE	ITEMS
U1	02/01/2016	A
U1	05/01/2016	B,C
U1	01/02/2016	D
U1	20/02/2016	A
U2	03/01/2016	A
U2	05/01/2016	B

(a)

SID	EID	ITEMS
U1	E1	A,B,C
U1	E2	D,A
U2	E1	A,B

(b)

Where, SID is a sequence ID. We are considering one user as a one sequence as we are finding sequences trending among all users, EID is an event ID. We are binding whole month transaction with the same event ID and ITEMS are the product purchased by the user in a month. In the above example A, B, C, D are the products. In Table 3:

- E1= Items purchase in January 2016
- E2= Items purchase in February 2016

Set the Event: Set the event such as week, month, year, etc. If we choose month as event, then we will assign the same event ID for that month and we get monthly sequences, e.g.,

$$A \to B$$

The user has purchased A then after some months B will be purchased by the user.

3.3   Sequence Mining Algorithm

Any sequence mining algorithm can be used to find out the sequences. Here we are using SPADE algorithm. Sequence mining is generally used for sequential or episodic data. Two types of sequence on a product:

1. **Same products repeating:** Users repeatedly buy the same items monthly (or weekly, yearly etc.)basis. This type of sequences falls in this type.

$$A \rightarrow A$$

   Example: Sequence found in a serial or episodic data, i.e.,books, TV serials, Movie series
2. **One after another**: If a user buys different items in a sequence, then this type of sequences will come under this category.

$$A \rightarrow B$$

   Example: Mobile phone $\rightarrow$ Mobile case

3.4   Intra-duration

There is one more important aspect of recommender system is when to recommend the recommended product. The efficient recommender system should recommended user when they need it. So time plays an important role in recommender system. Here we find out the time elapsed between the purchase of first product and the next sequential products. For example, if we have sequence $A \rightarrow B$ then we find after how many months the user is purchasing B once he purchased A. For this, we are finding mean and mode of the duration followed by all users. Here, mean gives the average time gap between products, whereas, mode gives the duration followed by most of the users.

4   Result

The algorithm for preprocessing data and finding sequences are implemented in Python. The algorithm was executed on a 64 core server having 64 GB of RAM. To evaluate the result we split our dataset into train dataset and test dataset as shown in Table 4. On train dataset we built our recommender system however, test dataset was used to check its performance.

Table 4. Train test split

Dataset	No. of record	No. of user	No. of product
Train Dataset	6,22,528	3,627	3,36,489
Test Dataset	2,66,240	1,555	1,74,561

Table 5. Frequent items

Sr.no	Frequent items (asin)	Support count
1	B00934WBRO	199
2	B0026ZYZ7Q	145
3	B00934WBRO → B00B9AAI9S	86
4	B0026ZYZ7Q → B00B9AAI9S	81
5	B001AIJZQ6, B0021YV8LS	57

Table 5 represents some of the frequent item sets returned by our system. The first and second row of the Table 5 contains one item set while row 5 contains 2 item sets brought together. Row three and four of Table 5 contains the sequence of two items brought in order A → B where A represents the first item and B represents the second item. The supports counts (Number of users bought the items) of the frequent items are also shown in column three. We were only interested in the sequences of the item that are purchased by the user. In our dataset we got 268 such sequences.

Table 6 represents the frequent sequence along with the duration between purchasing of first product and the next sequential products. The fourth column of Table 6 shows the average duration represented as *d1*. The next column of the same table shows duration followed by most of the user represented as *d2*. Both *d1* and *d2* represents duration in months (as described in Sect. 3.4).

Table 6. Sequences

Sr.no	Frequent items (asin)	Support count	d1	d2
1	B00934WBRO → B00B9AAI9S	86	3	3
2	B0026ZYZ7Q → B00B9AAI9S	81	2	2
3	B007FK3CVM → B00934WBRO	73	2	3
4	B00934WBRO → B00C88DV6M	71	4	4
5	B0013OQGO6 → B00B9AAI9S 65	57	4	5

4.1 Validation

To check the performance of the system, we used the following metrics. *Accuracy:* The accuracy of the recommendation is defined as the ratio of users who are purchasing products in a specific sequence to the users who purchase the product together or in different sequence. Say N1 number of users purchase products P1 and P2 either together or in any sequence. N2 is the number of users who are purchasing products P1 and P2 in the sequence P1 → P2. Then accuracy can be defined as

$$Accuracy = \frac{\sum \frac{N2}{N1}}{\hat{n}} \qquad (1)$$

Table 7. Test results

P1	P2	N1	N2	N2/N1
B00934WBRO	B00B9AAI9S	34	34	1
B00934WBRO	B00C88DV6M	30	30	1
B00934WBRO	B009FKNGGQ	26	26	1
B00934WBRO	B0021YV8LS	25	25	1
B00934WBRO	B001AIJZQ6	24	24	1
B00934WBRO	B001AIJZQ6	24	24	1
B0026ZYZ7Q	B00B9AAI9S	35	34	0.971428571
B007FK3CVM	B00934WBRO	28	27	0.964285714
B007FK3CVM	B00934WBRO	28	27	0.964285714
B007FK3CVM	B00934WBRO	28	27	0.964285714
B0026ZYZ7Q	B00C88DV6M	26	25	0.961538462

where, $\hat{n}$ be the number of the sequences followed by some users (at least one user). The accuracy measures on the scale of 0 to 1, where 1 refers 100% and 0 refers 0% accuracy. We calculated N1, N2 and N2/N1 for our test dataset and the details can be seen in Table 7. We got accuracy of 0.9 for our test dataset.

5   Discussion

Our proposed system extracted around 268 sequences that are found to be frequent for the dataset used. The system also calculated the mean and mode duration after which these sequences are followed. Our result includes most of the items listed in Amazon's *subscribe and save* option which supports our results. Since, Amazon's *subscribe and save* option includes single item which is repeated after specified month. The current proposal enhanced the recommendation system by recommending different items which are brought one after another after a gap of some months.

6   Conclusion

Sequential pattern mining has played an important role for accurate recommendation system. As, if we are able to find out the purchase sequence of users with respect to the time then we recommend, the more accurate product to the users that helps to minimize the user search time as well as improve the companies sell. In this article, we find out such purchase sequences of the user from amazon data set using SPADE algorithm and time duration within the sequences. So, we can recommend the next sequential product to user after some months. Here we evaluated those sequences which had a time gap of more than one month. We can decrease these time gaps to 1 day or a week. With this modification we would have more sequences which occur in short duration of time. There are some sequences which are common among all the users, so we have found only those sequences which are popular among all the users. However the future work can find sequences for specific user, or similar user by applying the same method. Future work can also include sequences which are followed by the user in different years.

References

1. Agrawal, R., Srikant, R., et al.: Fast algorithms for mining association rules. In: Proceedings 20th International Conference Very Large Data Bases, VLDB, vol. 1215, pp. 487–499 (1994)
2. Breese, J.S., Heckerman, D., Kadie, C.: Empirical analysis of predictive algorithms for collaborative filtering. In: Proceedings of the Fourteenth Conference on Uncertainty in Artificial Intelligence, pp. 43–52. Morgan Kaufmann Publishers Inc. (1998)
3. Burke, R.: Hybrid web recommender systems. In: Brusilovsky, P., Kobsa, A., Nejdl, W. (eds.) The Adaptive Web. LNCS, vol. 4321, pp. 377–408. Springer, Heidelberg (2007). doi:10.1007/978-3-540-72079-9_12
4. Cho, Y.H., Kim, J.K., Kim, S.H.: A personalized recommender system based on web usage mining and decision tree induction. Expert Syst. Appl. **23**(3), 329–342 (2002)
5. Choi, K., Yoo, D., Kim, G., Suh, Y.: A hybrid online-product recommendation system: combining implicit rating-based collaborative filtering and sequential pattern analysis. Electron. Commer. Res. Appl. **11**(4), 309–317 (2012)
6. Huang, C.-L., Huang, W.-L.: Handling sequential pattern decay: developing a two-stage collaborative recommender system. Electron. Commer. Res. Appl. **8**(3), 117–129 (2009)
7. Khandagale, S., Mallade, S., Kharat, K., Bansode, V.: Food recommendation system using sequential pattern mining. Imperial J. Interdiscip. Res. **2**(6), 912–915 (2016)
8. Liu, D.-R., Lai, C.-H., Lee, W.-J.: A hybrid of sequential rules and collaborative filtering for product recommendation. Inf. Sci. **179**(20), 3505–3519 (2009)
9. Lu, H.: Recommendations based on purchase patterns. Int. J. Mach. Learn. Comput. **4**(6), 501 (2014)
10. Mahmood, T., Ricci, F.: Improving recommender systems with adaptive conversational strategies. In: Proceedings of the 20th ACM Conference on Hypertext and Hypermedia, pp. 73–82. ACM (2009)
11. McAuley, J., Pandey, R., Leskovec, J.: Inferring networks of substitutable and complementary products. In: Proceedings of the 21th ACM SIGKDD International Conference on Knowledge Discovery and Data Mining, pp. 785–794. ACM (2015)
12. McAuley, J., Targett, C., Shi, Q., Van Den Hengel, A.: Image-based recommendations on styles and substitutes. In: Proceedings of the 38th International ACM SIGIR Conference on Research and Development in Information Retrieval, pp. 43–52. ACM (2015)
13. Zaki, M.J.: Spade: an efficient algorithm for mining frequent sequences. Mach. Learn. **42**(1–2), 31–60 (2001)

Industrial Management and Other Applications

Risk Assessment in a Parallel Production System with the Use of FMEA Method and Linguistic Variables

Anna Burduk[1]([⊠]) and Damian Krenczyk[2]

[1] Faculty of Mechanical Engineering, Wrocław University of Science
and Technology, Wrocław, Poland
anna.burduk@pwr.wroc.pl
[2] Faculty of Mechanical Engineering,
Silesian University of Technology, Gliwice, Poland
damian.krenczyk@polsl.pl

Abstract. Risk is a natural and common phenomenon in enterprises. Elimination of risk is impossible, because it affects every decision. In order to manage a company effectively, the risk level should be taken into account at the stage of production planning and manufacturing process control. The paper describes a method for analyzing and assessing the risk in a parallel production system. Under this method it was proposed to use Failure Mode and Effects Analysis (FMEA) in the classic method for assessing the risk in a production system with a parallel structure. Such a combination allows determining the level of risk in a system without laborious evaluation of the amount of losses caused by the occurrence of risk factors in individual elements of the system.

Keywords: Risk in production system · FMEA analysis

1 Introduction

Planning and decision-making processes in contemporary companies generally use deterministic methods, without taking into account the conditions of uncertainty [2, 6]. This increases the risk, because there is no information about the possible occurrence of threats and the resulting effects. To mitigate the risk and increase the probability of taking correct decisions, actions should be taken in order to identify the area of risk, its extent and the impact on the operations in the organization, as well to search for measures for eliminating the risk. The awareness of the omnipresence of various types of risk raises the need to identify it in terms of the place of its occurrence and the strength of its impact on the company.

As an answer to the lack of standards in understanding the risk and managing it, the International Organization for Standardization created a standard, which was translated into Polish in March 2012. ISO 31000 standard: 2012 "Risk Management - principles and guidelines" defines risk as "effect of uncertainty on objectives", while uncertainty is "the state, even partial, of deficiency of information related to understanding or knowledge of an event, its consequences, or likelihood" [8]. From the engineering

© IFIP International Federation for Information Processing 2017
Published by Springer International Publishing AG 2017. All Rights Reserved
K. Saeed et al. (Eds.): CISIM 2017, LNCS 10244, pp. 379–390, 2017.
DOI: 10.1007/978-3-319-59105-6_32

point of view, risk is the probability that the system, at a certain moment of time, will not perform the function, for which it has been designed [1]. Therefore, in order to identify a risk, the hazard that causes it should be located.

2 Risk in Production Systems

Failure is an unforeseen and undesirable phenomenon that occurs in every production process or technical object. It is a degree of malfunctioning which prevents a correct operation of a device or results in its complete shut-down of the device. The risk of failure cannot be completely eliminated – it is only possible to determine the risk level and the probability of occurrence as well as to prepare adequate preventive measures [7, 10, 13].

Reliability is a quantitative measure of the failure rate, which can be defined as the probability of correct operation of a technical object in specific operating conditions and over a specific period of time [11, 12, 14]. Reliability is not a constant value, as the probability of occurrence of a failure increases over time.

The specific character of today's production systems and, in particular, their complexity, allows treating them as operation systems, and then the reliability is one of their features measured by the extent of realization of determined indicators, parameters and characteristics. In turn, production systems must operate in an environment which continuously affects the system and causes its disturbances. This is a reason that the reliability in real conditions is of random nature [3, 12, 13].

The general reliability theory can be transposed to the sphere of production systems by treating the unreliability (Z), i.e. the opposite of the reliability, as a synonym of risk (R) [3]:

$$R = Z \tag{1}$$

The risk (unreliability) of a system (e.g. a production system) interpreted in this way will represent the probability that the system will not perform the functions, for which it has been designed, or the probability of occurrence of losses in this system. For this interpretation, the following equation should be true:

$$N + Z = 1 \tag{2}$$

The concept of the reliability engineering is often compared with the system survival ability. Reliability (N) can be represented by a reliability function $N_{(t)}$ which determines the probability that the system will be operational within a specified time interval [17].

Thus, in the interval from zero to infinity, the function is a decreasing function. If the variable $Z_{(t)}$ is adopted as a measure of unreliability, it can be concluded that the probability of malfunction is expressed by the formula [1]:

$$Z_{(t)} + N_{(t)} = 1 \tag{3}$$

From the viewpoint of the reliability engineering, an object can be treated as an element (selected from a system) or as a system (a set of interoperating elements). Individual elements in a system can be linked to each other, but it is usually assumed in practice that there are no links between them.

3   Classical Method for Determining the Risk in Systems with a Parallel Structure

The definition of the reliability according to the classical theory is that the system is fit for operation, if at least one of its objects is fit for operation, which means that a correct functioning of one element of the system is sufficient for functioning of the system. An example of a diagram of a parallel reliability structure of a system with n objects is shown in Fig. 1.

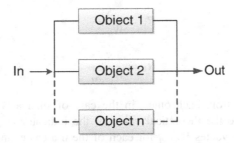

Fig. 1. An example of a parallel reliability structure of a system with *n* objects

Reliability of the system N_S, presented in Fig. 1 will be determined by the formula [4]:

$$N_S = 1 - [(1 - N_1) \cdot (1 - N_2) \cdot \ldots \cdot (1 - N_n)] \tag{4}$$

where $N_1, N_2, \ldots, N_n$ - reliability of individual objects/subsystems of the system.
R_c of the system can be determined based on the formulas (3) and (4):

$$R_C = R_1 \cdot R_2 \cdot \ldots \cdot R_n = \prod_{i=1}^{n} R_i \tag{5}$$

where R_1, R_2, R_n - the risk occurring in individual elements of the system.

Parallel structures occur in the production practice, however the nature of the production process does not allow for such an interpretation of the reliability structure. The classical theory of reliability considers 0/1 states of technical equipment. This means that (in the interpretation according to the classical theory) a production system would be recognized as reliable, if at least one element functioned correctly. In production systems, such a situation occurs only in redundant systems [4], i.e. with excess of elements functioning in the system. In reality, redundant systems occur very rarely, because excess of elements (e.g. machines, workers, means of transport, etc.) results in unused resources, which increases the costs.

Considering the structure of the system from Fig. 1 as a parallel production structure, the formula of the risk for this system should be as follows:

$$R_C = R_1 + R_2 + \ldots + R_n = \sum_{i=1}^{n} R_i \qquad (6)$$

where R_1, R_2, R_n - the risk occurring in individual objects/subsystems of the system.

If $R_C > 1$ is obtained as the result of such calculations, then:

$$R_C = maxR_i \qquad (7)$$

Individual risks R_i for n areas, depending on the amount of losses S_i incurred in these areas, will be as follows [3, 4]:

$$R_1 = \frac{S_1}{W_{teoret}} \qquad (8)$$

$$R_1 = \frac{S_2}{W_{teoret}} \qquad (9)$$

$$R_1 = \frac{S_n}{W_{teoret}} \qquad (10)$$

If the areas differ from each other, in the case of such a type of structure it is necessary to determine the theoretical value of the indicator (W_{teoret}) for each area. When determining the values W_{teoret} for each of the n areas examined, the individual losses S_i in these areas, depending on the time losses caused by the occurrence of risk factors in individual areas, will be as follows:

$$S_1 = W_{teoret}^1 \frac{\Delta t_1}{T} \qquad (11)$$

$$S_2 = W_{teoret}^2 \frac{\Delta t_2}{T} \qquad (12)$$

$$S_n = W_{teoret}^n \frac{\Delta t_n}{T} \qquad (13)$$

where: W_{teoret}^i - theoretical value of the indicator in individual areas of the system.

Δt_i - time losses in individual areas caused by risk factors.

Thus the total risk R_C for a system with n areas and a parallel structure of production will be as follows:

$$R_C = \frac{W_{teoret}^1 \Delta t_1 + W_{teoret}^2 \Delta t_2 + \ldots + W_{teoret}^n \Delta t_n}{W_{teoret} T} \qquad (14)$$

4   The Application of the FMEA Method and Linguistic Variables for Determining the Risk in Production Systems with a Parallel Reliability Structure

Failure Mode and Effects Analysis (FMEA) is one of many methods belonging to the group of quality control methods. It is described in the standard PN-IEC 812: 1994 – Procedure for Failure Mode and Effects Analysis – FMEA.

In order to reduce the level of risk in a production system, a series of actions must be taken. The first of them is the risk identification, which determines the threats that might occur during realization of company's goals. Due to a potential possibility that many risk factors may occur, it is important to find the source risk, which is the key cause of the problems. During the identification, it is important to search for the answers to the following questions: in which area of the production system the risk occurs and which area is affected by the highest risk.

The next step in reducing the risk level is measuring the risk and determining the extent of the impact on the production system. Failure Mode and Effect Analysis (FMEA) is one of the methods which allow determining the extent of risk in the designated area of a production process or in a product, as well as the resulting effects [9]. Thanks to this, corrective actions aiming at mitigation of the risk can be found subsequently [14]. *"One of the key factors in proper implementation of the FMEA program is to act before an event occurs and not to gain experience after the event. In order to obtain the best results, FMEA should be performed before a particular type of construction or process defect is "designed" for a given product."* [5].

When assessing the risk in a production process with the use of the FMEA method, the first step is to detail the operations in the process, then to identify the risk factors present in the process, determine the effects caused by their presence, and to find possible causes. The next step in the analysis is to assign numerical values to the following parameters shown in Table 1.

Table 1.   Characteristics of the parameters used in the FMEA method for determining RPN

Parameter symbol	Parameter name	Description
S	Severity	Whose value is the level of damage effects that occurs in the system
O	Occurrence	The value which represents the frequency of failure
D	Detectability	Ability of detecting a potential failure

The RPN number is a standard and most frequently used methodology and technique for the risk level analyzing of potential failures in the FMEA analysis [1, 17]. It is calculated for each of the selected areas of the production system using the formula [5]:

$$RPN = S(severity) x\, O(occurrence) x\, D(detectability) \tag{15}$$

The numerical values of S, O, and D represent the numerical values of the linguistic terms. They are usually in the range of 1–5 or 1–7 [15]. These criteria are defined by a team which conducts the analysis based on the data and the previous experience on the behavior of the system and the frequency of occurrence and the adverse effects of the machine parts failures on the system.

The value of RPN may be in the range between 1 and 343. So a high value of RPN corresponds to a high risk in the process. If the RPN value is high, efforts should be taken to mitigate the risk using corrective actions [5]. The corrective actions shall be taken first in the areas with the highest RPN level.

It is also needed to categorize the values of RPN and then, on the basis of the obtained values for RPN, take the measures necessary to reduce the risk level. Table 2 presents the range of five risk levels, with marginal values and measures to be taken to reduce the level of risk to an acceptable value.

Table 2. Matrix for RPN in the FMEA method

D (detectability)								
7	7	14	63	112	175	252	343
6	6	12	54	96	150	216	294
5	5	10	45	80	125	180	245
4	4	8	36	64	100	144	196
3	3	6	27	48	75	108	147
2	2	4	18	32	50	72	98
1	1	2	9	16	25	36	49
	1	2	9	16	25	36	49
	S (severity) x O (occurrence)							

It is also needed to categorize the values of RPN and then, on the basis of the obtained values for RPN, take the measures necessary to reduce the risk level. Table 3 presents the range of five risk levels with marginal values and measures to be taken to reduce the level of risk to an acceptable value.

Table 3. Measures to reduce the level of risk [15]

Risk level	Measures	RPN
Extreme	Reduce the risk to an acceptable level (Rank 2)	151–343
High	Reduce the risk to an acceptable level (Rank 2)	61–150
Moderate	Monitor the system and reduce the risk to an acceptable level (Rank 2)	31–60
Low	Monitor the system changes	16–30
Insignificant	Maintain the risk level on this level	1–15

Determination of a general limit for a high RPN value is not easy. Each FMEA analysis is unique and the risk estimation in this method cannot be compared with other analyses. This is caused by some sort of subjectivity, the dependence during the assessment, and the decisions made by the person performing the analysis. Therefore for each FMEA analysis a system of criteria should be developed and it should be determined from which values of RPN the corrective actions should be taken.

The values of risk in individual system elements defined in the FMEA method are greater than 1 and are within the range [1, 343] (see. Table 2). Therefore, in the next step of applying the method for estimating the risk in a parallel production system, normalization of RPN on the interval [0,1] should be carried out using the formula:

$$RPN' = \frac{RPN_i - RPN_{min}}{RPN_{max} - RPN_{min}} \tag{16}$$

where RPN_{max} is the maximum value obtained in the FMEA table based on the product of the values of parameters S, O, D, while RPN_{min} is the minimum value.

In order to determine the risk in a production system with a parallel structure using the FMEA method, a normalized RPN value should be substituted to the formula (6). Then the formula for the total risk of the system with n elements will be as follows:

$$R_C = RPN'_1 + RPN'_2 + \ldots + RPN'_n = \sum_{i=1}^{n} RPN'_i \tag{17}$$

If $R_C > 1$ is obtained as the result of such calculations, then:

$$R_C = maxRPN'_i \tag{18}$$

An advantage of the use of the FMEA method for determining the risk in a production system with a parallel structure is the possibility of assigning linguistic variables to values of individual parameters S, O, D by a team established for this purpose. Unlike in the case of the classical method presented in Sect. 3, there is no need to measure and determine the extent of losses (S_i) and increases of production times (Δt_i) caused by the occurrence of risk factors in a production system (compare the formulas 8–14).

5 Characteristics of the Production System and the Assessment of Risk with Use of the Method Proposed

The company whose production data were used to verify the proposed method manufactures steel products. The factory has 4 production lines with the layout shown in Fig. 2.

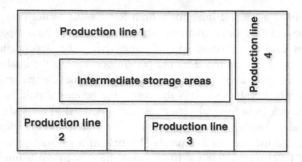

Fig. 2. Layout of production lines in the production floor

The production lines differ from each other by type and age of machines. Each production line consists of three workstations: a cutter, a press and a finishing workstation where quality control is also performed (Fig. 3).

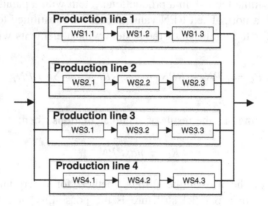

Fig. 3. Diagram of the production system

The factory makes products to individual orders, while individual production orders vary considerably in size of the products and the degree of their complexity. When planning the production, individual orders are assigned to different production lines depending on the size of products and the degree of their complexity. Table 4 summarizes the production lines and compares them in terms of the same parameters.

Table 4. Summary of basic parameters of production lines

Line number	Capacity [kW]	Max. metal plate thickness [mm]	Max. metal plate width [mm]	Age of the line [years]
PL 1	4 × 7	4	10–350	12
PL 2	4 × 4	3	10–350	10
PL 3	4 × 4	3	10–350	5
PL 4	4 × 7	4	10–350	3

LP1 and LP2 are the oldest production lines which are also most prone to failures. However, an inventory of spare parts for the elements that fail most frequently is kept there. Therefore, the time of repair of most failures on the LP1 and LP2 lines is relatively short. Repairs are performed by the maintenance department. A worse situation is in the case of the LP3 and LP4 production lines – in the event of a failure an external company is called to perform the service and thus the time of repair is much longer.

Due to the specific character of production described above, it is impossible to determine the average daily production volume for individual production lines. For example, the LP1 production line can manufacture products with a length from 2 to 14 m. The level of their complexity is also very different. Therefore, the potential losses in production volume caused by the occurrence of risk factors will vary considerably. In conjunction with the above, a decision was made to use the FMEA method.

In order to analyze and assess the risk in the factory with the use of the FMEA method, all 4 production lines have been subjected to detailed observation. Throughout July, the employees used forms prepared especially for this purpose to collect data on the random factors occurring in individual production lines and recorded the information on the type of risk factor as well as its severity (S), occurrence (O) and detectability (D).

For this purpose a team of production workers was set up. The task of this team was to assign values to the S, O, D (severity, occurrence and detectability) parameters and to determine the RPN value. In order to parameterize the values of individual risk factors, auxiliary tables were prepared, which are presented in brief in Table 5.

Table 5. Auxiliary table for determining the FMEA table in the company in question

Parameter name	Weight of parameter	Description
Severity (S)	1	Has a negligible impact on the course of the production process
	2 – 3	Has a weak impact on the course of the production process
	4 – 6	Has a negative impact on the course of the production process
	7	Has a very negative impact on the course of the production process
Occurrence (O)	1	Very rarely
	2 – 3	Rarely
	4 – 6	Often
	7	Very often
Detectability (D)	1	Very easy to detect
	2 – 3	Easy to detect
	4 – 6	Difficult to detect
	7	Very difficult to detect or undetectable

Then, FMEA tables were prepared for all the identified risk factors. The results from the FMEA tables obtained for all 3 machines located on the production lines have shown that the following factors are of key importance for the processes taking place in the factory:

- frequent failures of machines on the LP1 and LP2 production lines,
- long time of repair of the machines, and
- the necessity of additional setting or changeover of the machines.

Table 6 shows the synthetic values of RPN for these key risk factors. Since individual workstations at the production lines operate in a serial manner, the workstations with the largest RPN values were selected for the summary and further calculations.

Table 6. Abridged FMEA table

		S	O	D	RPN
LP1	Number of failures	6	7	5	210
	Duration of repair	4	3	4	48
	Necessity of additional setting of the machine	4	4	6	96
LP2	Number of failures	6	7	5	210
	Duration of repair	4	3	4	48
	Necessity of additional setting of the machine	4	4	6	96
LP3	Number of failures	3	2	6	36
	Duration of repair	6	5	4	150
	Necessity of additional setting of the machine	3	4	7	84
LP4	Number of failures	2	1	6	12
	Duration of repair	6	6	4	180
	Necessity of additional setting of the machine	3	4	7	84

In order to use the formula for the total risk of the system (6), the RPN value must be normalized first to the interval [0,1] using the formula (16).

$$R'_{LP1} = \frac{210 - 1}{343 - 1} = 0,61$$

$$R'_{LP2} = \frac{210 - 1}{343 - 1} = 0,61$$

$$R'_{LP3} = \frac{150 - 1}{343 - 1} = 0,44$$

$$R'_{LP4} = \frac{180 - 1}{343 - 1} = 0,52$$

The values of the resulting risks were substituted to the formula for the total risk (17):

$$R_C = R'_{LP1} + R'_{LP2} + R'_{LP3} + R'_{LP4} = 0,61 + 0,61 + 0,44 + 0,52 = 2,18$$

Since $R_C > 1$, then:

$$R_C = maxR_i = 0,61$$

The resulting value of the total risk in the production system indicates with a probability of 61% that it is not possible to execute the production plan in July. This result coincides with the extent of delays in the execution of production orders in the factory.

6 Summary

The paper presents a method for assessing the risk in a parallel production system with the use of the FMEA method and linguistic variables. It has many advantages as compared with the classical method described in Sect. 3. In order to assess the amount of losses caused by the occurrence of risk factors in individual elements of the system, it is enough to establish a team composed of employees who are familiar with the system. These employees provide verbally the information on the type of risk factor as well as its severity, occurrence and detectability. In the next step, values are assigned to individual parameters with the use of auxiliary tables of the FMEA method and the RPN is calculated. After normalization of RPN, the classical method for analyzing and assessing the risk in production systems with a parallel structure can be used.

References

1. Bowles, J.B., Pelaez, C.E.: Fuzzy logic prioritization of failures in a system failure mode, effects and criticality analysis. Reliab. Eng. Syst. Saf. **50**(2), 203–213 (1995)
2. Bożejko, W., Hejducki, Z., Rajba, P., Wodecki, M.: Project management in building process with uncertain tasks times. Manag. Prod. Eng. Rev. **2**(1), 3–9 (2011)
3. Burduk, A.: Evaluation of the risk in production systems with a parallel reliability structure taking into account its acceptance level. In: Corchado, E., Kurzyński, M., Woźniak, M. (eds.) HAIS 2011. LNCS, vol. 6679, pp. 389–396. Springer, Heidelberg (2011). doi:10. 1007/978-3-642-21222-2_47
4. Burduk, A., Chlebus, E.: Methods of risk evaluation in manufacturing systems. Arch. Civ. Mech. Eng. **9**(3), 17–30 (2009)
5. Chrysler Cooperation, Ford Motor Company, General Motors Cooperation: Potential Failure Mode and Effects Analysis (FMEA), First Edition Issued, February 1993
6. Grzybowska, K., Kovács, G.: The modelling and design process of coordination mechanisms in the supply chain. J. Appl. Logic (2016)
7. Grzybowska, K.: Selected activity coordination mechanisms in complex systems. In: Bajo, J., Hallenborg, K., Pawlewski, P., Botti, V., Sánchez-Pi, N., Duque Méndez, N.D., Lopes, F., Julian, V. (eds.) PAAMS 2015. CCIS, vol. 524, pp. 69–79. Springer, Cham (2015). doi:10.1007/978-3-319-19033-4_6

8. ISO 31000:2009: Risk management – Principles and guidelines (2012)
9. Jasiulewicz-Kaczmarek M.: Integrating lean and green paradigms in maintenance management. In: Proceedings of the 19th IFAC World Congress Cape Town, South Africa, 24–29, August 2014, vol. 47(3), pp. 4471–4476 (2014)
10. Jasiulewicz-Kaczmarek M.: Practical aspects of the application of RCM to select optimal maintenance policy of the production line. In: Nowakowski, T., Mlynczak, M., JodejkoPietruczuk, A. (eds.) Safety and Reliability: Methodology and Applications, Proceedings of the European Safety and Reliability Conference, ESREL Wroclaw, Poland, 14–18 September 2014, pp. 1187–1195 (2015)
11. Kłosowski, G., Gola, A., Świć, A.: Application of fuzzy logic in assigning workers to production tasks. In: Omatu, S., et al. (eds.) Distributed Computing and Artificial Intelligence, 13th International Conference. Advances in Intelligent Systems and Computing, vol. 474, pp. 505–513. Springer, Cham (2016)
12. Loska, A.: Exploitation assessment of selected technical objects using taxonomic methods. Eksploatacja i Niezawodnosc – Maintenance Reliab. 15(1), 1–8 (2013)
13. Mazurkiewicz, D.: Computer-aided maintenance and reliability management systems for conveyor belts. Eksploatacja i Niezawodnosc – Maintenance Reliab. 16(3), 377–382 (2014)
14. Sankar, N., Prabhu, B.: Modified approach for prioritization of failures in a system failure mode and effects analysis. Int. J. Qual. Reliab. Manag. 18(3), 324–336 (2001)
15. Petrovic, D.: V., Tanasijevic M., Milic V., Lilic N., Stojadinovic S., Svrkota I.: Risk assessment model of mining equipment failure based on fuzzy logic. Expert Syst. Appl. 41, 8157–8164 (2014)
16. Rojek, I., Studzinski, J.: Comparison of different types of neuronal nets for failures location within water-supply networks. Eksploatacja i Niezawodność – Maintenance Reliab. 16(1), 42–47 (2014)
17. Zhang, Z., Chu, X.: Risk prioritization in failure mode and effects analysis under uncertainty. Expert Syst. Appl. 38, 206–214 (2011)

The Multi Depot One-to-One Pickup and Delivery Problem with Distance Constraints: Real World Application and Heuristic Solution Approach

Olfa Chebbi[1(✉)] and Ezzeddine Fatnassi[2]

[1] Institut Supérieur d'Informatique et de Gestion de Kairouan,
Université de Kairouan, Avenue Khemais El Alouini, 3100 Kairouan, Tunisie
olfaa.chebbi@gmail.com
[2] Institut Supérieur de Gestion de Tunis, Université de Tunis,
41, Rue de la Liberté - Bouchoucha, 2000 Bardo, Tunisie

Abstract. This paper presents the development of the multi depot one-to-one pickup and delivery problem with distance constraints problem. This problem involve routing vehicles in a multi depot network topology to satisfy a set of pickup and delivery requests subject to a maximum allowable distance constraint. A problem definition is given and a real world application is proposed for that problem. An approximate solution approach which divides the problem into several subproblems and solve them to optimality is also proposed. Computational experiments show that the proposed solution approach reach good quality solutions is a reasonable computational time.

Keywords: Vehicle routing problem · Multi-depot · Pickup and delivery requests · Transportation problems

1 Introduction

Real-life urban on-demand passenger's transportation problems represent a high complex type of problems. In fact, these problems involve a variety of hard constraints which must not been violated. Such constraints involve multi-dimensional vehicle capacity, route duration restriction, time windows, exclusive travels and so on. These problems involve also several complex objective functions which are more complex than the classical distance minimization as several real life factors must be taken into account. However and despite the important interest of these problems, they have received little attention in the literature from an academic point of view.

Generally, real-life urban on-demand passenger's transportation problems are related to the theoretical vehicle routing problems. The vehicle routing problem (VRP) was first proposed by Dantzig and Ramser in 1959 [10]. VRP involves

© IFIP International Federation for Information Processing 2017
Published by Springer International Publishing AG 2017. All Rights Reserved
K. Saeed et al. (Eds.): CISIM 2017, LNCS 10244, pp. 391–401, 2017.
DOI: 10.1007/978-3-319-59105-6_33

a set of key decisions in order to find a least costs set of customers' sequences to be visited by each vehicle. VRP involves generally several constraints such as distance, capacity, time and cost constraints.

In the literature, several variants of VRP have been studied which meet and address condition of several real world applications of VRP. One could note for example the capacitated VRP(CVRP) [23], the heterogeneous VRP(HVRP) [8], VRP with time windows, VRP with pickup and delivery (PDP) [26], the multi depot VRP (MDVRP) [19] and so on. For a more clear survey on VRP and its extension, the reader is refereed to [2].

The PDP is the problem where the service required by a customer needs both pickup and delivery service. The PDP can be further subdivided to the many to many PDP, the one to many to one PDP and the one to one PDP. For a more classification of PDP the reader is referred to the survey paper of Berbeglia et al. [2].

The VRP and its several variants such as the PDP and the MDVRP could include several constraints and are known to be NP-Hard problems [2]. The relative complexity of these problem results on a long computational time to find optimal solution especially for large size problems. Consequently, heuristics and metaheuristics approaches have been widely applied and developed to solve large VRP problems. In fact, approximate methods have been able to provide good quality solutions within reasonable computational time.

Based on the works from the literature, relatively new variants of VRP could be proposed to tackle real world application of routing problems. For instance, we could note the works of Sombuntham and Kachitvichyanukul [17] where they proposed a particle swarm optimization algorithm for multi-depot vehicle routing problem with multiple pickup and delivery requests or the multi-depot pickup and delivery problem with a single hub and heterogeneous vehicles [16]. These works proves that the joint study of multiple depot and pickup and delivery problems is an interesting field to develop. However, one could note that none of the recent works in the literature of the multi-depot pickup and delivery problems proposed to add distance constraints related to VRP. Also, one could note that to the best of our knowledge the multi-depot variant of the one-to-one PDP has not been studied in literature before [2,18].

Consequently in this paper, we extends the works in the literature by focusing on the multi-depot one-to-one PDP with distance constraints problem. Starting from an urban on-demand passengers transportation problem related to automated transit system, we motivate the multi depot one-to-one PDP with distance constraints problem. We propose also an adapted linear programming heuristic in order to solve large size instances of the proposed problem in a fast computational time. Finally, the proposed solution approach is proved to be very effective by testing it on a carefully generated set of instances based on our real world context.

Consequently, Sect. 2 presents the real world application of the multi depot one-to-one PDP with distance constraints. Section 3 develops the problem formulation. Section 4 provides a description of the resolution methodology. Section 5 describes the computational results. Finally, Sect. 6 concludes the paper.

2   The Real World Application of the Multi Depot One-to-One PDP with Distance Constraints

In this paper, we focus on the multi depot one-to-one PDP with distance constraints by studying its real world urban on-demand passengers transportation application. In fact, there is several transportation systems that are designed to move people in urban areas. Examples of these systems include subway, bus, train, bus rapid transit (BRT), light rapid transit (LRT), automated transit network (ATN) and so on.

Fig. 1. ATN' vehicles (Source: http://www.ultraprt.net/multiVehicle.htm)

Among these system, one could focus on the ATN systems. ATN is designed as a public transportation tool to move passengers within urban areas. ATN offers an on-demand non-stop, origin-to-destination transportation service for its users over a dedicated network. ATN uses a set of fully automated vehicles carrying passengers from station to station. ATN'vehicles run on exclusive, grade-separated set of guideways (see Fig. 1). ATN offers an unique transportation service. In fact, ATN'stations are off-line. This feature allows vehicles to travel from origin to destination without any intermediate stops. Furthermore, ATN transportation service is done on-demand where users could choose their time and way of travel. Therefore, ATN offers a taxi-like transportation service. ATN transportation features are quite different from any other automated guideway transit service (AGN) such as LRT, BRT and streetcars.

In the literature, the main features of ATN are defined as follows:

– Small vehicles available for the moving an individual or small group traveling together by choice.
– direct origin-to-destination transportation service without any intermediate stops.
– on demand transportation service.
– fully automated driverless electric vehicles.

A literature review published in 2005 [9] states that there is more than 200 research papers related to ATN. More recently, several operational and strategic optimization studies related to ATN were published such as network design [25], station design [24], dynamic routing [4,13], simulation [7,14] energy minimization [22], passengers waiting time [20] total traveled distance [12,15], fleet size [5], optimized operational planning [6,11] and so on.

Starting from all these features, one could note that the transportation service for ATN consists on pickup passengers from a predefined station in order to deliver them to another station. Consequently, the ATN has a strong relation with the PDP problem. Also as the ATN uses a set of driverless vehicles with limited battery capacity, we could found distance constraints related to the routing of ATN vehicles. Finally, as the ATN'network could have multiple depots where initially the ATN vehicles are located, routing vehicles in the ATN context has also a strong relation with the Multi-depot VRP.

However and in the literature, routing problems related to ATN considered only the single depot network topology with different objective such as energy minimization [12], fleet size [5], waiting time of passengers [20] and so on. Consequently and based on all these features and this gap in the literature, we could state that routing driverless electric vehicles in the ATN'network has a strong relation with the multi depot one-to-one PDP with distance constraints.

In the next section, we detail the theoretical problem formulation related to the ATN.

3   Problem Formulation

In this section, we present the formal problem description and definition of the multi depot one-to-one PDP with distance constraints.

3.1   Problem Description

Generally in VRPs, a customer is described as a place that must be served by a vehicle from the depot. In this paper, the classic term of customer is replaced by a more general term of "travel". The travel reflects the pickup and delivery transportation service that must be done within the one-to-one PDP. For a PDP problem, a travel is represented by a commodities or a group of persons that must be collected from an origin location and must be delivered to a destination location. As we are treating the one-to-one PDP, the transportation service is done by direct shipment from origin to destination. As each travel has different physical locations, each location can play only one of these three roles: pickup location, delivery location, or depot. Consequently, each location may have several passengers or groups of passengers to be picked up and delivered to several other locations. The transportation situation happening in our problem can be depicted in Fig. 2.

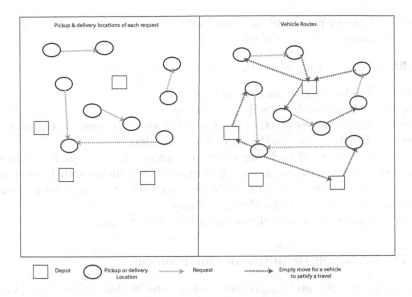

Fig. 2. The VRP with one to one transportation requests.

Our problem is based on the following assumptions:

- Let suppose to have a network composed of M different pickup/delivery location where passengers could embark or disembark from vehicles.
- The network is supposed to be fully connected. A vehicle could move between any pairs of pickup/delivery location.
- Our problem is primarily characterized by a set of travels T known in advance. $|T| = n$.
- Our problem suppose to have also an unlimited number of vehicles. The vehicles are initially located in one of the different depots in the simulated network. The vehicles need to satisfy the transportation demand.
- Each travel contains information concerning transportation demand. In order to satisfy travel i, the central control system must assign an empty vehicle in order to satisfy a transportation service from a pickup location DS_i to delivery location denoted AS_i. The service should be provided at the desired departure time, DT_i, and delays are not permitted. Each travel, i, has a specific arrival time AT_i.

Our objective is to design a set of least-cost journeys that start and end at the depot, are capable of accommodating all travel requests within the allocated time frame and under several constraints such as distance and time window constraints.

Generally, in our problem the vehicles routes have to be constructed in such a way that:

- The total energy consumption is minimized.
- All the travels must be fulfilled.

In addition, the following restrictions must be met:

- vehicles could serve only one travel at a time.
- Each travel is served by exactly one vehicle.
- The number of routes starting from a depot location must be equal to the number of route ending in the same depot location.
- The total duration of each route does not exceed a preset limit. As in our real world application we are using electric ATN'vehicles with limited electric battery capacity, the total route length must not exceed the maximum allowable travel time by the electric battery.
- Each request must be served exactly at its starting time.

3.2 Formal Graph Definition of Our Problem

More specifically, our problem is based on a non-directed graph $G = \{V, E\}$, where $V = \{1, 2, ..., n, d_1, d_2, ..., d_k\}$ is the set of vertices in the graph. $d_1, d_2, ..., d_k$ represent the different k depots in the network. Let the vertex set $V^* = \{1, ..., n\}$ corresponds to the set of travels. E represents the set of edges, with $e \in E = \{(i, j) \mid i, j \in V\}$. Note that $E^* = \{(i, j) \mid i, j \in V^*\}$.

We add edge e to set E when one of the following conditions is satisfied.

- for each nodes $(i, j) \in V^*$, we add an edge if and only if the departure date of travel j exceeds or equals the sum of the arrival time of travel i and the time needed to move from the arrival location of travel i to the departure location of travel j. The cost of this edge is the energy used for traveling from the arrival location of travel i to the departure location of travel j and of traveling from the departure location of travel j to the arrival location of travel j.
- for each node $i \in V^*$ and each depot $d \in D$, an edge (d, i) is added with the cost of moving from d to the departure location of travel i plus the cost of moving from the departure location of travel i to the arrival location of travel i.
- we add a final set of edges (i, d) for each node $i \in V^*$ and each depot $d \in D$. The cost of these edges includes the cost of moving from the arrival location of travel i to d.

4   The Resolution Methodology

In this section, we present our resolution methodology for the problem considered above which we call linear programming heuristic (LPH). Our LPH is based on the principles presented in Algorithm 1.

Based on Algorithm 1, we first solve a relaxed linear program in order to find set of roads starting and ending at one of the different depot in the network.

Algorithm 1. LPH(The network N, The set of travels T

1: Construct the graph G
2: Solve the relaxed Linear program (see Sect. 4.1)
3: **for** (each obtained routes R_i) **do**
4:    **if** R_i is a feasible route **then**
5:        Add R_i to the final solution
6:    **else**
7:        Construct a subproblem based on the nodes present in R_i.
8:        Solve the new small problem to optimality
9:        Add the obtained new roads to the final solution
10:    **end if**
11: **end for**
12: Return the final solution

The relaxed linear program founds unfeasible roads as we relaxed the distance constraints. Next our LPH and in order to find feasible roads and therefore feasible solution would use an optimal mathematical model to get feasible roads from the set of unfeasible roads. Next, we present more details of the implemented LPH.

4.1 The Relaxed Linear Program

This section presents the relaxed linear program that the LPH will use during its search process.

We first introduce the following integer variable:

$$x_{ij} = \begin{cases} 1 \text{ if arc } (i, j) \text{ is selected to match } i \text{ to } j \\ 0 \text{ otherwise} \end{cases}$$

In our heuristic, we first solve the following relaxed linear program.

$$: \text{Min} \sum_{(i,j) \in E} c_{ij} x_{ij}$$

$$\sum_{j \in \delta^+(i)} x_{ij} = 1 \forall i \in V^*$$

$$\sum_{j \in \delta^-(i)} x_{ji} = 1 \forall i \in V^*$$

$$\sum_{j \in \delta^+(i),\, k \in \delta^+(i)} x_{ij} = \sum x_{ki} \forall i \in D$$

$$x_{ij} \in \{0, 1\} \forall (i, j) \in E$$

Objective function 4.1 minimizes the total energy consumption of the system. Constraints 4.1 and 4.1 ensure that each travel node is served exactly once.

Constraints 4.1 ensure that the number of routes starting from a given depot is equal to the number of routes ending in that depot.

However solving this linear program could result on a set of infeasible tour as we do not include maximum distance constraint on it. To fix this dilemma, we propose a specific approach which is presented hereafter.

4.2 Approach

Our algorithmic approach is based on the fact that unfeasible routes which violate maximum allowable constraints could be corrected using a valid mathematical formulation of the proposed problem. In fact by solving the relaxed linear program, we could obtain two types of routes: feasible routes and unfeasible routes. Based on our approach, we consider the feasible routes as part of the final solution. The unfeasible routes would be corrected in order to make them respect the maximum allowable distance constraints. In fact from each unfeasible routes, we construct a small routing problem based on its nodes. This small problem would be solved to optimality using a valid mathematical formulation of our problem. This valid mathematical formulation is taken from the works in the literature of Almoustafa et al. [1] while adding the multiple depot constraints to it. Based on these principles, the final feasible solution would be constructed iteratively.

5   Computational Experiments

We now present the computational study performed to investigate the results of our LPH for solving the proposed optimization problem. An analysis of the obtained results is also performed to prove the efficiency of our algorithm.

5.1   Test Instances

The proposed algorithm is implemented using the C++ language and tested on a laptop with an Intel(R) Core (TM) i3 CPU M 380 2.53 GHz processor and 3 GB RAM (Windows 7 64-bit). Since we are treating a real world application of the GVRP–MDMPDRDC related to the ATN, we based the testing instances on recent works related to ATN [6]. In fact our instance generator is based on the Corby network which represents a real case of routing ATN'vehicles in urban areas. This network represents a realistic case study developed by Bly and Teycheene [3]. Corby is a town in Northampton, (UK) with a population of approximately 50 000. It offers a good example for testing the ATN feasibility in a relatively new town. This network has 14.2 km of ATN guideways. The Corby network has 15 stations and four depots.

Based on this network, we generated 100 instances where the number of travels varies between 10 and 100 in a steps of 10. Consequently and for each travel 'size, we generated 10 instances. The list of travels and its characteristics were based on the works from the literature of Mrad and Hidri [22] and Mrad et al. [21]. The maximum allowable time limit for each route was taken to be equal to 40 min [6]. We note also that all the mathematical models were solved using IBM-Cplex 12.2[1].

5.2 Computational Results

Results of our method are exposed in Table 1. To assert the quality of the obtained solutions we used the GAP metric. The GAP is obtained as follows:
$GAP = (\frac{(SOL-LB)}{LB}) \times 100$ We should note that LB is the linear relaxation of the presented mathematical formulation presented in the literature [1].

Table 1 illustrates that the LPH method provides good quality solutions. In fact, the LPH founds an average GAP of 2.435% in 0.132 s. As shown in Table 1, using the LPH method results on obtaining remarkable low GAPs which varies from 0.635 % to 5.075 %. Moreover, the GAP with respect to the lower bound values is below 6%. These results mean that the algorithm is capable to converge to a good solution even starting from an unfeasible one which is actually a good point for our algorithm. The good performance of the LPH is further compounded by the fact that it consume small computational time (less than 0.3 s). This is due mainly to the straightforward principles that the LPH uses. In fact by solving at each time a relaxed linear program, it has the ability to determine good parts of the final solution quickly.

Table 1. The obtained results

Number of travels	Average gap %	Average time (seconds)
10	0.635	0.037
20	0.800	0.050
30	1.649	0.067
40	1.641	0.071
50	2.655	0.099
60	2.682	0.124
70	3.782	0.151
80	2.774	0.212
90	2.655	0.234
100	5.075	0.271
Average	2.435	0.132

---

[1] Details about Cplex could be found in https://www-01.ibm.com/software/commerce/optimization/cplex-optimizer/.

6   Conclusions

The multi depot one-to-one PDP with distance constraints problem has been introduced and formalized in this paper. This is a new VRP that arises in real urban contexts. The goal of this problem is to carry a set of pickup and delivery operations at a minimum costs subject to different constraints related to the time windows and total traveled distance for vehicles. A real world application related to the multi depot one-to-one PDP with distance constraints was proposed. Our application arises in the context of ATN in order to carry a set of passengers from origin to destination locations. The proposed problem was formulated and a straightforward linear programming heuristic was proposed to solve it. Computational tests have been carried out on instances with different number of travels while representing realistic network contexts. The results obtained from computational tests show the efficacy and the effectiveness of the proposed approach. The most innovative aspect of this approach is its ability to extract goods part of the final solution while starting from an unfeasible solutions. Future developments in this field could address the introduction of stochastic travel time between locations of the treatment of the proposed routing problem in a dynamic context by the tool of simulation.

References

1. Almoustafa, S., Hanafi, S., Mladenovi, N.: New exact method for large asymmetric distance-constrained vehicle routing problem. Eur. J. Oper. Res. **226**, 386–394 (2012)
2. Berbeglia, G., Cordeau, J.F., Laporte, G.: Dynamic pickup and delivery problems. Eur. J. Oper. Res. **202**(1), 8–15 (2010)
3. Bly, P., Teychenne, R.: Three financial and socio-economic assessments of a personal rapid transit system. In: Proceedings of the Tenth International Conference on Automated People Movers, p. 39 (2005)
4. Chebbi, O., Chaouachi, J.: Modeling on-demand transit transportation system using an agent-based approach. In: Saeed, K., Homenda, W. (eds.) CISIM 2015. LNCS, vol. 9339, pp. 316–326. Springer, Cham (2015). doi:10.1007/978-3-319-24369-6_26
5. Chebbi, O., Chaouachi, J.: Optimal fleet sizing of personal rapid transit system. In: Saeed, K., Homenda, W. (eds.) CISIM 2015. LNCS, vol. 9339, pp. 327–338. Springer, Cham (2015). doi:10.1007/978-3-319-24369-6_27
6. Chebbi, O., Chaouachi, J.: Reducing the wasted transportation capacity of personal rapid transit systems: an integrated model and multi-objective optimization approach. Transp. Res. Part E Logistics. Transp. Rev. **89**, 236–258 (2015)
7. Chebbi, O., Chaouachi, J.: A decentralized management approach for on-demand transit transportation system. In: Abraham, A., Wegrzyn-Wolska, K., Hassanien, A.E., Snasel, V., Alimi, A.M. (eds.) Proceedings of the Second International Afro-European Conference for Industrial Advancement AECIA 2015. AISC, vol. 427, pp. 175–184. Springer, Cham (2016). doi:10.1007/978-3-319-29504-6_18
8. Coelho, V., Grasas, A., Ramalhinho, H., Coelho, I., Souza, M., Cruz, R.: An ils-based algorithm to solve a large-scale real heterogeneous fleet vrp with multi-trips and docking constraints. Eur. J. Oper. Res. **250**(2), 367–376 (2016)

9. Cottrell, W.D.: Critical review of the personal rapid transit literature. In: Proceedings of the 10th International Conference on Automated People Movers, pp. 1–4 (2005)
10. Dantzig, G.B., Ramser, J.H.: The truck dispatching problem. Manage. Sci. **6**(1), 80–91 (1959)
11. Fatnassi, E., Chaouachi, J., Klibi, W.: Planning and operating a shared goods and passengers on-demand rapid transit system for sustainable city-logistics. Transp. Res. Part B Methodol. **81**, 440–460 (2015)
12. Fatnassi, E., Chebbi, O., Chaouachi, J.: Discrete honeybee mating optimization algorithm for the routing of battery-operated automated guidance electric vehicles in personal rapid transit systems. Swarm Evol. Comput. **26**, 35–49 (2015)
13. Fatnassi, E., Chebbi, O., Siala, J.C.: Evaluation of different vehicle management strategies for the personal rapid transit system. In: 2013 5th International Conference on Modeling, Simulation and Applied Optimization (ICMSAO), pp. 1–5. IEEE (2013)
14. Fatnassi, E., Chebbi, O., Siala, J.C.: Two strategies for real time empty vehicle redistribution for the personal rapid transit system. In: 2013 16th International IEEE Conference on Intelligent Transportation Systems-(ITSC), pp. 1888–1893. IEEE (2013)
15. Fatnassi, E., Chebbi, O., Siala, J.C.: Comparison of two mathematical formulations for the offline routing of personal rapid transit system vehicles. In: The International Conference on Methods and Models in Automation and Robotics (2014)
16. Irnich, S.: A multi-depot pickup and delivery problem with a single hub and heterogeneous vehicles. Eur. J. Oper. Res. **122**(2), 310–328 (2000)
17. Kachitvichyanukul, V., Sombuntham, P., Kunnapapdeelert, S.: Two solution representations for solving multi-depot vehicle routing problem with multiple pickup and delivery requests via pso. Comput. Ind. Eng. **89**, 125–136 (2015)
18. Lahyani, R., Khemakhem, M., Semet, F.: Rich vehicle routing problems: from a taxonomy to a definition. Eur. J. Oper. Res. **241**(1), 1–14 (2015). http://www.sciencedirect.com/science/article/pii/S0377221714006146
19. Lalla-Ruiz, E., Expósito-Izquierdo, C., Taheripour, S., Voß, S.: An improved formulation for the multi-depot open vehicle routing problem. OR Spectrum **38**(1), 175–187 (2016)
20. Lees-Miller, J.D.: Minimising average passenger waiting time in personal rapid transit systems. Ann. Oper. Res. **236**(2), 405–424 (2016)
21. Mrad, M., Chebbi, O., Labidi, M., Louly, M.A.: Synchronous routing for personal rapid transit pods. J. Appl. Math. **2014** (2014)
22. Mrad, M., Hidri, L.: Optimal consumed electric energy while sequencing vehicle trips in a personal rapid transit transportation system. Comput. Ind. Eng. **79**, 1–9 (2015)
23. Prins, C.: A simple and effective evolutionary algorithm for the vehicle routing problem. Comput. Oper. Res. **31**(12), 1985–2002 (2004)
24. Won, J.M., Choe, H., Karray, F.: Optimal design of personal rapid transit. In: Intelligent Transportation Systems Conference 2006, ITSC 2006, pp. 1489–1494. IEEE (2006)
25. Zheng, H., Peeta, S.: Network design for personal rapid transit under transit-oriented development. Transp. Res. Part C Emerg. Technol. **55**, 351–362 (2015)
26. Zhu, Z., Xiao, J., He, S., Ji, Z., Sun, Y.: A multi-objective memetic algorithm based on locality-sensitive hashing for one-to-many-to-one dynamic pickup-and-delivery problem. Inf. Sci. **329**, 73–89 (2016)

Detection of 'Orange Skin' Type Surface Defects in Furniture Elements with the Use of Textural Features

Michał Kruk[1], Bartosz Świderski[1], Katarzyna Śmietańska[2], Jarosław Kurek[1], Leszek J. Chmielewski[1(✉)], Jarosław Górski[2], and Arkadiusz Orłowski[1]

[1] Faculty of Applied Informatics and Mathematics – WZIM, Warsaw University of Life Sciences – SGGW, ul. Nowoursynowska 159, 02-775 Warsaw, Poland
{michal_kruk,leszek_chmielewski}@sggw.pl
[2] Faculty of Wood Technology – WTD, Warsaw University of Life Sciences – SGGW, ul. Nowoursynowska 159, 02-775 Warsaw, Poland
http://www.wzim.sggw.pl
http://www.wtd.sggw.pl

Abstract. The accuracy of detecting the *orange skin* surface defect in lacquered furniture elements was tested. Textural features and an SVM classifier were used. Features were selected from a set of 50 features with the bottom-up feature selection strategy driven by the Fisher measure. The features selected were the Kolmogorow-Smirnow-based features, some of the Hilbert curve-based features, some of the maximum subregions features and also some of the thresholding-based features. The Otsu thresholding and percolation-based features were all rejected. The images of size 300 × 300 pixels cut from the original, larger images were treated as objects. There were three quality classes: *very good*, *good* and *bad*. In the cross-validation process where the testing sets consisted of 90 and the training sets of 910 objects the accuracies ranged from 90% to 98% and the average accuracy was 94%. The tests revealed that more research should be done on the choice of features for this problem.

Keywords: Orange skin · Surface defect · Detection · Quality inspection · Furniture · Textural features · Classification

1 Introduction

In the furniture manufacturing industry the shape accuracy is equally important as the visual quality of the products. In our previous papers we assessed the applicability of the image processing methods to measurements in the furniture industry [1]. It occurred that the problem of the surface defect called *orange skin* requires special attention due to that the dimensional variability introduced by this defect is minute. In [2] we found that this defect seems to be easily detectable with pure vision techniques and in [3] we stated that by using typical off-the-shelf textural features this defect is detectable in the majority of cases. In this paper we try to use some more advanced features already used by us in other, requiring applications [4, 5, 9].

As it was at the time of our previous publications, the literature on the application of image processing in the furniture industry seems to be extremely rare. As before, in the timber industry there is an entirely different situation: the structural and anatomical analysis is frequently performed with the image processing methods [6]. In the present paper we deal with painted surfaces, so the methods developed for raw materials [7] do not apply.

After positive experience with the detection of the *orange skin* defect treated with simple methods in [2] and some more advanced, but still well known ones in [3], now we shall assess the possibilities and limits of the application of relatively complex textural features from the groups of Kolmogorow-Smirnow features [9], maximum subregion-based features [4], features using the concept of percolation [4] and on the Hilbert curve [5].

We shall also try some features in which the main technique is a more or less advanced thresholding to finally check the usefulness of such simple features in the common setting with the advanced features, which proved their viability in demanding applications. These will be the thresholding-based features using the classical Otsu method [8] and some iteration-based features.

The remaining part of this paper is organized as follows. In the following Section we shall briefly characterize the considered surface defect. In the next Section we shall present the way we have prepared the images. Then, the features will be described together with an intermediate test aiming at feature selection with the classification accuracy as a criterion. In the following Section we shall report on the results obtained. Conclusions and outlook for further development will close the paper.

2   The Defect: *Orange Skin*

On the lacquered surfaces of furniture elements the defect called *orange skin* or *orange peel* can appear. It can emerge as small, shallow hollows, that is, an uneven structure of the hardened surface. The reasons for this defect are numerous: insufficient quantity or bad quality of dilutent, excessive temperature difference between the lacquer and the surface, bad distance or pressure of spraying, excessive air circulation during spraying or drying, and insufficient air humidity. On the lacquered surfaces the structure of wood is hidden, so *orange skin* is the only visible sign of surface unevenness.

A surface is considered good or defective for esthetic reasons. Moreover, it is not possible to point out a well-defined *defect* on the surface. The small valleys and holes are surrounded or gradually pass to the good regions. This is the presence or absence of the holes which make the whole surface *good* or *bad*. Also the *good* surface is not free from small deviations from planarity.

3   Measuring Setup and Images

The images were taken with the Nikon D750 24 Mpix camera equipped with the Nikon lens F/2.8, 105 mm. The distance from the focal plane to the object surface was 1 m and the optical axis of the camera was normal to the surface. The lighting was provided by a flash light with a typically small light emitting surface, located at 80 cm from the object, with the axis of the light beam inclined by 70° from the normal to the surface. In this way, the light was falling from a direction close to parallel to the surface, to emphasize the surface unevenness. The camera was fixed on a tripod and it was fired remotely to avoid vibration. The objects were painted with white lacquer in a typical technological process. The photographed surfaces belonged to several different objects. The surfaces were classified by the furniture quality expert as *very good*, *good* and *bad* in the terms of the orange skin defect, before the experiment. The photographs were made of a part of the object which was not farther than 30 cm from the center of the image. The elongated objects were moved in front of the camera between the images were taken, to encompass all of the surface of the objects in the experiment. The images were made in color mode, with lossless compression.

From these images, small non-overlapping images were cut, each of them of size 300 × 300 pix. There were 900 such images total. Each of these images was treated as a separate object and was classified independently of the other images. From these objects, the training and testing sets were chosen so that, in each choice, there were 90 images in the testing set, with equal numbers of images belonging to each class. The remaining 810 images formed the training set.

The way the small images were cut can be seen in Fig. 1. The examples of images belonging to the three classes are shown in Fig. 2.

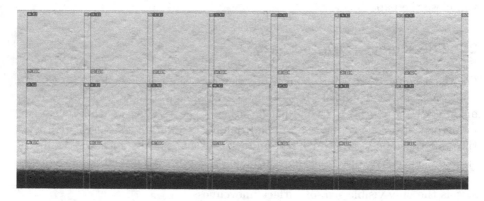

Fig. 1. Example of images of the surface of furniture elements. Small images of size 300 × 300 like those outlined with blue lines and marked with small dark blue icons were cut for the training and testing processes. Each of these images contained only the evenly illuminated surface of the object. (Color figure online)

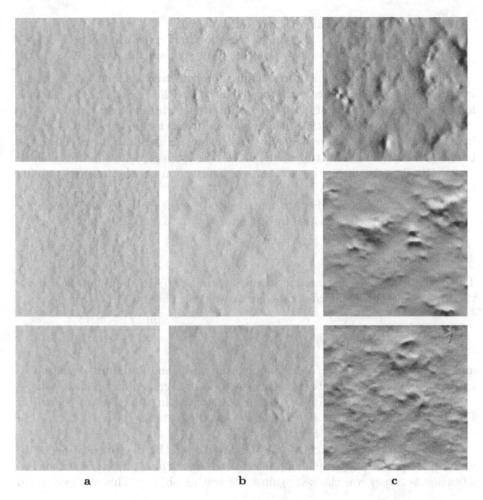

a   b   c

Fig. 2. Examples of images of the surfaces belonging to three classes: (**a**) very good, (**b**) good and (**c**) bad.

4 Features and Classification

4.1 Features

All the features were generated from the luminance component Y of the YIQ color model, $Y \in \{0, 1, ..., 255\}$.

The features for each small image were formed with the following methods:

- number of black fields after thresholding with Otsu method – 1 feature;
- Kolmogorow-Smirnow features [9] – 7 features;
- maximum subregions features [4] – 6 features;
- features based on the percolation [4] – 2;

– features based on the Hilbert curve (cf. [5]) – 16;
– features from iterative single-valued thresholding (explained below) – 9;
– features from iterative adaptive thresholding (explained below) – 9.

The iterative single-valued thresholding was performed as follows. The image was thresholded, in sequence, with thresholds: $i/10 \times 255, i = 1, 2, ..., 9$. The nine features are the numbers of black regions after each thresholding.

The iterative adaptive thresholding was performed as follows. Let A be the image after applying the averaging filter with the window 20×20 pix. Then, the image I_2 is calculated nine times as $I_2 = A - Y - i, i = 1, 2, ..., 9$ and thresholded at $255/10$. The feature is the number of black regions in the image I_2, giving 9 features.

The dimension of the feature matrix was then 900×50: there were 900 objects (images) each described by 50 features.

4.2   Feature Selection

The 50 features were calculated for the 810 training objects. For all these objects the Fisher measure of information content was calculated as

$$S(f) = \frac{1}{3} \sum_{i,j \in \{1,2,3\}, i \neq j} S_{ij}(f), \text{where } S_{ij}(f) = \frac{|m_i(f) - m_j(f)|}{\sigma_i(f) + \sigma_j(f)}, \quad (1)$$

and where $m_i(f)$ and $\sigma_i(f)$ are simply the mean and standard deviation of feature f in class i. The inter-class measures were averaged for all class pairs.

The Fisher measures for the classes calculated in this way are shown in Fig. 3. This measure made it possible to sort the features $f_k, k = 1, 2, ..., 50$ in the sequence of decreasing $S(f_k)$.

The support vector machine (SVM) classifier (to be described in Sect. 4.3) was used to perform the teaching process with the training objects, and the classification accuracy was checked against the testing objects. This was performed

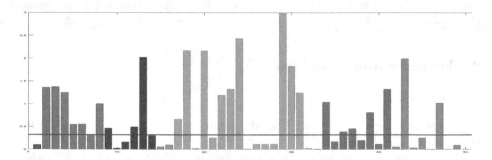

Fig. 3. Fisher measures for 50 features. Colors identify groups of features: blue: 1 Otsu feature; green: 7 Kolmogorow-Smirnow; red: 6 maximum subregions; bright blue: 2 percolation-based; yellow: 16 from Hilbert curve; magenta: 9 from single-valued thresholding; brown: 9 from adaptive thresholding. Threshold $S = 0.31$ obtained in the feature selection process marked with red line (see Sect. 4.2). (Color figure online)

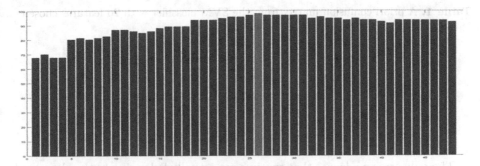

Fig. 4. Accuracy of classification for subsequent sets of features, containing from one to 50 features, chosen according to the decreasing Fisher measure S.

for different sets of features. The first feature set contained the first feature from the sequence with decreasing S (this was the 13th Hilbert feature, bearing the index 29 in the graph in Fig. 3 and having the largest S). The second set contained the first two features in the sequence (plus the 8th Hilbert feature), and so on, up to 50 features in the set. For each set, the attained classification accuracy was noted, as shown in Fig. 4. It can be seen that the accuracy increases for 26 features in the set, up to the value of 97.8%, and then decreases as the remaining 24 features are added. So, this was the bottom-up feature selection, controlled by the Fisher measure to avoid checking the accuracy attained after the addition of each of the features remaining at a given step of the feature adding process.

The result of this feature selection process is that the features having the Fisher measure $S > 0.31$ were chosen. This threshold is marked with the red line in Fig. 3. The chosen features were:

- All 7 Kolmogorow-Smirnow features (green in Fig. 3);
- 3 maximum subregions features (red);
- 9 features based on Hilbert curve (yellow);
- 5 features from single-valued thresholding (thresholds: $0.2, 0.4, 0.5, 0.7, 0.9$);
- 2 features from adaptive thresholding (thresholds: $0.2, 0.6$).

4.3 SVM Classifier

The used version and parameters of the SVM classifier were: radial-basis function kernel, cost $c = 300$, $\sigma = 0.1$. In this paper we paid attention rather to the problem of feature selection than to the choice of the classier. Therefore, we have used one of the classifiers typically applied to the problems of this kind. Extending the set of classifiers will be one of the next steps in our studies.

4.4 Accuracy of Classification

As described above, in the feature selection process, based upon one choice of the training and the testing set, the accuracy attained the highest value equal to 97.8%. The rates of a priori errors received in this case are shown in Table 1.

Table 1. A priori confusion matrix from the SVM classifier with 26 features chosen.

		Classified		
		very good	good	bad
Actual	very good	1.00	0.00	0.00
	good	0.0(6)	0.9(3)	0.00
	bad	0.00	0.00	1.00

The only error made was that two images actually belonging to the class *good* were misclassified and assigned to the class *very good*. In relation to 30 objects in each class (in the testing set) this gives the error rate 0.0(6). In relation to the whole 90 testing object this gives the already mentioned accuracy value of 97.8%.

The two images for which the errors were made are shown in Fig. 5a and b. In the case of these images the classification result was a false positive with respect to the class of the best quality, which should be avoided in quality inspection. However, it can be argued if each of these images really represents inferior quality, but this is beyond the scope of this technical study. It is positive that there are no errors between the two good classes and the bad one.

This result was further verified with the cross-validation with ten different divisions of the set of objects were used. As previously, in each division, 90 objects were chosen for testing, and the remaining 810 ones were used for training. The features were not changed with respect to those selected as described before. The first division was the one analyzed above. The results are shown in Fig. 6 and Table 2.

It can be clearly seen that for the first division the results were the most optimistic. In the remaining ones the results were worse. The average accuracy attained was 94.2%, but in the worst case it was 90%.

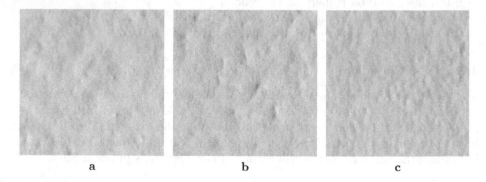

a   b   c

Fig. 5. Images for which the classifier made an error – subfigures (a) and (b). These are *good* objects but they were classified as *very good*. A truly *very good* object is shown for comparison in (c).

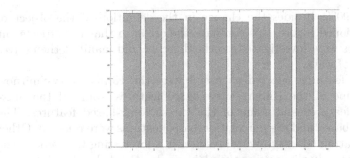

Fig. 6. Accuracy of classification for ten cross-validation cases.

Table 2. Accuracies and numbers of errors for ten cross-validation cases.

Case	Accuracy	No. of errors
1	97.8%	2
2	94.4%	5
3	93.3%	6
4	94.4%	5
5	94.4%	5
6	91.1%	8
7	94.4%	5
8	90.0%	9
9	96.7%	3
10	95.6%	4
Worst	90.0%	9
Average	94.2%	5.2

5   Discussion

Similar problem has been investigated in our previous publications [2,3]. Results obtained in those works suggested that the choice of features was not crucial to the classification result. Therefore, we did not pay much attention to this choice. However, the problem we investigated here was different from that described in [2], where as the classified object the whole product was considered, and there were only two classes: *good* and *bad* object. Now, we consider a small fragment of the product as the object to be classified. This is a more precise approach; accordingly, the choice of the feature should be more careful. Therefore, we have retained the features in which thresholding was used, but we augmented the set of features with a number of other ones, which were known for being useful in the problem of classification of the state of a surface.

The results obtained in this work did not reach the level of accuracy we expected. The average overall classification accuracy attained was 94% but the smallest one was 90%. Besides the change in the definition of the object of classification mentioned before, this can have the origin in that the objects cut from larger surfaces were investigated, so the defects could manifest themselves in a larger variety of ways.

The groups of features selected as useful were the Kolmogorow-Smirnow based features, some of the Hilbert curve-based features, some of the maximum subregions features and some of the thresholding-based features. The Otsu thresholding-based and the percolation-based features were rejected. Other groups of features attained less univocal results. It is interesting that among the simplest features, namely those using the plain single-valued thresholding, some were actually selected.

6   Summary and Prospects

The SVM classifier with features selected from a set of 50 features was successfully used to classify the surfaces affected by the *orange skin* surface defect. This defect appears at lacquered surfaces of furniture and causes these surfaces to belong to three classes: *very good*, *good* and *bad*, according to the furniture quality experts. The bottom-up feature selection strategy driven by the Fisher measure was applied. The features which performed the best were the Kolmogorow-Smirnow based features, some of the Hilbert curve-based features, some of the maximum subregions features and some of the thresholding-based features. The Otsu thresholding-based and the percolation-based features were all rejected. However, some of the simple thresholding-based features were selected.

This tend to confirm the usefulness of very simple methods in solving the problem of orange skin detection. However, such simple tools alone do not provide a sufficiently good result. It is clear that the problem of features should be investigated in depth. The variety of ways in which the surface defects manifest themselves in the lacquered furniture elements makes it necessary to broaden the range of features used in the classification. This will be the subject of our forthcoming papers.

References

1. Chmielewski, L.J., et al.: Defect detection in furniture elements with the hough transform applied to 3D data. In: Burduk, R., Jackowski, K., Kurzyński, M., Woźniak, M., Żołnierek, A. (eds.) Proceedings of the 9th International Conference on Computer Recognition Systems CORES 2015. AISC, vol. 403, pp. 631–640. Springer, Cham (2016). doi:10.1007/978-3-319-26227-7_59
2. Chmielewski, L.J., Orłowski, A., Śmietańska, K., Górski, J., Krajewski, K., Janowicz, M., Wilkowski, J., Kietlińska, K.: Detection of surface defects of type 'Orange Skin' in furniture elements with conventional image processing methods. In: Huang, F., Sugimoto, A. (eds.) PSIVT 2015. LNCS, vol. 9555, pp. 26–37. Springer, Cham (2016). doi:10.1007/978-3-319-30285-0_3

3. Chmielewski, L.J., Orłowski, A., Wieczorek, G., Śmietańska, K., Górski, J.: Testing the limits of detection of the 'Orange Skin' defect in furniture elements with the HOG features. In: Nguyen, N.T., Tojo, S., Nguyen, L.M., Trawiński, B. (eds.) ACIIDS 2017. LNCS, vol. 10192, pp. 276–286. Springer, Cham (2017). doi:10.1007/978-3-319-54430-4_27
4. Kruk, M., Świderski, B., Osowski, S., Kurek, J., et al.: Melanoma recognition using extended set of descriptors and classifiers. EURASIP J. Image Video Process. **2015**(1), 43 (2015). doi:10.1186/s13640-015-0099-9
5. Kurek, J., Świderski, B., Dhahbi, S., Kruk, M., et al.: Chaos theory-based quantification of ROIs for mammogram classification. In: Tavares, J.M.R.S., Natal, J.R.M. (eds.) Computational Vision and Medical Image Processing V. Proceedings of 5th Eccomas Thematic Conference on Computational Vision and Medical Image Processing VipIMAGE 2015, pp. 187–191. CRC Press, Tenerife, Spain, 19–21 October 2015. doi:10.1201/b19241-32
6. Longuetaud, F., Mothe, F., Kerautret, B., et al.: Automatic knot detection and measurements from X-ray CT images of wood: a review and validation of an improved algorithm on softwood samples. Comput. Electron. Agric. **85**, 77–89 (2012). doi:10.1016/j.compag.2012.03.013
7. Musat, E.C., Salca, E.A., Dinulica, F., et al.: Evaluation of color variability of oak veneers for sorting. BioResources **11**(1), 573–584 (2016). doi:10.15376/biores.11.1.573-584
8. Otsu, M.: A threshold selection method from gray-level histograms. IEEE Trans. Syst. Man Cybern. **9**(1), 62–66 (1979). doi:10.1109/TSMC.1979.4310076
9. Świderski, B., Osowski, S., Kruk, M., Kurek, J.: Texture characterization based on the Kolmogorov-Smirnov distance. Expert Syst. Appl. **42**(1), 503–509 (2015). doi:10.1016/j.eswa.2014.08.021

Smart Building Climate Control Considering Indoor and Outdoor Parameters

Batyrkhan Omarov[✉], Aigerim Altayeva, and Young Im Cho

Department of Computer Engineering, Gachon University, Seoul, Korea
batyahan@gmail.com, aikoshal703@gmail.com,
yicho@gachon.ac.kr

Abstract. Heating, ventilation, and air conditioning (HVAC systems) account for the majority of the energy used in buildings. Consequently, any business has the potential to realize significant cost savings by improving control of HVAC operations and increase the efficiency of the system it uses. Using a highly efficient HVAC equipment can lead to significant energy and emissions savings. The entire structure of the building in combination with the enhanced comfort zone can produce a much greater savings. Extended comfort includes the use of concepts such as providing a warm, but drier air using a desiccant dehumidification in the summer, or the colder air from the warm walls of windows and warm in winter. In addition, high efficiency HVAC can provide enhanced thermal comfort for people, as well as to contribute to the improvement of environmental quality in the room. The paper explores thermal process and the affecting parameters, and introduce fuzzy logic based energy consumption model based on controlling of HVAC devices.

Keywords: HVAC systems · Fuzzy logic · Thermal balance · Indoor microclimate

1 Introduction

Individuals spend most their time in an indoor environment and comfort is one of the most important issues with respect to staying indoors. Environmental quality of an interior environment is directly dependent on its organization and content. Therefore, the task of maintaining a comfortable environment is extremely important for health, good spirit, and human activity. Several parameters can be adjusted to achieve comfort in a room—air temperature, humidity, air quality, speed of movement of air throughout the room, oxygen content in the air, ionization of air, and noise level [2, 7]. A deviation of the aforementioned parameters could result in the deterioration of the normal state of an individual. This can lead to the disruption of thermal balance as well as result in a negative impact on health and productivity.

Prior to determining the microclimate of a room and determining any adjustments, it is necessary to find a certain method to determine the real condition of several parameters, i.e., to conduct a study of the microclimate.

An important stage in creating a system to manage temperature and humidity conditions involves the development of greenhouse facility models. This reflects the

K. Saeed et al. (Eds.): CISIM 2017, LNCS 10244, pp. 412–422, 2017.
DOI: 10.1007/978-3-319-59105-6_35

processes occurring within a system from two different standpoints, namely the synthesis of algorithms and the analysis of management quality [9, 11]. If the model requirements are adequate from the second standpoint, then the development of models with respect to the first class of problems should consider the satisfactory requirements as well as the current level of scientific support task synthesis algorithms. According to this classification key [1, 4] there are two groups of climate models as follows:

(a) A fundamental model aimed at solving problems of the object properties of analysis and quality control systems. The models in this group of physical phenomena are described by differential equations (usually in the state space). Parameters in the models of this group involve a physical interpretation.

(b) Black box models involve solution-oriented control algorithms synthesis problems. They are based on the specific synthesis problem using either static models (regression, polynomial, based on the use of neural networks, fuzzy sets) or dynamic models (usually in the form of differential equations in which the coefficients are determined from experimental data by identification methods, and a clear relationship is absent between the physical parameters and structural parameters of the greenhouse).

The present study used a schematic model of the microclimate as a basis for the development of both classes of models.

2 Indoor Microclimate Thermal Balance

Individuals only experience wellness and comfort within a narrow range of thermal conditions. Hence, the natural climate of a limited number of geographical locations is conducive for the comfort of individuals. In most regions, climate conditions are comfortable only for a limited time daily and for a limited time period annually. A building is an enclosure that protects individuals against external conditions. Thus, the interior of a building should provide a comfortable environment. Thermal balance is a principle in which the entire building is considered an entity with a number of energy sources and sinks. A thermal balance corresponds to the net amount of all gains and losses. The energy efficiency of a building is defined through its thermal balance.

Typically, energy flows in cold climates are either welcome gains (sources) or unwelcome losses (sinks) based on the time of year and external conditions [10]. It is necessary to balance the gains and losses that result in the residual energy to create comfortable indoor conditions.

Q_i – Internal heat gain corresponds to the total amount of internal energy gains. This includes heat emitted from human bodies, electrical devices, and artificial lighting.

$Q_{c,T}$ – Conductive heat loss corresponds to energy lost by the transmission of heat through the building envelope.

Q_s – Solar heat gain corresponds to the total amount of energy input induced by incoming solar radiation that heats indoor air and thermal mass in the building.

Q_v – Ventilation heat loss or gain is caused by supply of fresh air; removal of stale indoor air to remove smells, CO_2, and other contaminants; infiltration of cold air and exfiltration of warm indoor air through cracks in the building envelope; mixing of air from different temperature zones; and mechanical ventilation. This is expressed as follows:

Heat Losses: $Q_{Tv} + Q_{i,Sink} + Q_s = Q_{sink}$
Heat Sources: $Q_s + Q_T + Q_v + Q_{i,Source} = Q_{source}$
A thermal equilibrium exists when $Q_{sink} = Q_{source}$
If $Q_{sink} < Q_{source}$, then the temperature inside the building increases.
If $Q_{sink} > Q_{source}$, then the building cools down.

Additional systems and technologies are required for heating or cooling in buildings in which a thermal system is not naturally in equilibrium. It is necessary for the net heating energy to be provided by a heating system. The heating system experiences losses when heat is produced from a primary energy source. The total heating energy demand of a building corresponds to the sum of heating energy and heating equipment losses.

Parameters for sources and losses of energy can be categorized into building, environmental, legal, and usage parameters. The possibility of increasing the energy efficiency of a building exists when buildings are designed by considering given and fixed environmental and usage parameters.

How to ensure desired temperature in the room? An automatic temperature control system was used to formalize the description of the temperature regime of the process as the initial model. With respect to temperature control, it is necessary to consider the heat flows entering and exiting the system as well as the accumulation of thermal energy due to the cumulative capacity of the object. It is necessary to consider the existence of the following three thermal flows:

1. Q_{gain} – heat gain from the heating system.
2. Q_{env} – heat loss through the building envelope.
3. $Q_{fr.air}$ – heat loss for heating of fresh air.

Given the volume of the indoor air (V), air density (ρ), the specific heat capacity of air (C) and using the procedure of drawing up energy balance [1–3] results in the equation of heat that affects the change in air temperature inside a room as follows:

$$\rho VC \frac{dT(t)}{dt} = Q_{gain}(t) - \left(\sum Q_{env}(t) + Q_{fr.air}(t) \right) \tag{1}$$

where ρ – air density (kg/m^3); V – air volume (m^3); C – specific heat of air (J/°C·kg); (t) – indoor air temperature (°C); $Q_{gain}(t)$ – Heat proceeding from the heating system (W); $\Sigma Q_{env}(t)$ – heat loss through the building envelope (W); $Q_{fr.air}(t)$ – heat loss for heating of fresh air (W).

Define heat loss through the building envelope [4]:

$$Q_{env}(t) = \sum k \cdot F \cdot T_{air}(t) - T_{outdoor}(t) \tag{2}$$

where k – heat transfer coefficient of building envelope (J/(m^{2}s ·°C)); F – the building envelope square (m^2); $T_{air}(t)$ – air temperature inside the building (°C); $T_{outdoor}(t)$ – outdoor air temperature (°C).

Heat losses for heating fresh air [4] are given by the following expression:

$$Q_{fr.air}(t) = G_{fr.air}(t) \cdot C_{air} \cdot T_{indoor}(t) - T_{outdoor}(t) \qquad (3)$$

where $G_{fr.air}(t)$ – fresh air consumption for ventilation premises (kg/s); C_{air}– specific heat of air (J/kg·°C); T_{air} – air temperature inside the building (°C); $T_{outdoor}$ – outdoor air temperature (°C).

The initial Eq. (1) for the temperature change is specified as follows:

$$\rho VC \frac{dT(t)}{dt} = Q_{gain}(t) - \sum kF(T_{air}(t) - T_{outdoor}(t)) - G_{fr.air}(t)C_{air}\Delta T \qquad (4)$$

The $T_{outdoor}(t)$ is accepted for the current temperature in the room $T(t)$. Additionally, (t) is expressed as follows:

$$\rho VC \frac{dT(t)}{dt} + kFT(t) = Q_{gain}(t) + kFT_{outdoor}(t) - G_{fr.air}(t)C_{air}\Delta T \qquad (5)$$

Dividing both sides by kF results in the following expression:

$$\frac{\rho VC}{kF} \frac{dT(t)}{dt} + T(t) = \frac{1}{kF} Q_{gain}(t) + \frac{kF}{kF} T_{outdoor}(t) - \frac{1}{kF} G_{fr.air}(t)C_{air}\Delta T \qquad (6)$$

Equation (6) corresponds to a first order differential equation describing the temperature change as a function of defining and disturbances. It is assumed that $TT = \frac{\rho VC}{kF}$ is a time constant. The equation was expressed in operational form as follows:

$$(T_T p + 1)T(t) = \frac{1}{kF} Q_{gain}(t) + T_{outdoor}(t) - \frac{1}{kF} G_{fr.air}(t)C_{air}\Delta T \qquad (7)$$

Hence, it follows that T(t) was influenced by $Q_{gain}(t)$, $T_{outdoor}(t)$, and $G_{fr.air}(t)$. The next section investigates the influence of these parameters.

3 Algorithmic Process to Ensure Desired Air Temperature and Humidity

1. Specifically, $T_{outdoor}$ denotes the value of outdoor temperature. The average annual temperature was determined by the schedule for a particular geographic location premises [4, 5]. The transfer function to change the inside and outside temperatures specified in Eq. (7) is as follows:

$$W_{T1}(p) = \frac{T(p)}{T_{out}(p)} = \frac{1}{(T_T p + 1)} \qquad (8)$$

where $T(p)$ is the Laplace image for the indoor temperature, $T_{outdoor}(p)$ is the Laplace image for the outdoor temperature, and TT is the time constant.

Temperature changing process includes an inertia property and describes a typical inertial link. In the winter, the process can be characterized by cooling the building with no active heating system and other sources of heat flows affecting the temperature balance.

2. Component $\frac{1}{kF} Q_{gain}(t)$ considers the effect of the heating system that provides the heat necessary to maintain the heat balance of the room. The transfer function for adjusting the inside air temperature that is influenced by heat is as follows:

$$W_{T2}(p) = \frac{T(p)}{T_{gain}(p)} = \frac{k_1}{(T_T p + 1)} \tag{9}$$

where $T(p)$ is the Laplace image for the indoor air temperature, $Q_{gain}(p)$ is the Laplace transform for the heating system, and $k_1 = \frac{1}{kF}$ is the heating system efficiency factor, TT is the time constant.

This temperature change process also presents a typical inertial link.

3. Component $-\frac{1}{kF} G_{fr.air} C_{air} \Delta T$ considers the cost of heat that is caused by changes in temperature compensation ΔT supply and indoor air in the room. The consumption of fresh air $G_{fr.air}$ depends on the performance of the ventilation system and considers the value set by the control loop to stabilize the value of the qualitative composition of the air. The relationship between the change in air temperature $T(p)$ and the flow of fresh air $G_{fr.air}(p)$ is described with the following equation:

$$W_{T3}(p) = \frac{T(p)}{G_{fr.air}(p)} = \frac{k_2}{(T_T p + 1)} \tag{10}$$

where $T(p)$ – Laplace transform for the indoor air temperature, $G_{fr.air}(p)$ – Laplace image for fresh air consumption, $k_2 = -\frac{1}{kF} G_{air} \Delta T$ – ventilation system efficiency factor, and TT – time constant.

The process is inertial and presented by an inertial link. Increases in air flow led to decreases in air temperature, and vice versa, given a condition in which a positive temperature differential was present.

The complex influence of external factors on the indoor air temperature can be described by a block diagram as shown in Fig. 1.

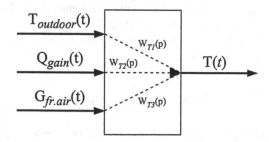

Fig. 1. The relationship structure between indoor temperature and influencing factors

Thus, the indoor air temperature T(t) is an object of control that can represent a dynamic system. It is influenced by three input values, namely a value controlling action $Q_{gain}(t)$ and two perturbing $T_{outdoor}(t)$ and $G_{fr.air}(t)$ values. The control action represented by the feed of heat from the heating system with the transfer function WT2 (p) described the transfer function of WT1(p), and heat loss during operation of the ventilation system for the preparation of fresh outdoor air. The control function was aimed at compensating disturbances in the form of heat loss through the building envelope (with a positive differential indoor $T_{indoor}(t)$ and the outside temperature Tout (t)). The consumption of fresh air $G_{fr.air}(t)$ was determined by the process of stabilizing loop air quality and its impact on the temperature T(t) as described by the WT3(p) transfer function.

The approach discussed above was used to describe the dynamic relationship between air humidity in the rooms with the control actions and influence disturbances. The initial equation involved using an equation given in a previous study [6] to describe the moisture content in the air as follows:

$$\rho V \frac{dX(t)}{dt} = G_{fr.air}(t)X_{fr.air}(t) - G_{outgoing\_air}(t)X_{outgoing\_air}(t) + G_{steam}(t) \qquad (11)$$

where

ρ – air density (kg/m^3); V – air volume (m^3); $X(t)$ – absolute humidity in the room ($\frac{m_{water}}{m_{air}}$); $G_{fr.air}(t)$ – fresh air consumption (kg/second); $X_{fr.air}(t)$ – absolute humidity of fresh air (kg$_{water}$/kg$_{air}$); $G_{outgoing\_air}(t)$ – outgoing air consumption (kg/s); $X_{outgoing\_air}(t)$ – absolute humidity of the outgoing air ($\frac{m_{water}}{m_{outgoing\_air}}$; kg$_{water}$/kg$_{air}$); $G_{steam}(t)$ – steam consumption (kg/s).

With respect to once-through ventilation systems, fresh air flow $G_{fr.air}(t)$ was approximately equal to that of the outgoing air flow $G_{outgoing\_air}(t)$ given that the air is not compressed and has a constant density ($\rho = const.$) and given that the size of the room was unchanged ($V = const.$)). As a first approximation, it was assumed that the humidity of the outgoing air from the room was equal to the actual value of the humidity $X_{outgoing\_air}(t) = X(t)$. The initial equation can then be expressed as follows:

$$\rho V \frac{dX(t)}{dt} = G_{outgoing\_air}(t)X(t) - G_{fr.air}(t)X_{fr.air}(t) + G_{steam}(t) \qquad (12)$$

The equation is transformed by dividing it into $G_{outgoing\_air}(t)$ as follows:

$$\frac{\rho V}{G_{outgoing\_air}} \frac{dX(t)}{dt} + X(t) = \frac{G_{fresh\_air}}{G_{outgoing\_air}} X_{fr.air}(t) + \frac{G_{steam}(t)}{G_{outgoing\_air}(t)} \qquad (13)$$

It is assumed that $\frac{\rho V}{G_{outgoing\_air}} = T_X$ and the equation is expressed in an operational form as follows:

$$(T_Xp + 1)X(t) = \frac{G_{fresh\_air}}{G_{outgoing\_air}} X_{fr.air}(t) + \frac{1}{G_{outgoing\_air}} G_{steam}(t) \qquad (14)$$

Air density $X(t)$ depends on the inflow of fresh air $\frac{G_{fresh\_air}}{G_{outgoing\_air}} X_{fr.air}(t)$ and the steam supply $\frac{1}{G_{outgoing\_air}} G_{steam}(t)$.

These relationships can be specified as follows:

The value of the air humidity is determined by climatic conditions of a region. The impact of a parameter is considered via a transfer function that follows from a differential equation as follows:

$$W_{X1}(p) = \frac{X(p)}{X_{fr.air}(p)} = \frac{1}{(T_Xp + 1)} \qquad (15)$$

where

(p) – Laplace image for indoor humidity,

$X_{fr.air}(p)$ – Laplace image for indoor humidity, and

$T_X = \frac{\rho V}{G_{outgoing\_air}}$ – time constant of humidifying process.

As observed from the transfer function, the process was described by the standard inertial and inertial element. The process involved room ventilation with outside air in the absence of external factors affecting the change in room humidity that led to indoor humidity values similar to the outdoor air humidity value.

Steam consumption is a reference variable that compensates for humidity deficit in the air. The parameter of the transfer function that binds air humidity (t) and exposure $G_{steam}(t)$ is considered as follows:

$$W_{X2}(p) = \frac{X(p)}{X_{steam}(p)} = \frac{k_3}{(T_Xp + 1)} \qquad (16)$$

Where:

$X(p)$ – Laplace image for indoor air humidity,

$X_{steam}(p)$ – Laplace image for steam consumption,

$T_X = \frac{\rho V}{G_{outgoing\_air}}$ – time constant of humidifying process, and

$k_3 = \frac{1}{G_{outgoing\_air}}$ – transformation coefficient of the steam consumption.

The process is also inertial and described by a typical inertial link.

The relationship between air humidity and air flow from the ventilation system is considered. It is assumed that $\frac{1}{G_{outgoing\_air}(t)}$ corresponds to $G`(t)$ and the transfer function for the relationship between air humidity and a flow rate of fresh air $G`(t)$ is derived as follows:

$$W_{X3}(p) = \frac{X(p)}{G'(p)} = \frac{k_4}{(T_X p + 1)} \qquad (17)$$

where $X(p)$ – Laplace image for indoor air humidity,

$G'(p)$ – Laplace image for fresh air consumption,

$k_4 = G_{steam}$ – the transformation coefficient for the fresh air consumption, and

$T_X = \frac{\rho V}{G_{outgoing\_air}}$ – time constant of humidifying process.

Based on the transfer functions, the dependence of air humidity on the influencing factors can be described by the structure shown in Fig. 2, which corresponds to a structure of multiple connected systems.

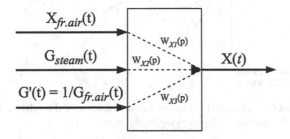

Fig. 2. Structure of the relations between the indoor humidity and influencing factors

The indoor air humidity $X(t)$ was represented by a dynamic system with three input variables, namely a manipulated variable $G_{steam}(t)$ and two perturbing variables $X_{fr.air}(t)$ and $G'(t)$. The control action described the transfer function $W_{X2}(p)$ and was aimed at compensating air humidity due to operation disturbances described by transformation functions $W_{X1}(p)$ and $W_{X3}(p)$, as a result of the ventilation system with $G_{fr.air}(t)$ performance and $X_{fr.air}(t)$ fresh outdoor air humidity.

4 Experiment Results

The experiments were conducted at the Artificial Intelligent and Smart City laboratory in Gachon University. In the laboratory space, an area of 3×6 m^2 with a height of 2.5 m on one of the outer walls included six work areas separated by translucent partition walls (with a height 1.5 m) with personal computers. Figure 3 illustrates the plan of the laboratory.

The room provided fresh air supply through the three dimension 400×400 mm windows. The experimental studies indicated that at an outside temperature below $T_{outdoor}$ ($-5°C$) during heating and ventilation operations, the air temperature significantly exceeded the critical temperature, and the relative humidity was in the range of 5–10%. Also, Fig. 4 shows the results of measurements of the relative humidity at elevations of 1.5 m above the floor space at $T_{outdoor} = -11°C$. The low relative

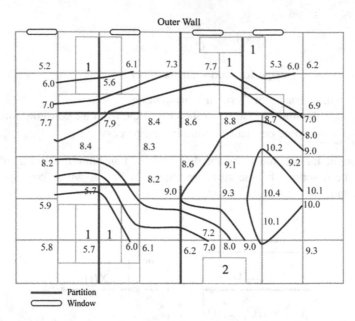

Fig. 3. The results of experimental studies of the distribution of the relative air humidity. 1 – desktops with PC; 2 – partitions; 3 – copying equipment

humidity primarily negatively affected the respiratory organs. Furthermore, humid air is a poor conductor of static electricity. This contributed to the accumulation of humid air on the surface, and this exceeded the performance of the electromagnetic field with respect to the remote control at the workplace with PC and led to failure of the electronic equipment. Humidification units were installed to ensure standardized relative humidity values in the installation of central air conditioning. Nevertheless, the generation of vapor or fine water required significant energy costs.

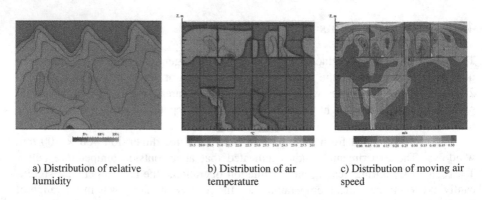

a) Distribution of relative humidity

b) Distribution of air temperature

c) Distribution of moving air speed

Fig. 4. Horizontal plane simulation results

Furthermore, as shown by field studies, the humidified air flowed in the duct and over obstacles (e.g., silencers, etc.). There were significant losses due to moisture condensation on solid surfaces. Thus, a power saving humidification process is necessary to determine the minimum amount of normal air and water supply wherein the relative humidity of indoor air was given. For this purpose, a numerical simulation of the spatial distribution of relative humidity in the room was initially conducted through corresponding field experiments.

In the study, the results indicated the minimum amount of moisture in the supply air by which it was possible to determine the rated value of relative humidity of internal air. The moisture content corresponded to $d = 5 \cdot 10^{-3}$.

The numerical simulation results shown in Fig. 4 include temperature field distribution, air velocity, and relative humidity in the horizontal plane data distance of 1.500 m from the room floor.

Field temperatures (Fig. 4b) confirmed the impact of rising convective flow from heating devices, individuals, and PCs. Accordingly, downward flows were also observed near the outer wall. All heat flows corresponded to limited translucent partitions. In the workplace, the temperature values and variations in the range of 20–22°C satisfied the requirements of regulatory documents [8].

Holistic project explores the specific climate of the building open state of the climate zone, as Fig. 4c illustrates distribution of moving air speed. In the workplace, air velocity satisfied the requirements of normative documents [8]. The rate of change of range of motion of air was in the range of 0.05–0.2 m/s, and it also satisfied the aforementioned requirements. The average values of relative humidity corresponded to the normal values. The range of changes in the relative humidity of the air in the occupied zone corresponded to 33–35%, as illustrated in Fig. 4c. Minimum relative humidity in the range 30–32% was observed in the zones of influence of convective flows and translucent structures.

5   Conclusion

Holistic project explores the specific climate of the building open state of the climate zone, as well as the cultural characteristics that lead to the development of specific requirements. Sustainable energy management requires a focus on the environment and economic efficiency of users. Combined monitoring of comfort and energy consumption is set to gain a better understanding of the reaction of the building to a particular climate, as well as user behavior and acceptance of users. It shows how the extreme conditions in the building can be designed and effectively as refrigeration and air conditioning can be optimized in view of the hot/cold temperatures and high/low humidity.

Acknowledgements. This paper is supported by NRF project "Intelligent Smart City Convergence Platform". Project number is 20151D1A1A01061271.

References

1. Chaouachi, A., Kamel, R.M., Andoulsi, R., Nagasaka, K.: Multiobjective intelligent energy management for a microgrid. IEEE Trans. Industr. Electron. **60**(4), 1688–1699 (2013)
2. Arcos-Aviles, D., Pascual, J., Marroyo, L., Sanchis, P., Guinjoan, F.: Fuzzy logic-based energy management system design for residential grid-connected microgrids. IEEE Trans. Smart Grid **PP**(99), 1 (2016). doi:10.1109/TSG.2016.2555245
3. Chuan, L., Ukil, A.: Modeling and validation of electrical load profiling in residential buildings in Singapore. IEEE Trans. Power Syst. **30**(3), 2800–2809 (2015)
4. Zhang, H., Ukil, A.: Framework for multipoint sensing simulation for energy efficient HVAC operation in buildings. In: 41st IEEE Annual Conference on Industrial Electronics-IECON, Yokohama, Japan, November 2015
5. Földváry, V., Bukovianska, H.P., Petráš, D.: Analysis of energy performance and indoor climate conditions of the slovak housing stock before and after its renovation. Energy Procedia **78**, 2184–2189 (2015). 6th International Building Physics Conference, IBPC 2015
6. Yu, T., Lin, C.: An intelligent wireless sensing and control system to improve indoor air quality: Monitoring, prediction, and preaction. Int. J. Distrib. Sens. Netw. **2015** (2015)
7. Abraham, S., Li, X.: A cost-effective wireless sensor network system for indoor air quality monitoring applications. Procedia Comput. Sci. **34**, 165–171 (2014)
8. Boduch, M., Finche, W.: Standards of human comfort: Relative and absolute. University of Texas at Austin School of Architecture (2016)
9. Omarov, B., Suliman, A., Kushibar, K.: Face recognition using artificial neural networks in parallel architecture. J. Theoret. Appl. Inf. Technol. **91**(2), 238–248 (2016). Islamabad
10. Altayeva, A., Omarov, B., Jeong, H.C., Cho, Y.I.: Multi-step face recognition for improving face detection and recognition rate. Far East J. Electron. Commun. **16**(3), 471–491 (2016)
11. Omarov, B., Altayeva, A., Suleimenov, Z., Cho. Y.I.: Design of fuzzy logic based controller for energy efficient operation in smart buildings. In: 2017 First IEEE International Conference on Robotic Computing, pp. 346–351, April 2017. doi:10.1109/IRC.2017.26

Service Strategies in Two-Server Tandem Configurations – Modeling and Investigation

Walenty Oniszczuk[✉]

Faculty of Computer Science, Bialystok University of Technology,
Bialystok, Poland
w.oniszczuk@pb.edu.pl

Abstract. In this document, two different service strategies in an Internet service station, which consists of with two separated servers (tandem), are investigated. At beginning the Internet tandem under study is first formulated as an open three-station queuing network with blocking assuming that there are finite capacity buffers at front of each server. For each Internet station configurations, the two-dimensional state graphs ware constructed and set of steady-state equations are created. These equations allow for calculating the state probabilities vectors for each tandem configurations, using an equation solving techniques. Many useful performance measures regarding the tandem configurations under study can be extracted from the steady-state probability vectors. The numerical part of this paper contains example for the investigation of different tandem configurations, where are presented the results of the calculation of the main measures of effectiveness and quality of service (QoS) parameters.

Keywords: Internet tandem configurations · Open queuing network · Blocking probabilities · Performance measures

1 Introduction

A traditional Internet server processes requests in FIFO manner. During a high load period, each task has to wait in a queue for a long time before getting serviced. Overhead from tasks competing for limited resources, such as open connections and network bandwidth, is increased. Retry from impatient clients worsens the load situation and causes the snowball effect. More elaborate resource allocation schemas, rather than best-effort service model, need to be adopted to provide predictable services during high load periods. The existing best-effort service with the FIFO scheduling mode and dropping tasks (requests) if the queue is full of the Internet servers leads to misallocation of scarce and expensive network and CPU resources during heavy load periods, causing unpredictable response delay.

The next generation Internet will demand differentiated services from Internet servers. The most important function of the future Internet is to support the provisioning of reliable real-time services on a wide scale. In order to achieve this goal, per-aggregate resource management is, nowadays, regarded as a mandatory choice. The classical example of the modern approach to service users tasks is divided they service processes onto several separated servers (for example, as mechanisms for resolving

K. Saeed et al. (Eds.): CISIM 2017, LNCS 10244, pp. 423–435, 2017.
DOI: 10.1007/978-3-319-59105-6_36

some security problems), which processes some independent parts of incoming tasks. In this paper, we analyze two different tandem configurations, which consists of with two separated servers, in specific way connected each other. At each server, FIFO multiplexing is in place, meaning that all tasks traversing the server are buffered in a single queue First-Come-First-Served. Nowadays the tandem networks have been studied extensively and applied in the evaluation of various systems as in design, capacity planning and performance evaluation of computer and communication systems, call centers, flexible manufacturing systems, etc. Some examples of their application in real systems (two transmitter communication networks with Dynamic Bandwidth Allocation, service facility with front and back room operations) can be found in [28], [1] respectively. The behavior of various systems, including communication and computer systems, as well as production and manufacturing procedures, can be represented and analyzed through queuing network models to evaluate their performance [11–13, 29, 30]. System performance analysis usually includes the queue length distribution and various performance indicators such as response time, throughput and utilization [2, 6, 7, 10].

The theory behind tandem queues is well developed, see, e.g. [3–5, 14, 26, 27]. However, there is still a great interest around more complicated setups involving blocking phenomena as well as different mechanisms for offering services. An excellent survey may be found in the well known of Perros [26] and Balsamo [3] books. Over the years high quality research has appeared in diverse journals and conference proceeding in the field of computer science, traffic engineering and communication engineering [4, 14, 26]. In particular, the two-node tandem queuing model with the Batch Markovian Arrival Process input flow and non-exponential service time distribution described in the paper [8]. Additionally, systems with finite capacity queues under various blocking mechanisms and scheduling constraints are analyzed by the author in [15–25]. In [15, 16], the closed type, multi-center computer networks with different blocking strategies are investigated and measures of effectiveness based on Quality of Service (QoS) are studied. Markovian and semi-Markovian approaches for analysis of open tandem networks with blocking are presented in [17, 19, 21, 23, 24, 25]. Some two-stage tandem queues with blocking and an optional feedback are presented in [20, 22]. In such systems, feedback is the likelihood of a task return, with fixed probability to the first server of the tandem immediately after the service at the second one [8]. Tandems with feedback are usually more complex than the ones without and they are mostly investigated given stationary Poisson arrival process and exponential service time distribution [1, 28]. Blocking and deadlocking phenomena in an open series, linked network model with HOL (head-of-line) priority feedback service was investigated and presented by the author in [18].

The remainder of this paper is organized as follows: Sect. 2 presents and explains the models specification and description. Section 3, analyzes a tandem as an open linked series three-station network with blocking. Section 4 explains a tandem as a linked rerouting two-server network the same with blocking. Section 5 describes the numerical results obtained using our solution technique, followed by the concluding remarks in Sect. 6.

2 Models Specification and Description

In this research, two different configuration of Internet tandem is presented. Each of these kinds of tandem networks has a single service line at the main server, and the other (additional) server with a single service line. Between these servers is a common waiting buffer with finite capacity, for example equal to $m2$. When this buffer is full, the accumulation of new tasks from the main server is temporarily suspended and a phenomenon called blocking occurs until the queue empties and allows new inserts. Similarly, if the first buffer (with capacity $m1$) ahead of the main server is full, then the Internet source node (station) is blocked. This is the classical mechanism for controlling the intensity of an arriving task stream, which comes from the Internet users to the servicing tandem. In this kind of network configuration, no more than $m1 + m2 + 2$ tasks can be processed simultaneously and the Internet tandem network becomes idle, if there are no tasks in both servers.

Let us consider the Internet two-server tandems with blocking, both configurations, as shown in Figs. 1 and 2. On these figures we present models of generalized Internet tandem networks and analyze the feasibility of service with blocking and rerouting. These networks contain of four major logical components:

1. Main server, for the first or the first and the second stage tasks processing with a task initiator, a task controller (realization ON-OFF strategy for incoming requests) and a task dispatcher.
2. Second sever – for the second stage tasks processing.
3. Communication channels.
4. Internet source and λ represents the request arrival process from the clients.

After processing the responses are sent back to the clients through the communication channels. To simplify the model, we assume that the tandem of servers connect to the client through a high speed network. We have ignored the channel delay and flow control on a client side as they are beyond the scope of the proposed study.

The input task stream comes from the Internet source to the main server. This server has a finite capacity buffer and it can accept only $m1 + 1$ tasks. A new task, which arrives at the full main server buffer, is forced to wait in the Internet source station and blocks it. For linked in series servers configuration of tandem (see Fig. 1), each task at the main server is processed on the service line and upon service completion sent to the second server. If there is a free service line on this server, the service process starts immediately, if not, the task must wait in the buffer. If the buffer is full, any task upon service completion at the main server is forced to wait and blocks this server. In case of tandem with rerouting configuration (see Fig. 2), after service completion at the main server, the task proceeds to the second server with probability $1 - \sigma$, and with probability σ the task departs from tandem. Tasks leaving the second server are always feed back to the main server. If the main server buffer is full, similarly as in the previous configuration, the tasks block the second server.

The general assumptions for these two-server tandem models are:

1. Internet tasks stream arriving to the main server is assumed to be a Poisson stream, with rate $\lambda = 1/a$, where a is the mean inter-arrival time,

2. a single service line is on the main server,
3. a single service line is available on the second server,
4. in both servers the service time represents exponentially distributed random variables, with mean $s^A = 1/\mu^A$ and $s^B = 1/\mu^B$, where μ is the mean service rate,
5. the buffers capacities are finite, for example equal to $m1$ and $m2$, respectively to the main and the second servers,
6. service strategies restrict and forbid tasks truncations, if the buffers are full in any case (**strategy network drop-tail is forbidden**) and tasks lose.

In this special type of multi-stage network with blocking a deadlock may occur. We assume that a deadlock is detected instantaneously and resolved without any delay time by simultaneously exchanging both blocked tasks [25].

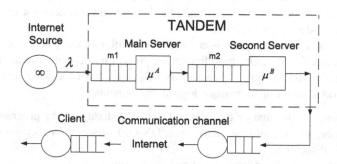

Fig. 1. Tandem configuration as open linked series servers.

Generally, blocking phenomena is a very important mechanism for controlling and regulating intensity of arriving tasks from the Internet source (users) to the Internet tandem servers. A blocking strategies in the main server are realized by a Controller mechanism, it means that controller temporarily suspend and resume (ON-OFF strategy) transfer process from users, because "**network drop-tail strategy is forbidden**" must be realized. The arrival rate to the main server depends on the state of the tandem and blocking factor that reduces the rate at which users are sending tasks to the tandems.

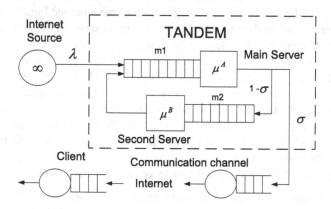

Fig. 2. Tandem configuration as rerouting networks.

3 Tandem as an Open Linked Series Servers

Let us consider the Internet two-server tandem shown in Fig. 1 as the three-station queuing network with blocking. Each queuing system can, in principle, be mapped onto an instance of a Markov process and then mathematically evaluated in terms of this process. According to general assumptions, a continuous-time homogeneous Markov chain can represent a tandem network. The queuing network model reaches a steady-state condition and the underlying Markov chain has a stationary state distribution. Also, such queuing network with finite capacity queues has finite state space. The solution of the Markov chain representation may then be computed and the desired performance characteristics, as queue length distribution, utilizations, and throughputs, obtained directly from the stationary probability vector.

In theory, any Markov model can be solved numerically. In particular, solution algorithm for Markov queuing networks with blocking is a five-step procedure:

1. Definition of the series network state space (choosing a state space representation).
2. Enumerating all the transitions that can possible occur among the states.
3. Definition of the transition rate matrix Q that describes the network evaluation (generating the transition rate).
4. Solution of linear system of the global balance equations to derive the stationary state distribution vector (computing appropriate probability vector).
5. Computation from the probability vector of the average performance indices.

In this type of an open series network we may denote its state by the pair (i,j), where i represents the number of tasks in main server and j denotes the number in second server, including all tasks in service and in blocking. Here some blocked tasks, physically, are located on the Internet source station or on the main server, but the nature of the service process in both servers, allows one to treat them as located in additional places in the buffers and they belong to the main server or the second server. In this case, there can be a maximum of $m1 + 2$ tasks assigned to the main server including the task in the Internet source that can be blocked. Similarly, there can be a maximum of $m2 + 2$ tasks assigned to second server with a task blocked in the main server. For any non-negative integer values of i and j, (i,j) represent a feasible state of this queuing network, and $p_{i,j}$ denotes the probability for that state in equilibrium. These states and the possible transitions among them are shown in Fig. 3. This state diagram of the series server network contains all possible non-blocked states (marked by ovals) as well as the blocking states (marked by rectangles).

Based on an analysis the state space diagrams, the process of constructing the corresponding differential-difference equations, differential equations in t, and difference in (i,j) state, can be divided into several independent steps, which describe some similar, repeatable schemas (see Fig. 3).

These equations are:

(a) for states without blocking factor:

$$p'_{0,0}(t) = -\lambda \cdot p_{0,0}(t) + \mu^B \cdot p_{0,1}(t)$$
$$p'_{0,j}(t) = -(\lambda + \mu^B) \cdot p_{0,j}(t) + \mu^A \cdot p_{1,j-1}(t) + \mu^B \cdot p_{0,j+1}(t) \quad \text{for } j = 1, \ldots, m2+1$$
$$p'_{i,0}(t) = -(\lambda + \mu^A) \cdot p_{i,0}(t) + \lambda \cdot p_{i-1,0}(t) + \mu^B \cdot p_{i,1}(t) \quad \text{for } i = 1, \ldots, m1+1$$
$$p'_{i,j}(t) = -(\lambda + \mu^B + \mu^A) \cdot p_{i,j}(t) + \lambda \cdot p_{i-1,j}(t) + \mu^A \cdot p_{i+1,j-1}(t) + \mu^B \cdot p_{i,j+1}(t) \quad \text{for } i = 1, \ldots, m1+1, j = 1, \ldots, m2+1$$

(1)

(b) for states with Main Server blocking:

$$p'_{0,m2+2}(t) = -(\lambda + \mu^B) \cdot p_{0,m2+2}(t) + \mu^A \cdot p_{1,m2+1}(t)$$
$$p'_{i,m2+2}(t) = -(\lambda + \mu^B) \cdot p_{i,m2+2}(t) + \lambda \cdot p_{i-1,m2+2}(t) + \mu^A \cdot p_{i+1,m2+1}(t) \quad \text{for } i = 1, \ldots, m1$$

(2)

(c) for states with both Internet source and Main Server simultaneous blocking:

$$p'_{m1+1,m2+2}(t) = -\mu^B \cdot p_{m1+1,m2+2}(t) + \lambda \cdot p_{m1,m2+2}(t) + \mu^A \cdot p_{m1+2,m2+1}(t) \quad (3)$$

(d) for states with Internet source blocking:

$$p'_{m1+2,0}(t) = -\mu^A \cdot p_{m1+2,0}(t) + \lambda \cdot p_{m1+1,0}(t) + \mu^B \cdot p_{m1+2,1}(t)$$
$$p'_{m1+2,j}(t) = -(\mu^A + \mu^B) \cdot p_{m1+2,j}(t) + \lambda \cdot p_{m1+1,j}(t) + \mu^B \cdot p_{m1+2,j+1}(t) \quad \text{for } j = 1, \ldots, m2$$
$$p'_{m1+2,m2+1}(t) = -(\mu^A + \mu^B) \cdot p_{m1+2,m2+1}(t) + \lambda \cdot p_{m1+1,m2+1}(t)$$

(4)

The solution for the equilibrium states (or the stationary states), if it exists, must satisfy:

$$\lim_{t \to \infty} p'_{i,j}(t) = 0 \tag{5}$$

and if we let

$$p_{i,j} = \lim_{t \to \infty} p'_{i,j}(t) \tag{6}$$

this leads to the set of equilibrium equations.

Here, a queuing network with blocking linked in series, under appropriate assumptions, is formulated as a Markov process and the stationary probability vector can be obtained using numerical methods for linear systems of equations. If there is a model network with finite number of states, its steady-state probabilities can be found directly from Eqs. (1)–(6) by using some iteration method and the normalizing condition for the sum of state probabilities.

Some specialized software for the solution of nonsymmetrical linear systems of equations by using iterative methods was created by the author. The package is written entirely in the C programming language, and data structures are managed dynamically.

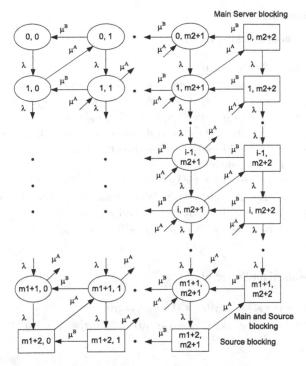

Fig. 3. State transmission diagram for linked series servers

This package allows efficiently calculate the steady-state probability vectors in Markovian models and automatically generates more than twenty different performance measures for analyzed linked series queuing network.

4 Tandem as Rerouting Networks

The same, as in the Sect. 3, let us consider the Internet two-server tandem shown in Fig. 2 as the three-station queuing network with blocking. The state diagram of this rerouting network is presented on the Fig. 4. Here are shown all possible non-blocked states (marked by ovals) as well as the blocking states (marked by rectangles). Based on an analysis this state space diagrams, the process of constructing the corresponding differential-difference equations, differential equations in t, and difference in (i,j) state, can be divided into several independent steps, which describe some similar, repeatable schemas.

These equations are:

(a) for states without blocking factor:

$$p'_{0,0}(t) = -\lambda \cdot p_{0,0}(t) + \mu^A \sigma \cdot p_{1,0}(t)$$
$$p'_{0,j}(t) = -(\lambda + \mu^B) \cdot p_{0,j}(t) + \mu^A(1-\sigma) \cdot p_{1,j-1}(t) + \mu^A \sigma \cdot p_{1,j}(t) \quad \text{for } j = 1,\ldots,m2+1$$
$$p'_{i,0}(t) = -(\lambda + \mu^A \sigma + \mu^A(1-\sigma)) \cdot p_{i,0}(t) + \lambda \cdot p_{i-1,0}(t) + \mu^B \cdot p_{i-1,1}(t) + \mu^A \sigma \cdot p_{i+1,0}(t) \quad \text{for } i = 1,\ldots,m1$$
$$p'_{i,j}(t) = -(\lambda + \mu^A \sigma + \mu^A(1-\sigma) + \mu^B) \cdot p_{i,j}(t) + \lambda \cdot p_{i-1,j}(t) + \mu^B \cdot p_{i-1,j+1}(t)$$
$$\qquad + \mu^A \sigma \cdot p_{i+1,j}(t) + \mu^A(1-\sigma) \cdot p_{i+1,j-1}(t) \quad \text{for } i = 1,\ldots,m1, j = 1,\ldots,m2+1$$
$$p'_{m1+1,0}(t) = -(\lambda + \mu^A \sigma + \mu^A(1-\sigma)) \cdot p_{m1+1,0}(t) + \lambda \cdot p_{m1,0}(t) + \mu^B \cdot p_{m1,1}(t)$$
$$\qquad + \mu^A \sigma \cdot p_{m1+2,0}(t) + \mu^A \sigma \cdot p_{m1+3,0}(t)$$
$$p'_{m1+1,j}(t) = -(\lambda + \mu^A \sigma + \mu^A(1-\sigma) + \mu^B) \cdot p_{m1+1,j}(t) + \lambda \cdot p_{m1,j}(t) + \mu^B \cdot p_{m1,j+1}(t)$$
$$\qquad + \mu^A \sigma \cdot p_{m1+2,j}(t) + \mu^A \sigma \cdot p_{m1+3,j}(t) + \mu^A(1-\sigma) \cdot p_{m1+3,j-1}(t) \quad \text{for } j = 1,\ldots,m2$$
$$p'_{m1+1,m2+1}(t) = -(\lambda + \mu^A \sigma + \mu^A(1-\sigma) + \mu^B) \cdot p_{m1+1,m2+1}(t) + \lambda \cdot p_{m1,m2+1}(t)$$
$$\qquad + \mu^B \cdot p_{m1,m2+2}(t) + \mu^A \sigma \cdot p_{m1+2,m2+1}(t) + \mu^A(1-\sigma) \cdot p_{m1+3,m2}(t)$$

$$(7)$$

(b) for states with Main Server blocking:

$$p'_{0,m2+2}(t) = -(\lambda + \mu^B) \cdot p_{0,m2+2}(t) + \mu^A(1-\sigma) \cdot p_{1,m2+1}(t)$$
$$p'_{i,m2+2}(t) = -(\lambda + \mu^B) \cdot p_{i,m2+2}(t) + \lambda \cdot p_{i-1,m2+2}(t) + \mu^A(1-\sigma) \cdot p_{i+1,m2+1}(t) \quad \text{for } i = 1,\ldots,m1$$

$$(8)$$

(c) for states with both Internet source and Main Server simultaneous blocking:

$$p'_{m1+1,m2+2}(t) = -\mu^B \cdot p_{m1+1,m2+2}(t) + \lambda \cdot p_{m1,m2+2}(t) + \mu^A(1-\sigma) \cdot p_{m1+2,m2+1}(t)$$

$$(9)$$

(d) for states with Source blocking:

$$p'_{m1+2,j}(t) = -(\mu^A \sigma + \mu^A(1-\sigma)) \cdot p_{m1+2,j}(t) + \lambda \cdot p_{m1+1,j}(t) \quad \text{for } j = 0,\ldots,m2$$
$$p'_{m1+2,m2+1}(t) = -(\mu^A \sigma + \mu^A(1-\sigma)) \cdot p_{m1+2,m2+1}(t) + \lambda \cdot p_{m1+1,m2+1}(t)$$
$$\qquad + \mu^B \cdot p_{m1+1,m2+2}(t)$$

$$(10)$$

(e) for states with Second Server blocking:

$$p'_{m1+3,j}(t) = -(\mu^A \sigma + \mu^A(1-\sigma)) \cdot p_{m1+3,j}(t) + \mu^B \cdot p_{m1+1,j+1}(t)$$
$$\text{for } j = 0,\ldots,m2$$

$$(11)$$

The solution of these equations for the equilibrium states, if it exists, must satisfy Formulas (5) and (6) and this leads to the set of stationary equations. In this case a queuing rerouting network with blocking is formulated as a Markov process and the stationary probability vector can be obtained using numerical methods for linear

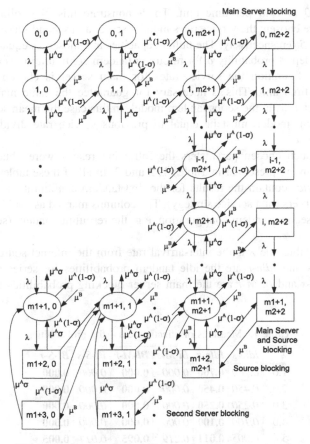

Fig. 4. State transmission diagram for rerouting network

systems of equations using Eqs. (7)–(11) with (5) and (6) and dedicated software for the solution of linear systems of equations was created by the author. This software allows efficiently calculate the steady-state probability vectors and automatically generates more than twenty different performance measures for analyzed queuing network.

5   Numerical Results

In this section, to demonstrate our analysis of two service strategies in the different Internet two-serves tandem configurations presented in Sects. 3 and 4, we have performed numerous calculations. We will concentrate on the several important performance descriptors, such as the probabilities that the different tandem configurations are blocked, it means how are blocked separated servers or blocked Internet sources or how are changed various time measures and how are changed buffers filling parameters if the inter-arrival rate λ from the Internet source (users) to tandems are changed within a range from *1.0* to *10.0* per time unit. To demonstrate this, the following tandem parameters were chosen: the service rates in main server and second server are equal to: $\mu^A = 8.0$, $\mu^B = 5.0$ respectively. The buffer capacities are chosen as equal to: $m1 = 40$, $m2 = 30$. The depart probability σ for rerouting tandem configuration is chosen as *0.5* and in this configuration the service rates for main server is chosen as equal to: $\mu^A = 16.0$ per time unit. This is necessary for guarantee the same main server utilization parameter, as in the series tandem model. In this case the mean service rate for tandem rerouting model, must be equal to previous service rate divided by depart probability, e.g. μ^A/σ.

Based on such chosen parameters the following results were obtained and the majority of them are presented in Tables 1, 2 and 3. In all of these tables the columns marked as "*italic*" contain the results for the first tandem configuration, e.g. the open linked series servers (first service strategy). The columns marked as "bold" contains the results for the second tandem configuration, e.g. the rerouting tandem (second service strategy).

In the first table, the λ is the inter-arrival rate from the Internet source to the both tandems, *Idle-s* and *Idle-r* are the idle tandem probabilities for series and rerouting tandems, *Bl-M-s* and *Bl-M-r* are the main server blocking probabilities for series and

Table 1. Measures of effectiveness – the probabilities

λ	Idle-s	Idle-r	Bl-M-s	Bl-M-r	Bl-S-s	Bl-S-r
1.0	*0.700*	**0.700**	*0.000*	**0.000**	*0.000*	**0.000**
2.0	*0.450*	**0.450**	*0.000*	**0.000**	*0.000*	**0.000**
3.0	*0.250*	**0.250**	*0.000*	**0.000**	*0.000*	**0.000**
4.0	*0.100*	**0.100**	*0.000*	**0.000**	*0.000*	**0.000**
5.0	*0.005*	**0.011**	*0.219*	**0.095**	*0.014*	**0.005**
6.0	*0.000*	**0.000**	*0.375*	**0.320**	*0.167*	**0.075**
7.0	*0.000*	**0.000**	*0.375*	**0.414**	*0.286*	**0.211**
8.0	*0.000*	**0.000**	*0.375*	**0.464**	*0.375*	**0.362**
9.0	*0.000*	**0.000**	*0.375*	**0.499**	*0.444*	**0.487**
10.0	*0.000*	**0.000**	*0.375*	**0.520**	*0.500*	**0.570**

rerouting tandems, *Bl-S-s* and *Bl-S-r* are the source blocking probabilities for series and rerouting tandems.

In the second table, the λ-*decl* is the declared inter-arrival input stream intensities from the Internet source to the tandems, λ-*s-eff* and λ-*r-eff* are effective input stream intensities for series and rerouting tandems, *w-s* and *w-r* are the mean waiting times for series and rerouting tandems, *ro-s* and *ro-r* are the second server utilization factors for series and rerouting tandems.

In the next table, the λ is the inter-arrival rate from the Internet source to the tandems, *v-M-s* and *v-M-r* are the number of tasks in the Main server buffer for series and rerouting tandems, *v-S-s* and *v-S-r* are the number of tasks in the Second server

Table 2. Measures of effectiveness – the responses (the time parameters)

λ-decl	λ-s-eff	λ-r-eff	w-s	w-r	ro-s	ro-r
1.0	1.000	**1.000**	0.010	**0.010**	0.200	**0.200**
2.0	2.000	**2.000**	0.053	**0.053**	0.400	**0.400**
3.0	3.000	**3.000**	0.180	**0.180**	0.600	**0.600**
4.0	4.000	**4.000**	0.640	**0.640**	0.800	**0.800**
5.0	4.992	**4.942**	3.331	**4.512**	0.972	**0.986**
6.0	5.836	**5.000**	5.469	**5.791**	0.999	**1.000**
7.0	6.408	**5.000**	5.829	**5.792**	1.000	**1.000**
8.0	6.774	**5.000**	5.928	**5.792**	1.000	**1.000**
9.0	7.064	**5.000**	5.978	**5.792**	1.000	**1.000**
10.0	7.372	**5.000**	6.004	**5.792**	1.000	**1.000**

Table 3. Measures of effectiveness – the occupation parameters

λ	v-M-s	v-M-r	v-S-s	v-S-r	ro-s	ro-r
1.0	0.018	**0.018**	0.050	**0.050**	0.125	**0.125**
2.0	0.083	**0.083**	0.267	**0.267**	0.250	**0.250**
3.0	0.225	**0.225**	0.900	**0.900**	0.375	**0.375**
4.0	0.504	**0.508**	3.198	**3.198**	0.500	**0.500**
5.0	12.531	**4.802**	22.562	**16.653**	0.836	**0.704**
6.0	35.948	**20.372**	28.955	**27.289**	1.000	**0.932**
7.0	38.302	**30.732**	28.958	**29.000**	1.000	**0.988**
8.0	39.028	**35.958**	28.958	**29.412**	1.000	**0.998**
9.0	39.363	**38.353**	28.958	**29.611**	1.000	**1.000**
10.0	39.548	**39.242**	28.958	**29.719**	1.000	**1.000**

buffer for series and rerouting tandems, *ro-s* and *ro-r* are the main server utilization factor for series and rerouting tandems.

The results of the experiments clearly show that the effect of the properly chosen service strategy in Internet tandem network must be taken into account when analyzing performance such computer networks. Also, results of these calculations evidently show that the blocking phenomena must be taken into account because variation of inter-arrival rate drastically changes the main performance parameters. Which tandem configurations and service strategies are better? It all depends, which measures or time parameters are more preferable during our analysis and obtained results applications.

6 Conclusions

An approach to compare the effectiveness of two service strategies in Internet servers linked to tandem with blocking has been presented. Tasks blocking probabilities and some other fundamental performance characteristics of such networks are derived, followed by numerical examples. The results confirm importance of a special treatment for the models with blocking, which justifies this research. Moreover, our proposal is useful in designing buffer sizes or channel capacities for a given blocking probability requirement constraint. The results can be used for capacity planning and performance evaluation of real-time computer networks where blocking are present.

References

1. Arivudainambi, D., Poongothai, V.: Analysis of a service facility with cross trained servers and optional feedback. Int. J. Oper. Res. **18**(2), 218–237 (2013)
2. Atencia, I.: A discrete-time system with service control and repairs. Int. J. Appl. Math. Comput. Sci. **24**(3), 471–484 (2014)
3. Balsamo, S., De Nito Persone, V., Onvural, R.: Analysis of Queueing Networks with Blocking. Kluwer Academic Publishers, Boston (2001)
4. Clo, M.C.: MVA for product-form cyclic queueing networks with blocking. Ann. Oper. Res. **79**, 83–96 (1998)
5. Economou, A., Fakinos, D.: Product form stationary distributions for queueing networks with blocking and rerouting. Queueing Syst. **30**(3/4), 251–260 (1998)
6. Gemikonakli, E., Mapp, G., Gemikonakli, O., Ever, E.: Exploring service and buffer management issues to provide integrated voice and data services in single and multi-channel wireless networks. In: 2013 IEEE 27th International Conference on Advanced Information Networking and Applications (AINA), pp. 1056–1063. IEEE Conference Publications (2013). doi:10.1109/AINA.2013.57
7. Itoh, H., Fukumoto, H., Wakuya, H., Furukawa, T.: Bottom-up learning of hierarchical models in a class of deterministic POMDP environments. Int. J. Appl. Math. Comput. Sci. **25**(3), 597–615 (2015)
8. Kim, C.S., Klimenok, V., Tsarenkov, G., Breuer, L., Dudin, A.: The BMAP/G/1- > /PH/1/M tandem queue with feedback and losses. Perform. Eval. **64**, 802–818 (2007)
9. Korolyuk, V.S., Korolyuk, V.V.: Stochastic Models of Systems. Kluwer Academic Publishers, Dordrecht (1999)
10. Kwiecień, J., Filipowicz, B.: Firefly algorithm in optimization of queueing systems. Bull. Pol. Ac. Tech. **60**(2), 363–368 (2012)
11. Legros, B., Jouini, O., Koole, G.: Optimal scheduling in call centers with a callback option. Perform. Eval. **95**, 1–40 (2016)
12. Malekian, R., Abdullah, A.H., Ye, N.: Novel packet queuing algorithm on packet delivery in mobile internet protocol version 6 networks. Appl. Math. Inf. Sci. **7**(3), 881–887 (2013)
13. Mangili, M., Martignon, F., Capone, A.: Performance analysis of content-centric and content-delivery networks with evolving object popularity. Comp. Netw. **94**, 80–98 (2016)
14. Martin, J.B.: Large tandem queueing networks with blocking. Queueing Syst. **41**(1/2), 45–72 (2002)
15. Oniszczuk, W.: Quality of service requirements in computer networks with blocking. In: Saeed, K., Pejas, J. (eds.) Information Processing and Security Systems, pp. 245–254. Springer, New York (2005)
16. Oniszczuk, W.: Modeling of dynamical flow control procedures in closed type queuing models of a computer network with blocking. Automat. Contr. Comput. Sci. **39**(4), 60–69 (2005)

17. Oniszczuk, W.: Tandem models with blocking in the computer subnetworks performance analysis. In: Saeed, K., Pejas, J., Mosdorf, R. (eds.) Biometrics, Computer Security Systems and Artificial Intelligence Applications, pp. 259–267. Springer, New York (2006)

18. Oniszczuk, W.: Blocking and deadlock factors in series linked servers with HOL priority feedback service. Pol. J. Environ. Stud. **16**(5B), 145–151 (2007)

19. Oniszczuk, W.: Analysis of an open linked series three-station network with blocking. In: Pejas, J., Saeed, K. (eds.) Advances in Information Processing and Protection, pp. 419–429. Springer, New York (2007)

20. Oniszczuk, W.: An intelligent service strategy in linked networks with blocking and feedback. In: Nguyen, N.T., Katarzyniak, R. (eds.) Studies in Computational Intelligence New Challenges in Applied Intelligence Technologies, SCI, vol. 134, pp. 351–361. Springer, Heidelberg (2008)

21. Oniszczuk, W.: Semi-Markov-based approach for analysis of open tandem networks with blocking and truncation. Int. J. Appl. Math. Comput. Sci. **19**(1), 151–163 (2009)

22. Oniszczuk, W.: Analysis of linked in series servers with blocking, priority feedback service and threshold policy. Int. J. Comput. Syst. Sci. Eng. **5**(1), 1–8 (2009)

23. Oniszczuk, W.: Loss tandem networks with blocking analysis – a semi-Markov approach. Bull. Pol. Ac. Tech. **58**(4), 673–681 (2010)

24. Oniszczuk, W.: Open tandem networks with blocking analysis – two approaches. Control Cybern. **43**(1), 111–132 (2014)

25. Oniszczuk, W.: Blocking and deadlocking phenomena in two-server tandem configuration with optional feedback – modeling and parameter sensitivity investigation. In: Saeed, K., Homenda, W. (eds.) CISIM 2016. LNCS, vol. 9842, pp. 441–452. Springer, Cham (2016). doi:10.1007/978-3-319-45378-1_39

26. Onvural, R.: Survey of closed queuing networks with blocking. Comput. Surv. **22**(2), 83–121 (1990)

27. Perros, H.G.: Queuing Networks with Blocking. Exact and Approximate Solution. Oxford University Press, New York (1994)

28. Raghavendran, C.H.V., Naga Satish, G., Rama Sundari, M.V., Suresh Varma, P.: Tandem communication network model with DBA having non homogeneous poisson arrivals and feedback for first node. Int. J. Comput. Technol. **13**(9), 4922–4932 (2014)

29. Sunitha, G.P., Kumar, S.M.D., Kumar B.P.V.: A pre-emptive multiple queue congestion control for different traffic classes in WSN. In: 2014 International Conference on Circuits, Communication, Control and Computing, pp. 212–218. IEEE Conference Publications (2014). doi:10.1109/CIMCA.2014.7057793

30. Tikhonenko, O., Kempa, W.M.: On the queue-size distribution in the multi-server system with bounded capacity and packet dropping. Kybernetika **49**(6), 855–867 (2013)

Image-Driven Decision Making with Application to Control Gas Burners

Ewaryst Rafajłowicz$^{(\boxtimes)}$ and Wojciech Rafajłowicz

Faculty of Electronics, Wrocław University of Technology, Wrocław, Poland
`ewaryst.rafajlowicz@pwr.wroc.pl`

Abstract. Our aim is to propose a model-free approach to decision making that is based on the direct use of images. More, precisely, a content of each image is used – without further processing – in order to cluster them by the K-medoids method. Then, decisions are attached to each cluster by an expert. When a new image is acquired, it is firstly classified to one of the clusters and the corresponding decision is made. The approach is conceptually rather simple, but its success in on-line applications depends on the way of organizing learning and decision phases. We illustrate the approach by the example of a decision-making system for industrial gas burners.

Keywords: Camera in the loop · Image-based control · Gas burner

1 Introduction

Most decisions made by human beings and animals are based on images provided by the eyes. In most cases these decisions are made on an intuitive level as when we are walking or grasping a cup of tea. In somewhat more complicated situations, e.g., when we see a red light at a crossroads, our decisions are more consciously made. Even more image interpretation work is necessary when a policeman is governing the traffic at a crossroads[1].

The number of cases when processing images and their interpretation in decision making is so broad that it is impossible to consider all of them in one paper. We concentrate on image-driven decision making in industrial applications. At least the following three classes of problems can be distinguished:

1. simple signals given by workers to each other (start, stop, go on etc.) and safety monitoring by monitoring the presence in dangerous areas – we skip discussing these topics, since they are relatively simple and well-developed,

---

[1] By the way, it would be of interest to know how researchers working on autonomous vehicles take such cases into account. More broadly, one can imagine an emergency situation (road accident or a fire), when warnings are even less standarized (hand waving, using a flashlight or a handkerchief).

© IFIP International Federation for Information Processing 2017
Published by Springer International Publishing AG 2017. All Rights Reserved
K. Saeed et al. (Eds.): CISIM 2017, LNCS 10244, pp. 436–446, 2017.
DOI: 10.1007/978-3-319-59105-6_37

2. quality monitoring of produced items,
3. on-line control of continuously running industrial processes.

Quality monitoring of a produced item is also relatively well developed (see [3] and extensive bibliography cited therein and [10,11] for more recent contributions). However, there are still large areas of potential applications of machine vision techniques in quality control both of item by item and continuously running industrial processes. In particular, the approach proposed in this paper can also be used for these purposes. The distinguishing feature of machine vision techniques in quality monitoring is that the resulting decision are in the most cases binary – confirms requirements or not. The second feature that differentiates them from problems of on-line control with camera in the loop is that in quality monitoring usually there is no automatic feedback in order to improve a production process. Instead, experts analyse past data, trying to find reasons of poor quality.

In this paper we concentrate on item 3. of the above list. Advanced applications of control systems with camera in the loop are described rather rarely (see [2,5,5,6,12] for several more recent examples).

Approaches to control systems with a camera in the loop can roughly be classified as follows:

model-based – a mathematical model of a system to be controlled is known and a camera provides information that is inaccessible by classic sensors (see [9]),

model-free – a mathematical model of a process is not available and images provided by a camera are either:

> **intensively processed** in order to extract problem-specific features usefull in decision-making [8,14]
>
> **OR**
>
> **roughly clustered** using only a general (dis-)similarity measure between images in order to cluster them into system states that require the same (or similar) decision (action).

The latter approach is the main topic of this paper. We shall call this approach model-free, image-driven decision making (IDDM). As far as we know, the approach that is completely model-free decision making, which is solely based on images, but without their intensive processing, does not have its counterpart in the literature. For this reason we shall not provide comparisons of the IDDM with other methods that require much more a priori information.

Its main advantages of the IDDM are the following:

- the IDDM approach is relatively fast, since the learning (clusterization) phase can be separated from an on-line decision making,
- the decision-making phase can be implemented as a low-cost microprocessor system,
- a low level of a priori knowledge is necessary in order to design a IDDM system.

The IDDM is based on K-medoids clustering, but other clustering methods might also be used. It is worth mentioning that K-medoids clustering in image processing was used mainly for clustering pixels of one image (see [1] and the bibliography cited therein), while the proposed version aims to cluster images as whole entities.

The paper is organized as follows:

- in the next section we provide a general description of the IDDM approach,
- then, this approach is applied to design a decision-making system for control industrial gas burners using a camera,
- finally, we discuss possible extensions of the IDDM approach.

We remark that the problem of decision-making for industrial gas burners using a camera is an area of recent active research: [8, 13, 14, 16], but the approach proposed here is different. Namely, we do not use time-consuming image processing operations other than verifying to which cluster acquired images belong.

2   Image-Driven Decision Making – a General Idea and Algorithm

The proposed approach consists of the following two phases:

- off-line clustering phase,
- on-line decision making.

Below we describe these phases in more details.

2.1   Off-Line Clustering Phase

The first step of this phase is collecting a large number of images that are representative for the system states. We shall call these images the set of representative images (SRI). This step is crucial for a proper functioning of a decision system. The SIR must contain images that represent all important system states. The number of images illustrating each group of important states should be sufficiently large.

A strategy of clustering images and decisions. The second step is to cluster the set of images into an appropriate number of clusters (see below for details). The third step is to attach decisions (control actions) to each cluster. We discuss steps two and three in common, since one can consider the following two strategies of attaching (linking) decisions and images.

Cluster and attach decisions. The SRI is firstly clustered into, say, $K > 1$ disjoint sets of similar states represented by images. Then, an expert attaches control actions (decisions) to each of them. We shall use this strategy in the present paper.

Attach decisions and cluster. This strategy is more laborious for the expert, since he/she has to attach a decision to each image in the SRI. Then, pairs (*image, decision*) are clustered, using a (dis-)similarity function (metric) that takes into account both the similarity of images as well as the similarity of decisions. This requires that decisions can be in some sense ordered or their closeness can be defined. After clustering pairs (*image, decision*) one may find some inconsistencies, since it may happen that two images that are attached to the same cluster have different decisions attached. Thus, before using this approach it is necessary to unify decisions. This can be done by the majority voting among decision labels in each cluster. However, if in a given cluster we have, e.g., two decision labels in almost equal proportions, then it is expedient to consider splitting this cluster into two and further join it with another cluster (sub-cluster) with the same decision label. As one can notice, this strategy needs to be carefully elaborated in order to avoid decision clashes.

Distance functions for clustering images. Images can formally be clustered in the same way as other objects. The only specificity is in selecting a similarity measure between images that should take into account both the correspondence of pixels in space as well as different contents and ways of coding images. We require that a similarity function $\rho(A, A')$ is a metric (distance function) that is defined on the Cartesian product of an appropriate space of images $A, A', \ldots$, as it is illustrated by examples listed below.

It is assumed that all images in the SRI are of the same type (binary, gray levels or color) and of the same dimensions $I \times J$, say. Concerning color images we additionally assume that all of them use the same color coding scheme (e.g., RGB or HSI).

Color RGB images. Color images, coded as RGB (red, green, blue) channels, are represented as: $C = [c_{ij\gamma}]$, $C' = [c'_{ij\gamma}]$, where $\gamma \in \{R, G, B\}$. Again, $c_{ij\gamma}$ and $c'_{ij\gamma}$ are usually restricted to $[0, 1]$ or to $[0, 255]$ for each channel. Later on we shall use the following distance function for RGB color images:

$$\rho_C(C, C') = \sum_{i=1}^{I} \sum_{j=1}^{J} \sum_{\gamma \in \{R, G, B\}} (c_{ij\gamma} - c'_{ij\gamma})^2. \tag{1}$$

Clearly, gray-level and binary counterparts of (1) can also be used.

Details of clustering images – K-medoids. Having selected a distance function between images, one can cluster SRI using the well known K-means algorithm. However, for our purposes the method of K-medoids (see [4,7] for recent implementations of this algorithm) seems to be better suited. The reason is in that it returns – as its output – K images which are present in SIR. This would be of special interest when the second strategy (attach decisions to images and cluster) would be used. However, also when the first strategy is preferred (as in our case study), the K-medoids approach works better than the K-means for the following reasons:

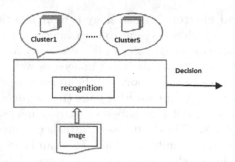

Fig. 1. A general scheme of on-line, image-driven decision making after the learning phase that provides clusters.

1. the K-medoids method is more robust to noise and outliers (as it has features similar to the one-dimensional median),
2. the distances between images are calculated only once (important for large images),
3. for a long sequence of images the K-medoids method can be faster than the K-means method.

Denote by $C^{(n)}$, $n = 1, 2, \ldots, N$ the images in the SRI and let $\mathcal{C}$ be the collection of them. An image $\hat{C} \in \mathcal{C}$ is called the medoid of this set (see, e.g., [15] and the bibliography cited therein), if it minimizes the following distance function:

$$\sum \rho_C(\hat{C}, C^{(n)}), \qquad (2)$$

where the sum in (2) is taken over all $C^{(n)} \in \mathcal{C}$ such that $\hat{C} \neq C^{(n)}$. We shall use this definition also for subsets of $\mathcal{C}$.

For arbitrarily selected $C_k \in \mathcal{C}$, $k = 1, 2, \ldots, K$ define clusters $\mathcal{C}_k$, $k = 1, 2, \ldots, K$ by attaching to $\mathcal{C}_k$ all the images $C^{(n)}$, $n = 1, 2, \ldots, N$ such that they are closer to C_k than to other C_l, $k \neq l$ in ρ_C distance. Define the total distance as follows:

$$L(C_1, C_2, \ldots, C_K) = \sum_{k=1}^{K} \sum_{C^{(n)} \in \mathcal{C}_k} \rho_C(C_k, C^{(n)}). \qquad (3)$$

We are looking for $\hat{C}_k \in \mathcal{C}$ and $\hat{\mathcal{C}}_k$ $k = 1, 2, \ldots, K$ that minimize (3).

Below we provide a skeletal version of the K-medoids algorithm that is adapted to split all images from $\mathcal{C}$ into K disjoint clusters. It can also serve as the definition of the K-medoids method.

Algorithm 1 – K-medoids algorithm for clustering images.

Step 0. Calculate and store a $N \times N$ distance matrix $D = [d_{nm}]$, where $d_{nm} = \rho_C(C^{(n)}, C^{(m)})$. Select initial medoids C_k, $k = 1, 2, \ldots, K$ by drawing them at random from $\mathcal{C}$ and insert them into a collection, $\mathcal{CCM}$ say, of considered candidates for medoids.

Step 1. Form clusters C_k, $k = 1, 2, \ldots, K$ by attaching to C_k all the images from C that are closer C_k than to other temporary medoids C_l, $k \neq l$.

Step 2. Calculate the total distance L between images and their temporary clusters as follows:

$$L(C_1, C_2, \ldots, C_K) = \sum_{k=1}^{K} \sum_{C^{(n)} \in \mathcal{C}_k} \rho_C(C_k, C^{(n)}), \qquad (4)$$

where $\rho_C(C_k, C^{(n)})$ is read out from the appropriate element of matrix D.

Step 3. Select at random an image, say $C^{(*)}$, from C, which is different than those in $\mathcal{CCM}$. $C^{(*)}$ is a candidate for a new medoid center. Using distances from matrix D find the medoid $C(j)$, say, that is closest to $C^{(*)}$ among all current medoids $C_1, C_2, \ldots, C_K$.

Step 4. Calculate the total distance function with $C(j)$ replaced by $C^{(*)}$:

$$L_{trial} \overset{def}{=} L(C_1, C_2, \ldots \underbrace{C^{(*)}}_{j-th} \ldots, C_K)$$

in the same way as in (4).

Step 4a. If $L_{trial} < L(C_1, C_2, \ldots, C_K)$, then: replace $C(j)$ by $C^{(*)}$, insert $C^{(*)}$ into $\mathcal{CCM}$ and go to Step 1.

Step 4b. $L_{trial} \geq L(C_1, C_2, \ldots, C_K)$, insert $C^{(*)}$ into $\mathcal{CCM}$. If $\mathcal{CCM} = C$ or if Step 4b was visited a large (prescribed) number of times in subsequent iterations, then STOP and provide current medoids $C_1, C_2, \ldots, C_K$ and the corresponding clusters $\mathcal{C}_k$, $k = 1, 2, \ldots, K$ as the output of the algorithm. Otherwise, go to Step 3.

If the algorithm stops at Step 4b, then we consider its output either as the optimal solution $\hat{C}_k \in C$ and $\hat{C}_k$ $k = 1, 2, \ldots, K$ or its its approximation.

A faster implementation of K-medoids clustering of images, more in the spirit of the K-means algorithm, can be elaborated using general guidelines provided in [7]. In [4] one can find a survey of approaches to K-medoids clustering that are based on evolutionary algorithms.

2.2   On-Line Decision Making

Medoids and clusters $\hat{C}_k \in C$ and $\hat{C}_k$ $k = 1, 2, \ldots, K$ form a base for on-line decision making, when a new image, C_{cur} say, is captured by a camera. As it was mentioned earlier, at this stage an expert has to attach decisions, d_k, $k = 1, 2, \ldots, K$ say, to each cluster. Thus, we have the sequence $(\hat{C}_k, d_k)$ $k = 1, 2, \ldots, K$ at our disposal.

Algorithm 2 – On-line decision making algorithm.

Step 1. Image acquisition: provides C_{cur} image.

Step 2. Recognition: find cluster label $k_{cur} \in \{1, 2, \ldots, K\}$ such that C_{cur} fits best $\hat{C}_{k_{cur}}$ among all clusters.

Step 3. Decision: read out the corresponding decision $d_{k_{cur}}$ and go to the step Image acquisition.

An outline of this algorithm is presented in Fig. 1.

Recognition (Step 2) of this algorithm can be formalized in a number of ways. At least three of them are worth mentioning.

(R1) Features can be extracted from medoids $\hat{C}_k$ $k = 1, 2, \ldots, K$ and compared with the same features extracted from C_{cur}.

(R2) Among medoids $\hat{C}_k$ $k = 1, 2, \ldots, K$ find the one that is closest to C_{cur} in ρ_C metric.

(R3) Calculate representative images, $\tilde{C}_k$ say, for clusters $\hat{C}_k$ $k = 1, 2, \ldots, K$, other than $\hat{C}_k$'s and find $\tilde{C}_k$ that is closest to C_{cur}.

In the case study presented in the next section we have selected the arithmetic means of images contained in $\hat{C}_k$'s as the representative images $\tilde{C}_k$, $k = 1, 2, \ldots, K$. Notice that this way is different than using K-means, since at the first stage we use the more robust K-medoids method for defining clusters and only after that – they are averaged.

For (R3) approach (applicable also to (R2)), one can estimate the probabilities $\tilde{p}_1, \tilde{p}_2, \ldots, \tilde{p}_K$ of the events: C_{cur} is from k-th cluster. A natural, compatible with ρ_C, way of doing this is as follows.

Algorithm 3 – Estimating probabilities

Step 1. If for a certain cluster label $\check{k}$, say, we have $\rho(C_{cur}, \tilde{C}_k)=0$, then set $\tilde{p}_{\check{k}} = 1$ and $\tilde{p}_k = 0$ for $k \neq \check{p}$.

Step 2. Otherwise, calculate $l_k = 1/\rho(C_{cur}, \tilde{C}_k)$ and set $M = \sum_{k=1}^{K} l_k$.

Step 3. Set $\tilde{p}_k = l_k/M$, $k = 1, 2, \ldots, K$.

Remark 1. *By construction, the largest $\tilde{p}_k$ corresponds to that $\check{k}$, for which $\rho(C_{cur}, \tilde{C}_k)$ is the smallest one. However, values of $\tilde{p}_k$'s still have diagnostic properties. Namely, if $\tilde{p}_{\check{k}}$ is not too much larger than (a) certain other(s) $\tilde{p}_k$'s, then we may consider this classification as uncertain. In the next section the following rule is applied: if for at least one k $0.8\,\tilde{p}_{\check{k}} < \tilde{p}_k$, then the classification is uncertain and – instead of taking decision $d_{\check{k}}$ – one may consider other actions.*

3   Image-Driven Control of a Gas Burner – A Case Study

In this section we apply the methodology of image-driven control (Sec. 2) to support the decision on the rate of air supply to a gas burner. We refer the reader to [8,14] for the problem statement and specific features of industrial gas burners control using a camera. For an alternative approach see [13].

Images of flames of an industrial gas burner ($N = 100$) are clustered into $K = 5$ groups using ρ_C similarity measure between images. The clustering was

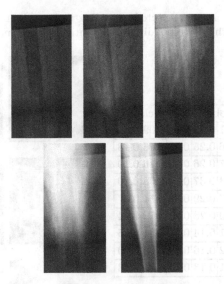

Fig. 2. Representative images – obtained by averaging K-medoid clusters. Classes labelled 1-5, row-wise from the upper left.

done according to general rules of K-medoid clustering (see Algorithm 1), implemented in Wolfram's Mathematica ver. 11. Then, representative images for each class were calculated, according to R3) – by averaging. The resulting images are shown in Fig. 2. In order to test the resulting cluster-based classifier a testing sequence containing 54 images (other than those in the learning sequence) was passed as its input. According to the rule described in Remark 1, nine images displayed in Table 1 (right panel) are selected as those that are potentially incorrectly classified. This means that about 84% of them were classified without doubts. A more careful analysis of the probabilities corresponding to potentially misclassified images (see Table 1 – right panel) reveals that six of them have been classified to class labelled as 2, while possible misclassifications were to classes 1 or 3. As we shall see, these potential misclassifications do not lead to essential problems. Thus, we can say that we have a sufficiently reliable and fast tool for the direct recognition of images.

Now, it remains to attach decisions to clusters and then, one can apply Algorithm 2 on-line. The analysis of Fig. 2 indicates that a proper mode of operating the burner is somewhere between Class 1 and Class 2, since Class 1 flames are blue, but it happens that the burner is loudly roaring. Flames from Class 2 indicate a slightly too low air supply. In order to ensure that the decisions are not too frequently changed, we assume that Class 2 is the proper one. Images from Classes 3–5 indicate a too low or much too low air supply. Thus, as decisions attached to each class, one may consider the following:

d_1 – slightly reduce the air supply rate,
d_2 – keep the air supply rate at this level,

Table 1. Right panel – images selected according to Remark 1 – as potentially misclassified. Left panel – the corresponding probabilities of class matching.

No	Cl	probabilities of classes				
18.	2.	0.31	0.35	0.13	0.09	0.11
20.	2.	0.16	0.25	0.24	0.16	0.18
21.	2.	0.17	0.26	0.22	0.16	0.19
22.	2.	0.33	0.37	0.12	0.08	0.10
23.	2.	0.17	0.29	0.23	0.14	0.17
25.	2.	0.20	0.28	0.25	0.12	0.14
32.	4.	0.11	0.14	0.19	0.31	0.25
34.	5.	0.12	0.16	0.19	0.23	0.30
42.	5.	0.11	0.13	0.18	0.25	0.33

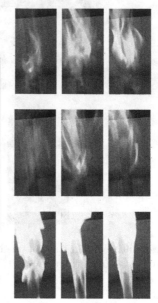

d_3 – slightly increase the air supply rate,
d_4 – largely increase the air supply rate,
d_5 – highly increase the air supply rate.

The above decisions are of a qualitative nature. Providing quantitative decisions would require much broader experimental data than we had at our disposal. Notice that the reason that leads to changes of decisions stems from fluctuations of methane contents in natural gas. A specific feature of gas burners of a moderate size that made it possible to apply the proposed approach is their almost immediate response for changing the air supply rate.

4   Concluding Remarks

A direct approach to image-driven decision making has been proposed. It consists of the clustering phase – that can be time-consuming – and a decision-making phase, which is sufficiently fast for on-line applications, since no image processing is necessary. This approach has a wide range of possible applications. One of them, namely, air supply rate control of an industrial gas burner is reported in the paper. The approach is flexible and may have many variants that differ in the way of selecting the method of clustering and the similarity function as well as by forming images representative for classes.

Being widely applicable, the IDDM cannot be universal. Its applicability is limited to cases when relatively large portions of images are changing. It can be extended to certain classes of dynamic systems when one has to take into account that a memory of older states is present in the system, but the extension is outside the scope of this paper.

Acknowledgements. The research of the first author has been supported by the National Science Center under grant: 2012/07/B/ST7/01216.

References

1. Cai, W., Chen, S., Zhang, D.: Fast and robust fuzzy c-means clustering algorithms incorporating local information for image segmentation. Pattern Recogn. **40**(3), 825–838 (2007)
2. Chapman, K.W., Carroll Johnson, W., McLean, T.J.: A high speed statistical process control application of machine vision to electronics manufacturing. Comput. Ind. Eng. **19**(1), 234–238 (1990)
3. Davies, E.R.: Machine Vision: Theory, Algorithms, Practicalities. Elsevier, Amsterdam (2004)
4. Hruschka, E.R., Campello Ricardo, J.G.B., Freitas, A.A., et al.: A survey of evolutionary algorithms for clustering. IEEE Trans. Syst. Man Cybern. Part C Appl. Rev. **39**(2), 133–155 (2009)
5. King, T.: Vision-in-the-loop for control in manufacturing. Mechatronics **13**(10), 1123–1147 (2003)
6. O'Leary, P.: Machine vision for feedback control in a steel rolling mill. Comput. Ind. **56**(8), 997–1004 (2005)
7. Park, H.-S., Jun, C.-H.: A simple and fast algorithm for k-medoids clustering. Expert Syst. Appl. **36**(2), 3336–3341 (2009)
8. Rafajłowicz, E., Pawlak-Kruczek, H., Rafajłowicz, W.: Statistical classifier with ordered decisions as an image based controller with application to gas burners. In: Rutkowski, L., Korytkowski, M., Scherer, R., Tadeusiewicz, R., Zadeh, L.A., Zurada, J.M. (eds.) ICAISC 2014. LNCS, vol. 8467, pp. 586–597. Springer, Cham (2014). doi:10.1007/978-3-319-07173-2_50
9. Rafajłowicz, E., Rafajłowicz, W.: Iterative learning in repetitive optimal control of linear dynamic processes. In: Rutkowski, L., Korytkowski, M., Scherer, R., Tadeusiewicz, R., Zadeh, L.A., Zurada, J.M. (eds.) ICAISC 2016. LNCS (LNAI), vol. 9692, pp. 705–717. Springer, Cham (2016). doi:10.1007/978-3-319-39378-0_60
10. Rafajłowicz E., Wietrzych J., Rafajłowicz, W.: A computer vision system for evaluation of high temperature corrosion damages in steam boilers. In: Korbicz, J., Kowal, M. (eds.) Intelligent Systems in Technical and Medical Diagnostics. AISC, vol 230, pp. 391–402. Springer, Heidelberg (2014)
11. Rafajłowicz, E., Wnuk, M., Rafajłowicz, W.: Local detection of defects from image sequences. Int. J. Appl. Math. Comput. Sci. **18**(4), 581–592 (2008)
12. Rigelsford, J.: Industrial image processing: visual quality control in manufacturing. Sens. Rev. **21**(2) (2001)
13. Skubalska-Rafajłowicz, E.: Sparse random projections of camera images for monitoring of a combustion process in a gas burner. In: Saeed, K., Homenda, W., Chaki, R. (eds.) CISIM 2017. LNCS, vol. 10244, pp. 447–456. Springer, Heidelberg (2017)

14. Wójcik, W., Kotyra, A.: Combustion diagnosis by image processing. Photonics Lett. Pol. **1**(1), 40–42 (2009)
15. Xu, R., Wunsch, D.: Survey of clustering algorithms. IEEE Trans. Neural Netw. **16**(3), 645–678 (2005)
16. Yan, H., Paynabar, K., Shi, J.: Image-based process monitoring using low-rank tensor decomposition. IEEE Trans. Autom. Sci. Eng. **12**(1), 216–227 (2015)

Sparse Random Projections of Camera Images for Monitoring of a Combustion Process in a Gas Burner

Ewa Skubalska-Rafajłowicz[✉] [ID]

Department of Computer Engineering, Faculty of Electronics,
Wrocław University of Science and Technology, Wrocław, Poland
ewa.rafajlowicz@pwr.edu.pl

Abstract. In this paper we present a fast and easy method of quality monitoring for processes observed by cameras. A process of combustion in an industrial gas burner is used as an example. It is shown that we can observe only a small randomly chosen part of subsequent camera images. We propose a few, working in parallel manner, quality control charts. These Shewart type charts operate on squared norms of sparse partial image projections. Each chart is used for monitoring only a part of the whole camera image. The charts provide a partial decision about the state of the monitored system. A final decision is the logical product of these partial decisions. A simulation study based on 144 images of a working gas burner is presented.

Keywords: Image processing · Process monitoring · Random projections · Parallel processing

1 Introduction

Camera-based process monitoring is a recently very popular method of supervising a production process. Quality control of products [11,12], controlling processes [14,15], object fault detection [5,6,16,18] or anomaly detection [7] are good examples.

In this paper we propose a methodology of quality monitoring for processes observed by cameras. We illustrate its applicability by monitoring a process of combustion in an industrial gas burner. Subsequent camera images of the process under consideration are used for the process analysis.

A gas burner is a device which is used to generate a flame, in order to heat up products using a gaseous fuel such as acetylene, natural gas, or propane. In the case under consideration it is a natural gas (which is mainly methane) burner. The burner has an air inlet to mix the fuel gas with air, to enable complete combustion. Burner flames depend on air flow and we can register four states of burning process:

© IFIP International Federation for Information Processing 2017
Published by Springer International Publishing AG 2017. All Rights Reserved
K. Saeed et al. (Eds.): CISIM 2017, LNCS 10244, pp. 447–456, 2017.
DOI: 10.1007/978-3-319-59105-6_38

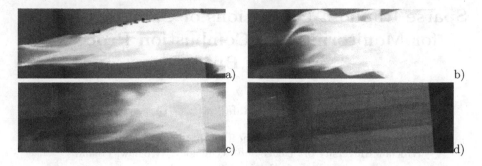

Fig. 1. Different states of a gas burner. (a) Laminar and lighting flame when the air hole is closed. (b) (c) Orange-yellow turbulent flame and yellow-blue flame when the air hole is slightly open or is not sufficiently open. (d) Roaring blue flame (normal state) when the air hole is sufficiently open (Color figure online).

1. when the air hole is closed (yellow-white, laminar and lighting flame, see Fig. 1a)
2. the air hole is slightly open (orange-yellow, more turbulent flame, see Fig. 1b)
3. the air hole is not sufficiently open (yellow-blue flame, see Fig. 1c)
4. the air hole fully open (roaring blue flame see Fig. 1d).

We assume that a blue flame (hardly visible on the camera image) means that the process is an in-control state.

In contrast to the other approaches (see for example [14]) the presented method is based on computing only the energy of a set of sub-images. Energy of an image is defined as a sum of image pixel values squared. In other words, the energy of an image is the squared Frobenius norm of this image treated as a matrix, or is the squared Euclidean norm of the image if it is represented as a vector.

Thus each image frame can be considered as a set of highly multidimensional observations. In the case of an appropriate partition of every frame, the same for every image, the proposed approach can be sufficiently informative in monitoring the state of the process under consideration.

A partition of each camera image is always the same and in fact it is fully content-dependent. In this paper we assume that the image partition is given (is performed by an expert). When a large set of image data is available, designing an adequate partition can be also stated as a learning problem.

Due to the very high dimensionality of image data the dimensionality reduction is rather necessary. Random projections seems to be a good choice in the case of image energy monitoring. Random projections based approaches have been widely used in computer science and machine learning applications and in image processing [1–4,9,17–20].

If sub-images are sufficiently large it is possible to estimate their energy using only a part of image pixels. Sparse random projections [1,9] allows us to retrieve only $1/3$ of whole image pixels whilst retaining an adequate precision of computations.

In this paper we propose to use simple monitoring charts of the Shewart type [13] based on squared norms of sparse image projections in normal state (i.e., in-control).

In the next Section we provide some information about random projections. Section 3 presents the Shewart-type control chart used in our monitoring system. Section 4 describes a simulation study performed on 144 images of a working gas burner. Finally, in Sect. 5 some brief conclusions are presented.

2 Random Projections

Random projections are closely related to the Johnson-Lindenstrauss lemma [8], which states that any set of N points in an Euclidean space can be embedded in an Euclidean space of lower dimension ($\sim O(\log N)$) with relatively small distortion of the distances between any pair of points from the set of points. The Johnson-Lindenstrauss-lemma has been shown to be useful in many applications in computer science [1–4, 9, 20], among many others.

The main idea of a random linear projection is that we can estimate the distance between two points (two vectors), let say u and z, in a d-dimensional Euclidean space $D^2(u, z) = ||u - z||^2 = (u - z)^T (u - z)$, $u,\ z \in \mathcal{R}^d$ from the sample squared distances as follows:

$$\hat{D}^2(u, z) = \frac{1}{k} \sum_{j=1}^{k} (s_j(u - z))^2 = \frac{1}{k} ||Su - Sz||^2, \tag{1}$$

where s_j is the j-th row of S, i.e., individual projection.

Thus, for any chosen pair of vectors $u, v \in \mathcal{R}^d$ $E(\hat{D}^2) = D^2$, $var(\hat{D}^2) = \frac{2}{k} D^4$ and $\frac{k\hat{D}}{D^2} \sim \chi_k^2$. These facts lead to the conclusion that

$$\Pr\left\{ \frac{|\hat{D}^2 - D^2|}{D^2} \geq \varepsilon \right\} \leq 2 \exp\left(-\frac{k}{4}\varepsilon^2 + \frac{k}{6}\varepsilon^3 \right), \tag{2}$$

where $\varepsilon \in (0, 1)$ (see for example [4, 20] for details). The same inequalities one can obtain for norms of vectors defined by the set of points under consideration.

2.1 Sparse Random Projections

We do not have to use $s_{ij} \sim \mathcal{N}(0, 1)$ for dimension reduction in the space with Euclidean norm. For example, we can sample s_{ij} from any subgaussian tails distributions [2, 9]. Sparse random projections proposed by Achlioptas [1] belong to this class.

Thus, to speed up the computations, one can generate a sparse random projection matrix for data dimensionality reduction. It is proved that the entries of projection matrix S can be chosen as independent $+1$, 0, -1 random variables.

A projection matrix composed from independent entries of the form:

$$s_{ij} = \begin{cases} 1 & \text{with probability } \frac{1}{2c} \\ 0 & \text{with probability } 1 - \frac{1}{c} \\ -1 & \text{with probability } \frac{1}{2c} \end{cases} \tag{3}$$

with common factor $\sqrt{c}$ leads to the projection distribution with subgaussian tails (at least up to a suitable threshold) [9].

An Achlioptas variant of this result (with $c = 3$) has the entries attaining value 0 with probability $2/3$ and values $+1$ and -1 with probability $1/6$ each. This setting allows for computing the projection about 3 times faster than the Gaussian projection. Since S is sparse, only about one third of the entries are nonzero numbers.

This kind of sparse projection, i.e., with $c = 3$, we have used for processing a sequence of working gas burner images. Furthermore, the rows of the projection matrix were orthonomalized. This fact is not important from the point of our goals in this work, but it will be useful in a further more theoretical research on the topic of sparse random projections.

Let S_O denote such an orthonormalized matrix. It is easy to show that for any vector $x \in \mathcal{R}^d$

$$E\{\|S_O x\|^2\} = \frac{k}{d}\|x\|^2.$$

It should be emphasized that after random construction of the projection matrix, let us say S_O, it is treated as unique, non-random projection matrix. Thus, further in the paper S_O will be represented an ordinary matrix.

3   Control Charts for Monitoring a Process Using Random Projections of Camera Images

Let $p_1, p_2, \ldots, p_N$, denote a sequence of historical images (sub-images) in a normal (in-control) state. Each $p_i \in [0, 1]^d$ is a vector consisting of pixel intensity values and d is the number of pixels forming the image under consideration.

Let

$$x_i = \frac{1}{k}\|S_O p_i\|^2, \tag{4}$$

for $i = 1, 2, \ldots, N$.

Now $X_h = (x_1, x_2, \ldots, x_N)$ denote a sequence of historical observations in a normal (in-control) state. Each observation $x_i \in [0, 1]$ is a real (non-negative) value obtained according to (4).

Although we do not make any assumption about distribution of X_h, it is presumed that X_h is a sequence of independent observations taken from the same distribution. However, we suppose that X_i (i.e., observations treated as random variables) are approximately Gaussian. It is not clear how large (or may be small) should be projection dimension k. On the one hand, if k is large we can use the Central Limit Theorem as a an argument for a Gaussianity of X_i, but on the other hand it is postulated [10] that typical k-dimensional projections of probability measures on R^d are approximately Gaussian when k is sufficiently small. It is in our opinion an open problem.

3.1   A Shewart Type Chart for Monitoring Energy of Images

Let m_h denote the mean value of X_h and s_h its standard deviation. The upper control limit (UCL) is computed as

$$UCL = m_h + 3\,s_h$$

and the lower control limit (LCL) is given by

$$LCL = m_h - 3\,s_h.$$

Let p be any observed image. The Shewart control chart for individual observations [13] allows us to decide that if

$$x = \frac{1}{k}||S_O p||^2 > UCL$$

or

$$x = \frac{1}{k}||S_O p||^2 < LCL,$$

then the system state connected with x (i.e., with image p) is not normal (is out-of-control). This simple test will be further used for monitoring separate parts of the whole burning process image. Thus, the final decision will be in conjunction with partial tests (the logical conjunction will be used). More technical details will be provided in the next section.

4   Simulation Study

A data set used for experiments consists of 144 images similar to that shown in Fig. 1. Each image has 120×352 pixels, i.e., its vector dimension is 42240. Each image is assigned by an expert to one of the four classes (see Fig. 1). The overall quality of images is rather poor. We decided to not rely on color representation of the images since color-based segmentation of these images is too time-consuming. It occurred that pixel intensity in the gray scale is sufficient for the images analysis. As an alternative one can use red color channel (R) as very similar in the intensity values to the gray level image representation in this particular case. Each image in the sequence is divided into four sub-images consisting of $0 - -120 \times 0 - 88$ (sub-image type A), $0 - 120 \times 89 - 176$ (sub-image type B), $0 - 120 \times 177 - 264$ (sub-image type C) and $0 - 120 \times 265 - 352$ (sub-image type D) pixels of the original image.

The first ten images from the data set, which present normal gas burner state (see Fig. 1d), was used as historical data. The first image in this set indicates the state in-between normal state and some lack of air state. It was included into the normal state learning sequence, because we want to obtain a decision system robust to a very small shortage of air. On the basis of this subset the levels of alarm for the 4-dimensional chart were computed. Furthermore, the last ten images, which present "no-air" state (see Fig. 1a), was also used for providing the additional alarm levels for this state. Thus, the remainder of images (from 11 till 134) were used as a testing sequence.

Figure 2 shows mean energy of sub-images (A, B, C, D) for all images in the data set. Corresponding mean energy of the images estimated using 10 and 100 random projections are drawn in Figs. 3, 4 and 5, respectively. One can observe, that estimated mean energy of the images (blue lines) is very close to its true values (yellow lines) even if dimensionality of the projection k is low.

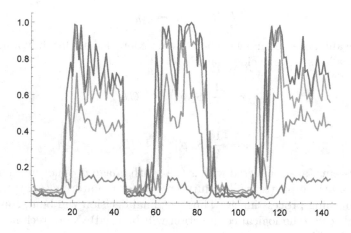

Fig. 2. Mean energy of images A (blue line), B (yellow line), C (green line) and D (red line) (Color figure online).

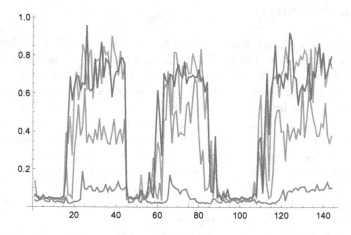

Fig. 3. Mean energy of images A (blue line), B (yellow line), C (green line) and D (red line) estimated using $k = 10$ sparse random projections (Color figure online).

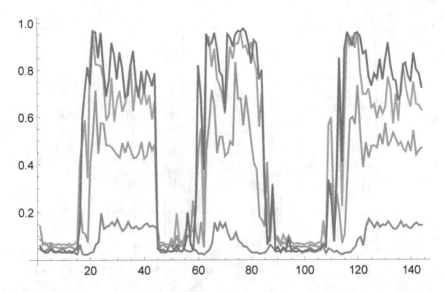

Fig. 4. Mean energy of images A (blue line), B (yellow line), C (green line) and D (red line) estimated using $k = 100$ sparse random projections (Color figure online).

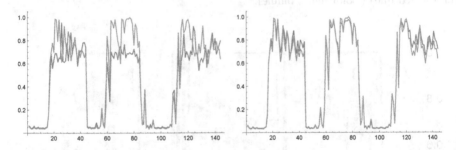

Fig. 5. Mean energy of images D – true values (yellow lines) and estimated using $k = 10$ (left panel) and $k = 100$ (right panel) sparse random projections (Color figure online).

The number of case images was rather restricted, but despite this we have obtained satisfactory results. We expect that larger image data sets allow us to design decision systems which could be used in practice.

Figure 6 illustrates decisions about alarm for the whole image sequence (144 items). The red line on zero level indicates the in-control state (the air inlet is sufficiently open). The red line on 1 level shows the out-of-control state (the air hole is too small). The alarming system works almost perfectly. It does not accept as normal positions 45, 50 and 53 very similar (but slightly lighter) to the mentioned earlier position 1 in the learning sequence. Removing testing based on sub-images type A results in no alarms at positions 45, 50 and 53 (see Fig. 7).

In a similar way as previously we can design a decision system which produces an additional alarm signal for the no-air state (see Fig. 1a). The system based

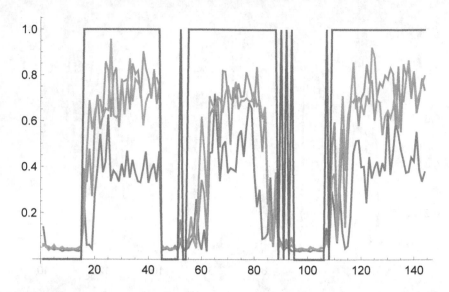

Fig. 6. Mean energy of images A, B,C, D – (violet, blue, yellow and green lines respectively) and estimated using $k = 10$ sparse random projections and a global alarm decision (red line) (Color figure online).

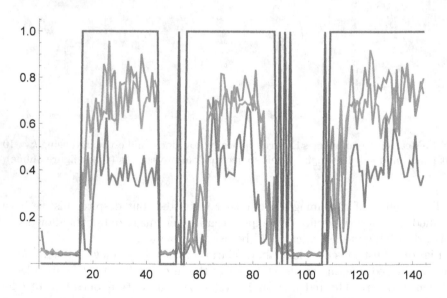

Fig. 7. Mean energy of images B,C, D – (blue, yellow and green lines respectively) and estimated using $k = 10$ sparse random projections and a global alarm level (red line) (Color figure online).

on A, B, C and partial images and the last ten images labeled by an expert as connected with no-air state (closed air hole) indicates correctly all such cases. Additionally 6 images characterized by slightly turbulent flow (positions 24, 66, 74, 75 and 120, 121 also produce this kind of alarm. In fact this occurred when the air inlet was almost closed.

5   Comments and Conclusion

The method proposed here can be applied to other processes observed using a camera when relatively large image changes are important. The proposed control chart may also be used without dimensionality reduction by random projections. Our motivation behind applying a sparse random projection are twofold. First, we want to obtain simultaneously a really simple and fast algorithm. Second, it is suggested [10] that typical k-dimensional projections of probability measures on R^d are approximately Gaussian when k is sufficiently small. The problem of obtaining an adequate statistical model of the monitored sequence of images is outside the scope of this paper.

Acknowledgments. This research has been supported by the National Science Center under grant: 2012/07/B/ST7/01216.

References

1. Achlioptas, D.: Database-friendly random projections: Johnson-Lindenstrauss with binary coins. J. Comput. Syst. Sci. **66**, 671–687 (2003)
2. Ailon, N., Chazelle, B.: The fast Johnson-Lindenstrauss transform and approximate nearest neighbors. SIAM J. Comput. **39**(1), 302–322 (2009)
3. Arriaga, R.I., Vempala, S.: An algorithmic theory of learning: robust concepts and random projection. In: Proceedings of the 40th Annual Symposium Foundations of Computer Science, pp. 616–623 (1999)
4. Dasgupta, S., Gupta, A.: An elementary proof of the Johnson-Lindenstrauss lemma. Random Struct. Algorithms **22**(1), 60–65 (2002)
5. Davies, E.R.: A comparison of methods for the rapid location of products and their features and defects. In: McKeown, P.A. (ed.) Proceedings of the 7th International Conference on Automated Inspection and Product Control, Birmingham, AL, 26–28 March, pp. 111–120 (1985)
6. Davies, E.R.: Machine Vision: Theory, Algorithms, Practicalities. Morgan Kaufmann Publishers Inc., San Francisco (2005)
7. Fowler, J.E., Du, Q.: Anomaly detection and reconstruction from random projections. IEEE Trans. Image Process. **21**(1), 184–195 (2012)
8. Johnson, W.B., Lindenstrauss, J.: Extensions of Lipshitz mapping into Hilbert space. Contemp. Math. **26**, 189–206 (1984)
9. Matoušek, J.: On variants of the Johnson-Lindenstrauss lemma. Random Struct. Algorithms **33**(2), 142–156 (2008)
10. Meckes, E.: Approximation of projections of random vectors. J. Theor. Probab. **25**(2), 333–352 (2012)

11. Megahed, F.M., Woodall, W.H., Camelio, J.A.: A review and perspective on control charting with image data. J. Qual. Technol. **43**(2), 84–98 (2011)
12. Megahed, F.M., Wells, L.J., Camelio, J.A., Woodall, W.H.: A spatiotemporal method for the monitoring of image data. Qual. Reliab. Eng. Int. **28**, 967–980 (2012)
13. Montgomery, D.C.: Introduction to Statistical Quality Control, 3rd edn. Wiley, New York (1996)
14. Rafajłowicz, E., Pawlak-Kruczek, H., Rafajłowicz, W.: Statistical classifier with ordered decisions as an image based controller with application to gas burners. In: Rutkowski, L., Korytkowski, M., Scherer, R., Tadeusiewicz, R., Zadeh, L.A., Zurada, J.M. (eds.) ICAISC 2014. LNCS (LNAI), vol. 8467, pp. 586–597. Springer, Cham (2014). doi:10.1007/978-3-319-07173-2_50
15. Scheitler, C., et al.: Experimental investigation of direct diamond laser cladding in combination with high speed camera based process monitoring. J. Laser Appl. **28**, 022304 (2016)
16. Skubalska-Rafajłowicz, E.: Local correlation and entropy maps as tools for detecting defects in industrial images. Int. J. Appl. Math. Comput. Sci. **18**(1), 41–47 (2008)
17. Skubalska-Rafajłowicz, E.: Detection and estimation translations of large images using random projections. In: 7th International Workshop on Multidimensional (nD) Systems (nDs), Poitiers, 5–7 September (2011). doi:10.1109/nDS.2011.6076838
18. Skubalska-Rafajłowicz, E.: Random projections and Hotelling's T^2 statistics for change detection in high-dimensional data stream. Int. J. Appl. Math. Comput. Sci. **23**(2), 447–461 (2013)
19. Tsagkatakis, G., Savakis, A.: A random projections model for object tracking under variable pose and multi-camera views. In: Proceedings of the Third ACM/IEEE International Conference on Distributed Smart Cameras, ICDSC 2009, pp. 1–7 (2009). doi:10.1109/ICDSC.2009.5289384
20. Vempala, S.: The Random Projection Method. American Mathematical Society, Providence (2004)

Modelling and Optimization

Rough Sets in Imbalanced Data Problem: Improving Re–sampling Process

Katarzyna Borowska[✉] and Jarosław Stepaniuk

Faculty of Computer Science, Bialystok University of Technology,
Wiejska 45A, 15-351 Bialystok, Poland
{k.borowska,j.stepaniuk}@pb.edu.pl
http://www.wi.pb.edu.pl

Abstract. Imbalanced data problem is still one of the most interesting and important research subjects. The latest experiments and detailed analysis revealed that not only the underrepresented classes are the main cause of performance loss in machine learning process, but also the inherent complex characteristics of data. The list of discovered significant difficulty factors consists of the phenomena like class overlapping, decomposition of the minority class, presence of noise and outliers. Although there are numerous solutions proposed, it is still unclear how to deal with all of these issues together and correctly evaluate the class distribution to select a proper treatment (especially considering the real–world applications where levels of uncertainty are eminently high). Since applying rough sets theory to the imbalanced data learning problem could be a promising research direction, the improved re–sampling approach combining selective preprocessing and editing techniques is introduced in this paper. The novel technique allows both qualitative and quantitative data handling.

Keywords: Data preprocessing · Class imbalance · Rough sets · SMOTE · Oversampling · Undersampling

1 Introduction

With the growing interest of knowledge researchers and increasing number of proposed solutions, the imbalanced data problem becomes one of the most significant and challenging issues of the last years. The main reason of this particular attention given to the underrepresented data is the fundamental importance of untypical instances. Considering medical diagnosis, it is obvious that the cost of not recognizing patient that suffers from a rare disease might lead to serious and irreversible consequences. Apart from this example, there are numerous domains in which imbalanced class distribution occurs, such as [14, 21, 25]: fraudulent credit card transactions, detecting oil spills from satellite images, network intrusion detection, financial risk analysis, text categorization and information filtering. Indeed, the wide range of problem occurrences increases its significance and explains the efforts put into finding effective solution.

© IFIP International Federation for Information Processing 2017
Published by Springer International Publishing AG 2017. All Rights Reserved
K. Saeed et al. (Eds.): CISIM 2017, LNCS 10244, pp. 459–469, 2017.
DOI: 10.1007/978-3-319-59105-6_39

Initially, the major cause of the classifier performance depletion was merely identified with not sufficient number of examples representing minority data. However, recent comprehensive studies carried on the nature of imbalanced data revealed that there are other factors contributing to this undesirable effects [7,14,21]. Small disjuncts [13], class overlapping [15] and presence of noise as well as outliers [25] were especially considered as the most meaningful difficulties. Despite lots of suggested solutions (discussed briefly in the next section), there are still many open issues, particularly regarding the flexibility of proposed methods and tuning their parameters. We decided to focus on the data–level approach as it is classifier–independent and therefore more universal. However, it is worth to mention that besides this kind of concept, there are also numerous algorithm–level and cost–sensitive methods [11].

Although many re–sampling methods were proposed to deal with imbalanced data problem, only few incorporate the rough set theory. The standard rough sets approach was developed by Pawlak (1926–2006) in 1982 [16]. Objects characterized by the same information (identical values of the provided attributes) are treated as indiscernible instances [17,18,23]. Hence, the idea of indiscernibility relation is introduced. Since the real–life problems are often vague and contains inconsistent information, the rough (not precise) set concept can be replaced by a pair of precise concepts, namely the lower and upper approximations. We claim that this methodology could be very useful both in preprocessing step and cleaning phase of the algorithm (see [3]). Especially the extended version, which allows the continuous values of attributes by involving the similarity relation. Therefore, we propose the adjusted VIS_RST algorithm, dedicated for both qualitative and quantitative data. What is more, new mechanisms for careful oversampling are introduced.

2   Related Works

In this paper we focus only on the data–level methods addressing imbalanced data problem, as it was declared in the previous section. This category consists of classifier–independent solutions which transform the original data set into less complex and more balanced distribution using techniques such as oversampling and undersampling [11,21]. The major algorithm representing this mentioned group is Synthetic Minority Oversampling Technique [6]. Since the approach of generating new minority samples based on the similarities between existing minority examples became very successful and powerful method, it was an excellent inspiration for researchers to develop numerous extensions and improvements. Some of them properly reduce the consequences of SMOTE drawbacks, such as over–generalization and variance [11]. Preparing the overview of related techniques, two main subjects were considered. Firstly, methods which handle additional difficulty factors are discussed. Secondly, we show the applications of rough set notions in imbalance data problem.

2.1 SMOTE–Based Methods Dealing with Complex Imbalanced Data Distribution

Highly imbalanced datasets, especially characterized by the complex distribution, require dedicated methods. Even such groundbreaking algorithm as SMOTE turns out as insufficiently effective in some specific domains. Indeed, the most recent researches revealed that technique of dividing minority data into some categories that reflect their local characteristics is a proper direction of development. The main reason of this conclusion is the nature of real–world data. Assuming that minority class instances placed in relatively homogeneous regions of feature space are named safe, we should consider the fact that these safe examples are uncommon in real–life data sets [21]. In order to deal with complex imbalanced data distributions, many sophisticated methods were proposed:

- MSMOTE (Modified Synthetic Minority Oversampling Technique) [12] - the strategy of generating new samples is adapted to the local neighbourhood of the instance. Safe objects are processed similarly as in standard SMOTE technique. For border instances only the nearest neighbour is chosen. Latent noise representatives are not taken into consideration in undersampling.
- Borderline-SMOTE [9] - method that strengthens the area of class overlapping. Only borderline examples are used in processing.
- SMOTE-ENN [2] - technique combining oversampling and additional cleaning step. Standard SMOTE algorithm is enriched by the Edited Nearest Neighbour Rule (ENN) approach, which removes examples from both classes as long as they are misclassified by their three nearest neighbours.
- Selective Preprocessing of Imbalanced Data (SPIDER) [15] - method that identifies noisy minority data using the k–NN technique and continues processing in a way depending on the selected option: weak, relabel or strong. Chosen condition determines if only minority class examples are amplified or also majority objects are relabeled. After oversampling, noisy representatives of majority class are removed.
- Safe–Level SMOTE [5] - the algorithm applies k–NN technique to obtain the safe levels of minority class samples. New synthetic instances are created only in safe regions in order to improve prediction performance of classifiers.

2.2 Rough Sets Solutions for Imbalanced Data Problem

The occurrence of noisy and borderline examples in real–domain data sets is the fact that need to be acknowledged in most cases. Hence, the relevancy of methods dealing with these additional difficulties should be emphasized. The rough set notions appears as a promising approach to reduce data distribution complexity and understand hidden patterns in data. Before describing existing algorithms based on the rough sets approach, basic concepts of this theory are introduced.

Let U denote a finite non-empty set of objects, to be called the universe. The fundamental assumption of the rough set approach is that objects from a set U described by the same information are indiscernible. This main concept is source of the notion referred as indiscernibility relation $IND \subseteq U \times U$, defined on the set U. The indiscernibility relation IND is an equivalence relation on U. As such, it induces a partition of U into indiscernibility classes. Let $[x]_{IND} = \{y \in U : (x, y) \in IND\}$ be an indiscernibility class, where $x \in U$. For any subset X of the set U it is possible to prepare the following characteristics [18]:

- the lower approximation of a set X is the set of all objects that can be certainly classified as members of X with respect to IND:

$$\{x \in U : [x]_{IND} \subseteq X\}, \tag{1}$$

- the boundary region of a set X is the set of all objects that are possibly members of X with respect to IND:

$$\{x \in U : [x]_{IND} \cap X \neq \varnothing \ \&[x]_{IND} \nsubseteq X\}. \tag{2}$$

The most known preprocessing methods directly utilizing the rough set theory are the following:

- filtering techniques (relabel and remove) [22] - depending on the method: majority class examples belonging to the boundary region (defined by the rough sets) are either relabeled or removed,
- SMOTE–RSB$_*$ [19] - method combining SMOTE algorithm with rough set theory by introducing additional cleaning phase of processing.

3   Proposed Algorithm VISROT - Versatile Improved SMOTE Based on Rough Set Theory

Comprehensive studies on imbalanced data problem and analysis of foregoing solutions revealed that there are many open issues and the need of more general approach dealing with wide range of different data characteristics is still actual [21]. Since most of the real–world data sets have complex distribution, researchers should pay particular attention to careful assortment of oversampling strategy [14]. In [20] two main types of SMOTE–based preprocessing algorithms are specified:

- *change–direction* methods - new instances are created only in specific areas of the input space (especially close to relatively large positive examples clusters)
- *filtering–based* techniques - SMOTE algorithm integrated with additional cleaning and filtering methods that aim to create more regular class boundaries.

The authors of this categorization claim that the first group may suffer from noisy and borderline instances. The necessity of additional cleaning phase was indicated. Since our VIS_RST [3] algorithm meets this requirement, but it is not directly suitable for quantitative data, we decided to improve the existing approach and enable processing of any attributes' types.

The code generalization for both qualitative and quantitative data involved many adjustments and handling specific cases. The main modification concerns usage of weaker similarity concept instead of the strict indiscernibility relation [10]. We applied the HVDM distance metrics [26] as a generator of similarity measure.

The algorithm flexibility is obtained by two approaches dedicated to different types of problems. Analysis of local neighbourhood of each example enables to evaluate the complexity of data distribution. Based on the studies from [15] we assume that the occurrence of 30% of borderline and noisy instances indicates that the problem is difficult. Identification of these specific examples is performed by applying the k–NN algorithm. Continuing the categorization introduced in VIS algorithm [4], we distinguish between three types of objects, namely SAFE, DANGER and NOISE. SAFE examples are relatively easy to recognize, they are main representatives of minority class. DANGER instances are placed in the area surrounding class boundaries, they typically overlap with majority class examples. NOISE instances are rare, probably incorrect, individuals located in areas occupied by the majority class objects. The mechanism of categorization into mentioned groups is described below.

Let $DT = (U, A \cup \{d\})$ be a decision table, where U is a non-empty set of objects, A is a set of condition attributes and d is a decision attribute and $V_d = \{+, -\}$. The following rules enable labeling minority data $X_{d=+} = \{x \in U : d(x) = +\}$:

Definition 1. *Let $k > 0$ be a given natural number. Let $x \in X_{d=+}$ be an object from minority class. We define $Label : X_{d=+} \rightarrow \{NOISE, DANGER, SAFE\}$ as follows:*

- *$Label(x) = NOISE$ if and only if all of the k nearest neighbors of x represent the majority class $X_{d=-} = \{x \in U : d(x) = -\}$,*
- *$Label(x) = DANGER$ if and only if half or more than half of the k nearest neighbors of x belong to the majority class $X_{d=-}$ or the nearest neighbour of x is majority class representative,*
- *$Label(x) = SAFE$ if and only if more than half of the k nearest neighbors represent the same class as the example under consideration and the nearest neighbour of x is minority class representative.*

The explained approach involves three modes of processing of DT. None of them creates new samples using NOISE examples. The first one is defined below:

Definition 2. *HighComplexity mode: $DT \longmapsto DT_{balanced}$*

- *DANGER: the number of objects is doubled by creating one new example along the line segment between half of the distance from DANGER object and one of its k nearest neighbors. For nominal attributes values describing the object under consideration are replicated,*

- *SAFE: assuming that these concentrated instances provide specific and easy to learn patterns that enable proper recognition of minority samples, a plenty of new data is created by interpolation between SAFE object and one of its k nearest neighbors. Nominal attributes are determined by majority vote of k nearest neighbors' features.*

The second option is applied when most of examples belong to the relatively homogeneous areas:

Definition 3. *LowComplexity mode: $DT \longmapsto DT_{balanced}$*

- *DANGER: the most of synthetic samples are generated in these borderline areas, since numerous majority class representatives may have greater impact on the classifier learning, when there are not enough minority examples. Hence, many new examples are created closer to the object under consideration. One of the k nearest neighbor is chosen for each new sample when determining the value of numeric feature. Values of nominal attributes are obtained by the majority vote of k nearest neighbors' features,*
- *SAFE: there is no need to increase significantly the number of instances in these safe areas. Only one new object per existing minority SAFE instance is generated. Numeric attributes are handled by the interpolation with one of the k nearest neighbors. For the nominal features, new sample has the same values of attributes as the object under consideration.*

The third option is specified as follows:

Definition 4. *noSAFE mode: $DT \longmapsto DT_{balanced}$*

- *DANGER: all of the synthetic objects are created in the area surrounding class boundaries. This particular solution is selected in case especially complex data distribution, which do not include any SAFE samples. Missing SAFE elements indicates that most of the examples are labeled as DANGER (there are no homogeneous regions). Since only DANGER and NOISE examples are available, only generating new instances in neighborhood of DANGER objects would provide sufficient number of minority samples.*

Omitting NOISE examples in oversampling phase is explained by the idea of keeping data distribution complexity as low as possible. Generating new synthetic samples by utilisation of objects surrounded only by the majority class representatives may introduce more inconsistencies. However, there is no guarantee that objects labeled as NOISE are truly effects of errors or they are only outliers which are untypical since no other similar objects are provided in the imbalanced data set [21]. Hence, we do not remove any of these instances, but we also do not create new examples similar to them.

Even when examples considered as noise are excluded from the oversampling process, generating new samples by combining features of two chosen instances still may contribute to creation of noisy examples. Thus some filtering and cleaning mechanisms are advisable [20]. In order to resolve problem of introducing additional inconsistencies we propose the technique of supervise preprocessing. The main idea of this approach is based on the lower approximation. After obtaining the threshold, algorithm identifies newly created objects that do not belong to the lower approximation of the minority class. The correctness of each element is obtained iteratively (by means of similarity relation rather than the strict indiscernibility relation). The expected proper number of new samples is assured by the increased limit of generated objects. The proposed solution consists of steps described in provided algorithm.

Algorithm. VISROT

INPUT: All instances from both classes defined as $DT = (U, A \cup \{d\})$;
  Number of minority class samples $M = card(\{x \in U : d(x) = +\}) > 0$;
  Number of nearest neighbors $k \geq 3$.
OUTPUT: $DT_{balanced}$: minority and majority class instances after preprocessing.

 1: **Step I:** Compare feature values of minority and majority instances. Remove all negative objects ($d = -$) identical to the positive ($d = +$) ones regarding all attributes.
 2: **Step II:** Calculate the HVDM ($Heterogeneous Value Distance Metric$) distance between each minority class example and every instance from majority class. Use $k - NN$ algorithm. Assign positive objects into categories (namely SAFE, DANGER and NOISE) considering rules specified in definition 1. Save numbers of instances belonging to each group (variables: $safeN$, $dangerN$, $noiseN$).
 3: **Step III:** Select the strategy of processing utilizing the accomplished categorization as follows:
 4: **if** $safeN == 0$ **then**
 5:   $mode := noSAFE$
 6: **else if** $dangerN \geqslant 0.3 \cdot M$ **then**
 7:   $mode := HighComplexity$
 8: **else**
 9:   $mode := LowComplexity$
10: **end if**
11: **Step IV:** Obtain the threshold (t) that enable to evaluate which minority instances belong to the lower approximation. The threshold is established by the analysis of the average objects distance. It is set to 0.25 of calculated average distance.
12: **Step V:** Compute the number of required minority class instances to even classes' cardinalities (N variable). The expected result should be increased by the 30%. Save the obtained number in $redundN$ variable.
13: **Step VI:** Over–sampling. Generate $redundN$ minority instances considering rules specified in Definitions 2, 3 and 4. Save the result in $syntheticSamples$ list. Randomize the order of new elements stored in list.
14: **Step VII:** From newly created minority examples ($syntheticSamples$) select N elements belonging to the lower approximation of minority class and add them to the $DT_{balanced}$. Assume that all objects that are insufficiently far apart from the majority class instances (their distance from any negative object is less than calculated threshold t) should not be included in the $DT_{balanced}$, since they belong to the rough set boundary region.

Generating redundant instances in Step VI protects from filtering out too many positive synthetic samples in cleaning phase. The method of determining additional objects number should be evaluated in the further research - the impact on the computing performance need to be especially investigated. We suggest that this number should be related to the complexity of the considered specific problem.

4   Experiments

The results of experimental study are presented in this section. We decided to compare our algorithm with five oversampling methods considered as successful in many domains. All of these techniques are described in Sect. 2. Widely used C4.5 decision tree was chosen as a classifier, since it is one of the most effective data–mining methods [7]. Very important parameter of k–NN processing, namely k, was set to 5 as it was proven that this is the most suitable value for wide range of problems [8]. The HVDM metric was applied to measure the distances between objects, because it properly handles both quantitative and qualitative data [26].

Six data sets were selected to perform described experiments. They are highly–imbalanced real–life data sets obtained from the UCI repository [24]. All of them were firstly divided into training and test partitions to ensure that the results of fivefolds cross-validation would be correct. We used partitioned data available in the KEEL website [1]. The analyzed data sets are presented in Table 1.

Table 1. Characteristics of evaluated data sets

Dataset	Objects	Attributes	IR	Boundary region
glass-0-1-6_vs_5	184	9	19.44	empty
ecoli-0-1-3-7_vs_2-6	281	7	39.14	nonempty
glass5	214	9	22.78	empty
ecoli-0-1_vs_5	240	6	11	nonempty
led7digit-0-2-4-5-6-7-8-9_vs_1	443	7	10.97	nonempty
ecoli-0-1-4-6_vs_5	280	6	13	nonempty

The existence of boundary region defined by the rough set notions is emphasized to verify the impact of data inconsistencies on the classifier performance preceded by the particular preprocessing techniques.

Table 2 presents the results of experiments. The area under the ROC curve (AUC) was used to evaluate classifier performance. This measure discloses the dependency between sensitivity (percentage of positive instances correctly classified) and percentage of negative examples misclassified.

VISROT algorithm introduced in this paper was evaluated in comparison with five other preprocessing techniques which performance was measured in [19].

Table 2. Classification results for the selected UCI datasets - comparison of proposed algorithm VISROT with five other techniques and classification without preprocessing step (noPRE).

Dataset	noPRE	SMOTE	S–ENN	Border–S	SafeL–S	S–RSB$_*$	VISROT
glass016_vs_5	0.8943	0.8129	0.8743	0.8386	0.8429	0.8800	0.8943
ecoli0137_vs_2-6	0.7481	0.8136	0.8209	0.8445	0.8118	0.8445	0.8445
glass5	0.8976	0.8829	0.7756	0.8854	0.8939	0.9232	0.9951
ecoli01_vs_5	0.8159	0.7977	0.8250	0.8318	0.8568	0.7818	0.8636
led7digit02456789_vs_1	0.8788	0.8908	0.8379	0.8908	0.9023	0.9019	0.8918
ecoli0146_vs_5	0.7885	0.8981	0.8981	0.7558	0.8519	0.8231	0.8366

The results revealed that proposed method outperforms other algorithms in two cases (glass5, ecoli01_vs_5), one of whom has non–empty boundary region. For two data sets VISTROT has similar result as the most effective techniques. In the remaining two cases applying VISROT approach was slightly less beneficial than SMOTE and SMOTE–ENN or Safe–Level SMOTE and SMOTE–RSB$_*$. The experiments proved that the proposed algorithm is suitable to deal with real–life complex data distributions, even highly–imbalanced.

5   Conclusions and Future Research

In this paper we introduced new preprocessing method dedicated to both quantitative and qualitative attributes in imbalanced data problems. The described approach considers significant difficulties that lead to the misclassification of many minority class samples. Since not enough number of examples representing positive class is not the main reason of performance depletion, other factors were also considered. Especially occurrence of sub–regions, noise and class overlapping were examined as they indicates the high data complexity. Performed experiments confirms that oversampling preceded by the analysis of local neighborhood of positive instances is proper approach. Moreover, the need of additional cleaning step that removes the inconsistencies is emphasized. The VISROT results showed that rough set notions can be successfully applied to the imbalanced data problems.

We suggest that proposed algorithm should be adjusted to handle Big Data problems in future research. The values of minimal allowed distance defining weaken low approximation rule (threshold) can also be investigated.

Acknowledgments. This research was supported by the grant S/WI/3/2013 of the Polish Ministry of Science and Higher Education.

References

1. Alcala-Fdez, J., Fernandez, A., Luengo, J., Derrac, J., Garca, S., Sanchez, L., Herrera, F.: KEEL data-mining software tool: data set repository, integration of algorithms and experimental analysis framework. J. Multiple-Valued Logic Soft Comput. **17**(2–3), 255–287 (2011)
2. Batista, G.E.A.P.A., Prati, R.C., Monard, M.C.: A study of the behavior of several methods for balancing machine learning training data. SIGKDD Explor. Newsl. **6**(1), 20–29 (2004)
3. Borowska, K., Stepaniuk, J.: Imbalanced data classification: a novel re-sampling approach combining versatile improved SMOTE and rough sets. In: Saeed, K., Homenda, W. (eds.) CISIM 2016. LNCS, vol. 9842, pp. 31–42. Springer, Cham (2016). doi:10.1007/978-3-319-45378-1_4
4. Borowska, K., Topczewska, M.: New data level approach for imbalanced data classification improvement. In: Burduk, R., Jackowski, K., Kurzyński, M., Woźniak, M., Żołnierek, A. (eds.) Proceedings of the 9th International Conference on Computer Recognition Systems CORES 2015. AISC, vol. 403, pp. 283–294. Springer, Cham (2016). doi:10.1007/978-3-319-26227-7_27
5. Bunkhumpornpat, C., Sinapiromsaran, K., Lursinsap, C.: Safe-level-SMOTE: safe-level-synthetic minority over-sampling technique for handling the class imbalanced problem. In: Theeramunkong, T., Kijsirikul, B., Cercone, N., Ho, T.-B. (eds.) PAKDD 2009. LNCS, vol. 5476, pp. 475–482. Springer, Heidelberg (2009). doi:10.1007/978-3-642-01307-2_43
6. Chawla, N.V., Bowyer, K.W., Hall, L.O., Kegelmeyer, W.P.: SMOTE: synthetic minority over-sampling technique. J. Artif. Int. Res. **16**(1), 321–357 (2002)
7. Galar M., Fernandez A., Barrenechea E., Bustince H., Herrera F.: A review on ensembles for the class imbalance problem: bagging-, boosting-, and hybrid-based approaches. IEEE Trans. Syst. Man Cybern Part C Appl. Rev. **42**(4), 463–484 (2012)
8. Garca, V., Mollineda, R.A., Snchez, J.S.: On the k-NN performance in a challenging scenario of imbalance and overlapping. Pattern Anal. Appl. **11**(3–4), 269–280 (2008)
9. Han, H., Wang, W.-Y., Mao, B.-H.: Borderline-SMOTE: a new over-sampling method in imbalanced data sets learning. In: Huang, D.-S., Zhang, X.-P., Huang, G.-B. (eds.) ICIC 2005. LNCS, vol. 3644, pp. 878–887. Springer, Heidelberg (2005). doi:10.1007/11538059_91
10. Krawiec, K., Słowiński, R., Vanderpooten, D.: Learning decision rules from similarity based rough approximations. In: Polkowski, L., Skowron, A. (eds.) Rough Sets in Knowledge Discovery 2. STUDFUZZ, vol. 19, pp. 37–54. Springer, Heidelberg (1998). doi:10.1007/978-3-7908-1883-3_3
11. He, H., Garcia, E.A.: Learning from Imbalanced Data. IEEE Trans. Knowl. Data Eng. **21**(9), 1263–1284 (2009)
12. Hu, S., Liang, Y., Ma, L., He, Y.: MSMOTE: improving classification performance when training data is imbalanced, computer science and engineering. In: Second International Workshop on WCSE 2009, Qingdao, pp. 13–17 (2009)
13. Jo, T., Japkowicz, N.: Class imbalances versus small disjuncts. SIGKDD Explor. Newsl. **6**(1), 40–49 (2004)
14. Napierała, K., Stefanowski, J.: Types of minority class examples and their influence on learning classifiers from imbalanced data. J. Intell. Inf. Syst. **46**, 563–597 (2016)

15. Napierała, K., Stefanowski, J., Wilk, S.: Learning from imbalanced data in presence of noisy and borderline examples. In: Szczuka, M., Kryszkiewicz, M., Ramanna, S., Jensen, R., Hu, Q. (eds.) RSCTC 2010. LNCS, vol. 6086, pp. 158–167. Springer, Heidelberg (2010). doi:10.1007/978-3-642-13529-3_18
16. Pawlak, Z.: Rough sets. Int. J. Comput. Inform. Sci. **11**(5), 341–356 (1982)
17. Pawlak, Z., Skowron, A.: Rough sets: some extensions. Inf. Sci. **177**(1), 28–40 (2007)
18. Pawlak, Z., Skowron, A.: Rudiments of rough sets. Inf. Sci. **177**(1), 3–27 (2007)
19. Ramentol, E., Caballero, Y., Bello, R., Herrera, F.: SMOTE-RSB*: a hybrid pre-processing approach based on oversampling and undersampling for high imbalanced data-sets using SMOTE and rough sets theory. Knowl. Inf. Syst. **33**(2), 245–265 (2011)
20. Saez, J.A., Luengo, J., Stefanowski, J., Herrera, F.: SMOTEIPF: addressing the noisy and borderline examples problem in imbalanced classification by a re-sampling method with filtering. Inf. Sci. **291**, 184–203 (2015)
21. Stefanowski, J.: Dealing with data difficulty factors while learning from imbalanced data. In: Matwin, S., Mielniczuk, J. (eds.) Challenges in Computational Statistics and Data Mining. SCI, vol. 605, pp. 333–363. Springer, Cham (2016). doi:10.1007/978-3-319-18781-5_17
22. Stefanowski, J., Wilk, S.: Rough sets for handling imbalanced data: combining filtering and rule-based classifiers. Fundam. Inf. **72**(1–3), 379–391 (2006)
23. Stepaniuk J.: Rough-Granular Computing in Knowledge Discovery and Data Mining. SCI, vol. 152. Springer, Heidelberg (2008)
24. UC Irvine Machine Learning Repository. http://archive.ics.uci.edu/ml/, (Accessed 03 Feb 2017)
25. Weiss, G.M.: Mining with rarity: a unifying framework. SIGKDD Explor. Newsl. **6**, 7–19 (2004)
26. Wilson, D.R., Martinez, T.R.: Improved heterogeneous distance functions. J. Artif. Intell. Res. **6**, 1–34 (1997)

A Model of Machine Learning Based Interactive E-business Website

Germanas Budnikas[1,2(✉)]

[1] Faculty of Economics and Informatics in Vilnius,
University of Białystok, Białystok, Poland
german.budnik@uwb.edu.pl
[2] Faculty of Informatics, Kaunas University of Technology, Kaunas, Lithuania

Abstract. Current online businesses usually contain supporting tools for an instant acquiring offered services and goods. Electronic web site solutions that guide a potential user to a successful finalization of browsing activities, i.e. to purchase finalization play an important role in trading. The proposed in the paper approach presents a model aiming at an assistance in transaction finalization using browsing activity data and personal information. The model is capable to discover missing personal data and to use forecasted values in the research. Results of the applied machine learning techniques are compared while using the whole set of the collected browsing activity data and the data with a reduced number of dimensions.

Keywords: Support vector machines · K-means · Artificial neural network · Principal component analysis · Online customer behavior tracking

1 Introduction

Practically all of nowadays businesses rely on web sites and web services. Their interaction structure with a visitor can be represented as a two-phase process. During the first phase a user gets some information about a service, during the second phase the user may finalize a transaction with a web site. A transaction finalization is a web site content depended process – it might be a service ordering, commenting, liking something in fb, etc. It is extremely important for business owners to know how web site guests behave online and is it possible to influence their actions. This paper topic addresses these issues and presents results of the research.

Analysis and understanding of web user behavior is a key topic of a behavioral targeting. Behavioral targeting is an evolving area of a web mining that deals with optimization of web online ads based on an analysis of web user behaviors. The research presented in the paper has some similarities to works in the considered field of the study. Methods of behavioral analysis investigate web surfing data gathered mainly from log files. The topic is actively investigated; examples of similar works could be papers by [1–3].

Approach by [3] suggests a method for monitoring user's online behavior. The method is implemented based on data pulled from log files where HTTP/GET requests are saved when a user clicks a hyperlink. These data are gathered using agent devices

K. Saeed et al. (Eds.): CISIM 2017, LNCS 10244, pp. 470–480, 2017.
DOI: 10.1007/978-3-319-59105-6_40

installed on user computers. The approach uses Open Directory Project [4] for a categorization of visited web sites. The research emphasizes a creation of behavior profiles with respect to web page visitation event, frequencies and probability distributions, and causality relations or time-dependencies.

Technique by [2] describes the problem of predicting behavior of web users based on real historical data. The data are gathered from user cookie files. An analysis is performed using a statistical decision theory.

Paper by [1] presents a method for modelling and analysis of user behavior in online communities that include personal profiles, wiki, blogs, file sharing, and a forum. The approach implements behavior modelling, role mining and role inference and is based on a statistical clustering.

The approach proposed in the current paper differs from the works listed above by its application area – it operates at Internet level, while [1, 3] approaches operate at Intranet level. The approach proposed is similar to [1] because they both use a dynamical update of estimations with respect to new data.

The given paper is a continuation of research started in [5] where e-business website data on visitor behavior were collected and used for creation of the model for forecasting online activities of a new visitor. The offered paper differs from the previous one by a wider range of machine learning techniques applied for model creation as well as by taking into a consideration new attributes like user profile data and page or product category visited by a user that are being estimated in case of it absence. Another difference is as follows – since the overall number of tracked attributes had increased, a dimension reduction technique has been employed in order to use the most important components in model analysis. A scoring of the developed model that uses two types of data – original and reduced ones has been prepared in order to evaluate a usability of Principal Component Analysis technique in classification task aiming to discover whether a visitor is willing to finalize a transaction.

The paper is structured in the following way. The second section presents a general architecture of a web site used in the approach. The third section presents a sketch of a procedure of statistical data collecting from a web site. Model creation steps along with the results of machine learning experiments are given in the fourth section. The fifth section briefly outlines a website interaction process based on the proposed machine learning model. Conclusion summarizes an accomplished research.

2 Web Site Architecture Considered in the Research

Surfing on web sites usually differs with respect to types of these sites. Open Directory Project (ODP) differentiates the following web site types: Arts, Business, Computers, and 13 more instances. These types generalize manually selected web sites in different languages and are used in various kind of research including the suggested in this paper. Classification of web sites into types helps in understanding of possible kinds of behavior. Specification of sub-types and its instances is crucial for understanding behavior cases. The paper considers an instance of the Consumer Goods and Services sub-type of a business type with respect to ODP classification. Each browsing activity on web sites, especially on business sites, can be logically divided into two parts – introductory that usually includes list of services, descriptions, etc., and (transaction) finalization that could be expressed by paying for services, commenting, fb likes and so on. According to Fig. 1, an introductory logical part of a browsing activity may consist of Product Category Selection, Product Selection, Product Related Information Viewing, Delivery and Company Information Viewing; while Check-out and Payment browsing activity corresponds the logical part – transaction finalization.

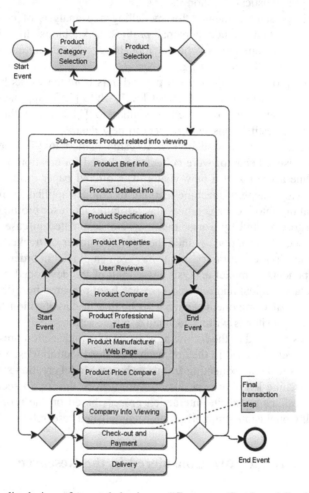

Fig. 1. A generalized view of a user behavior on "Consumer Goods and Services" sites using business process modelling notation (Source: [5])

Specification of web site surfing activity makes possible to understand a visitor online behavior that can be monitored by using various techniques, e.g., Google Analytics [6] tracking function.

The following 7-tuple could be used for such a specification to define a data-set that is used to monitor customer behavior on an analyzed web site:

$$< e, y, g, a, u, t, m >,$$

Where

e is a user browsing *session* during which web site pages are visited;
y is a *category* of a product, viewed by a user. As e-commerce web site may contain a huge number of products (even of the same category), products are differentiated only if they belong to the different categories;
g, a, u correspond to a user gender, age interval and identifier correspondingly set by a cookie file – a tiny text file that contains user visiting information. In case of a new user or not logging to own account, user specific information can be entered in a pop-up window;
t is a kind of an activity or a *task* performed by a user on the web site page like "Product Category Selection", "Viewing Product Price Comparison" (see Fig. 1);
m is activity t start time *moment* that is used to differentiate between different browsing sessions.

3 Online Visitor Behavior Tracking

To understand new web site visitor online action, it is needed to track an actual behavior of online visitors. It can be caught using numerous techniques like Open Web Analytics [7] or Google Analytics Event Tracking [8]. Such techniques enable recording user interaction with website elements, such as web page, embedded AJAX page element, page gadgets, and Flash-driven element and so on. Additionally to tracking function, a cookie file is used for unique user identification [9].

Data about actual on-site surfing is gathered and saved in a form like this

$$\langle e, y, g, a, u, t_1, \ldots, t_{n-1}, t_f \rangle,$$

where t_f corresponds the final task. For example, record R_1 (see Table 1) represents situation that a user during the first session has visited Product Properties (t_4), Product Price Compare (t_9) and Delivery (t_{11}) web pages and has not finalized the transaction – Check-out and Payment task (t_f) has not been accomplished. Task designations have the following meanings: 0 means a web page has not been visited (i.e., a task has not been accomplished) and 1 means that a web page has been visited. Customer gender information is encoded as 0 for females and 1 for males and 2 for other, age interval has only two intervals – up to 50 and over 50 (surely, that could be expanded onto more detailed parts). User next session (see record R_2 of Table 1) consists of visits to the same pages that are marked by grey background color in the table and which ended with a finalization of a transaction. Please note two conflicting records in Table 1. They are handled by removing entries that are not ending with transaction finalization while entries with an opposite outcome and the same premises are left. A detailed and formalized description of removing conflicting issues can be found in [5]. An abstract web site, which browsing activity diagram is presented in Fig. 1, was used for an illustration of the proposed technique and up to 3000 visitor behavior data records were used.

Table 1. Illustration of tracked data fragment read off from a web site (Source: self-made)

Record number	Session	Product category	Gender	Age interval	User ID	Brief Info	Detailed info	Specification	Properties	User Reviews	Compare	Professional Tests	Manufacturer Web page	Price Compare	Company Info	Delivery	Check-out and Payment
	e	y	g	a	u	t_1	t_2	t_3	t_4	t_5	t_6	t_7	t_8	t_9	t_{10}	t_{11}	t_f
R_1	1	1	0	1	1	0	0	0	1	0	0	0	0	1	0	1	0
R_2	2	1	0	1	1	0	0	0	1	0	0	0	0	1	0	1	1

4   Model Creation Steps

Model construction steps can be divided onto 4 parts as depicted on Fig. 2. At the initial step, visitor activities on a web site are tracked and recorded. Website surfers may be logged or not that means visitor profile data – gender and age information may not be accessible. That later fact requires model developing for such data forecasting based on logged in surfers with filled in personal data.

The first step additionally covers data preparation and processing activities. They include removal of redundant and ambivalent records. An algorithm for processing

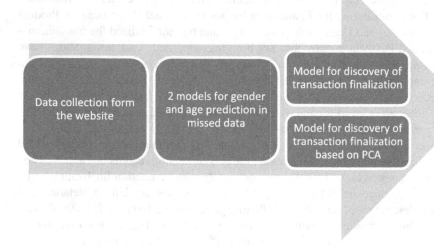

Fig. 2. Model creation steps (Source: self-made)

such records has been given in [5]. During that phase data for the models to be explained further are being prepared.

As there exists a correlation between visitor age, gender and their browsing patterns ([10, 11], it is important to discover such an information in case of missing data. That could be implemented by building supervised machine learning model based on web surfing activities of registered users.

Binary classification methods were employed for easiness of implementation of female, male and *other* gender discovery. Target classes female/none, male/none were used. A winner class is chosen based on the higher prediction value except the both classes scored greater than 65% (value set experimentally) – an *other* gender is chosen then. The last approach is also applicable in situations when e.g. mother searches for her son's products. The following table summarizes 10-fold cross validation experiments on a discovery of visitor gender in case of anonymous user surfing using three machine learning techniques – artificial neural networks [12], k-means [13, 14] and support vector machines [15] (Table 2).

A classification technique with a highest score obtained based on a given training data set should be employed in the model. In the similar way, two age intervals could be derived. The following table depicts 10-fold cross validation results (Table 3).

At the fourth stage, a model for discovering whether a given transaction will be finalized was created. The approach for the model creation at that stage was twofold. The model used all the data taken form the first step (see Fig. 2), namely – number of session, visited types of pages including product categories and personal data (real ones either discovered using aforementioned classification methods). All these data (16 in total) were used as inputs for classification methods. The following table depicts results of cross validation of the applied classification techniques (Table 4).

Next, architecture and performance characteristics concerning the best scored classification method are presented (Fig. 3, Table 5).

Table 2. 10-fold cross validation results for gender discovery (female, male, other) (Source: self-made)

Artificial neural network	K-means	Support vector machines
0.9112	0.8796	0.8612

Table 3. 10-fold cross validation results for age interval discovery (up to 50, 50 +) (Source: self-made)

Artificial neural network	K-means	Support vector machines
0.6275	0.6288	0.5530

Table 4. 10-fold cross validation results for transaction finalization discovery (Source: self-made)

Artificial neural network	K-means	Support vector machines
0.9761	0.9402	0.8126

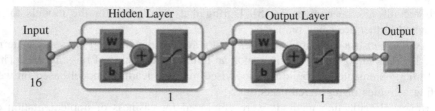

Fig. 3. Artificial neural network architecture used to discover whether a web transaction will be finalized (Source: self-made using Matlab)

Table 5. Performance characteristics of artificial neural network used to discover whether a web transaction will be finalized (Source: self-made using Matlab)

	Samples	MSE	%E
Training	2392	2.61098e-2	2.50836e-0
Validation	149	9.58289e-3	6.71140e-1
Testing	448	2.27893e-2	2.23214e-0

Another competitive approach was applied in order to evaluate how dimension reduction affects classification accuracy. For that purpose, Principal Component Analysis [16] technique was applied. 16 principal components were obtained and the first three of them are depicted on the figure below (Fig. 4).

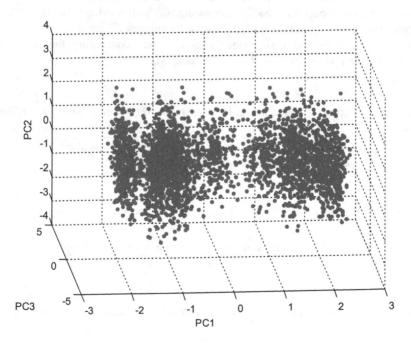

Fig. 4. First three principal components derived from data on website visitor browsing activities using PCA technique (Source: self-made using Matlab)

Table 6. Variances for all 16 principal components (Source: self-made using Matlab `princomp` function from the Statistics Toolbox)

PC#	Variance
PC1	2.0906
PC2	1.0905
PC3	1.0851
PC4	1.0718
PC5	1.0461
PC6	1.0239
PC7	0.9980
PC8	0.9886
PC9	0.9819
PC10	0.9694
PC11	0.9533
PC12	0.9494
PC13	0.9080
PC14	0.8862
PC15	0.8215
PC16	0.1357

Below in Table 6, variance values are given for samples of web surfing data to which Principal Components were applied.

A number of experiments was conducted seeking to discover an appropriate number of principal components to be used as inputs for classification models. The following table presents the best results of the research on dimension reduction while solving classification task (Table 7).

Table 7. 10-fold cross validation results for discovering an appropriate number of principal components (Source: self-made)

PC#	Artificial neural network	K-means	Support vector machines
10	0.3868	0.8329	0.8658
11	0.4020	0.8734	0.8883
12	0.4857	0.9012	0.9016
13	0.4943	0.9092	0.8695

The table below (see Table 8) summarizes results of application of selected machine learning techniques to two groups of tracked web site visitor data: in original form and to the data with reduced number of dimensions using PCA technique.

Table 8. Estimation of transaction finalization based on original data and data with reduced number of dimensions (Source: self-made)

	Artificial neural network	K-means	Support vector machines
Original data	**0.9761**	**0.9402**	0.8126
Data with dimension reduction (12 principal components)	0.4857	0.9012	**0.9016**

5   E-business Web Site Interaction with a Visitor

A purpose of web site interaction is in providing an assistance for a visitor aiming at influence their willingness to finalize a transaction. Such an interaction has been activated after the visitor had browsed some predefined number of pages or page sections. Based on the constructed models a personal information has been forecasted (see Tables 9 and 10) and used in later forecasting tasks defining a willingness of a visitor concerning their final decision.

Additionally, the same model has evaluated an influence of each unvisited web page to successful transaction finalization using the machine learning technique that earned best score – artificial neural network without dimension reduction (see Table 11).

Table 9. Gender prediction for an anonymous visitor based on a partial page visits (7 of 9) (Source: self-made)

Gender	Artificial neural network	K-means	Support vector machines
Female	0.6447	0.5982	0.6109
Male	0.5232	0.5146	0.4932
Resulting predicted gender:			Female

Table 10. Age interval prediction for an anonymous visitor based on a partial page visits (7 of 9) (Source: self-made)

Age interval	Artificial neural network	K-means	Support vector machines
up to 50	0.5167	0.4973	0.5014
50+	0.4692	0.4618	0.4734
Resulting predicted age interval:			up to 50

Table 11. Prediction of impact levels on the finalization of transaction by anonymous user with predicted personal information for unvisited web pages (Source: self-made)

Unvisited web page	Artificial neural network	K-means	Support vector machines
User reviews	0.7517	0.7347	0.7453
Compare	0.6383	0.6228	0.6364
Professional tests	0.7894	0.7629	0.7712

A page (namely – Professional tests), which had been characterized with the highest impact on the finalization, has been advised to visit.

6 Conclusion and Discussion

The paper describes a model of machine learning based interactive e-business website. The model is illustrated by an example. The model comprises of a usage of three classification techniques that estimate a visitor age interval and a gender, which in their turn used in forecasting the web page with the highest impact on transaction finalization along with actual behavior data. The three machine learning techniques – artificial neural networks, k-means and support vector machines were used to increase credibility of results.

Dimension reduction technique – principal component analysis was used to investigate a possibility to increase a performance of classification techniques. This was reasonable only for support vector machines – an increase of prediction performance was by 8.9%. However, prediction scoring of the three machine learning techniques that used visitor behavior data with the reduced number of dimensions was less than the performance by techniques that used the original learning data.

References

1. Angeletou, S., Rowe, M., Alani, H.: Modelling and analysis of user behaviour in online communities. In: The Semantic Web – ISWC 2011 (2011)
2. Dembczyński, K., Kotłowski, W., Sydow, M.: Effective prediction of web user behaviour with user-level models. J. Fundam. Informaticae **89**(2–3), 189–206 (2009)
3. Robinson, D.J., Berk, V.H., Cybenko, G.V.: Online behavioural analysis and modeling methodology (OBAMM). In: Liu, H., Salerno, J., Young, M.J. (eds.) Social Computing, Behavioural Modeling, and Prediction, pp. 100–109. Springer, Heidelberg (2008)
4. Xian, X., Chen, F., Wang, J.: An insight into campus network user behavior analysis decision system, Taichung (2014)
5. Budnikas, G.: Computerised recommendations on e-transaction finalisation by means of machine learning. Stat. Trans. New Ser. **16**(2), 309–322 (2015)
6. Clifton, B.: Advanced Web Metrics with Google Analytics, 3rd edn. Wiley, Indianapolis (2012)
7. Jarvinen, J., Karjaluoto, H.: The use of Web analytics for digital marketing performance measurement. Ind. Mark. Manage. **50**, 117–127 (2015)
8. Weber, J.: Practical Google Analytics and Google Tag Manager for Developers. Apress, New York (2015)
9. Aldekhail, M.: Application and significance of web usage mining in the 21st century: a literature review. Int. J. Comput. Theory Eng. **8**, 41–47 (2016)
10. Richard, M.O., Chebat, J.-C., Yang, Z., Putrevu, S.: A proposed model of online consumer behavior: assessing the role of gender. J. Bus. Res. **63**(9–10), 926–934 (2010)
11. Thanuskodi, S.: Gender differences in internet usage among college students: a comparative study. Libr. Philos. Pract. (e-journal). Paper 1052 (2013)

12. Russell, S., Norvig, P.: Artificial Intelligence: A Modern Approach, 3rd edn. Pearson, Upper Saddle River (2010). International Version
13. Lloyd, S.P.: Least squares quantization in PCM. Technical report RR-5497, Bell Lab (1957)
14. MacQueen, J.B.: Some methods for classification and analysis of multivariate observations. In: Le Cam, L.M., Neyman, J. (eds.) Proceedings of the Fifth Berkeley Symposium on Mathematical Statistics and Probability, vol. 1, pp. 281–297. University of California Press, California (1967)
15. Steinwart, I., Christmann, A.: Support Vector Machines. Springer, New York (2008)
16. Jolliffe, I.: Principal Component Analysis. Springer Series in Statistics. Springer, New York (2002)

Towards Golden Rule of Capital Accumulation: A Genetic Algorithm Approach

Sankhadeep Chatterjee[1], Rhitaban Nag[2], Soumya Sen[3], and Amitrajit Sarkar[4(✉)]

[1] Department of Computer Science and Engineering,
University of Calcutta, Kolkata, India
chatterjeesankhadeep.cu@gmail.com
[2] Department of Economics, Raja Peary Mohan College,
Hooghly, Uttarpara, India
nag.rhitaban@gmail.com
[3] A.K.Choudhury School of Information Technology,
University of Calcutta, Kolkata, India
soumyasen1@acm.org
[4] Department of Computing, Ara Institute of Canterbury,
Christchurch, New Zealand
sarkara@cpit.ac.nz

Abstract. The current study deals with maximizing consumption per worker in connection with the economic growth of society. The traditional Solow model based approach is well-studied and computationally complex. The present work proposes a Genetic Algorithm (GA) based consumption maximization in attaining the Golden rule. An objective function derived from traditional Solow model based on depreciation rate and amount of accumulated capital is utilized. The current study considered a constant output per worker to incorporate a constant efficiency level of labor. Different ranges of Depreciation rate and accumulated capital are tested to check the stability of the proposed GA based optimization process. The mean error and standard deviation in optimization process is utilized as a performance metric. The experimental results suggested that GA is very fast and is able to produce economically significant result with an average mean error 0.142% and standard deviation 0.021%.

Keywords: Accumulated capital · Depreciation rate · Golden rule · Genetic algorithm · Metaheuristic · Solow model

1 Introduction

Economic growth of society directly impacts economy of a country. Economic growth depends on several factors; one of them is consumption. Thus, consumption maximization is an imperative task to ensure ever growing economic stability. Solow model [11] deals with the growth of the economy in terms of basic production, investment and depreciation. The steady level of capital plays a vital role in the same. Maximization of consumption is traditionally done by employing a long time consuming and computationally complex Solow model based mathematical approach. Motivated by this,

© IFIP International Federation for Information Processing 2017
Published by Springer International Publishing AG 2017. All Rights Reserved
K. Saeed et al. (Eds.): CISIM 2017, LNCS 10244, pp. 481–491, 2017.
DOI: 10.1007/978-3-319-59105-6_41

in the current work we consider Genetic Algorithm (GA) to maximize consumption. Typically, the economic problems can be framed as an optimization problem, such as cost minimization, and revenue maximization. Thus, efficient optimization methods are required to deliver accurate results. Consequently, several optimization algorithms can be involved to solve the required maximum profit level, such methods include the genetic algorithm (GA), particle swarm optimization (PSO), firefly algorithm, and cuckoo search algorithm (CS). Several studies have established the ingenuity and accuracy of GA [1–4]. Generally, the GA has numerous advantages including its flexibility to model the problem's constraints, and its easy convergence to the optimal solution inspired by Darwinian principle [6]. Nicoară [12] revealed about the GA relevance compared to the traditional methods for manufacturing structure optimization. Geisendorf [13] employed the GA to solve Resource Economic problem using two different assumptions to calculate the optimal extraction rate in order to achieve optimal benefits. Arifovic [14] solved decision rules of future production and sales by employing the GA in a competitive cobweb model in a market of single product. The simulation results indicated that the GA is capable of capturing different features from the experimental nature of the subjects under consideration. Riechmann [15] established that the GA can be connected with the evolutionary game theory. Hommes et al. [16] reveled that GA can converge to a series of near Nash equilibrium solutions, where the heterogeneous agent behavior has been modeled using GA.

The rest of the work is arranged as follows; first in Sect. 2 the basic economic background is introduced and mathematically explained. Next in Sect. 3 the economical steady state is introduced and explained. In Sect. 4 Golden rule of capital based on the Solow model is formulated. The appropriateness of choosing the objective function is mathematically established. Section 5 introduces the GA based proposed method. Section 6 reported the experimental set up of GA and finally, Sect. 7 reveals experimental results. It discusses the economic significance of the obtained results as well.

2 Basic Economic Background

The Solow model deals with growth of economy. It includes the living standard of every citizen currently living in the economy. Their living standard depends on various kinds of determinant; one of them is their income. The consumption increases with increasing earning of citizens thereby raising the overall consumption of economy. These results in potential growth in economic systems as the consumption rate of citizens have increased inside that economy. Consequently, consumption turns out to be a major indicator of growth. At maximum consumption rate, economic growth will take place. The golden rule of capital accumulation is a tool which has used to maximize the consumption. Golden rule actually indicates steady state with maximum consumption. The aforesaid formalism is mathematically established using a basic Coubb-Douglaus production function [11].

$$Q = f(L, K)$$
$$\frac{Q}{L} = f(\frac{L}{L}, \frac{K}{L})$$
$$y = f(1, k) \tag{1}$$
$$y = f(k)$$

Where, 'k' denotes capital per worker, 'y' denotes output per worker, 'c' is consumption per worker, 'i' is investment per worker, 'Q' is total output, 'L' denotes total labor and 'K' is total capital.

Suppose, a firm earns 'y' and saves 's' fraction of 'y'. $(1 - s)$ fraction of 'y' goes to its consumption. Hence;

$$c = (1-s) * y \tag{2}$$

Where, 'y' is income per worker. And the relation between income per worker and consumption is given by;

$$y = c + i \tag{3}$$

From (2) and (3) we get;

$$y = (1-s) * y + i$$
$$i = s * y \tag{4}$$
$$i = s * f(k)$$

Investment per worker depends on the savings rate of the firm (s). There is a positive relationship between investment per worker and savings rate. As saving rate rises, investment per worker also rises. An increasing savings rate shifts the investment per worker vs. capital per worker curve upward as depicted in Fig. 2.

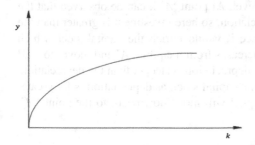

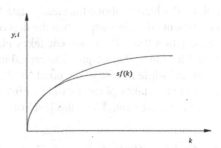

Fig. 1. Capital per worker vs. output per worker curve

Fig. 2. Combining output per worker and investment per worker curve. Where, $sf(k)$ denotes investment per worker curve

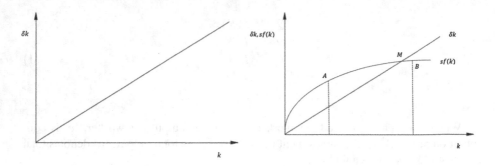

Fig. 3. Relationship between capital and total depreciation

Fig. 4. Combining Figs. 1 and 3. Depicting economic steady state

The relationship between change in capital per worker and depreciation is given as;

$$\Delta k = i - \delta * k \qquad (5)$$

From Eq. (4) we get;

$$\Delta k = s * f(k) - \delta * k$$

Figure 3 depicts that depreciation is increased with increased capital per worker.

3   Economical Steady State

From the Fig. 4 we depict how the economy approaches the steady level of capital. In Fig. 4 we have shown the steady level is at point 'M'. Now, to examine whether at point 'M' the economy reached steady state level of capital or not we take two points. The first point is point 'A' which is below the steady state level. And the second point is point 'B' which is above the steady state level. At point 'A' it can be observed that the investment curve is steeper than the depreciation, so here investment is greater than depreciation thus, if investment takes place it would enrich the capital stock which would lead to higher output. The capital increases from the point 'A' and moves toward point 'M' while in case of the point 'B' the depreciation is steeper than the depreciation. If investment takes place it would shrink the capital stock as depreciation is far greater than the investment. Thus, the level of capital will move downward to the point 'M'.

4   Golden Rule Level of Capital

After achieving the steady state level of capital, there is a state where we maximize the consumption per worker that is generally known as the Golden rule level of capital [11, 18]. The Golden rule addresses the question of presence of any growth in an

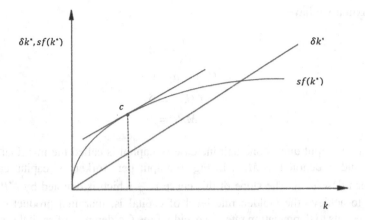

Fig. 5. Golden rule level of capital accumulation. At point 'c' $MP_k = \delta$ which indicates that the rate of change of output with respect to capital (MP_k) is equal to the slope of the depreciation line. Thus it is achieving the Golden rule of capital accumulation.

economy. There are many factors which decide the growth of an economy. The current study focuses on the consumption. Maximization of consumption is an imperative task in order to achieve economic growth. The Golden rule of capital indicates a state (a unique value of depreciation rate and amount of capital accumulated) that ensures maximum consumption level, thereby assures a strong economic growth [18].

From Eq. 3 and 5 we get;

$$c = y - i$$
$$\Delta k = i - \delta * k \qquad (6)$$
$$i = \delta * k$$

As, the difference between output and depreciation curve is zero (At point 'M' of Fig. 4). Hence, $\Delta k = 0$

$$c = f(k^*) - \delta * k^* \qquad (7)$$

Here, $i = \delta * k^*$ as stated in Golden rule of Capital [11]. Now differentiating with respect to k^* we get (Fig. 5);

$$\frac{dc}{dk^*} = f'(k^*) - \delta$$

At maxima we have;

$$\frac{dc}{dk^*} = 0$$
$$f'(k^*) - \delta = 0 \qquad (8)$$
$$f'(k^*) = \delta$$
$$MP_k = \delta$$

Change in output due to one unit increase of capital is called the marginal product of capital and is denoted as MP_k. In Fig. 1 output per worker vs. capital curve has already been described. The slope of this curve is $\frac{dy}{dk}$ which is denoted by MP_k. Initial condition to achieve the Golden rule level of capital is; marginal product of capital should be equals to depreciation rate. To decide if the Golden rule of capital is steady or not; we consider two different cases.

i. **Case 1**

$$MP_k - \delta < 0$$

Where, if one unit of capital is added, output will increase less than the depreciation. If level of capital is increased consumption will fall.

ii. **Case 2**

$$MP_k - \delta > 0$$

Where, if one unit of capital is added, output will increase more than the depreciation. If level of capital is increased consumption will rise. As none of Case 1 and 2 produces a steady state hence, Eq. 8 is only condition which satisfy Golden rule level of capital.

5 Genetic Algorithm Based Methodology

The GA is a parallel optimization procedure that relies on evolution for optimizing a group of solutions at once [5]. The model is highly inspired from Darwinian principle of Natural Evolution, and involves a population which participates in finding the solution of a particular problem under consideration. In the proposed work, the GA is applied to determine the optimal consumption value, where the GA proves its effectiveness for superior convergence toward global optimization compared to other global search algorithm. The overall GA algorithm is as follows [6] mentioning types of different operators. Each chromosome represents a potential solution in mating pool. The chromosome representation considered in the current study is as follows;

Algorithm: Genetic Algorithm
Start
Generate random chromosomes' population that represents solutions
Evaluate the population-fitness
Create new population using the following steps:
Select two parent chromosomes form the population based on their fitness (Roulette)
Crossover the parents to generate new offspring (Single Point)
Mutate new offspring at each locus (Gaussian)
Place new offspring in the new population
Use new generated population
Test: If the end condition is satisfied, stop, and return the best solution in present population
Stop

A binary coded chromosome representation technique is adapted. The chromosome has two major parts. The first part depicts δ (depreciation rate) and the next part depicts k^* (amount of capital accumulated). The chromosome representation is depicted in Fig. 6. Each part is numerically a sequence of binary digits. The length of each such part is n. The length depends on the search range of the corresponding variable.

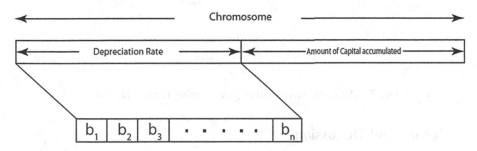

Fig. 6. Chromosome representation of Genetic algorithm

As reported in the preceding algorithm, it is clear that each member of the population represents a potential solution of the problem under concern. Further, each of them is associated with a fitness value indicating the superiority of that particular solution. The fitness value is calculated by following Eq. 7 described in Sect. 4.

Solutions at any stage participate in Darwinian reproduction, survival of the fittest and other genetic operations to produce successors. The GA tries to find out the best solution at every generation by breeding the best solutions from the previous generation. The candidate solutions under consideration are actually artificial chromosomes which are inspired from the DNA structure. In practice, these chromosomes have fixed length strings (binary/real coded), where each location (gene) holds information about one of the variables associated in the problem. In the current study real coded fixed length formalism is utilized. Each chromosome has two different components one depicting δ (Depreciation rate) and another is k^* (amount of capital accumulated). The range of each of the components varies from context to context [18].

GA the population (initially random) by applying genetic operators already defined to generate new solutions from them. The genetic operators such as crossover, mutation and several other versions of these two are popular [7, 8]. Crossover can be of different types; broadly Single point or multi point. The current study used a single point crossover [9] method. A Gaussian type mutation strategy is adopted [10] and employed. The probability value of mutation is determined by a simple trial and error method and is described in next section. Based on the preceding genetic algorithm procedure, Fig. 7 demonstrated the proposed approach for consumption maximization in achieving Golden rule of capital accumulation using the GA.

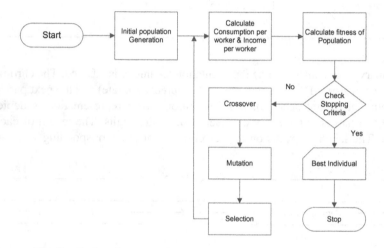

Fig. 7. The profit maximization process using Genetic algorithm

6   Results and Discussion

The experiments are carried out using Intel Core i3 4 GB Machine. A real coded Genetic algorithm is implemented using the algorithmic set up which are obtained by running the GA 100 times with different parameters and is described in Table 1. Depending on the difficulty of the problem being solved the initial size of population is set to 200 and maximum number of generation is set to 500. The selection procedure during iteration is Roulette. Single point cross over strategy is adopted with a crossover probability of 0.15 which indicates that a significantly low probability would be sufficient to ensure the better quality population, while it is kept low in order to prevent the process from being trapped in local optima. The solution generated by the proposed system is a pair of values consisting δ (depreciation rate) and k^* (amount of capital accumulated) with in the given range of search. The output is approximate a point in search space for which the objective function is highly close to global optima.

Table 1. Genetic algorithm setup for consumption maximization

Size of population	200
Maximum number of generation	500
Type of selection	Roulette
Type of crossover	Single point crossover
Crossover probability	0.15
Mutation type	Gaussian
Stall time limit	25 s

The experiments are run for 50 times for each set up of input ranges and the best results are reported. The objective function is already described and explained in Sect. 4 (Eq. 7). $f(k^*)$ denotes output per worker. This is kept constant to ensure constant efficiency level of labor [18] and in the current study this is set to 2000. δ denotes depreciation rate and k^* denotes amount of capital accumulated.

7 Experimental Results

Table 2 reports the performance of Genetic Algorithm. Performance analysis is done using the Mean Error and Standard Deviation. The results are tabulated in form mean error (%) ± standard deviation (%). Different ranges of δ and k is used. The ranges are written in form [lower bound, upper bound]. As suggested in [11] the range of δ is kept low and k is kept high. The mean error for ranges [0.01, 0.1], [1, 1000] of δ and k respectively the mean error is 0.257% and standard deviation is 0.005%. Next for ranges [0.1, 0.9] and [1, 1000] the achieved mean error and standard deviation are 0.192% and 0.043% respectively. The average of these different set up is reported as well. Average mean error achieved is 0.142% and standard deviation is 0.021%.

Table 2. Performance analysis of GA

Range of δ	Range of k^*	Mean error (%) ± Standard deviation (%)
[0.01, 0.1]	[1, 1000]	0.257% ± 0.005%
[0.1, 0.9]	[1, 1000]	0.192% ± 0.043%
[0.25, 1]	[250, 750]	0.048% ± 0.003%
[0.01, 0.9]	[250, 850]	0.072% ± 0.036%
Average		0.142% ± 0.021%

Figure 8 depicts the convergence graph of Genetic Algorithm for ranges of δ and k [0.01, 0.1] and [1, 1000] respectively. GA took 52 iterations to converge. Figure 8 depicts a similar plot with ranges [0.1, 0.9] and [1, 1000] of δ and k respectively. It took 54 iterations to converge. The plots reveal that GA is extremely fast in maximizing the objective function and is better than traditional methods [18] because these involve calculation of mathematical differentiation of complex functions and is proved to be NP - Hard (exponential complexity) [17]. GA is faster as it takes polynomial time

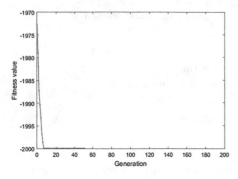 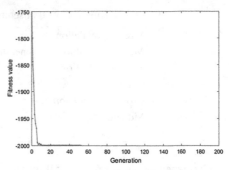

Fig. 8. GA convergence plot with ranges of δ and k being [0.01–0.1] and [1–1000]

Fig. 9. GA convergence plot with ranges of δ and k being [0.1–0.9] and [1–1000]

to converge [3, 4]. This is supported by the experimental results and it establishes that GA based method to be faster than traditional method as well (Fig. 9).

7.1   Economic Significance

The results obtained by Genetic algorithm are economically significant. The optimum results indicated that in maximizing the consumption per worker the value of depreciation rate (δ) tends to the lower bound of the given range which indicates a lower depreciation rate. From economical point of view lower depreciation rate is expected [11] and in addition the capital accumulation tends to the higher bound of given range that indicates an increased accumulated capital that is equally significant [18].

8   Conclusion

Economic growth takes a vital role in sustainable development of a society and impacts the economic stability of a country to a greater extent. The current study considered the consumption maximization problem which is a major factor in economic growth. The traditional Solow model based approach is time consuming and computationally complex due to high involvement of mathematical operations and is proved to be NP-Hard. In the current study a well-known Darwinian principle inspired metaheuristic Genetic Algorithm is employed in maximizing the consumption (The Golden rule of capital accumulation) in terms of depreciation and capital accumulation. Experimental results have indicated that the proposed GA based method is highly fast and produces economically significant results in achieving the Golden rule of capital accumulation.

References

1. Reeves, C.R.: A genetic algorithm for flowshop sequencing. Comput. Oper. Res. **22**(1), 5–13 (1995)
2. Beasley, J.E., Chu, P.C.: A genetic algorithm for the set covering problem. Eur. J. Oper. Res. **94**(2), 392–404 (1996)
3. Orero, S.O., Irving, M.R.: Economic dispatch of generators with prohibited operating zones: a genetic algorithm approach. IEEE Proc. Gener. Transm. Distrib. **143**(6), 529–534 (1996)
4. Shin, K.-S., Lee, Y.-J.: A genetic algorithm application in bankruptcy prediction modeling. Expert Syst. Appl. **23**(3), 321–328 (2002)
5. Goldberg, D.E., Holland, J.H.: Genetic algorithms and machine learning. Mach. Learn. **3**(2), 95–99 (1988)
6. Malhotra, R., Singh, N., Singh, Y.: Genetic algorithms: concepts, design for optimization of process controllers. Comput. Inf. Sci. **4** (2011). doi:10.5539/cis.v4n2p39
7. Walters, D.C., Sheble, G.B.: Genetic algorithm solution of economic dispatch with valve point loading. IEEE Trans. Power Syst. **8**(3), 1325–1332 (1993)
8. Azadeh, A., Ghaderi, S.F., Nokhandan, B.P., Sheikhalishahi, M.: A new genetic algorithm approach for optimizing bidding strategy viewpoint of profit maximization of a generation company. Expert Syst. Appl. **39**(1), 1565–1574 (2012)
9. Chatterjee, S., Ghosh, S., Dawn, S., Hore, S., Dey, N.: Forest type classification: a hybrid NN-GA model based approach. In: Satapathy, S.C., Mandal, J.K., Udgata, S.K., Bhateja, V. (eds.) Information Systems Design and Intelligent Applications. AISC, vol. 435, pp. 227–236. Springer, New Delhi (2016). doi:10.1007/978-81-322-2757-1_23
10. Hore, S., Chatterjee, S., Santhi, V., Dey, N., Ashour, A.S., Balas, V.E., Shi, F.: Indian sign language recognition using optimized neural networks. In: Balas, V.E., Jain, L.C., Zhao, X. (eds.) Information Technology and Intelligent Transportation Systems. AISC, vol. 455, pp. 553–563. Springer, Cham (2017). doi:10.1007/978-3-319-38771-0_54
11. Mankiw, N.G.: Principles of Macroeconomics. Cengage Learning, Boston (2014)
12. Nicoară, E.S.: Applying genetic algorithms to optimization problems in economics. Petroleum-Gas University of Ploiesti Bulletin. Technical Series 67, no. 3 (2015)
13. Geisendorf, S.: Genetic algorithms in resource economic models. Santa Fe Institute, NM, USA, Working Papers, 99-08 (1999)
14. Arifovic, J.: Genetic algorithm learning and the cobweb model. J. Econ. Dynamics Control **18**(1), 3–28 (1994)
15. Riechmann, T.: Genetic algorithms and economic evolution. Fachbereich Wirtschaftswiss., Univ. (1998)
16. Hommes, C., Makarewicz, T., Massaro, D., Smits, T.: Genetic algorithm learning in a new keynesian macroeconomic setup (2015)
17. Kaltofen, E.: Computational differentiation and algebraic complexity theory. In: Workshop Report on First Theory Institute on Computational Differentiation, Argonne, Illinois, USA, pp. 28–30 (1993)
18. De La Croix, D., Ponthiere, G.: On the golden rule of capital accumulation under endogenous longevity. Math. Soc. Sci. **59**(2), 227–238 (2010)

A Multi-agent System Model for the Personal Rapid Transit System

Ezzeddine Fatnassi[✉] and Hadhami Kaabi

Institut Supérieur de Gestion de Tunis, Tunis University,
41, Rue de la Liberté - Bouchoucha, 2000 Bardo, Tunisie
ezzeddine.fatnassi@gmail.com

Abstract. This research concerns a routing and dispatching problem in the context of the on-demand Personal Rapid Transit transportation system. The objective of the problem is to efficiently optimize the total empty movement related to the vehicles as well as the waiting time of passengers in a dynamic settings. To achieve this, a multi-agent model is developed to manage efficiently the Personal Rapid Transit system. The proposed model involves three types of agent as well as the implementation of an efficient decentralized management strategy in order to handle demand of the passengers. Tests are made on a realistic use'case and results reveal the viability of the proposed model and strategy.

Keywords: Multi-agent system modeling · On demand transportation system · Pubic transportation · Simulation

1 Introduction

Personal Rapid transit (PRT) is an on-demand urban transit transportation system. It is generally organized in a fully connected network' shape that covers some parts of a large urban area, or a multi-terminal airport. The network is composed by a set of PRT'stations and dedicated guideways.

The system is fully automated. In fact, the PRT uses a set of driverless electric vehicles (i.e. system controlled) that move along a set of dedicated elevated guideways. This feature allows the separation of the PRT traffic from the conventional urban traffic. PRT vehicles could carry an individual passenger or a small group of individuals up to 6 persons. PRT offers a personalized transportation service as the users of such a system determine on their own the departure time, the departure and the destination of their trip freely. The control system determines based on the current demand the vehicle that should satisfies the demand of users as well as its route and movements within the PRT' network.

The PRT control system needs also to determine the set of empty moves of vehicles within the system. In fact, as the demand from a PRT station does not equal to the demand to this specific PRT station, the PRT control system would need to balance the flow of empty available vehicles in order to meet perfectly

K. Saeed et al. (Eds.): CISIM 2017, LNCS 10244, pp. 492–501, 2017.
DOI: 10.1007/978-3-319-59105-6_42

the demand of its users while minimizing their waiting time as well as the total energy consumption of the system. This problem is known in the literature by the empty vehicle redistribution problem. The reader should refer to [12] for more details about this problem.

In the literature, many algorithms have been developed for the empty vehicle management of PRT' vehicles which focused mainly on the optimal reallocation of the empty vehicles within the system. In fact, this strategy could significantly reduce the waiting time of passengers within the PRT system by increasing the set of empty vehicles displacement. Generally, reallocation algorithms to manage empty moves of PRT vehicles are based on the available historical data related to the incoming of passengers as well as the estimation and prediction of future demands. These approaches use a form of a centralized data base containing past demand and historical data. Due to the central repository, these algorithms are implemented in a centralized manner which they mainly refer to the empty vehicle reallocation. Consequently, these algorithms are hard to be developed in a distributed decentralized way.

Based on this context, implementing simulation tools could be useful in order to analyze and implement effective empty vehicles strategies for PRT system. In fact, simulation could be seen as an abstraction of a complex system in order to study its behavior. In the literature, there exists several simulation approaches such as discrete event simulation, dynamic system and agent-based simulation approach (ABS).

Recently, an increasing interest on using multi-agent systems for innovation transportation applications have been proposed in the literature. In fact, Multi agent systems is a very convenient way to model complex urban transportation system composed of a large number of homogenous and heterogeneous individuals interacting within each other and with their environment. Generally, in this kind of system vehicles are modeled as an autonomous agents which aim to find a sequence of moves in order to optimize their operational cost. However, there are only few works in the literature that proposed efficient algorithms for computing approximate solutions in order to optimize transportation system.

The ABS presents the advantage of being able to study various complex system from the perspective of individual point of view. In the literature, ABS have been implemented and applied to model many logistics and transportation systems [13,15]. Consequently, it would be interesting to implement an ABS based on the context of PRT in order to reduce its empty vehicles movement and waiting time of passengers.

In the literature, several simulation model and dynamic strategies have been implemented for the PRT context. One could note [12] where authors studied to minimize waiting time of passengers. However, these latter works does not consider battery issues related to the electric PRT vehicles.

One could note also [14]where authors proposed a discrete event simulation approach to model the PRT system. ABS have been proposed within the PRT context in [2,5,6]. However, in [2,5] authors focused on the activities related to vehicles rather than the stations and in [6] authors does not consider battery issues related to PRT vehicles.

Based on these gaps in the literature, we propose in this paper a distributed management algorithm and ABS for PRT systems. The novelty of our approach resides on the fact that we model stations in PRT as an independent actors (i.e. Agents) that are capable of making decisions and ask for empty PRT vehicles. In fact, we give a special focus on implementing a decentralized management algorithm where the set of decisions is distributed on the stations rather than the vehicles. This feature offers several advantages:

- Eliminating the need for a central control system as the decisions are made autonomously by the stations.
- A high flexibility for the PRT system as it would be able to cope with uncertain and unusual demand and traffic condition.

Consequently, the contributions of this paper is threefold:

- We propose an ABS where stations acts as an independent and autonomous actors in the PRT system.
- We propose a decentralized management strategy for minimizing waiting time of passengers and the set of empty moves in the system.
- We test our approach based on a realistic case study of Corby in the United Kingdom.

The structure of this paper is as follows. In Sect. 2, the problem definition is presented. Section 3 explains the proposed ABS as well as the implemented decentralized strategy. The computational results and analysis of our simulation model are presented in Sect. 4. Finally, Sect. 5 concludes and gives directions for future research.

2   Problem Definition

In this section, we present the formal problem definition related to PRT. The proposed problem considers to have a PRT network N with a set of finite PRT stations denoted M. Groups or individual PRT'users come at the different PRT stations to ask a specific transportation service from their current location to a specific PRT'station. We suppose that passengers arrives based on a specific poisson process of rate λ. The transportation requests should be served immediately. Rejection of transportation demand is not allowed in the system. The PRT system has a set of electric driverless vehicles that the system would use to satisfy the transportation demand. The PRT'vehicles are constrained by its limited battery capacity B. This limited battery capacity would allow the vehicle to travel for a limited distance before returning to the charging location to recharge their batteries.

We consider also to have a predefined matrix distance that determine the cost of moving between each pair of stations. The vehicles are initially located at the charging location. The vehicles in the PRT system are driverless that move without any human intervention. Our problem consider to find a set of dispatching decisions in order to satisfy the transportation demand. We should note that dispatching decisions refer to the assignment of a vehicle to a specific transportation request. As soon as the system receives transportation demand, dispatching decisions need to be made as soon as possible in order to reduce the waiting time of passengers and to increase the efficiency of the system. The dispatching decisions within a PRT system should be made while knowing the current state of the network. That is why effective strategies should be made while evaluating several possibilities in order to optimize the current state of the system.

Our problem is a dynamic one. In fact, the information related to the coming of the transportation requests is known gradually as the PRT system serves its passengers. This characteristic represents an important feature to our problem as the driverless vehicles could not serve all the transportation requests at the same time due to the limited battery capacity and fleet size.

The objective of our problem is to find the set of dispatching decisions related to PRT system that would minimize the total energy consumption and the waiting time of passengers. These two objectives are of a high interest as they would increase the efficiency and the appealing of such a transportation system.

3 The Simulation Model

In this section, we present the proposed ABS model to tackle the proposed problem related to PRT. For this purpose, we present the multi-agent system modeling of PRT. Then, we present the proposed decentralized strategy.

3.1 The Multi-agent System Modeling of PRT

Generally, coordination in on-demand transportation systems (i.e. PRT) could be in two distinctive forms: (i) Centralized in which the central control system tends to improve the performance of the global system by exploring all the different alternatives related to the current situation related to the transportation network by the use of coordination and information sharing. (ii) Decentralized in which coordination could be found at an inter-urban zone only, which could causes conflicting practices that need to be managed.

As a result of the high level of transportation service that the PRT aims to offer to its users, PRT could be modeled as a decentralized system in which independent agents could take their own decisions. This feature would ensures a highly reactive system to the upcoming demand of passengers. Consequently, the PRT could be modeled by using multi-agent system modeling approach. Multi-agent system modeling approach consists of a set of different agents interacting with each other's in order to solve a specific problem, compete for a finite set of shared resources (i.e. the PRT vehicles) or coordinating with each other in order to avoid conflicts.

In the literature [1], the term agent defines a software or a hardware based computer system that has specific characteristics such as reactivity and pro-activity, autonomy, and social ability. Muti-agents systems offer the advantage of being simple to implement and understand [15]. Also when the problem and the modeled systems is itself distributed, multi-agent system models offer more flexibility in term of dealing with the different constraints of the simulated system.

As complex systems such the PRT are generally a decentralized and distributed ones with many interactions between its different components, it is rather difficult to model and analyze each possible interaction at the earlier design process of a multi-agent model. In fact, multi-agent systems modeling approach handles this complexity by decomposing the system into smaller and rather simple autonomous agents. Consequently and based on this feature, there is no need to define all the possible control reaction and interaction in the simulated system. Therefore, an autonomous agent in a multi-agent system would act and update its state according to its own environment and interaction with the other different agents. Based on this feature, the complexity of the whole simulated system is reduced [11].

In the literature, PRT is considered as a complex and distributed system [4]. PRT is composed by different interacting actors and a network of complex subsystems that together provide a high level of transportation service. Thus, PRT can be modeled as a network of agents. Agents in PRT would try to maximize their own gain rather than the whole system gain. Each agents would act autonomously by being able to interact with its dynamic environment and taking pro-active and reactive decisions [13]. In this sense, it exists numerous studies that proposed to tackle on-demand transportation systems modeling by the use of a multi-agent system modeling approach.

In [2,5], authors proposed to model PRT using multi-agents based approach where vehicles act as an independent agents. In [6], authors proposed to use multi-agent simulation approach for the PRT context where stations act as independent agent but without tackling many hard constraints related to PRT such as the limited distance constraints. Other works on PRT includes discrete event simulation [8,9], static energy consumption minimization [7,10], fleet sizing [3], network design [16], and so on. The novelty on our approach is to consider stations as independent agents while taking into account various constraints and limitation related to the PRT vehicles.

3.2   The Proposed Modeling Approach

As we proposed to use Multi-agents simulation approach for our PRT system, one could argue that the driverless vehicles would be used as the only agent types in our model. However, we used in our model three type of agents: (i) Vehicles, (ii) Passengers, (iii) Stations.

This different agents would communicate with each other and their own environment. The passengers agents arrive at specific PRT station and ask to be transported to another PRT station. Consequently, the passengers agents send a transportation request to its current departure station. The transportation request is represented by a triplet: (i) Departure station (ii) Arrival station (iii) Departure time.

This transportation request would be treated by the specific agent that represents the departure station. In fact, the station agent and based on the transportation demand characteristic would select the best available vehicle agent available at the departure station based on the total traveled distance and the available electric battery charge. Consequently, we could consider that the environment in our simulated system represents all the information available at the different nodes of the network.

In the following subsections, the role of each type of agent is explained.

3.3   Vehicle Agent

The vehicle agents in our model has four different functions:

- They transport passenger' agents in order to satisfy their transportation requests.
- They interact with the station agents in order to know what passengers request they could satisfy.
- They interact with the specific charging station agent in order to perform charging operation.
- They gather different statistics in order to evaluate the performance of the whole system.

Every vehicle can be in four principal states: waiting empty, moving empty, moving with passengers, charging state.

3.4   Passenger Agent

The passenger agent is composed of a set of passengers or an individual one with the same departure and destination stations, and whose number does not exceed the capacity of the PRT vehicle in term of number of passengers (e.g. six passengers). This agent interacts with the station agent in order to inform it about its related transportation request. Then, after a vehicle agent pick up the passenger agent it sends a message to the station agent in order to inform it about its waiting time which would be needed to gather statistics related to the system.

3.5   Station Agent

In our simulation model, the station agents are the most important ones. In fact, the dispatching decisions related to the PRT system are implemented as an integral part of the station agents. Thus, the station agents would receive all the different passengers arriving at their locations. Each station agent would evaluate the available transportation requests. Based on the current situation of the system, the station agent would interact with the vehicles agent available at its location in order to perform the transportation request. The station agent would choose from the available empty vehicle the best one able to perform the transportation request. This decision is based on the traveled distance related to the transportation request as well as the available electric energy in the different vehicles. If no empty vehicles are available, the station agent would communicate with the other station agents in order to ask for a specific number of vehicles. For example, if a station agent has four waiting transportation requests that could not be satisfied by the available vehicle agent in the station, it would ask all the other stations agents to send four different empty PRT vehicles. The different other station agents would evaluate the demand and would accept or reject the demand in empty vehicles. In the case of acceptance a conflict could arise if more than one station would satisfy the need of empty vehicles of a specific station agent. In this case, the station agent asking for empty vehicle would accept only the vehicles coming from the closest distance possible. Finally, we should note that periodically the station agent would evaluate the available empty vehicle agent available at its location. If a vehicle has waited empty for too long, it would be sent to the charging location.

Details about PRT station agents are shown in Algorithm 1. We should note that station agents treat the transportation demand based on the principle of first come first serve in order to minimize the total waiting time.

Algorithm 1. Station Agent Algorithm()

1: **for all** Waiting Passengers P_i in this.CurrentStation **do**
2:   **for all** Waiting empty vehicles V_i in this.CurrentStation **do**
3:     **if** $V_i.Batterylevel$ Allows the vehicle to serve P_i **then**
4:       Assign P_i to Vehicle V_i
5:       Exit FOR
6:     **end if**
7:   **end for**
8:   **if** P_i isn't satisfied by an empty vehicles **then**
9:     Ask other station agents to send empty vehicle to satisfy P_i
10:     Evaluate the offers in term of empty vehicles from the other station agents and assign the best alternative to P_i.
11:   **end if**
12: **end for**
13: Evaluate the number of empty vehicles in the station
14: **if** the number of empty waiting vehicles is less than a certain reserve value **then**
15:   Ask other station agents to send empty vehicle to balance the number of waiting empty vehicles
16: **end if**

Finally, we should note from Algorithm 1 that a proactive behavior is implemented as a part of the general behavior of the station agent. In fact, we propose that each station should have a fixed number of empty vehicle waiting for passengers to come in order to reduce the total waiting time of passengers. Periodically and after serving the different waiting passengers, the station agent would look for the number of empty waiting vehicles in its current location and ask other station agents to send empty vehicles if the station is at a deficit of empty vehicles (e.g. number of empty vehicles is less than the reserve value).

4   Computational Results

The proposed simulation model was written in C++ language with the intention of analyzing the proposed decentralized strategy. The written computer program was written with the intention to predict the service level for the system using several statistics related to the waiting time of passenger, consumed energy, etc.

In this section, we present the computational results related to our multi-agent model for the PRT system. For the testing bed, we choose the one from the literature [9]. The testing bed is based on the Corby real use case which represents a realistic PRT network. The network is composed of 15 stations and 4 depots. As we are treating the case of a single depot topology, we proposed

Table 1. Results of the proposed strategy

Network	Scenario	Waiting time in min	Empty movement in %	Full movement in %
1	1	2.552	37.634	62.366
1	2	2.920	38.725	61.275
1	3	3.145	40.158	59.842
1	4	2.931	41.787	58.213
1	5	2.827	40.840	59.160
2	1	3.286	43.977	56.023
2	2	3.891	44.474	55.526
2	3	3.610	43.713	56.287
2	4	3.981	47.605	52.395
2	5	3.816	46.748	53.252
3	1	4.338	54.576	45.424
3	2	4.599	52.304	47.696
3	3	4.039	51.145	48.855
3	4	4.478	52.770	47.230
3	5	4.750	55.088	44.912
4	1	4.143	51.331	48.669
4	2	4.770	51.513	48.487
4	3	4.634	53.284	46.716
4	4	4.295	53.729	46.271
4	5	3.936	52.134	47.866
Average		3.847	47.677	52.323

to generate four different networks where each one of them contain only one different depot.

As for the simulated scenarios related to the PRT transportation requests, we used scenarios adapted from the literature [4]. More specifically, the generated scenarios are based on the data available in the ATS/CityMobil software[1]. The ATS/CityMobil presents the rates λ_{ij} of a poisson process for traveling from any station i to any other station j in the Corby network. We should note that $\lambda_{ij} \in [0.789, 17.902]$. We used in this paper 5 different scenarios. Also, we supposed that the total number of fleet is equal to 200 vehicles. The reserve value related to the number of empty vehicles that should be present in each station is equal to 2 vehicles. We should note that we supposed that the battery would make the vehicles run for 40 min before to be needed to recharge it [4]. Results are presented in Table 1. Table 1 presents the percentage of empty movements as well as the full movement (movement of a vehicles with passengers) of the total movement of vehicles in the system. We also present the mean waiting time of passengers for each scenario in minutes (Min). We should note that the waiting time of a passengers is the difference between the arrival time of the passengers to their arrival station and the time of the fulfillment of their demand.

Results shows the good performance of our decentralized strategy as we found a mean waiting time of 3.847 min and a mean empty movement of 47.677 % which means that the vehicles move in 47.677 % empty without taking passengers.

5 Conclusions

In this study, a multi-agent system model is proposed for the PRT system. Unlike the majority of the previous studies, a decentralized management strategy with complex relationships between the different agents is proposed. This study differs from the previous studies for PRT in that it considers stations as an autonomous agent as well as battery issues within a multi agent simulation model. The validity and reliability of the proposed model are evaluated through simulation experiments by using a real world application related to an urban use case from the United Kingdom.

The next step of this study is to integrate the proposed model within a decision support system related to PRT in order to evaluate the best strategy among many others for the system. In future studies, the effect of other external factors on the performance of the different agents could be studied Finally, the development of learning algorithms for the stations and vehicles agents could be a promising field of study.

References

1. Avci, M.G., Selim, H.: A multi-agent system model for supply chains with lateral preventive transshipments: application in a multi-national automotive supply chain. Comput. Ind. **82**, 28–39 (2016)

---

[1] ATS/CityMobil PRT source: http://www.ultraprt.com/prt/implementation/simulation/.

2. Chebbi, O., Chaouachi, J.: Modeling on-demand transit transportation system using an agent-based approach. In: Saeed, K., Homenda, W. (eds.) CISIM 2015. LNCS, vol. 9339, pp. 316–326. Springer, Cham (2015). doi:10.1007/978-3-319-24369-6_26

3. Chebbi, O., Chaouachi, J.: Optimal fleet sizing of personal rapid transit system. In: Saeed, K., Homenda, W. (eds.) CISIM 2015. LNCS, vol. 9339, pp. 327–338. Springer, Cham (2015). doi:10.1007/978-3-319-24369-6_27

4. Chebbi, O., Chaouachi, J.: Reducing the wasted transportation capacity of personal rapid transit systems: an integrated model and multi-objective optimization approach. Transp. Res. Part E Logistics Transp. Rev. (2015)

5. Chebbi, O., Chaouachi, J.: A decentralized management approach for on-demand transit transportation system. In: Abraham, A., Wegrzyn-Wolska, K., Hassanien, A.E., Snasel, V., Alimi, A.M. (eds.) Proceedings of the Second International Afro-European Conference for Industrial Advancement AECIA 2015. AISC, vol. 427, pp. 175–184. Springer, Cham (2016). doi:10.1007/978-3-319-29504-6_18

6. Daszczuk, W.B., Mieścicki, J., Grabski, W.: Distributed algorithm for empty vehicles management in personal rapid transit (PRT) network. J. Adv. Transp. **50**, 608–629 (2016)

7. Fatnassi, E., Chebbi, O., Chaouachi, J.: Discrete honeybee mating optimization algorithm for the routing of battery-operated automated guidance electric vehicles in personal rapid transit systems. Swarm Evol. Comput. (2015)

8. Fatnassi, E., Chebbi, O., Siala, J.C.: Evaluation of different vehicle management strategies for the personal rapid transit system. In: 2013 5th International Conference on Modeling, Simulation and Applied Optimization (ICMSAO), pp. 1–5. IEEE (2013)

9. Fatnassi, E., Chebbi, O., Siala, J.C.: Two strategies for real time empty vehicle redistribution for the personal rapid transit system. In: 2013 16th International IEEE Conference on Intelligent Transportation Systems-(ITSC), pp. 1888–1893. IEEE (2013)

10. Fatnassi, E., Chebbi, O., Siala, J.C.: Comparison of two mathematical formulations for the offline routing of personal rapid transit system vehicles. In: 2014 19th International Conference on Methods and Models in Automation and Robotics (MMAR), pp. 554–559. IEEE (2014)

11. Jennings, N.R.: On agent-based software engineering. Artif. Intell. **117**(2), 277–296 (2000). http://www.sciencedirect.com/science/article/pii/S0004370299001071

12. Lees-Miller, J.D.: Empty vehicle redistribution for personal rapid transit. Ph.D. thesis, Liverpool John Moores University (2011)

13. Moyaux, T., Chaib-Draa, B., D'Amours, S.: Supply chain management and multiagent systems: an overview. In: Chaib-draa, B., Müller, J.P. (eds.) Multiagent based supply chain management, vol. 28, pp. 1–27. Springer, Heidelberg (2006)

14. Mueller, K., Sgouridis, S.P.: Simulation-based analysis of personal rapid transit systems: service and energy performance assessment of the masdar city prt case. J. Adv. Transp. **45**(4), 252–270 (2011)

15. Wen, G., Zhao, Y., Duan, Z., Yu, W., Chen, G.: Containment of higher-order multi-leader multi-agent systems: a dynamic output approach. IEEE Trans. Autom. Control **61**(4), 1135–1140 (2016)

16. Zheng, H., Peeta, S.: Network design for personal rapid transit under transit-oriented development. Transp. Res. Part C Emerg. Technol. **55**, 351–362 (2015)

Fractional-Order Linear Systems Modeling in Time and Frequency Domains

Wiktor Jakowluk[(✉)]

Faculty of Computer Science, Bialystok University of Technology,
Wiejska 45a, 15-351 Bialystok, Poland
w.jakowluk@pb.edu.pl
http://wi.pb.edu.pl/pracownicy/

Abstract. Non-integer order calculus is a very helpful tool, which is used in modeling and control applications. Many real processes display fractional order dynamics and their behavior is described by fractional-order differential equation. In this paper we quantify fitting the Oustaloup filter to the approximated transfer functions for given non-integer systems. The goal of this paper is to verify the accuracy of the Outsaloup filter to the fractional inertial system parameter approximation in a specified narrow frequency range and order. The pertinence of the compared models, in both time and frequency domains, is verified. Finally, the approximated model can be used to design the fractional order differentiation operator in an integer order state-space form. The presented methodology could be utilised for a general class of systems and is illustrated using numerical examples.

Keywords: Fractional calculus · Oustaloup filter · Fractional dynamic systems · Parameter estimation

1 Introduction

Fractional-order calculus was not especially popular in previous decades when its concepts have a lot of attention in various scientific fields, including more accurate system modeling and automatic control assignment [1, 2]. Utilising the notion of non-integer order should be more appropriate step because real-life processes appear to be fractional [3, 4]. The fractional-order calculus is the generalisation of the classical calculus, where the order of integration and differentiation is not an integer index [5]. There have been some reports on non-integer calculus, applied to various areas of the applications, e.g.: bioengineering [6], physics [7, 8], chaos theory [9], control systems [1, 10, 11] and fractional signal processing [12, 13].

It is clear that the rise of interest in the fractional calculus domain is related to the increasing availability of high-performance and advanced computational tools. Fractional order calculus was applied in robotics and automation, taking into account system identification and automatic control [2]. The control performance assessment has a large influence on the economic aspect of the real-life processes. It was reported that conventional PID controller, in industrial applications, is worse than fractional order PID controller according to the tuning flexibility [14].

© IFIP International Federation for Information Processing 2017
Published by Springer International Publishing AG 2017. All Rights Reserved
K. Saeed et al. (Eds.): CISIM 2017, LNCS 10244, pp. 502–513, 2017.
DOI: 10.1007/978-3-319-59105-6_43

For fractional order system analysis one of existing packages for non-integer order modeling and controller synthesis tasks, such as CRONE, Ninteger or FOMCON [15], can be employed. Above packages are implemented in Matlab environment and have effective tools for solving various fractional order problems and can be easily connected with other Matlab facilities (e.g. simulation of models in Simulink environment utilising graphical interface).

The non-integer order differentiation is equivalent to infinite dimensional filter that is why the selection of appropriate approximation factors is very important. The goal of this study is to verify fitting the Outsaloup filter to the fractional inertial model approximation in a specified narrow frequency range. The proper Oustaloup's approximation could be then used for modelling the non-integer order differentiation operator in an integer order state-space form. The fractional order control problem would be then reformulated to solve optimal input signal design task [16, 17]. For non-integer order system modeling in frequency and time domains the Fomcon toolbox was utilised [15].

2 Fractional Calculus

The idea of the differentiation operator is a fundamental tool in the study of the ordinary differential equations. Fractional calculus is a special case of integration and differentiation to non-integer order operator $_aD_t^\alpha$ as follows:

$$_aD_t^\alpha = \begin{cases} \frac{d^\alpha}{dt^\alpha} & \Re(\alpha) > 0 \\ 1 & \Re(\alpha) = 0, \\ \int\limits_a^t (d\tau)^{-\alpha} & \Re(\alpha) < 0 \end{cases} \tag{1}$$

where: a, t - denote the limits of the process and α is the set for all complex numbers.

There are different definitions of the fractional derivative operator [1].

The Riemann-Liouville fractional derivative ($\alpha > 0$) of a function $f(t)$ is defined as:

$$_aD_t^\alpha f(t) = \frac{d^\alpha f(t)}{dt^\alpha} = \frac{1}{\Gamma(m-\alpha)} \left(\frac{d}{dt}\right)^m \int\limits_a^t \frac{f(\tau)}{(t-\tau)^{\alpha+1-m}} d\tau, \tag{2}$$

where: $\Gamma(\cdot)$ stands for Euler's gamma function and $m - 1 < \alpha \le m, m \in \mathbb{N}$, for $\alpha \in (0, 1)$. Such a definition can also be reformulated to fractional-order derivative in the form:

$$_aD_t^\alpha f(t) = \frac{d^\alpha f(t)}{dt^\alpha} = \frac{1}{\Gamma(1-\alpha)} \frac{d}{dt} \int\limits_a^t \frac{f(\tau)}{(t-\tau)^\alpha} d\tau, \tag{3}$$

The Laplace transform of the Riemann-Liouville derivative (2) for $a = 0$ is:

$$L\{_0D_t^\alpha f(t)\} = s^\alpha F(s) - \sum_{k=1}^{m} s^{k-1} f^{(a-k)}(0^+), \tag{4}$$

where: $F(s) = L\{f(t)\}$.

The Caputo's definition of fractional-order derivative ($\alpha > 0$) is defined as follows:

$$_aD_t^\alpha f(t) = \frac{d^\alpha f(t)}{dt^\alpha} = \frac{1}{\Gamma(m-\alpha)} \int_0^t \frac{f^{(p)}(\tau)}{(t-\tau)^{\alpha+1-m}} d\tau, \tag{5}$$

where: $f^{(m)}(t) = (d^m/dt^m)f(t)$, $m-1 < \alpha \leq m$. This definition for $\alpha \in (0, 1)$ can be reformulated to fractional-order derivative in the following form:

$$_aD_t^\alpha f(t) = \frac{d^\alpha f(t)}{dt^\alpha} = \frac{1}{\Gamma(1-\alpha)} \int_0^t \frac{f(\tau)}{(t-\tau)^\alpha} d\tau. \tag{6}$$

The Laplace transform of the Caputo derivative (5) for $a = 0$ is:

$$L\{_0D_t^\alpha f(t)\} = s^\alpha F(s) - \sum_{k=1}^{m} s^{\alpha-k} f^{(k-1)}(0^+). \tag{7}$$

It was reported that for real functions, the fractional-order derivative from the Riemann-Liouville and Grünwald-Letnikov definitions are identical [10].

Finally, the Grünwald-Letnikov definition would be considered:

$$_aD_t^\alpha f(t) = \lim_{h \to 0} \frac{1}{h^\alpha} \sum_{j=0}^{k} (-1)^j \binom{\alpha}{j} f(t-jh), \tag{8}$$

where: $\omega_j^\alpha = (-1)^j \binom{\alpha}{j}$ describes polynomial factors, which can be received recursively from:

$$\omega_0^\alpha = 1, \omega_j^\alpha = \left(1 - \frac{\alpha+1}{j}\right) \omega_{j-1}^\alpha, j = 1, 2, \ldots, \tag{9}$$

Utilising Eq. (9) the fractional-order derivative (8) can be suitably modified as:

$$_aD_t^\alpha f(t) \approx \frac{1}{h^\alpha} \sum_{j=0}^{k} \omega_j^\alpha f(t-jh), \tag{10}$$

where $a = 0$, $t = kh$ is the step number and h is the step duration. The Laplace transform assuming zero initial conditions of derivative (8) with $\alpha \in R^+$ is as follows [1]:

$$L\{_0D_t^{\alpha}f(t)\} = s^{\alpha}F(s). \tag{11}$$

Linear fractional-order continuous-time SISO dynamic system can be expressed by a fractional-order differential equation [1, 2]:

$$\sum_{k=0}^{n} a_k D_t^{\alpha_i} y(t) = \sum_{k=0}^{m} b_k D_t^{\beta_i} u(t), \tag{12}$$

where: a_k, b_k are real numbers. The discrete-time version for various orders one can find in [18]. Applying the Laplace transform to (12) with zero initial conditions the input-output description of the fractional-order system can be expressed in the transfer function form:

$$G(s) = \frac{Y(s)}{U(s)} = \frac{b_m s^{\beta_m} + b_{m-1} s^{\beta_{m-1}} + \ldots + b_0 s^{\beta_0}}{a_n s^{\alpha_n} + a_{n-1} s^{\alpha_{n-1}} + \ldots + a_0 s^{\alpha_0}}. \tag{13}$$

The transfer function (13) is commensurate order if all orders of the fractional operator s are integer multiples of base order q in such a way: $q \in R^+$, $0 < q < 1$, $\alpha_k, \beta_k = kq$. The above continuous-time transfer function can be modified to give to the pseudo-rational function $H(\lambda)$ in the form:

$$H(\lambda) = \frac{\displaystyle\sum_{k=0}^{m} b_k \lambda^k}{\displaystyle\sum_{k=0}^{n} a_k \lambda^k}, \tag{14}$$

where: $\lambda = s^q$. Using the pseudo-rational notation a fractional-order linear time-invariant system can be easily expressed by a state-space model given by:

$$\begin{aligned}
_0D_t^{\alpha} x(t) &= Ax(t) + Bu(t), \\
y(t) &= Cx(t) + Du(t).
\end{aligned} \tag{15}$$

For system parameters identification purposes the difference equation representing input-output dynamic of the system is more convenient than the state-space description. However the state-space model notation provides of multiple input and multiple output (MIMO) fractional-order systems representation.

3 Oustaloup Filter to Approximation of Fractional-Order Operators

The potentiality of approximating the fractional-order plant model by an integer-order one is presented in [1]. For linear fractional-order model identification purposes the Oustaloup filter method, which is often used in practical applications, should be considered. We focus our attention on the classical Oustaloup approximation algorithm.

To solve the problem of approximation of a fractional differentiator or a fractional integrator the following equations should be used:

$$s^{\alpha} \approx K \prod_{k=1}^{N} \frac{s + \omega_k'}{s + \omega_k},$$ (16)

where: poles, zeros and gain of the filter can be obtained from:

$$\omega_k' = \omega_b \cdot \omega_u^{(2k-1-\alpha)/N},$$ (17)

$$\omega_k = \omega_b \cdot \omega_u^{(2k-1+\alpha)/N},$$ (18)

$$K = \omega_h^{\alpha},$$ (19)

$$\omega_u = \sqrt{\frac{\omega_h}{\omega_b}},$$ (20)

where: N is the order of approximation and (ω_b, ω_h) is the expected frequency fitting range. The order of the resulting filter is $2N + 1$, taking into account a higher orders of N the resulting approximation should be more accurate.

The Oustaloup filter provides very good approximation results of fractional operators in an expected fitting range and a wide orders interval. Thus, for the fractional order operators where $\alpha \geq 1$ the following equation should be adopted:

$$s^{\alpha} = s^n s^{\gamma},$$ (21)

where: $n = \alpha - \gamma$ indicates the integer part of α and s^{γ} is evaluated according to (16) utilising Oustaloup filter method.

4   Problem Formulation

To illustrate the properties of the above approach to fractional-order system parameter estimation, using the Oustaloup filter, we have selected FOMCON toolbox, which provides time-domain and frequency-domain non-integer order system analysis, as well as system stability checking [15]. The goal of this study is to verify the accuracy of the Oustaloup filter to the fractional inertial system transfer function parameters estimation in a specified frequency range $\omega = [\omega_b, \omega_h]$ and order of the filter $2N + 1$.

To justify the idea of this approach to integer model parameter estimation, an inertial object was selected as:

$$G(s) = \frac{k}{s^{\alpha}T + 1}, \quad \alpha > 0.$$ (22)

The fractional-order linear time invariant system can be then described by the following single input, single output state-space model:

$$_0D_t^\alpha x(t) = Ax(t) + Bu(t),$$
$$y(t) = x(t),$$
(23)

with assumed values of the matrix parameters: $A = -1$, $B = 1$ and zero initial conditions. The specified wide bandwidth would cause a large computational burden as N is increased. Therefore, the choice of N is based on following rule:

$$N = \log(\omega_h) - \log(\omega_b).$$
(24)

The results of the Oustaloup filter approximation of the fractional transfer function (22) for different values α from the interval $0.5 \leq \alpha \leq 1.9$ and arbitrary selected bandwidth $\omega = [10^{-1}, 10^1]$ with $N = 2$ according to (24), are displayed by transfer functions $G_o(s)$ given by:

$$G(s) = \frac{1}{s^{0.5}+1}, \quad G_o(s) = \frac{0.24s^5 + 3.14s^4 + 11.5s^3 + 14.48s^2 + 6.26s + 0.76}{s^5 + 9.4s^4 + 25.98s^3 + 25.98s^2 + 9.4s + 1},$$
(25)

$$G(s) = \frac{1}{s^{0.7}+1}, \quad G_o(s) = \frac{0.17s^5 + 2.38s^4 + 9.57s^3 + 13.21s^2 + 6.27s + 0.83}{s^5 + 8.65s^4 + 22.78s^3 + 22.78s^2 + 8.65s + 1},$$
(26)

$$G(s) = \frac{1}{s^{0.99}+1}, \quad G_o(s) = \frac{0.09s^5 + 1.52s^4 + 6.97s^3 + 11.01s^2 + 5.97s + 0.91}{s^5 + 7.49s^4 + 17.99s^3 + 17.99s^2 + 7.49s + 1},$$
(27)

$$G(s) = \frac{1}{s^{1.3}+1}, \quad G_o(s) = \frac{0.50s^5 + 5.97s^4 + 19.95s^3 + 22.91s^2 + 9.04s + 1}{s^6 + 9.54s^5 + 22.88s^4 + 39.91s^3 + 28.88s^2 + 9.54s + 1},$$
(28)

$$G(s) = \frac{1}{s^{1.5}+1}, \quad G_o(s) = \frac{0.32s^5 + 4.13s^4 + 15.14s^3 + 19.05s^2 + 8.24s + 1}{s^6 + 8.56s^5 + 23.19s^4 + 30.27s^3 + 23.19s^2 + 8.56s + 1},$$
(29)

$$G(s) = \frac{1}{s^{1.7}+1}, \quad G_o(s) = \frac{0.20s^5 + 2.86s^4 + 11.48s^3 + 15.85s^2 + 7.52s + 1}{s^6 + 7.72s^5 + 18.71s^4 + 22.96s^3 + 18.71s^2 + 7.72s + 1},$$
(30)

$$G(s) = \frac{1}{s^{1.9}+1}, \quad G_o(s) = \frac{0.02s^5 + 1.97s^4 + 49.18s^3 + 289.6s^2 + 402.9s + 112.2}{s^6 + 35.9s^5 + 260s^4 + 487.5s^3 + 465.4s^2 + 417s + 112.2}.$$
(31)

As it can be seen the resulting filters can be displayed in the Laplace domain, as reasonable approximations of the non-integer order operators. Additionally, this method exhibit practical property: it has zeros and poles interlaced on the negative real axis of the s plane, and the length between following poles and zeros decreases as the estimation is improved by increasing the order of the polynomials' numerator and denominator, as it is displayed in Fig. 6.

5   The Experimental Results for Time and Frequency Domains

The time-domain simulation of the evaluated model of the fractional system, utilising step input signal, is based on the Grünwald-Letnikov definition shown in Eq. (8). The solution of the numerical problem (22) is performed utilising modified Grünwald-Letnikov definition [2]:

$$
y_t = \frac{1}{\sum\limits_{i=0}^{n} \frac{a_i}{h^{\alpha_i}}} \left[u_t - \sum_{i=0}^{n} \frac{a_i}{h^{\alpha_i}} \sum_{j=1}^{t/h} \omega_j^{(\alpha_j)} y_{t-jh} \right],
\tag{32}
$$

where $h = 0.01$ is the numerical step-size. The frequency-domain simulation is executed by replacing $s = j\omega$. This substitution was applied to Eqs. (25), (27), (29–31) to obtain frequency domain diagrams. In order to verify the stability of the approximated

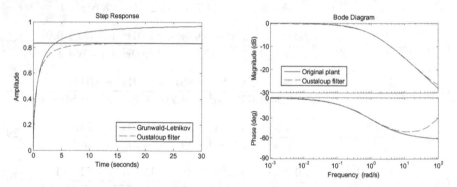

Fig. 1. Step and frequency responses comparison for inertial ($\alpha = 0.5$) system

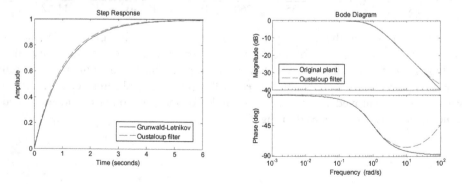

Fig. 2. Step and frequency responses comparison for inertial ($\alpha = 0.99$) system

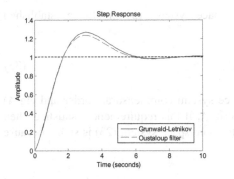
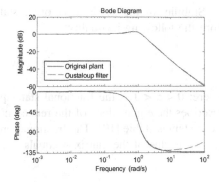

Fig. 3. Step and frequency responses comparison for inertial ($\alpha = 1.5$) system

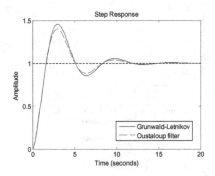
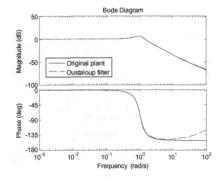

Fig. 4. Step and frequency responses comparison for inertial ($\alpha = 1.7$) system

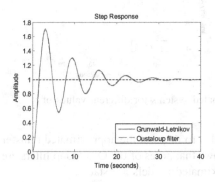
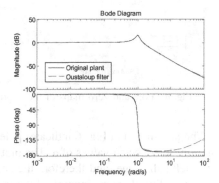

Fig. 5. Step and frequency responses comparison for inertial ($\alpha = 1.9$) system

systems we obtained a step responses (at $t = [0, t_{end}]$ with $dt = 0.1$) and Bode diagrams (for frequency axis range $\omega = [10^{-3}, 10^2]$ and $N = 2$) shown in Figs. 1, 2, 3, 4 and 5.

The Figs. 1, 2, 3, 4 and 5 show the Oustaloup filter step responses compared with the exact fractional inertial model step responses and frequency plots (Bode diagrams) of the real plant and obtained approximations.

Stability of the non-integer order state-space system (15) should be established from the following inequality:

$$|\arg(\text{eig}(A))| > \alpha\frac{\pi}{2}, \tag{33}$$

where: $0 < \alpha < 1$ is the fractional state-space system commensurate order and $\text{eig}(A)$ describes the eigenvalues of the related matrix A. If this requirement is satisfied, then the system is stable [19]. The fractional order state-space system (23) is stable because the eigenvalue of the matrix A equals -1.

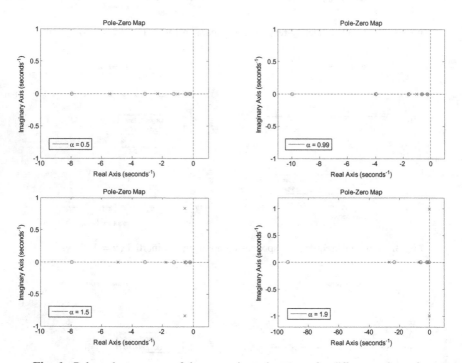

Fig. 6. Pole and zero maps of the approximated systems for different values of α

The plot shown in Fig. 6 indicates pole and zero maps of the approximated transfer functions for selected values of α. The plot shows that poles of the Oustaloup filters are in the left half-plane, and therefore the approximated models are stable.

The quality of approximation of the fractional inertial system in the response space can be expressed by following errors and factors:

$$\Delta y^{(w)} = |y - \breve{y}|, \tag{34}$$

$$e^{(w)} = \frac{\Delta y}{|y|} \cdot 100\% \,;\, y \neq 0, \tag{35}$$

$$M = \sqrt{\frac{1}{n}\sum_{w=1}^{n}(\Delta y)^2}, \tag{36}$$

$$R^2 = \frac{\sum_{w=1}^{n}\left[\bar{y}^{(w)} - \bar{y}\right]^2}{\sum_{w=1}^{n}\left[y^{(w)} - \bar{y}\right]^2}, \tag{37}$$

Table 1. The comparision of the approximation errors and factors.

α	0.5	0.7	0.9	1.0	1.1	1.3	1.5	1.7	1.9
$\Delta y_{min}^{(w)}$	0.016	0.013	0.008	0.000	0.000	0.000	0.000	0.000	0.000
$\Delta y_{max}^{(w)}$	0.139	0.133	0.106	0.018	0.017	0.020	0.035	0.060	0.080
$e_{min}^{(w)}$ [%]	3.26	4.50	3.83	0.00	0.00	0.00	0.04	0.00	0.00
$e_{avg}^{(w)}$ [%]	11.13	11.02	9.72	0.25	0.55	0.75	0.68	0.93	0.97
$e_{max}^{(w)}$ [%]	15.48	13.77	10.70	4.45	6.04	4.99	6.71	7.43	7.59
M	0.101	0.106	0.096	0.004	0.006	0.009	0.010	0.017	0.018
R^2	0.942	0.973	0.995	0.999	0.999	0.998	0.997	0.996	0.965

where $\Delta y^{(w)}$, $e^{(w)}$, M and R^2 are respectively: absolute error, relative error, root-mean-square error and coefficient of determination. The comparison of the performance indices for Oustaloup filter approximation are displayed in Table 1.

The estimated transfer functions parameters and obtained indices show high accuracy of the Oustaloup filter approximation. The slight fitting errors could be observed in the range of fractional order from the interval $0.9 \leq \alpha \leq 1.7$.

In some applications, a zero-pole transfer functions (25–31) as a result of fractional order systems approximation are not helpful. Instead of this, the state-space realisation (23) is desirable. The examples of the approximated integer order state-space matrices for $\alpha = 0.5$ and $\alpha = 1.5$ are given by:

$$\check{A} = \begin{bmatrix} -9.4 & -26.0 & -26.0 & -9.4 & -1.0 \\ 1.0 & 0 & 0 & 0 & 0 \\ 0 & 1.0 & 0 & 0 & 0 \\ 0 & 0 & 1.0 & 0 & 0 \\ 0 & 0 & 0 & 1.0 & 0 \end{bmatrix}, \check{B} = \begin{bmatrix} 1 \\ 0 \\ 0 \\ 0 \\ 0 \end{bmatrix}, \check{C} = [0.9 \ \ 5.3 \ \ 8.2 \ \ 4.0 \ \ 0.5], \check{D} = [0.2],$$

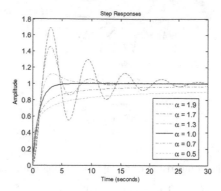

Fig. 7. Step responses comparison for inertial system with different order values α

$$\tilde{A} = \begin{bmatrix} -8.6 & -23.2 & -30.3 & -23.2 & -8.6 & -1.0 \\ 1.0 & 0 & 0 & 0 & 0 & 0 \\ 0 & 1.0 & 0 & 0 & 0 & 0 \\ 0 & 0 & 1.0 & 0 & 0 & 0 \\ 0 & 0 & 0 & 1.0 & 0 & 0 \\ 0 & 0 & 0 & 0 & 1.0 & 0 \end{bmatrix}, \tilde{B} = \begin{bmatrix} 1 \\ 0 \\ 0 \\ 0 \\ 0 \\ 0 \end{bmatrix}, \tilde{C} = [0.3 \quad 4.1 \quad 15.1 \quad 19.0 \quad 8.2 \quad 1.0].$$

A step responses of the fractional inertial system (22) in the time duration $t = [0, 30]$ seconds with a step size of $h = 0.01$ are obtained utilising the Grünwald-Letnikov method (32). The step responses for $\alpha \leq 1$ are aperiodic (Fig. 7), however conventional first order inertial system step response can be observed for $\alpha = 1$. The step responses are oscillating for non-integer system orders $\alpha \geq 1$.

6   Conclusions

In this paper the accuracy of the approximation of the Outsaloup filter yielding transfer functions for a given fractional-order inertial model have been verified. The results of the Oustaloup filter approximation of the non-integer inertial model for different values α from the interval $0.5 \leq \alpha \leq 1.9$ and arbitrary selected narrow bandwidth $\omega = [10^{-1}, 10^1]$ was presented. The simulation results in time and frequency domains confirm high accuracy of the Oustaloup estimation to the selected frequency range and order. The comparison of the performance indices for the Oustaloup approximation model and original plant shows a slight fitting errors for fractional order from the interval $0.9 \leq \alpha \leq 1.8$. The pole and zero diagrams show that for different values of α, obtained integer order models are stable. The choice of the approximation method depends on established requirements (e.g. accurate frequency behavior or precise time response). The proper Oustaloup's approximation can be utilised for modelling the fractional order operator in an integer order state-space form. Then, it is possible to use one of the existing optimal control packages to solve fractional order optimal input problem.

Acknowledgment. The present study was supported by a grant S/WI/1/13 from Bialystok University of Technology and founded from resources for research by Ministry of Science and Higher Education.

References

1. Monje, C.A., Chen, Y., Vinagre, B., Xue, D., Feliu, V.: Fractional-Order Systems and Controls: Fundamentals and Applications. Advances in Industrial Control. Springer, London (2010)
2. Chen, Y.Q., Petráš, I., Xue, D.: Fractional order control - a tutorial. In: Proceedings of American Control Conference, ACC 2009, pp. 1397–1411 (2009)
3. Torvik, P.J., Bagley, R.L.: On the appearance of the fractional derivative in the behaviour of real materials. Trans. ASME **51**(4), 294–298 (1984)
4. Oustaloup, A., Levron, F., Mathieu, B., Nanot, F.: Frequency-band complex noninteger differentiator: characterization and synthesis. IEEE Trans. Circ. Syst. Fundam. Theory Appl. **47**(1), 25–40 (2000)
5. Miller, K., Ross, B.: An Introduction to the Fractional Calculus and Fractional Differential Equations. Wiley, New York (1993)
6. Magin, R.L.: Fractional Calculus in Bioengineering. Begell House Publishers, Redding (2006)
7. Hilfer, R.: Applications of Fractional Calculus in Physics. World Scientific, Singapore (2000)
8. West, B., Bologna, M., Grigolini, P.: Physics of Fractal Operators. Springer, New York (2003)
9. Petras, I.: Fractional-Order Nonlinear Systems. Springer, New York (2011)
10. Podlubny, I.: Fractional Differential Equations. Academic Press, San Diego (1999)
11. Valério, D., Costa, J.: An Introduction to Fractional Control. IET, London (2013)
12. Sheng, H., Chen, Y.D., Qiu, T.S.: Fractional Processes and Fractional-Order Signal Processing. Springer, London (2012)
13. Mozyrska, D., Torres, D.F.M.: Modified optimal energy and initial memory of fractional continuous-time linear systems. Sig. Process. **91**(3), 379–385 (2011). Special Issue: SI
14. Monje, C., Vinagre, B., Feliu, V., Chen, Y.: Tuning and auto-tuning of fractional order controllers for industry applications. Control Eng. Pract. **16**(7), 798–812 (2008)
15. Tepljakov, A., Petlenkov, E., Belikov, J.: FOMCON: a MATLAB toolbox for fractional-order system identification and control. Int. J. Microelectron. Comput. Sci. **2**(2), 51–62 (2011)
16. Jakowluk, W.: Plant friendly input design for parameter estimation in an inertial system with respect to D-efficiency constraints. Entropy **16**(11), 5822–5837 (2014)
17. Jakowluk, W.: Optimal input signal design for a second order dynamic system identification subject to D-efficiency constraints. In: Saeed, K., Homenda, W. (eds.) CISIM 2015. LNCS, vol. 9339, pp. 351–362. Springer, Cham (2015). doi:10.1007/978-3-319-24369-6_29
18. Mozyrska, D.: Multiparameter fractional difference linear control systems. Discrete Dyn. Nat. Soc. **2014**, 8 (2014)
19. Matignon, D.: Generalized fractional differential and difference equations: stability properties and modeling issues. In: Proceedings of Mathematical Theory of Networks and Systems Symposium, pp. 503–506 (1998)

Maximization of Attractiveness EV Tourist Routes

Joanna Karbowska-Chilinska$^{(\boxtimes)}$ (iD) and Pawel Zabielski (iD)

Faculty of Computer Science, Bialystok University of Technology, Białystok, Poland
`j.karbowska@pb.edu.pl`

Abstract. This paper presents model and an algorithmic approach for the problem of generation optimal tourist route for electric vehicles (EVs). In the discussed problem a starting and a final point of a route are EV charging stations where tourist could charge the battery and then continue a journey. The main objective is to select to the route points of interests (POIs) which maximizing tourist attractiveness. Furthermore maximum length of the route is limited by the number of kilometers that the car can travel on a single battery charge. The model applied by us is the graph routing problem named as the Orienteering Problem with Time Windows (OPTW). In OPTW each location has positive score and a specific time interval in which a location can be visited. The solution of OPTW is a route (from the given starting to the ending point) with a fixed limit of length including a subset of locations. Moreover the route maximizes the total score of the locations visited in the predefined time intervals. As a solution we present the evolutionary algorithm with combines path relinking method instead crossover. Computational experiments are conducted on realistic database POIs and EV charging stations of Podlasie region in Poland. Tests results and execution time of the algorithm shows that the described solution could be a part of EV software module with generates the most interesting route.

Keywords: Orienteering problem with time windows · Tourist trip generation · Electric vehicles · Evolutionary algorithm

1 Introduction

Nowadays carbon dioxide emissions have rapidly increased due to cities development and population growth. Transport has a high negative impact, on the environment degradation. In this reason in last years Green Logistics (GL) has received increasing attention in business as well as in a research field [3]. The main goals of GL are: maximum utilization of means of transport, development of green intelligent transportation systems which reduces the energy consumption, promotion of alternative fuels and vehicles with electric engines. Environmental aspects has been included to the optimization problem of vehicle routing problems (VRP) and also green vehicle routing problem is developed (G-VRP) [13].

© IFIP International Federation for Information Processing 2017
Published by Springer International Publishing AG 2017. All Rights Reserved
K. Saeed et al. (Eds.): CISIM 2017, LNCS 10244, pp. 514–525, 2017.
DOI: 10.1007/978-3-319-59105-6_44

In modern transportation system the electrical vehicles (EVs) are beneficial to the environment. EVs are more silent in operation and emission free
compared to gasoline powered cars. However the driving range of a car depends
largely on the capacity of the battery. It is important constraint which affect into
routing planning for EVs. Batteries need to be charged a significant amount of
time extending the route time. Literature describes some problems such as Electric Vehicle Scheduling Problem (E-VSP) [23], Electric Vehicle Routing Problem (EVRP) [1], Electric Vehicles Routing problem with Time Windows and
Recharging Stations(E-VRPTW) [15] which solutions minimizing total traveled
distance and give possibility of recharging batteries.

In many touristic regions when clear air and national parks are important
e.g. US [5] (California, Arizona, Orlando), Europe (Goms and Haslital region of
the Swiss Alps [4]) the Electric Vehicle Tourism is popularized. Especially EV
rental cars services are developed in those touristic regions. Tourist that use EV
are satisfied when they could choose the most interesting POIs for each trip day
and have not to care about charging the battery. It is comfortable if the battery
charging can take place during e.g. an accommodation or the other break in a
tour. The opening and closing time assigned to each POIs is additional constraint
considered in a tour scheduling.

To the best our knowledge any web, mobile and cars applications (e.g. rang
assistant in BMW i3, EV TripPlanner for Tesla S users [6]) do not select the
set of POIs maximizing tourist satisfaction and taking into account the trip
constraints such as: driving range of a car battery as well as POIs visiting hours.

In this regard, this article presents the suitable model for the described problem. Moreover the effective evolutionary algorithm with path relinking instead
crossover developed by us in [12] is used to generate the most satisfying tourist
trip for EVs user with the aforementioned limitations. The graph optimisation
routing problem called Orienteering Problem with Time Windows (OPTW) [20]
is used by us as the model. The considered graph have vertices with assigned
score/profit which was interpreted by us as a vertex attractiveness.

An extension of OPTW is Team Orienteering Problem with Time Windows
(TOPTW) where the given number of optimal routes (the parameter m) are
generated, each one not exceeded the same constraint. Methods for the TOPTW
could also be applied to the OPTW because the solution OPTW is only one
optimal route ($m = 1$). Both these problems belongs to the class NP- hard [22]. In
literature there are many meta-heuristic approaches giving satisfactory solutions
e.g. local search methods [21], tabu search [19], ant colony optimisation [16],
variable neighbour search [14], evolitionary inspired algorithms [17].

The remainder of the paper is organized as follows. The OPTW problem
definition and its transformation to the problem of generation optimal tourist
routes of EVs are presented in Sect. 2. In Sect. 3, we describe the concept of our
evolutionary algorithm for solving the problem. The computational experiments
run on realistic database POIs and EV charging stations of Podlasie region in
Poland are discussed in Sect. 4. Finally the paper is concluded in Sect. 5. In this
section we also lay the groundwork for further research.

2   The Problem Definition

In this work the optimization of an EV tourist route is modeled by the known graph problem called OPTW [10,22]. In OPTW a set of the fixed locations is given. Each location i has a positive score S_i, which is added after the visit of the location and a visiting time T_i as well as a time window $[O_i, C_i]$, where O_i and C_i denote the opening and closing time, respectively. Service of a location must begin and end within this interval. It is permissible to wait before the opening time in order to visit profitable locations and maximize the total score. Each edge between locations i and j has a fixed cost t_{ij} which is interpreted as distance needed to travel between locations. The OPTW goal is to determine a single route from the fixed starting to the ending point, that visits some of vertices within the fixed time windows and maximizes the total score. Moreover, the total cost of the edges on the route must be less than the threshold t_{max}, and any vertex on the path can only be visited once. A feasible solution not violate any time window constraint on the fixed travel time limit (or travel length) of the route.

In the case of the optimization of a tourist route of EV the set A of n POI(s) and the set B of m EV charging stations are given. Each POI i has assigned interval $[O_i, C_i]$ in which a visit can last and the fixed visiting time T_i. The distances between each pair of POIs and each POI and EV charging station are denoted by t_{ij} for $i, j \in \{1, ..., n + m\}$. Each POI i has a score $S_i \geq 0$ interpreted as its attractiveness. The EV charging stations have profits equal to zero. Moreover t_{max}- the number of kilometers that the consider model of car can travel on a single battery charge is known. The starting and ending points, denoted by s and e respectively are selected among the points from the set B and their distance does not exceed the limit t_{max}. The optimization goal is the generation a route from starting to the ending point that maximizes the total collected score (connected with attractiveness of the route), each POI is visited at most once in the predefined time interval and the length of the route does not exceed the limit t_{max}. The problem can be formulate as a mixed integer problem with the decision variable: $x_{ij} = 1$ if the direct link between i and j is included in a route, and $x_{ij} = 0$ otherwise. Moreover $start_i$ denotes the start of service time at vertex i and M is a large constant.

The objective function (1) maximizes the total collected profit of the route:

$$max \sum_{i=1}^{n+m-1} \sum_{j=2}^{n+m} S_i x_{ij}. \tag{1}$$

The constraint in (2) guarantees that the path starts at vertex 1 and ends at vertex $n + m$:

$$\sum_{j=2}^{n+m} x_{1j} = \sum_{i=1}^{n+m-1} x_{in+m} = 1. \tag{2}$$

Constraint (3) requires that there may be at most one visit to any vertex:

$$\sum_{i=1}^{n+m-1} x_{ik} = \sum_{j=2}^{n+m} x_{kj} \leq 1 \quad \forall k \in \{2, ..., n+m-1\}. \tag{3}$$

The constraint in (4) ensures that the distance of the route is limited by t_{max}:

$$\sum_{i=1}^{n+m-1} \sum_{j=2}^{n+m} t_{ij} x_{ij} \leq t_{max}. \tag{4}$$

Constraint (5) ensures the timeline of the route:

$$start_i + T_i + t_{ij} - start_j \leq M \cdot (1 - x_{ij}). \tag{5}$$

The start of the service is restricted by a time window as in (6):

$$O_i \leq start_i \leq C_i \quad \forall i = 1, ..., n+m. \tag{6}$$

3   Evolutionary Algorithm

To solve the presented problem, the evolutionary algorithm (EA) is used, previously developed by us to solve OPTW [12]. The EA for OPTW gives about 2% better results in comparison to other metaheuristics like iterated local search or greedy randomized adaptive search procedure [12]. In this reason we decide to use EA also to solve the presented in this paper problem. In the algorithm instead of the crossover a path relinking (PR) strategy is used. PR starts from selecting initial and guiding solutions to represent the starting and the ending points of the route [7]. Attributes from the guiding solution are gradually introduced into the intermediate solutions, so that these solutions contain less characteristics from the initial solution and more from the guiding solution. As a result, the selective moves between initial and guiding solutions provide the better routes than the input routes. In the literature PR significantly improves the different metaheuristics solving different optimization problems e.g. greedy randomized adaptive search procedure (GRASP) [2], variable neighbor search (VNS) [18], genetic algorithms (GA) [8] and tabu search (TS) [9].

Let N_g denotes a number of the algorithm generations, P_{size} describes the number of routes in the initial population.

The basic structure of the EA is given as follows:

```
compute initial P_size routes;
  iter=0; not_imp=0; stop= false
while  (iter< Ng) and (stop =false) do
      iter++;
      evaluate the fitness value of each route;
      make a tournament grouping selection;
      perform path relinking;
```

```
        perform mutation;
        if no improvements in an attractiveness after 100 iterations
        then stop= true;

    od
    return the route with the highest profit value;
```

The subsequent steps of the EA are described in detail in the following subsections.

3.1   Initialization

In our approach a route is coded as a sequence of POIs but the starting (s) and ending (e) points are the fixed among EV charging stations. First the route is initialized by s and e stations. Then the following values are assigned sequentially to a POI selected to route: $arrival_i$ - arrival time at POI i, $wait_i$ - waiting time, if the arrival at a POI i is before opening time, $start_i$ and end_i - starting and ending service time at POI i. Moreover, the maximum time the a visit i can be delayed without making other visits infeasible is calculated for each POI in the route as follows [21]:

$$MaxShift_i = Min(C_i - start_i - T_i, wait_{i+1} + MaxShift_{i+1}) \qquad (7)$$

Let POI l be the predecessor of charging station e in the route. In the subsequent steps a set of POIs is included. Each location v from this set is adjacent to location l and the station e and will satisfy the following conditions after insertion: (a) $start_v$ and end_v are within the range $[O_v, C_v]$; (b) the locations after v could be visited in the route; and (c) the current travel length of the route does not exceed the given t_{max}. A random location v is chosen from this set. The values $arrival_v$, $wait_v$, $start_v$ and end_v are calculated and the location v is inserted. After the insertion, the values $arrival_e$, $wait_e$, $start_e$ and end_e are updated. Moreover, for each POI in the tour (from vertex e to s) the $MaxShift$ value is updated as well. The route generation is continued for as long as POIs that have not been included are present and t_{max} is not exceeded.

3.2   Selection

We use tournament grouping selection used by us in [24] and in [11]. This selection yields better adapted individuals than standard tournament selection. In this method a set of P_{size} routes is divided into k groups and the tournaments are carried out sequentially in each of the groups. t_{size} routes are removed from the group, the chromosome with the highest value for the fitness function in the form:

$$\frac{TotalProfit^3}{TravelTime} \qquad (8)$$

is copied to the next population, and the t_{size} previously chosen individuals are returned to the old group. $TotalProfit$ denotes sum of POI's profits in the route and $TravelTime$ is the time connected with the visit of the POI's as well as length of the route. After repetition of P_{size}/k selection from the group currently analyzed, P_{size}/k routes are chosen for a new population. Finally, when this step has been repeated in each of the remaining groups, a new population is created, containing P_{size} routes.

3.3 Path Relinking

In this paper PR is used by us as alternative to the crossover. The method was developed by us with good results on benchmarks in the case of OPTW solution in [12]. Let $V_{R_1-R_2}$ be the set of POIs present in a route R_1 and not presented in R_2, and let $V_{R_2-R_1}$ denotes the set of POIs present in R_2 and not in R_1. During $PR(R_1, R_2)$ we attempt to insert POIs from $V_{R_2-R_1}$ into R_1 in the best possible positions. The total consumption time associated with inserting a POI j between i and k is calculated in the following way:

$$Shift_j = t_{ij} + wait_j + T_j + t_{jk} - t_{ik}. \tag{9}$$

In addition, we check whether the shift resulting from the new insertion exceeds the constraints associated with the previously calculated $wait$ and $MaxShift$ values for the vertices located directly after the newly inserted one. If the shift exceeds the constraints the vertices from $V_{R_1-R_2}$ are removed to restore the possibility of inserting new POIs. For each vertex u from this set a ratio is calculated as follows:

$$RemovalRatio = \frac{(p_u)^2}{end_u - arrive_u}. \tag{10}$$

After this computation the POI with the smallest value for $RemovalRatio$ is removed. This removal is repeated until we can insert some vertices into the path. Finally the vertex u with the highest value:

$$InsertionRatio = \frac{(p_u)^2}{Shift_u} \tag{11}$$

is selected for insertion if not exceed the mentioned constraints. After u is inserted, the values of $arrive_u$, $wait_u$, $start_u$ and end_u are calculated. For each location in the route after u the arrival time, waiting time, start and end of service are updated. $MaxShift$ values are also updated for the locations from the starting point to the ending point of the route. The process is repeated for as long as t_{max} is not exceeded and the set $V_{R_2-R_1}$ is not empty. Similarly, $PR(R_2, R_1)$ is performed by inserting vertices from $V_{R_1-R_2}$ into R_2. In result two new routes are created. If the fitness values of the new routes are higher than the fitness value of R_1 and R_2, they replace them.

3.4   Mutation

In mutation phase a random route is selected from all routes. Two types of mutation are used by us – a gene insertion or gene removal (the probability of each is 0.5). The mutation process is repeated on the selected route N_m times, where N_m is the parameter of the algorithm. In *insertion mutation*, all possibilities for inclusion of each new POI not presented in the route are considered. We check whether the shift resulting from the new insertion exceeds the constraints associated with the previously calculated *wait* and *MaxShift* values of the POIs located directly after the newly inserted one. The location u with the highest value of $(p_u)^2/TravelTimeIncrease(u)$ is selected for insertion. $TravelTimeIncrease(u)$ is defined as the increased travel and visit time when POI u is included. After the insertion POI u into the route the values of $arrival_u$, $wait_u$, $start_u$ and end_u are calculated. For each location after u the arrival time, waiting time, start and end of service are updated. The *MaxShift* value is updated for each location in the tour.

In the *deletion mutation* we remove a randomly selected POI in order to shorten the travel length. After the gene is removed, all locations after the removed gene are shifted towards the beginning of the route. Furthermore, the locations before and after the removed POI should be updated.

4   Computational Experiment

The EA was implemented in C++ and run on an Intel Core i7, 1.73 GHz CPU (turbo boost to 2.93 GHz). The computational experiments were carried out on realistic database 531 POIs and EV charging stations Podlasie region (Poland). Each POI is specified by coordinates, profit (determined on the basis of the votes of Internet users on the given object), time window and visiting time (randomly assigned). Shortest car distance between each pair of POIs and between POIs and battery charging stations were determined on the basis of the queries to Bing Map Service (Routes API).

For comparison results we also tests another version of EA having crossover instead path relinking process. The version with crossover is denoted by EA CR and the version with path relinking by EA PR. In the crossover we selected two routes and in these routes we determine all genes which could be replaced without violating time windows conditions and the limit of route length. Finally a random pair is selected from all similar pairs of genes and this is a point of crossover. The new routes are created by exchange chromosome fragments from both parents from crossover point to the end of route.

Many tests were carried out to establish the evolutionary algorithms parameters and determine convergence and sensitivity. The parameter values which represent the best trade-off between the quality of the solutions and the computational time are as follows: the number of routes in the initial population- $P_{size} = 150$, the number of groups in the tournament selection- $k = 15$, the number of routes removed from the group $t_{size} = 10$, the mutation process is repeated on the selected route $N_m = 15$ times. In tests we take different limit of routes length (t_{max}) because of different number of kilometers possible to drive on a single battery charge (this value depends on an EV brand and do not exceed 500 km).

We recall that by the attractiveness we mean sum of scores connected with POI's included to the route. The attractiveness of routes balance (see Fig. 1) because of removing POI in deletion mutation. It can be notice that the attractiveness is not higher after 1000 iterations so the maximum number of algorithm generations was set to 1000. Additionally after each 100 generations the current population is checked and the algorithm is stopped if no improvements in attractiveness of route have been found.

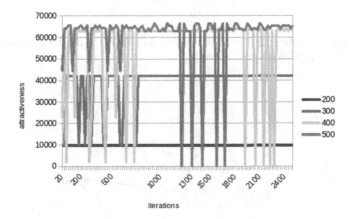

Fig. 1. Convergence of the GA PR for $t_{max}=$ 200-500 value

The comparison of the results according to the EA CR (the version with crossover) as well as EA PR (the version with the path relinking) are outlined in Tables 1 and 2. In tables the length is given in kilometers, execution time of the algorithm in seconds. The algorithm is run 15 times and in tables we place the best results from all runs. The execution time is calculated as a sum from 15 runs of algorithm. Results indicate that both algorithms give results in the comparable execution time (about 0.2 s). In the case when the starting and ending points are different (see Table 1) both versions give the same results in the length of route and attractiveness. The exception is $t_{max} = 300$ where EA PR gives better result in attractiveness than EA CR about 2%. When the starting and ending point is the same for $t_{max} = 400, 500$ (see Table 2) the length of routes is higher in case of EA PR than EA CR. However, in case of $t_{max} = 400$ for EA CR the attractiveness of a route is higher about 0.7% in comparison to EA PR. Both algorithms for $t_{max} = 200, 300$ give the same attractiveness and the length. For $t_{max} = 500$ results EA PR outperform EA CR about 0.1%. Figures 1 and 2 illustrate generated routes by EA PR marked on Podlasie region map. In figures green points denotes POIs and their size depend on POI attractiveness. The starting and ending points (battery charging stations) are blue (Fig. 3).

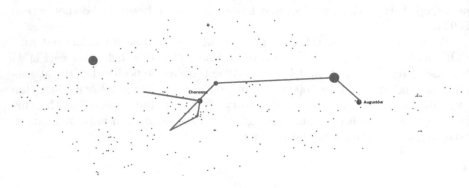

Fig. 2. EV route example: 1-352-24-370-56-344-441- 442-5-2 (the battery charging stations are different). (Color figure online)

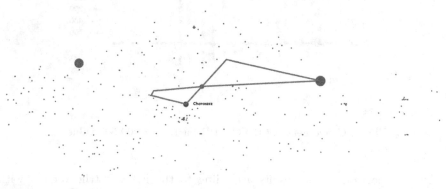

Fig. 3. EV route example:1-2-357-442-344-433-381- 431-23-1. (the battery charging station is the same) (Color figure online)

Table 1. Comparison EA CR and EA PR routes (starting and ending charge stations are different)

t_{max}	EA CR			EA PR		
	Length	Attractiveness	Time	Length	Attractiveness	Time
200	198.970	1427	0.164	198.970	1427	0.168
300	287.640	42629	0.154	296.420	43497	0.159
400	393.224	51206	0.177	393.224	51206	0.174
500	499.152	65460	0.221	499.152	65460	0.187

Table 2. Comparison EA CR and EA PR routes (the starting and the ending charge station is the same)

t_{max}	EA CR			EA PR		
	Length	Attractiveness	Time	Length	Attractiveness	Time
200	198.324	9695	0.165	198.324	9695	0.164
300	285.147	42103	0.166	285.147	42103	0.160
400	382.272	64014	0.171	386.839	63569	0.171
500	488.931	66411	0.193	497.797	66466	0.209

5   Conclusions and Further Work

In this paper we describe the problem of generation EV tourist routes which maximizing the attractiveness of a trip and the length do not exceeded the number of kilometers that a car can travel on a single battery charge. The problem is transformed to the graph routing problem named the Orienteering Problem with Time Windows. The evolutionary algorithm is presented by us as the solution of the problem. The tests on the real dates show that two versions of algorithm generate routes with similar attractiveness. The execution time of the algorithm is relatively short to use them in practice.

Modern electric vehicles like BMWi3, Tesla S have navigation system to make driving easy and convenient. For example the range assistant with dynamic range map indicate the maximum distance that the vehicle can achieve in all directions from current location and the route is modified in real time. The navigation system in these cars do not select the set of POIs maximizing tourist satisfaction and do not take into account the trip constraints such as: driving range of a car as well as POIs visiting hours. In this regard the evolutionary algorithm described in this paper could be a module of the software application which suggest a driver the most attractiveness trip and the length of the route do not exceed a battery range.

It easy notice that OPTW model allows describe route which are only one stage (i.e. the route ends when a battery is discharged). In our further research it is our intention to generate multistage route i.e. we want maximize the attractiveness of EV tourist routes which be continue after charging battery. In this case Team Orienteering Problem with Times Windows models such problem [14].

Acknowledgements. The authors gratefully acknowledge support from the Polish Ministry of Science and Higher Education at the Bialystok University of Technology (grant S/WI/1/2014 and S/WI/2/2013).

References

1. Afroditi, A., Boile, M., Theofanis, S., Sdoukopoulos, E., Margaritis, D.: Electric vehicle routing problem with industry constraints: trends and insights for future research. Transp. Res. Procedia **3**, 452–459 (2014). doi:10.1016/j.trpro.2014.10.026
2. Campos, V., Marti, R., Sanchez-Oro, J., Duarte, A.: Grasp with path relinking for the orienteering problem. J. Oper. Res. Soc. (2013). doi:10.1057/jors.2013.156
3. Dekker, R., Bloemhof, J., Mallidis, I.: Operations research for green logistics - an overview of aspects, issues, contributions and challenges. Eur. J. Oper. Res. **219**(3), 671–679 (2012). doi:10.1016/j.ejor.2011.11.010
4. EV rentals in Alps. www.greencarcongress.com/2010/08/think-and-migros-teamup-with-swiss-ecotourism-group-to-offer-ev-rentals-in-alps.html Last Access 16 Feb 2017
5. EV Tourism in US. http://fresh-energy.org/wp/wp-content/uploads/2014/08/White-Paper-EV-Tourism-2014.pdf. Last Access 16 Feb 2017
6. EV trip planner. https://www.evtripplanner.com. Last Access 16 Feb 2017
7. Glover, F.: A template for scatter search and path relinking. In: Hao, J.-K., Lutton, E., Ronald, E., Schoenauer, M., Snyers, D. (eds.) AE 1997. LNCS, vol. 1363, pp. 13–54. Springer, Heidelberg (1998). doi:10.1007/BFb0026589
8. Huang, Y.H., Ting, C.K.: Genetic algorithm with path relinking for the multi-vehicle selective pickup and delivery problem. IEEE Congr. Evol. Comput. (CEC), 1818–1825 (2011). doi:10.1109/CEC.2011.5949836
9. Jia, S., Hu, Z.H.: Path-relinking Tabu search for the multi-objective flexible job shop scheduling problem. Comput. Oper. Res. **47**, 11–26 (2014). doi:10.1016/j.cor.2014.01.010
10. Kantor, M., Rosenwein, M.: The orienteering problem with time windows. J. Oper. Res. Soc. **43**, 629–635 (1992). doi:10.2307/2583018
11. Karbowska-Chilinska, J., Zabielski, P.: Genetic algorithm solving the orienteering problem with time windows. In: Swiątek, J., Grzech, A., Swiątek, P., Tomczak, J.M. (eds.) Advances in Systems Science. AISC, vol. 240, pp. 609–619. Springer, Cham (2014). doi:10.1007/978-3-319-01857-7_59
12. Karbowska-Chilinska, J., Zabielski, P.: Genetic algorithm with path relinking for the orienteerig problem with time widows. Fundam. Informaticae **135**(4), 419–431 (2014). doi:10.3233/FI-2014-1132
13. Lin, C., Choy, K.L., Ho, G.T.S., Chung, S.H., Lam, H.Y.: Survey of green vehicle routing problem: past and future trends. Expert Syst. Appl. **41**(4), 1118–1138 (2014). doi:10.1016/j.eswa.2013.07.107
14. Labadi, N., Mansini, R., Melechovsky, J., Calvo, R.W.: The team orienteering problem with time windows: an LP-based granular variable neighborhood search. Eur. J. Oper. Res. **220**(1), 15–27 (2012). doi:10.1016/j.ejor.2012.01.030
15. Schneider, M., Stenger, A., Goeke, D.: The electric vehicle routing problem with time windows and recharging stations. Transp. Sci. **48**(4), 500–520 (2014). doi:10.1287/trsc.2013.0490
16. Montemanni, R., Gambardella, L.M.: Ant colony system for team orienteering problems with time windows. Found. Comput. Decis. Sci. **34**, 287–306 (2009)
17. Ostrowski, K., Karbowska-Chilinska, J., Koszelew, J., Zabielski, P.: Evolution-inspired local improvement algorithm solving orienteering problem. Ann. Oper. Res., 1–25 (2016). doi:10.1007/s10479-016-2278-1
18. Perez, M.P., Rodríguez, F.A., Moreno-Vega, J.M.: A hybrid VNS-path relinking for the p-hub median problem. J. Manage. Math. **18**(2), 157–171 (2007). doi:10.1093/imaman/dpm013

19. Tang, H., Miller-Hooks, E.: A Tabu search heuristic for the team orienteering problem. Comput. Oper. Res. **32**(6), 1379–1407 (2005). doi:10.1016/j.cor.2003.11.008

20. Tsiligirides, T.: Heuristic methods applied to orienteering. J. Oper. Res. Soc. **35**(9), 797–809 (1984). doi:10.1057/jors.1984.162

21. Vansteenwegen, P., Souffriau, W., Vanden Berghe, G., Van Oudheusden, D.: Iterated local search for the team orienteering problem with time windows. Comput. O.R. **36**, 3281–3290 (2009). doi:10.1016/j.cor.2009.03.008

22. Vansteenwegen, P., Souffriau, W., Van Oudheusden, D.: The orienteering problem: a survey. Eur. J. Oper. Res. **209**(1), 1–10 (2011). doi:10.1016/j.ejor.2010.03.045

23. Wen, M., Linde, E., Ropke, S., Mirchandani, P., Larsen, A.: An adaptive large neighborhood search heuristic for the electric vehicle scheduling problem. Comput. Oper. Res. **76**, 73–83 (2016). doi:10.1016/j.cor.2016.06.013

24. Zabielski, P., Karbowska-Chilinska, J., Koszelew, J., Ostrowski, K.: A genetic algorithm with grouping selection and searching operators for the orienteering problem. In: Nguyen, N.T., Trawiński, B., Kosala, R. (eds.) ACIIDS 2015. LNCS, vol. 9012, pp. 31–40. Springer, Cham (2015). doi:10.1007/978-3-319-15705-4_4

Synthesis Method of Finite State Machines Based on State Minimization for Low Power Design

Adam Klimowicz[(⊠)]

Bialystok University of Technology, Bialystok, Poland
a.klimowicz@pb.edu.pl

Abstract. A new method for the synthesis of finite state machines (FSMs) is proposed. In this method, such optimization criterion as the power consumption is taken into account already at the stage of minimizing internal states. In addition, the proposed method allows one to minimize the number of transitions and input variables of the FSM. The method is based on sequential merging of two internal states. For this purpose, the set of all pairs of states that can be merged is found, and the pair that best satisfies the optimization criteria is chosen for merging. The sequential algorithm is used for low power state encoding. Experimental results show, that the dissipated power is less by 7% comparing to traditional methods.

Keywords: Finite state machine (FSM) · State minimization · Logic synthesis · Low power design

1 Introduction

In recent years digital systems appears in all spheres of human activities. Reducing the power consumption of digital devices has become more important due to especially for battery powered mobile devices. Depending on specific conditions, this parameter can be the major factor to be optimized. There are several approaches to the solution of this problem: technological, logical, system level etc. A some way of solving this problem is to reduce the power consumption of finite state machines (FSMs).

The finite state machine (FSM) provides a mathematical model that is widely used for designing digital systems, which are often designed as sequential circuits. For that reason, the optimization of FSMs with respect to the power consumption parameter is an important task.

The conventional approach to the synthesis of FSMs includes the following stages, which are executed sequentially: minimization of the number of internal states, state assignment and synthesis of the combinational part of the FSM. Under the conventional approach, a developer has only two methods of optimizing the FSM: minimization of the number of internal states and state assignment.

Often, even the exact minimization of the number of internal states does not make it possible to solve the optimization problems at the stage of logic synthesis.

K. Saeed et al. (Eds.): CISIM 2017, LNCS 10244, pp. 526–535, 2017.
DOI: 10.1007/978-3-319-59105-6_45

In work [1], the problem of minimization and state assignment was considered for asynchronous FSMs. The method proposed in [2] is applicable only to FSMs with the number of states not exceeding 10. In [3], a program for concurrent state reduction and state encoding was presented, which made it possible to build incompletely specified state codes.

The power consumption of an FSM can be directly reduced by special encoding of internal states [4–6]. In [7–9], the implementation cost is minimized simultaneously with the minimization of the power consumption at the stage of state assignment. In the majority of these works, genetic algorithms are used. In [10], the minimization of power consumption and delay is considered for asynchronous FSMs. The concept of a low power semi-synchronous FSM operating on a high frequency is proposed that can be implemented and tested as an ordinary synchronous FSM. In [11], the conventional approach to the synthesis of FSMs is considered, under which the number of internal states is first minimized, then the internal states are encoded; next, the program ESPRESSO is used to build disjunctive normal forms (DNFs) of the functions to be realized and, finally, the cost, power consumption, and speed of operation are estimated. A set of algorithms is proposed to select the best state assignment so as to minimize the parameters mentioned above.

The analysis of available studies showed that the number of internal states and power consumption are not simultaneously minimized. The methods that claim to simultaneously take into account several optimization criteria actually reduce to the conventional approach in which several different algorithms are proposed for each stage. In the present paper, we propose a heuristic method for the minimization of incompletely specified FSMs that makes it possible to optimize a power consumption already at the stage of minimization of the number of internal states. In addition the method of synthesis also applies a special state assignment method called sequential encoding algorithm [12] designed for low power optimization. The proposed approach suits well for the implementation of FSMs on programmable logic devices (PLDs).

2 Idea of the Proposed Approach

A FSM behavior can be described by the *transition list*. The transition list is a table with four columns: a_m, a_s, $X(a_m, a_s)$, and $Y(a_m, a_s)$. Each row of the transition list corresponds to one FSM transition. The column a_m contains the present, the column a_s contains the next state, the column $X(a_m, a_s)$ contains the set of values of the input variables that initiates this transition (*a transition condition* or *an input vector*), and the column $Y(a_m, a_s)$ contains the set of values of the output variables that is generated by FSM at this transition (*an output vector*).

The proposed approach is based on the method for the minimization of the number of internal states of incompletely specified FSMs (ISFSM) proposed in [13]. An ISFSM output vector is represented by ternary vector. For example, $Y(a_m, a_s) =$ "01-0", where 0 denotes zero value, 1 denotes unity value, and dash ("-") denotes a don't care value of the corresponding output variable.

The idea of the method [13] is to sequentially merge two states. For this purpose, the set G of all pairs of internal states of the FSM satisfying the merging condition is found at each step. Then, for each pair in G, a trial merging is done. Next, the pair (a_i, a_j) that leaves the maximum possibilities for merging other pairs in G is chosen for real merging.

In distinction from [13], in the present paper we chose for merging at each step the pair (a_i, a_j) that best satisfies the optimization criteria in terms of power consumption, and leaves the maximum possibilities for merging other pairs in G. This procedure is repeated while at least one pair of states can be merged.

After procedure of state minimization, the sequential algorithm of state assignment [12] is performed to provide encoding which minimizes the power consumption.

Let (a_s, a_t) be a pair of states in G, where P_{st} is the estimate of power consumption, and M_{st} is the estimate of the possibility to merge other states. Then, with regard to the above considerations, the FSM synthesis algorithm can be described as follows.

Algorithm 1 (general algorithm for FSM synthesis)

1. Using the method described in [13], form the set G of pairs of states that can be merged. If $G = \varnothing$ (no pairs can be merged), go to step 5.
2. For each pair of states (a_s, a_t) in set G, calculate the estimates P_{st}, and M_{st} of the optimization criteria.
3. According to the specified order of optimization criteria, choose a pair of states (a_i, a_j) for merging. Among all the pairs in G, choose a pair (a_i, a_j) for which $P_{ij} = \min$; if there are several such pairs, then choose among them the one for which $M_{ij} = \max$.
4. Merge the pair of states (a_i, a_j). Store the results of minimization (transition list and corresponding P_{st} value). Go to step 1.
5. Among all saved results of minimization select one with minimal P_{st} value.
6. Minimize the number of transitions in the FSM.
7. Minimize the number of input variables in the FSM.
8. Perform state assignment using sequential algorithm [12].
9. Stop.

Algorithms of minimization of the number of transition an input variables are based on some observations. Suppose, for instance, that one transition from a state a_1 under condition x_1 leads to a state a_2 and the second transition from a_1 under condition $\bar{x}_1$ leads to another state a_3 and on each of these transitions not orthogonal output vectors are formed ($\bar{x}_1$ is an inversed form of the variable x_1). Suppose that the states a_2 and a_3 can be merged. After merging a_2 and a_3, a new state a_{23} is formed. Now two transitions lead from a_1 to a_{2_3}, one under condition x_1 and the second under condition $\bar{x}_1$. The latter means that the transition from a_1 to a_{23} is unconditional and two transitions can be replaced by one unconditional transition. Notice that in general transition conditions from a state a_1 can be much more complicated.

At minimization of the number of FSM transitions one can arrive at a situation when certain input variables have no impact on the transition conditions. Suppose, for instance, that one transition from a state a_1 under condition x_1 leads to a state a_2 and another transition from a_1 under condition $\bar{x}_1$ leads to a state a_3 and the variable x_1 does not meet anywhere else in transition conditions of the FSM. Suppose that after the states a_2 and a_3 have been merged, the transition from the state a_1 to the state a_{23} becomes unconditional, i.e. it does not depend on values of input variables. The latter means that the variable x_1 has no impact on any FSM transition and therefore it is redundant.

3   Estimation of Optimization Criteria

To estimate the optimization criteria, all pairs of states in G are considered one after another. For each pair of states (a_s, a_t) in G, a trial merging is performed. Next the internal states are encoded using sequential algorithm and the system of Boolean functions corresponding to the combinational part of the FSM is built. Next, for the pair (a_s, a_t), power consumption P_{st}, and the possibility of minimizing other states M_{st} are estimated. The optimization criteria for each pair of states (a_s, a_t) in G are estimated at step 2 of Algorithm 1 using the following algorithm.

Algorithm 2 (estimation of optimization criteria)

1. Sequentially consider the elements of the set G.
2. For each pair of states $(a_s, a_t) \in G$, make a trial merging.
3. Encode the internal states using sequential algorithm.
4. Estimate the power consumption P_{st}.
5. Estimate the possibility of other states minimization M_{st}.
6. Return to the original FSM (before merging at step 2).
7. Execute steps 2–9 for all pairs of states in G.
8. Stop.

The estimate M_{st} is determined by the number of pairs of the FSM that can be merged after merging the pair (a_s, a_t). To provide the best possibilities for merging other states, M_{st} should be maximized. Using the method described in [13], the set G_{st} of pairs of states that can be merged upon merging the pair (a_s, a_t) must me find. After that, the parameter M_{st} can be calculated as the cardinality of the set $G_{st}(M_{st} = |G_{st}|)$.

To estimate the power consumption of an FSM, we use the method given in [14] because it is the quite universal and suitable for any hardware components built using the CMOS technology. The procedure described in [14] makes it possible to calculate the dynamic power consumption of an FSM taking into account the encoding of its internal states and the probability of occurrence of ones at FSM inputs.

According to [14], the power consumption of the FSM is determined by the rule:

$$P = \sum_{r=1}^{R} P_r = \frac{1}{2} V_{DD}^2 f C \sum_{r=1}^{R} N_r \tag{1}$$

where P_r is the power consumed by the trigger r, V_{DD} is the supply voltage, f is the frequency at which the FSM operates, C is the capacity of trigger output, and N_r is the activity of the trigger r.

Let k_i be a binary code of a state a_i. Denote by k_r^i the value of the bit r in the code k_i of the state a_i. Then, the activity N_r of switching the memory element r of the FSM satisfies the following equation

$$N_r = \sum_{m=1}^{M} \sum_{s=1}^{M} P(a_m \rightarrow a_s)\left(k_m^r \oplus k_s^r\right) \tag{2}$$

where $P(a_m \rightarrow a_s)$ is the probability of transition from the state a_m to the state a_s and $\oplus$ is the XOR operation. The FSM has to be encoded first to determine the activity of each trigger.

The probability $P(a_m \rightarrow a_s)$ of transition from the state a_m to the state a_s is given by the following equation:

$$P(a_m \rightarrow a_s) = P(a_m)P(X(a_m, a_s)) \tag{3}$$

where $P(a_m)$ is the probability of the FSM to be in the state a_m and $P(X(a_m, a_s))$ is the probability of appearing the vector $X(a_m, a_s)$ initiating the transition from a_m to a_s at the input of the FSM.

The probability $P(X(a_m, a_s))$ of the vector $X(a_m, a_s)$ to appear at the input of the FSM is given by the rule:

$$P(X(a_m, a_s)) = \prod_{b=1}^{L} P(x_b = d) \tag{4}$$

where $d \in \{0, 1, \text{'-'}\}$ and $P(x_b = d)$ is the probability that the input variable x_b in the input vector $X(a_m, a_s)$ takes the value d. We make an assumption that 0 and 1 appear at each input of the FSM with the same probability; therefore, $P(x_b = 0) = P(x_b = 1) = 0.5$ and $P(x_b = \text{'-'}) = 1$ (the probability that 0 or 1 appear at each input of the FSM is equal one because symbol '-' means logic zero or logic one and any other values cannot appear at input). For a specific FSM, $P(x_b = 0)$ and $P(x_b = 1)$ may be different; however, it must hold that $P(x_b = 0) + P(x_b = 1) = 1$.

The probability $P(a_i)$ to find the FSM in each state a_i can be determined by solving the system of equations

$$P(a_i) = \sum_{m=1}^{M} P(a_m)P(X(a_m, a_i)), \quad i \in [1, M] \tag{5}$$

If there are no transitions between the states a_m and a_i, then we set $P(X(a_m, a_i)) = 0$. If there are several transitions, then $P(X(a_m, a_i))$ is the sum of the probabilities of appearing each input vector initiating the transition from a_m to a_i.

System (5) is a system of M linear equations with M unknowns $P(a_1), \ldots, P(a_M)$, which can be solved by any available method, for example, by the Gauss method. Since the FSM is always in one of its internal states, it holds that

$$\sum_{m=1}^{M} P(a_m) = 1 \tag{6}$$

To simplify the solution of system (5), one equation in (5) can be replaced with (6). With regard to the above considerations, the algorithm for estimating the FSM power consumption is as follows.

Algorithm 3 (estimation of the power consumption)

1. According to (4), for each input vector $X(a_m, a_s)$ $(a_m, a_s \in A)$, calculate the probability $P(X(a_m, a_s))$ of its appearance at the input of the FSM.
2. Solve system of Eq. (5) to find the probabilities $P(a_i)$ of the FSM to be in each state $a_i \in A$.
3. Using (3), calculate the probabilities of transitions $P(a_m \rightarrow a_s)$ of the FSM for $a_m, a_s \in A$.
4. Based on the encoding of internal states, find the activity N_r $(r \in [1, R])$ of each trigger using (3).
5. Using (1), calculate the power consumption P of the FSM for the following values of the parameters: $V_{DD} = 5$ V, $f = 10$ MHz, and $C = 3$ pF (these are typical values for most chips manufactured using the CMOS technology). Set $P_{st} := P$.
6. Stop.

4   State Assignment Procedure

The encoding of internal states is proposed to be made with the sequential algorithm more precisely described in [12]. In this method assigning the code to the state depends on states assigned earlier. It needs to define the set K^R of the all state codes that can be assigned, where $R = [\text{int} \log_2 M, M]$.

An FSM can be described by a state transition graph (STG), where the states are defined by the vertices and the transitions are defined by the edges. STG is a directed graph but for the power computations purpose we can convert it to an undirected graph because the transition from a_i to a_j causes that the same number of the flip-flops changes the output value as the transition from a_j to a_i. Weights of the edges can be expressed by:

$$w_{i,j} = P(a_i \rightarrow a_j) + P(a_j \rightarrow a_i) \tag{7}$$

Every state a_i must be assigned a code c_i. Thus internal states set A is connected with states codes set $C = \{c_1, c_2, ..., c_M\}$. Every code must be orthogonal with the all other states codes. The code width R can be any value from the range $[\text{int} \log_2 M, M]$.

Let c_i^l denote l-th bit of the code of the state a_i. Hamming distance $H(c_i, c_j)$ is defined as the number of bits in the same position with the opposite phase:

$$H(c_i, c_j) = \sum_{i=1}^{R} c_i^l \oplus c_j^l \tag{8}$$

Then, with regard to the above considerations, the sequential encoding algorithm can be described as follows.

Algorithm 4 (sequential low power encoding)

1. Select two states a_i and a_j, for which $w_{i,j}$ is highest.
2. Assign two codes from the K^R, such that Hamming distance $H(c_i, c_j) = 1$. Remove the assigned state codes from K^R.
3. Repeat steps 4–5 until all states are assigned.
4. Select the unassigned state a_i, such that sum of the weights of the edges connected with the already assigned states is highest.
5. Assign the state a_i unassigned code from K^R with the lowest value of the function γ.

$$\gamma(c_i) = \sum_{j=1}^{M} w_{i,j} \cdot H(c_i, c_j) \tag{9}$$

6. Remove the code from the K^R.
7. Stop.

5   Experimental Results

The method for synthesis of finite state machines was implemented in a program called ZUBR. To estimate the efficiency of the offered method we used MCNC FSM benchmarks [15] and well-known STAMINA minimization program [16] for comparison. The experiments were performed using Altera Quartus Prime version 16.0 EDA tool. All benchmarks in all three cases (without minimization, minimized with STAMINA and synthesized with proposed method) were implemented using identical design flow optimization parameters. Three parameters were taken from report files for further analysis: Core Dynamic Power (P), Total Logic Elements (C) and Maximum Clock Frequency - Fmax (F). For an implementation author has chosen the EP4CE115F29I8L device – a popular low cost FPGA from the Cyclone IV E family.

The experimental results for Core Dynamic Power are presented in Table 1, where M_0 and P_0 are, respectively, the number of internal states and dissipated power (in mW) of the initial FSM (without minimization); M_1 and P_1 are, respectively, the number of internal states and dissipated power (in mW) after minimization using STAMINA and M_2, and P_2 are, respectively, the number of internal states and dissipated power (in mW) after synthesis using proposed method. P_0/P_2 and P_1/P_2 are ratios of the corresponding parameters. *Average* row contains the mean values.

The analysis of Table 1 shows that application of the proposed method allows to reduce the number of internal states of the initial FSM. Similarly, the average reduction of the power consumption of the FSM makes 1.07 times, and on occasion (example *S832*) 1.19 times. In comparison to STAMINA the number of states is higher in 4 cases but the average reduction of the power consumption of the FSM makes 1.06 times, and on occasion (example *S208*) 1.13 times.

The experimental results for cost (Total Logic Elements) and speed (Fmax) are presented in Table 2, where C_0 and F_0 are, respectively, the number used logic element and maximum frequency of the initial FSM (without minimization); C_1 and F_1 are,

Table 1. The experimental results for power and number of states

Name	M_0	P_0	M_1	P_1	M_2	P_2	P_0/P_2	P_1/P_2
LION9	9	0.21	4	0.2	5	0.20	1.05	1.00
PLANET	48	0.29	48	0.29	48	0.26	1.12	1.12
S208	18	0.27	18	0.27	18	0.24	1.13	1.13
S27	6	0.21	5	0.2	5	0.20	1.05	1.00
S386	13	0.22	13	0.22	13	0.21	1.05	1.05
S420	18	0.26	18	0.26	18	0.25	1.04	1.04
S820	25	0.35	24	0.38	25	0.34	1.03	1.12
S832	25	0.37	24	0.32	25	0.31	1.19	1.03
SAND	32	0.34	32	0.34	32	0.32	1.06	1.06
TMA	20	0.23	18	0.24	19	0.23	1.00	1.04
Average	21.4	0.28	20.4	0.27	20.8	0.26	1.07	1.06

Table 2. The experimental results for cost and speed

Name	C_0	F_0	C_1	F_1	C_2	F_2
LION9	20	490.20	6	587.2	11	504.80
PLANET	134	369.96	134	369.96	126	457.25
S208	150	171.94	150	171.94	115	193.12
S27	22	388.50	18	450.65	18	420.34
S386	46	358.29	46	358.29	44	289.44
S420	135	177.43	135	177.43	127	175.62
S820	227	141.38	238	152.74	209	157.88
S832	247	148.92	228	143.55	204	159.92
SAND	221	164.12	221	164.12	189	194.10
TMA	84	389.41	96	237.76	84	418.41
Average	128.6	280.02	127.2	281.36	112.7	297.09

respectively, the same parameters after minimization using STAMINA [16] and C_2, and F_2 are, respectively, the same parameters after synthesis using proposed method. *Average* row contains the mean values.

The analysis of Table 2 shows that application of the proposed method also allows to reduce the number of used logic elements in 9 of 10 cases in relation to FSMs without any minimization and in 8 of 10 cases in relation to FSMs minimized by STAMINA. In addition the maximum clock frequency in benchmarks realized with proposed method was higher than in base FSMs in 8 of 10 cases and higher than in STAMINA minimized benchmarks in 6 of 10 cases. Of course, there are examples where the cost and the speed were worse in relation to initial machines or FSMs minimized with STAMINA. It is related to fact, that in minimization method with power consumption criterion, the full minimization of states is not performed. There is always selected a result with lower power dissipation, which is not always the same as one with minimal number of states.

6 Conclusion

In this paper we presented an efficient method for FSM synthesis. In contrast to traditional approaches, the proposed method allows to minimize not only the number of FSM states and consumed power, but also the number of FSM transitions and input variables what has an influence the cost and the speed of synthesized circuits. Using the proposed method there are always obtained machines with less or the same power consumption as the initial machines or STAMINA minimized FSMs.

Presented method is the part of future work on the complex minimization method, where not only power consumption, but also speed and area parameters are taken in consideration. In the general case, the problem of choosing the group of states for merging is a multicriteria discrete optimization problem, which can be solved by various algorithms.

In future, the complex synthesis method will serve to minimize power and cost and increase speed for FSM realization on programmable logic devices.

Acknowledgements. The research has been done in the framework of the grant S/WI/1/2013 and financed from the funds for science by MNiSW.

References

1. Hallbauer, G.: Procedures of state reduction and assignment in one step in synthesis of asynchronous sequential circuits. In: Proceedings of the International IFAC Symposium on Discrete Systems, Riga, Pergamons, pp. 272–282 (1974)
2. Lee, E.B., Perkowski, M.: Concurrent minimization and state assignment of finite state machines. In: Proceedings of the IEEE International Conference on Systems, Man and Cybernetics, Minneapolis. IEEE Computer Society (1984)
3. Avedillo, M.J., Quintana, J.M., Huertas, J.L.: SMAS: a program for concurrent state reduction and state assignment of finite state machines. In: Proceedings of the IEEE International Symposium on Circuits and Systems (ISCAS), pp. 1781–1784. IEEE, Singapore (1991)
4. Benini, L., De Micheli, G.: State assignment for low power dissipation. IEEE J. SolidState Circuits 30(3), 259–268 (1995)
5. Chattopadhyay, S.: Low power state assignment and flipflop selection for finite state machine synthesis - a genetic algorithmic approach. IEE Proc. Comput. Digital Techn. 148 (45), 147–151 (2001)
6. Koegst, M., Franke, G., Feske, K.: State assignment for FSM low power design. In: Proceedings of Conference on European Design Automation, Geneva, pp. 28–33 (2003)
7. Gören, S., Ferguson, F.: On state reduction of incompletely specified finite state machines. Comput. Electr. Eng. 33(1), 58–69 (2007)
8. Xia, Y., Almaini, A.E.A.: Genetic algorithm based state assignment for power and area optimization. IEE Proc. Comput. Digital Techn. 149(4), 128–133 (2002)
9. Aiman, M., Sadiq, S.M., Nawaz, K.F.: Finite state machine state assignment for area and power minimization. In: Proceedings of the IEEE International Symposium on Circuits and Systems (ISCAS), pp. 5303–5306. IEEE Computer Society (2006)

10. Lindholm, C.: High frequency and low power semi-synchronous PFM state machine. In: Proceedings of the IEEE International Symposium on Digital Object Identifier, pp. 1868–1871. IEEE Computer Society (2011)

11. Shiue, W.-T.: Novel state minimization and state assignment in finite state machine design for low-power portable devices. Integr. VLSI J. **38**, 549–570 (2005)

12. Grzes, T.N., Solov'ev, V.V.: Sequential algorithm for low-power encoding internal states of finite state machines. J. Comput. Syst. Sci. Int. **53**(1), 92–99 (2014)

13. Klimowicz, A., Solov'ev, V.V.: Minimization of incompletely specified Mealy finite-state machines by merging two internal states. J. Comput. Syst. Sci. Int. **52**(3), 400–409 (2013)

14. Tsui, C.-Y., Monteiro, J., Devadas, S., Despain, A.M., Lin, B.: Power estimation methods for sequential logic circuits. IEEE Trans. VLSI Syst. **3**, 404–416 (1995)

15. Yang, S.: Logic synthesis and optimization benchmarks user guide, version 3.0. Technical report, North Carolina, Microelectronics Center of North Carolina (1991)

16. Rho, J.-K., Hachtel, G., Somenzi, F., Jacoby, R.: Exact and heuristic algorithms for the minimization of incompletely specified state machines. IEEE Trans. Comput.-Aided Des. **13**, 167–177 (1994)

Self-organizing Traffic Signal Control with Prioritization Strategy Aided by Vehicular Sensor Network

Marcin Lewandowski[✉], Bartłomiej Płaczek, and Marcin Bernas

Institute of Computer Science, University of Silesia,
Będzińska 39, 41-200 Sosnowiec, Poland
marcin.lewandowski@us.edu.pl, placzek.bartlomiej@gmail.com,
marcin.bernas@gmail.com

Abstract. Preemption strategies are necessary for traffic signal control at intersections in a road network to ensure minimum delay of priority vehicles, such as ambulances or police cars. This paper introduces a decentralized algorithm, which extends the self-organizing signal control to provide preemption for the priority vehicles. The introduced algorithm enables effective utilisation of real-time data collected in vehicular sensor network (VSN). Results of simulation experiments show that the proposed approach ensures a quick passage of the priority vehicles and minimizes the negative effect of signal preemption on delays of non-priority vehicles. The new VSN-aided preemption strategy improves performance of the state-of-the-art methods that are based on road-side vehicle detectors and simple vehicle-to-infrastructure communication systems.

Keywords: Vehicular sensor networks · Self-organizing systems · Traffic signal control · Priority vehicles

1 Introduction

Effective traffic signal control is a key element of intelligent transport systems, which improves utilization of the existing road infrastructure and increases its capacity [1]. State-of-the-art traffic control approaches are based on centralized techniques that require global information about traffic conditions in the considered road network. The centralized traffic control methods are computationally complex and inherently non-scalable. Low scalability of the centralized control algorithms has motivated the current interest in decentralized self-organizing traffic control [2,3]. The self-organizing traffic signals are controlled independently for each intersection in the network on the basis of real-time traffic information obtained from local measurements. The information required by self-organizing traffic control describes current traffic conditions at road segments connected to a particular intersection.

© IFIP International Federation for Information Processing 2017
Published by Springer International Publishing AG 2017. All Rights Reserved
K. Saeed et al. (Eds.): CISIM 2017, LNCS 10244, pp. 536–547, 2017.
DOI: 10.1007/978-3-319-59105-6_46

Recent advances in vehicular sensor networks (VSNs) facilitate wireless data transfer between vehicles and infrastructure [4–6]. The vehicles in VSN can collect detailed and useful information regarding their current positions and velocities. The collected data can be then transmitted via wireless communication to a control unit at the nearest intersection. This technology enables cost-effective collection of the local traffic information in real-time. The increased availability of detailed real-time traffic information results in high application potential of the VSN-aided self-organizing traffic control.

This paper focuses on performance analysis of the self-organizing traffic control with a preemption strategy. The aim of signal preemption strategies is to efficiently clear the paths for priority vehicles, such as ambulances, police cars, fire engines, transit buses, light rail vehicles, snow ploughs, etc. [7–9]. Preemption interrupts normal signal operations to serve the priority vehicle as soon as possible with little or no delay [10]. An algorithm is proposed in this paper, which extends the self-organizing signal control to provide preemption for priority vehicles. The objective of the proposed algorithm is to ensure a quick passage of the priority vehicles and minimize the negative effect of signal preemption on delays of non-priority vehicles.

Performance of the proposed algorithm was examined in a simulation environment with application of different self-organizing control strategies from the literature. Two scenarios for the preemption strategy were considered during the simulation experiments. In the first scenario a priority vehicle sends preemption request to the traffic control unit as it approaches the intersection and the control unit responds immediately by switching traffic lights. This scenario corresponds to the current solutions that utilize the vehicle-to-infrastructure (V2I) communication [11,12]. The new approach with VSN-aided preemption is considered in the second scenario. In this case, the traffic lights are not switched immediately, when the request from priority vehicle is received. Instead, the traffic control unit evaluates time of preemption operation, which allows the priority vehicle to pass the intersection without stopping. This evaluation is based on real-time information about vehicles position delivered from VSN.

The paper is organized as follows. Related works are discussed in Sect. 2. Section 3 introduces the proposed method. Results of simulation experiments are presented in Sect. 4. Finally, conclusions are given in Sect. 5.

2   Related Works

Several decentralized control approaches for the self-organizing traffic signals have been proposed in the related literature. An advantage of the self-organizing methods discussed in this section is high scalability, which is ensured as these methods do not require any central controller and do not involve communication between local control units at intersections.

A simple algorithm for self-organizing traffic lights (SOTL) was presented in [13]. According to this algorithm, a preference is given to vehicles that have been waiting longer, and to larger groups of vehicles (platoons). The experimental results reported in [14] show that SOTL can achieve higher performance and increase the network capacity in comparison to the conventional Sydney Coordinated Adaptive Traffic System.

A more sophisticated self-organizing traffic control method was introduced by Lämmer and Helbing [15]. This method takes into account priorities that correspond to expected number of vehicles entering the intersection during a given time horizon. The expected numbers of vehicles are determined in this method by short-term traffic flow prediction based on a macroscopic fluid-dynamic model. Experimental comparison of this method with conventional adaptive control in a real-world road network revealed higher effectiveness of the self-organizing approach. Another work along these lines [16] introduces a self-organizing traffic signal system, where an interval microscopic traffic model is used to predict effects of possible control actions in a short time horizon.

Back-pressure [17] is a control strategy for the self-organizing traffic signals, which takes into account differences in traffic load on the road leading into the intersection and those leading out. The back-pressure method was originally proposed for routing algorithms in wireless networks as a decentralized scheme, which can provide maximum network throughput under the assumptions that all links in the network have infinite capacities. This concept was then adapted to urban road networks for signal control.

In [18] a cellular automata model of self-organizing traffic signal system was proposed, which enables evolutionary optimization of control rules that rely on adaptation to local variations in traffic state and enable effective coordination of the vehicular traffic at a network level. Fitness function, which guides the evolution of control rules, is evaluated in this approach via traffic simulation by using a microscopic cellular automata model.

A physic-based self-organizing control scheme for traffic signals was proposed in [2]. This method uses "virtual impulses" given by red signals or preceding cars, which are defined in a similar manner as the impulses used in physics. The virtual impulses are calculated at each traffic signal by using an optimal velocity model. They characterize to what extent vehicles will slow down owing to the existence of the preceding cars or red signals. The traffic signals are switched to reduce these virtual impulses.

A considerable research has also been devoted to signal preemption strategies that utilize V2I communication. Such strategies allow priority vehicles to send green light requests to traffic control units when approaching signalized intersections. The ZigBee communication was used in [19] for emergency vehicle clearance. According to that simple solution, the control unit at an intersection switches the traffic signals immediately, when it receives a preemption request from the emergency vehicle. The traffic lights are switched back to the normal operation once the priority vehicle passes through, and the control unit no longer receives the ZigBee signal.

Another simple preemption strategy was studied in [11] with application of the WAVE standard (IEEE 802.11p). According to this method the distance between the emergency car and the traffic lights is calculated in discrete time steps. If the distance is less than the specified value (which is defined in advance), the traffic light status changes to green for the emergency vehicle and red for the other cars. After the emergency vehicle passes the traffic light (with a distance of 20 m) the traffic light status returns to its original state.

In [20] a signal control strategy was proposed, which decreases response time of emergency vehicles by employing V2I communication and a beaconing concept based on the WAVE standard as well as the prediction of queue length. According to that strategy, the traffic signals are adjusted adaptively to provide an early green at the right time so that the queue at the downstream intersections can be served just in time for the arrival of an emergency vehicle.

When using the V2I communication, it is possible that multiple priority vehicles will send requests such that there may be multiple active requests at the same time. An optimisation problem was formulated in [21] to explicitly accommodate the multiple priority requests from different modes of vehicles while simultaneously considering signal coordination and vehicle actuation.

In this paper a decentralized algorithm is proposed, which combines the self-organizing signal control with a preemption strategy. The introduced algorithm enables effective utilisation of real-time position and speed data collected from particular vehicles in VSN.

3   Proposed Approach

This section introduces an algorithm, which allows the self-organizing signal control to provide preemption for priority vehicles. The objective of the preemption procedure is to serve the priority vehicles as soon as possible with minimum negative impact on the delay of non-priority vehicles. To this end, the proposed procedure utilizes data collected in VSN. The considered VSN is composed of vehicle nodes and control units that take control decisions and manage traffic signals at intersections by using the self-organizing strategy. Vehicles are equipped with sensors that collect speed and position data. The collected information is periodically transmitted from vehicles to control units.

Pseudocode of the self-organizing traffic signal control algorithm with preemption is presented in Algorithm 1. The input data of this algorithm consists of parameters that describe the traffic streams passing through an intersection. Output of the algorithm is a control decision that determines which traffic lane (or lanes) should get a green signal for a subsequent time interval. The consecutive control decisions are taken in constant time steps. In order to take control decision, priorities are assigned to the traffic lanes approaching the intersection. The priorities for traffic lanes are calculated dynamically based on current traffic data delivered from VSN.

According to the proposed algorithm, a *preemption_condition* function is used to verify if a priority vehicle for which the preemption has to be executed immediately is present in given traffic lane (line 5 of the pseudocode). The preemption condition takes into account expected time in which the priority vehicle will reach the traffic signal (t_R) and the predicted time, which is necessary to clear the queue of vehicles in the considered lane (t_C). This condition is defined as follows:

$$t_R \leqslant t_G + t_C, \tag{1}$$

where t_G is required intergreen time between the green period terminating for traffic lanes that are losing right of way and the start of the green period for the lane where priority vehicle is detected. The intergreen time has to be introduced to ensure traffic safety. Signal reaching time is calculated as:

$$t_R = d/v_F, \tag{2}$$

where d denotes distance of the priority vehicle to traffic signal and v_F is desired speed of the priority vehicle, which is observed in low traffic (free flow) conditions and in the absence of traffic signals. The vehicle node calculates the desired speed based on collected historical sensor readings and reports it to the control unit. Queue clearance time is estimated by using the formula:

$$t_C = n/s + t_0, \tag{3}$$

where n denotes number of vehicles in a queue ahead of the priority vehicle, s is saturation flow rate, i.e. the maximum number of vehicles that can pass through the intersection during a time unit, when the traffic signal is green, t_0 is the time lost at the beginning of green light, when vehicles are accelerating.

Algorithm 1. Self-organizing traffic signal control with preemption

---

```
 1: for each time step do
 2:     if not setup time then
 3:         preemption = false
 4:         for each lane do
 5:             if preemption_condition(lane) = true then
 6:                 preemption = true
 7:                 priority[lane] = preemption_priority(lane)
 8:             else
 9:                 priority[lane] = 0
10:             end if
11:         end for
12:         if preemption = false then
13:             for each line do
14:                 priority[lane] = regular_priority(lane)
15:             end for
16:         end if
17:         provide green signal for lane with the highest priority
18:     end if
19: end for
```

If preemption condition is satisfied for a given lane, then a priority of the preemption is calculated using the *preemption_priority* function. The preemption priority is useful for taking control decision when priority vehicles are approaching in two or more conflicting traffic lanes (that cannot get the right of way in the same time). This priority is calculated as follows:

$$preemption\_priority = \frac{m}{t_G^{start} + t_S + t_G^{end}},$$ (4)

where m is number of priority vehicles in the given lane, t_G^{start} is intergreen time, which has to be introduced before giving green signal for the considered lane ($t_G^{start} = 0$ if the considered lane already has the green signal), t_S is the green time necessary for the m priority vehicles to leave the intersection, and t_G^{end} denotes intergreen time after green signal for the considered lane. The above definition of the preemption priority is based on the approach presented in [15].

If the preemption condition is not satisfied for all traffic lanes, then the proposed algorithm uses the *regular_priority* function to calculate the priority of each lane in accordance with a selected state-of-the-art traffic control method. The *regular_priority* function also assures that all traffic lanes at the intersection will get the green signal at least once in a predetermined time period. In this study different definitions of the *regular_priority* function are taken into consideration, as discussed in the next section. These definitions correspond to various self-organizing traffic control methods from the literature.

During setup time, which includes the intergreen time and a minimum green time, the priority computation and decision making procedure is skipped because the service cannot be switched to another traffic lane.

4   Experiments

Simulation experiments were performed to compare effectiveness of the proposed VSN-aided preemption strategy with the state-of-the-art methods. Application of various self-organizing traffic control methods was considered in this study. The experimental results presented in this section concern delay and average speed of both the priority and non-priority vehicles. Based on these results, impact of priority vehicles on the performance of different self-organizing traffic control strategies is analysed.

4.1   Simulation Setup

In this study the simulation experiments were conducted in SUMO (Simulation of Urban MObility) [22]. SUMO is a widely recognized open-source traffic simulation package including a traffic simulator as well as supporting tools. The simulator is microscopic, space-continuous and time-discrete, providing a fair approximation of real world traffic scenarios. Topology of the simulated network is a lattice of 8 bidirectional roads with 16 signalized intersections. Schema of the simulated road network and an intersection example are presented in Fig. 1. During single run of simulation, the traffic intensity was changed from 0.02 to 0.14 vehicles per second. The vehicles were generated with the same intensity at each entrance of the road network. One simulation run corresponds to one hour. Percentage of the priority vehicles was changed between 0% and 3.5%.

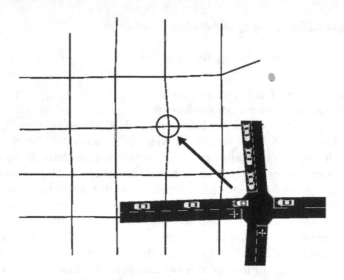

Fig. 1. Simulated road network. (Color figure online)

This percentage was determined for each one-hour simulation run. Two types of the priority vehicles were considered: slow, with maximum speed of 60 km/h, and fast, with the maximum speed of 72 km/h. Maximum speed of the non-priority vehicles was equal to 60 km/h. Results of the simulation include stop delays and average speeds of vehicles. The results were collected for four intersections in centre of the simulated road network.

Traffic signals at the simulated intersections were controlled by using decentralized self-organizing algorithms. Six different signal control algorithms were implemented in the simulation environment (Table 1). These algorithms use three control strategies (SOTL, LH, and BP) to calculate the regular priorities for traffic lanes, when priority vehicles are absent.

The SOTL (Self-Organizing Traffic Lights) strategy [15] takes into account current counts of vehicles approaching an intersection. Each traffic signal has a counter, which is set to zero when the signal turns red and then it is incremented

Table 1. Compared algorithms

Algorithm	SOTL1	LH1	BP1	SOTL2	LH2	BP2
Source of information about non-priority vehicles	RSD	VSN	Road-side detectors (RSD)		VSN	RSD
Source of information about priority vehicles	RSD or V2I communication			VSN		
Preemption condition	Distance to signal			Time to reach signal		
Preemption priority	Order of requests			Minimum delay		

at each time step by the number of vehicles approaching this red signal. When the counter reaches a predetermined threshold, the traffic lane gets the highest priority. In order to prevent the traffic signals from switching too frequently, the minimum green time constraint is used. Another constraint in the SOTL strategy keeps the small groups of vehicles (platoons) together and allows for dividing the large platoons that would excessively block the traffic flow of intersecting streets. Pseudo-code of the SOTL strategy can be found in [13].

In case of LH strategy [16], which is based on the method introduced by Lämmer and Helbing, two control rules are used: optimization rule, and stabilisation rule. According to the optimization rule, a cost associated with providing green signal for a particular lane is predicted as a total increase of vehicle delay. The prediction is performed by using a microscopic traffic model, which is based on cellular automata. The traffic lane with minimum cost gets the highest priority. The objective of the stabilisation is to assure that all traffic lanes will get a green signal at least once in a maximum time period. More detailed information about the optimization and stabilisation rules can be found in [15].

The idea of BackPressure (BP) strategy [17] is to compute pressures at every intersection of the network based on queue lengths and to give priority for traffic lanes with a high upstream pressure and a low downstream pressure. This strategy uses priorities that are proportional to the difference of queue lengths in traffic lanes leading into the intersection and those leading out. Pseudo-code of the BP strategy can be found in [17].

The LH strategy uses a microscopic cellular automata model to map current positions and velocities of particular vehicles. Thus, this strategy can fully utilize the detailed data from VSN. In contrast, the SOTL and BP strategies are designed for cooperation with state-of-the-art road-side detectors that deliver information about vehicle counts and queue lengths in traffic lanes.

The signal control algorithms in Table 1 are categorized into two groups with regard to the preemption method. For the first group (SOTL1, LH1, and BP1) the state-of-the-art preemption method is used, which means that the preemption request is registered when the distance of priority vehicle to intersection is below a predetermined threshold. In case of many requests, the highest priority is assigned to the first registered request. This scenario corresponds to the current solutions that utilize the V2I communication or the road-side detectors. Utilization of the detailed VSN data (i.e., current position and speed of the priority vehicles) for preemption purposes is possible for the second group of algorithms (SOTL2, LH2, and BP2). These algorithms include the preemption condition and the preemption priority functions that were proposed in Sect. 3.

4.2   Experimental Results

A signal preemption strategy should enable a quick passage of the priority vehicles with a minimum negative effect for the non-priority vehicles. The traffic simulations were conducted to evaluate average speed and stop delay of vehicles for the compared algorithms. In this section the simulation results are analysed to determine the impact of signal preemption on speed and delay of the non-priority vehicles.

Average delay and speed of non-priority vehicles for the considered algorithms are compared in Fig. 2. The lowest delay and the highest speed were observed for the LH algorithm, which utilizes the detailed data delivered from VSN. The algorithms designed for the state-of-the-art road-side detectors (SOTL and BP) have achieved a lower performance. When comparing the algorithms that employ the state-of -the-art preemption strategy (denoted by the suffix 1) with those implementing the proposed VSN-aided signal preemption (denoted by the suffix 2), it can be observed that the proposed approach ensures lower delay and increased speed of the vehicles. The introduced preemption strategy has decreased the average delay by 11% for algorithm LH, 6% for algorithm SOTL, and 2% for algorithm BP (Fig. 2a). Moreover, the average speed was increased by 2% for LH and 1% for SOTL. In case of algorithm BP, the average speed remains at the same level (Fig. 2b).

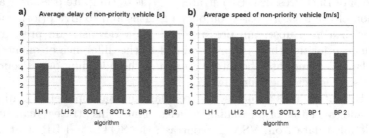

Fig. 2. Average delay and average speed of non-priority vehicles for the compared algorithms.

The chart in Fig. 3 compares average speed of priority vehicles for the considered algorithms. These results show that the proposed VSN-aided preemption strategy does not decrease the average speed of priority vehicles for the LH algorithm. It means that the LH2 algorithm, which utilizes the data collected from VSN to the largest extent, allows the delay of non-priority cars to be reduced and at the same time ensures high speed of the priority vehicles. In case of SOTL and BP algorithms the reduced delay of non-priority cars is obtained at the cost of lower speed of the priority vehicles.

Detailed results of the simulation for LH and SOTL algorithms are presented in Figs. 4 and 5. Each data point in these charts corresponds to results of one-hour traffic simulation. For particular runs of the simulation, the model settings were adjusted in order to obtain different percentages of the priority vehicles. The results show that average delay of non-priority vehicles increases with the percentage of the priority vehicles. In contrary, average speed of non-priority cars decreases as the percentage of priority vehicles increases. Such dependencies have been observed for all analysed algorithms.

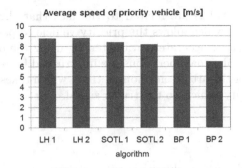

Fig. 3. Average speed of priority vehicles for the compared algorithms.

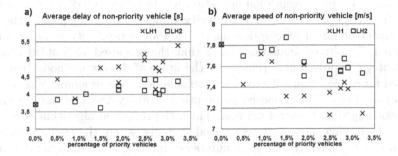

Fig. 4. Average delay and average speed of non-priority vehicles for the LH algorithms.

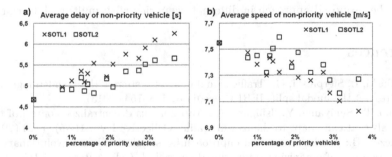

Fig. 5. Average delay and average speed of non-priority vehicles for the SOTL algorithms.

Comparison of the results obtained for algorithm LH1 with those of algorithm LH2 (Fig. 4) confirms that the VSN-aided preemption strategy decreases the negative impact of priority vehicles on delay and speed of the non-priority vehicles. This effect can be observed for a wide range of percentages of priority vehicles. Similar observations are made when comparing the results of algorithms SOTL1 and SOTL2 (Fig. 5). The better results for the proposed preemption strategy (LH2 and SOTL2) are related to the fact that the required time of preemption operation, which allows the priority vehicle to pass the intersection without stopping, can be accurately evaluated by using the detailed data from VSN. Thus, the normal signal operations are interrupted for a shorter time than in case of the state-of-the-art preemption method, which takes into account only the distance of priority vehicle to the traffic signal.

5   Conclusion

The introduced traffic control algorithm with preemption strategy enables effective utilisation of the data collected from VSN, which describe positions and velocities of particular vehicles. These data allow the control unit to accurately decide when a signal preemption operation has to be executed in order to clear the path through intersection for a priority vehicle. As a consequence, the negative impact of signal preemption on the flow of non-priority vehicles can be minimized. Results of simulations show that the proposed VSN-aided preemption strategy improves performance of the state-of-the-art methods that were designed for cooperation with road-side vehicle detectors or simple V2I communication solutions. The proposed preemption strategy was combined with the self-organizing signal control method. Thus, the proposed algorithm is scalable and can be implemented in decentralized systems, where the traffic signals are controlled independently for a large number of intersections. Moreover, the input data for this algorithm have to be collected locally from vehicles at road segments connected directly to a particular intersection. It means that the cost of data collection in VSN can be kept at a low level. Further research is necessary to test the proposed approach in different scenarios with multimodal priority.

References

1. Celiński, I., Sierpiński, G.: Traffic signal control system with extended logic in the context of the modal split. IERI Procedia 4, 148–154 (2013)
2. Kano, T., Sugiyama, Y., Ishiguro, A.: Autonomous decentralized control of traffic signals that can adapt to changes in traffic. Collective Dyn. 1(A5), 1–18 (2016)
3. Płaczek, B.: A cellular automata approach for simulation-based evolutionary optimization of self-organizing traffic signal control. J. Cell. Automata 11(5–6), 475–496 (2016)
4. Younes, M.B., Boukerche, A.: Intelligent traffic light controlling algorithms using vehicular networks. IEEE Trans. Veh. Technol. 65(8), 5887–5899 (2016)
5. Płaczek, B.: Selective data collection in vehicular networks for traffic control applications. Data Manage. Veh. Netw. 23, 14–28 (2012)
6. Płaczek, B., Bernas, M.: Optimizing data collection for object tracking in wireless sensor networks. Commun. Comput. Inf. Sci. 370, 485–494 (2013)
7. Nellore, K., Hancke, G.P.: Traffic management for emergency vehicle priority based on visual sensing. Sensors 16(11), 1892 (2016)
8. Zhanga, Z., Hea, Q., Gouc, J., Lid, X.: Performance measure for reliable travel time of emergency vehicles. Transp. Res. Part C Emerg. Technol. 65, 97–110 (2016)

9. Yang, M., Wang, W., Han, J.: Performance of the priority control strategies for bus rapid transit: comparative study from scenario microsimulation using VISSIM. Discrete Dyn. Nat. Soc. **2013**, 1–9 (2013)

10. Zamanipour, M., Head, K.L., Feng, Y.: Efficient priority control model for multi-modal traffic signals. Transp. Res. Rec. J Transp. Res. Board **2557**, 89–99 (2016)

11. Noori, H.: Impact of VANET-based traffic signal control on the response time of emergency vehicles in realistic large scale urban area. In: IEEE International Conference on Communication Workshop, (2013)

12. Bernas, M.: VANETs as a part of weather warning systems. Commun. Comput. Inf. Sci. **291**, 459–466 (2012)

13. Cools, S.B., Gershenson, C., D'Hooghe, B.: Self-organizing traffic lights: a realistic simulation. In: Prokopenko, M. (ed.) Advances in Applied Self-Organizing Systems. Advanced Information and Knowledge Processing, pp. 45–55. Springer, London (2013). doi:10.1007/978-1-4471-5113-5_3

14. Zhang, L., Garoni, T.M., de Gier, J.: A comparative study of macroscopic fundamental diagrams of arterial road networks governed by adaptive traffic signal systems. Transp. Res. Part B Methodol. **49**, 1–23 (2013)

15. Lämmer, S., Helbing, D.: Self-control of traffic lights and vehicle flows in urban road networks. J. Stat. Mech. Theory Exp. **2008**(4), 4–19 (2008)

16. Płaczek, B.: A self-organizing system for urban traffic control based on predictive interval microscopic model. Eng. Appl. Artif. Intell. **34**, 75–84 (2014)

17. Wongpiromsarn, T., Uthaicharoenpong, T., Wang, Y., Frazzoli, E., Wang, D.: Distributed traffic signal control for maximum network throughput. In: 15th International IEEE Conference on Intelligent Transportation Systems, ITSC 2012, pp. 588–595. IEEE (2012)

18. Placzek, B.: A cellular automata approach for simulation-based evolutionary optimization of self-organizing traffic signal control. J. Cell. Automata **11**(5/6), 475–496 (2016)

19. Sundar, R., Hebbar, S., Golla, V.: Implementing intelligent traffic control system for congestion control, ambulance clearance, and stolen vehicle detection. IEEE Sens. J. **15**(2), 1109–1113 (2015)

20. Noori, H., Fu, L., Shiravi, S.: A connected vehicle based traffic signal control strategy for emergency vehicle preemption. In: 2016 95th Transportation Research Board, vol. 16, p. 6763 (2016)

21. He, Q., Head, K.L., Ding, J.: Multi-modal traffic signal control with priority, signal actuation and coordination. Transp. Res. Part C Emerg. Technol. **46**, 65–82 (2014)

22. Behrisch, M., Bieker, L., Erdmann, J., Krajzewicz, D.: SUMO simulation of urban mobility: an overview. In: The Third International Conference on Advances in Syston, Proceedings of SIMUL 2011. ThinkMind (2011)

Infinite Impulse Response Approximations to the Non-integer Order Integrator Using Cuckoo Search Algorithm

Shibendu Mahata[1], Suman Kumar Saha[2], Rajib Kar[1(✉)],
and Durbadal Mandal[1]

[1] Department of Electronics and Communication Engineering,
NIT Durgapur, Durgapur, India
shibendu.mahata@gmail.com, rajibkarece@gmail.com,
durbadal.bittu@gmail.com
[2] Department of Electronics and Telecommunication Engineering,
NIT Raipur, Raipur, India
namus.ahas@gmail.com

Abstract. A popular metaheuristic global optimization technique called Cuckoo Search Algorithm (CSA) is employed to design non-integer order integrators (NOIs) in terms of the Infinite Impulse Response (IIR) templates in this paper. Extensive comparisons on the basis of design quality robustness, error convergence, and optimization time of the CSA-based NOIs are carried out with the Particle Swarm Optimization (PSO) based designs. Results demonstrate the efficient performance of CSA in exploring the multimodal, non-linear, and non-uniform error surface for this optimization problem. The CSA-based designs also outperform the recent literature by 9.67 decibel (dB) and 19.26 dB in terms of mean absolute relative magnitude error (MARME) and maximum absolute magnitude error (MAME) metrics, respectively.

Keywords: Non-integer order integrator · Cuckoo search algorithm · Particle swarm optimization · Metaheuristic optimization

1 Introduction

An important application area of fractional calculus [1] is in the realm of control systems and signal processing [2, 3] where the additional degrees-of-freedom provided by the non-integer (fractional) operators have resulted in the design of fractional order controllers (FOCs) [4] which can outperform the traditional controller designs based on the integer order operators. The non-integer order integrators (NOIs) are one of the fundamental building blocks of the FOCs. The frequency response of an ideal NOI is described by $H(\omega) = (1/\omega^r)\angle - (90° \times r)$, where, $r \in (0, 1)$ is the fractional order, and ω is the angular frequency. Note that $r = 1$ results in the conventional (integer order) integrator. Thus, it is easy to realize that NOIs are more generalized and provides superior design flexibility than the conventional integrator. However, since the ideal NOI is an infinite dimensional structure, hence, its practical realization can only be of finite dimensions. Thus, the implementation of NOIs can be regarded as an

K. Saeed et al. (Eds.): CISIM 2017, LNCS 10244, pp. 548–556, 2017.
DOI: 10.1007/978-3-319-59105-6_47

approximation problem with the objective of designing accurate designs with smaller dimensions. Since the digital implementations of the NOIs based on infinite impulse response (IIR) filter structures as compared with the finite impulse response filters are preferred for real-time applications for various reasons such as power consumption and latency, the primary objective of this paper is to design digital NOIs in terms of IIR filters of third order such that it accurately meets the ideal frequency response. It is worth noting that achieving both stable and minimum phase IIR designs makes this design problem even more challenging.

Design of IIR NOIs based on series expansion methods [5–9], least square technique [10], Chebyshev polynomials [11], indirect discretization [12], Particle Swarm Optimization (PSO) [13], and Colliding Bodies Optimization algorithm [14] are published in the literature. An excellent survey dealing with the design of NOIs is reported in [15].

Literature survey reveals that metaheuristics have shown promising results in the field of digital filter design [16–18]. Hence, more research effort should be directed towards the design of NOIs based on the nature-inspired optimization algorithms. This paper employs a popular swarm-intelligence based global optimizer called Cuckoo Search Algorithm (CSA) [19] to design an IIR filter based digital NOI with accurate magnitude response. Further comparisons are also carried out with PSO optimized NOIs with respect to the frequency response performance, robustness, and convergence. Comparison with the latest literature further demonstrates the superiority of the CSA-based designs.

The arrangement of the rest of the paper is as follows. In Sect. 2, the problem formulation is shown. CSA is briefly presented in Sect. 3. The MATLAB simulations are carried out on i3 CPU (1.70 GHz) with 2 GB RAM and the results are shown in Sect. 4. Finally, Sect. 5 concludes the paper.

2 Optimization Problem Formulation

The IIR filter based representation of the digital NOI is given by (1).

$$H_P(z) = \frac{\sum_{j=0}^{M} q_j z^{-j}}{\sum_{j=0}^{M} p_j z^{-j}} \tag{1}$$

where, M is the order of $H_P(z)$; q_j and p_j, $j = 0, 1, ..., M$, are the coefficients of $H_P(z)$. The transfer function in the frequency domain of $H_P(z)$ is given by (2).

$$H_P(\omega) = \frac{\sum_{j=0}^{M} q_j e^{-j\omega}}{\sum_{j=0}^{M} p_j e^{-j\omega}} \tag{2}$$

The purpose of the optimization procedure based on PSO and CSA is find out the set of coefficient values of $H_P(\omega)$ such that the cost function f as defined by (3) is minimized.

$$f = \sum_{i=1}^{L} [H_P(\omega_i) - H(\omega_i)]^2 \qquad (3)$$

where, L is the total number of points where the frequency responses are determined. Here, $0.1 \leq \omega \, (radians/sec) \leq \pi$, $M = 3$, $L = 1000$, and $r = 0.5$ are chosen.

Note that this particular optimization problem is a multidimensional (dimension, $D = 8$) and multimodal one.

3   Cuckoo Search Algorithm (CSA)

CSA [19, 20] is a nature-inspired optimization technique which mimics the parasitism behavior of some species of the cuckoo bird. The efficient nature of CSA lies in employing Levy flights as compared with the simple random walks used in PSO. CSA is based on the following rules: (a) each cuckoo bird can lay only one egg which is dumped in a randomly chosen nest, (b) only the best nests containing eggs of superior quality are carried over to the following generation, (c) a fixed number of host nests is only available, (d) the probability of identifying the egg laid by the cuckoo on the host nest by the host bird is given by a probability p_a, where, $p_a \in (0, 1)$.

The control parameter p_a allows efficient switching between the global and the local random walks. The local random walk is given by (4).

$$x_i^{t+1} = x_i^t + \alpha s \otimes H(p_a - \varepsilon) \otimes (x_j^t - x_k^t) \qquad (4)$$

where, x_j^t and x_k^t are two solutions chosen in a random manner by permutation, $H(.)$ is the Heaviside function, ε is a random number which is chosen from a uniform distribution, α is the step-size scaling factor, and s is the step size. The entry-wise product is denoted by $\otimes$.

The Levy flight based global random walk is defined by (5).

$$x_i^{t+1} = x_i^t + \alpha \otimes L(s, \lambda) \qquad (5)$$

where, $L(s, \lambda) = \frac{\lambda \Gamma(\lambda) \sin(\lambda \pi / 2)}{\pi} \frac{1}{s^{1+\lambda}}$.

After performing 50 runs of the algorithm for each set of values of n (= 20, 50, 100, 200) and p_a (= 0.10, 0.25, 0.40, 0.50, 0.80), the following parameters of CSA which produced the best design results are: $n = 50$ and $p_a = 0.25$. The random numbers with the distribution L is drawn using the Mantegna algorithm.

Define fitness function $f(x)$, $x=(x_1, ..., x_{2M+2})^T$
Randomly generate n number of host nests x_i
while ($t<1000$)
    Randomly select a cuckoo
    Generate a solution as per (5)
    Determine its fitness (f_i)
    Randomly select a nest (say, the jth nest)
        if ($f_i<f_j$)
                Substitute the jth solution with the ith
        end if
    Abandon p_a fraction of host nests
    Generate new nests as per (4)
    Retain the best nests
    Determine the current best nest
    Increment t
end while
Declare the best nest as the optimal solution

Fig. 1. Pseudo code of CSA.

The pseudo code of CSA is shown in Fig. 1.

4   Simulation Results and Discussions

The optimal non-integer order ($r = 0.5$) integrators based on CSA and PSO are given by (6) and (7), respectively.

$$H_p(z) = \frac{0.9495 - 0.9436z^{-1} + 0.0646z^{-2} + 0.0563z^{-3}}{1.0270 - 1.6080z^{-1} + 0.6006z^{-2} + 0.0055z^{-3}} \tag{6}$$

$$H_p(z) = \frac{0.8008 + 0.5178z^{-1} - 0.1260z^{-2} - 0.0594z^{-3}}{0.8818 + 0.0936z^{-1} - 0.4763z^{-2} - 0.0652z^{-3}} \tag{7}$$

The comparison of the magnitude responses of the designed NOIs with the ideal half integrator is shown in Fig. 2. The MARME and the MAME values attained for CSA are −52.19 dB and −28.94 dB, respectively, which is better than PSO based design by 6.97 dB and 25.62 dB, respectively. The absolute relative magnitude error (ARME) response of PSO and CSA based designs are shown in Fig. 3. The better frequency domain fitting to the continuous-time domain for the CSA-based NOI can be credited to the alternating arrangement of zeros and poles in the real axis of the z-plane as shown in the pole-zero diagram in Fig. 4. Furthermore, this diagram also demonstrates that the CSA based half integrator is stable and exhibits a minimum-phase response which is an essential requirement for control and signal processing applications.

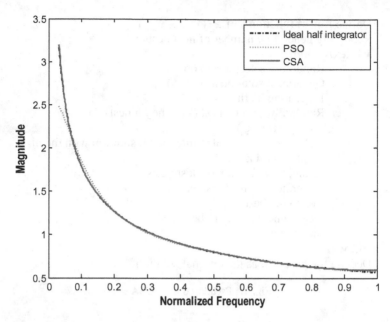

Fig. 2. Magnitude response of the digital half integrators designed using PSO and CSA.

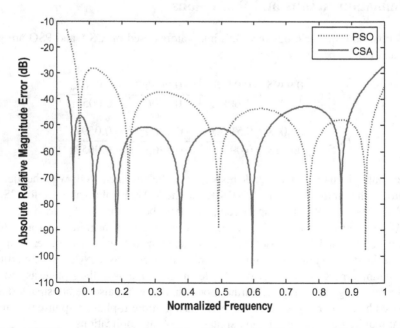

Fig. 3. ARME response comparison of the CSA based half integrator with the literature.

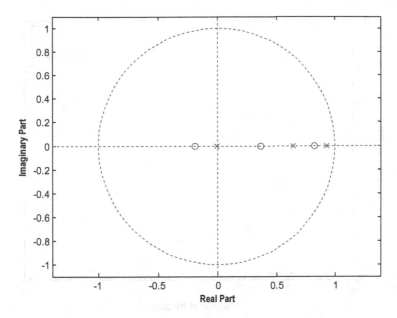

Fig. 4. Pole-zero diagram of the CSA based digital half integrator.

Table 1. Performance of CSA based designs based on different performance metrics.

Optimizer	Metric	Best	Worst	Mean	SD
PSO	MARME (dB)	−45.22	−30.88	−38.02	3.13
	MAME (dB)	−3.32	14.75	5.56	3.89
	Iterations to converge	146	222	181	14
	Optimization time (s)	88.652	89.691	89.092	0.205
CSA	MARME (dB)	−52.19	−36.24	−45.24	2.99
	MAME (dB)	−28.94	−16.03	−21.23	2.74
	Iterations to converge	84	123	106	10
	Optimization time (s)	85.789	86.648	86.215	0.188

After conducting 100 runs for PSO and CSA, the performance of the designs are analyzed on the basis of best, worst, mean, and standard deviation (SD) for the MARME and MAME metrics, and the results are shown in Table 1. The proposed CSA based design achieves a small SD, which exemplify the robust performance of CSA as compared with PSO for solving this multimodal optimization problem.

The fitness convergence of PSO and CSA for the design of half integrator is shown in Fig. 5 which shows a faster convergence rate with respect to iterations for CSA. A further study based on 100 trial runs is carried out to determine the mean and SD

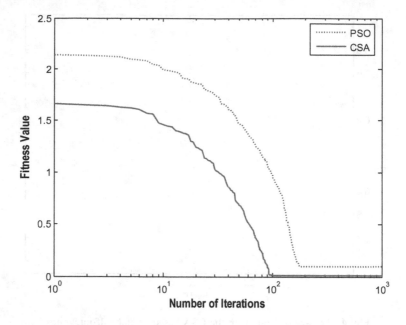

Fig. 5. Convergence curves of PSO and CSA.

Table 2. Comparison with the literature.

Reference	Approach	MARME (dB)	MAME (dB)
[6]	Direct discretization	−42.52	−9.02
[13]	Linear interpolation	−29.71	−6.77
[13]	Particle swarm optimization	−31.85	−9.68
Proposed	Cuckoo search algorithm	−52.19	−28.94

performances of convergence characteristics and the optimization time (in seconds) of PSO and CSA and the results are shown in Table 1. CSA outperforms PSO in achieving a faster convergence speed and a smaller execution time as highlighted by the mean and the SD values.

Table 2 shows the comparison of the CSA based NOI with the literature based on the MARME and MAME metrics. Compared with the designs based on direct discretization [6], interpolation [13], and PSO [13], the proposed designs achieve improvements of 22.74%, 75.66%, and 63.86%, respectively, in terms of MARME, and 220.84%, 327.47%, and 198.96%, respectively, in terms of MAME. Thus, CSA yields the most accurate optimal NOIs. The ARME responses of CSA-based NOI with the literature are shown in Fig. 6.

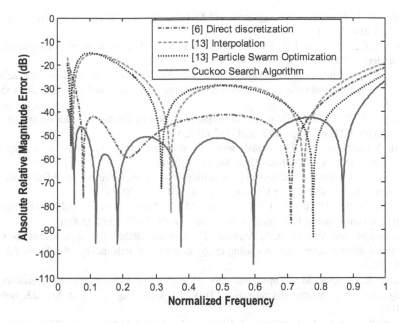

Fig. 6. ARME response comparison of the CSA based half integrator with the literature.

5   Conclusions

Cuckoo Search Algorithm is used to design IIR non-integer order integrator with a wideband frequency response in this work. Magnitude response, speed of convergence, and optimization time are considered to compare among the PSO and CSA based designs. The CSA based model outperforms the PSO based designs for all the afore-mentioned parameters. The proposed CSA based half integrator achieves 22.74% and 198.96% improvement for MARME and MAME metrics, respectively, over the reported literature.

Acknowledgments. This work is financially supported by the Visvesvaraya Young Faculty Fellowship, Govt. of India (Grant No. PhD-MLA-4(29)/2015-16).Query ID="Q3" Text="Reference [1] is given in the list but not cited in the text. Please cite it in text or delete it from the list." –>

References

1. Oldham, K.B., Spanier, J.: The Fractional Calculus. Academic Press, New York (1974)
2. Monje, C.A., Chen, Y.Q., Vinagre, B.M., Xue, D., Feliu, V.: Fractional-Order Systems and Controls - Fundamentals and Applications. Springer, London (2010)
3. Das, S., Pan, I.: Fractional Order Signal Processing - Introductory Concepts and Applications. Springer, New York (2012)

4. Podlubny, I.: Fractional-order systems and $PI^\lambda D^\mu$-controllers. IEEE Trans. Autom. Control **44**, 208–214 (1999)
5. Chen, Y.Q., Moore, K.L.: Discretization schemes for fractional-order differentiators and integrators. IEEE Trans. Circuits Syst. – I **49**, 363–367 (2002)
6. Chen, Y.Q., Vinagre, B.M., Podlubny, I.: Continued fraction expansion approaches to discretizing fractional order derivatives – an expository review. Nonlinear Dyn. **38**, 155–170 (2004)
7. Valerio, D., Costa, J.S.: Time-domain implementation of fractional order controllers. IEE Proc. Control Theor. Appl. **152**, 539–552 (2005)
8. Ferdi, Y.: Computation of fractional order derivative and integral via power series expansion and signal modeling. Nonlinear Dyn. **46**, 1–15 (2006)
9. Maione, G.: Continued fractions approximation of the impulse response of fractional-order dynamic systems. IET Control Theor. Appl. **2**, 564–572 (2008)
10. Barbosa, R.S., Machado, J.A.T., Silva, M.F.: Time domain design of fractional differ-integrators using least-squares. Sig. Process. **86**, 2567–2581 (2006)
11. Romero, M., de Madrid, A.P., Manoso, C., Vinagre, B.M.: IIR approximations to the fractional differentiator/integrator using chebyshev polynomials theory. ISA Trans. **52**, 461–468 (2013)
12. Yadav, R., Gupta, M.: Approximations of higher-order fractional differentiators and integrators using indirect discretization. Turk. J. Electr. Eng. Comput. Sci. **23**, 666–680 (2015)
13. Yadav, R., Gupta, M.: New improved fractional order integrators using PSO optimization. Int. J. Electron. **102**, 490–499 (2015)
14. Mahata, S., Saha, S.K., Kar, R., Mandal, D.: Optimal design of wideband infinite impulse response fractional order digital integrators using colliding bodies optimisation algorithm. IET Sig. Process. **10**, 1135–1156 (2016)
15. Krishna, B.T.: Studies of fractional order differentiators and integrators: a survey. Sig. Process. **91**, 386–426 (2011)
16. Mahata, S., Saha, S.K., Kar, R., Mandal, D.: Optimal design of wideband digital integrators and differentiators using harmony search algorithm. Int. J. Numer. Model.: Netw. Devices Fields (2016). doi:10.1002/jnm.2203
17. Mahata, S., Saha, S.K., Kar, R., Mandal, D.: Optimal and accurate design of fractional order digital differentiator – an evolutionary approach. IET Sig. Process. (2016). doi:10.1049/iet-spr.2016.0201
18. Mahata, S., Saha, S.K., Kar, R., Mandal, D.: Enhanced colliding bodies optimisation-based optimal design of wideband digital integrators and differentiators. Int. J. Bio-Inspired Comput. (in press)
19. Yang, X.-S., Deb, S.: Cuckoo search via levy flights. In: IEEE World Congress Nature & Biologically Inspired Computing, pp. 210–214 (2009)
20. Yang, X.-S., Deb, S.: Cuckoo search: recent advances and applications. Neural Comput. Appl. **24**, 169–174 (2014)

Designing Moore FSM with Transformation of State Codes

Kamil Mielcarek[✉], Alexander Barkalov, and Larisa Titarenko

Institute of Metrology, Electronics and Computer Science, Faculty of Computer,
Electrical and Control Engineering, University of Zielona Góra,
ul. Prof. Z. Szafrana 2, 65-516 Zielona Góra, Poland
{K.Mielcarek,A.Barkalov,L.Titarenko}@imei.uz.zgora.pl

Abstract. A design method is proposed for FPGA-based Moore FSMs. The method is based on transformation of state codes into codes of collections of output functions and classes of pseudoequivalent states. Example of design and results of investigations are given.

Keywords: Moore FSM · FPGA · Look-up table · EMB · Design · Pseudoequivalent states

1 Introduction

The model of Moore finite state machine (FSM) is often used during the design of control units [2]. One of the important problems of FSM synthesis is need to reduce the hardware consumed by FSM logic circuit [3,12]. The methods of solution of this problem depend strongly on features of logic elements used for designing the circuits [6,8]. In this article we discuss the case when field-programmable gate arrays (FPGA) are used to implement the Moore FSM logic circuit.

To implement the FSM logic circuit, it is enough to use two components of FPGA fabric. These components are logic elements (LE) and a matrix of programmable interconnections [1,21]. An LE consists of a look-up table (LUT) element, a programmable flip-flop and multiplexers. A LUT can be viewed as a random access memory block having S address inputs and a single output. One LUT can keep a truth table of an arbitrary Boolean function having up to S arguments. The flip-flop of LE could be bypassed. It means that the output of LE could be either combinational or registered.

A LUT has rather small number of inputs ($S \leq 6$) [1,21]. This peculiarity leads to necessity of functional decomposition [14,16] for Boolean functions having more than S arguments. It results in multilevel logic circuits with complex interconnections. To reduce the hardware amount, it is necessary to diminish the numbers of arguments in Boolean functions representing an FSM logic circuit. We propose one of possible approaches for solution of this problem. Our approach is based on: (1) using the classes of pseudoequivalent states of Moore FSM [6] and (2) encoding of the collections of output functions [4].

© IFIP International Federation for Information Processing 2017
Published by Springer International Publishing AG 2017. All Rights Reserved
K. Saeed et al. (Eds.): CISIM 2017, LNCS 10244, pp. 557–568, 2017.
DOI: 10.1007/978-3-319-59105-6_48

2   Theoretical Background

A Moore FSM is characterised by the following sets: $A = \{a_1, ..., a_M\}$ is a set of internal states; $X = \{x_1, ..., x_L\}$ is a set of input variables; $Y = \{y_1, ...y_N\}$ is a set of output functions. Transitions between the states could be represented by a state transition graph (STG) [12]. There is an STG of Moore FSM S_1 shown in Fig. 1.

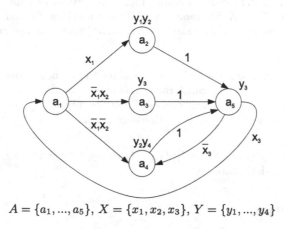

$$A = \{a_1, ..., a_5\}, \ X = \{x_1, x_2, x_3\}, \ Y = \{y_1, ..., y_4\}$$

Fig. 1. State transition graph for Moore FSM S_1

The vertices of STG correspond to states $a_m \in A$, while the edges to transitions between the states. The transitions are determined by inputs $X_h (h = \overline{1, H})$ equal to conjunctions of some elements $x_e \in X$ (or their complements). There is a collection of output functions (COF) $Y_q \subseteq Y$ marked above a vertex $a_m \in A$. It means that the COF $Y_q ((q = \overline{1, a})$ is generated while an FSM is in the state $a_m \in A$.

The states $a_m \in A$ are encoded using state variables $T_r \in T$, where $T = \{T_1, ..., T_R\}$ is a set of state variables. State codes $K(a_m)$ are assigned during the step of state assignment [12]. The number R is determined as

$$R = \lceil log_2 M \rceil, \tag{1}$$

where $\lceil a \rceil$ is a minimum integer not less than a. To change contents of flip-flops, input memory functions are used forming the set $\Phi = \{D_1, ..., D_R\}$.

To design the Moore FSM logic circuit, it is necessary to find the following systems of Boolean functions:

$$\Phi = \Phi(T, X), \tag{2}$$

$$Y = Y(T). \tag{3}$$

Systems (2)–(3) determine the structural diagram of Moore FSM S_1 (Fig. 2a). This diagram targets the FPGA chips.

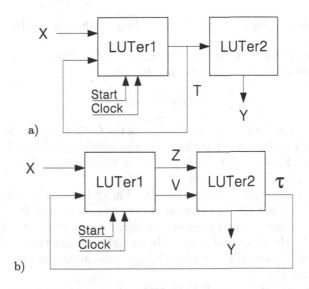

Fig. 2. Structural diagrams of Moore FSM U_1 (a) and U_2 (b)

We use the name "LUTer" to denote a logic circuit consisting from LUTs. If there are flip-flops in a circuit, they are controlled by pulses $Start$ and $Clock$. The pulse $Start$ loads the zero code into a register formed by these flip-flops. It corresponds to the initial state $a_1 \in A$. The pulse $Clock$ allows changing content of flip-flops. It corresponds to a transition between the states.

The LUTer1 implements the system (2), the LUTer2 the system (3). Let the following condition take place:

$$R \leq S. \tag{4}$$

In this case, it is enough a single LUT to implement any function $y_n \in Y$. If the condition (4) is violated, then the number of LUTs exceeds N in the circuit of LUTer2. In this case, the circuit of LUTer2 is multilevel.

In this article, we discuss a design method for reducing the number of LUTs in LUTer2 if the condition (4) is violated. Also, we propose to use pseudoequivalent states [6] to decrease the hardware

3   Main Idea of Proposed Method

The states $a_m, a_s \in A$ are pseudoequivalent states (PES) if identical inputs result in identical next states for both states $a_m, a_s \in A$. For example, there are PES $a_2, a_3, a_4 \in A$ for Moore FSM S_1 (Fig. 1). Let $\Pi_A = \{B_1, ..., B_I\}$ be a partition of the set A by the classes of PES $(I \leq M)$.

In the case of S_1, there is $I = 3$. There are the following classes of PES: $B_1 = \{a_1\}$, $B_2 = \{a_2, a_3, a_4\}$, $B_3 = \{a_5\}$.

Let us encode the classes $B_i \in \Pi_A$ by binary codes $K(B_i)$ having R_I bits:

$$R_I = \lceil log_2 I \rceil. \tag{5}$$

Let us use the variables $\tau_r \in T$ for encoding of the classes $B_i \in \Pi_A$, where $T = \{\tau_1, ..., \tau_{RI}\}$.

Let it be Q different COF $Y_q \subseteq Y$ for a Moore FSM. Let us encode each COF Y_q by a binary code $K(Y_q)$ having R_Q bits:

$$R_Q = \lceil log_2 Q \rceil. \tag{6}$$

Let us use the variables $z_r \in Z$ for encoding of the COF $Y_q \subseteq Y$, where $|Z| = R_Q$.

Analysis of Fig. 1 shows that there are the following COF in FSM S_1: $Y_1 = \emptyset, Y_2 = \{y_2, y_3\}, Y_3 = \{y_3\}, Y_4 = \{y_2, y_4\}$. So, there is $Q = 4$. It gives $R_Q = 2$ and $Z = \{z_1, z_2\}$.

The COF Y_1 corresponds to the class B_1. The collections Y_2 and Y_3 determine the class B_2. But the COF Y_4 determines two classes, B_2 and B_3. It means that it is necessary to have some identifiers to distinguish the classes B_2 and B_3 for the COF Y_4. In the discussed case, it is enough two identifiers (I_1 and I_2) to distinguish the classes. Let the pair $\langle Y_4, I_2 \rangle$ determine the class B_2, whereas $\langle Y_4, I_2 \rangle$ the class B_3.

In common case, it is enough K identifiers forming the set $ID = \{I_1, ..., I_K\}$. Let us encode them using R_K variables where

$$R_K = \lceil log_2 K \rceil. \tag{7}$$

Let us use variables $v_r = V$ for encoding of identifiers where $|V| = R_K$.

Basing on these preliminaries, we propose the structural diagram of Moore FSM U_2 (Fig. 2b). In U_2, the LUTer1 generates functions

$$Z = Z(\tau, X); \tag{8}$$

$$V = V(T, X). \tag{9}$$

The LUTer2 implements the systems

$$Y = Y(Z); \tag{10}$$

$$T = T(Z, V). \tag{11}$$

Our analysis of the library of standard benchmarks [11] shows that the following conditions take places:

$$R_Q < R; \tag{12}$$

$$R_I < R; \tag{13}$$

$$H(U_2) < H(U_1). \tag{14}$$

We use the symbol $H(U_i)$ to denote the number of terms in the system Φ of $U_i(\overline{1, 2})$.

Basing on (12)–(14), we can expect that logic circuits obtained for FSM U_2 consume less.

Let us point out that a state of transition $a_s \in A$ is represented by a pair $\langle Y_q, I_k \rangle$, where $A_s \in B_i$ and $Y_q \subseteq Y$ is generated in the state $a_s \in A$. It means that the code $K(a_s)$ is represented as

$$K(a_s) = K(Y_q) * K(I_k). \tag{15}$$

In (15), the symbol $K(Y_q)$ stands for the code of COF Y_q, the symbol $K(I_k)$ for the code of identifier $I_k \in ID$. So, the code $K(a_s)$ should be transformed into corresponding codes from (15).

4   Proposed Design Method

In this article, we propose a design method for U_2. It includes the following steps:

1. Constructing partition Π_A and collections $Y_q \subseteq Y$ for a given STG.
2. Constructing the pairs $\langle Y_q, I_k \rangle$ for states $a_s \in A$.
3. Encoding of classes $B_i \in \Pi_A$, collections $Y_q \subseteq Y$ and identifiers $I_k \in ID$.
4. Transforming initial STG into class transition graph (CTG).
5. Finding systems (8)–(11).
6. Implementing FSM logic circuit using LUTs of a particular FPGA chip.

Let us apply this method for the Moore FSM S_1. As it is mentioned before, there are the partition $\Pi_A = \{B_1, B_2, B_3\}$ with classes $B_1 = \{a_1\}$, $B_2 = \{a_2, a_3, a_4\}$ and $B_3 = \{a_5\}$ and the collections $Y_1 = \emptyset$, $Y_2 = \{y_1, y_2\}$, $Y_3 = \{y_3\}$ and $Y_4 = \{y_2, y_4\}$. It gives $I = 3$ and $Q = 4$.

There are the following pairs $\langle Y_q, I_k \rangle$ in the discussed case: $\langle Y_1, \emptyset \rangle = a_1, \langle Y_2, \emptyset \rangle = a_2, \langle Y_3, \emptyset \rangle = a_3, \langle Y_4, I_1 \rangle = a_4$ and $\langle Y_4, I_2 \rangle = a_5$. So, there is $K = 2$ and $I = \{I_1, I_2\}$.

Using (1), (5), (6) and (7), we can find that $R = 3$, $R_I = 2$, $R_Q = 2$ and $R_K = 1$. Using (15), we can find that the codes $K(a_s)$ should include $R_Q + R_K = 3$ bits. It gives the set $\Phi = \{D_1, D_2, D_3\}$. Functions D_1, D_2 determine the variables z_1 and z_2. Function D_3 determines the variable v_1. So, there are the following sets: $Z = \{z_1, z_2\}$, $V = \{v_1\}$ and $T = \{\tau_1, \tau_2\}$.

Let us encode in the trivial way the classes $B_i \in \Pi_A$, the collections $Y_q \subseteq Y$ and identifiers $I_k \in I$. It gives the following codes: $K(B_1) = K(Y_1) = 00$, $K(B_2) = K(Y_2) = 01$, $K(B_3) = K(Y_3) = 10$, $K(Y_4) = 11$, $K(I_1) = 0$ and $K(I_2) = 1$.

Using these codes, we can find the codes $K(a_s)$ corresponding to (15). There are the following codes: $K(a_1) = 00*, K(a_2) = 01*, K(a_3) = 10*, K(a_4) = 110$ and $K(a_5) = 111$. The symbol "*" corresponds to the element $\emptyset$ in the pairs $\langle Y_q, I_K \rangle$.

To construct a CTG, let us replace the states $a_m \in B_i$ by a single vertex $B_i \in \Pi_A$. In the discussed case, the CTG is shown in Fig. 3.

If some class $B_i \in \Pi_A$ has more than one state, then these states are shown inside a particular vertex of CTG. We did it for the class B_2.

There are the following columns in the structure table of U_2: B_i, $K(B_i)$, a_s, $K(a_S)$, X_h, Φ_h, h. This table is constructed on the base of CTG. The column $K(a_s)$

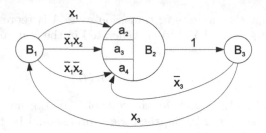

Fig. 3. Class transition graph for Moore FSM S_1

includes a code of the state of transition (12). The column X_h contains an input signal determining a transition from a state $a_m \in B_i$ into a state $a_s \in A$. The column Φ_h contains input memory functions $D_r \in \Phi$ equal to 1 to load the codes $K(Y_q)$ and $K(I_K)$ into the distributed state register.

The column h contains the number of transition ($h = \overline{1, H(U_2)}$). In the case of S_1, this table has $H(U_2) = 6$ rows (Table 1). We use the combination 11 to optimize the codes of B_2 and B_3. We replace all "*" in state codes by zeros.

Table 1. Structure table of Moore FSM S_1

B_i	$K(B_i)$	a_s	$K(a_s)$	X_h	Φ_h	h
B_1	00	a_2	010	x_1	D_2	1
		a_3	100	$\bar{x}_1 x_2$	D_1	2
		a_4	110	$\bar{x}_1 \bar{x}_2$	$D_1 D_2$	3
B_2	*1	a_5	111	1	$D_1 D_2 D_3$	4
B_3	1*	a_1	000	x_3	–	5
		a_4	110	$\bar{x}_3$	$D_1 D_2$	6

The ST is used to derive the functions (8) and (9). In the discussed case, there are the following functions:

$$z_1 = D1 = \bar{\tau}_1 \bar{\tau}_2 \bar{x}_1 \vee \tau_2 \vee \tau_1 \bar{x}_3;$$
$$z_2 = D_2 = \bar{\tau}_1 \bar{\tau}_2 x_1 \vee \bar{\tau}_1 \bar{\tau}_2 \bar{x}_2 \vee \tau_2 \vee \tau_1 \bar{x}_3; \tag{16}$$
$$v_1 = D_3 = \tau_2.$$

To find the functions (10), we should find disjunctions of COF $Y_q \subseteq Y$ for each function $y_n \in Y$. In the discussed case, there are the following functions:

$$y_1 = Y_2 = \bar{z}_1 z_2;$$
$$y_2 = Y_2 \vee Y_4 = z_2;$$
$$y_3 = Y_3 = z_1 \bar{z}_2; \tag{17}$$
$$y_4 = Y_4 = z_1 z_2.$$

To find the functions (11), we should find disjunctions of state codes $a_s \in B_i$ for each class B_i: $B_1 = A_1, B_2 = A_2 \vee A_3 \vee A_4$ and $B_3 = A_5$. It gives the following functions: $B_1 = \bar{z}_1 \bar{z}_2, B_2 = \tau_2 = \bar{z}_1 z_2 \vee z_1 \bar{z}_2 \vee z_1 z_2 v_1; B_3 = \tau_1 = z_1 z_2 v_1$.

To execute the last step of the proposed design method, such problems should be solved as the mapping, placing and routing [10]. To do it, some industrial packages should be used [1,21]. In our research, we use program tools of Xilinx to implement the FSM logic circuits.

5   Replacement LUTs by EMBs

It is possible to improve the characteristics of FSM replacing LUTs by embedded memory blocks (EMB) [5,7,9,15,18–20]. The EMBs of modern FPGA chips [2,13] have a property of configurability. It means that such parameters as the number of cells and their outputs can be changed. There are the following typical configurations of EMBs: $32K \times 1$, $16K \times 2$, $8K \times 4$, $4K \times 8$, $2K \times 16$, $1K \times 32$ and 512×64 (bits) [2,13]. So, modern EMBs are very flexible and can be tuned to meet a particular design.

It is possible to implement an FSM circuit using only a single EMB [20]. It can be done if the following condition takes place:

$$(N + R) \cdot 2^{L+R} \leq V_0. \tag{18}$$

In (18), the symbol V_0 stands for the number of cells in the configuration of EMB having $t_F = 1$ outputs. Of course, the condition (18) has place only for rather simple FSMs.

To improve the characteristics of U_1, we propose to replace the LUTer2 by EMBer. The symbol EMBer stands for the circuit implemented with EMBs. Such a replacement leads to the FSM U_3 (Fig. 4).

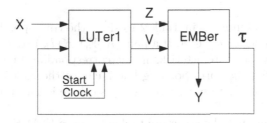

Fig. 4. Structural diagram of Moore FSM U_3

In this FSM, the EMBer implements the systems (10) and (11). Our analysis of the library [11] shows that the following condition takes place for all standard benchmarks [11]:

$$2^{R_Q + R_K}(N + R_I) \leq V_0. \tag{19}$$

It means that only a single EMB is enough for implementing FSM circuits based on the model U_3. This model can be used till the following condition takes place:

$$S_A \geq R_Q + R_K. \tag{20}$$

In (20), the symbol S_A stands for the number of address bits for some configuration of EMB.

There are the same steps 1–5 in design methods for U_2 and U_3. But there is a difference in the executing the step 6. In the case of U_2 it is necessary to construct the table of EMBer. It includes the following columns: $K(Y_q)$, $K(I_K)$, Y, T, h. The first two columns determine an address of a memory cell. The table includes H_E lines where

$$H_E = 2^{R_Q + R_K}. \tag{21}$$

In the discussed case, there is $R_Q = 2$ and $R_K = 1$. So, there is $H_E = 8$. Table 2 represents the table of EMBer for Moore FSM S_1.

Table 2. Table of EMBer of Moore FSM S_1

$K(Y_q)$	$K(I_K)$	Y	T	h	a_m
$z_1 z_2$	v_1	$y_1 y_2 y_3 y_4$	$\tau_1 \tau_2$		
00	0	0000	00	1	a_1
00	1	****	**	2	*
01	0	1100	01	3	a_2
01	1	****	**	4	*
10	0	001*	01	5	a_3
10	1	****	**	6	*
11	0	0001	01	7	a_4
11	1	0001	10	8	a_5

We added the column a_m in Table 2 to show the correspondence among the pairs $\langle Y_q, I_K \rangle$ and states $a_m \in A$. If a pair $\langle K(Y_q), K(I_K) \rangle$ does not correspond to any state, then there are asterisks in the corresponding lines of Table 2. If a state $a_m \in B_i$, then the corresponding line includes the code of this class. For example, there is the relation $a_2, a_3, a_4 \in B_2$, so there is the code 01 in the lines 3,5 and 7 of Table 2.

Let us point out that the structure table of Moore FSM S_1 in the case of U_3 is the same as for U_2 (Table 1). It means that systems (8)–(9) are represented as the system (16) for both models U_2 and U_3 of FSM S_1.

6   Results of Investigations

We use the standard benchmarks [11] to investigate efficiency of proposed method. The library LGSynth93 includes 48 finite-state machines represented in the KISS2 format.

To use the benchmarks, we worked out the CAD tool named K2F. It translates the KISS2 file into VHDL model of the Moore FSM. We use Active-HDL environment to synthesize and simulate the FSM. To implement the FSM circuits, we use Xilinx ISE 14.1 package. We choose the FPGA device XC5vex30ff324 by Virtex-5 of Xilinx as a target platform. Some results of investigations are shown in Table 3.

Table 3. Results of investigation for FSM U_2

BM	U_1 auto	U_1 compact	JEDI	DEMAIN	U_2
cse	74	72	57	63	42
dk16	72	59	49	67	36
ex1	96	111	90	86	56
keyb	84	98	70	74	52
kirkman	77	85	68	70	50
planet	152	208	145	154	105
S1488	210	212	183	185	134
S298	542	495	443	465	315
scf	269	303	232	260	174
styr	178	191	156	158	114
Total	1754	1834	1482	1582	1078
Percentage	163%	170%	137%	147%	100%

There are the numbers of LUTs necessary for implementing logic circuits of different FSMs for given benchmarks in Table 3. There is the name of a benchmark in the column BM. The following methods were taken for comparison with U_2: (1) FSM U_1 designed with method "Auto" of ISE 14.1; (2) FSM U_1 designed with method "Compact" of ISE 14.1; (3) Moore FSM used the state assignment by JEDI from SIS [17]; (4) Moore FSM designed by DEMAIN [13].

We show the most complex benchmarks from [11] into Table 3. As follows from Table 3, the FSM U_2 always produces the best results. The row "Total" gives the overall numbers of LUTs for all benchmarks (for the given design method). The row "Percentage" shows the percentage of the total number of LUTs regarding the FSM U_2. We have taken the total number of LUTs for U_2 as 100%.

Our approach gives better results for 60% of all benchmarks from [11]. If an FSM has less than 20 states, then better results belong to JEDI. Our methods produces better results because: (1) we take into account the existence of PES and (2) we encode the collections of output functions. The JEDI uses PES but there is no encoding of COF for this method. Also, the JEDI uses state variables $T_r \in T$ for representing classes of PES. We use some additional variables $\tau_r \in \mathcal{T}$. Due to these two features, our method produces better circuits than JEDI (and all other methods from Table 3).

We also investigated the efficiency of the model U_3. The same FSMs were taken for comparison with U_3 as it was for the case of U_2. The results of investigations for FSM U_3 are shown in Table 4.

Our analysis of the library [16] shows that it is enough a single EMB to implement output functions in the cases of U_1 auto, U_1 compact, JEDI and DEMAIN. The same is true for the case of U_3. So, there are only numbers of LUTs shown in Table 4.

As follows from Table 4, our approach gives better results for all complex benchmarks from [16]. The reasons for it are stated during the analysis of Table 3. But if EMBs are used, then there is a gain exceeds the gain for the case of LUT-based FSMs. It follows from comparison the rows "Percentage" from Tables 3 and 4.

Table 4. Results of investigation for FSM U_3

BM	U_1 auto	U_1 compact	JEDI	DEMAIN	U_3
cse	64	62	47	53	32
dk16	65	52	42	60	29
ex1	84	99	78	74	44
keyb	73	87	59	63	41
kirkman	68	76	59	61	41
planet	128	185	122	131	82
S1488	184	186	157	159	108
S298	529	482	430	452	302
scf	241	275	204	232	146
styr	164	177	142	144	100
Total	1601	1681	1329	1429	925
Percentage	173%	182%	144%	154%	100%

To explain this conclusion, let us construct a table with comparison of numbers of LUTs necessary in the case of LUT-based and EMB-based FSMs. It is Table 5. There is a ratio of numbers of LUTs for corresponding cells of Tables 3 and 4.

In all cases, practically the same number of LUTs is replaced by a single EMB. It is equal to N for U_1 auto, U_1 compact, JEDI and DEMAIN. It is equal to $N + R_I$ for U_2 and U_3. So, the less number of LUTs in LUTer1 (or LUTer), the better results can be obtained due to replacement LUTer2 by EMBer. For example, in the case of U_1 auto saving is equal to 12%. But transition from U_2 to U_3 saves in average 22% of LUTs (see the last column of Table 4).

Table 5. Relations between Tables 3 and 4

BM	U_1 auto	U_1 compact	JEDI	DEMAIN	U_2/U_3
cse	1,16	1,16	1,21	1,19	1,31
dk16	1,11	1,13	1,16	1,12	1,24
ex1	1,14	1,12	1,15	1,16	1,27
keyb	1,15	1,13	1,19	1,17	1,27
kirkman	1,13	1,12	1,15	1,15	1,22
planet	1,18	1,12	1,19	1,17	1,28
S1488	1,14	1,15	1,17	1,16	1,24
S298	1,02	1,03	1,03	1,03	1,04
scf	1,11	1,10	1,14	1,12	1,21
styr	1,09	1,08	1,10	1,10	1,14
Total	11,23	11,14	11,49	11,37	12,22
Average	1,12	1,11	1,15	1,14	1,22

7   Conclusion

The proposed method is based on representing state codes as concatenations of class codes and codes of collections of output functions. It targets LUT-based FSM circuits. Our investigation shows that the method produces FSM circuits having fewer LUTs than the methods used by SIS, DEMAIN and ISE 14.1. The method could be applied for rather complex Moore FSMs having more than 20 states.

The future direction of our research is the development of a method for encoding of collections of output functions. It is necessary if the following condition is violated:

$$R_Q > S. \tag{22}$$

The method should diminish the number of arguments in Boolean function (8). It allows hardware reduction in the circuit of block LUTer2.

References

1. Altera: http://www.altera.com. Accessed Jan 2016
2. Baranov, S.: Logic Synthesis of Control Automata. Kluwer Academic Publishers, Boston (1994)
3. Barkalov, A., Titarenko, L.: Logic Synthesis for FSM-Based Control Units. Springer, Berlin (2009)
4. Barkalov, A., Titarenko, L., Barkalov, A.: Structural decomposition as a tool for the optimization of an FPGA-based implementation of a mealy FSM. Cybern. Syst. Anal. **48**(2), 313–322 (2012)
5. Barkalov, A., Titarenko, L., Kołopieńczyk, M.: EMB-based design of Mealy FSM. In: 12th IFAC Conference on Programmable Devices and Embedded Systems, Velké Karlovice, Czechy, pp. 215–220 (2013)

6. Barkalov, A., Titarenko, L., Kołopieńczyk, M., Mielcarek, K., Bazydło, G.: Logic synthesis for FPGA-based Finite State Machines. Studies in Systems, Decision and Control, vol. 38. Springer International Publishing, Cham (2015). http://link.springer.com/book/10.1007/978-3-319-24202-6
7. Cong, J., Yan, K.: Synthesis for FPGAs with embedded memory blocks. In: Proceedings of the 2000 ACM/SIGDA 8th International Symposium on FPGAs, pp. 75–82 (2000)
8. Czerwinski, R., Kania, D.: Area and speed oriented synthesis of FSMs for PAL-based CPLDs. Microprocess. Microsyst. **36**(1), 45–61 (2012). http://dx.doi.org/10.1016/j.micpro.2011.06.004
9. Garcia-Vargas, I., Senhadji-Navarro, R., Jiménez-Moreno, G., Civit-Balcells, A., Guerra-Gutierrez, P.: ROM-based finite state machine implementation in low cost FPGAs. In: IEEE International Symposium on Industrial Electronics ISIE 2007, pp. 2342–2347. IEEE (2007)
10. Grout, I.: Digital Systems Design with FPGAs and CPLDs. Elsevier Science, Oxford (2008)
11. LGSynth93: International Workshop on logic synthesis benchmark suite (LGSynth93). TAR, Benchmarks test (1993). http://www.cbl.ncsu.edu:16080/benchmarks/LGSynth93/LGSynth93.tar
12. Micheli, G.D.: Synthesis and Optimization of Digital Circuits. McGraw-Hill, New York (1994)
13. Nowicka, M., Łuba, T., Rawski, M.: FPGA-based decomposition of Boolean functions. Algorithms and implementation. In: Proceedings of Sixth International Conference on Advanced Computer Systems, pp. 502–509 (1999)
14. Rawski, M., Selvaraj, H., Łuba, T.: An application of functional decomposition in ROM-based FSM implementation in FPGA devices. J. Syst. Archit. **51**(6–7), 423–434 (2005)
15. Rawski, M., Tomaszewicz, P., Borowski, G., Łuba, T.: Logic Synthesis Method of Digital Circuits Designed for Implementation with Embedded Memory Blocks on FPGAs. In: Adamski, M., Barkalov, A., Węgrzyn, M. (eds.) Design of Digital Systems and Devices. LNEE, vol. 79, pp. 121–144. Springer, Berlin (2011)
16. Scholl, C.: Functional Decomposition with Application to FPGA Synthesis. Kluwer Academic Publishers, Boston (2001)
17. Sentowich, E., Singh, K., Lavango, L., Moon, C., Murgai, R., Saldanha, A., Savoj, H., Stephan, P.R., Bryton, R.K., Sangiovanni-Vincentelli, A.L.: SIS: a system for sequential circuit synthesis. Technical report, University of California, Berkely (1992)
18. Sklyarov, V.: Synthesis and implementation of RAM-based finite state machines in FPGAs. In: Hartenstein, R.W., Grünbacher, H. (eds.) FPL 2000. LNCS, vol. 1896, pp. 718–727. Springer, Heidelberg (2000). doi:10.1007/3-540-44614-1_76
19. Sutter, G., Todorovich, E., Lopez-Buedo, S., Boemo, E.: Low-power FSMs in FPGA: encoding alternatives. In: Hochet, B., Acosta, A.J., Bellido, M.J. (eds.) PATMOS 2002. LNCS, vol. 2451, pp. 363–370. Springer, Heidelberg (2002). doi:10.1007/3-540-45716-X_36
20. Tiwari, A., Tomko, K.: Saving power by mapping finite-state machines into embedded memory blocks in FPGAs. In: Proceedings of the Conference on Design, Automation and Test in Europe, vol. 2, pp. 916–921. IEEE Computer Society (2004)
21. Xilinx: http://www.xilinx.com. Accessed Jan 2016

Efficient Simulation of Interacting Particle Systems in Continuous Space and Time

Tomasz Ożański[✉]

Department of Electronics, Wrocław University of Technology, Wrocław, Poland
tomasz.ozanski@pwr.edu.pl

Abstract. Interacting particle systems models became an increasingly important tool for modeling complex real-world phenomena with applications ranging from ecology, classical physics to tumor evolution. The need for efficient algorithm for simulations becomes therefore apparent. The existing simulation ideas and frameworks mostly make use of lattice models with discrete time. The work presents an efficient algorithm allowing simulation of complicated models while allowing particles positioned in continuous space with continuous timing between events.

Keywords: Interacting particle system · Event driven simulation · Birth and death process · Tumor evolution

1 Introduction

The original motivation for interacting particle systems comes from statistical mechanics, with the first models being investigated in XIX century, focusing mainly on dynamics of particles representing real atoms and molecules interacting by physical forces and following Newton's Laws. The notable results obtained by such formulation include Boltzmann's kinetic gas theory and Navier-Stokes equations.

Another class of models were later developed to investigate phenomena in crystal lattice. One of such models was the Ising model. The particles represented magnetic spins, each in one of two possible states -1 or 1 arranged in a grid structure representing metallic lattice. The dynamics of the system was driven by a Hamiltonian function including nearest-neighbor interactions between spin and optional external magnetic field.

While it was still possible to analyze Ising model in one and two dimensions using mathematical tools and characterize a phase transition precisely, it quickly became apparent that answering more complicated questions regarding dynamics of the system becomes difficult with the available mathematical tools.

Spin models can be reinterpreted by assigning an existence of a particle to one of the states and an empty spot to the other to obtain a birth and death process where flipping a spin means creation (birth) or removal (death) of a particle from the system. Such processes can be used to model biological systems.

© IFIP International Federation for Information Processing 2017
Published by Springer International Publishing AG 2017. All Rights Reserved
K. Saeed et al. (Eds.): CISIM 2017, LNCS 10244, pp. 569–579, 2017.
DOI: 10.1007/978-3-319-59105-6_49

One of the first famous models of this type was Conway's Game of Life, it's aim was to emulate spreading of species on a two-dimensional space approximated by a spin lattice and a set of simple rules: a birth occurs when an empty spots has exactly 3 neighbors and a death occurs if an existing particle has less than two or more than three neighbors [3].

The growing computational power of the first computers allowed to run simulations allowing the direct observation of system dynamics, leading to development of new tools to analyze such models like Markov Chain Monte Carlo algorithms for the Ising model [4]. Another framework developed at that time to broaden classes of problem that could be analyzed were cellular automata. In the classical cellular automaton the dynamics usually happens in generations, i.e. all the cells are updated simultaneously and the next state of a cell depends only on the state of its nearest neighbors.

Lattice models have their strength in straightforward implementation as a computer program which can be as simple as a loop iterating over an array. However, the simplicity also has its drawbacks – enforcing all particles to lie on a grid is only suitable for models where particles are inherently distributed on a grid, otherwise it produces an unnecessary interference into model's dynamics. Another drawback comes from limitation on simulation space, because of limited memory of a computer the space also becomes limited, this problem becomes especially evident for higher dimensions. For example in a 3D model of length 1024 in each dimension where one byte is required per lattice site one needs 1 GB of memory just for storing the grid irregardless of how many particles there exist in the system.

For more advanced models the underlying lattice can be replaced with graph providing generalized neighborhoods for interaction. Many times the state transition rules can also be substituted by a probabilistic ones, what is a standard setting for both Contact Process or Voter Model, making them a Markov Processes. For a biological model more closely resembling nature, one would prefer to avoid using lattice models, but allow the particles to be in an Euclidean space.

Apart from continuous space, the Birth and Death Processes are usually also defined as continuous time processes. In the simplest case the state-changes are Markov process meaning only one event happens during a state change and the temporal spacing between two consecutive events is given as a rate for exponential distributions and depends on interactions between particles.

For simulation of an ecological system one usually considers two-dimensional continuous space with each particle representing an individual on a surface. The birth and death events of a particles directly correspond to start and end of life of modeled individual. The competition for resources between individuals and efficient spreading on large distances requires interactions to be long-ranged with close-ranged component emulating direct interactions between individuals.

Another area of applications which can be described by Birth and Death processes is dynamics of cell ensembles, especially in connection with models solid tumor evolution. In such models a cell is modeled as a particle, the birth and death event becomes a cell division and a cell death respectively. There are both short- and long-range interactions that can be considered here, the first type comes from mechanical pressure and local competition for glucose and oxygen and the second corresponds to the signals carried over by various chemicals.

Allowing different types of particles and adding intrinsic variables can simulate changes of the genetic profile of the cells. Such simulations would provide a important tool for understanding Darwinian forces between different subclones of a heterogeneously composed tumors. Better understanding of complex processes in tumor evolution would hopefully also advance the search for a cure for a cancer.

2 System Description

The system is defined on a set of particles, each having its position in D-dimensional euclidean space (with D being usually 2 or 3) and a set of other model-specific intrinsic parameters (attributes). The evolution of the class of systems can be described as a sequence of events each of them representing a single change to the state. The base events that can occur are:

- birth – creation of a particle to the configuration set
- death – removal of a particle from the configuration set

More complex events can be constructed as a combination of more than one base events, for example:

- jump – removal of a particle and creation of an identical one elsewhere
- division – removal of a particle and creation of two identical ones nearby
- mutation – removal of a particle and a creation of a new different one in the same place

While mutation is listed as complex event, for convenience and performance reasons it is better to consider it as another base event. In many models mutation would usually immediately follow any of the standard events to update the intrinsic parameters.

It is also worth noting that not all the dynamics can be captured by combining finite number of events and has to be approximated by a such, e.g. a continuous time motion can be replaced by a chain of shorter jumps.

The dynamics of the system is entirely described by timings between events which on the other hand depend on interactions between particles. In the deterministic case it means that the waiting time till the next event for a particle can be computed knowing the position of all the other particles and their intrinsic values. It is only required that no two events happen exactly at the same time, i.e. the order of the events is determined.

It is also possible to use stochastic timing where the distribution of the waiting time is known and depends on positions of all particles and their intrinsic values. In the simplest case the distribution is an exponential distribution with probability density function $f(x) = \lambda \exp(-\lambda x)$ with event intensity parameter λ dependent on interaction through functions called kernels.

The simplest death kernel is just a constant making lifespan exponentially-distributed with the rate of dying being same at any moment. An example of a death kernel with rate dependent on local density is

$$m(x; \gamma_t) = \sum_{y \in \gamma_t} e^{-\mathrm{dist}(x,y)}, \tag{1}$$

where γ_t is a configuration of all particles in the system at time t and $\mathrm{dist}(x, y)$ is Euclidian distance between particles x and y. In the presented kernel each neighbor contribution to local density is given by a Gaussian function.

A kernel describing an event in which a parent particle gives a birth to an offspring particle in principle can depend on both positions, however, it is easier to consider only the kernels where the placement of the offspring does not depend on the birth rate. For example a kernel

$$b(x, x'; \gamma) = \frac{1}{\sigma\sqrt{2\pi}} e^{\frac{-(\mathrm{dist}(x,x'))^2}{2\sigma^2}} \sum_{y \in \gamma} e^{-dist(x,y)} \tag{2}$$

describes a birth rate in position x' by particle x under configuration γ. The rate depends on local density around x and the offspring particle x' is placed according to a normal distribution centered around x' with standard deviation σ. For more examples of kernels see for instance [1] or the references therein.

3   Simulation Algorithm

3.1   Naive Algorithm

A naive algorithm which is capable of simulating the above process can be as follows

>   **while** configuration not empty **do**
>   >   **for** every particle P from configuration **do**
>   >   >   compute next event time
>   >
>   >   **end for**
>   >   decide which event comes first in time
>   >   execute event
>
>   **end while**

The algorithm as presented above is not very efficient. Several measures which can be taken to improve the situation are described below.

3.2   Partial Updates

There is no need to do a full update of the event list at each iteration, it is only necessary to update those events which could have possibly been changed by the executed event. Unfortunately not much can be done in a case when every event depends on all particles in the configuration set.

However, very often this is not the case, in many systems one might expect that a particle will have a very little effect on what is happening in a distant location. This is the case if long-range correlations are not present or not important for the evolution of the system.

Assume that the maximum range of interaction is known to be r_{max}. For an event which takes place at position x it is only needed to update all the events which have at least one dependency in ball with radius r_{max} centered at x.

3.3 Neighborhood Structure

To efficiently decide which events needs update the algorithm must be able to quickly find particles close to the place where the event occurred, therefore a special data structure is required to achieve this goal.

The space is subdivided into tiles, each representing a D-dimensional cube of fixed side-length approximately equal to r_{max}. All particles which spatially belong to the given tile are compactly stored together in a resizeable array. This approach fulfills the need for an efficient way to access all the particles in the given volume, but without an additional structure it does not provide an efficient way to find a single particle within the tile.

Non-empty ones are stored in a hash table with keys being their positions in D-dimensional space. Empty tiles are simply non-present elements in the hash table. This approach allows for having virtually no restrictions on simulation space while allowing constant-time tile access.

In contrast to other space-partitioning data structures like octrees or kd-trees an advantage of hash-based structure, apart from not having logarithmic access cost, is simplicity of implementation for multidimensional spaces. To access all the neighbors of a given point it is enough to visit a bounded number of tiles surrounding the point. In a two-dimensional case with tile size equal to r_{max} one has to visit up to 9 tiles.

3.4 Time Ordering

The update algorithm requires ability to quickly find the next event to be executed. To perform the operation efficiently a priority queue for all the events is required. The existing tile structure is extended with additional features allowing it to maintain a heap property.

For every tile it is enough to keep a pointer to a particle which event comes first within the tile. Whenever a new particle is added to the tile a single check is required to restore the pointer. One of the costly operations is removal of the particle from the tile which requires a linear search. However, in most use cases both insertion or removal is accompanied by an update to all the neighboring particles including those inside the tile. Both the incremental search and particle visitation have the same linear complexity in number of particles in tile therefore doing an incremental search does not increase the overall complexity. In fact an incremental search can be performed during particle visitation.

All the tiles are organized in a efficient heap structure namely a pairing heap which is believed to provide amortized logarithmic asymptotic complexity for all single-particle operations [2]. Adding all costs together a single event execution is linear in size of the neighborhood and has the same complexity in number of tiles as pairing heap.

3.5   Update Algorithm Examples

This subsection summarizes the ideas for an efficient simulation by giving example algorithms for the two basic events: birth and death.

Helper Functions. The helper functions used in the example algorithm are explained below

- HASHFINDTILE(p) – finds and returns a tile to which position p belongs to
- CREATETILE(p) – creates tiles to which position p will belong and inserts the tile to the hash table and heap-of-tiles
- REMOVETILE(T) – removes tile T from hash table and heap-of-tiles and destroys the tile
- PUSH(T,P) – adds particle P to tile T
- POP(T) – removes last particle from tile T
- RESETFIRSTEVENTPOINTER(T) – resets first event pointer in tile T
- INCLUDEINTERACTION(P,Q) – update particle P by including interaction with particle Q
- EXCLUDEINTERACTION(P,Q) – update particle P by excluding interaction with particle Q
- SAMPLENEWEVENT(P) – samples a new realization of an event for a particle P
- UPDATEFIRSTEVENTPOINTER(T,P) – checks whether particle T would now be the one with first event in tile T and updates the first event pointer accordingly
- HEAPOFTILESUPDATE(T) – updates position of tile T in heap-of-tiles structure
- SWAPCONTENTS(Q,R) – exchanges data of both particles including their positions.

Birth Event. A simple case of execution of a birth event requires updating all the interaction between newly-created particle and its neighbors it is possible to perform all the updates of the time-ordering structure at the same time. An example step-by-step algorithm for executing birth of a particle at position x is presented below:

function EXECUTEBIRTH(position x)
    $T \Leftarrow$ HASHFINDTILE(x)
    if T not found **then**
        $T \Leftarrow$ CREATETILE(x)

   end if
$P \Leftarrow$ PARTICLE(x)
PUSH(T,P)
for non-empty tile $U \neq T$ which can have particles within $r_{\max}$ from P **do**
   RESETFIRSTEVENTPOINTER(U)
   for every particle Q within tile U **do**
      if DISTANCE(P,Q) $< r_{\max}$ **then**
         INCLUDEINTERACTION(P,Q)
         INCLUDEINTERACTION(Q,P)
         SAMPLENEWEVENT(Q)
      end if
      UPDATEFIRSTEVENTPOINTER(U,Q)
   end for
   HEAPOFTILESUPDATE(U)
end for
RESETFIRSTEVENTPOINTER(T)
for every particle Q in T except the last one **do**
   if DISTANCE(P,Q) $< r_{\max}$ **then**
      INCLUDEINTERACTION(P,Q)
      INCLUDEINTERACTION(Q,P)
      SAMPLENEWEVENT(Q)
   end if
   UPDATEFIRSTEVENTPOINTER(T,Q)
end for
GENERATENEWEVENT(P)
UPDATEFIRSTEVENTPOINTER(T,P)
HEAPOFTILESUPDATE(T)
end function

Death Event. An execution of a death event requires excluding the interaction with the particle to be removed. Again it is possible to update time-ordering structures at the same time. In an example step-by-step algorithm for executing a death of a particle P is the following:

  function EXECUTEDEATH(particle P)
   $T \Leftarrow$ HASHFINDTILE(P)
   for non-empty tile $U \neq T$ which can have particles within $r_{\max}$ from P **do**
      RESETFIRSTEVENTPOINTER(U)
      for every particle Q within tile U **do**
         if DISTANCE(P,Q) $< r_{\max}$ **then**
            EXCLUDEINTERACTION(Q,P)
            SAMPLENEWEVENT(Q)
         end if
         UPDATEFIRSTEVENTPOINTER(U,Q)
      end for
      HEAPOFTILESUPDATE(U)

      end for
      RESETFIRSTEVENTPOINTER(T)
      for every particle Q in T except the last one **do**
        if $P = Q$ **then**
          $R \Leftarrow$ LAST(T)
          SWAPCONTENTS(Q,R)
        end if
        if DISTANCE(P,Q) $< r_{\max}$ **then**
          EXCLUDEINTERACTION(Q,P)
          SAMPLENEWEVENT(Q)
        end if
        UPDATEFIRSTEVENTPOINTER(T,Q)
      end for
      POP(T)
      if $T = \emptyset$ **then**
        REMOVETILE(T)
      end if
    end function

4 Summary and Outlook

The running time of the algorithm greatly depends on ratio of tile size with to $r_{\max}$.

On one side too large tiles would result in unnecessary visitations of neighboring particles on the other side having too small tiles would mean large number of updates to heap-of-tiles structure. To find the optimal value for tile size one has to perform an empirical search since results might vary for different models and hardware. The optimal tile size search results for an example model are presented on Fig. 1.

The example model has the timings between events given by rates for exponential distributions – birth rate and death rate depend on intrinsic parameters of each cell and local density measured by a Gaussian kernel. The relation between density and birth rate and expected lifespan is given by a normalized Gaussian function. The placement of new particles is normally distributed with respect to the parent particle. After each birth event, with small probability both parent and child particle undergo a mutation modifying particle's intrinsic parameters.

The cost of updating of heap-of-tiles structure increases as number of tiles in the system becomes larger. Due to that fact the time needed for execution of a single event in a growing model also increases. The results for the example model are presented on Fig. 2.

During a run, a simulation gives access to all the particles' positions and their intrinsic values which can be used to produce snapshots of the data for viewing or static analysis. A render of a configuration from a sample cancer evolution model where each particle represents a tumor cell is presented on Fig. 3.

The program can be also configured to produce a stream containing all the events in the chronological order which can be used for further analysis. While

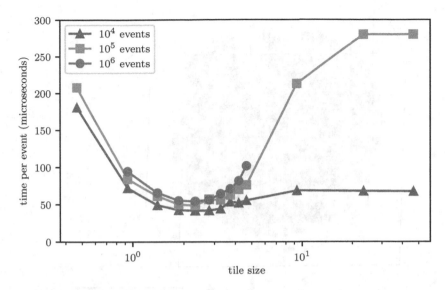

Fig. 1. Execution time per event in relation tile size (in multiplicities of interaction range r_{max}). Tests were performed for runs of different lengths: 10^4, 10^5 and 10^6 events

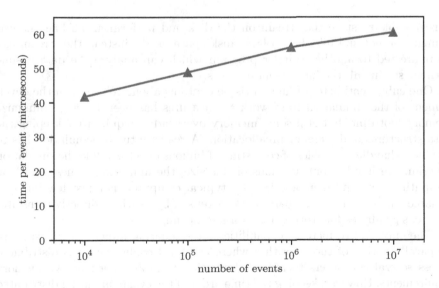

Fig. 2. Execution time per event in relation to number of events executed measured for on IntelCore i5 processor clocked at 2.6 GHz. The execution of a million of events requires about one minute

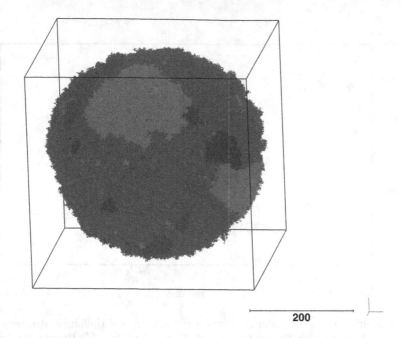

200

Fig. 3. Render of a sample 3D configuration having about 8.2 million points. Different colors correspond to different values of particles' intrinsic parameters. The render was created using CloudCompare software

it is possible to store the stream on the disk and perform an off-line analysis it might be not suitable due to large disk space needs, instead the stream can be redirected to another simpler program which can analyze the data on-line without storing all the intermediate events.

One cubic centimeter of human tissue contains about 10^9 cells. In the development of the simulation framework all measures has been taken to minimize memory footprint, but still some memory overhead is required for keeping the data structures and memory preallocation. A realistic tumor simulation has to be able to handle ensembles of consisting of billions of cells. While the simulation program can handle configurations of this size, the limitation comes from long computing time and memory size of a typical computer. For just few intrinsic variables the size of a single particle takes tens of bytes which directly translates into tens gigabytes for storing a billion-sized configuration.

The only way to increase capabilities for simulating larger systems seem to be parallelization of the algorithm where the total configuration is distributed across several computers to reduce simulation time and per-machine memory requirements. However, keeping the time order of the events in during distributed computations seems to be major difficulty.

Acknowledgements. I thank my supervisor Tyll Krüger for guidance and corrections to this work. I grateful to Ewaryst Rafajłowicz and Ewa Skubalska-Rafajłowicz for valuable discussions and support during my PhD program at Wrocław University of Technology. This research was supported in part by PL-Grid Infrastructure.

I thank for the support of Yuri Kondratiev and hospitality and financial support for several visits in Bielefeld University. I'm thankful to Center for Interdisciplinary Research (ZiF) in Bielefeld where part of the work was carried out in ZiF cooperation group *Multiscale Modelling of Tumour Initiation, Growth and Progression: From Gene Regulation to Evolutionary Dynamics.*

I thank my colleagues Mykola Lebid, Viktor Bezborodov and Marcin Bodych for many discussions on the topic.

References

1. Finkelshtein, D., Kondratiev, Y., Kutoviy, O.: Individual based model with competition in spatial ecology. SIAM J. Math. Anal. **41**(1), 297–317 (2009)
2. Fredman, M.L., Sedgewick, R., Sleator, D.D., Tarjan, R.E.: The pairing heap: a new form of self-adjusting heap. Algorithmica **1**(1–4), 111–129 (1986)
3. Gardner, M.: Mathematical games: the fantastic combinations of john conways new solitaire game life. Sci. Am. **223**(4), 120–123 (1970)
4. Liggett, T.: Interacting Particle Systems, vol. 276. Springer, Heidelberg (2012)

Sampling Method for the Flow Shop with Uncertain Parameters

Paweł Rajba and Mieczysław Wodecki[✉]

Institute of Computer Science, University of Wrocław,
Joliot-Curie 15, 50-383 Wrocław, Poland
{pawel.rajba,mieczyslaw.wodecki}@uwr.edu.pl

Abstract. In the classic approach for optimization problems modelling well defined parameters are assumed. However, in real life problems we find ourself very often in a situation where parameters are not defined precisely. This may have many sources like inaccurate measurement, inability to establishing precise values, randomness, inconsistent information or subjectivity.

In this paper we propose a sampling method for solving optimization problems with uncertain parameters modeled by random variables. Moreover, by applying confidence intervals theory, the execution time has been significantly reduced. We will also show an application of the method for the flowshop problem with deadlines and parameters modeled by random variables with the normal distribution.

Keywords: Flowshop with deadlines · Uncertain parameters · Tabu search · Normal distribution

1 Introduction

Practical machine scheduling problems are numerous and varied. They arise in diverse areas such as flexible manufacturing systems, production planning, communication, computer design, etc. A scheduling problem consists in finding sequences of jobs on given machines with the objective of minimizing some function. In a simpler version of the problem, the flow shop scheduling, all jobs pass through all machines in the some order. In this paper, we deal with another specific version of the problem called a permutation flow shop scheduling problem where each machine processes the jobs in the same order ($F||w_i U_i$).

Research concerning problems of algorithms arrangement refers mainly to deterministic models [1]. To solve such problems, which belong in the majority of cases to the NP-strongly hard class, rough algorithms are applied successfully [2, 6, 8]. They are mainly based on local optimalization methods: simulated annealing, tabu search and a genetic algorithm. Determined by these algorithms, solutions only slightly differ from best solutions. However, in practice, in the course of a process realisation (according to the fixed schedule) very often it

© IFIP International Federation for Information Processing 2017
Published by Springer International Publishing AG 2017. All Rights Reserved
K. Saeed et al. (Eds.): CISIM 2017, LNCS 10244, pp. 580–591, 2017.
DOI: 10.1007/978-3-319-59105-6_50

appears that certain parameters (e.g. the task completion time) are different from the initial ones. By the lack of the solutions stability in the fixed schedule there may occur a big mistake, which makes such a schedule unacceptable. That's why a necessity exists to construct such models and methods of their solutions that would take into account potential changes in the course of parameters process realisation and generate stable solutions [4,9,15].

Problems of arrangements with uncertain data may be solved using methods based on elements of probability calculus [5,13,14]. In this work we deal with the flow shop problem of tasks arrangement with the latest completion times and the minimalisation of the costs sum of tardy tasks [7,10]. On the basis of this problem the resistance to a random variable of constructive solutions of parameters according to tabu search metaheuristics is examined.

In this study, permutation flow shop scheduling problem of the typical situation of the flexible production systems which occupy a very important place in recent production systems are taken into consideration with random variables due dates.

2   Flowshop Problem

Let $\mathcal{J} = \{1, \ldots, N\}$ be a set of jobs to be executed on M machines from the set $\mathcal{M} = \{1, \ldots, m\}$. At any given moment a specific machine can execute at most one job and all jobs needs to be executed without the preemption. Any job $j \in \mathcal{J}$ needs to be executed in sequence on every machine and if a job is being executed on the machine k then it means that it has been executed on machine the $k - 1$ ($k = 2, 3, \ldots, M$). Jobs are executed in a given order determined by a permutation with a constraint that the permutation is applied on all machines. The execution of a job on a machine is named operation. In this section we consider flowshop problem with due dates defined as a set $(p_{i,j}, w_i, \widetilde{d_i})$ ($i = 1, \ldots, N$, $j = 1, \ldots, M$) where $p_{i,j}$ are processing times of operations, w_i are weights for all jobs and $\widetilde{d_i}$ are due dates for all jobs, but they are defined as random variables with the distribution $N(d_i, c \cdot d_i)$.

Let Π be the set of all permutations of the set $\mathcal{J}$. For every permutation $\pi \in \Pi$ we define

$$
C_{\pi(i),j} = \begin{cases} \sum_{k=1}^{i} p_{\pi(i),j}, & \text{dla } j = 1, \\ C_{\pi i, j-1} + p_{\pi(i),j}, & \text{dla } i = 1, j > 1, \\ \max\{C_{\pi i, j-1}, C_{\pi i-1, j}\} + p_{\pi(i),j}, & \text{dla } i > 1, j > 1, \end{cases}
$$

as a completion time of execution job i on machine j in reference to permutation π.

The cost of execution of operations determined by permutation π is as follows

$$
\sum_{i=1}^{n} w_{\pi(i)} \widetilde{U}_{i\pi(i)}.
$$

where

$$\tilde{U}_{i\pi(i)} = \begin{cases} 0 & \text{dla} \quad C_{\pi(i)} \leqslant \tilde{d}_{i\pi(i)}, \\ 1 & \text{dla} \quad C_{\pi(i)} > \tilde{d}_{i\pi(i)}. \end{cases}$$

We consider the optimization problem where the goal is to find a permutation $\pi^* \in \Pi$ which minimizes cost of execution of all operations:

$$\widetilde{W}(\pi^*) = \min_{\pi \in \Pi} \left(\sum_{i=1}^{n} w_{\pi(i)} \tilde{U}_{i\pi(i)} \right).$$

3   Tabu search

Rough algorithms are used mainly to solve NP-hard problems of discrete optimization. Solutions determined by these algorithms are found to be fully satisfactory (very often they differ from the best known solutions approximately less than a few percent). One of realizations of constructive methods of these algorithms is the tabu search, whose basic elements are

- *movement* – a function which transforms one task into another,
- *neighborhood* – a subset of acceptable solutions set,
- *tabu list* – a list which contains attributes of a number of examined solutions.

Let $\pi \in \Pi$ be a starting permutation, L_{TS} a tabu list and π^* the best solution found so far.

Algorithm 1. Tabu Search

1: **repeat**
2:     Determine the neighborhood $\mathcal{N}(\pi)$ of permutation π
3:     Delete from $\mathcal{N}(\pi)$ permutations forbidden by the list L_{TS}
4:     Determine a permutation $\delta \in \mathcal{N}(\pi)$, such that $\mathcal{F}(\delta) = \min\{\mathcal{F}(\beta): \beta \in \mathcal{N}(\pi)\}$
5:     **if** $\mathcal{F}(\delta) < \mathcal{F}(\pi^*)$ **then**
6:         $\pi^* := \delta$
7:     Place attributes δ on the list L_{TS}
8:     $\pi := \delta$
9: **until** the completion condition

3.1   Movement and Neighborhood

Let $\pi = (\pi(1), \ldots, \pi(n))$ be any permutation from the set Π. By π_l^k ($l = 1, 2, \ldots, k-1, k+1, \ldots, n$) we denote the permutation obtained from π by a change of positions $\pi(k)$ with $\pi(l)$. We say, in such a case, that a π_l^k permutation was generated from π by a type of a swap move s_l^k (i.e. a permutation $\pi_l^k = s_l^k(\pi)$). Then, let $M(\pi(k))$ be a set of swap moves of an element $\pi(k)$, a set of all such movements

$$\mathcal{M}(\pi) = \bigcup_{\pi(k) \in L(\pi)} M(\pi(k)).$$

The neighborhood of an element $\pi \in \Pi$ is a set of permutations

$$\mathcal{N}(\pi) = \left\{ s_l^k(\pi) \colon s_l^k \in \mathcal{M}(\pi) \cap L(\pi) \right\},$$

where $L(\pi) = \{\pi(i) \colon C_{\pi(i)} > d_{\pi(i)}\}$ is a set of delay solutions in π.

By implementing an algorithm from the neighborhood permutations whose attributes are on the tabu list L_{TS} are removed.

3.2   The Tabu Moves List

To prevent a cycle from arising some attributes of each movement are put on the list of tabu moves. It's served by means of the FIFO queue. Performing a movement $s_j^r \in \mathcal{M}(\pi)$ (i.e. generating it from $\pi \in \Pi$ the π_j^r permutation) on the tabu list L_{TS} attributes of this movement, i.e. the triple $\left(\pi(r), j, \mathcal{F}(\pi_j^r)\right)$ are put down.

Assuming that we examine a movement $s_l^k \in \mathcal{M}(\beta)$ generating from $\beta \in \Pi$ a permutation β_l^k. If on the list L_{TS} there is a triple (r, j, Ψ) such that $\beta(k) = r$, $l = j$ and $\mathcal{F}(\beta_l^k) \leq \Psi$, then such a movement is forbidden and removed from the set $\mathcal{M}(\beta)$.

4   Robustness

Due to the fact that we consider uncertain environment and the actual values are not known at the moment of the algorithm execution, we need a way to measure the quality of solutions. We assume that we have a set of reference test data and there are two algorithms: the examined one and the reference one (classic in our paper). The scenario of verification is as follows. For a specific test instance both algorithms propose solutions π_p (examined) and π_d (reference) which we expect to be robust. Then we generate a set of disturbed subinstances based on the test instance and for every subinstance we calculate the cost of execution with reference to π_p (cost w_p) and π_d (cost w_d). We also calculate an "almost optimal" solution for the subinstance w^*. Having that we calculate a relative error for all subinstances, then calculate relative error for all instances and by that we are able to take conclusion about the algorithm. We do that for both algorithms and compare the final values.

More formally, let define the basic robustness coefficient as a relative distance between examined and the reference solution, i.e. let w be a cost of "robust" solution (w_p or w_d) and w^* be the reference "almost optimal" solution cost. Then relative error

$$\delta = \frac{w - w^*}{w^*} 100\%$$

and it shows how many percent w is worse than w^*.

In some scenarios we need to compare the sets of values based on the disturbed data, so we propose an extension to the basic error definition. Let consider s disturbed data instances, $w_1, \ldots, w_s$ be cost values obtained by examined algorithm and $w_1^*, \ldots w_s^*$ be reference cost values. Then we define extended relative error as follows:

$$\Delta = \frac{\frac{w_1 + \ldots + w_n}{n} - \frac{w_1^* + \ldots + w_n^*}{n}}{\frac{w_1^* + \ldots + w_n^*}{n}} = \frac{(w_1 + \ldots + w_n) - (w_1^* + \ldots + w_n^*)}{w_1^* + \ldots + w_n^*}$$

Let ψ be a data instance, $\mathfrak{D}(\psi)$ be a set of disturbed data subinstances obtain from ψ based on the random variable $\tilde{d}_i$ and

- A_{ref} be an algorithm which find the reference solution,
- A be the examined algorithm,
- $\pi_{M,x}$ be a solution obtained by algorithm $M \in \{A, A_{ref}\}$ for the problem instance x,
- $W(\pi_{M,x}, y)$ be the cost of instance y calculated by applying a solution $\pi_{M,x}$.

Then

$$\Delta(A, \psi, \mathfrak{D}(\psi)) = \frac{\sum_{\varphi \in \mathfrak{D}(\delta)} W(\pi_{A,\psi}, \varphi) - \sum_{\varphi \in \mathfrak{D}(\delta)} F(\pi_{A_{ref},\varphi}, \varphi)}{\sum_{\varphi \in \mathfrak{D}(\delta)} W(\pi_{A_{ref},\varphi}, \varphi)},$$

we define as solution robustness $\pi_{A,\psi}$ (obtained by the algorithm A for instance ψ) based on set of disturbed data $\mathfrak{D}(\psi)$.

Let Ω be a set of test data for the examined problem. Then by

$$\mathbb{S}(A, \Omega) = \frac{1}{\Omega} \sum_{\psi \in \Omega} \Delta(A, \psi, \mathfrak{D}(\psi)) \tag{1}$$

we define as the robustness coefficient for the algorithm A on the set of test data Ω. The less the value is, the better the algorithm is, i.e. solutions obtained by the examined algorithm are more robust and random changes in the actual data don't affect significantly the final execution cost.

5   Sampling Method

The idea of the method is as follows. In every tabu search algorithm iteration we are testing different candidate solutions from the neighbourhood to find the best one and improve the current global best solution. Let assume an instance $(p_{i,j}, w_i, \tilde{d}_i)$ and that we examine the candidate solution, a permutation π. Due to the fact that $\tilde{d}_i$ is defined as random variable, we don't know the actual data that may come. What we propose in the sampling method is to simulate this actual scenario by testing the candidate solution on a sample of disturbed data generated from $\tilde{d}_i$. We can describe the method in the following main steps:

1. Generate l vectors $\overline{d}^k = (\overline{d}_1^k, \ldots, \overline{d}_N^k)$, where $k \in \{1, \ldots, l\}$. By that we get l deterministic instances $(p_{i,j}, w_i, \overline{d}^k)$.

2. For every deterministic instance a cost is calculated based on the candidate solution π. By that we obtain sample $W_1^\pi, \ldots, W_l^\pi$.
3. We calculate a mean $\bar{x}$ and a standard deviation from s the sample which are used in the comparison by tabusearch. Of course less is better.

One can easily notice that in the above description we are missing the size of the sample, i.e. the value of l. We want the l to be as small as possible and meaningful on the other hand. To determine that we apply confidence intervals theory with the standard significance level $\alpha = 5\%$. Please note that we don't know the distribution of the sample $W_1^\pi, \ldots, W_l^\pi$. By that we apply the following variant of significance level formula:

$$\bar{x} - \mu_\alpha \frac{s}{\sqrt{l}} < m < \bar{x} + \mu_\alpha \frac{s}{\sqrt{l}}$$

where l is a sample size (at least 30), $\bar{x}$ is the sample mean, s is the sample standard deviation and μ_α is the value of random variable $N(0,1)$ under the condition:

$$\Phi(\mu_\alpha) = 1 - \frac{\alpha}{2}$$

what, according to the assumptions, provide $\mu_\alpha = 1,96$.

To sum up, the comparison criteria in the tabusearch method needs to be extended by the following code:

Function 2. Extention for comparison criteria in tabu search

1: $z \leftarrow 0$ ▷ current number of generated vectors
2: $l \leftarrow 30$
3: Generate $l - z$ vectors $(\vec{d}^k = (\vec{d}_1^k, \ldots, \vec{d}_N^k)$, where $k \in \{1, \ldots, l\}$. By that we have l instances $(p_{i,j}, w_i, \vec{d}^k)$
4: For every new instance calculate cost in context of candidate solution π. We obtain sample $W_1^\pi, \ldots, W_l^\pi$.
5: Calculate mean $\bar{x}$ and standard deviation s from sample.
6: $z \leftarrow l$
7: **if** $d \leqslant 5\%\bar{x}$ or $l > N \cdot M$ **then**
8:      return $(\bar{x}, s)$
9: **else**
10:     $l \leftarrow l + 10\%l$
11:     Go to point 3

A remark: random sample don't need to be generated with every calculation of comparison criteria function. It is enough to generate it once for a specific data instance and this way it has been implemented in the computational experiments.

6 Computational Experiments

In this section we describe the method for generating random data and elaborate the efficiency of the proposed method. The tabu search algorithm presented in Sect. 3 has been appropriately applied. As a reference algorithm we use classic deterministic implementation of tabusearch which we compare with the adaptation of tabusearch for the sampling method. Moreover, the following customization has been applied:

- start permutation: $\pi = (1, 2, \ldots, n)$,
- tabu list size: n,
- algorithm's iterations count: n.

In order to measure the efficiency of the proposed method we examine the computational complexity by checking samples' size and the robustness.

6.1   Test Data

Both implemented algorithms have been examined on the commonly used reference test data which comes from [12] where he hired variants with jobs' numbers $N = 20, 50, 100$ and machines' numbers $M = 5, 10, 20$ what give 9 combinations. For every combination 10 examples are available so in total we have 90 test examples. Due to the fact that published examples consist of only processing times we needed to complete those examples by generating weights (w_i) and due dates (d_i). We applied the following schema: w_i has been generated uniformly from the range $[1, 10]$ and d_i has been generated uniformly from the range $[P(1 - T - R/2), P(1 - T + R/2)]$ where P denotes the best known value for the makespan for the $C_{\max}$ problem, $T = 0.3$ and $R = 0.3$ [11].

Based on the reference data we create the random instances $(p_{i,j}, w_i, \widetilde{d}_i)$ as formulated in the problem definition in Sect. 2 where $p_{i,j}$ and w_i values come from previously described examples and $\widetilde{d}_i \sim N(d_i, c \cdot d_i)$ where $c \in \{0.05, 0.1, 0.15, 0.2, 0.25, 0.3\}$. Having that for every random instance we generated 100 disturbed deterministic subinstances according to distribution of the random variable $\widetilde{d}_i$, in total we obtained $90 \cdot 5 \cdot 100 = 54000$ subinstances. The robustness coefficient (1) has been determined for both algorithms and results are presented in the next section.

6.2   Results

Before performing the complete set of tests we have checked whether sample measure on the mean only is good enough or is it worth introduce the standard deviation as well. It turned out the introducing standard deviation has a negligible influence on the final result, so all the tests have been executed with applying the mean only.

We executed tests for two main algorithms, but we examined the proposed method in more details to have a better insight into value that it brings. In the Tables 1, 2, 3, 4, 5, 6, 7, 8 there is a complete summary of all tested variants with main results. A quick observation leads to the conclusion that the proposed method gives much better results than the classic approach. Moreover, in all cases the results obtained by applying the sampling method are better in the sense of statistical significance than results obtained by the classic way.

Table 1. Complete results summary for confidence intervals sample size

c	Classic	Sampling	Relatively	Sample size	#Better
0,05	0,79	0,26	2,04	75,48	89
0,10	1,36	0,66	1,08	79,26	89
0,15	2,00	1,14	0,75	83,17	89
0,20	2,62	1,64	0,59	90,16	89
0,25	3,31	2,27	0,46	89,54	88
0,30	3,66	2,60	0,41	91,67	88
Average	2,29	1,43	0,89	84,88	88,7

Table 2. Complete results summary for NM sample size

c	Classic	Sampling	Relatively	Sample size	#Better
0,05	0,82	0,25	2,25	661,11	90
0,10	1,38	0,63	1,21	661,11	90
0,15	1,99	1,08	0,85	661,11	89
0,20	2,63	1,59	0,66	661,11	90
0,25	3,24	2,11	0,53	661,11	90
0,30	3,61	2,47	0,46	661,11	88
Average	2,28	1,35	0,99	661,11	89,5

Table 3. Complete results summary for $0.3 \cdot NM$ sample size

c	Classic	Sampling	Relatively	Sample size	#Better
0,05	0,82	0,26	2,11	198,33	87
0,10	1,37	0,64	1,14	198,33	90
0,15	2,00	1,11	0,80	198,33	89
0,20	2,66	1,66	0,60	198,33	90
0,25	3,25	2,15	0,51	198,33	89
0,30	3,63	2,50	0,45	198,33	88
Average	2,29	1,39	0,94	198,33	88,8

The only thing which is puzzling is the fact that the more value c is the less advantage of sampling method is.

Another general observation is that for almost all test instances the sampling method gives better robustness than the classic approach. When the sample size is based on confidence intervals theory, we obtain the level $98,5\%$ of advantage. The best one is for the sample size $N \cdot M$ when we have the value $99,4\%$. Even for a small sample size $N \cdot M \cdot 0.03$ the sampling method gives the level $92,3\%$ of advantage, finally we lose the advantage for a very small sample size $N \cdot M \cdot 0.01$.

Table 4. Complete results summary for $0.15 \cdot NM$ sample size

c	Classic	Sampling	Relatively	Sample size	#Better
0,05	0,81	0,27	2,00	99,22	89
0,10	1,37	0,65	1,12	99,22	90
0,15	2,00	1,14	0,75	99,22	89
0,20	2,64	1,69	0,57	99,22	89
0,25	3,25	2,21	0,47	99,22	88
0,30	3,67	2,60	0,41	99,22	88
Average	2,29	1,43	0,89	99,22	88,8

Table 5. Complete results summary for $0.1 \cdot NM$ sample size

c	Classic	Sampling	Relatively	Sample size	#Better
0,05	0,80	0,28	1,86	66,11	87
0,10	1,36	0,67	1,03	66,11	90
0,15	1,98	1,17	0,70	66,11	89
0,20	2,63	1,70	0,55	66,11	89
0,25	3,26	2,26	0,44	66,11	87
0,30	3,69	2,67	0,38	66,11	86
Average	2,29	1,46	0,83	66,11	88

Table 6. Complete results summary for $0.05 \cdot NM$ sample size

c	Classic	Sampling	Relatively	Sample size	#Better
0,05	0,79	0,30	1,66	33,11	88
0,10	1,36	0,72	0,89	33,11	88
0,15	1,99	1,26	0,58	33,11	85
0,20	2,68	1,84	0,46	33,11	85
0,25	3,30	2,41	0,37	33,11	83
0,30	3,77	2,89	0,30	33,11	83
Average	2,32	1,57	0,71	33,11	85,3

Let's take a closer look at the relationship between the classic approach, the sampling one with sample size NM and the sampling one with sample size based on confidence intervals based sample size. On the chart one can see the robustness level (Fig. 1). We can easily observe that for all values of parameter c the advantage of the sampling method is indisputable. We can also observe that we can get the best robustness when the sample size is NM.

Finally, let's discuss the relationship between the algorithms' results with different sample size with reference to the robustness level (Fig. 2). We can see that

Table 7. Complete results summary for $0.03 \cdot NM$ sample size

c	Classic	Sampling	Relatively	Sample size	#Better
0,05	0,78	0,33	1,38	19,89	87
0,10	1,36	0,77	0,76	19,89	85
0,15	1,99	1,31	0,52	19,89	82
0,20	2,66	1,92	0,39	19,89	84
0,25	3,32	2,53	0,31	19,89	84
0,30	3,77	3,00	0,26	19,89	80
Average	2,31	1,64	0,6	19,89	83,7

Table 8. Complete results summary for $0.01 \cdot NM$ sample size

c	Classic	Sampling	Relatively	Sample size	#Better
0,05	0,74	0,48	0,52	6,67	73
0,10	1,33	1,01	0,32	6,67	72
0,15	1,98	1,61	0,23	6,67	70
0,20	2,66	2,26	0,18	6,67	71
0,25	3,31	2,96	0,12	6,67	65
0,30	3,82	3,52	0,08	6,67	62
Average	2,31	1,97	0,24	6,67	68,8

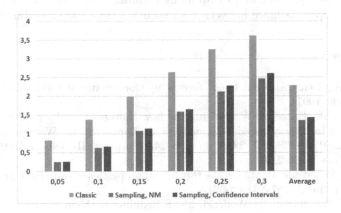

Fig. 1. Comparison of the robustness level with reference to the main methods

within the range $[1..0.1] \cdot NM$ the robustness levels are very close to each other. Only when the sample size is getting smaller (from $0.05NM$), the robustness level is getting significantly worse.

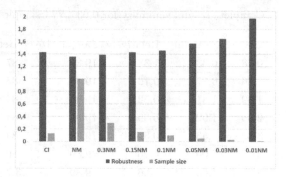

Fig. 2. Comparison of the robustness level with reference to the sample size

7 Conclusions

In this paper we proposed a sampling method to solve optimization problems with uncertain parameters modeled by random variables. By applying confidence intervals we wanted to keep a very good balance between the execution time and the robustness level. We have seen an application of the method for the flowshop problem with deadlines and parameters modeled by random variables with the normal distribution. Based on the performed computational experiments we can conclude that the proposed method gives substantially more robust solutions than the classic approach and by applying confidence interval theory we achieve the goal of keeping balance between the execution time and the robustness level.

References

1. Aarts, A., Lenstra, J.K.: Local Search in Combinatorial Optimization. Wiley, New York (1997)
2. Wodecki, M., Bożejko, W.: Solving the flow shop problem by parallel simulated annealing. In: Wyrzykowski, R., Dongarra, J., Paprzycki, M., Waśniewski, J. (eds.) PPAM 2001. LNCS, vol. 2328, pp. 236–244. Springer, Heidelberg (2002). doi:10.1007/3-540-48086-2_26
3. Bożejko, W., Wodecki, M.: On the theoretical properties of swap multimoves. Oper. Res. Lett. **35**(2), 227–231 (2007)
4. Bożejko, W., Rajba, P., Wodecki, M.: Scheduling problem with uncertain parameters in just in time system. In: Rutkowski, L., Korytkowski, M., Scherer, R., Tadeusiewicz, R., Zadeh, L.A., Zurada, J.M. (eds.) ICAISC 2014. LNCS, vol. 8468, pp. 456–467. Springer, Cham (2014). doi:10.1007/978-3-319-07176-3_40
5. Dean B.C.: Approximation algorithms for stochastic scheduling problems. Ph.D. thesis, MIT (2005)
6. Grabowski, J., Wodecki, M.: A very fast tabu search algorithm for the permutation flow shop problem with makespan criterion. Comput. Oper. Res. **31**, 1891–1909 (2004)
7. Jang, W., Klein, C.M.: Minimizing the expected number of tardy jobs when processing times are normally distributed. Oper. Res. Lett. **30**, 100–106 (2002)

8. Nowicki, E., Smutnicki, C.: A fast tabu search algorithm for permutation flow shop problem. Eur. J. Oper. Res. **91**, 160–175 (1996)
9. Rajba, P., Wodecki, M.: Stability of scheduling with random processing times on one machine. Applicationes Mathematicae **39**(2), 169–183 (2012)
10. Righter R., Stochastic scheduling. In: Shaked, M., Shandhkumar (eds.) Stochastic Orders. Academic Press, San Diego (1994)
11. Sioud, A., Gagné, C., Gravel, M.: Minimizing total tardiness in a hybrid flexible flowshop with sequence dependent setup times. In: INFOCOMP 2014: The Fourth International Conference on Advanced Communications and Computation 2014, pp. 13–18 (2014)
12. Taillard, E.: Benchmarks for basic scheduling problems. EJOR **64**(2), 278–285 (1993)
13. Van den Akker, M., Hoogeveen, H.: Minimizing the number of late jobs in a stochastic setting using a chance constraint. J. Sched. **11**, 59–69 (2008)
14. Vondrák, J.: Probabilistic methods in combinatorial and stochastic optimization. Ph.D. thesis, MIT (2005)
15. Zhu, X., Cai, X.: General stochastic single-machine scheduling with regular cost functions. Math. Comput. Modell. **26**(3), 95–108 (1997)

State Assignment of Finite-State Machines by Using the Values of Input Variables

Valery Salauyou$^{(\boxtimes)}$ and Michal Ostapczuk

Faculty of Computer Science, Bialystok University of Technology,
Bialystok, Poland
valsol@mail.ru

Abstract. In this paper, we propose the method of FSM synthesis on field programmable gate arrays (FPGAs) when input variables are used for state assignment. For this purpose we offer a combined structural model of class A and class E FSMs. This paper also describes in detail the algorithms for synthesis a class AE FSM which consists of splitting of internal states for performance of necessary conditions for synthesis of the class E FSM and state assignment of the class AE FSM. It is shown that the proposed method reduces the area for all families of FPGAs by a factor of 1.19–1.39 on average and by a factor of three for certain families. Practical issues concerning the method and the specific features of its use are discussed, and possible directions of the elaboration of this approach are proposed.

Keywords: Finite state machine (FSM) · Field programmable gate array (FPGA) · State assignment · Area minimization · State splitting · Look up table

1 Introduction

In the general case, a digital system can be represented by a set of combinational circuits and finite state machines (FSMs). FSMs are also widely used as individual units as controllers and control devices. Usually, when working on a project, the designer has to develop new FSMs each time. It is clear that the parameters of FSMs used in a digital system to a large extent determine the success of the whole project. For this reason, the issue of minimization of FSMs is very important. As the FSM optimization criteria, one typically uses area, delay, and power consumption. Presently, field programmable gate arrays (FPGAs) are widely used in digital systems; for this reason, many FSM optimization methods are designed for the implementation of FSMs based in FPGAs.

The idea of using the values of the input and output variables of the FSM for encoding its internal states was first proposed in [1]. Later, this approach was elaborated in [2], where various combinations of the input and output variables that can be used for encoding the internal states are considered. The choice of the minimum number of input and output variables for encoding is an NP-hard problem. In [3], it was proposed to use the values of the output variables of the Moor FSM as the codes of the internal states.

© IFIP International Federation for Information Processing 2017
Published by Springer International Publishing AG 2017. All Rights Reserved
K. Saeed et al. (Eds.): CISIM 2017, LNCS 10244, pp. 592–603, 2017.
DOI: 10.1007/978-3-319-59105-6_51

In [4], structural models of FSMs based on the architectural capabilities of FPGAs were proposed; these models make it possible to use the values of the FSM input and output variables as internal state codes. A new classification of structural models of FSMs is given. Here the class A and B FSMs are traditional of Mealy and Moore FSMs accordingly. In the class C (Mealy) and the class D (Moore) FSMs the value of an output vector completely coincides with the code of the present state of the FSM. In the class E (Mealy) and class F (Moore) FSMs the value of an input vector completely coincides with the code of the next state of the FSM.

In [5], the synthesis method of Mealy FSMs was proposed, where the values of output variables are used as the codes of FSM states. In this paper, we present the method of FSM synthesis which allows, unlike [5], to use the values of input variables as the codes of FSM states. For this purpose, the structural model of the class E FSM [4] is used.

2 Structural FSM Models

The most general model of the Mealy FSM can be described by means of following equations:

$$a_{t+1} = \Phi(z_t, a_t);$$
$$w_t = \Psi(z_t, a_t),$$

where Φ is the transition function, Ψ is the output function, a_t is the present state of the FSM at time t ($t = 1, 2, 3, \ldots$), a_{t+1} is the next state of the FSM, z_t is a collection of values of the input variables (the input vector) on the FSM input at time t, and w_t is a collection of values of the output variables (the output vector) formed at time t.

The Mealy FSM in classification [4] received a title the *class A FSM*. The structural model of the Mealy FSM show on Fig. 1a, where CL_Φ is the combinational circuit

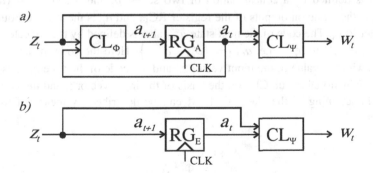

Fig. 1. The structural models of FSMs: a – the class A FSM; b – the class E FSM

forming the values of the transition functions, CL_Ψ is the combinational circuit forming the values of the output functions, and RG is the FSM's memory.

In the *class E FSM* the value of the input vector z_t determines the code of the next state a_{t+1}; therefore, the equations of functioning of the class E FSM have the following view:

$$a_{t+1} = z_t;$$
$$w_t = \Psi(z_t, a_t),$$

In contrast to the Mealy FSM, the structure of the class E FSM does not include the combinational circuit CL_Φ (Fig. 1*b*) that allows to build FSMs of a low cost (an area) and a high-speed performance.

However in practice, the "pure" type of the class E FSM meets very rarely. Therefore, in the present work we offer the combined model of the *class AE FSM*. In the class AE FSM the codes of internal states are divided on two parts: one part is defined by the value of input variables, and the second part is formed the same as in the class A FSM, by means of combinational circuit CL_Φ (Fig. 2).

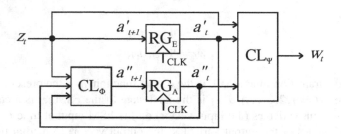

Fig. 2. The structural model of the class AE FSM

The memory of the class AE FSM is presented by two registers RG_A and RG_E which correspond to the class A and the class E FSMs. The internal state a_t of the class AE FSM is defined by a concatenation of two states: a'_t and a''_t, i.e. $a_t = \{a'_t, a''_t\}$, where a'_t is the value on outputs of the register RG_E, and a''_t is the value on outputs of the register RG_A. The code of the next state a_{t+1} also is defined by the concatenation of two states: a'_{t+1} and a''_{t+1}, i.e. $a_{t+1} = \{a'_{t+1}, a''_{t+1}\}$. Here the code of the state a'_{t+1} coincides with the value of the input vector z_t, and the code of the state a''_{t+1} is formed by the combinational circuit CL_Φ on the basis of the input vector z_t and the code of the state a_t. Functioning of the class AE FSM can be described by means of following equations:

$$a'_{t+1} = z_t;$$
$$a''_{t+1} = \Phi(z_t, a_t);$$
$$w_t = \Psi(z_t, a_t).$$

3 The Synthesis Method of the Class AE FSM

Let us present the class AE FSM by the structural diagram on Fig. 3 that consists of two registers RG_A and RG_E, and the combinational circuit CL. Here, in contrast to the structure on Fig. 2, the combinational circuits CL_Φ and CL_Ψ are united in one circuit CL. The combinational circuit CL receives the values of the input variables $X = \{x_1, \ldots, x_L\}$, the values of the variables $G = \{g_1, \ldots, g_L\}$, which define the state a'_t code, and the values of the feedback variables $E = \{e_1, \ldots, e_R\}$, which define the state a''_t code. Based on FSM algorithm functioning and arriving the values of the variables, the combinational circuit CL forms values of the output functions $Y = \{y_1, \ldots, y_N\}$ and the transition functions $D = \{d_1, \ldots, d_R\}$ which define the state a''_{t+1} code.

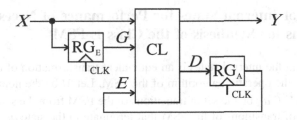

Fig. 3. The structural diagram of the class AE FSM

Let A is a set of internal states of the FSM. Let us denote by $U(a_i)$ the set of all the transition conditions in the state a_i, $a_i \in A$:

$$U(a_i) = \{X(a_m, a_i) | a_m \in B(a_i)\}, \tag{1}$$

where $X(a_m, a_i)$ is a collection of values of the input variables (a transition condition or an input vector) that initiates the transition from the state a_m to the state a_i, $B(a_i)$ is the set of states, transitions from which terminate in the state a_i.

The state a_i, $a_i \in A$, is a state of the class E FSM, i.e. $a_i \in A_E$, if next conditions are satisfied:

$$|U(a_i)| = 1 \tag{2}$$

$$U(a_i) \cap U(a_j) = \varnothing \text{ at } i \neq j \text{ for all } a_j \in A, \tag{3}$$

where $|M|$ is the cardinality (the number of elements) of the set M, $\varnothing$ is an empty set.

A performance of the condition (2) guarantees that all transitions to the state a_i are carried out by the same transition condition (i.e. the state a_i has only one code), and a performance of the condition (3) provides a determinacy of a FSM behavior (i.e. the transition condition in some state a_i does not initiate passages to other FSM states).

The FSM is the class E FSM if all its states are states of the class E FSM, i.e. $A_E = A$. In other words, the finite state machine is the class E FSM if for all its states conditions (2) and (3) are satisfied.

The satisfaction of the conditions (2) is carried out by splitting of FSM states. Let, for example, for some state a_i, $a_i \in A$, takes place $|U(a_i)| = Q > 1$. It is possible to split a state a_i on states $a_{i\_1}, \ldots, a_{i\_Q}$ so that the transitions in each state a_{i_q} were defined only by one transition condition, i.e. was fulfilled $|U(a_{i\_q})| = 1$, $q = \overline{1, Q}$. Now instead of one state a_i, we have Q states for which conditions (2) are satisfied.

In case of violations of the conditions (3), the synthesis of the class E FSM is impossible, since the determinacy of the FSM behavior is broken. In this case, it is offered to use the combined model of the class AE FSM (Fig. 2). For this purpose, the second part of the code of the class A FSM is added to the code of each internal state of the class E FSM, which corresponds to the states a''_t and a''_{t+1}. The last is carried out by special state assignment of the FSM.

4   Splitting of Internal States for Performance of Necessary Conditions for Synthesis of the Class E FSM

Note that splitting the internal states is an equivalent transformation of the FSM and it does not change the operation algorithm of the FSM. Let M be the number of internal states of the FSM, $P(a_i)$ be the set of transitions of the FSM from the state a_i, $i = \overline{1, M}$, $C(a_i)$ be the set of transitions of the FSM that terminate in the state a_i, $a_i \in A$, and X (a_i) be some a transition condition to the state a_i, $X(a_i) \in U(a_i)$. Then the algorithm splitting of internal states for performance of necessary conditions for synthesis of the class E FSM has the following view.

Algorithm 1

1. For each internal state a_i, $a_i \in A$, according to (1) the set $U(a_i)$ is defined.
2. In the set A, find a state a_i for which condition (2) are not satisfied. If such a state is found, then go to Step 3; otherwise, go to Step 7.
3. Put $Q := |U(a_i)|$. Introduce Q new states $a_{i\_1}, \ldots, a_{i\_Q}$.
4. Determine the subsets $C(a_{i\_1}), \ldots, C(a_{i\_Q})$ of transitions to the states $a_{i\_1}, \ldots, a_{i\_Q}$. Each subset $C(a_{i\_q})$ is assigned transitions which is initiated by the condition $X^q(a_m, a_i) \in U(a_i)$, $a_m \in B(a_i)$, $q = \overline{1, Q}$.
5. The subsets $P(a_{i\_1}), \ldots, P(a_{i\_Q})$ of transitions from the states $a_{i\_1}, \ldots, a_{i\_Q}$ are determinated in the following way: $P(a_{i\_q}) := P(a_i)$ for all $q = \overline{1, Q}$.
6. Put $A := A \backslash \{a_i\}$, $A := A \cup \{a_{i\_1}, \ldots, a_{i\_Q}\}$, and $M := M + Q - 1$; go to Step 2.
7. Stop.

5   State Assignment of the Class AE FSM

The main purpose of encoding the internal states when designing the class AE FSMs is to ensure the mutual orthogonality of these codes. To encode the internal states of a class AE FSM, a ternary matrix W is constructed in which the rows correspond to the internal states and the columns correspond to the variables of the set G. A unit is put on intersection of the row i and the column j of the matrix W, if the input variable x_j has the value 1 in the condition $X(a_i)$, a zero, if the input variable x_j has the value 0 in the condition $X(a_i)$, and an undetermined value (the dash), if the variable x_j does not influence on the transition condition $X(a_i)$. Later, the rows of the matrix W will determine the codes of the internal states of the class AE FSM.

To make the codes of internal states of the class AE FSM orthogonal it is necessary to solve the following task.

Task 1. To add in matrix W the minimum number of the columns, which corresponding to the variables $e_1, \ldots, e_R$, and to encode the rows of the matrix W by binary values of the variables $e_1, \ldots, e_R$ so that all the rows of the matrix W were mutually orthogonal.

In order to solve the Task 1 and to encode the internal state of the class AE FSM the following algorithm is offered.

Algorithm 2

1. The graph H for the orthogonalization of the rows of the matrix W is constructed. The vertices of H correspond to the rows of W (internal states of the FSM). Two vertices of H are connected by an edge if the corresponding rows of W are orthogonal.
2. The vertices connected to all other vertices (the rows of W corresponding to these vertices are orthogonal to all other rows) are removed from H.
3. The graph H is decomposed into the minimum number of complete subgraphs $H_1, \ldots, H_T$ using Algorithm 3.
4. The subgraphs $H_1, \ldots, H_T$ are encoded by binary codes of the minimum length $R = intlog_2 T$ using Algorithm 5.
5. R columns that correspond to the variables $e_1, \ldots, e_R$ of the codes of the subgraphs $H_1, \ldots, H_T$ are added to the matrix W. In row i of W, the positions of the additional columns are filled by the code of the subgraph H_t, $t = \overline{1,T}$, containing the vertex a_i, $i = \overline{1,M}$. The other positions of the additional columns in W are filled by zeros.
6. The contents of the row i of W is used as the code of the internal state a_i, $i = \overline{1,M}$.
7. Stop.

The decomposition of the graph H into the minimum number of complete graphs $H_1, \ldots, H_T$ (at Step 3 of Algorithm 2) is made by the following algorithm.

Algorithm 3

1. Set $T := 0$.
2. Set $T := T + 1$. In the graph H, find a complete graph H_T with the maximum number of vertices.
3. Remove the vertices of H_T from the graph H.
4. If the set of vertices of H is not empty, the go to Step 2; otherwise, go to Step 5.
5. Stop.

The maximal complete subgraph H_t, $t = \overline{1,T}$, at Step 2 of Algorithm 3 can be found using the following algorithm.

Algorithm 4

1. Find a vertex a_i in H with the greatest local degree.
2. Include a_i into the graph H_t.
3. Among all the vertices of H not included in H_t, find a node a_i connected to all the nodes of the subgraph H_t. If several such nodes are found, choose a node with the greatest local degree among them.
4. If a vertex connected to all the vertices of the subgraph H_t was found at Step 3, then go to Step 2; otherwise, go to Step 5.
5. Stop.

To encode the subgraphs $H_1, \ldots, H_T$ (Step 4 of Algorithm 2) the following algorithm is used to minimize the area of implementing the transition functions.

Algorithm 5

1. Calculate the length R of the codes of the subgraphs $H_1, \ldots, H_T$: $R = intlog_2T$.
2. Form the set K of binary codes of length R.
3. The subgraph containing the initial state a_1 is encoded by the zero code from K.
4. If all the subgraphs $H_1, \ldots, H_T$ are encoded, then go to Step 5; otherwise, find among the not yet encoded subgraphs $H_1, \ldots, H_T$ a subgraph H_t for which $\sum |C(a_i)| = $ max for all $a_i \in H_t$.
   To encode the subgraph H_t, the code with the minimum number of unities is chosen in the set K. Go to Step 4.
5. Stop.

Example. Let us apply the proposed method for designing the FSM described by the state diagram shown in Fig. 4. The vertices correspond to the internal states $a_1, \ldots, a_5$

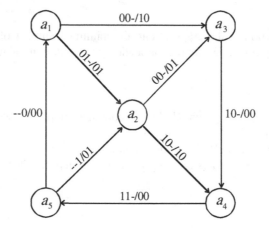

Fig. 4. The state diagram of the initial FSM

of this FSM, and the arcs correspond to the FSM transitions. Beside each arc, the value of the input vector that initiates the transition and, separated by a slash, the value of the output vector that formed on this transition are indicated. In this example, the FSM has five states, three input variables, and two output variables.

In this example, conditions (2) are violated for the state a_2 because $U(a_2) = \{01\text{-},-1\}$, i.e. $|U(a_2)| = 2$, therefore, a_2 is split into two states a_{2_1} and a_{2_2}. The state diagram of the FSM obtained upon splitting the state a_2 is shown in Fig. 5.

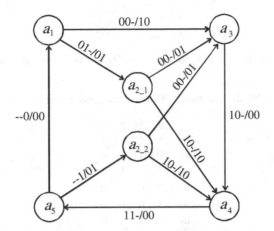

Fig. 5. The state diagram of the FSM after splitting the state a_2

The encoding of the internal states begins with constructing the matrix W (Table 1). Figure 6 shows the orthogonality graph H of the rows of W. The graph H is decomposed into two complete subgraphs H_1 and H_2. As the number of subgraphs T is equal 2, then one variable e_1 has enough for coding of two subgraphs. According to Step 4 of algorithm 5, the subgraph H_1 is encoded by binary code "1", and the subgraph H_2 is encoded by the code "0". The matrix W with an additional column e_1 for orthogonalization of rows is resulted in Table 2.

Table 1. The matrix W for state assignment of a class AE FSM

	g_1	g_2	g_3
a_1	–	–	0
a_{2_1}	0	1	–
a_{2_2}	–	–	1
a_3	0	0	–
a_4	1	0	–
a_5	1	1	–

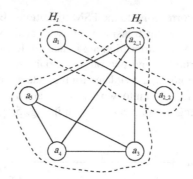

Fig. 6. The graph H for orthogonality of rows of the matrix W

Table 2. The matrix W after orthogonalization of rows

	g_1	g_2	g_3	e_1
a_1	–	–	0	1
a_{2_1}	0	1	–	0
a_{2_2}	–	–	1	1
a_3	0	0	–	0
a_4	1	0	–	0
a_5	1	1	–	0

The logical equations implemented by combinative circuit CL (Fig. 3) for our example have the following view:

$$d_1 = g_1 g_2 \bar{e}_1;$$
$$y_1 = \bar{g}_3 e_1 \bar{x}_1 \bar{x}_2 + \bar{g}_1 g_2 \bar{e}_1 x_1 \bar{x}_2 + g_3 e_1 x_1 \bar{x}_2;$$
$$y_2 = \bar{g}_3 e_1 \bar{x}_1 x_2 + \bar{g}_1 g_2 \bar{e}_1 \bar{x}_1 \bar{x}_2 + g_3 e_1 \bar{x}_1 \bar{x}_2 + g_1 g_2 \bar{e}_1 x_3.$$

As it is possible to see from the resulted equations, the transition functions for the class AE FSM are very simple. The implementation cost of the given system of Boolean functions (it is traditionally defined as the number of inputs of the necessary for implementation gates) is equal 40, while at traditional implementation of the class A FSM, the implementation cost is equal 74. Thus, for the considered example usage of structural model of the class AE FSM, in comparison with the traditional approach, allowed to reduce the implementation cost by a factor of 1.85 or by 54%.

The efficiency of the proposed method for designing the class AE FSMs was tested by implementing the FSM described in the example above in the FPGAs manufactured by Altera using the CAD tools Quartus Prime version 16.0. It is the synthesis parameters by default of CAD Quartus were used. The initial FSM of class A and the synthesized FSM of class AE have been described in language Verilog.

Table 3 show the results of experiments for various FPGA families manufactured by the companies Altera, where LE_A and LE_{AE} are the numbers of the logical elements

Table 3. Results of experimental researches at implementation on FPGA of the FSMs from the considered example

FPGA	LE_A	F_{maxA}	LE_{AE}	F_{maxAE}	LE_A/LE_{AE}	F_{maxAE}/F_{maxA}
MAX II	12	517.06	10	417.19	1.20	0.807
MAX V	12	261.57	10	260.15	1.20	0.996
MAX 10	13	592.42	11	581.40	1.18	0.981
Arria II	8	1025.64	4	1022.49	2.00	0.997
Cyclone IV E	12	738.01	10	801.92	1.20	1.085
Cyclone IV GX	12	726.74	10	727.27	1.20	1.001
Cyclone V	6	640.20	4	640.20	1.50	1.000
mid					1.35	0.981

(functional generators LUT — look-up table) used in the implementation of the class A FSM and the class AE FSM, F_{maxA} and F_{maxAE} are the maximum operation frequencies (in MHz) of these FSMs, LE_A/LE_{AE} and F_{maxAE}/F_{maxA} are the ratio of the corresponding parameters, and *mid* is the mean value of the parameter. The data in Table 3 show that the proposed method for designing the class AE FSM reduced the implementation area of the FSM from the example on the Altera FPGAs by a factor of 1.35 on average and by a factor of 3.00 for the Arria II family. Thus the maximum operation frequency of the class AE FSM concedes to the maximum operation frequency of the class A FSM a little.

6 Experimental Study

The synthesis method of the class AE FSM was researched at implementation on FPGA for the FSM benchmarks MCNC [6]. For this purpose to each benchmark of the FSM the considered synthesis method was applied. Both finite state machines, the initial class A FSM and synthesized the class AE FSM, were described in language Verilog. Then standard implementation on FPGA of FSMs by means of CAD Quartus II version 13.1 was fulfilled. It is the synthesis parameters by default of CAD Quartus were used. As criteria of optimization the implementation cost (C), defined by the number of used logical elements LUT, and the maximum operation frequency (F) was considered.

In Tables 4 and 5, the parameter relations are presented for eleven FSM benchmarks for which usage of the synthesis method of the class AE FSM is the most effective. Here relation C_A/C_{AE} shows in how many time the synthesis method of the class AE FSM, in comparison with the class A FSM, improves the implementation cost; F_{AE}/F_A – the frequency.

The analysis of Tables 4 and 5 shows that the synthesis method of the class AE FSM allows to reduce a implementation cost by a factor of 3.00 for the benchmark shiftreg for all FPGA families, a time delay by a factor of 1.60 for the benchmark lion for family Cyclone, and an operation frequency by a factor of 2.93 for the benchmark train4 for family Stratix.

Table 4. Results of experimental researches of the synthesis method of the class AE FSM for families Arria GX and Cyclone

FSM	Arria GX		Cyclone		Cyclone II		Cyclone III	
	C_A/C_{AE}	F_{AE}/F_A	C_A/C_{AE}	F_{AE}/F_A	C_A/C_{AE}	F_{AE}/F_A	C_A/C_{AE}	F_{AE}/F_A
dk15	0.86	1.55	0.71	1.45	0.71	1.18	0.71	1.06
dk16	1.31	0.85	0.63	0.80	0.55	0.74	0.55	0.69
dk17	1.67	1.06	0.96	0.70	0.96	0.91	0.96	1.12
dk27	1.33	1.05	1.25	0.97	1.25	0.99	1.25	1.04
dk512	1.42	0.82	0.68	0.91	0.78	0.82	0.78	0.77
ex5	0.79	0.61	0.64	0.67	0.64	0.68	0.64	0.69
lion	1.00	0.65	0.71	0.54	0.77	0.63	0.77	0.64
lion9	1.43	0.81	1.82	1.16	1.82	1.08	1.82	0.91
shiftreg	3.00	0.62	3.00	0.55	3.00	0.75	3.00	0.64
train4	0.75	1.77	1.00	1.60	1.00	1.45	1.00	1.56
train11	1.71	1.49	1.71	1.56	1.92	0.94	1.92	0.84
mid	1.39	1.03	1.19	0.99	1.22	0.92	1.22	0.91
max	3.00	1.77	3.00	1.60	3.00	1.45	3.00	1.56

Table 5. Results of experimental researches of the synthesis method of the class AE FSM for families MAX II and Stratix

FSM	MAX II		Stratix		Stratix II		Stratix III	
	C_A/C_{AE}	F_{AE}/F_A	C_A/C_{AE}	F_{AE}/F_A	C_A/C_{AE}	F_{AE}/F_A	C_A/C_{AE}	F_{AE}/F_A
dk15	0.70	1.18	0.71	1.07	0.86	1.02	0.86	0.66
dk16	0.63	0.83	0.63	0.73	1.31	0.77	1.31	0.82
dk17	1.39	0.98	0.96	0.75	1.67	1.21	1.67	1.02
dk27	1.25	1.20	1.25	0.95	1.33	0.89	1.33	1.00
dk512	0.70	0.89	0.68	0.98	1.42	1.03	1.42	0.78
ex5	0.62	0.77	0.64	0.63	0.79	0.48	0.79	0.68
lion	0.71	0.77	0.71	0.84	1.00	0.66	1.00	0.54
lion9	1.82	0.82	1.82	0.75	1.43	0.95	1.43	0.87
shiftreg	3.00	1.14	3.00	0.31	3.00	0.66	3.00	0.71
train4	1.00	0.95	1.00	2.93	0.75	1.77	0.75	1.91
train11	1.77	0.97	1.71	2.15	1.71	1.74	1.71	1.65
mid	1.24	0.95	1.19	1.10	1.39	1.02	1.39	0.97
max	3.00	1.20	3.00	2.93	3.00	1.77	3.00	1.91

An average improving is of a cost by a factor from 1.19 (Cyclone, Stratix) to 1.39 (Arria, Stratix II, (III)), of a time delay – from 0.97 (Cyclone II) to 1.05 (Cyclone), of a frequency – from 1.92 (Cyclone II) to 1.10 (Stratix).

7   Conclusions

The considered method of synthesis of the class AE FSM showed the high efficiency at minimization of implementation cost of FSMs for various FPGA families, by a factor of 1.19–1.39 on average and by a factor of 3.00 for certain families. Besides, in certain cases the method allows to increase the FSM performance (by a factor of 2.93 for benchmark train4 for family Sratix). An application of the given method is the most effective for FSMs with the many of input variables, especially when the transitions in the various states are initiated by different transition conditions.

The proposed method for the minimization of FSMs based on the use of the structural model of the class AE FSM is universal because it is applicable to Mealy FSMs (i.e., to arbitrary FSMs), does not change the operational algorithm of the FSM, and is efficient for all FPGA families. Therefore, this method can be recommended for inclusion in industrial CAD tools in order to minimize the area of implementation. The given method can be used not only at implementation of FSMs on FPGA, but also on other an element basis, for example on ASIC (Application Specific Integrated Circuit). We see perspective a direction of the further researches when values of input and output variables of the FSM are shared for states assignment.

Acknowledgments. The present study was supported by a grant S/WI/1/2013 from Bialystok University of Technology and founded from the resources for research by Ministry of Science and Higher Education.

References

1. McCluskey, E.J.: Reduction of feedback loops in sequential circuits and carry leads in iterative networks. Inf. Control **2**, 99–118 (1963)
2. Pomeranz, I., Cheng, K.T.: STOIC: state assignment based on output/input functions. IEEE Trans. CAD **8**, 613–622 (1993)
3. Forrest, J.: ODE: output direct state machine encoding. In: European Design Automation Conference (EURO-DAC 1995), Brighton, UK, pp. 600–605 (1995)
4. Solovjev, V.: Synthesis of sequential circuits on programmable logic devices based on new models of finite state machines. In: Euromicro Symposium on Digital Systems Design (DSD 2001), Warsaw. Poland, pp. 170–173 (2001)
5. Solov'ev V.V.: Minimization of mealy finite-state machines by using the values of the output variables for state assignment. J. Comput. Syst. Sci. Int. **1**, 96–104 (2017)
6. Yang, S.: Logic synthesis and optimization benchmarks user guide, version 3.0. Microelectronics Center of North Carolina (MCNC), North Carolina (1991)

Nonnegative Matrix Factorization Based Decomposition for Time Series Modelling

Tatjana Sidekerskienė[1], Marcin Woźniak[3],
and Robertas Damaševičius[2(✉)]

[1] Department of Applied Mathematics,
Kaunas University of Technology, Kaunas, Lithuania
[2] Department of Software Engineering,
Kaunas University of Technology, Kaunas, Lithuania
robertas.damasevicius@ktu.lt
[3] Faculty of Applied Mathematics, Institute of Mathematics,
Silesian University of Technology, Gliwice, Poland

Abstract. We propose a novel method of time series decomposition based on the non-negative factorization of the Hankel matrix of time series and apply this method for time series modelling and prediction. An interim (surrogate) model of time series is built from the components of the time series using random cointegration, while the best cointegration is selected using a nature-inspired optimization method (Artificial Bee Colony). For modelling of cointegrated time series we use the ARX (AutoRegressive with eXogenous inputs) model. The results of modelling using the historical data (daily highest price) of S&P 500 stocks from 2009 are presented and compared against stand-alone ARX models. The results are evaluated using a variety of metrics (RMSE, MAE, MAPE, Pearson correlation, Nash-Suttcliffe efficiency coefficient, etc.) as well as illustrated graphically using Taylor and Target diagrams. The results show a 51–98% improvement of prediction accuracy (depending upon accuracy metric used). The proposed time series modelling method can be used for variety applications (time series denoising, prediction, etc.).

Keywords: Time series modelling · Time series decomposition · ARX · Random cointegration

1 Introduction

Modelling of time series (including the prediction of any future values) is an important problem with many areas of application, including problems in bioinformatics [1], medical diagnosis [2], air pollution forecasting [3], industrial machine condition monitoring [4], environmental modelling [5], financial investment [6], production planning [7], sales forecasting [8] and stock portfolio management [9]. In the domain of financial investment management, to invest and take proper decision, a more precise forecasting of financial environments is an important issue.

Financial time series originate from real-world systems (such as stock exchanges) and represent the outcome of complex multi-layer dynamic interactions between

© IFIP International Federation for Information Processing 2017
Published by Springer International Publishing AG 2017. All Rights Reserved
K. Saeed et al. (Eds.): CISIM 2017, LNCS 10244, pp. 604–613, 2017.
DOI: 10.1007/978-3-319-59105-6_52

multiple agents [10]. Real-world systems have mostly nonlinear and non-stationary behaviour. A nonlinear time series is a signal generated by a nonlinear dynamic process, in which the output is not directly proportional to the input, i.e. even a small change in input may lead to large change in output. Moreover, real-world systems often operate under transient non-stationary conditions, characterized by time-changing statistics. These properties prevent from acquisition of an effective predictive model and its reliable application. Therefore, the researchers are motivated to explore new data modelling methods.

Time series can be represented by different patterns of behaviour. Sometimes it is useful to decompose time series into several components, each representing some pattern or class of behaviour. It is common to decompose the economical time series data into trend (long term variation), cyclical (repeated but non-periodic fluctuations), seasonal and irregular (or noise) components [11]. Predictability can be used as a criterion to decomposing a times series into deterministic and non-deterministic components (Wold decomposition [12]). STL (Seasonal Trend decomposition using Loess) [13] can be used to estimate seasonal effects on time series and to predict future seasonally adjusted values. When they have time varying properties, the Holt-Winters decomposition [14] uses exponential to derive the decomposition model, which also includes error corrections in forecasting future values of the time series. Wavelet decomposition [15] decomposes a time series using the scaling function and wavelet functions (i.e. mother wavelet). Second generation wavelets can be used to generate wavelet functions in the spatial domain and to deal with complex structure, arbitrary boundary conditions, and irregular sampling intervals of time series [16].

Empirical Mode Decomposition (EMD) [17] initially has been developed for natural and engineering sciences for analysing nonlinear and non-stationary data such as sea wave data and earthquake signals, but has been applied to financial data as well [18]. EMD decomposes any time series into a finite number of intrinsic mode functions (IMF). Since the decomposition is based on the local characteristic time scale of the data, it is applicable to non-linear and non-stationary processes, and also can extract variability on different time scales. By performing clustering [19] or remixing [20] of IMFs one can identify different structural patterns of a time series and further analyze them with respect with their orthogonality and cross-correlation properties. However, the application of EMD has many important problems such as the end effect [21] and the IMF stopping criterion [22]. Extensions of EMD such as BoostEMD [23] try to alleviate these problems and improve the characteristics of IMF.

Despite long history and the availability of many time series decomposition algorithms and models, in many cases they are unable to account for complex structure (such as multiple or fractional seasonality) of time series.

We propose a novel method of time series decomposition based on the non-negative factorization of the Hankel matrix of time series in Sect. 2. In Sect. 3 we apply the method for time series prediction using the random cointegration approach. We describe the results of experiments using the historical stock data in Sect. 4. Finally, conclusions and discussion of future work are presented in Sect. 5.

2 Decomposition Method

We propose a new EMD-like signal decomposition method, called Nonnegative Hankel Matrix Factorization based Decomposition (NHMFD). The task is to decompose signal $x(t)$ into long term (trend), cyclical, and irregular components:

$$x(t) = \sum_{j=1}^{k} c_j + r_T + r_R \tag{1}$$

here c_j is a cyclical component (or Intrinsic Mode Function, IMF), and r_T is a trend, and r_R is the irregular (random) component.

The steps for proposed decomposition are as follows:

1. **Normalization:** the signal $x(t)$ is represented as time series X and normalized to $[0, 1]$ as follows:

$$\hat{X} = \frac{X - X_{min}}{X_{max} - X_{min}}, \tag{2}$$

   here X_{min} and X_{max} are the smallest and largest values of the time series.
2. **Construction of Hankel matrix:** Hankel matrix H of the normalized time series $X = \{x_1, x_2, x_3, \cdots, x_l\}$ is a square matrix:

$$H = \begin{bmatrix} x_1 & x_2 & x_3 & \cdots \\ x_2 & x_3 & x_4 & \cdots \\ x_3 & x_4 & x_5 & \cdots \\ \vdots & \vdots & \vdots & \ddots \end{bmatrix}, \quad h_{i,j} = x_{i+j-1} \tag{3}$$

   The size of Hankel matrix H is $n = \left\lfloor \frac{l+1}{2} \right\rfloor$ here l is the length of X.
3. **Nonnegative matrix factorization:** performs factorization of the form $H \approx V \times W$, here $V = \Re^{n \times k}$ and $W = \Re^{k \times n}$ are positive matrices, and k is the number of factors. Factorization is not exact: matrices V and W are chosen to minimize the residual D between H and $V \times W$:

$$D = \|H - V \times W\| \tag{4}$$

4. **Reconstruction of Hankel matrix:** The signal is reconstructed as

$$H' = V \times W + E \tag{5}$$

   here H' is the reconstructed Hankel matrix, E is the reconstruction error.
5. **Reconstruction of signal:** The signal is reconstructed from the reconstructed Hankel matrix H' by taking the means of matrix elements along its minor (secondary) diagonals as follows:

$$X' = \{x'_1, x'_2, x'_3, \ldots, x'_l\}, \quad x'_i = \sum_{i=j+k-1} h'_{j,k} \Big/ i. \tag{6}$$

The reconstruction of a signal is not exact, i.e. $X = X' + \varepsilon$, here ε is the reconstruction error. Linear regression is performed to find the fitting coefficients α and β such as to minimize error $\sum (X - \alpha - \beta X')^2$.

6. **Calculation of intrinsic mode:** the mode of a signal is calculated as follows. Let fitted reconstructed signal be: $\tilde{X} = \alpha + \beta X'$. Then the first component of the signal is defined by centering the fitted reconstructed signal as: $\hat{C}_l = \tilde{X} - \sum \tilde{X}/l$, and the decomposition residue is $\hat{R}_l = \hat{X} - \hat{C}_l$.

7. **Iterative decomposition of residue:** decomposition is continued with residue until the desired number of extracted modes is reached.

8. **Denormalization.** Extracted modes and residue are denormalized as follows:

$$C = \hat{C}(X_{max} - X_{min}), \quad R = \hat{R}(X_{max} - X_{min}) + X_{min} \tag{7}$$

9. **Extraction of trend and irregular component.** Finally, the residue is decomposed into trend and irregular (random or noise) component by computing the least-squares fit of a straight line to the residue and subtracting the resulting function from the residue as follows:

$$r_T = at + b, r_R = R - r_T \tag{8}$$

here a and b minimize error $\sum_t \left\{ [(at + b) - R(t)]^2 \right\}$.

Figure 1 shows an example of decomposition for a time series (1st subplot). The series was decomposed into two cyclical components, irregular residue and trend residue.

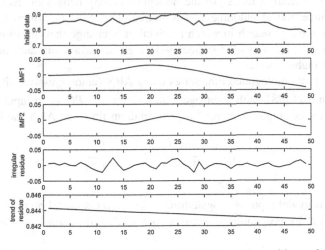

Fig. 1. Example of decomposition: sample signal, IMFs, irregular residue and trend residue

3 Modelling Methodology

To derive a model of a time series, we use a combination of several methods:

(1) Nonnegative Hankel Matrix Factorization based Decomposition (NHMFD) proposed in Sect. 2 to derive Intrinsic Mode Functions (IMFs) (see Sect. 2).

(2) Random cointegration of IMFs. A random vector P is generated that is multiplied
by the IMF component matrix C to obtain a surrogate time series S. Cointegration
is defined as the existence of a stationary linear combination of nonstationary time
series [24]. This indicates that there is a long run equilibrium relationship between
the series. While stationarity in a strict statistical sense may not be always
achieved, cointegration is considered to improve the statistical characteristics of
time series [25], which is good for predictability. The cointegrated series can be
considered as surrogate data series [26], which inherit the statistical properties of
the original data but may have some desired properties such as predictability. The
original time series can be restored as a sum of IMFs with unitary weights as
given by Eq. 1. The cointegrated (surrogate) time series S can be generated by
summing time series components c_j with random weights p_j as follows:

$$S = \sum_{j=1}^{k} p_j c_j = PC \qquad (9)$$

(3) Selection of best fitting random cointegration vector $\hat{P}$ using a nature-inspired
optimization method. We use Artificial Bee Colony (ABC) [27] algorithm to find
a cointegration vector that ensures the lowest RMSE of 1-step ahead prediction
using the ARX model on surrogate testing data. ABC is based on a model of
foraging behaviour of a honeybee colony. This model consists of three essential
components: food sources, employed foragers, and unemployed foragers, and
defines two leading modes of the honeybee colony behaviour: recruitment to a
food source and abandonment of a source. The ABC algorithm implements a
population-based search in which artificial bees change their positions aiming to
discover the places of food sources with high nectar amount and finally the one
with the highest nectar.

(4) Modelling of cointegrated time series using ARX (autoregressive with exogenous
inputs) model [28], with a surrogate time series $\hat{S} = \hat{P}C$ as an input and original
time series as output. The input-output relationship of an ARX model is:

$$X(t) = \frac{B(q^{-1})}{A(q^{-1})} \hat{S}(t) + \frac{1}{A(q^{-1})} e(t) \qquad (10)$$

here $\hat{S}(t)$ is model input (surrogate time series), $X(t)$ is model output (original time
series), A and B are polynomials, q^{-1} is a backward shift operator, and $e(t)$ is noise.

4 Experiments and Results

We use the historical data (2009) of S&P 500 stocks (245 days, 379 stocks with non-zero value). Here we analyze the daily highest price value. The dataset is separated into 3 subsets: train (40%), test (40%) and validate (20%). Train subset is used for decomposition, test subset for finding best co-integration vector and validate subset for calculating prediction accuracy. We decompose each time series into 4 components (2 cyclical, trend and irregular residues). For the ABC algorithm, we use 100 bees (colony size), maximum number of iterations is 200. Algorithm is run 20 times and the best solution is retained.

We model the 1-day ahead value of time series and evaluate model accuracy using a variety of metrics (RMSE (Root Mean Square Error), MAE (Mean Absolute Error), MAPE (Mean Absolute Percentage Error), MSE (Mean Squared Error), Pearson correlation, Nash-Suttcliffe (NS) efficiency coefficient, MSPE (Mean Squared Prediction Error), RMSPE (Root Mean Square Percentage Error)) as well as illustrate graphically using Taylor diagram and target diagram.

Figure 2 shows the mean values of RSME, MAPE, MAE and MSE. In all cases, the model of a time series derived using the proposed method is better (error is smaller).

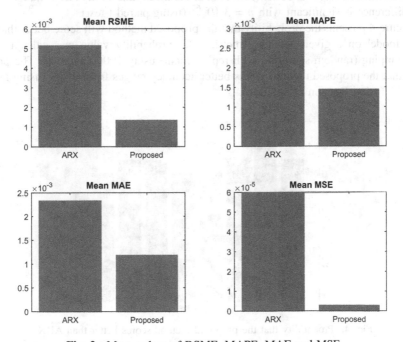

Fig. 2. Mean values of RSME, MAPE, MAE and MSE

Figure 3 shows the mean values of Pearson correlation, NS coefficient as well as the mean rank. Mean rank was calculated by ranking the modelling results of each stock (better = 1, worse = 2) based on the RMSE value. The mean rank of the

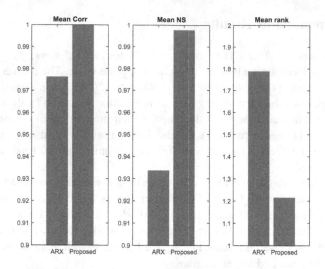

Fig. 3. Mean values of correlation, Nash-Suttcliffe (NS) efficiency coefficient, and rank

proposed method (1.21) is better (lower) than the mean rank of the ARX model (1.79). The difference is significant with $p = 3 \cdot 10^{-67}$ (using paired t-test).

Figure 4 presents the probability that the proposed method will score better than the ARX model on a given accuracy metric. The probability value was calculated by bootstrapping (random sampling with replacement) using 10000 samples. The probability that the proposed method yields better accuracy ranges from 0.709 (using MAE) to 0.916 (using Pearson correlation).

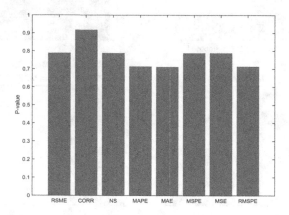

Fig. 4. Probability that the proposed method scores better than ARX

Taylor diagram (Fig. 5, left) is used to perform the comparative assessment of several different models and to quantify the degree of correspondence between the modelled and observed behaviour in terms of three statistics: Pearson correlation, RMSD (Root Mean Square Deviation), and the standard deviation [29]. The model that

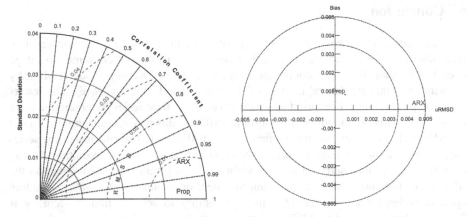

Fig. 5. Taylor diagram (left) and target diagram (right)

is located lower on the diagram is considered to represent the reality better. Note that the proposed model (*Prop*) is lower than the ARX model.

Target diagram (Fig. 5, right) [30] summarizes and visualizes information regarding the bias and the error between a model and real observations. The Y-axis corresponds to the normalized bias (Bias) and the X-axis corresponds to the normalized unbiased RMSD (uRMSD). Variables located in the upper part of the diagram ($Y > 0$) are overestimated by the model. The standard deviation of a model is larger than the standard deviation for the observations when variables are located in the right part of the target diagram ($X > 0$). The distance between any point and the origin is the value of the total RMSD. Note that while the proposed model performs better than the ARX model in terms of uRMSD ($5 \cdot 10^{-4}$ vs $5 \cdot 10^{-3}$) and total RSMD ($1.3 \cdot 10^{-3}$ vs $5.1 \cdot 10^{-3}$), it has a larger bias ($8.1 \cdot 10^{-3}$) than the ARX model ($1.6 \cdot 10^{-3}$).

The results are summarized in Table 1. Mean values of accuracy metrics are given and a relative improvement of the proposed method over ARX. Overall, the proposed method has improved the prediction accuracy of 78.6% of stocks (by RMSE).

Table 1. Summary of results

Metric	ARX	Proposed	Improvement, %
RMSE	0.0051	0.0013	74.51
RMSPE	0.0029	0.0014	51.72
MSE	$6 \cdot 10^{-5}$	$2.7 \cdot 10^{-6}$	95.43
MAE	0.0023	0.0012	47.83
MAPE	0.0029	0.0014	51.72
MASE	0.2270	0.1141	49.74
MSPE	$8.5 \cdot 10^{-5}$	$4.1 \cdot 10^{-6}$	95.19
NS	0.9335	0.9976	96.39
corr	0.976	0.9997	98.75
rank	1.786	1.214	72.77

5 Conclusion

We have introduced a new signal decomposition method based on the non-negative factorization of the Hankel matrix of a time series. The method offers some advantage over its conceptually similar counterpart, Empirical Mode Decomposition (EMD), by allowing to obtain the desired number of Intrinsic Mode Functions (IMF). The results of decomposition have been used to generate surrogate time series by prediction error minimization driven random cointegration of IMFs. In this paper, cointegration, to our knowledge, has been applied for the first time to IMFs, ever. The surrogate time series used as input allows for more accurate prediction of time series than predicting directly from the original time series. The results obtained using historical stock data and the ARX prediction model show a mean improvement of accuracy of 51–98% depending upon considered accuracy metric, while probability to achieve higher accuracy is 70–91% when compared to ARX prediction using the original time series only.

Future work will focus on the application of the proposed method on other datasets as well as on comparison with other time series modelling and prediction methods.

References

1. Castellini, A., Paltrinieri, D., Manca, V.: MP-GeneticSynth: inferring biological network regulations from time series. Bioinformatics 31(5), 785–787 (2015)
2. Maharaj, E.A., Alonso, A.M.: Discriminant analysis of multivariate time series: application to diagnosis based on ECG signals. Comput. Stat. Data Anal. 70, 67–87 (2014)
3. Nunnari, G.: Modelling air pollution time-series by using wavelet functions and genetic algorithms. Soft. Comput. 8(3), 173–178 (2004)
4. Messaoud, A., Weihs, C., Hering, F.: Nonlinear time series modelling: monitoring a drilling process. In: From Data and Information Analysis to Knowledge Engineering. Studies in Classification, Data Analysis, and Knowledge Organization, vol. 31, pp. 302–309 (2006)
5. Soubeyrand, S., Morris, C.E., Bigg, E.K.: Analysis of fragmented time directionality in time series to elucidate feedbacks in climate data. Environ. Model Softw. 61, 78–86 (2014)
6. Soto, R., Núñez, G.: Soft modelling of financial time series. Model. Simul. 2003, 537–542 (2003)
7. Wei, B., Pinto, H., Wang, X.: A symbolic tree model for oil and gas production prediction using time-series production data. In: IEEE International Conference on Data Science and Advanced Analytics (DSAA), pp. 272–281 (2016)
8. Hülsmann, M., Borscheid, D., Friedrich, C.M., Reith, D.: General sales forecast models for automobile markets based on time series analysis and data mining techniques. In: Perner, P. (ed.) ICDM 2011. LNCS, vol. 6870, pp. 255–269. Springer, Heidelberg (2011). doi:10.1007/978-3-642-23184-1_20
9. Chen, Y.-S., Cheng, C.-H., Tsai, W.-L.: Modeling fitting-function-based fuzzy time series patterns for evolving stock index forecasting. Appl. Intell. 41(2), 327–347 (2014)
10. Cheng, C., Sa-Ngasoongsong, A., Beyca, O., Le, T., Yang, H., Kong, Z., Bukkapatnam, S.T. S.: Time series forecasting for nonlinear and non-stationary processes: a review and comparative study. IIE Trans. 47(10), 1053–1071 (2015)
11. Dagum, E.B.: Time series modeling and decomposition. Statistica 4, 433–457 (2010)

12. Wold, H.: A Study in the Analysis of Stationary Time Series. Almqvist & Wiksell, Stockholm (1954)
13. Cleveland, R.B., Cleveland, W.S., McRae, J.E., Terpenning, I.: Stl: a seasonal-trend decomposition procedure based on loess. J. Official Stat. **6**(1), 3–73 (1990)
14. Winters, P.R.: Forecasting sales by exponentially weighted moving averages. Manage. Sci. **6**, 324–342 (1960)
15. Wozniak, M., Napoli, C., Tramontana, E., Capizzi, G.: A multiscale image compressor with RBFNN and Discrete Wavelet decomposition. In: International Joint Conference on Neural Networks (IJCNN), pp. 1219–1225 (2015)
16. Capizzi, G., Napoli, C., Bonanno, F.: Innovative second-generation wavelets construction with recurrent neural networks for solar radiation forecasting. IEEE Trans. Neural Netw. Learn. Syst. **23**(11), 1805–1815 (2012)
17. Huang, N.E., Shen, Z., Long, S.R., Wu, M.C., Shih, H.H., Zheng, Q., Yen, N.C., Tung, C.C., Liu, H.H.: The empirical mode decomposition and the Hilbert spectrum for nonlinear and nonstationary time series analysis. Proc. Roy. Soc. Lond. A **454**, 903–995 (1998)
18. Tiwari, A.K., Dar, A.B., Bhanja, N., Gupta, R.: A historical analysis of the US stock price index using empirical mode decomposition over 1791–2015. Economics Discussion Papers, no 2016–9, Kiel Institute for the World Economy (2016)
19. Xu, M., Shang, P., Lin, A.: Cross-correlation analysis of stock markets using EMD and EEMD. Phys. A Stat. Mech. Appl. **442**, 82–90 (2016)
20. Damasevicius, R., Napoli, C., Sidekerskiene, T., Wozniak, M.: IMF remixing for mode demixing in EMD and application for jitter analysis. In: IEEE Symposium on Computers and Communication (ISCC), pp. 50–55 (2016)
21. Deng, Y., Wang, W.: Boundary processing technique in EMD method and Hilbert transform. Chin. Sci. Bull. **46**(11), 257–263 (2001)
22. Wu, Q., Riemenschneider, S.D.: Boundary extension and stop criteria for empirical mode decomposition. Adv. Adapt. Data Anal. **2**(2), 157–169 (2010)
23. Damaševičius, R., Vasiljevas, M., Martišius, I., Jusas, V., Birvinskas, D., Woźniak, M.: BoostEMD: an extension of EMD method and its application for denoising of EMG signals. Electron. Electr. Eng. **21**(6), 57–61 (2015)
24. Engle, R.F., Granger, C.W.J.: Co-integration and error correction: representation, estimation and testing. Econometrica **55**(2), 251–276 (1987)
25. Barghouthi, S.A., Rehman, I.U., Rawashdeh, G.: Testing the efficiency of Amman Stock Exchange by the two step regression based technique, the Johansen multivariate technique cointegration, and Granger causality. Electron. J. Appl. Stat. Anal. **9**(3), 572–586 (2016)
26. Schreiber, T., Schmitz, A.: Surrogate time series. J. Phys. D Appl. Phys. **142**(3–4), 346–382 (2000)
27. Karaboga, D., Basturk, B.: A powerful and efficient algorithm for numerical function optimization: artificial bee colony (ABC) algorithm. J. Global Optim. **39**, 459–471 (2007)
28. Box, G., Jenkins, G.M., Reinsel, G.C.: Time Series Analysis: Forecasting and Control, 4th edn. Wiley, Chichester (2008)
29. Taylor, K.E.: Summarizing multiple aspects of model performance in a single diagram. J. Geophys. Res. **106**, 7183–7192 (2001)
30. Jolliff, J.K., Kindle, J.C., Shulman, I., Penta, B., Friedrichs, M.A.M., Helber, R., Arnone, R. A.: Summary diagrams for coupled hydrodynamic-ecosystem model skill assessment. J. Mar. Syst. **76**, 64–82 (2009)

Various Aspects of Computer Security

Evil-AP - Mobile Man-in-the-Middle Threat

Kamil Breński, Maciej Chołuj, and Marcin Luckner(✉)

Faculty of Mathematics and Information Science, Warsaw University of Technology,
ul. Koszykowa 75, 00–662 Warszawa, Poland
{brenskik,cholujm}@student.mini.pw.edu.pl, mluckner@mini.pw.edu.pl

Abstract. Clients of public hotspots are exposed to various threats including a man–in–the–middle attacks. To stress existing threats we created the Evil-AP application for demonstrating a man–in–the–middle attack. The application, installed on an Android phone with root permissions, turns on hotspot services and performs network redirection. We tested as the proposed techniques can be used to eavesdrop, redirect, inject, and strip the Internet traffic. A mobility of the created solution together with the wide functionality creates an extremely dangerous tool. Therefore, we concluded our work with good practices that allow the users to avoid similar threats as described in our work.

1 Introduction

The users of mobile devices utilise various access points to connect with the Internet including public hotspots. They are exposed on various penetration tests [2] including man–in–the–middle (MITM) attack [12]. Such dangerous should be examined and a proper tools for that must be created.

In this work we presented the Evil-AP application developed for demonstration purposes. It sets up a MITM attack using an Android phone with root permissions, turns on hotpot services and preforms network redirection.

The performed tests showed that the proposed technique creates extremely dangerous mobile trap for careless public hotspots users. The Evil-AP can eavesdrop, redirect, inject, and strip the Internet traffic.

Similarly, as in works [3, 9–11, 13] the main aim of this document is to raise awareness of the dangers of MITM attacks. We demonstrated the methods that could be used by attackers, and provided appropriate methods and things to consider in order to stay safe, and keep our information private.

The rest of the paper is structured as follows. Section 2 contains information on a man-in-the middle attack and network protocols. Section 3 presents related works. Section 4 describes the Evil-AP application. Section 5 presents the tests of the application. Finally, Sect. 6 presents brief conclusions.

2 Preliminaries

A man-in-the middle attack intercepts communication between two systems. The focus of this work were Hypertext Transfer Protocol (HTTP) transactions.

© IFIP International Federation for Information Processing 2017
Published by Springer International Publishing AG 2017. All Rights Reserved
K. Saeed et al. (Eds.): CISIM 2017, LNCS 10244, pp. 617–627, 2017.
DOI: 10.1007/978-3-319-59105-6_53

In this case the target is the Transmission Control Protocol (TCP) connection between a client and a web server. Using different techniques, the attacker splits the original TCP connection into 2 new connections, one between the client and the attacker and the other between the attacker and the server. Once the TCP connection is intercepted, the attacker acts as a proxy, being able to read, insert and modify the data in the intercepted communication. MITM attacks can also be done over Hypertext Transfer Protocol Secure (HTTPS) connections. The only difference consists in the establishment of two independent Secure Socket Layer (SSL) sessions, one over each TCP connection. The browser sets up a SSL connection with the attacker, and the attacker establishes another SSL connection with the web server. In general the browser warns the user that the digital certificate used is not valid, but the user may ignore the warning because he does not understand the threat. In some specific contexts it is possible that the warning does not appear, as for example, when the Server certificate is compromised by the attacker or when the attacker certificate is signed by a trusted Certificate Authority (CA) and the Common Name (CN) is the same of the original web site [8].

Since the developed Evil-AP proxy is an HTTP proxy, an overview of HTTP is presented. The HTTP protocol has always been a popular protocol [1]. It is the foundation of data communication in the world wide web. HTTP functions as a request-response protocol in the client-server computing model [7]. In the usual scenario a web browser like Firefox or Chrome is the client which makes the request to the web server for some particular resource like an HTML, CSS, or JavaScript file, along with any other resources needed to properly render a website. HTTP typically works over TCP which is a stateful protocol which provides a reliable connection. TCP is a transport layer protocol of the OSI model, while HTTP is an application layer protocol. For the purposes of this work we designed a HTTP proxy which will be between client and server communication. The HTTP protocol that is in common use today was developed in 1999 and is defined in RFC 2616 [4].

There are various requests that the client can make to the server, popular ones being the GET and POST requests. The GET request is used to retrieve remote data from a host server. Yet it is not uncommon to pass variables from one page to another by using the URL query string. On the other hand a POST request is used to insert or update remote data. Such data might include a comment or a block of data that is the result of submitting a web form. This data is sent in the body of the request and not clearly visible like variables in the URL of GET requests. There is a common misconception among new web developers that data sent in POST requests is safer than data sent in GET requests. That is not true as someone using a proxy can easily modify any part of the request, just like Evil-AP does. The data found in a POST request is quite commonly originating from a web form, this makes the contents of the body particularly interesting to someone with malicious intent as it might contain personal information or login credentials. There are various other requests like the OPTIONS, HEAD, or TRACE requests but they are usually used less often. Evil-AP application supports the GET and POST requests.

3   Related Work

Several works described MITM attacks. The high-level overview of what penetration tests are and what tools are used can be found in [2]. Some concrete examples of certain activities that might be performed during a penetration test are discussed, yet only a small section is devoted to MITM attacks. That section only describes MITM attack as Address Resolution Protocol (ARP) poisoning [5]. Work [12] identified the lack of a good taxonomy of MITM attacks against HTTPS. It established such a taxonomy in order to improve the SSL/TLS protocols by providing a better understanding of such attacks. It did not provide details on any concrete MITM attack implementation. Work [3] presented various security vulnerabilities that occur in WiFi networks. It focused on showing various ways that a malicious party can in fact monitor network traffic that various other legitimate users are generating. The work presented more attack types than MITM, yet it focused on sniffing private information like passwords of email and bank accounts, along with facebook activity, without editing any of the existing network traffic. The issue of encrypted traffic was not raised.

Several works discussed similar issues as presented in this work. We prepared a brief description of those works and stressed differences between our approach and other propositions. Work [13] presented a possible method of establishing a secure point-to-point connection using a shared secret derived from the fluctuations in a radio environment. Creating such a secure connection between two points would effectively render MITM attacks unlikely as someone who is not in close proximity to the two points that want to establish a connection will not have the same radio environment from which a token was derived. This work did not take into consideration the security and privacy of clients using a shared LAN network. Work [10] presented an epidemiological approach to simulate the spread of malware over poorly protected Wi–Fi Access Points. It focused on the aspect of compromising a LAN network, which gives the attacker the ability to perform MITM attacks. The work touched on the topic of compromising typical home routers and re-flashing them with new firmware which would give the attacker total control over the device. Its aim was to show the possible coverage and time needed in order to infect as many APs as possible. Work [6] presented a detection scheme for discovering Evil-Twin attacks on WiFi networks. The Evil-Twin attack is a certain type of MITM attack where the attacker poses as a legitimate Access Point and intercepts communication. Using appropriate hotspot configuration Evil-AP can also be used in an Evil Twin attack. Unfortunately the scheme discussed in this work only functioned in attacks that use a single ISP gateway, where Evil-AP uses a different ISP gateway, the one provided when using a mobile data plan. Extra steps are needed to ensure that the detection scheme works for both scenarios. Work [9] demonstrated how Android applications can be exploited using MITM attacks with DNS spoofing. It also pointed out various security holes in the Android security model. Unlike Evil-AP this work used a laptop to set up a rouge access point, and focuses on editing the contents of a WebView that is displayed by an application. Finally, work [11] discussed a vulnerability found on Apple iOS devices, affected version being iOS

3 to iOS 5. The vulnerability occurs when an Apple device joins an open WiFi network, the device then automatically makes a request to one of the Apple's servers to test network connectivity. If the response is not what the device was expecting it makes the assumption that there is a captive portal and it automatically opens a UIWebView for the user to accept the terms of service. Problems begin when that response contains malicious content like a hook used to control browsers like the one that can be generated using the BEEF framework. This work focused on attacking client devices and not on security and privacy of data transferred on a LAN.

4   Evil-AP

At the core of the Evil-AP application there is a proxy server which listens for incoming HTTP and HTTPS connections. Furthermore this proxy can be seen as having two parts. The private network (LAN) facing part which will be a server that accepts connections from clients connected the hotspot and a public network (Internet) facing part which will send requests to web servers in our client's name. A request will have to go through our proxy server in order to be processed, logged, and perhaps modified by it. Similar rules apply to responses from web server. This scheme is represented in Fig. 1. Internally the proxy server is implemented as an android service which uses two thread pools, one for handling HTTP connections and the other one for handling HTTPS connections.

4.1   Applied Technology and Requirements

The Evil-AP application is implemented in the Java programming language using Android Studio IDE. Since the application also requires interaction with the

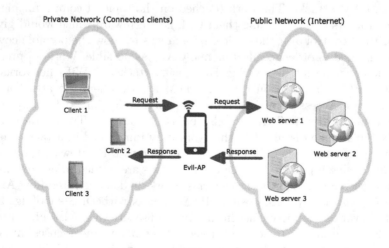

Fig. 1. Architecture overview.

underlying Linux kernel of the rooted phone, UNIX commands from within Java are used to accomplish certain tasks. These tasks include applying new firewall traffic redirection rules or reading certain system files in order to gather information about connected clients.

As the project requires at least a partial implementation of the HTTP protocol an external library is used to help with this. The library is called *okhttp* [14] and it is used to make requests to web servers.

The application requires the following permissions:

ACCESS_CHECKIN_PROPERTIES Allows read/write access to the "properties" table in the checkin database, to change values that get uploaded. Application requires these permissions in order to configure the hotspot properties.

ACCESS_NETWORK_STATE Allows application to access information about networks.

CHANGE_NETWORK_STATE Allows application to change network state.

ACCESS_WIFI_STATE Allows application to access information about Wi-Fi networks.

CHANGE_WIFI_STATE Allows application to change Wi-Fi state.

READ_EXTERNAL_STORAGE Allows application to read from external storage. Necessary for SQLite database to function properly.

WRITE_EXTERNAL_STORAGE Allows application to write to external storage. Necessary for SQLite database to function properly.

INTERNET Allows application to open network sockets.

The phone itself needs to give the application root permissions which allows it to redirect traffic using the Linux firewall called iptables. In order to do this the phone itself needs to be rooted. The specific rule used for HTTP redirection looks as such `iptables -t nat -I PREROUTING -i wlan0 -p tcp --dport 80 -j REDIRECT --to-port 1337`, a similar rule is used in the case of HTTPS. The application also uses the phones mobile data plan in order to connect to the Internet, this is because the wireless interface that could be used to connect to an existing WiFi is already being used by the hotspot. Another assumption that is made by the application is the fact that all requests made by the clients will have the host header present since it is needed in order to construct the okhttp request.

4.2 Evil-AP Functionality

To describe the functionality of the Evil-AP application we defined two roles.

The first role is the Evil-AP user. The user configures the hotspot. The configuration consists of a service set identifier (SSID), a password, and a security method.

Next, the user can define how the network traffic will be edited. There are three modes. In the first mode, the user selects the image to use as a replacement to all images in an HTTP response. In the second mode, the user writes the JavaScript code he wants to inject to an HTTP response. For security reasons, the JavaScript code is limited to an alert box and the user can only modify the presented text.

In the last mode, the user enables SSL Strip. In the last mode the application forces a client's browser into communicating in plain-text over HTTP. All https:// URLs are striped and turned into http:// URLs.

Additionally, the user can ban clients, view the client log and redirect HTTP(S).

The client, which is unaware, can only connect to the hotspot, browse the Internet, and disconnect.

4.3   Proxy Architecture

The core of the Evil-AP application is a set of proxy components. The components handle HTTP requests. The flow of a request through the proxy components is shown in Fig. 2.

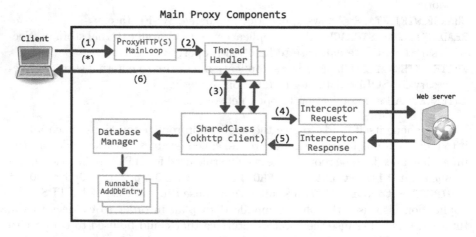

Fig. 2. Overview of main proxy components

The client sends a request and it is rerouted to our application (1). Next, the `ProxyHTTP(S)MainLoop` accepts the connection and passes it to a thread from the thread pool (2). The `ThreadHandler` reads the client request and parses it into an okhttp request. While parsing the string request it uses the `SharedClass` object to insert new entries into the SQLite database. Internally `SharedClass` uses a thread pool to run SQL INSERT commands in order to avoid further delaying the handling of client connections. It then accesses the okhttp client found in `SharedClass` to make the request to the web server (3). Before forwarding the request to the web server `InterceptorRequest` removes any security related headers like "Upgrade-Insecure-Requests" or "Strict-Transport-Security" (4). The response from the web server is edited by `InterceptorResponse`. The status-line of the response has a hard-coded "HTTP/1.1" string in order to avoid using HTTP/2.0.

This is also where various actions like injecting JavaScript or replacing the bytes of images take place (5). After receiving the response `ThreadHandler` forwards it to the client (6). When the client makes a regular HTTP request it will originally be destined for port 80. This scheme still applies if the client makes an HTTPS request, the only difference is that it will be destined for port 443 and before any data is exchanged the SSL/TLS handshake will take place. When that happens the proxy server will present the client with a self-signed certificate and the client should have an option to either add an exception for the untrusted certificate or be denied access to the web resource he is requesting (*).

5   Tests

In this section results of various Evil-AP configurations are shown. A single connected client was used to make a request for the faculty of Mathematics and Information Science website found at "http://www.mini.pw.edu.pl/tikiwiki". The Firefox browser was configured to not use its cache by changing entries.

The application was started as a hotspot and tested in several configurations as it is shown in Fig. 3. The following configurations of Evil-AP were tested:

- Evil-AP not redirecting traffic (*no redirection*)
- Evil-AP only redirecting and logging traffic (*redirection*)
- Redirection with JavaScript injection (*js*)
- Redirection with image replacement and SSL Strip (*ir + issl*)
- Redirection with image replacement, SSL Strip, and JavaScript injection (*ir + ssl + js*)

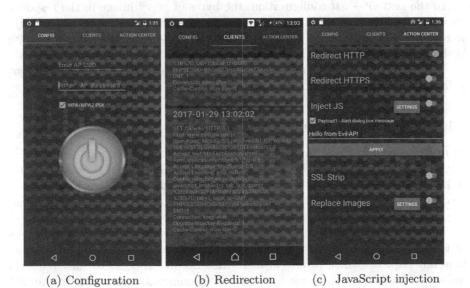

(a) Configuration   (b) Redirection   (c) JavaScript injection

Fig. 3. Evil-AP configuration and tests

Evil-AP with *no redirection* did not establish a MITM attack between connected clients. The requests were not logged or edited. The hotspot worked normally, just as if Evil-AP would not have been installed. Figure 4a shows the faculty website rendered normally.

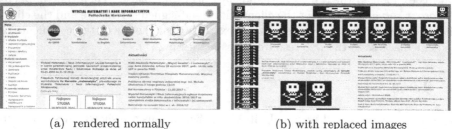

(a) rendered normally   (b) with replaced images

Fig. 4. Faculty website

In the *redirection* configuration Evil-AP proxy established a MITM attack and logged client's requests. The requests were sent and the response was forwarded back without any editions. Figure 3b shows the logged initial request that was made by the client.

In the *js* configuration, the Evil-AP injected a small piece of JavaScript in the HTML response. The used script was `alert("Hello from Evil-AP!");`. As a result the alert box was displayed. Figure 3c shows configuration of the injection.

In the next *ir + ssl* configuration, the bytes of every image in the response were swapped, and all HTTPS links were changed to HTTP ones. All images were replaced by the image currently loaded in Evil-AP. The rendered website is shown in Fig. 4b.

In the last configuration all features of Evil-AP were turned on. The user got a JavaScript alert and all images were swapped like in Fig. 4b.

5.1   Performance Comparison

In order to test how the proxy impacts performance, 10 requests for the faculty website were made in each configuration. The amount of time for the initial request and the amount of time needed to render the entire website were recorded. For the final chart the average for those times was taken. To fully load the website 58 requests were made in total.

Figure 5 shows the performance comparison between various configurations of Evil-AP. It is visible that enabling various features causes some delay while handling requests which results in more time needed in order to fully render a website. The delay is there yet it is not that significant mostly due to the fact that HTTP persistent connection is implemented inside the application. This allows the browser to use a single TCP connection to make multiple requests,

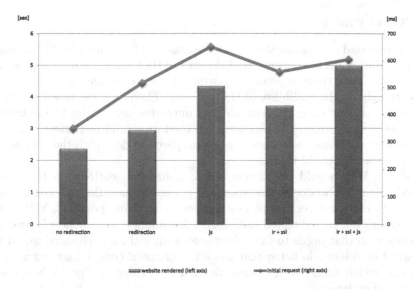

Fig. 5. Network performance for different configurations of Evil-AP

without the overhead of setting up and tearing down each TCP connection for each individual request.

6   Conclusions

In our work, we have shown that the usage of untrusted access points can be extremely dangerous. Our mobile application Evil-AP can change, inject, or redirect HTTP and HTTPS traffic. The Avast free Wi-Fi experiment at Mobile World Congress[1] has shown that even experts are careless using unknown hotspots with a free Internet. And by its mobility, our solution is even more dangerous.

Maliciously performing MITM attacks like the ones discussed in this paper is not only wrong, it is illegal. The goal of this paper is not to enable attacks on hotspots clients, but rather to make people aware of the real dangers that exist to an individual's privacy so that better care can be taken in order to secure ourselves against these threats. We honestly hope that the information contained here will be used in good-faith by aspiring penetration-testers and security enthusiasts. According to our aim it is good to stress several good practises that allow the users to avoid dangers connected with the attacks as one described in this work.

---

[1] https://blog.avast.com/2016/02/24/avast-free-wi-fi-experiment-fools-mobile-world-congress-attendees/.

6.1   Good Practises

Since a generated self-signed SSL certificate was used to set up a MITM attack on HTTPS connections for websites that do not use HSTS, a warning was presented to the client that there is something wrong with the connection. This attack relies strongly on the gullibility of the end-user. Therefore, the best thing to do is to never add any exceptions or add any untrusted certificates to the browser certificate store. If we do add an exception, then we should be perfectly aware of the real reason behind the message, or be prepared to deal with the very serious consequences that could result.

Using a VPN would circumvent traffic redirection entirely, in the case of Evil-AP. Since VPNs do not use standard ports, and no other rules exist other then the two that redirect traffic destined for port 80 and port 443, VPN traffic would never even be redirected to Evil-AP. Assuming that somehow it was. The authentication that needs to take place before any data is exchanged would fail. The worst case scenario being that the attacker could cut off connectivity with the VPN, which would be a clear indication that there is a proxy between us and the public Internet.

Modern browsers always give us an indication of what kind of connection is established with the host server. HTTPS connections are usually represented with a green lock somewhere around the address of the website we have connected to The lack of this green lock or a crossed out lock indicates a regular HTTP connection. This should raise our suspicion and we should be aware that anything we send or receive over this type of connection can be easily intercepted, monitored, or transformed.

In the case of the Evil-AP proxy there are a few indicators that could hint that network traffic is being intercepted. The biggest one being that the HTTP protocol is only partially implemented, meaning requests other than GET and POST will not work. This means that websites that rely on other methods will not render properly.

6.2   Possible Improvements and Future Work

The Evil-AP application does not work in the case of servers configured with HSTS. This is because the browser has an entry saved that says it should only connect to this server using HTTPS and it stops the user from easily adding certificate exceptions for this host. While it is always nice for servers to be configured this way, it should not be treated as a final cure for MITM attacks. That is because a malicious actor could control the entire traffic flow, including DNS traffic. An upgraded version of SSL Strip can be therefore constructed. Instead of only changing all occurrences of https:// into http:// a small part of the hostname could also be changed, like adding an extra w in www, it would not really matter that such a host might not exists as the attacker is the one that is doing the name resolution anyway. By doing DNS resolution on edited hostnames an attacker will be able to slip past already existing HSTS entries saved in the browser. Another possible improvement that would add potency to Evil-AP is the ability to inject forged 802.11 frames. This would allow for better execution of the Evil-Twin attack since the configuration of a legitimate AP can be copied, then the attacker would send forged 802.11 deauthentication frames with the spoofed address of the client that will be disconnected from the legitimate AP and perhaps re-connect to Evil-AP if the communication from the malicious AP is faster then the one from the legitimate AP.

References

1. Raggett, D., Arnaud Le Hors, I.J.: HTML 4.01 specification (1999). https://www.w3.org/TR/html4/. Accessed 28 Jan 2017
2. Denis, M., Zena, C., Hayajneh, T.: Penetration testing: concepts, attack methods, and defense strategies. In: 2016 IEEE Long Island Systems, Applications and Technology Conference (LISAT), pp. 1–6, April 2016
3. Fahmy, S., Nasir, A., Shamsuddin, N.: Wireless network attack: raising the awareness of kampung wifi residents. In: 2012 International Conference on Computer Information Science (ICCIS), vol. 2, pp. 736–740, June 2012
4. Fielding, R.T., Gettys, J., Mogul, J.C., Nielsen, H.F., Masinter, L., Leach, P.J., Berners-Lee, T.: Hypertext transfer protocol - http/1.1. RFC 2616, RFC Editor. http://www.rfc-editor.org/rfc/rfc2616.txt
5. King, J., Lauerman, K.: ARP poisoning attack and mitigation techniques (2016). http://www.cisco.com/c/en/us/products/collateral/switches/catalyst-6500-series -switches/white_paper_c11_603839.html. Accessed 28 Jan 2017
6. Nakhila, O., Zou, C.: User-side wi-fi evil twin attack detection using random wireless channel monitoring. In: MILCOM 2016 - 2016 IEEE Military Communications Conference, pp. 1243–1248, November 2016
7. IoT ONE: Hypertext Transfer Protocol. http://www.iotone.com/term/hypertext-transfer-protocol-http/t557. Accessed Dec 2016
8. OWASP: Man-in-the-middle attack (2015). https://www.owasp.org/index.php/Man-in-the-middle_attack. Accessed 28 Jan 2017
9. Park, M.W., Choi, Y.H., Eom, J.H., Chung, T.M.: Dangerous wi-fi access point: attacks to benign smartphone applications. Pers. Ubiquitous Comput. 18(6), 1373–1386 (2014). http://dx.doi.org/10.1007/s00779-013-0739-y
10. Sanatinia, A., Narain, S., Noubir, G.: Wireless spreading of wifi aps infections using wps flaws: an epidemiological and experimental study. In: 2013 IEEE Conference on Communications and Network Security (CNS), pp. 430–437, October 2013
11. Spaulding, J., Krauss, A., Srinivasan, A.: Exploring an open wifi detection vulnerability as a malware attack vector on ios devices. In: 2012 7th International Conference on Malicious and Unwanted Software, pp. 87–93, October 2012
12. Stricot-Tarboton, S., Chaisiri, S., Ko, R.K.L.: Taxonomy of man-in-the-middle attacks on https. In: 2016 IEEE Trustcom/BigDataSE/ISPA, pp. 527–534, August 2016
13. Varshavsky, A., LaMarca, A., de Lara, E.: Enabling secure and spontaneous communication between mobile devices using common radio environment. In: Eighth IEEE Workshop on Mobile Computing Systems and Applications, pp. 9–13, March 2007
14. Wilson, J.: Okhttp wiki, May 2014. https://github.com/square/okhttp/wiki

Intention to Adopt the Cash on Delivery (COD) Payment Model for E-commerce Transactions: An Empirical Study

Mohanad Halaweh[(⊠)]

Al Falah University, Dubai, United Arab Emirates
Mohanad.halaweh@afu.ac.ae

Abstract. The cash on delivery (COD) model has been increasingly used in the last few years as a method of payment for e-commerce transactions. However, little research has empirically investigated the factors that influence customers' intention to adopt this method as opposed to traditional electronic payment methods. As a result, this paper aims to predict and test the factors that influence the customer's intention to adopt the cash on delivery (COD) model for e-commerce transaction payments. A research model of key influencing factors and three hypotheses was developed based on previous conceptual research. To test these hypotheses, a questionnaire was designed to collect the data, which were analysed using the partial least squares (PLS) method in SmartPLS software. The results of this study supported the hypothesis that perceived security, privacy and trust exerted significant influence on the customers' intention to adopt a COD payment system. The interpretation of the results and implications for practise and future research are also discussed.

Keywords: E-commerce · Online payment methods · Cash on Delivery (COD) · Adoption

1 Introduction

Since the appearance of the first e-commerce website in 1995, various methods of online payment for e-commerce purchases have been used, including credit cards, debit cards, smart cards, e-cash, e-checks, e-wallet, and micropayment. However, during the past few years, a new method of payment called cash on delivery (COD) has been increasingly used. COD is different from all other methods of payment in terms of its processing, the time and place that the payment is made, the parties involved, and many other issues, including its security and privacy assurance. COD enables customers to make a payment in cash at the time a product is delivered to any location the customers choose. The use of this method is increasing in some countries. For example, in Vietnam, COD is accepted by 24 out of the 33 (73%) surveyed e-commerce companies [18]. In India, COD accounts for 50–80% of online transaction payments [8], while in the United Arab Emirates, this number is about 60% [12]. However, although it has gained more popularity in the last few years, little empirical research has investigated the reasons that influence customers' intention to adopt this method of payment or what

© IFIP International Federation for Information Processing 2017
Published by Springer International Publishing AG 2017. All Rights Reserved
K. Saeed et al. (Eds.): CISIM 2017, LNCS 10244, pp. 628–637, 2017.
DOI: 10.1007/978-3-319-59105-6_54

factors make customers favour COD over other methods. This research aims to fill this gap by developing a model of factors that might influence the customers' intention to use this method. It is worth mentioning that no previous empirical research study exists, which makes it impossible to compare these results with previous research. However, the predicted factors were revealed in a prior literature review but in a different context, which was used in this study to predict whether these factors are the reasons that motivate customers to accept it as an alternative to existing e-payment methods. In other words, this research suggested that the concerns that make customers reluctant to adopt e-payment methods are predicted to be the motivating factors for adopting COD for e-commerce transaction payments.

The remainder of the paper is organized as follows: Section 2 provides a literature review on e-commerce payment methods and related concerns, which led to developing the current research model and hypothesis. Section 3 describes the employed research method. Section 4 presents the research results. Section 5 provides a discussion and the practical implications followed by the research conclusion.

2 Literature Review

An electronic payment (e-payment) is a payment that is initiated, processed and received electronically over the Internet. Multiple methods of e-payment are used for e-commerce transactions, such as credit cards, prepaid cards or smart cards, e-cash (digital cash) and e-checks (digital checks). Among these, the credit card method is considered the most common e-payment method [20]. According to much previous research, perceived privacy, security and trust were the main critical factors or reasons that make customers reluctant to adopt existing e-commerce and e-payment methods [1, 2, 6, 13, 19, 21, 22, 25].

E-payments generate information that can be used to analyse customer purchasing behavior or to conduct other investigations, which can be used for purposes that violate customers' privacy. Chellappa [3] defined perceived privacy as the 'the subjective probability with which consumers believe that the collection and subsequent access, use, and disclosure of their private and personal information is consistent with their expectations' (p. 12). Dinev, Xu, Smith, and Hart [7] defined it as 'an individual's self-assessed state in which external agents have limited access to information about him or her' (p. 299). Customers might have more control of their privacy when they use COD as a payment method because they do not have to release too much information about themselves and their purchases. Banks and e-commerce websites are unable to track the history of their cash transactions. The customers simply need to provide their mobile phone numbers to receive the product at any location (e.g., at work, at home or in any public place) to protect their privacy and avoid tracking. In contrast, when a customer uses a credit card, every single transaction is recorded; banks, merchants or third parties can obtain this information and compile data about consumer purchasing behaviours, interests or preferences, which is an invasion of customer privacy for (Reference removed).

Security is still a consistent concern that prevents customers from engaging in e-commerce. Perceived security can be defined as 'the subjective probability with which consumers believe that their personal information (private and monetary) will not be viewed, stored, and manipulated during transit and storage by inappropriate parties in a manner consistent with their confident expectations [3]. The COD method provides customers with a more convenient way not only to ensure the security of their payment, as they do not have to release their credit cards online, but also to inspect the quality of the product itself at the time of delivery so they can confirm they have received the same product that they ordered, which also helps to build trust between the customer and the e-commerce company. In this situation, as opposed to an online payment transaction, two processes are checked and ensured: receiving the product as expected, which helps to build trust, and payment by cash, which gives the feeling of security and eliminates the Internet's risks/threats. Obviously, this method provides advantages over payments transmitted over the Internet (online payment methods).

Distrust might exist in e-commerce contexts as there is no direct face-to-face interaction between the seller and buyer and uncertainty exists all the time because of both parties' unpredictable actions and opportunistic behaviours [10]. Therefore, the key to removing this type of uncertainty and making successful e-commerce transactions is avoiding opportunistic behaviour [17], a situation that can be enabled through COD because the payment is made after the customer has received and inspected the ordered item. As pointed out by Li, Kim, and Park [23], trust can only exist if the consumer believes that the seller has the ability to provide and deliver goods of expected or better quality, which can be easily verified though COD payment.

Because of all these concerns that exist regarding online payments for e-commerce transactions, COD payment has been increasingly popular in the last few years in some countries, such as India, Gulf Cooperation Council (GCC) countries, Thailand, Vietnam, and Poland (4, 13, 19, 26, 28). The aforementioned e-commerce concerns can be predicted to be the same factors that motivate customers to adopt COD. In other words, a customer feels that he is not vulnerable to any security threats, privacy invasions or opportunistic behaviours when he uses COD payment for e-commerce transactions. Thus, the following hypotheses are expected:

H1. Perceived security will positively influence the customer's intention to adopt COD for e-commerce payment transactions.
H2. Perceived trust will positively influence the customer's intention to adopt COD for e-commerce payment transactions.
H3. Perceived privacy will positively influence the customer's intention to adopt COD for e-commerce payment transactions.

3   Research Method

The aim of this paper was to predict and test the factors that influence customers' intention to use COD for e-commerce payment transactions. Thus, three hypotheses were formulated, as presented in the previous section. A questionnaire instrument was designed that included the constructs shown in Table 1. All items were assessed using a five-point Likert scale (I strongly agree (5), I agree (4), Neutral (4), I disagree (2) and I strongly disagree (1)). The questionnaire was distributed to 100 participants from UAE.

Table 1. Survey constructs and measurements

Construct	Code	Item
Security	**SE1**	I feel that my private information is secure when I use COD for e-commerce payment transactions
	SE2	When I use COD, I am not vulnerable to any internet security threats
Privacy	**PR1**	COD keeps my identity anonymous so that banks and other third parties cannot track me
	PR2	My sensitive information can be protected when COD is used for e-commerce payment transactions
	PR3	COD reduces the amount of personal information that I need to share with e-commerce websites
Trust	**TR1**	COD gives me the chance to check/test the product before I make the payment
	TR4	COD ensures the identity of the e-commerce company
Adoption of COD	**AD1**	I intend to use COD when I purchase products from e-commerce websites

In total, 88 participants filled out and returned the survey, and their responses were deemed appropriate for analysis. The data were analysed using partial least squares (PLS) [a form of structural equation modelling] with SmartPLS software. PLS-SEM has experienced increasing dissemination in recent years in a variety of fields, including Information Systems [16]. PLS is typically recommended in situations in which there are no stable, well-defined theories to be tested in a confirmatory research setting, when the objective is prediction and when the sample size is small [4, 5, 11, 16, 26]. For all these reasons, PLS was an appropriate approach for the purpose of the current research. The model of factors and relationships (depicted in Fig. 1) was developed based on conceptual research, yet there is no established theory to explain the factors that influence the customers' intention to adopt COD for e-commerce payment transactions. The model contains constructs that were not previously tested in the context of using COD for e-commerce payment transactions. In addition, the sample size was appropriate for the PLS technique. Furthermore, the condition of minimum sample size was met, as Chin [4] and Hair et al. [16] proposed, in which the minimum sample size should be 10 times the largest number of structural paths directed at a particular latent construct in the structural model. The research model (Fig. 1 or 2) has only one dependent (latent) variable, 'adoption of COD', which has three paths directed to it. Thus, the sample size of this study should be a minimum of 30, and this condition has been met (the sample was 88). As shown in the questionnaire and research model (Fig. 2), the constructs were measured by a small number of items (n = 2 or 3) where, for example, the intention to adopt COD is measured with one overall reflective item. However, as pointed out by Hair et al. [16], PLS-SEM can easily handle reflective and formative measurement models, as well as single-item constructs, with no identification problems or additional constraints. In addition, it is a good way to shorten the questionnaire.

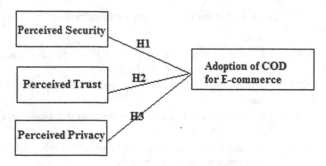

Fig. 1. Proposed theoretical model with hypotheses

4 Results Analysis

This section assesses the measurement and structural equation models.

4.1 Measurement Assessment

The measurement model was assessed using reliability and convergent and discriminant validity. Reliability was tested using Cronbach's alpha. According to Hair et al. [14, 15], items have high reliability if the Cronbach's alpha value is greater than 0.7. As shown in Table 2 (fourth column), the Cronbach's alpha value of all the constructs was greater than 0.7, so they had high reliability. The convergent validity was assessed by factor loadings, composite reliability and average variance extracted (AVE). The loadings for all items exceeded the recommended value of 0.6 (Table 2 and Fig. 2). All of the constructs exceeded the threshold for composite reliability, as they were greater than 0.70 [14, 15] (Table 4), ranging from 0.885–1.000. All values of average variance extracted were higher than 0.5 (Hair et al. [15], with a range from 0.855–1.000.

Discriminant validity was assessed by examining whether the square root of the AVE for each construct was higher than the squared correlation between that construct and all other constructs [9]. Table 3 shows that discriminant validity was met. The

Table 2. Summary of construct and validity and item loading

Construct	Items	Factor loading	Cronbach's alpha	Composite reliability	AVE
Adoption of COD for e-commerce	**AD1**	1.000	1.000	1.000	1.00
Perceived privacy	**PR1**	0.928	0.878	0.923	0.801
	PR2	0.857			
	PR3	0.898			
Perceived security	**SE1**	0.900	0.741	0.885	0.794
	SE2	0.882			
Perceived trust	**TR1**	0.943	0.833	0.922	0.855
	TR2	0.907			

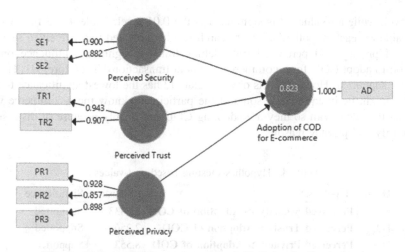

Fig. 2. PLS structural equation mode (with factor loading values)

Table 3. Correlation between Constructs (the diagonal represents the square roots of average variance extracted)

	Adoption of COD	Perceived Privacy	Perceived Security	Perceived Trust
Adoption of COD	1.000			
Perceived privacy	−0.667	0.895		
Perceived security	−0.870	0.894	0.891	
Perceived trust	0.251	−0.004	−0.108	0.925

square root of the AVE for each construct was greater than the correlation between constructs. As a result, the measurement model demonstrated adequate reliability, convergent validity and discriminant validity.

4.2 Structure Equation Model

Two measures were used to assess the structural model: the statistical significance (t-tests) of the estimated path coefficients and the ability of the model to explain the variance in the dependent variables (R square). The R square attempts to measure the explained variance of the dependent variable relative to its total variance. Values of approximately 0.670 are considered substantial; values around 0.333 are moderate, while values of approximately 0.190 are weak [4]. As shown in Fig. 2, the R square of the research model was 0.823, indicating that 80% of the variance in the adoption of COD for e-commerce was explained by the independent variables, which is a high variance. Figure 2 shows the R square for the dependent variable (adoption of COD for e-commerce). To test the significance of the hypotheses, the rule proposed by Martinez-Ruiz and Aluja-Banet [24] was followed. A t-value >1.65 is significant at the

0.05 level, while a t-value >2 is significant at the 0.01 level. Table 4 and Fig. 3 show the t-value for each hypothesis. The research results indicated that perceived security, perceived privacy and perceived trust demonstrated a significant influence on the intention to adopt COD for e-commerce payment transactions. Therefore, H1, H2 and H3 were supported. However, it is obvious that H2 has the lowest significance t-value and this might be interpreted as some of the participants know the e-commerce websites that they deal with so they are adopting COD not mainly because of distrust but for security and privacy reasons.

Table 4. Hypothesis testing based on t-values

H No.	Hypothesis	t Statistics	Significance
H1	**Perceived Security -> Adoption of COD**	18.433	Supported
H2	**Perceived Trust -> Adoption of COD**	2.256	Supported
H3	**Perceived Privacy -> Adoption of COD**	8.553	Supported

Note: A t-value >1.65 is significant at the 0.05** level; a t-value >2 is significant at the 0.01* level.

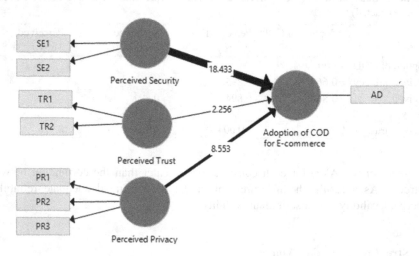

Fig. 3. Factors' relationship with the adoption of COD by t-values Using SmartPLS (the level of significance is indicated by bold arrow)

5   Research Implications and Conclusion

This paper aimed to predict the factors that influence customers' intention to adopt COD as a method of payment for e-commerce transactions. As expected, the perceived security was a significant factor that motivated customers to adopt COD for e-commerce payment transactions. Since Internet security threats continue to increase and there are no guaranteed solutions, some customers still prefer to pay in cash at the time of delivery instead of taking the risk of using a credit card or other payment method over the Internet. Our results indicated that customers intend to adopt this method of payment and might prefer it to other e-payment methods. Thus, considering the results, e-commerce companies need to provide this service to customers and should also clearly indicate this option on their websites. For example, e-commerce companies could create a special logo that reflects the COD service and display this logo on their homepage to attract customers' attention and encourage them to purchase from the website.

Consistent with our predictions, perceived privacy had an impact on customer intention to adopt COD. Customers do not want to share too much information about themselves and would prefer to keep their identities anonymous when they conduct transactions online. They believe that this privacy can be obtained with a COD payment method. For the last few decades, e-commerce companies have failed to show respect for customer privacy by using their information, by annoying them with calls, texts or emails promoting products or services, or by following their personal life due to the ability to track every single purchase made using a credit card transaction.

As expected, customers perceive e-commerce websites as more trustworthy when COD is used as they can verify whether the item is exactly as they expected before purchasing it. Consumers do not have this advantage when they make a payment using a credit card in advance of receiving the ordered item. Customers might have negative past experiences with e-commerce websites, such as receiving incorrect, fake or unexpected products, so COD offers a solution as it enables them to verify if the e-commerce company is credible and trustworthy.

This paper is considered original because it is the first academic paper to the author's knowledge that empirically investigated the COD payment method for e-commerce transactions from a customer's perspective. COD could continue to grow as an e-commerce payment method because it offers an alternative to other e-payment methods, which have many problems, including security, privacy risk and credibility and other issues. COD could be one of the best options for certain customers in specific situations, but it should be accepted along with other traditional e-payment methods. It is not advisable to rely only on COD as there might also be customers who prefer the convenience of other methods and are concerned about COD for reasons such as cash availability and exchange issues.

For practitioners in the e-commerce industry, this study provides e-commerce companies with statistical data that show a customer preference for paying using COD. It also indicates the reasons that prompt them to adopt this method. E-commerce companies have two options to tackle these reasons: (1) accepting COD besides other methods of e-payment. (2) Providing solutions that address the concerns and problems regarding existing traditional e-payment methods, including security, privacy and trust issues, which are not yet 100% guaranteed. Thus, option 1 could help e-commerce companies increase sales and convince customers to pay online. It also might give e-commerce websites that accept this method of payment an advantage over others that do not.

One limitation of this study is that it tested only three main constructs. There could be other constructs, such as cost, convenience and simplicity, that impact a customer's decision to adopt this method of payment for e-commerce transactions. Thus, future research might consider empirically testing other factors. Second, the data were collected from a context where around 40% of e-commerce transactions involved COD, and the results supported our prediction that three constructs influenced customers' intention to adopt COD. However, if data were collected from other contexts and countries where this method has not been used or is rarely accepted by e-commerce websites, the results might differ. Thus, further investigation of these constructs and hypotheses in a different context can help to generalize the results. Finally, it is not known whether the questionnaire respondents had prior experience purchasing products and paying online using a credit card, using COD, using both methods, or using none of them.

Therefore, the research findings might be different for consumers who have never purchased online using a credit card, for example.

The current study predicted factors that influenced the adoption of COD from the customers' perspective. Future research will be required to investigate empirically if e-commerce companies are also willing to accept COD payments and what reasons might motivate them to do so. Future research is also needed to identify whether using COD will enable e-commerce companies to gain a competitive advantage and increase sales over other e-commerce companies that do not accept this payment method.

References

1. Barkhordari, M., Nourollah, Z., Mashayekhi, H., Mashayekhi, Y., Ahangar, S.M.: Factors influencing adoption of e-payment systems: an empirical study on Iranian customers. ISeBM **15**(1), 89–116 (2017)
2. Bolt, W., Humphrey, D., Uittenbogaard, R.: The effect of transaction pricing on the adoption of electronic payments: A cross-country comparison. Working paper, Federal Reserve Bank of Philadelphia (2005)
3. Chellappa, R.K.: Consumers' trust in electronic commerce transactions: The role of perceived privacy and perceived security (2008). http://www.bus.emory.edu/ram/Papers/sec-priv.pdf
4. Chin, W.W.: The partial least squares approach to structural equation modeling. In: Marcoulides, G.A. (ed.) Modern Methods for Business Research, pp. 1295–1336. Lawrence Erlbaum Associates, Mahwah (1998)
5. Chin, W., Newsted, P.: Structural equation modeling analysis with small samples using partial least squares. In: Hoyle, R. (ed.) Statistical Strategies for Small Sample Research, pp. 307–341. Sage Publications (1999)
6. Daştan, İ., Gürler, C.: Factors affecting the adoption of mobile payment systems: an empirical analysis. Emerg. Markets J. **6**(1), 17–24 (2016)
7. Dinev, T., Xu, H., Smith, J., Hart, P.: Information privacy and correlates: an empirical attempt to bridge and distinguish privacy related concepts. Eur. J. Inf. Syst. **22**, 295–316 (2013)
8. Ernst & Young: Rebirth of e-commerce in India (2013). http://www.ey.com/Publication/vwLUAssets/Rebirth_of_eCommerce_in_India/%24FILE/EY_RE-BIRTH_OF_ECOMMERCE.pdf
9. Fornell, C., Larcker, D.F.: Evaluating structural equation models with unobservable variables and measurement error. J. Mark. Res. **18**(1), 39–50 (1981)

10. Jang, H.Y., Jeong, K.H., Jeong, D.Y.: The consequences of customer trust and the determinants of purchasing intention in Internet shopping malls. J. MIS Res. **15**(2), 23–49 (2005)
11. Haenlein, M., Kaplan, A.: A beginner's guide to partial least squares analysis, understanding statistics. Stat. Issues Psychol. Soc. Sci. **3**(4), 283–297 (2004)
12. Hamid, T.: Cash on delivery: The biggest obstacle to e-commerce in UAE and region (2014). http://www.thenational.ae/blogs/plugged-in/cash-on-delivery-the-biggest-obstacle-to-e-commerce-in-uae-and-region
13. Hamid, N., Cheng, A.: A risk perception analysis on the use of electronic payment systems by young adults. WSEAS Trans. Inf. Sci. Appl. **10**(1), 26–35 (2013)
14. Hair, J.F., Sarstedt, M., Hopkins, L., Kuppelwieser, G.: Partial least squares structural equation modeling (PLS-SEM): an emerging tool in business research. Eur. Bus. Rev. **26**(2), 106–121 (2014)
15. Hair, J.F., Black, W.C., Babin, B.J., Anderson, R.E., Tatham, R.L.: Multivariate Data Analysis, 6th edn. Pearson Prentice Hall, Upper Saddle River (2006)
16. Hair, J.F., Tomas, G.M., Ringle, C., Sarstedt, M.: A Primer in Partial Least Squares Structural Equation Modeling (PLS-SEM). Sage, Thousand Oaks (2014)
17. Hosmer, L.T.: Trust: the connecting link between organizational theory and philosophical ethics. Acad. Manag. Rev. **20**(2), 379–403 (1995)
18. International Finance Corporation. E- and m-commerce and payment sector development in Vietnam (2014). http://www.ifc.org/wps/wcm/connect/67a0740047f652aab0d3f5299ede9589/EMcommerce.pdf?MOD=AJPERES
19. Kim, C., Tao, W., Shin, N., Kim, K.S.: An empirical study of customers' perceptions of security and trust in e-payment systems. Electron. Commer. Res. Appl. **9**(1), 84–95 (2010)
20. Kou, W.: Payment Technologies for E-commerce. Springer, US (2013)
21. Lee, Z., Yu, H., Ku, P.: An analysis and comparison of different types of electronic payment systems. Manag. Eng. Technol. **2**, 38–45 (2001)
22. Lim, B., Lee, H., Kurnia, S.: Exploring the reasons for a failure of electronic payment systems: a case study of an Australian company. J. Res. Pract. Inf. Technol. **39**(4), 231–243 (2007)
23. Li, R., Kim, J.J., Park, J.S.: The effects of Internet shoppers' trust on their purchasing intention in China. J. Inf. Syst. Technol. Manag. **4**(3), 269–286 (2007)
24. Martinez-Ruiz, A., Aluja-Banet, T.: Toward the definition of a structural equation model of patent value: PLS path modelling with formative Constructs. Revstat Stat. J. **7**(3), 265–290 (2009)
25. Ozkan, S., Bindusara, G., Hackney, R.: Facilitating the adoption of e-payment system: theoretical constructs and empirical analysis. J. Enterp. Inf. Manag. **23**(3), 305–325 (2010)
26. Urbach, N., Ahlemann, F.: Structural equation modeling in information systems research using partial least squares. J. Inf. Technol. Theor. Appl. **11**(2), 5–40 (2010)

A Signature Scheme Based on Implicit and Explicit Certificates Against k-Traitors Collusion Attack

Tomasz Hyla$^{(\boxtimes)}$ and Jerzy Pejaś

Faculty of Computer Science and Information Technology,
West Pomeranian University of Technology in Szczecin, Szczecin, Poland
{thyla, jpejas}@zut.edu.pl

Abstract. In 2002, Mitsunari, Sakai and Kasahara formulated the Collusion Attack Algorithm with k traitors (known as k-CAA problem) and used it to develop the first traitor tracing scheme based on the bilinear pairings. Traitor tracing scheme is needed to discourage legitimate subscribers from sharing their secret keys to construct pirate decoders. In this paper, we propose a first signature scheme (IE-CBS-kCAA) based on k-CAA problem, which belongs to the fourth category of PKC schemes: the public key cryptography schemes based on an implicit and explicit certificates. The security analysis proves that our IE-CBS-kCAA scheme is secure against two game attacks in the random oracle model. The security is closely related to the difficulty of solving the modified k-CAA and discrete logarithm problems.

Keywords: ID-based signature schemes · Implicit and explicit certificates-based public key cryptography · Bilinear pairing · Security analysis · k-CAA problem

1 Introduction

Collusion Attack Algorithm with k traitors (k-CAA problem) is one of many hard computational problems used in public key cryptography based on bilinear pairings. Problem of k cooperating traitors has a great significance in group signature and encryption schemes. In this schemes, it is assumed that some unauthorized users (adversaries) may obtain some decryption or signature keys from a group of one or more authorized users (traitors). Then the adversaries can decrypt or sign data that they are not entitled to.

In 2002 S. Mitsunari *et al.* [1] proposed an interesting traitor tracing scheme. The scheme was a first traitor tracing scheme using bilinear mappings. Also, in this paper they formulated k-CAA problem. The problem and its variants developed later [2] were useful during construction of many new encryption or signature schemes. The idea of encryption and digital signature schemes based on k-CAA problem is very similar to the idea of k cooperating traitors in global networking systems. In both cases, it is assumed, that if a group containing less then k traitors exists, who disclose their private keys and other secret information, then it is computationally infeasible to recreate or to

© IFIP International Federation for Information Processing 2017
Published by Springer International Publishing AG 2017. All Rights Reserved
K. Saeed et al. (Eds.): CISIM 2017, LNCS 10244, pp. 638–651, 2017.
DOI: 10.1007/978-3-319-59105-6_55

generate another private key belonging to an entity from outside the group. This condition in case of a traitor tracing system means that system is k-collusion resistant, if tracing succeeds and the adversary has fewer than k user keys at his disposal.

Sakai and Kasahara [3] in 2003 proposed one of the first encryption schemes based on k-CAA problem. Almost at the same time, in 2004 Zhang et al. [4] proposed an efficient ID-based short signature scheme (ZSS), which security relies on k-CAA problem. The ZSS scheme plays an important role in many pairing-based cryptographic systems (e.g. P. Barreto et al. [5]) and it is a starting point for security proofs in new signature schemes. ZSS scheme is existentially unforgeable under an adaptive chosen message in the random oracle model, although B.C. Hu et al. [6] demonstrated that the scheme is vulnerable to an attack called *message-and-key replacement attack*. Another example of ZSS extension was given by Du and Wen [7] in 2007.

The basic problem of ID-based schemes is the key escrow of a user's private key. Certificateless signature scheme (CLS scheme) introduced by S. Al-Riyami and K. Paterson [8] is a practical solution of the key escrow problem. However, most of the ID-based schemes do not satisfy Girault's level-3 security [9], which conventional public key infrastructure (PKI) can achieve. Such drawback has also a certificateless short signature scheme proposed in 2009 by Du and Wen [10], which is an extended version of their ID-based signature scheme [7]. This scheme was the first concrete certificateless signature construction based on k-CAA problem with Sakai-Kasahara key construction method.

In 2011, J.K. Liu et al. [16] and J. Li et al. [14] presented certificate-based signature schemes and claimed their scheme are proven secure in the random oracle model using k-CAA assumption or its variations. In both schemes, Sakai-Kasahara construction of key generation is not used. Unfortunately, Cheng et al. [18] showed that J.K. Liu et al.[17] scheme is insecure against a Type I adversary under a security model defined in [14], i.e., a Type I adversary can obtain a partial private key of a targeted user. Subsequently, Hung [15] reported how a Type I adversary (i.e. an uncertified entity) can successfully attack Li et al. scheme and extract singer's secret key and certificate of a target entity.

Recently, T. Hyla et al. [19] have introduced a new paradigm called Implicit and Explicit Certificates-Based Public Key Cryptography (IEC-PKC) and proposed a concrete implicit and explicit certificates-based encryption scheme (IE-CBE). In the IE-CBE construction, the implicit and explicit certificates are based on a short signature scheme given in [11, 16], which security depends on a k-CAA hard problem. To our best knowledge, an implicit and explicit certificates-based signature scheme based on k-CAA problem or its modification still does not exist. Hence, it is challenge and open problem to design such secure signature schemes under the proper security model.

Our contribution. In this paper, inspired by T. Hyla et al. [20] results, we propose the first IE-CBS-kCAA signature scheme using Sakai-Kasahara key construction with provable security against k-traitors Collusion Attack. The proposed scheme belongs to the public key cryptography schemes based on an implicit and explicit certificates. The main features of our scheme are presented below.

Firstly, a signature verification in IE-CBS-kCAA scheme can be carried out in two modes: in a first mode using an explicit certificate and in a second mode with an implicit certificate; in the first mode, the verification can be made like in the PKI certificates. The verification in the second mode is similar to many cases of the certificate-based signature schemes and it is carried out without referencing to an explicit certificate. This type of dual nature of IE-CBS-kCAA scheme is a unique feature among other IEC-PKC (see T. Hyla *et al.* [21]) signature schemes.

Secondly, the proposed scheme possesses existential unforgeability against adaptive chosen-message and identity attacks (EUF-CMA) under the variation of the collusion attack algorithm with k-traitors (*k*-mCAA) and the discrete logarithm (DL) assumptions. Thirdly, the explicit and implicit certificates in IE-CBS-kCAA scheme are generated in two different algebraic groups. It is similar solution to the work [19], where implicit and explicit certificates belongs to the different groups. However, in both cases it is computationally hard to recreate implicit certificate using only explicit certificate and *vice versa*.

Lastly, the *Sign* algorithm in our scheme uses a random number. Therefore, IE-CBS-kCAA scheme is a randomized scheme. Randomization protects the scheme from known attacks. Definitely, the proposed scheme does not belong to short signature schemes, but it is computationally more efficient and has a similar signature length comparing to another (implicit) certificate-based signature schemes in [16, 20] with the similar security level.

Paper Organisation. The rest of this paper is organized as follows. In the next section, we briefly review some basic knowledge. Before presenting our results, we first present the notion of an implicit and explicit certificates-based signature scheme and its security model against two different types of attacks (see Sect. 3). In Sect. 4, the IE-CBS-kCAA randomized signature scheme from pairings is proposed, whose security in the random oracle, is analysed in Sect. 4. The efficiency of our scheme is discussed in Sect. 5. At last, we present our concluding remarks.

2 Preliminaries

In this section, we will review hard mathematical problems and security assumptions required in this paper. The definition and notation for an asymmetric bilinear map $\hat{e} : G_1 \times G_2 \to G_T$ can be found in [5].

Definition 1 (Discrete Logarithm (DL) problem). Given the generator $P \in G_1$ and $T \in G_1^*$ compute $a \in Z_p^*$ such that $T = aP$. The DL is (t, ε_{DL}) – hard if the success probability of any probabilistic t-polynomial-time algorithm A_{DL} solving the DL problem in G_1 is defined to be:

$$Adv_{DL}^A = \Pr\left\{A_{DL}(P, aP) = a \mid a \in Z_p^*\right\} < \varepsilon_{DL} \qquad (1)$$

The DL assumption states that the probability Adv_{DL}^A is negligible for every probabilistic polynomial – time algorithm A.

Definition 2 (*k*-CAA problem, S. Mitsunari *et al.* [1]). For a positive integer k and $s \in Z_p^*$, $Q \in G_2$, given

$$\left\{ \begin{array}{l} Q, Q_0 = sQ, h^*, h_1, \ldots, h_k \in Z_p^*, h^* \notin \{h_1, \ldots, h_k\}, \\ \frac{1}{h_1+s}Q, \ldots, \frac{1}{h_k+s}Q \end{array} \right\},$$

compute a new pair $\left\{h^*, \frac{1}{h^*+s}Q\right\}$. We say that the k-CAA is $(t, \varepsilon_{k\text{-}CAA})$-hard if, for all t-time adversaries $A_{k\text{-}CAA}$, we have

$$Adv^A_{k\text{-}CAA} = Pr\left\{ \begin{array}{l} A_{k\text{-}CAA}\left(Q, Q_0, \frac{1}{h_1+s}Q, \ldots, \frac{1}{h_k+s}Q\right) = \frac{1}{h^*+s}Q \\ \left| s \in Z_p^*, Q \in G_2, h^*, h_1, \ldots, h_k \in Z_p^*, h^* \notin \{h_1, \ldots, h_k\} \right. \end{array} \right\} < \varepsilon_{k\text{-}CAA}$$

The k-CAA problem is believed to be hard, i.e., there is no polynomial time algorithm to solve it with non-negligible probability. For the needs of this paper we define a new variant of k-CAA problem hereinafter referred to as the k-mCAA problem (compare [22]).

Definition 3 (k-mCAA problem). For randomly picked values $s, r^*, h^*, r_1, h_1, \ldots, r_k, h_k \in Z_p^*, Q \in G_2$, given

$$\left\{ \begin{array}{l} Q, Q_0 = sQ, h^*, h_1, \ldots, h_k \in Z_p^*, h^* \notin \{h_1, \ldots, h_k\}, \\ r^*Q, r_1Q, \ldots, r_kQ, r^*Q \notin \{r_1Q, \ldots, r_kQ\}, \frac{1}{r_1h_1+s}Q, \ldots, \frac{1}{r_kh_k+s}Q \end{array} \right\},$$

compute a new pair $\left\{h^*, \frac{1}{r^*h^*+s}Q\right\}$. We say that the k-mCAA problem is $(t, \varepsilon_{k\text{-}mCAA})$-hard if, for all t-time adversaries $A_{k\text{-}mCAA}$, we have

$$Adv^A_{k\text{-}mCAA} = Pr\left\{ \begin{array}{l} A_{k\text{-}mCAA}\left(\begin{array}{l} Q, Q_0, r_1Q, \ldots, r_kQ, \\ \frac{1}{r_1h_1+s}Q, \ldots, \frac{1}{r_kh_k+s}Q \end{array} \right) = \frac{1}{r^*h^*+s}Q \\ \left| s \in Z_p^*, Q \in G_2, h^*, h_1, \ldots, h_k \in Z_p^*, \right. \\ h^* \notin \{h_1, \ldots, h_k\}, r^*Q \notin \{r_1Q, \ldots, r_kQ\} \end{array} \right\} < \varepsilon_{k\text{-}mCAA}.$$

The k-mCAA assumption states that the probability $Adv^A_{k\text{-}mCAA}$ is negligible for every probabilistic polynomial-time algorithm A. It is worth to noting that the k-mCAA is hard to break, because even if h is known, the probability for finding a number $x \in Z_p^*$ such that $x = (s + r^*h)^{-1} \mod p$ with two unknowns s and r^* is negligible and equal to $(p(p-1))^{-1})$.

Definition 3 was derived from the k-CAA3 problem definition, formulated by S.H. Islam et al. [22]. In contrast to the original definition, it was assumed that the values $r^*P, r_1P, \ldots, r_kP$ are input to the k-mCAA problem.

Let assume that $r^* = 1$ and $r_i = 1, (i = 1, \ldots, k)$. Then the k-mCAA problem is transformed into k-CAA problem. Thus, k-CAA problem can be seen as a special case of the k-mCAA problem. Similar, if $r_i = r^*, (i = 1, \ldots, k)$, then the k-mCAA problem is equivalent to the original k-CAA3 problem form [22].

3   Security Model of IE-CBS-kCAA Scheme

In this paper, we consider only one kind of security notion, existential unforgeability (EUF) under chosen-message attack (CMA) in the random oracle model (EUF-CMA). In this attack, an adversary, allowed to ask the signer to sign any message of its choice adaptively according to previous answers, should not be able to generate a new valid message-signature pair.

3.1   Adversaries and Oracles

The security model of the proposed IE-CBS-kCAA scheme, hereinafter referred to as EUF-IECBS-kCAA-CMA, is defined by two games between challenger C and adversary A, assuming that the adversary chooses which game to play. In both cases, adversary $A = (A_1, A_2)$ is trying to break the EUF-CMA security of the IE-CBS-kCAA scheme, i.e., the formal model describing existential unforgeability. To describe these games, we use the widely accepted two types of adversaries with different capabilities: **Type I Adversary** and **Type II Adversary** (e.g., T. Hyla *et al.* [20]).

Type I Adversary (A_1) is able to compromise the user's secret key or replace the user's public key, but is unable to gain TA's master secret key nor the user's partial private key issued by TA. We assume that adversary A_1 models the security against non-certified users and eavesdroppers, i.e., against the users, who are not registered and do not have certificates issued by the TA.

Type II Adversary (A_2) can obtain TA's master secret key and the user's implicit certificate, but cannot compromise the user's secret key nor replace her/his target public key. In this case, it is reasonable to consider attack scenarios that targets certified users, i.e., users who come into possession of a private/public key pair and explicit certificates before the master key s becomes known to the adversary.

The formal security model of the implicit and explicit certificates-based signature schemes divides the potential adversaries according to their attack power and classified the Type I/II adversary into three kinds (see Li, J., *et al.* [14] and Huang, X., *et al.* [12]): Normal Adversary, Strong Adversary and Super Adversary. The most power attacks are related to Super Type I/II Adversary, which may issue the following queries:

Create-User-Query. If a user identity ID has already been created, nothing is carried out by the oracle. Otherwise, challenger C runs the algorithms **Create-User** to obtain the secret value s_{ID} and the partial public key Pk_{ID}. Then it adds $\langle ID, s_{ID}, Pk_{ID}\rangle$ to the L_U list. In this case, the user with identity ID is said to be created. In both cases, Pk_{ID} is returned.

Public-Key-Replacement-Query. If ID is created, the oracle takes as input a query $(CI_{ID}, Pk_{ID}, Pk'_{ID})$, finds the user ID in the list L_U and replaces the original user public key Pk_{ID} with $Pk'_{ID} = s'_{ID}P$. Otherwise, no action will be taken. Note that the adversary is not required to provide the secret value s'_{ID}.

Corruption-Query. This oracle takes as input a query *ID*. It browses the list L_U and if *ID* denotes the identity which has been created, the oracle outputs the secret key s_{ID}.

Implicit-Cert-Gen-Query. On input of an identity index (ID, Pk_{ID}), this oracle returns an implicit certificate $\overline{Sk}_{ID}$ whenever the user with identity index (ID, Pk_{ID}) has been created. Otherwise, a symbol $\perp$ is returned.

Explicit-Cert-Gen-Query. For a certificate request for a user with identity index (CI_{ID}, Pk_{ID}), this oracle returns an explicit certificate $Cert_{ID}$ and two additional components $(\underline{R}_{ID}, \underline{\underline{R}}_{ID})$. If the user with $CI_{ID}.ID^1$ is not created, the symbol $\perp$ is returned.

Super-Sign-Query. If *ID* has not been created, the oracle returns $\perp$. Otherwise, it takes as input a query $\left(m, CI_{ID}, Pk_{ID}, \underline{R}_{ID}, \underline{\underline{R}}_{ID}\right)$, where m denotes the message to be signed, and then returns a valid signature σ_{ID} such that **Verify** $(params, m, \sigma, CI_{ID}, Pk_{ID}, \underline{R}_{ID}, \underline{\underline{R}}_{ID}, Cert_{ID}) \rightarrow true$. Here Pk_{ID} denotes the user ID_S's current public key in the list L_U and can be replaced by A_I or returned from the oracle **Create-User-Query**.

Remark 1. A Super Type II Adversary, who simulates the malicious certifier, is not allowed to make any requests to **Implicit-Cert-Gen-Query** and **Explicit-Cert-Gen-Query**.

3.2 Games Against a Super Type I/II Adversary

To investigate the existential unforgeability of IE-CBS-kCAA scheme against Super Type I/II Adversary (A_1/A_2 in short) we can now define two games (**Game I** and **Game II**) between a challenger C and the two types of adversaries (A_1 and A_2, respectively).

Game I. This game is executed between challenger C and an adversary A_1 under an adaptively chosen message and chosen user's identity *ID*.

Setup. Challenger C executes algorithm **Setup** $(1^k) \rightarrow (s, params)$ in the IE-CBS-kCAA scheme to obtain the public parameter *params* and master secret key s. Adversary A_1 is given *params*, but the challenger C keeps the master secret key s secret.

Queries. In this phase, A_1 can adaptively submit queries to following oracles defined in Sect. 3.1: **Create-User-Query**, **Implicit-Cert-Gen-Query**, **Explicit-Cert-Gen-Query**, **Public-Key-Replacement-Query**, **Corruption-Query** and **Super-Sign-Query**.

Forgery. Eventually, after some or all queries, adversary A_1 outputs a forgery $\left(\hat{m}, \hat{\sigma} = (\hat{h}, \hat{w}_1, \hat{w}_2, \hat{\Sigma}), ID, CI_{ID}, Pk_{ID}, \underline{\hat{R}}_{ID}, \underline{\hat{\underline{R}}}_{ID}, Cert_{ID}\right)$.

Constrains. Adversary A_1 wins the game if the forgery satisfies the following requirements:

---

[1] This notation means the filed *ID* of the user's certificate information *CIID*.

(a) $\hat{\sigma}$ is a valid signature on the message $\hat{m}$ under the public key Pk_{ID} and the explicit certificate $Cert_{ID}$, i.e. **Verify** $(params, \hat{m}, \hat{\sigma}, CI_{ID}, Pk_{ID}, \hat{R}_{ID}, \hat{\underline{R}}_{ID}, Cert_{ID}) \rightarrow true$. Here, Pk_{ID} is chosen by A_1 and might not be the one returned from **Create-User-Query** oracle.

(b) (ID, Pk_{ID}) and (CI_{ID}, Pk_{ID}) has never been submitted to respective oracles **Implicit-Cert-Gen-Query** and **Explicit-Cert-Gen-Query**.

(c) ID has never appeared as one of **Corruption-Query**.

(d) $(\hat{m}, CI_{ID}, Pk_{ID}, \hat{R}_{ID}, \hat{\underline{R}}_{ID})$ has never been submitted to oracle **Super-Sign-Query**.

The success probability that an adaptive chosen message and adversary A_1 with chosen identity index (ID, Pk_{ID}) wins the above game is defined as $Adv^{A_1}_{\text{IE–CBS–kCAA}}$.

Game II. In this Game an adversary A_2 with chosen identity index (ID, Pk_{ID}) interacts with its challenger C under an adaptively chosen message.

Setup. Challenger C executes algorithm **Setup** $(1^k) \rightarrow (s, params)$ in the IE-CBS-kCAA scheme to obtain the public parameter $params$ and master secret key s. C then sends $(params, s)$ to the adversary A_2.

Queries. In this phase, challenger C runs adversary A_2 can adaptively access the following oracles: **Create-User-Query**, **Public-Key-Replacement-Query**, **Corruption-Query** and **Super-Sign-Query**. The oracles **Implicit-Cert-Gen-Query** and **Explicit-Cert-Gen-Query** are not accessible and no longer needed, as adversary A_2, which simply holds the master key s, can now generate all user partial keys and certificates.

Forgery. At the end of this phase, after some or all queries, adversary A_2 outputs the forgery $\left(\hat{m}, \hat{\sigma} = (\hat{h}, \hat{w}_1, \hat{w}_2, \hat{\Sigma}), ID, CI_{ID}, Pk_{ID}, \hat{R}_{ID}, \hat{\underline{R}}_{ID}, Cert_{ID}\right)$.

Constrains. Adversary A_2 wins the game if the forgery satisfies the following requirements:

(a) $\hat{\sigma}$ is a valid signature on the message $\hat{m}$ under the public key Pk_{ID} and the explicit certificate $Cert_{ID}$, i.e. **Verify** $(params, \hat{m}, \hat{\sigma}, CI_{ID}, Pk_{ID}, \hat{R}_{ID}, \hat{\underline{R}}_{ID}, Cert_{ID}) \rightarrow true$. Here, Pk_{ID} is the output returned by **Create-User-Query** oracle for ID.

(b) ID has never appeared as one of **Corruption-Query**.

(c) $(\hat{m}, CI_{ID}, Pk_{ID}, \hat{R}_{ID}, \hat{\underline{R}}_{ID})$ has never been submitted to oracle **Super-Sign-Query**.

In this game, adversary A_2 may call the **Public-Key-Replacement-Query** oracle and obtain all secrets corresponding to identity indices other than (ID, Pk_{ID}).

The success probability that an adaptive chosen message and adversary A_2 with chosen identity index (ID, Pk_{ID}) wins the above game is defined as $Adv^{A_2}_{\text{IE–CBS–kCAA}}$.

Definition 4. An implicit and explicit certificate signature scheme IE-CBS-kCAA has existential unforgeability against chosen message attacks (EUF-IECBS-kCAA-CMA), if no probabilistic polynomial-time adversary has non-negligible probability to win Game I and Game II.

4 A New Implicit and Explicit Certificates-Based Signature Scheme IE-CBS-kCAA

The IE-CBS-kCAA scheme contains seven polynomial time algorithms: **Setup, Create-User, Implicit-Cert-Gen, Explicit-Cert-Gen, Set-Private-Key, Sign** and **Verify**. A detailed description of all algorithms of IE-CBS-kCAA scheme is presented below:

1. **Setup:** the system parameters are $params = \{G_1, G_2, G_T, \hat{e}, p, P, P_0, Q, Q_0, H_1, H_2\}$, where $|G_1| = |G_2| = |G_T| = p$ for some prime number $p \geq 2^k$ (k is the system security number), (P, Q) - generators of respectively G_1 and G_2 such that $\hat{e}(P, Q) = g$, $P_0 = sP$ and $Q_0 = sQ$ - system's master public keys with the master secret key $s \in Z_p^*$, $H_1, H_2 : \Gamma \times \{0, 1\}^* \to Z_p$ are two secure cryptographic hash functions. The $\Gamma \in (0, 1)^*$ means a string space that can be used to define a user with the identity ID. In the cases, when ID contains more information other than the identity we will mark it as CI (see below).

2. **Create-User** $(params, ID_S)$: the user ID_S chooses a random number $s_{ID_S} \in Z_p^*$, sets s_{ID_S} as the secret key and produces the corresponding public key $Pk_{ID_S} = s_{ID_S}P$; the resulting public key is widely and freely distributed, e.g., the TA publishes them in its public repository.

3. **Implicit-Cert-Gen** $(params, s, ID_S, Pk_{ID_S})$: given ID_S presenting S's identity, his public key Pk_{ID_S}, the trust authority TA:
   (a) composes the user's certificate information CI_{ID_S}, including the TA's public keys (P_0, Q_0), identifiers ID_S and ID_{TA} of the user S and the TA, respectively, and the time period τ for which the information CI_{ID_S} is valid;
   (b) randomly selects $r_{ID_S} \in Z_p^*$ and computes $\left(R_{ID_S}, \underline{R}_{ID_S}\right) = (r_{ID_S}P, r_{ID_S}Q)$;
   (c) for Pk_{ID_S} and $\left(R_{ID_S}, \underline{R}_{ID_S}\right)$
   (d) computes $q_{ID_S} = H_1\left(CI_{ID_S}, Pk_{ID_S}, R_{ID_S}, \underline{R}_{ID_S}\right)$, generates S's private key as:

$$\overline{Sk}_{ID_S} = \frac{1}{s + r_{ID_S}q_{ID_S}}Q \tag{2}$$

   and transmits it to the user S secretly; in addition, TA sends also $\left(CI_{ID_S}, \underline{R}_{ID_S}, \underline{R}_{ID_S}\right)$.

4. **Explicit-Cert-Gen** $(params, ID_S, s, r_{ID_S}, q_{ID_S})$: TA authority, using parameters received from S and values calculated during execution **Implicit-Cert-Gen** algorithm, generates an explicit certificate $Cert_{ID_S}$ of a signer S:
   (a) TA generates the explicit certificate for an entity S, which binds its identity with the public key components:
   (b) TA sends $Cert_{ID_S}$ to an entity S.

$$Cert_{ID_S} = \frac{1}{s + r_{ID_S}q_{ID_S}}P \tag{3}$$

5. **Set-Private-Key** $(params, CI_{ID_S}, s_{ID_S}, Pk_{ID_S}, \underline{R}_{ID_S}, \underline{R}_{ID_S}, \overline{Sk}_{ID_S})$: the user S checks if $\hat{e}(q_{ID_S}R_{ID_S} + P_0, \overline{Sk}_{ID_S}) = \hat{e}(P, Q) = g$, and then formulates his private key in the form $Sk_{ID_S} = (s_{ID_S}, \overline{Sk}_{ID_S})$.

6. **Sign** $(params, m, CI_{ID_S}, (Sk_{ID_S}, Pk_{ID_S}, \underline{R}_{ID}, \underline{R}_{ID}))$: to sign a message $m \in \{0,1\}^*$, a signer S performs the following steps:

   (a) pick two random numbers $k_1, k_2 \in_R Z_p^*$;

   (b) computes a hash value $q_{ID_S} = H_1\left(CI_{ID_S}, Pk_{ID_S}, \underline{R}_{ID_S}, \underline{R}_{ID_S}\right)$ and then generates the signature $\sigma = (h, w_1, w_2, \sum)$, where $h = H_2(m, k_1 P, U, q_{ID_S})$,

$$\sum = \frac{k_1 - k_2^{-1} h}{k_1 h + s_{ID_S}} \overline{Sk}_{ID_S} \tag{4}$$

   $w_1 = k_1 - hs_{ID_S} (\bmod p)$, $w_2 = k_2(k_1 h + s_{ID_S})(\bmod p)$, while $U = g^{k_1 k_2}$.

7. **Verify** $(params, m, \sigma, CI_{ID}, Pk_{ID}, \underline{R}_{ID}, \underline{R}_{ID}, Cert_{ID})$: to verify the message/signature/certificate triple, i.e. $(m, \sigma = (h, w_1, w_2, \sum), Cert_{ID_S})$, V performs the following steps:

   (a) computes a hash $q_{ID_S} = H_1\left(CI_{ID_S}, Pk_{ID_S}, \underline{R}_{ID_S}, \underline{R}_{ID_S}\right)$ and then the values

$$U' = \hat{e}(q_{ID_S}R_{ID} + P_0, \sum)^{w_2} \hat{e}\left(Cert_{ID_S}, q_{ID_S}\underline{R}_{ID} + Q_0\right)^h, \overline{k_1 P} = w_1 P + h P_{ID_S};$$

   (b) if $h \equiv H_2\left(m, \overline{k_1 P}, U', q_{ID_S}\right)$ and $\hat{e} = \left(Cert_{ID_S}, q_{ID_S}\underline{R}_{ID} + Q_0\right) \equiv g$, then returns *accept*, else *reject*.

4.1   Correctness of the IE-CBS-kCAA Scheme

Assume that digital signature σ and an explicit certificate $cert_{ID_S}$ have been generated using the **Sign** and **Explicit-Cert-Gen** algorithms, respectively. Therefore, σ is a valid signature on message m because it is accepted by the verification algorithm **Verify**:

$$U' = \hat{e}\left(q_{ID_S}R_{ID} + P_0, \sum\right)^{w_2} \hat{e}\left(Cert_{ID_S}, q_{ID_S}\underline{R}_{ID} + Q_0\right)^h$$

$$= \hat{e}\left(q_{ID_S}R_{ID} + P_0, \frac{k_1 - k_2^{-1} h}{k_1 h + s_{ID_S}} \overline{Sk}_{ID_S}\right)^{k_2(k_1 h + s_{ID_S})} \hat{e}\left(Cert_{ID_S}, q_{ID_S}\underline{R}_{ID} + Q_0\right)^h$$

$$= \hat{e}\left(q_{ID_S}R_{ID} + P_0, (k_1 k_2 - h)\overline{Sk}_{ID_S}\right)\hat{e}\left(Cert_{ID_S}, q_{ID_S}\underline{R}_{ID} + Q_0\right)^h$$

$$= \hat{e}\left((s + r_{ID_S}q_{ID_S})P, (k_1 k_2 - h)\frac{1}{s + r_{ID_S}q_{ID_S}}Q\right)\hat{e}\left(\frac{1}{s + r_{ID_S}q_{ID_S}}P, h(s + r_{ID_S}q_{ID_S})Q\right)$$

$$= \hat{e}(P, Q)^{k_1 k_2}$$

$$= U$$

$$\tag{5}$$

Hence,

$$h' = H_2\left(m, \overline{k_1 P}, U', q_{ID_s}\right)$$
$$= H_2(m, wP + hP_{ID_s}, U, q_{ID_s}) \tag{6}$$
$$= h$$

Furthermore, it is now easy to prove the correctness of the explicit certificate:

$$g' = \hat{e}\left(Cert_{ID_s}, q_{ID_s}\underline{R_{ID}} + Q_0\right)$$
$$= \hat{e}\left(\frac{1}{s + r_{ID_s}q_{ID_s}}P, (s + r_{ID_s}q_{ID_s})Q\right) \tag{7}$$
$$= \hat{e}(P, Q)$$
$$= g$$

4.2 Security Analysis of IE-CBS-kCAA Scheme

We prove the security of IE-CBS-kCAA scheme by using the approach of reducing the security of a higher-level construction to a lower-level primitive. More precisely we reduce the existence of an adversary breaking the protocol into an algorithm that was able to solve the respective k-mCAA or a discrete logarithm (DL) problem with non-negligible probability. In our reductions, we use the multiple forking lemma, proposed by Boldyreva and et al. [23], in the way similar to [20].

Lemma 1 Suppose that the hash functions H_1 and H_2 are random oracles, and in Game 1 against IE-CBS-kCAA scheme, adversary A_1 plays the role of an uncertified user. The proposed implicit and explicit certificates signature scheme IE-CBS-kCAA is existential unforgeable against a Super Type I adversary A_1 under the k-mCAA assumption.

Proof (sketch). Similarly to approach given in [20], our reduction was proceed into two steps. First, we described an intermediate algorithm B_1 (i.e. the wrapper) that interacts with the adversary A_1 and returned a side output. Second, we showed how to build a reduction algorithm R_1 that has launched the forking game $MF_{B,1}$ on the wrapper B_1. As a result, an algorithm R_1 was obtained one pairing equation with one unknowns and indeed returned the correct solution to the k-mCAA problem instance.

Algorithm R1 obtains two valid signature forgeries, each of them in the form $\hat{\sigma}_i = \left(\hat{m}, \hat{h}_i, \hat{w}_{1,i}, \hat{w}_{2,i}, \hat{\Sigma}_i, Pk_{ID}, \underline{R_{ID}}, \underline{R_{ID}}, Cert_{ID}\right), (i = 0, 1)$ for the same message $\hat{m}$, the public key Pk_{ID}, the explicit certificate $Cert_{ID}$ and $(\underline{R_{ID}}, \underline{R_{ID}})$. If both forgeries are valid, then R_1 obtains two sets of side-outputs σ_0, σ_1, where σ_i (for $i = 0, 1$) is of the form $(\hat{h}_i, \hat{U}_i, \hat{\Sigma}_i, \hat{w}_{2,i}, Pk_{ID}, \underline{R_{ID}}, \underline{R_{ID}})$. Additionally, we assume that $(\hat{U}_0 = \hat{U}_1)$. Based on these two sets of side-outputs σ_0, σ_1, the following equation is fulfilled

$$\hat{e}\left(q_{ID}\underline{R}_{ID} + P_0, \hat{\sum}_0\right)^{\hat{w}_{2,0}} \hat{e}\left(Cert_{ID}, q_{ID}\underline{\underline{R}}_{ID} + Q_0\right)^{\hat{h}_0}$$
$$= \hat{e}\left(q_{ID}\underline{R}_{ID} + P_0, \hat{\sum}_1\right)^{\hat{w}_{2,1}} \hat{e}\left(Cert_{ID}, q_{ID}\underline{\underline{R}}_{ID} + Q_0\right)^{\hat{h}_1} \tag{8}$$

By making the suitable arrangements, the Eq. (10) can be converted to the form:

$$\hat{e}\left(q_{ID}\underline{R}_{ID} + P_0, \hat{w}_{2,0}\hat{\sum}_0 + \hat{h}_0\overline{Sk}_{ID}\right) = \hat{e}\left(q_{ID}\underline{R}_{ID} + P_0, \hat{w}_{2,1}\hat{\sum}_0 + \hat{h}_1\overline{Sk}_{ID}\right) \tag{9}$$

Finally, we get the solution to the k-mCAA problem challenge (see Definition 4):

$$\overline{Sk}_{ID} = \frac{\left(\hat{w}_{2,0}\hat{\Sigma}_0 - \hat{w}_{2,1}\hat{\Sigma}_1\right)}{\left(\hat{h}_0 - \hat{h}_1\right)} \tag{10}$$

Now, for the Game 2 implemented with Super Type 2 adversary, in which the adversary models a certified entity, we demand that a signer is honest and his tuple $(ID, Pk_{ID}, Cert_{ID})$ has been previously registered with the TA. For this assumption, the following lemma can be proved in the random oracle model:

Lemma 2 Suppose that the hash functions H_1 and H_2 are random oracles. The proposed implicit and explicit certificates signature scheme IE-CBS-kCAA is existentially unforgeable against a Super Type II adversary under the *DL* problem.

The proof is similar to the proof of [20] and is omitted here.

5 Performance Comparison

In this section, we compare our implicit and explicit certificates-based signature scheme IE-CBS-kCAA to other existing schemes with similar constructions. The comparison is based on results presented in [20]. Operations like: hashing, operations in Z_p^* (inversion, addition, multiplication), multiplication in G_T and addition in G_1 or G_2 can be omitted in efficiency comparison, because they are several orders of magnitude faster when compared with pairings, scalar multiplications in G_1 or G_2 and exponentiations in G_T. In Table 1, proposed IE-CBS-kCAA is compared to other schemes ($|G_1|$ and $|Z_p|$ is the bit length of an element in G_2 and Z_p, M_G is a scalar multiplication in G_1 or G_1 and $\hat{e}$ is a bilinear pairing on $G_1 \times G_2$ and P_{GT} is exponentiation in G_T). Our proposed scheme has the same security level as WMSH Scheme II and IE-CBHS scheme. It requires the similar number of time-intensive operation when comparing to other schemes and is slightly faster than IE-CBHS scheme.

Table 1. Performance comparison (based on [20])

Scheme	Type	Public key size	Signature size	Sign	Verify	Security level
LHMSW (J. Li et al. [14])	I-CBS	$|G_1|$	$2|G_1|$	$3\,M_G$	$3\hat{e}$	Normal A_1 and Normal A_2
LHZX (J. Li et al. [24])	I-CBS	$2|G_1|$	$|G_1|$	M_G	$\hat{e}+M_G$	Normal A_1 and Super A_2
CBSa (Kang et al. [13])	I-CBS	$|G_1|$	$3|G_1|$	$3\,M_G$	$3\hat{e}+2M_G$	Strong A_1 and Strong A_2
WMSH Scheme II (Wu, W., et al. [16])	I-CBS	$|G_1|$	$|G_1|+2|Z_p|$	$\hat{e}+4M_G$	$2\hat{e}+3M_G$	Super A_1 and Super A_2
IE–CBHS scheme (Hyla, T., et al. [20])	IE-CBS	$|G_1|$	$|G_1|+2|Z_p|$	$\hat{e}+3M_G$	$2\hat{e}+7M_G$	Super A_1 and Super A_2
Our IE-CBS-kCAA scheme	IE-CBS	$|G_1|$	$|G_2|+3|Z_p|$	$2M_G+P_{GT}$	$2\hat{e}+6M_G$	Super A_1 and Super A_2

6 Conclusions

The paper contains the IE-CBS-kCAA signature scheme that has been built on a new paradigm called Implicit and Explicit Certificates-Based Public Key Cryptography (IEC-PKC) [19]. Using this paradigm we propose the first signature scheme based on the implicit and explicit certificates resistant against k-traitors collusion attacks with Sakai-Kasahara key construction. We proved that our scheme is existential unforgeable against the adaptive chosen message and identity attacks based on the variation of Collusion Attack Algorithm with k traitors (k-mCAA) and discrete logarithm (DL) assumptions in the random oracle model with Super Type I/II Adversaries.

The most time-consuming operation in a signature scheme from pairings is the computation of the pairing. Our scheme contains no one pairing operation in the signing phase and two pairing operation in the signature verification phase. Therefore, IE-CBS-kCAA scheme, when compared with other signature schemes (Table 1), has similar efficiency and is both more flexible, and more useful in practice.

References

1. Mitsunari, S., Sakai, R., Kasahara, M.: A new traitor tracing. IEICE Trans. **E85-A**(2), 481–484 (2002)
2. Chen, L., Cheng, Z.: Security proof of Sakai-Kasahara's identity-based encryption scheme. In: Smart, N.P. (ed.) Cryptography and Coding 2005. LNCS, vol. 3796, pp. 442–459. Springer, Heidelberg (2005). doi:10.1007/11586821_29

3. Sakai, R., Kasahara, M.: ID based Cryptosystems with Pairing on Elliptic Curve (2003). http://eprint.iacr.org/2003/054

4. Zhang, F., Safavi-Naini, R., Susilo, W.: An efficient signature scheme from bilinear pairings and its applications. In: Bao, F., Deng, R., Zhou, J. (eds.) PKC 2004. LNCS, vol. 2947, pp. 277–290. Springer, Heidelberg (2004). doi:10.1007/978-3-540-24632-9_20

5. Barreto, P.S.L.M., Libert, B., McCullagh, N., Quisquater, J.-J.: Efficient and provably-secure identity-based signatures and signcryption from bilinear maps. In: Roy, B. (ed.) ASIACRYPT 2005. LNCS, vol. 3788, pp. 515–532. Springer, Heidelberg (2005). doi:10. 1007/11593447_28

6. Hu, B.C., Wong, D.S., Zhang, Z., Deng, X.: Certificateless signature: a new security model and an improved generic construction. Des. Codes Cryptogr. 42, 109–126 (2007)

7. Du, H., Wen, Q.: An efficient identity-based short signature scheme from bilinear pairings. In: 2007 International Conference on Computational Intelligence and Security (CIS 2007), pp. 725–729 (2007)

8. Al-Riyami, S.S., Paterson, K.G.: Certificateless public key cryptography. In: Laih, C.-S. (ed.) ASIACRYPT 2003. LNCS, vol. 2894, pp. 452–473. Springer, Heidelberg (2003). doi:10.1007/978-3-540-40061-5_29

9. Girault, M.: Self-certified public keys. In: Davies, D.W. (ed.) EUROCRYPT 1991. LNCS, vol. 547, pp. 490–497. Springer, Heidelberg (1991). doi:10.1007/3-540-46416-6_42

10. Du, H., Wen, Q.: Efficient and provably-secure certificateless short signature scheme from bilinear pairings. Comput. Stand. Interfaces 31(2), 390–394 (2009)

11. Huang, X., Susilo, W., Mu, Y., Zhang, F.: On the security of certificateless signature schemes from Asiacrypt 2003. In: Desmedt, Y.G., Wang, H., Mu, Y., Li, Y. (eds.) CANS 2005. LNCS, vol. 3810, pp. 13–25. Springer, Heidelberg (2005). doi:10.1007/11599371_2

12. Huang, X., Mu, Y., Susilo, W., Wong, D.S., Wu, W.: Certificateless signatures: new schemes and security models. Comput. J. 55(4), 457–474 (2011)

13. Kang, B.G., Park, J.H., Hahn, S.G.: A certificate-based signature scheme. In: Okamoto, T. (ed.) CT-RSA 2004. LNCS, vol. 2964, pp. 99–111. Springer, Heidelberg (2004). doi:10. 1007/978-3-540-24660-2_8

14. Li, J., Huang, X., Mu, Y., Susilo, W., Wu, Q.: Certificate-based signature: security model and efficient construction. In: Lopez, J., Samarati, P., Ferrer, J.L. (eds.) EuroPKI 2007. LNCS, vol. 4582, pp. 110–125. Springer, Heidelberg (2007). doi:10.1007/978-3-540-73408-6_8

15. Hung, Y.-H., Huang, S.-S., Tseng, Y.-M.: A short certificate-based signature scheme with provable security. Inf. Technol. Control 45(3), 243–253 (2015)

16. Wu, W., Mu, Y., Susilo, W., Huang, X.: Certificate-based signatures revisited. J. Univ. Comput. Sci. 15(8), 1659–1684 (2009)

17. Liu, J.K., Bao, F., Zhou, J.: Short and efficient certificate-based signature. In: Casares-Giner, V., Manzoni, P., Pont, A. (eds.) NETWORKING 2011. LNCS, vol. 6827, pp. 167–178. Springer, Heidelberg (2011). doi:10.1007/978-3-642-23041-7_17

18. Cheng, L., Xiao, Y., Wang, G.: Cryptanalysis of a certificate-based on signature scheme. Procedia Eng. 29, 2821–2825 (2012)

19. Hyla, T., Maćków, W., Pejaś, J.: Implicit and explicit certificates-based encryption scheme. In: Saeed, K., Snášel, V. (eds.) CISIM 2014. LNCS, vol. 8838, pp. 651–666. Springer, Heidelberg (2014). doi:10.1007/978-3-662-45237-0_59

20. Hyla, T., Pejaś, J.: A hess-like signature scheme based on implicit and explicit certificates. Comput. J. 60(4), 457–475 (2017). doi:10.1093/comjnl/bxw052, http://comjnl.oxfor djournals.org/cgi/reprint/bxw052

21. Hyla, T., Pejaś, J.: Non-standard certification models for pairing based cryptography. In: Kobayashi, S.-Y., Piegat, A., Pejaś, J., El Fray, I., Kacprzyk, J. (eds.) Hard and Soft Computing for Artificial Intelligence, Multimedia and Security. AISC, vol. 534, pp. 167–181. Springer, Cham (2017). doi:10.1007/978-3-319-48429-7_16

22. Islam, S.H., Biswas, G.P.: An efficient and provably-secure digital signature scheme based on elliptic curve bilinear pairings. Theor. Appl. Inf. 24(2), 109–118 (2012)

23. Boldyreva, A., Palacio, A., Warinschi, B.: Secure proxy signature schemes for delegation of signing rights. J. Cryptology 25(1), 57–115 (2012)

24. Li, J., Huang, X., Zhang, Y., Xu, L.: An efficient short certificate-based signature scheme. J. Syst. Soft. 85, 314–322 (2012)

Netflow-Based Malware Detection and Data Visualisation System

Rafał Kozik[✉], Robert Młodzikowski, and Michał Choraś

Institute of Telecommunication and Computer Science,
UTP University of Science and Technology, Bydgoszcz, Poland
rafal.kozik@utp.edu.pl

Abstract. This paper presents a system for network traffic visualisation and anomalies detection by means of data mining and machine learning techniques. First, this work describes and analyses existing solutions in the field of network anomalies detection in order to identify adapted techniques in that area. Afterwards, the system architecture and the adapted tools and libraries are presented. Particularly, two different anomalies detection methods are proposed.

The key experiments and analysis focus on performance evaluation of the proposed algorithms. In particular, different setups are considered in order to evaluate such aspects as detection effectiveness and computational complexity.

The obtained results are promising and show that the proposed system can be considered as a useful tool for the network administrator.

Keywords: Cyber security · Anomaly detection · Botnet · NetFlow · Visualisation

1 Introduction

Nowadays, one of the cybersecurity challenges is to counter the malicious software [1]. Usually, malware samples are carefully crafted pieces of computer programs that aim at staying dormant while performing detailed surveillance of infected infrastructures and assets. Infected computers commonly connect together over the telecommunication network and form so-called botnet that can be easily centrally controlled by the cybercriminals for different malicious purposes such as DDoS attacks, SPAM distribution, sensitive data thefts, extortion attacks, etc.

In order to combat such cyber threat, one may use different solutions. However, commonly used anti-virus software may not be efficient enough to protect the network. An example is the case of the polish financial sector problem that happened in 2017 [2]. During that attack, the largest system hack in the country's history took place and several banks in Poland have been infected with malware. This particular malware was a new strain of malicious software which

K. Saeed et al. (Eds.): CISIM 2017, LNCS 10244, pp. 652–660, 2017.
DOI: 10.1007/978-3-319-59105-6_56

has never been seen before in live attacks and it had a zero detection rate on
VirusTotal.

The advancements in machine learning and data mining techniques in the
area of Big Data introduces new tools supporting the fight against the malware.
Therefore, in this research, we analyse existing techniques for botnet detection.
Moreover, we propose the system that adapts different pattern extraction techniques, classification and visualisation methods.

The main contribution of this work is a proposal of a tool enhancing the cyber
security of local area network. The tool intends to support network administrator
in network traffic analysis by providing visualisation, data mining and feature
extraction capabilities. In the current version of the system we have provided
(i) two different pattern extraction algorithms, (ii) a variety of data mining
algorithms available via Weka [3] library, (iii) a visualisation module.

The paper is structured as follows. First, we provide an overview of existing
solutions and methods for botnets detection. Next, we propose system architecture and different pattern extraction and classification methods for NetFlow
analysis. The experiment section presents evaluation methodology and obtained
results. This paper is concluded with final remarks and plans for the future work.

2   Related Work

Commonly the signatures (in form of reactive rules) of an attack for a software
like Snort [4] are provided by experts from a cyber community. Typically, for
deterministic attacks, it is fairly easy to develop patterns that will clearly identify
the particular attack. It often happens when given malicious software (e.g. worm)
uses the same protocol and algorithm to communicate trough network with
command and control centre or other instance of such software. However, the
task of developing new signatures becomes more complicated when it comes to
polymorphic worms or viruses. Such software commonly modifies and obfuscates
its code (without changing the internal algorithms) in order to be less predictive
and hard to detect.

The development of an efficient and scalable method for malware detection is
currently challenging also due to the general unavailability of raw network data.
Therefore, this aspect while being related to users privacy and administrative
and legal reasons causes additional difficulties for research and development [5,6].

Currently, the common alternative is so-called NetFlow [7] data that is often
captured by ISPs for auditing and performance monitoring purposes. Since Net-
Flow samples do not contain any sensitive data they are widely available. However, the fact that this kind of samples is lacking raw content of network packets
is the disadvantage.

In the literature, there are different approaches focusing on the analysis
of NetFlow data. In [8,9] authors focused on computational paradigms (e.g.
MapReduce) for NetFlow data analysis and malware detection. On the other
hand, in [10,11] author proposed statistical techniques for feature extraction
from groups of network flows.

The BClus [12] method uses behavioural approach for botnet detection. It aggregates NetFlows for specific IP addresses and clusters them according to statistical characteristics. The properties of the clusters are described and used for further botnet detection. Another approach is used in BotHunter [13] tool. It monitors the two-way communication flows between hosts within internal network and the Internet. BotHunter employs Snort intrusion detection system. It models an infection sequence as a composition of participants and a loosely ordered sequence of network information exchanges.

3   Proposed System Architecture

In the Fig. 1 the general overview of the system design is presented. The collected raw data is processed in order to extract the NetFlows. The NetFlow is a standardised format for describing bidirectional communication and contains such information as IP source and destination address, destination port, amount of bytes exchanged, etc. The extracted NetFlows are stored in the database for further processing, so that the data mining and feature extraction methods currently work in the batch processing mode. However, in the future, we plan to allow the system to analyse directly the streams of data containing the raw NetFlows.

The single NetFlow usually does not provide enough evidence to decide whenever the particular machine is infected or if the particular request has malicious symptoms. Therefore, it is quite common [12] that NetFlows are aggregated in

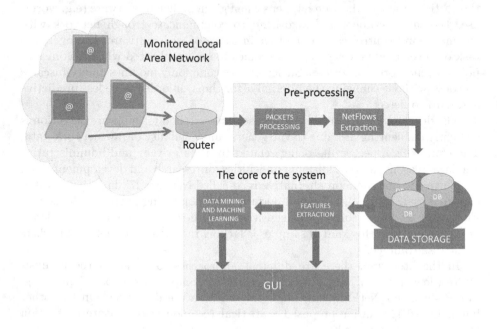

Fig. 1. System architecture diagram

so-called time windows so that more contextual data can be extracted and malicious behaviour recorded (e.g. port scanning, packet flooding effects, etc.). In order to do that different statistics can be extracted for each time window. In the current version of the proposed system, we have implemented two different methods for pattern extraction (the Feature Extraction block on the diagram). These methods have been described in the consecutive subsections. In general, these methods produce the feature vectors that are further used to learn different ML algorithms (the Data Mining and Machine Learning block on the diagram). The machine learning algorithms are available via the Weka [3] library.

The system is also facilitated with graphical user interface (indicated as GUI on the diagram) which allows the network administrator to visualise different statistical properties of the analysed traffic (e.g. amount of data generated by specific IP addresses or the most active ones) as well as classification results. Some aspects of the visualisation process have also been described in separate section.

In order to evaluate the effectiveness of different algorithms, we have used CTU-13 dataset. It contains different scenarios representing different infections and malware communication schemes with command and control. Therefore, in this paper, we do not consider the problem of the realistic testbed construction.

3.1 Method 1

The first feature extraction method aggregates NetFlows in a time window (in this approach we use 1-minute long time windows). One of the reasons behind the aggregation process is the context identification in order to capture relevant behaviours of different hosts. For each time window the following statistics are calculated:

- number of NetFlows
- total sum of transferred bytes
- average sum of transferred bytes per NetFlow
- number of unique destination IP addresses

One of the advantages of this approach is the fact that the number of features vectors is equal to the number of time windows. Therefore, for the short scenarios the size of the resulting dataset will be small and thus the machine learning process will be faster.

However, one of the obvious drawbacks is the fact that for this approach it is impossible to identify the IP address of the infected machine because the system will only signal that particular time window should be considered anomalous.

3.2 Method 2

The second feature extraction method, similar to the previous one, aggregates NetFlows in the time windows. However, for each time window, we additionally group the NetFlow by IP source addresses. For each group (time window, IP source address) we calculate the following statistics:

- number of flows
- sum of transferred bytes
- average sum of bytes per NetFlow
- average communication time between unique IPs
- number of unique IP addresses
- number of unique destination ports
- most frequently used protocol (e.g. TCP, UDP) by specific IP source address

In contrast to the previous method, the advantage of this approach it the fact that it allows the network administrator to identify the possibly infected IP addresses.

3.3 Machine-Learning Module

In our research, we have selected different machine learning algorithms available in the WEKA software package [3]. We have considered such algorithms as Naive-Bayes, Logistic, MultilayerPerceptron, SimpleLogistic, IBk, ClassificationViaRegression, LogitBoost, RandomCommittee, RandomizableFilteredClassifier, JRip, PART, J48, RandomForest, RandomTree. During the experiments, we have used different configurations of the algorithms in order to obtain optimal results.

4 Data Visualisation

The visualisation module is dedicated for network administrator in order to facilitate the in-depth analysis of network traffic. Different figures allow for visual

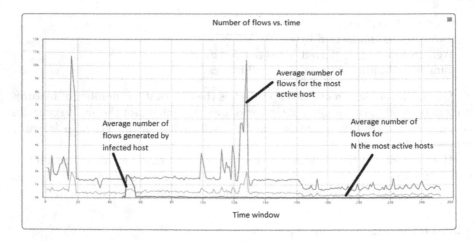

Fig. 2. An example of the proposed system visualisation capabilities for the selected scenario. The figure presents the amount of traffic generated on average by all hosts (green line), by the most active hosts (orange line), and the infected host (red line). (Color figure online)

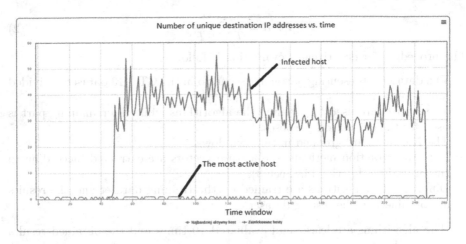

Fig. 3. The figure presents the number of established connection by different hosts for the analysed scenario. It can be noticed that the infected host establishes suspiciously high number of connections.

detection of possibly anomalous network situations (e.g. port scanning). The examples of GUI screenshots (for the same scenario) has been shown in Figs. 2 and 3. The system allows also the administrator to visualise:

- number of NetFlows for different time windows
- amount of bytes transferred for specific search criteria
- destination port utilisation
- results of classification process
- dependencies analysis between possibly infected hosts and other ones

5   Experiments

5.1   Validation Methodology

For the evaluation purposes, we have adapted stratified 10-fold cross-validation methodology. The method was used to assess the TPR - true positives, and FPR - false positives rates.

True Positives Ratio (TPR) is defined as the number samples (feature vectors) identified correctly as infected (True Positives - TP) divided by the number of all samples that are infected (True Positives + False Negatives).

$$TPR = \frac{TP}{TP + FN} \tag{1}$$

False Positives Ratio (FPR) is defined as the number of samples identified wrongly as infected (False Positives - FP) divided by the number of all clean samples (True Negatives + False Positives).

$$FPR = \frac{FP}{TN + FP} \tag{2}$$

The procedure for effectiveness evaluation is following:

- The dataset representing particular scenario in the CTU-13 dataset is divided into 10 parts.
- The 9 parts are used for training the algorithms while the remaining part is used for the evaluation purposes.
- The NetFlows are grouped in time windows.
- For two extraction methods, the feature vectors are extracted (according to the procedure described in Sect. 3).
- Different ML algorithms are trained on the training dataset and the results are obtained on the testing dataset.

The algorithms are learnt and evaluated 10 times and the obtained results are averaged.

5.2   Evaluation Dataset

For the evaluation purposes we have used CTU-13 dataset [12]. This dataset includes different scenarios, which represents different types of attack scenarios including a different type of botnets. Each of these scenarios contains collected traffic in form of NetFlows. As it is explained in [12], the data was collected for the realistic testbed. We have presented the results and the discussion for one of the most problematic scenarios. Each of the scenarios has been recorded in a separate file as NetFlow using CSV notation. Each of the row in a file has 15 attributes (columns):

- StartTime - Start time of the recorded NetFlow,
- Dur - Duration,
- Proto - IP protocol (e.g. UTP, TCP),
- SrcAddr - Source address,
- Sport - Source port,
- Dir - Direction of the recorded communication,
- DstAddr - Destination Address,
- Dport - Destination Port,
- State - Protocol state,
- sTos - Source type of service,
- dTos - Destination type of service,
- TotPkts - Total number of packets that have been exchanged between source and destination,
- TotBytes - Total bytes exchanged,
- SrcBytes - Number of bytes send by source,
- Label - Label - label assigned to this NetFlow (e.g. Background, Normal, Botnet)

It must be noted that the "Label" field is an additional attribute provided by authors of the dataset. Normally, the NetFlow will have 14 attributes and the "Label" will be assigned by the classifier.

Table 1. Effectiveness of different algorithms for Rbot malware activity detection.

Algorithms	Feature extraction method			
	Method 1		Method 2	
	TPR	FP	TP	FP
NaiveBayes	60,0%	33,3%	50,0%	0,2%
Logistic	40,0%	50,0%	33,3%	0,0%
MultilayerPerceptron	40,0%	25,0%	33,3%	0,0%
SimpleLogist	0,0%	0,0%	25,0%	0,0%
IBk	20,0%	41,7%	58,3%	0,0%
CVR	40,0%	25,0%	33,3%	0,0%
LogitBoost	40,0%	16,7%	33,3%	0,0%
RandomCommitte	20,0%	33,3%	66,7%	0,0%
JRip	0,0%	16,7%	50,0%	0,0%
PART	60,0%	50,0%	50,0%	0,0%
J48	60,0%	50,0%	50,0%	0,0%
RandomForest	40,0%	25,0%	66,7%	0,0%
RandomTree	20,0%	16,7%	58,3%	0,0%

5.3   Results

The proposed methods have been evaluated on the scenario concerning the Rbot malware. According to the scenario description, the malware realises ICMP DDoS attack.

The values of TPR and FPR ratios have been presented in Table 1. The results obtained with the second method for feature extraction have achieved better results. The average effectiveness of botnet detection for all the classifiers for the first method is 47.0% while for the second method is 63.0%. However, the classifiers combined with the first method for pattern extraction yielded high FP ratios.

The conclusion from this experiment is that the second feature extraction method combined with RandomForest (or RandomCommittee) allowed us to achieve 66.7% of malware detection while having no false positives.

6   Conclusions

In this paper, we have proposed preliminary results of the malware detection method. Our approach relies on the analysis of malware network activity that is captured by means of NetFlows. We have presented the architecture of the proposed system. The current implementation includes two methods for pattern extraction that analyses the NetFlows in disjoint time windows. The extracted feature vectors have been used to train different machine learning algorithms.

The methods have been evaluated on the publicly available dataset. Future work will be dedicated to the evaluation of scalability of the proposed methods and further improvements towards online machine learning.

References

1. Choras, M., Kozik, R., Renk, R., Holubowicz, W.: A practical framework and guidelines to enhance cyber security and privacy. In: Herrero, A., Baruque, B., Sedano, J., Quintan, H., Corchado, E. (eds.) International Joint Conference CISIS 2015 and ICEUTE 2015. AISC, pp. 485–496. Springer, Heidelberg (2015). ISBN: 978-3-319-19712-8
2. The Hacker News web page. Polish Banks Hacked using Malware Planted on their own Government Site. http://thehackernews.com/2017/02/bank-hacking-malware.html
3. WEKA Data Mining Software. http://www.cs.waikato.ac.nz/ml/weka/
4. SNORT. Project homepage. http://www.snort.org/
5. Andrysiak, T., Saganowski, Ł., Choraś, M., Kozik, R.: Network traffic prediction and anomaly detection based on ARFIMA model. In: Puerta, J.G., Ferreira, I.G., Bringas, P.G., Klett, F., Abraham, A., Carvalho, A.C.P.L.F., Herrero, Á., Baruque, B., Quintián, H., Corchado, E. (eds.) International Joint Conference SOCO 2014-CISIS 2014-ICEUTE 2014. AISC, vol. 299, pp. 545–554. Springer, Cham (2014). doi:10.1007/978-3-319-07995-0_54
6. Choras, M., Kozik, R., Puchalski, D., Holubowicz, W.: Correlation approach for SQL injection attacks detection. In: Herrero, A., et al. (eds.) International Joint Conference CISIS 2012-ICEUTE 2012-SOCO 2012 Special Sessions. AISC, vol. 189, pp. 177–186. Springer, Heidelberg (2012)
7. Claise, B.: Cisco Systems NetFlow Services Export Version 9. RFC 3954 (Informational) (2004)
8. Francis, J., Wang, S., State, R., Engel, T.: Bottrack: tracking botnets using netflow and pagerank. In: Proceedings of IFIP/TC6 Networking (2011)
9. Dean, J., Ghemawat, S.: MapReduce: simplified data processing on large clusters. In: Symposium on Operating Systems Design and Implementation (OSDI). USENIX Association (2004)
10. Lakhina, A., Crovella, M., Diot, C.: Diagnosing network-wide traffic anomalies. ACM SIGCOMM Comput. Commun. Rev. **34**, 357–374 (2004)
11. Lakhina, A., Crovella, M., Diot, C.: Mining anomalies using traffic feature distributions. ACM SIGCOMM Comput. Commun. Rev. **35**, 217–228 (2005)
12. Garcia, S., Grill, M., Stiborek, J., Zunino, A.: An empirical comparison of botnet detection methods. Comput. Secur. J. **45**, 100–123 (2014). Elsevier
13. BotHunter homepage. http://www.bothunter.net/about.html

Application of XGBoost Algorithm in Fingerprinting Localisation Task

Marcin Luckner[✉], Bartosz Topolski, and Magdalena Mazurek

Faculty of Mathematics and Information Science, Warsaw University of Technology,
ul. Koszykowa 75, 00–662 Warszawa, Poland
mluckner@mini.pw.edu.pl, {topolskib,mazurekm}@student.mini.pw.edu.pl

Abstract. An Indoor Positioning System (IPS) issues regression and classification challenges in form of an horizontal localisation and a floor detection. We propose to apply the XGBoost algorithm for both tasks. The algorithm uses vectors of Received Signal Strengths from Wi–Fi access points to map the obtained fingerprints into horizontal coordinates and a current floor number. The original application schema for the algorithm to create IPS was proposed. The algorithm was tested using real data from an academic building. The testing data were split into two datasets. The first data set contains signals from all observed access points. The second dataset consist of signals from the academic network infrastructure. The second dataset was created to eliminate temporary hotspots and to improve a stability of the positioning system. The tested algorithm got similar results as reference methods on the wider set of access points. On the limited set the algorithm obtained the best results.

1 Introduction

Creation of an effective Indoor Positioning System (IPS) is an open issue. Commonly known and usage methods based on the Global Positioning System (GPS) are great outdoor but fail inside the buildings.

A fingerprinting based on Wi–Fi signals is a popular method that replaces GPS localisation. In this method, vectors of Received Signal Strengths (RSS) are mapped into horizontal coordinates by a regression method.

However, expectations for the localisation system are greater in the case of the IPSs. The acceptable accuracy of an outdoor localisation system is measured in dozens of meters when an expected error of IPS should not be greater than few meters.

Moreover, the indoor localisation raises floor detection issue that does not exist in an outdoor localisation task. An RSS vector should be mapped into a current floor by a classification method. It is extremely important to obtain a high accuracy in this classification task. A localisation with minimal horizontal error is useless if an object is localised on the wrong floor.

The research is supported by the National Centre for Research and Development, grant No PBS2/B3/24/2014, application No 208921.

K. Saeed et al. (Eds.): CISIM 2017, LNCS 10244, pp. 661–671, 2017.
DOI: 10.1007/978-3-319-59105-6_57

Therefore, we are still looking for new classification and regression methods that can be applied in fingerprinting localisation task.

In this paper, we applied the XGBoost algorithm [2] in fingerprinting localisation task. The XGBoost algorithm is a scalable tree boosting system that can be used both for classification and regression tasks. According to our knowledge, the algorithm was not applied in fingerprinting localisation task before. The original schema of the application was proposed.

The algorithm was tested on real data collected in an academic building. The localisation results were compared with a reference method. As a reference methods kNN and random forest were used.

The algorithm was tested on two data sources. The first source contains signals from all access points observed during the data collection. However, it was stressed [5] that such data may contain temporary access points. If such access points are present only in the learning set the accuracy obtained on the testing set will be decreased. Therefore, the second data source was limited to well–known access points that create the academic infrastructure.

The rest of the paper is structured as follows. Section 2 contains information on a fingerprinting method and measures of errors. Section 3 presents related work. Section 4 describes the XGBoost algorithm and its application for IPS. Section 5 presents the obtained localisation results. Finally, Sect. 6 presents brief conclusions.

2   Preliminaries

In this section we briefly describe a general fingerprinting method and the measures of an error used in this paper.

The fingerprinting approach to indoor localisation requires a model based on a dataset of measured Received Signal Strengths (RSS), which is later used to predict user's location on the base of the current RSS measurements. Our analysis was based on the data collected from a six-floor academic building. The building had an irregular shape and its outer dimensions were around 50 by 70 m and its height was 24 m.

The signals were measured using the following models of mobile phones: LG Nexus 4, Sony Xperia Z, and HTC One mini. All phones were working with Android 4.2 Jelly Bean and dedicated application for data collection [11].

The data were collected into the two independent series, used later as the training and the testing subset. Each subset consists of the vectors of the signal strengths from $\mathbb{R}^{570}$ labelled by the position of a point in which those signals were measured. The position information contains x and y - the horizontal coordinates, and f - the floor number. The training set contains the measurements from 1401 points gathered in a 1.5×1.5 m grid, and the test set contains the measurements from 1461 points gathered on another day in the grid shifted by 0.75 m in each horizontal direction. There were 40 measurements for each point, giving us 56020 training fingerprints and 58440 test fingerprints.

The quality of models was evaluated by two measures: a horizontal median error (**HME**) and an accuracy of the floor detection (**ACC**). The horizontal error for fingerprint $m \in \mathbb{R}^{570}$ was defined as

$$he(m) = \sqrt{(x_m - h_x(m))^2 + (y_m - h_y(m))^2)} \tag{1}$$

where x_m and y_m were the horizontal coordinates of the point where the fingerprint m was taken, and $h_x(m)$ and $h_y(m)$ were coordinates predicted for the fingerprint m. The floor error for fingerprint $m \in \mathbb{R}^{570}$ was defined as

$$fe(m) = |f_m - h_f(m)| \tag{2}$$

where f_m was the floor number where the fingerprint m was taken, and $h_f(m)$ was a floor number predicted by the model.

We defined a horizontal median error for the test set $\mathcal{T}$ as

$$\mathbf{HME} = \frac{\sum_{m \in \mathcal{T}} he(m)}{|\mathcal{T}|} \tag{3}$$

and an accuracy of the floor detection as

$$\mathbf{ACC} = \frac{\sum_{m \in \mathcal{T}} (1 - \text{sgn}(fe(m)))}{|\mathcal{T}|} \tag{4}$$

3   Related Work

The comparison of indoor positioning system can be found in [3,4].

In [3] the authors presented an overview of the current trends in this localisation using a Wireless Sensor Network (WSN) with an introduction of the mathematical tools used to determine position.

Work [4] compared different methods of creating IPS model for a given radio map. The authors defined two categories: deterministic and probabilistic. The deterministic methods are based on distances between RSS vectors while probabilistic ones use the estimation of the probability that we are in a given localisation while a particular RSS vector was measured.

There were several works that discussed a usage of machine learning methods to create IPS for the same building but not necessary on the same data as used in this paper.

In work [10], the Particle Swarm Optimisation (PSO) algorithm was applied to the training process of a Multilayer Perceptron (MLP). In work [8] the k Nearest Neighbours (kNN) algorithm was used to estimate a current floor. In work [12] a localisation method for moving terminal was implemented with the usage of the Particle Filter method.

Finally, in works [5,7] the authors used the random forest. The authors built the independent models for the estimation of each coordinate (x, y, f).

The nature of the given problem justifies the usage of a random tree-based method [1]. The interference in a signal strength caused by walls and irregular access point locations disallows any assumptions about the distribution of signal strengths. Moreover, those characteristics also imply highly non-linear interactions between variables, which are very well-handled by tree-based methods. Having this in mind we decided to use XGBoost algorithm and check if it can improve the results obtained with the random forest.

4   XGBoost Algorithm

In this section we show basics of tree boosting methods, and we discuss XGBoost algorithm, a scalable machine learning system for tree boosting.

The main difference between Random Forest (RF) and Gradient Boosted Machines (GBM) is that while in RF trees are built independent of each other, GBM adds a new tree to complement already built ones.

Assume we have data $\mathcal{D} = \{(x_i, y_i) : i = 1 \ldots n, \ x_i \in \mathbb{R}^m, \ y_i \in \mathbb{R}\}$, so we have n observations with m features each and with a corresponding variable y. Let us define $\hat{y}_i$ as a result given by an ensemble represented by the generalised model

$$\hat{y}_i = \phi(x_i) = \sum_{k=1}^{K} f_k(x_i) \tag{5}$$

In our case f_k is a regression tree, and $f_k(x_i)$ represents the score given by the k-th tree to the i-th observation in data. We want to minimise the following regularised objective function in order to choose functions f_k.

$$\mathcal{L}(\phi) = \sum_i l(y_i, \hat{y}_i) + \sum_k \Omega(f_k) \tag{6}$$

l is the loss function. To prevent too large complexity of the model the penalty term Ω is included as follows:

$$\Omega(f_k) = \gamma T + \frac{1}{2}\lambda\|w\|^2, \tag{7}$$

where *gamma* and *lambda* are parameters controlling penalty for, respectively, the number of leaves T and magnitude of leaf weights w.

This penalty term is the first feature that is unique to XGBoost in comparison to general tree boosting methods. Its purpose is to prevent over-fitting and to simplify models produced by this algorithm.

In order to minimise the objective function an iterative method is used. In j-th iteration we want to add f_j, which minimises the following objective function:

$$\mathcal{L}^j = \sum_{i=1}^{n} l(y_i, \hat{y}_i^{(j-1)} + f_j(x_i)) + \Omega(f_j). \tag{8}$$

Using the Taylor expansion we can simplify this function, and derive a formula for loss reduction after the tree split from given node:

$$\mathcal{L}_{split} = \frac{1}{2}\left[\frac{\left(\sum_{i\in\mathcal{I}_L} g_i\right)^2}{\sum_{i\in\mathcal{I}_L} h_i + \lambda} + \frac{\left(\sum_{i\in\mathcal{I}_R} g_i\right)^2}{\sum_{i\in\mathcal{I}_R} h_i + \lambda} - \frac{\left(\sum_{i\in\mathcal{I}} g_i\right)^2}{\sum_{i\in\mathcal{I}} h_i + \lambda} \right] - \gamma, \tag{9}$$

where $\mathcal{I}$ is a subset of the observations available in the current node, and $\mathcal{I}_L$, $\mathcal{I}_R$ are subsets of the observations available in the left and right nodes after the split. The functions g_i and h_i are defined as follows: $g_i = \partial_{\hat{y}_i^{(j-1)}} l(y_i, \hat{y}_i^{(j-1)})$, $h_i = \partial^2_{\hat{y}_i^{(j-1)}} l(y_i, \hat{y}_i^{(j-1)})$. This formula is used for finding the best split at any given node. It depends only on the loss function (through the first and second-order gradients) and the regularisation parameter γ. It is easy to see that this algorithm can optimise any loss function given by the user, as long as he can provide the first and second-order gradients.

In addition to introducing the regularised loss function, XGBoost provides two additional (compared to general GBM) features to prevent over-fitting. First, the weights of each new tree can be scaled down by a given constant η. It reduces an impact of a single tree on the final score, and leaves more room for next trees to improve the model. The second feature is a column sampling. It works in a similar way as random forests – each tree is built using only a column-wise sample from the training dataset.

Besides those improvements in terms of the algorithm, XGBoost also performs better than other tree boosting methods. It supports an approximate split finding, which improves the process of the building trees and scales very well with the number of CPU cores.

For our purposes we used regression with least squares objective for the horizontal localisation task and a multi–class classification using a softmax objective function for the floor detection. Both objectives are implemented in the 'xgboost' package for the 'R' language provided by the creators of the algorithm.

4.1 Application for IPS

Our task was to estimate of the coordinates (x_m, y_m, f_m) of the point where the fingerprint m was taken by predictions $(h_x(m), h_y(m), h_f(m))$. It was done by an ensemble of XGBoost models.

A straightforward application uses three models to estimate each of the coordinates separately. We proposed the different process for the training models. Instead of using two models for estimation of the horizontal coordinates in the whole building, we build two models for each floor of the building. By making each model more specific than the generic one we can make more accurate predictions on each floor. However, we are aware that this approach can lead to horizontal location errors caused by wrong floor prediction.

The application of XGBoost models for IPS was done using the following schema. The first model ϕ^f estimated the current floor

$$h_f(m) = \phi^f(m). \tag{10}$$

For each floor separate models were created for estimation of the horizontal coordinates. The coordinates x_m and y_m were estimated by the models ϕ_i^x and ϕ_i^y respectively, where $i \in [\min(f_m), \ldots, \max(f_m)]$.

According to recognised floor the x_m coordinate was estimated as

$$h_x(m) = \phi^x_{h_f(m)}(m). \tag{11}$$

Similarly, the y_m coordinate was estimated as

$$h_y(m) = \phi^y_{h_f(m)}(m). \tag{12}$$

5   Results

While the data provided measurements from 570 access points, work [5] concluded that it is not necessary to use all variables in the learning process. Therefore, we selected only 46 access points from the academic Wi–Fi network. The selection expelled all mobile and temporary access points (which was desirable from the practical point of view) but also made the models building and the predictions making much faster. However, for the sake of comparison we also tested the model based on all access points.

We compared the XGBoost model with random forests – using results from [5] – and with the kNN algorithm implemented for the need for the reference method in this work. It should be stressed that the model of the horizontal localisation in [5] was created for the whole building contrary to our model where the horizontal localisation was modelled for each floor separately.

5.1   Tests on Full Set of Access Points

In the first test all access points were taken into consideration. The number of trees in the model was fixed to 450 and the other parameters were adjusted to achieve the best performance on the learning set.

Table 1. Results of localisation on all 570 access points

Model	HME			ACC
	Median	Mean	80%	
XGBoost (2 models)	2.44	3.32	4.54	0.95
XGBoost (12 models)	2.34	3.37	4.42	0.95
Random forest	2.78	3.80	5.14	0.94
kNN	2.39	3.00	4.19	0.93

Table 1 compares the results obtained by the XGBoost algorithm, the kNN method, and the random forests. A quality of the algorithms is measured by the mean, median, and 80th percentile values of the horizontal error (**HME**) and by the accuracy (**ACC**).

The XGBoost algorithm was tested in two forms. The straightforward application used two models for the horizontal localisation and the application described in Sect. 4.1 used 12 models in order to do the same localisation.

We can notice that on the full dataset the kNN algorithm performs better than the XGBoost algorithm in terms of the horizontal error. We can also see

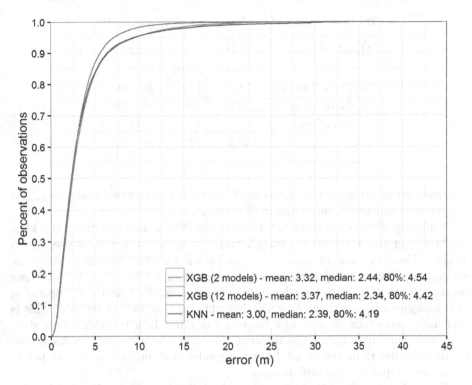

Fig. 1. Results of horizontal localisation on all access points

that using the XGBoost algorithm improves the horizontal median error over random forest by about 12%.

Figure 1 shows the distribution of the horizontal errors for the XGBoost and kNN models. The kNN algorithm reduced the number of errors from the range 4 to 20 m. Therefore, the differences between the means and gross errors are visible when the median error are nearly the same. The differences between two application schema of the XGBoost algorithm are ambiguous because one model has a lower median error when the other wins a comparison of the rest of the measures.

The XGBoost algorithm obtained the best accuracy in the floor detection task. Mostly, the classification error was not greater than one floor. However, we should remember that even such small error keeps us from correct localisation. Therefore, it is not unambiguous that the kNN method – with the smaller horizontal error – should be preferred over the XGBoost algorithm.

5.2 Tests on Access Points from Academic Infrastructure

In the second test, the number of the access points used to build a model was limited to 46 access points from the academic network. The number of trees

Table 2. Results of localisation on 46 access points

Model	HME			ACC
	Median	Mean	80%	
XGBoost(2 models)	2.92	4.13	5.30	0.93
XGBoost(12 models)	2.81	3.99	5.22	0.93
Random forest	-	4.47	-	0.93
kNN	3.13	4.73	5.76	0.91

was reduced to 50 since the reduction in the number of the columns made it unnecessary to use a higher number of the trees.

Table 2 groups the results obtained by the XGBoost algorithm, the kNN method, and the random forests. The same error measures were used as in Table 1. However, not all measures were known for the random forest. Still, we can see that the improvement over the random forest is greater when we use only signals from the academic Wi–Fi network. The XGBoost algorithm also performed better than the kNN algorithm on this smaller dataset. This is especially important because of a reduction of data. In a practical application the reduction can improve the learning time and the obtained results should be more stable than the result from the model that utilises all access points including temporary and mobile ones.

Figure 2 shows the distribution of the horizontal errors on the test data for three algorithms: the XGBoost algorithms with two models for the horizontal location, the XGBoost algorithm with twelve models for the horizontal location and the kNN algorithm. For the kNN algorithm the optimal value of the parameter k was 20. We can see that for the shorter length of input data the XGBoost algorithm provides an improvement over the kNN method. The kNN method fails with the gross errors mostly. The difference for 80th percentile error exceeds half of meter.

The usage of 12 models benefited in the reduction of the horizontal errors. We can observe the reduction of the gross errors specifically. To prove that there is a significant difference between results obtained by the 12 models and 2 models, we performed Wilcoxon's Signed–Rank test for paired scores [9].

For both estimator we created a vector that contains the six **HME** errors presented in Tables 1 and 2.

Wilcoxon's Signed–Rank test rejected the null hypothesis ($p = 0.062500$), which stated that the results obtained by the two estimators were not significantly different, at the 0.1 level. Moreover, the modified test accepted ($p = 0.984375$), at the 0.1 level, the alternate hypothesis that the differences between errors of the XGB(2) and the XGB(12) come from a distribution with median greater than 0. Therefore, the results obtained by XGB(12) model are statistically better.

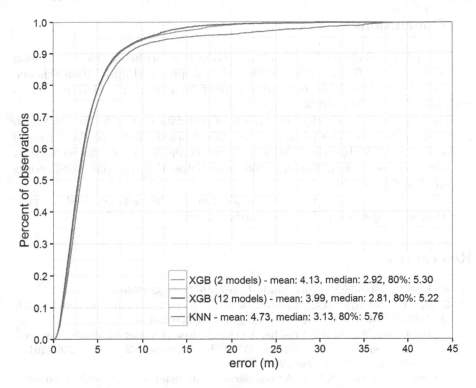

Fig. 2. Results of horizontal localisation on 46 access points

All algorithms – except the kNN method – obtained the same accuracy in the floor detection task. Once again, the classification error was not greater than one floor mostly.

The obtained results are worse than the results obtained for all 570 access points. However, it can be better to use the limited number of the access points in a practical case. The well–known access points are under control and other access points can be switch off without any notification. It may reduce the localisation quality significantly. At the same time a localisation based on the infrastructure can work several years keeping good localisation results [6].

In practical application, XGBoost and Random Forest may be easier to use than kNN method. The implementation itself is not a problem in any case since all algorithms are commonly available in many libraries. However, the prediction in kNN requires constantly referring to the training set, which must be kept available during localisation phase. On the other hand, estimating location with tree-based models is much easier and only requires checking a certain number of logical conditions without the need to access any large volume of data.

6   Conclusions

We have presented the application of the XGBoost algorithm for the localisation task based on the fingerprinting method. In the proposed application schema, we have used one model to estimate a current floor number and 12 models to estimate a horizontal position.

The application was tested on two sets of real data that varied in the length of the input vectors. The proposed algorithm worked similar to the reference method – the kNN algorithm – on longer vectors and better on shorter vectors. For both data sets, the obtained results were better than the published results obtained on the same data sets.

In future work we want to test the algorithm on other data sets and compare it with a wider spectrum of the localisation systems.

References

1. Breiman, L.: Random forests. Mach. Learn. **45**(1), 5–32 (2001)
2. Chen, T., Guestrin, C.: Xgboost: a scalable tree boosting system. CoRR abs/1603.02754 (2016). http://arxiv.org/abs/1603.02754
3. Dalce, R., Val, T., van den Bossche, A.: Comparison of indoor localization systems based on wireless communications. Wirel. Eng. Technol. **2**(4), 240–256 (2011). http://dx.doi.org/10.4236/wet.2011.24033
4. Dawes, B., Chin, K.W.: A comparison of deterministic and probabilistic methods for indoor localization. J. Syst. Softw. **84**(3), 442–451 (2011). http://www.sciencedirect.com/science/article/pii/S0164121210003109
5. Górak, R., Luckner, M.: Malfunction Immune wi–fi localisation method. In: Núñez, M., Nguyen, N.T., Camacho, D., Trawiński, B. (eds.) ICCCI 2015. LNCS, vol. 9329, pp. 328–337. Springer, Cham (2015). doi:10.1007/978-3-319-24069-5_31
6. Górak, R., Luckner, M.: Long term analysis of the localization model based on wi-fi network. In: Król, D., Madeyski, L., Nguyen, N.T. (eds.) Recent Developments in Intelligent Information and Database Systems. SCI, vol. 642, pp. 87–96. Springer, Cham (2016). doi:10.1007/978-3-319-31277-4_8
7. Górak, R., Luckner, M.: Modified random forest algorithm for wi–fi indoor localization system. In: Nguyen, N.-T., Manolopoulos, Y., Iliadis, L., Trawiński, B. (eds.) ICCCI 2016. LNCS, vol. 9876, pp. 147–157. Springer, Cham (2016). doi:10.1007/978-3-319-45246-3_14
8. Grzenda, M.: On the prediction of floor identification credibility in RSS-based positioning techniques. In: Ali, M., Bosse, T., Hindriks, K.V., Hoogendoorn, M., Jonker, C.M., Treur, J. (eds.) IEA/AIE 2013. LNCS, vol. 7906, pp. 610–619. Springer, Heidelberg (2013). doi:10.1007/978-3-642-38577-3_63
9. Japkowicz, N., Shah, M.: Evaluating Learning Algorithms: A Classification Perspective. Cambridge University Press, New York (2011)
10. Karwowski, J., Okulewicz, M., Legierski, J.: Application of particle swarm optimization algorithm to neural network training process in the localization of the mobile terminal. In: Iliadis, L., Papadopoulos, H., Jayne, C. (eds.) EANN 2013. CCIS, vol. 383, pp. 122–131. Springer, Heidelberg (2013). doi:10.1007/978-3-642-41013-0_13

11. Korbel, P., Wawrzyniak, P., Grabowski, S., Krasinska, D.: Locfusion api - programming interface for accurate multi-source mobile terminal positioning. In: 2013 Federated Conference on Computer Science and Information Systems (FedCSIS), pp. 819–823, September 2013
12. Okulewicz, M., Bodzon, D., Kozak, M., Piwowarski, M., Tenderenda, P.: Indoor localization of a moving mobile terminal by an enhanced particle filter method. In: Rutkowski, L., Korytkowski, M., Scherer, R., Tadeusiewicz, R., Zadeh, L.A., Zurada, J.M. (eds.) ICAISC 2016. LNCS, vol. 9693, pp. 512–522. Springer, Cham (2016). doi:10.1007/978-3-319-39384-1_45

Developing Countermeasures against Cloning of Identity Tokens in Legacy Systems

Pavel Moravec[1,2](✉) and Michal Krumnikl[1,2]

[1] Department of Computer Science, FEECS, VŠB - Technical University of Ostrava,
17. listopadu 15/2172, 708 33 Ostrava-Poruba, Czech Republic
{pavel.moravec,michal.krumnikl}@vsb.cz
[2] IT4Innovations, VŠB - Technical University of Ostrava,
17. listopadu 15/2172, 708 33 Ostrava, Czech Republic

Abstract. During the development of a new access system based on modern RFID technologies it was found that companies producing access control systems for residential and office buildings still prefer the use of existing cheap solutions instead of incorporating new technologies. This is mainly due to the additional costs new systems require.

The used legacy technologies are however prone to identity token cloning which allows easy access of unauthorized people to buildings. In previous paper, we have already briefly described a way how to detect cloned RFID tokens in 125 kHz RFID system.

This paper lists the risks of the legacy access systems and offers ways how to detect a cloned 125 kHz tag, 13.56 MHz RFID MIFARE Classic card or Dallas Semiconductors iButton access token and how to pro-actively disable them.

Keywords: RFID · Legacy access systems · Identity token · DS1990 · EM4100 · MIFARE classic · Cloning

1 Introduction

During the last year, we have developed an access system using the state-of-the-art technologies. This however meant that the production costs of the final device exceeded \$ 50 mark. The company we have done this research for then tried to offer the solution to their partners as a drop-in replacement for legacy modules, but was not successful due to the production costs being considered too high. The companies still prefer the use of legacy solutions which are known to be unsafe, and users may create clones of the access tokens in a relatively simple way. This means that the physical security of such buildings, lifts or restricted areas is compromised and the access may be presently gained by making a cheap clone of an access token, sometimes requiring as little as taking a photograph of the token or reading the RFID token wirelessly and creating its clone later on.

Nowadays, there is a huge variety of tags and labels used in modern access systems. Tags can be either passive or active and they differ in size, casing, storage capacity and used microcontrollers. The functions they provide range from

K. Saeed et al. (Eds.): CISIM 2017, LNCS 10244, pp. 672–684, 2017.
DOI: 10.1007/978-3-319-59105-6_58

transmitting read-only factory-assigned serial number to bi-directional communication with high-end cryptographic features.

Most electronic access systems use radio-frequency identification chips (RFID) as they provide simple use for end users. As the number of RFID applications increases, attacks against both tags and readers are getting more and more frequent. We may say that the price of solution usually reflects the level of security. Nevertheless, even more expensive RFID solutions do not always guarantee higher level of security. In the past, MIFARE Classic provided sufficient protection against attacks for reasonable price. Despite the fact that they are nowadays considered insecure and there are several easy to implement attacks against them [7,10], they are still being used. An improved and more secure version, MIFARE DESFire tags were broken few years later using a non-invasive power analysis and template attacks [18].

In other tokens, like HID iClass similar flaws were found [5]. Insecure RFID technologies were also found in Hitag2 car keys [20]. More practical approaches of eavesdropping, unauthorized scanning and relay attacks on ISO 14443-A tokens and radio layer were described in [8,9,14].

Wired technologies, like iButtons are vulnerable to similar attacks. One of the first hacking attempt on iButtons was presented on CCC Conference [2] followed by other presentations on this topic [6]. Secure iButtons that are using a SHA-1 enabled DS1963S chips were broken as well [3]. In order to maintain the same level of security over the years, manufacturers would have to replace the broken technologies in their installations. This is expensive and hard to manage.

Our goal is to provide a cheap drop-in module for present solutions, which will detect – and disable – cheap clones without their user gaining physical access to the building or restricted area. The resulting solution must be cheap (less than $ 10), provide a drop-in replacement for original module and be able to detect at least the commercially available tokens used for cloning. Ideally, the solution may also combine some of the legacy technologies, to provide an added value for the company whilst being compatible with the original module.

The paper will be organized as follows: First, we will describe the technologies with access tokens, which are still being sold for new installations. Second, we will discuss the possibilities of cloning such tokens and commercially available solutions for token cloning and their prices. Third, we will discus the possibilities of detecting these commercially available counterfeit access tokens and provide a framework to disable them. Further, we will offer solutions for individual technologies and provide the costs and comparison with the original solution.

2 Electronic Access Control Systems

In this section, we will discuss the electronic access control systems with identity token technologies used mainly in residential buildings, which are presently sold in Czech Republic. There are generally two areas:

- contact system sold nowadays solely with support of Dallas Semiconductors iButton Serial number tags of DS1990 [12] series,
- passive proximity cards offering contactless operation with the reader supplying power needed to operate the device. These systems are operating either on 125 kHz or 13.56 MHz band.

2.1   Dallas Semiconductors DS1990 iButton Serial Number

The iButton serial number (SN) is a widespread technology which is used for both gaining access to the residential buildings or restricted areas and for allowing special operation inside the lifts (access to some floors, operation of the lift only with the tag).

Each tag contains a unique 56-bit serial number and its 8-bit checksum, which the manufacturer presents as a 64-bit unique registration number. The chip is encased in a stainless steel case with the value of serial number laser-printed in a hexadecimal format on the positive pole of the case, which is typically mounted on a plastic keychain fob. The identification can be obtained through 1-Wire serial protocol by momentary contact. Communication with the bus master is performed by transmitting a 16.3 kbps signal on a wire used to power the device [12].

2.2   EM Microelectronic Passive Proximity EM41xx RFID Transponder

EM4100/4102/4105 tags are low frequency tags manufactured by EM Microelectronic. It is a RFID transponder containing 64 bits of read only memory programmed to store a 40-bit long unique ID. Remaining bits are used for the header and parity bits. The output is modulated using the Manchester coding on 125 kHz carrier with ASK modulation [4]. EM41xx tags are passive, drawing power from the RF field created by the reader. These tags cannot be rewritten, however there are other types that can be programmed to emulate original behavior.

2.3   Contactless RFID Tokens for Access Management

These tokens typically operate in 13.56 MHz frequency range and may be capable of storing user data. They either provide just a factory-set ID, or several kB of additional memory with read/write capability and ISO 14443 compliance. They use either a 4 byte non-unique ID or a 7 byte unique ID. Recently, tags with a 10 byte unique ID have been also introduced.

Each ISO 14443 Type A compatible tag with 7 byte ID should contain a 56-bit globally unique serial number [15], since each manufacturer is being assigned their own specific prefix. However, this does not take into account the situation, where counterfeit products exist on the market, duplicating the unique numbers assigned to legit manufacturers.

Fig. 1. RW1990 timing diagram during read and write operations [13]. Due to a different timing of write mode, the time axis is not to scale. The reader periodically checks the 1-Wire bus for the presence of iButton (1). When the iButton tag is detected, search ROM command is triggered. The tag responds with its family code, ROM code and CRC (2). Write operation is triggered after the reset (3), followed by a special command (4). Writing a new serial number is performed in a non-standard way. Each written bit is followed by 10 ms high state delay on the bus (5). The whole procedure is finished in about 680 ms.

Typical example of such smart card ICs is the NXP Semiconductors MIFARE card family, which offer in their MIFARE Classic [16,17] variant either a 32-bit ID or unique 56-bit ID, and an EEPROM with 1 kB to 4 kB storage capacity. The ID is stored in the first 7 bytes of EEPROM memory, however for most functions we use only the first 4 bytes of the UID. These cards were superseded by NXP MIFARE DESFire card family in many applications, but remain still used in the legacy systems used for access management – especially where storing additional data on the card, e.g. the number of accesses, electronic waller, or time limit when the entry is permitted.

3   Identity Token Cloning Using Commercially Available Tags

Unfortunately, it is possible to clone almost any identification (ID) tag used in present installations of the electronic access control systems (EACS), which use solely the IDs stored on tokens as the method to gain entry. Such tokens may be emulated by a suitable hardware, either by running a software on a microcontroller which mimics the identity token behavior, or by designing a copy of the identity token and intentionally removing the limitations enforced by the original identity token's manufacturer.

Originally, the emulation of identity tokens was limited to laboratory conditions [10] or specialized hardware [11,21] which required an experienced user and often hard-coding the ID in the source code. However, in recent years the alternatives to genuine tokens emerged, which are easy to use and do not require any prior user knowledge. We will concentrate on such devices and tokens, since they provide the easiest way to gain unauthorized access.

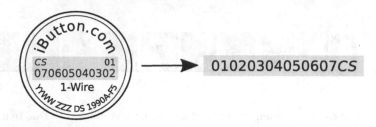

Fig. 2. iButton (DS1990) serial number extraction for programming of a RW1990 clone using the Arduino librarys (CS indicates the CRC8 checksum value)

3.1   Dallas Semiconductors DS1990 iButton Serial Number Clone – RW1990

For quite some time, there was no official clone which would make it possible to emulate the iButton SN. However, during the last year, it became possible to order RW1990 chips encased in a steel case compatible with DS1990. The device comes with an empty ID, which must be programmed manually by cloning an existing DS1990 ID. Writing to the tags is done by a specialized 1-Wire protocol, for details see Fig. 1.

On one hand, the commercial programmers for these tags are still expensive and can clone only the iButton SN which we have physical access to, on the other hand a generic solution can be implemented by uploading a publicly available sketch to Arduino and use it to program the RW1990 chip. Moreover, since the ID of each iButton SN is laser-printed on its case, a simple photograph of the iButton is enough for its duplication by reversing the order of the bytes in the serial number (see Fig. 2 for an example how the token ID may be read directly from a photo).

3.2   Passive Proximity EM41xx RFID Transponder Clone – EM4305

Tags used by so-called "card cloners" (Fig. 3) are based on E5550-compatible OTP identification circuit (Atmel ATA5557/5567/5577, etc.) These tags operate in 125 kHz range and provide bi-directional communication with the base station. Tags can be programmed to operate with different modulations and encodings, supporting also Manchester with ASK modulation used by the original EM4100 tags. The programming is performed by short interrupts in the RF field (on-off carrier keying) [1]. A simplified timing diagram of normal operation (reading mode) and programming mode is depicted in Fig. 4.

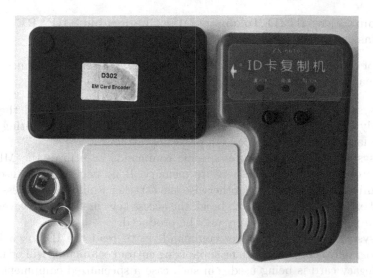

Fig. 3. Cloning of EM proximity 125 kHz tokens – from top-left corner clockwise: a USB writer, a hand-held copier, a blank card and a blank tag (with protective cover removed)

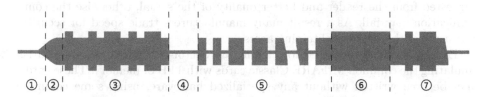

Fig. 4. Simplified ATA5577C [1] timing diagram during read and write operations. When the tag enters the RF field (1), the power-on reset circuit remains active until the internal capacitor is charged and an adequate voltage threshold is reached (2). After a default initialization delay (usually about 3 ms after entering the RF field), the tag enters regular read mode. In the normal mode, data is encoded according the configuration registers of ATA5577C and transmitted from the first stored data block (3). Most configurations use Manchester ASK modulation. To switch the tag from reading to writing mode, the card reader must interrupt the RF field for a short time (4), typically for 64–400 µs. After the successful mode switch, the tag enables (by default) the damping. A sequence of operational code, lock bits, address and data block must follow (5). Data bits are encoded by an on-off modulation with write gaps of 64–160 µs. The programming sequence is terminated with the programming delay of 5.6 ms. This delay is necessary for correct programming. After programming, the tag returns to block-read mode and transmits last written block (7).

3.3   Contactless RFID Tokens – UID Changeable MIFARE Classic Cards

In case of contactless RFID cards, there are several possible outcomes, which may or may not prevent successful cloning of the ID tag:

- The system uses ISO 14443 commands to read the tag ID and the ID is directly used for user access. In this case, a tag which allows writing of the UID may be used for cloning by a proximity attack.
- The system uses manufacturer-specific commands or utilizes the MIFARE classic cards and writes data to its memory. If no encryption is used, the proximity attack is possible, otherwise the attacker would need access to the ID token for several minutes to break the access keys first [10]. However, after that, a perfect one-to-one copy may be produced.
- The system uses manufacturer command set to read the ID token but its cryptography is broken – a clone supporting custom commands will be needed.
- Non-legacy card is being used – in such case a specialized equipment [18] is required to obtain the identity or duplication is not yet possible at all.

However, from our experience accessing the encrypted on-card memory with the reader significantly increases the processing time and requires more power harvested from the reader and better quality of the signal, otherwise the communication may fail. As a result many manufacturers trade speed for security and use just the UID for obtaining access.

Examples of the tags used for cloning are Sector-0/Block-0 writable cards, emulating the common MIFARE Classic cards with 1 kB of memory. These cards may be even written without any specialized hardware, using some common Android phones with NFC support or USB readers/writers. There are two types of such cards on market. The older ones are either directly writable, or they include specific commands which unlock the whole memory for reading and writing and bypass the security mechanisms. The more recent ones behave like standard MIFARE Classic cards, but allow to write the block in which the card ID is stored.

3.4   Overview of the Cloning Costs

The costs for cloning the ID tokens have presently become very low and the devices are easily available on popular auction sites with free delivery worldwide. The devices used to write data into cloned tags may be more expensive in some cases, but a cheap hardware may be used as an alternative and guides how to do that exist on Internet. In Table 1, we can see the overview of prices for such tags and programming devices.

Table 1. Approximate lowest prices of tags or cards (based on 5 pieces per lot) and devices used for identity token cloning – Q1/2017

Technology	Single tag/Card	Standalone copier	USB writer	Custom built
DS1990 iButton	$ 1.4	$ 72 (TM1[a])	—	< $ 2
EM proximity 125 kHz	$ 0.5	$ 7 (ZX-6610)	$ 12	Not needed
13.56 MHz RFID	$ 0.6/$ 0.9	$ 50[b]	$ 28 (ACR-122U)	< $ 7

[a] It also supports cloning of EM proximity 125 kHz cards.
[b] We may use some smart-phones with NFC support which are still compatible with MIFARE Classic family instead.

4   Proposed Detection and Disabling Methods

In this section, we will propose the way how to detect or semi-permanently disable the cloned identity tokens and prevent the entry of unauthorized personnel. Generally, we will use the same techniques utilized for ID programming to detect such tokens. The hardware used for this task will be very cheap (less than $ 10 and for most cases less than $ 2), with the possibility to update the detection code and optional support for two different technologies (EM proximity 125 kHz tokens and iButtons) which should satisfy the manufacturers' requirements for minimal additional costs whilst improving the security.

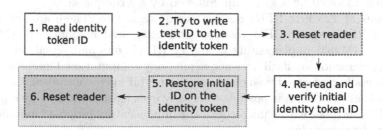

Fig. 5. Cloned token general detection method overview

The general mechanism is shown in Fig. 5. Step one is typically necessary to detect the presence of an ID token, step two tries to use mechanism normally reserved for cloning (which original, read-only tokens will just ignore). Steps 3 and 6 may not be necessary in some implementations (we may write a gap instead in case of EM 125 kHz proximity cards). In step 4, the verification takes place and we check if the ID of the token has changed, indicating counterfeit token.

The fifth step is not compulsory for genuine tokens and may not be necessary for clones as well. On one hand, we may want to restore the original ID without letting the user know how the detection worked, on the other hand if this reader is used together with the original legacy readers, we may decide to semi-permanently disable the ID token and skip the restoration of the original ID altogether.

4.1   iButton RW1990 Clone

The detection follows steps 1–4 (or 1–6) shown in Fig. 5 directly, the reader must be reset and chip initialized between reading and writing. Once the original iButton is detected, we reset the bus, change from the standard protocol to a lower-speed pulse-width modulation and send ID bytes to the tag, see Fig. 1. Then we reset, switch back to the standard 1-Wire protocol and verify if the ID has changed. Optionally we may restore the original ID by step 5, resetting the bus before writing original ID again.

4.2   Passive Proximity RFID Transponder EM4305 Clone

The method used for detecting the most widespread clones of EM4100 tokens maintains the previous scheme. Proposed RFID reader (base station) reads the content of the tag memory and then tries to switch into the programming mode. As read only tags do not support this switch they will either continue in the reading sequence and resume sending the unique ID or will reset and start from the beginning if the write gap was long enough to trigger the reset. Both situations are easily recognizable. In case of programmable tag, the reader can rewrite (erase) the content of the tag and thus efficiently block it for later use or leave the content and just indicate that the tag is programmable and probably cloned. Figure 4 depicts such pattern. At first, normal read operation is performed, followed by a write gap, followed by a write phase.

Designs of 125 kHz RFID readers are quite simple. There are several off the shelf RFID reader OEM modules and integrated circuits (e.g. U2270B, HTRC110, IM283) implementing necessary RF circuits and signal processing. As the implementation itself does not require any computational intensive tasks, it can be easily performed even on the smallest 8-bit microcontrollers, like Atmel AVRs. Thanks to this, it is possible to modify even existing designs by replacing the RFID controller with a microcontroller implementing proposed modification of the reading procedure.

4.3   UID Changeable MIFARE Classic Tags

For the MIFARE Classic clones, we have three different approaches how to detect the clone, however not all of them must be executed. In the first step, we read the token ID. Then we have three ways how to detect an unofficial ID token:

1. Issue the Request for Answer To Select (RATS) command and check the result. If the command is supported by the tag, a response is returned. We check the response for a special identification code (0xdabc1910) [19], if it is found, the token is an emulation token and we may ignore it (or write a special ID to it).
2. Issue special commands (7-bit value 0×40, then a single byte 0×43) [19]. If they are accepted, the token contains backdoor for unprotected access and we ignore the token by the reader (or write a special ID to it).

3. Try to write into first 16-byte block of the token (block-0/0), rewriting the original ID with a test one. After resetting the reader, we again check the ID of the token and if it has been changed to our test ID, we may either restore the token ID, or keep the test ID.

Tokens which were mentioned in the first and second cases were more expensive special emulation ones, which never became widespread due to their price. However, the first two detection methods may also be included, as they will prolong the test by approximately 150 ms in our test setup.

It should be noted that during the tests we have verified, that it is possible to semi-permanently disable the UID-writable tokens by writing zeros into the block-0/0, which will prevent tokens from being used by standard readers and from being detected by smart phones with NFC support (which can otherwise write to them). It is still possible to write a special software which recovers the token, but it is not easily available.

5   Experimental Evaluation of Our Approach

For the evaluation of our proposal for iButton and EM4100 clones, we have used a cheap hardware based on ATMega328p microcontroller, which is easily available for less than $ 2 due to its popularity in Arduino clones. It also provides serial output for potential readers. However, it is also possible to use cheaper processors such as ATtiny25/45/85.

The implementation of reading the 1-Wire iButton was straightforward as there are publicly available libraries implementing all necessary functions. The writing phase was implemented based on the Maxim's application note [13] and RW1990 descriptions available on Internet forums. Reading the token without the clone detection takes approximately 16 ms, while checking the clone by performing the write phase takes additional 680 ms. The whole procedure of clone detection (as described in Sect. 4) takes approximately 712 ms. This is significantly longer time than the simple read, but still fast enough to not bother the end users.

Detecting EM4100 clones is much faster, mainly due to faster write operations. The normal reading is finished in about 33 ms and the writing phase takes approximately 90 ms. The cloned card can be detected even sooner, since the full write phase is not necessary. The decision can be made immediately after the reader generates the write gap (see Fig. 4).

The most complex task was the evaluation of MIFARE Classic clones, which requires a specialized reader (e.g. with the PN532 chipset), already available in some devices. To simulate the solution we have written a tool using standard NFC libraries, executed on a PC with USB reader/writer.

In our test setup, it takes approximately 20 ms to select the token after initialization and obtain its UID (which would have to happen anyway). The actual detection methods from Sect. 4.3 take approximately:

1. 25 ms for (unsuccessful) RATS query for our test tokens[1].
2. 65 ms for initial setup of the second test with special command sequence and
   - either 26 ms for successfully executed second test which identifies the token of this type.
   - or 63 ms for in case we use this test on and token incompatible with special commands (a genuine token or a token of the third type).
3. 30 ms for the test consisting of: authentication (8 ms), reading the block-0/0 backup (9 ms) and writing of the new block-0/0.

The reset step and following reinitialization of the token took 123 ms.

So even when we combine all of the abovementioned methods (in case of the genuine MIFARE Classic), the whole process still takes less than $\frac{1}{3}$ s, which is indistinguishable by the user. Whilst these times may be influenced by actual reader chipset and hardware setup, the total time should not be significantly higher.

To conclude the evaluation, all proposed clone detection mechanisms extend the ID tag processing times to some degree, but our observations have shown that the majority of users do not notice any change in reader behavior as it usually takes a few seconds to gain access using these technologies.

6   Conclusion

In this paper, we have shown some common, commercially available products used for identity token cloning. We have described the ways by which the cloning is achieved for three common legacy electronic access systems and presented a general framework and individual solutions for these systems, which would not significantly increase the time needed for a user to be verified by the system or the manufacturing costs, but which would provide an additional protection against cloned identity tokens. We have also discussed the time needed for our approach compared to normal verification time.

In future, we may extend this detection framework by methods which check for other non-standard behavior of cloned ID tokens. This could, however, introduce situations, where counterfeit tags or generic tags from other manufacturers (which do not permit identity cloning) would be detected as false positives, preventing their use in such systems.

Acknowledgment. This work has been supported in part by Grant of SGS No. SP2017/61, VŠB – Technical University of Ostrava, Czech Republic, and by The Ministry of Education, Youth and Sports from the Large Infrastructures for Research, Experimental Development and Innovations project "IT4Innovations National Supercomputing Center – LM2015070".

---

[1] We were not able to obtain a sample of an emulated card with these parameters for our testing.

References

1. Atmel Corporation: ATA5577C Read/Write LF RFID IDIC 100 to 150 khz, technical datasheet, rev. 9187H-RFID-07/14 (2014)
2. Brandt, C.: Hacking iButtons. Presentation at 27c3 (2010)
3. Brandt, C., Kasper, M.: Don't push it: breaking iButton security. In: Danger, J.-L., Debbabi, M., Marion, J.-Y., Garcia-Alfaro, J., Zincir Heywood, N. (eds.) FPS -2013. LNCS, vol. 8352, pp. 369–387. Springer, Cham (2014). doi:10.1007/978-3-319-05302-8_23
4. EM Microelectronic-Marin SA: EM4100 read only contactless identification device, technical datasheet (2004)
5. Garcia, F.D., Koning Gans, G., Verdult, R., Meriac, M.: Dismantling iClass and iClass elite. In: Foresti, S., Yung, M., Martinelli, F. (eds.) ESORICS 2012. LNCS, vol. 7459, pp. 697–715. Springer, Heidelberg (2012). doi:10.1007/978-3-642-33167-1_40
6. Grand, J., Studio, G.I.: Can You Really Trust Hardware? Exploring Security Problems in Hardware Devices. The Black Hat Briefings (2005)
7. Hancke, G.: A practical relay attack on ISO 14443 proximity cards. Technical report (2005)
8. Hancke, G.: Practical attacks on proximity identification systems. In: 2006 IEEE Symposium on Security and Privacy, pp. 328–333, May 2006
9. Issovits, W., Hutter, M.: Weaknesses of the ISO/IEC 14443 protocol regarding relay attacks. In: 2011 IEEE International Conference on RFID-Technologies and Applications (RFID-TA), pp. 335–342, September 2011
10. Koning Gans, G., Hoepman, J.-H., Garcia, F.D.: A practical attack on the MIFARE classic. In: Grimaud, G., Standaert, F.-X. (eds.) CARDIS 2008. LNCS, vol. 5189, pp. 267–282. Springer, Heidelberg (2008). doi:10.1007/978-3-540-85893-5_20
11. Krumnikl, M.: Unique (EM4001) RFID emulator. Technical report, Department of Computer Science. VŠB - Technical University of Ostrava (2007)
12. Maxim Integrated Products, Inc.: DS1990A serial number iButton, technical datasheet (2008)
13. Maxim Integrated Products, Inc.: Software methods to achieve robust 1-Wire communication in iButton applications, application Note 159 (2008)
14. Mitrokotsa, A., Rieback, M., Tanenbaum, A.: Classifying RFID attacks and defenses. Inf. Syst. Front. 12(5), 491–505 (2010). http://dx.doi.org/10.1007/s10796-009-9210-z
15. NXP Semiconductors: AN10927 MIFARE and handling of UIDs, application note, rev. 4.0
16. NXP Semiconductors: MF1S50yyX/V1 MIFARE Classic EV1 1K - Mainstream contactless smart card IC for fast and easy solution development, product data sheet, rev. 3.0
17. NXP Semiconductors: MF1S70yyX/V1 MIFARE Classic EV1 4K - Mainstream contactless smart card IC for fast and easy solution development, product data sheet, rev. 3.1
18. Oswald, D., Paar, C.: Breaking Mifare DESFire MF3ICD40: power analysis and templates in the real world. In: Preneel, B., Takagi, T. (eds.) CHES 2011. LNCS, vol. 6917, pp. 207–222. Springer, Heidelberg (2011). doi:10.1007/978-3-642-23951-9_14
19. Tools, N.: Platform independent Near Field Communication (NFC) library (2017). https://github.com/nfc-tools/libnfc

20. Verdult, R., Garcia, F.D., Balasch, J.: Gone in 360 seconds: Hijacking with Hitag2. In: Proceedings of the 21st USENIX Conference on Security Symposium, Security 2012, USENIX Association, Berkeley, CA, USA, p. 37–37 (2012). http://dl.acm.org/citation.cfm?id=2362793.2362830
21. Verdult, R., de Koning Gans, G., Garcia, F.D.: A toolbox for RFID protocol analysis. In: 2012 Fourth International EURASIP Workshop on RFID Technology (EURASIP RFID), pp. 27–34. IEEE (2012)

Analysis of Specific Personal Information Protection Assessment in the Social Security and Tax Number System of Local Governments in Japan

Sanggyu Shin[✉], Yoichi Seto, Mayumi Sasaki, and Kei Sakamoto

Advanced Institute of Industrial Technology, 1-10-40, Higashiooi,
Shinagawa-Ku, Tokyo 140-0011, Japan
{shin,seto.yoichi}@aiit.ac.jp

Abstract. A law in Japan has been established concerning the *My Number* system or the use of numbers for identifying specific individuals in administrative procedures in local governments. The law requires local governments to implement the specific personal implementation protection assessment for social security and tax number systems. In this paper, we analyzed the assessment reports of the specific personal information protection assessments conducted by local governments. We did the analysis in two directions: (1) adequacy of risk assessment and measures, and (2) reuse of the assessment report. Our analysis shows that there was a description of assessment on the risk assessment items, but there were many assessment reports with missing assessment on some operations.

Keywords: Risk assessment · Privacy impact assessment · Privacy risk · Social security and tax number system · Specific personal information protection assessment

1 Introduction

On May 24, 2013, the *Act on the Use of Numbers to Identify a Specific Individual in the Administrative Procedure*, also known as the *My Number* law, was raised. From this law, the Social Security and Tax Number System or the *My Number* system came in.

The *My Number* system is used to confirm that information on individuals possessed by multiple agencies such as administrative agencies and local governments are information of the same person. This system advocates a fairer and more just society, enhanced public convenience and improved administrative efficiency [1].

From October 2015, the government has enforced the *My Number* law, and notified the residents of their *My Number* numbers. The personal information including *My Number* is called *Specific Personal Information*.

Protection Assessment is done to prevent infringement of privacy of personal information and ensure the trust and protect the rights of citizens and residents [2]. After protection assessment, each local government unit must conduct their risk assessment as assessment report [3].

© IFIP International Federation for Information Processing 2017
Published by Springer International Publishing AG 2017. All Rights Reserved
K. Saeed et al. (Eds.): CISIM 2017, LNCS 10244, pp. 685–696, 2017.
DOI: 10.1007/978-3-319-59105-6_59

In this paper, we analyzed the report published by the local governments in the following perspectives:

1. Adequacy of risk items, and
2. Re-use of the Assessment report.

In other countries, privacy impact assessment (from now on referred to as PIA) has been carried out to preliminarily assess the influence on privacy when introducing or repairing a system involving the acquisition of personal information, and taking measures to avoid or mitigate privacy risk [4].

In the PIA, there are two studies on the validity of impact assessment: one is the assessment of the suitability of the PIA applied to the biometrics system. The other is a study evaluating the effectiveness of the PIA itself.

Officials in charge of the administrative organization self-evaluate the *Specific Personal Information Protection Assessment* about the system and operation. On the other hand, the *PIA* does not include the operation, but only the system is assessed by a specialized neutral third party. The government has published protection assessment as equivalent to PIA, but as stated above, PIA and protection assessment are fundamentally different.

This paper analyzes and assesses whether the *Specific Personal Information Protection Assessment* prescribed by the *My Number* law is properly implemented by local governments based on the assessment report issued by the local governments.

2   Related Works

There are two similar researches on the appropriateness of risk assessment in conjunction with PIA. Protection assessment concerning specific personal information was implemented in 2015, and no case study on the protection assessment was found. The protection assessment is conducted only in Japan, while the PIA is an assessment method that has international standards and is implemented in other countries. In the PIA, there are two cases of research on the appropriateness.

First, Kush Wadhwa et al. applied PIA to biometric systems then assessed the appropriateness of the procedures for PIA by ranking [5]. They assumed that the PIA method is useful and evaluated its adequacy as to whether the implementation procedure is appropriate for the case of PIA. For example, their work assessed whether the report release procedure is appropriate or not. The other related work is a case study where Sakamoto et al. conducted the effectiveness assessment of PIA itself [6]. They assessed the effect of how much privacy risk could be reduced by implementing PIA using the risk assessment method developed based on the international standard ISO 22307. In other words, the effectiveness of PIA is quantitatively assessed from two viewpoints: visualization of privacy risk on personal information and improvement of awareness of stakeholders concerning personal information protection.

The protection assessment to be implemented in Japan is stipulated by the guidelines so that risk assessment is carried out in a mixture of system and operation by self-evaluation of officials in charge of the administrative organizations who have used the system [4, 7]. Due to these reasons, the two assessment methods are completely different, and it's hard to apply the assessment method implemented in the PIA to the *Specific Personal Information Protection Assessment*.

In our work, we evaluate whether the assessment is done properly by analyzing the assessment report which is the result of the protection assessment of the specific personal information.

3 Specific Personal Information Protection Assessment

3.1 Outline of Specific Personal Information Protection Assessment

In the case of the *My Number* system, it was imperative to implement the protective assessment as one of the protective measures against the task of handling specific personal information [1]. Figure 1 shows an overview of protective assessment.

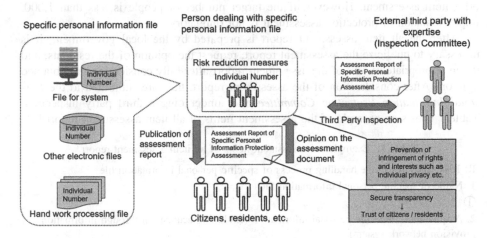

Fig. 1. Overview of specific personal information protection assessment

Protection assessment for specific personal information aims to prevent the leakage of specific personal information and other accidents beforehand by ensuring proper handling of specific personal information files such as the *My Number* number, to prevent and protect rights and interests of residents. That is the basic idea of the protection assessment. Its purpose lies in the following.

1. Preventing infringement of rights and interests such as personal privacy by prior response, and
2. Ensuring the confidence of citizens and residents through appropriate disclosure of information.

3.2 Procedure of the Specific Personal Information Protection Assessment

In the protection assessment, it is obligatory to carry out either essential item assessment, priority item assessment, or all item assessment by threshold judgment.

Indicators of threshold judgments include the number of people to be handled, the number of persons dealing with specific personal information files (from now on referred to as the number of handlers), and the occurrence or not of a serious accident concerning specific personal information at the assessment executing agency.

For example, if the target number of people is 300,000 or more, all items are assessed. For more than 100,000 or more are less than 300,000 people, priority item assessment is required. For less than 100,000 people, only the essential item assessment is obliged.

If the number of handlers is 500 or more or a serious accident related to protection of specific personal information has occurred within the past year, it switches from priority item assessment to all item assessment, and essential item assessment to priority item assessment. However, if the target number of people is less than 1,000, implementation of protection assessment is not obligatory.

After the all item assessment report is prepared by the local government, it is necessary to publicize the assessment report, request the opinion of the residents, and do an appropriate review of the assessment report after fully considering the obtained opinion. After consideration of the assessment report, they are submitted to the *Personal Information Protection Committee* after undergoing a third party inspection. Table 1 shows an example of the assessment items of all item assessment report [8].

Table 1. Examples of assessment items of all item assessment report

III Risk measures in the handling process of specific personal information file	
1. Name of specific personal information file	
①	
2. Acquisition of specific personal information (excluding acquisition through information provision network system)	
Risk 1: Risk of obtaining non-purpose acquisition	
The content of measures to prevent the acquisition of information other than the target peoples	②
The content of measures to prevent obtaining non-necessary information	③
Contents of other measures	④
Is the measure of risk sufficient?	[⑤] < Option> (1) Putting particular emphasis (2) Enough (3) Issues remain
Hereinafter omitted	Hereinafter omitted

The method of describing the assessment report includes the method of writing an outline in the blanks shown in ① to ④ in Table 1 and the selection description method shown in ⑤. For example, in ②, actions that correspond systematically such as "restrict accessible terminals" and measure concerning operation (human/organizational) such as "to verify identification based on notification/application details or identification documents" are described. In other words, it is necessary to assess both system and operation for every item and describe each measure without omissions. In the selection description, chooses one from options such as (1) Putting particular emphasis, (2) Enough, and (3) Issues remain, etc. In the case of PIA, risk assessment targets are not administrative (operations) but systems. The privacy commissioner issued the standard guideline and risk assessment carries out the assessment based on this guidance. Also, risk assessment is not classified by the number of personal information handled [4].

3.3 Issues of Specific Personal Information Protection Assessment

Although protection evaluation is said to be equivalent to PIA adopted in other countries, there are the following differences when compared with PIA.

1. The assessment object is "clerical work handling specific personal information file," the definition of administrative tasks is unclear, and the system and operation related to the target functions (organizational and human) are mixed.
2. While PIA is evaluated by a third-party organization with neutrality and expertise, protection evaluation is a self-assessment by the system operator (officials such as administrative agencies) and self-declaration by the chief, etc.
3. Risk assessment manual etc. for protection evaluation still has not been sorted out. Therefore, administrative agencies are preparing assessment reports by individual risk analysis methods.

As described above, there is a possibility that the risk assessment is not properly implemented in the protection assessment on specific personal information. Therefore, using all the item assessment reports released by the local governments, we analyze whether the risk assessment is properly implemented from the two following viewpoints.

1. Adequacy of risk assessment and measures: assess the excess and deficiency of assessment standard and safety control measures created separately for system and operation.
2. Reuse of the assessment report: We analyze the assessment report published by the local governments and assess the situation on reuse.

4 Analysis of All Item Assessment Report

4.1 Analysis Method

As described in Sect. 3.3, protection assessment and PIA have different targets and procedures. For this reason, we analyzed whether protection assessment deals with the protection of specific personal information in the My Number system based on the two following points.

Adequacy of risk assessment and measures

In the protection assessment, for example, each local government implements measures of risk countermeasure against the risk items described in the all item assessment report. However, there is a possibility that risk assessment and safety control measures will not be considered sufficiently in the protection evaluation. From this issue, three issues 1 to 3 are conceivable.

1. For risk countermeasures, since risks (threats and vulnerabilities) are different in the system and operation, they should be evaluated and described separately, but many local governments expressed mixed opinions about systems and operational risk mitigation measures.
2. The basis for the content of the description for the risk item is unclear. Although the risk item shown in Table 1 is presented from the central government, there is no explanation about its basis.
3. Risk items in the assessment reports are uniform entries and the specific level when the local governments consider the risk countermeasure is not indicated. For that reason, it is conceivable that local governments differ in the way of grasping risks and the level of description. There are issues such as whether adequacy judgment is carried out is subjective, such as "adequate measures" for risks in situations where countermeasure standards are not presented. As a result, the local governments that assess can select "Enough" etc. depending on their personal opinions.

Reuse of assessment reports

Reuse of the assessment report has two viewpoints. One is to reuse assessment reports of other local governments that precede the same affairs, or samples provided by the central government. The second one is to reuse the content of the assessment report of the administrative office that was previously assessed in the same local government in the assessment of another office work.

4.2   Selection of Analysis Targets

As described in Sect. 3.2, the protection assessment is classified into three assessments based on threshold judgment, essential item assessment, priority item assessment, and all item assessment.

In this paper, we focused the assessment report of all items. Many officials deal with a lot of specific personal information in the all items assessment. Therefore, the risk of leakage of specific personal information and other accidents is high thus more detailed and accurate risk measures are required.

As of June 2015, 221 assessment reports of all items have been released by the *Personal Information Protection Committee*. We investigated 10 cases of all item assessment reports.

Selection criteria for the all item assessment report to be investigated are as follows.

1. Official assessment report released by the Personal Information Protection Committee.
2. Assessment report for the same affairs, that is, "affairs concerning the basic resident register."

3. Selection from local governments in various parts of Japan that do not depend on locality: 9 assessment reports corresponding to approximately 10% of all item assessment documents (80 cases).
4. Select the description procedure that is presented from the central government as a criterion to compare with all the item assessment reports of the local government.

Table 2 shows the basic data of the local governments that were selected as assessment targets [9].

Table 2. Basic data of local governments Unit (people)

Local government	Basic data		Assessment description contents	
	Number of inhabitants	Number of staff	Number of people handled specific personal information	Number of handled specific personal information
A city	967,679	7,260	Over 300,000	500+
B city	355,467	5,495	Over 300,000	Less than 500
C city	446,286	3,198	Over 300,000	Less than 500
D district	879,658	5,057	Over 300,000	Less than 500
E city	1,946,540	14,360	Over 300,000	Less than 500
F city	182,843	994	Over 100,000 Below 300,000	500+
G city	1,536,499	14,701	Over 300,000	500+
H city	323,240	2,332	Over 300,000	Less than 500
I district	710,970	4,313	Over 300,000	500+

5 Assessment Analysis of All Items Assessment Report

5.1 Adequacy of Risk Assessment and Measures

In the protection assessment, there is no procedural manual on risk assessment, so the assessment is left to the administrative agencies and local governments. Also, the skill level of the person in charge who performs the assessment is not stipulated. In this section, we analyze whether each local government described appropriate risk response for risk assessment.

The evaluation criteria were prepared according to the safety measure standards shown in the *(Separate) Safety Management Measures for Specific Personal Information (Operator's Guide)*. We prepared assessment criteria by classifying risk correspondence to be implemented for each risk item into systematic correspondence and human organizational correspondence [10].

We analyzed to compare each risk items which are assessment criteria classified into system-related measures and measures concerning the operation of the "*III Risk measures in the handling process of specific personal information*" about the basic resident register file with all item assessment reports to be analyzed which published by local governments. Figure 2 show the example of the comparative assessment.

Assessment report (Example)

System risk   Compare   Operational risk

Assessment standard (Example)

Fig. 2. Comparison of all item assessment report and assessment standard

The result of the comparison is indexed in Table 3 to confirm the excess or deficiency for each corresponding risk item. We roughly distinguished that the assessment index of risk to three stages (Table 3) because it is hard to fix the index based on a logical basis. This assessment index was decided based on a discussion with the expert on PIA.

Table 3. The category of assessment of the risk response.

Assessment results	Assessment index
The risk correspondence indicated by the evaluation standard is being satisfied. Furthermore, the risk described corresponding to the evaluation criteria is supported	3
The only parts of the risk management that are shown in the assessment criteria are described	2
The risk correspondence indicated by the assessment standard isn't mentioned	1
Risk correspondence isn't indicated in the assessment standard	- (Excluded from assessment)

Table 4 shows the distribution and the assessment value of the assessment index concerning the risk correspondence on the system in each local government.

The assessment value is calculated by adding the value of multiplying risk number by the assessment index and dividing by the number obtained by subtracting the number of items not subject to evaluation from the total number of items (49).

Table 4. The situation of corresponding to the risk (System).

All 49 items	System				Assessment index
	3	2	1	0	(Average of all item)
A city	7	12	5	25	2.08
B city	11	10	5	23	2.23
C city	7	12	6	24	2.04
D district	11	8	8	22	2.11
E city	9	13	3	24	2.24
F city	10	13	1	25	2.38
G city	11	12	1	25	2.42
H city	5	16	3	25	2.08
I district	24	0	0	25	3.00

For example, in the case of City A, it is calculated as follows.

$$\text{Assessment value} = (3 \times 7 + 2 \times 12 + 1 \times 5) \div (49 - 25) = 2.08$$

The assessment index when not mentioning the risk correspondence indicated by the assessment standard at all is 1 point. Also, since the assessment index when only a part of the risk correspondence is indicated in the assessment criteria is described is 2 points. When the average value of the assessment index is 2 points or less, there is a possibility that proper risk response could not be made. The fact that the average value of the assessment index is 2 points or less means that many risk items did not cope with the risk indicated by the assessment criteria.

Table 5 shows the distribution and the assessment value of the assessment index concerning the risk correspondence on the operation in each local government. As for the

Table 5. The situation of corresponding to the risk (Operation).

All 49 items	Operation				Assessment index
	3	2	1	0	(Average of all item)
A city	11	17	7	14	2.11
B city	12	21	2	14	2.29
C city	9	16	11	13	1.94
D district	12	12	12	13	2.00
E city	8	17	11	13	1.92
F city	12	14	10	13	2.06
G city	8	16	12	13	1.89
H city	11	13	12	13	1.97
I district	36	0	0	13	3.00

operation, the assessment index is lower as a whole compared to the system. This is because local governments do not mention countermeasures concerning operations. They only describe the risk correspondence concerning the system in risk countermeasures.

5.2   Reuse of Assessment Reports

Many descriptions of all items assessed by local governments are similar to the *Procedure for Specific Personal Information Protection Evaluation Procedure (draft) on affairs related to basic residential ledger* (from now on referred to as the Procedure) exemplified by the Ministry of Internal Affairs and Communications [11, 12].

In other words, there is a possibility that the all item assessment report announced previously was reused by simply copying and pasting. In the case of preparing the all items evaluation document by reuse, it may be considered that the examination of risk assessment is inappropriate and it is possible that the existing reason of the system itself will be gone. We analyzed the identity confirmation information file of all items assessment report selected in Sect. 4.2. We compared the corresponding items in the description procedure and its similarities concerning the "*III Risk measures in the handling process of specific personal information.*"

Specifically, we count the number of characters for which the *Description* of the assessment report and the statement of description are identical and then calculate the ratio. The higher the reuse rate, the higher the likelihood of reuse. Table 6 shows the reuse rate by the local governments.

Table 6. Local government reuse rate.

	A city	B city	C city	D district	E city	F city	G city	H city	I district	Average
Reuse rate	52.1	64.4	38.5	75.9	44.0	47.2	55.6	43.5	32.7	50.5

All item assessment report in which the reuse rate exceeded 50% is 44% (4 out of 9: A/B/C City and D District). All item assessment report in which mistook the incorrect legal number is 89% (8 out of 9: local governments excluding B City). All item assessment report in which misprinted typographical errors similarly is 67% (6 out of 9: A/B/C/G City and D/I District).

For reasons that the reuse rate for each local government exceeds 50%, there may be uniformity in the description format of all item assessment reports. Thus, the description contents are similar. Therefore, it can't be said that there is a problem in reuse and it can be said that it is effective means to reuse to improve efficiency. However, it is important that proper risk assessment and countermeasures are implemented, and confirming this is the responsibility of third party inspection. If the inspection committee (or the personal information council) functions properly, it can be confirmed whether or not there is a problem with reuse.

6   Conclusion

In this paper, we analyzed from the viewpoint of all items assessment report the specific personal information protection assessment system for all item assessment. As a result of the analysis, the following problems were found out.

1. Since risk assessment guidelines do not exist, cases were found where appropriate risk assessment was not conducted for each local government.
2. Because the legal status of third-party inspection is unclear, there are local governments whose third-party inspections are not functioning effectively.

To deal with these problems, it is necessary to consider countermeasures from both the improvement in the current system and the review of the institutional design. Improvement measures in the current system are to prepare guidelines for common evaluation of local governments [13]. By conducting assessment and inspection according to the guidelines, we believe that appropriate correspondence without missing will be possible, and variations in responses among local governments will be improved. Also, the load on the evaluator can be reduced.

Acknowledgments. This research carried out in the Project Based Learning in the Advanced Institute of Industrial Technology. In advancing the PBL, we got the cooperation of Kazuhiro Midorikawa, Yuta Kurosawa, Okimura Seiji, and Xiaofei Ma. We would like to express our appreciation here.

References

1. Act on the Use of Numbers to Identify a Specific Individual in Administrative Procedures (2013). http://law.e-gov.go.jp/htmldata/H25/H25HO027.html. Last accessed 17 Mar 2017
2. The Specific personal information protection committee.: Description of the specific personal information protection evaluation guidelines (2014). http://www.ppc.go.jp/files/pdf/explanation.pdf. Last accessed 17 Mar 2017
3. Takashi, M.: Improper specific personal information protection evaluation shakes "My number" system. NikKei Comput. **5**(14), 6–10 (2015)
4. Yoichi, S.: Practical privacy risk assessment technique, Kindaikagaku, Tokyo, pp. 21–24 (2014)
5. Wadhwa, K.: SAPIENT project supporting fundamental rights, privacy and ethics in smart surveillance technologies, Biometrics (2011)
6. Sakamoto, M., Yoichi, S., Okazakim, M., Okamoto, N., Kawaguchi, H., Nagano, S.: Assessment of effectiveness of personal information impact assessment. J. Digital Pract. **7** (1), 52–60 (2016)
7. Supervised by Yoichi S.: Specific personal information protection practice guidelines for local governments. Gyosei, pp. 38–156 (2015)
8. Cabinet Secretariat, Specific personal information protection evaluation guidelines (draft Cabinet Secretariat), Attached document 3: All items evaluation sheet, December 2013. http://www.cas.go.jp/jp/seisaku/bangoseido/kojinjoho/pdf/tkjhh-3.xls
9. From demographics by each local government (Web site of each local government as of June 2015)

10. Personal Information Protection Commission, Guidelines on proper handling of specific personal information (Operator's edition). http://www.ppc.go.jp/files/pdf/160101_guideline_jigyousya.pdf. Last accessed 17 Mar 2017
11. Personal Information Protection Commission, My number protection assessment Web. http://www.ppc.go.jp/mynumber/evaluationSearch/. Last accessed 17 Mar 2017
12. Personal Information Protection Commission, Proposed guidelines for prescribing specific personal information protection assessment on affairs related to basic resident register (draft). http://www.ppc.go.jp/files/pdf/260624siryo1.pdf. Last accessed 17 Mar 2017
13. Advanced Institute of Industrial Technology: Related manual of Specific Personal Information Protection Assessment (2015). http://aiit.ac.jp/master_program/isa/professor/y_seto.html. Last accessed 17 Mar 2017

The Implementation of Electronic Document in Transaction Execution

Gerard Wawrzyniak[1] and Imed El Fray[1,2(✉)]

[1] Faculty of Computer Science and Information Technology,
West Pomeranian University of Technology, Szczecin, Poland
gwawrzyniak@wi.zut.edu.pl, imed_el_fray@sggw.pl
[2] Faculty of Applied Informatics and Mathematics,
Warsaw University of Life Sciences – SGGW, Warsaw, Poland

Abstract. The article presents the implementation of an electronic document in the form of electronic forms that can be used in legally binding way in transactions execution regardless of the field of application, the type of entity involved in the transaction or their local information systems. Paper also presents the concept of the form in which the data layer, the presentation and the logic is encapsulated in a one single XML file, whose syntax is described using XML schema (XSD). Presentation of the document is done on the background of the discussion about the general concept of the document and the transaction. Authors present also the ways of implementation a few basic types of transactions, from which more complex solutions can be composed. The vision of the further research and development of the electronic document towards the use of crypto - currency, smart contracts, block chains and distributed autonomous organization is outlined in this paper.

Keywords: Electronic document · Transaction · XML · XSD

1 Introduction

1.1 The Transaction

Activity understood as a series of structured activities carried out to achieve a specific goals is called a transaction. The transaction [1–3] can be understood as:

- Commercial operation associated with the purchase or sale of material assets, intangible assets or services and agreement associated with this operation,
- Transfer of material goods, services or intangible goods between the parties resulting from variety of relations binding the parties, may be economic, commercial, financial, social or any other relations,
- An agreement (contract) between the parties the subject of which are good, services or other agreements and commitments.

It should be emphasized that the subject of this article are not transaction in the sense of database transaction or other related to information technology.

© IFIP International Federation for Information Processing 2017
Published by Springer International Publishing AG 2017. All Rights Reserved
K. Saeed et al. (Eds.): CISIM 2017, LNCS 10244, pp. 697–708, 2017.
DOI: 10.1007/978-3-319-59105-6_60

The concept of transaction is general and applies to essentially all human activities regardless of: form of organization, activity, type of transaction or sector.

Transaction is always related to: creation, processing, transfer (flow), collection (gathering) and store of information [4].

1.2   The Document in the Transactions

It can be found, that information is in a immanent way is accompanied by a transactions and often is the subject of the transaction. However if information is to be useful in the implementation of transaction in secure manner, it must have some certain features:

- Authenticity – sure of the veracity of the information,
- Non-repudiation of origin – sure the origin of information,
- Durability – possibility to use of information after the time.

If the information meets the above characteristics, then we can talk about the document [5], which can be used as evidence in explanatory proceedings.

It should be noted that the role of the document has been extended through the use of electronic document as mean of supporting the transactions realization. The essence of the electronic document as a special form of a document is presented in the paper [5]. Here it should be noted that the electronic document must have all the features of the traditional document.

An important aspect of the electronic document is the need to ensure the interoperability of electronic document in a wide range, namely:

- the ability to use regardless of the maturity of IT used by users,
- document format must be independent of industry or activity sector of the economy,
- document format and software to use the document must be technology-neutral,
- ease of integration with various user's systems,
- autonomy - the ability to use a document on a device without access to network,
- the ability to interpret the document both:
  - automatically (the integration with information systems,
  - by human and automatically.

2   Expected Features of an Electronic Document and Proposal

2.1   Expectations vs. Possibilities of Existing Solutions

To be able to support transactions or to be a subject of transactions, electronic document must be provided with the following features:

A. Non-repudiation, integrity, authenticity – legal effectiveness
B. Autonomy – the ability to use document without access to the network,
C. Intelligibility for people – visualization based on universal commonly known rules,
D. Interoperability – ease of automatic processing, ease of data exchange with information systems (XML),

E. Ability to define and execute the logic – validation rules, calculation rules, rules of dynamic presentation of objects in the document, build – in cryptography and public key infrastructure functions, build – in mechanisms for communication via SMTP/POP3, SOAP, REST, HTTP GET/POST,

F. Ability to integrate and use emerging technologies like: cryptocurrency, block chains, distributed autonomous organizations, session initialization protocols.

Solution	Feature					
	A	B	C	D	E	F
PDF	+	+	+	–	–	–
Packages (MS Office, Libre Office)	–	+	+	–	–	–
SMTP/POP3/IMAP	–	+	+	–	–	–
Fax	–	+	+	–	–	–
Centralized IT systems	+	–	–	–	–	+

PDF (Portable Document Format) – the biggest problem in using it to document the transaction is complicated structure of the file what makes automatic processing difficult and requires dedicated libraries. Also the logic layer doesn't exist what makes this format less useful. It is at least difficult to use it to exchange legally binding data between systems (with automatic processing) [6].

Office packages (MS Office, Libre Office and similar) – in the case of those solutions the problem of parsing and interpreting data can be observed – similar to PDF. Non repudiation of origin, integrity and authenticity cannot be ensured. Also definition and execution of the logic does not exist [7].

E-Mail approach (SMTP/POP3/IMAP) – it is possible to sign e-mail message, but doubts appear if it is fully legal. Processing the mail message is embarrassing It is at least difficult to use it to support transaction execution [8].

Fax – it is the image of the document only. It is not possible to exchange legally binding information using the image of document.

Centralized IT systems – allow to support transactions in efficient way but it is limited to the space of specific system only. The information exchange with other systems requires specific preparations for all systems involved in the information flow [9].

2.2 Proposal

The solution which meets all needs/features/requirements considered above is electronic document (electronic form), in the form of XML file, with syntax defined using XML schema (XSD) [10–13]. To use the form, the dedicated application or standard commonly known XML parsers should be applied.

The extension of electronic documents application is to integrate and use them with the implementation of concepts: Cryptocurrency, Smart Contracts, Block Chains, Distributed Autonomous Organizations.

3 ebForm – Electronic Form

3.1 ebForm

The concept of the electronic form that meets all of the above features has been implemented as ebForm forms.

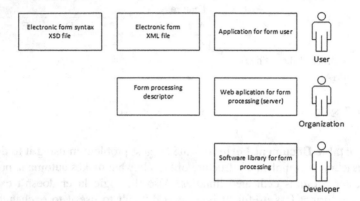

Fig. 1. Key elements of the electronic forms solution

The whole solution consists of (Fig. 1):

- Electronic form in the form of XML file with syntax defined using XSD,
- The application designed to use ebForm forms – interprets and executes visualization (presentation) data input, signature operations and form logic,
- ebFormProcessor server – application server:
  - communicates with the ebForm application (ebCommunicator), using SOAP protocol according to the logic defined in the logic layer of the form, and
  - processes the form – downloads data from the form and records data to the organization's internal systems, verifies the document authenticity, writes data into the form, generates signature in the form, returns the form to the ebCommunicator application, all above in accordance with logic defined in the ebFormProcessor.xml file.
- ebFormAPI library – library designed for developers to create solutions based on, and using ebForm. The library allows reading and writing data from/to the form as well as execution and verification signatures.

ebForm contains the following conceptual layers of the document (Fig. 2):

- visualization (presentation) layer – a description of the visual shape of components of the form,
- data layer – the data entered into the form is not separated from the presentation layer, but with other layers (visualization and logic) is a single entity in the form of file,

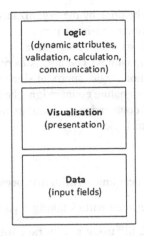

Fig. 2. Conceptual layers of electronic forms

- logic layer – these are non – visual elements not existing in traditional paper forms, this layer allows to:
  - define the validity rules for data entered into particular fields of the form,
  - define the dynamic behavior of graphical components and other calculations depending on the status of individual forma fields,
  - define the activities initiated as a result of interaction with the user.

ebForm syntax description is a specific description language for forms and can be regarded as the implementation of the concept of declarative programming. In particular, ebForm includes:

- **Graphical components** – graphical elements of the form. Each element (text, text field etc.) has a defined list of attributes that determine the way of presentation. Attributes can take the values depend on the values of input field/s or current referred function value/s.
- **Expressions** – default values can be calculated and assigned to individual fields. Calculations are performed using various expressions using appropriate type (string, integer or decimal etc.). It allows to determine values of attributes of components.
- **Actions** (Activities) – special component is a push button that can be assigned to a sequence of actions, to be performed by the application ebCommunicator. These actions include: construction of a signature, the removal of a signature, writing to the file, sending a mail, calling the Web service SOAP RPC calling to a SOAP Web Service MSG, updating values in a component, verifying the value of the component opening the specified web site.
- **Signatures** – four types of signatures are implemented in the form:
  - **Resource signatures** – signatures of resources, files located in the global network and pointed by URL, which are in logical relations with the form,
  - **Approval signatures** – designed to legally approve the form to use. Signatures cover the blank (empty) form and countersign resource signature(s) if exists.

Approval signature is to be done by the organization (or organizations) that uses the form to support its (their) business process.

- **Form signature** – single mandatory signature, covers blank form, countersigns resource and approval signatures. The aim is to protect the whole form against tampering (the visualization, logic, approval signatures and resource signatures)
- **Users signatures** – user signature countersigns the form signature and signs data entered by the user and countersigns signatures of other users as specified for that signature in the form logic.

3.2   Forms Transfer and Processing - ebFormProcessor

The form can be transferred between parties taking a part in the transaction:

- Simple transfer of the XML file using any storage media (disk, pen drive etc.)
- The use of electronic mail (SMTP server, Fig. 3) – the recipients list and encryption information, the mail content text, mail subject can be defined in the logic for send mail action. ebCommunicator application, builds and sends a mail message with ebForm file attached to the message. The mail message does not constitute a document (document is attached as file)
- The form can also be the content of the SOAP-Envelope structure and transferred to the server pointed by address specified in the logic layer for action Send SOAP.

The third way it is the web application (servlet running on the server). It gives wide possibilities to define processing of received forms. The form is:

- received by the application (servlet) as a structure of HTTP SOAP Request, then
- processed according to the logic described in the process descriptor file, where the treatment of different types of the ebForm form is defined. Form processing consists of tasks performed in the order specified in the processes descriptor file, for example:
  - full verification of indicated signatures in the form,
  - read the indicated data from the form and write it to the internal system,

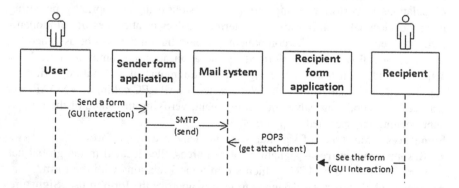

Fig. 3. UML sequence diagram for mail transport of electronic form

- generate and write data to the form,
- generate digital signature in the form,
- construct a mail message and send it to intended recipients,
- save the form in the local file system or internal information system,
- build the SOAP Response structure with the form included (Envelope) and return it to the application ebCommunicator.

Use ebFormProcessor server allows to build solutions that implement the support of transactions in a distributed manner - without the use of the central system with the need to register and then login and verify the logged user.

4   The Transaction with Use of Electronic Forms

Electronic forms in accordance with the requirements described above must reflect the traditional paper forms. Traditional forms can/should reflect all steps of the transaction in the various areas of the form. In the same manner – electronic form should document stages of its processing e.g.:

- Undeniable delivery of a document to the recipient:
  - Using SOAP Protocol – the sequence of actions executed is presented in the Figs. 4 and 5.
  - Using electronic mail – the sequence of actions executed is presented in the Figs. 3 and 6.
- Document (form) flow

  It is possible to implement the document flow between the participants in the transaction. It is possible to implement:
  - automated document flow, with the use of document processing server (ebFormProcessor),

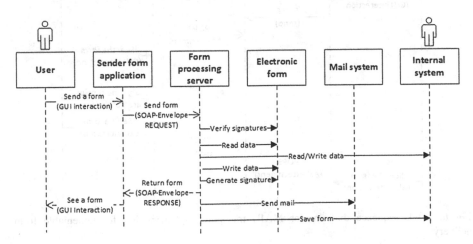

Fig. 4. UML sequence diagram for SOAP transport and processing of electronic form

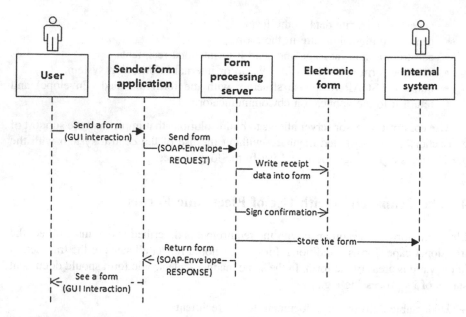

Fig. 5. UML sequence diagram for SOAP transport implementation for undeniable form delivery

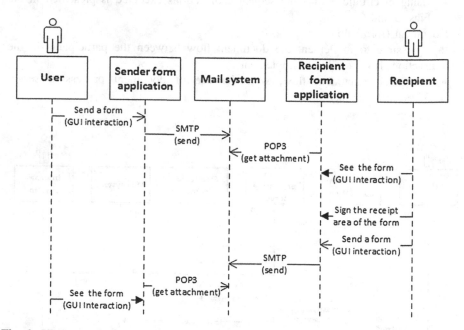

Fig. 6. UML sequence diagram for MAIL transport implementation for undeniable form delivery

- non-automatic flow process, in which the role of the server serve the people and the email is used to transport the document between the parties.

The transfer of the form is executed according to sequence diagrams for SOAP and Mail transport presented in Figs. 3 and 4.

- It is possible to implement support for transaction associated with payment, money transfer and other sophisticated transactions.

5   Implementation, Applications

In the following part of this paper real implementation of the ebForm forms are presented.

Hundreds of traditional paper forms has been implemented in the shape of ebForm forms in about 50 Municipal authorities. Also ebFormProcessor integrated with internal (local) IT systems has been installed. The integration was implemented to store values of data fields in RDBMS SQL Systems, Lotus Notes Server and a few local document flow systems. The experience proofed the usability of the ebForm solution in wide area of applications regardless of the sector, area or social environment. Here only few forms are presented (Figs. 7, 8 and 9).

Fig. 7. Example of the form delivered to Municipal Authority in Szczecin. Non deniable receipt is shown in the violet table.

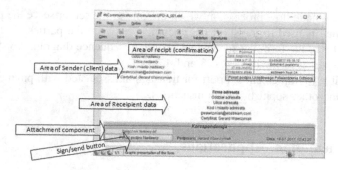

Fig. 8. Example of the form implementing the concept of the envelope with non-deniable delivery to the server.

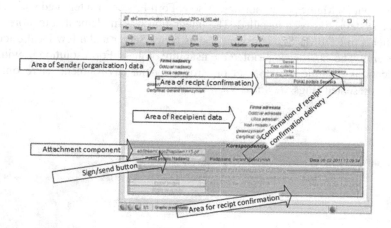

Fig. 9. Example of the form implementing the concept of the envelope with non-deniable delivery to the client.

6   Discussion

As stated above, the document as useful mean for transaction support, must meet features discussed in Sect. 2 of this paper. All popular and widely known and being used solutions doesn't fit to those requirements.

In contrast to approaches presented above, ebForm (XML) proposal provides:

- ease automatic processing, data manipulation, data exchange between information systems thanks to use XML [3] format as the base
- legal effectiveness by through the use of standard XML Signature in accordance with the W3C specification [1, 2],
- intelligibility for people by possibility to visualize the document based on universal, defined with XML Schema [X], syntax and semantic of the document,
- possibility to define and execute the logic defined in the document file and executed by application in accordance to defined syntax and semantics of the form format,

- autonomy – the document can be used by people and systems regardless of network or other systems connection,
- the ability of emerging technologies (cryptocurrency, block chains, smart contracts distributed autonomous organizations) integration in a rapid way. It is not necessary to wait until new technologies are implemented in other approaches in a way required for documents in transactions.

It seems that presented XML form though the generic approach meets expectations and requirements of different kind of transactions and business processes involving those transactions. I does not require to use complex centralized systems and transactions can be executed in totally distributed (decentralized) way.

7 Conclusions

It was found and presented in the paper that the immanent features of electronic document, useful for processing, presentation for human and transaction support are:

- visualization integrated with data and
- the possibility of automatic processing and use by humans,
- the independence that allows to use a document without a network connection,
- while ensuring authenticity, non-repudiation and integrity [14].

As far as presented features apply to all documents (both traditional, paper and electronic), the logic layer, is specific for digital documents (form) only, and provide the ability to define: validation rules, dynamic presentation of graphic components, communication mechanisms calculation rules. In this layer the integration and implementation of concepts of emerging technologies are to be included.

Further development of electronic document capabilities should be anticipated. For example:

- further integration with the communication environment, the dynamic relation between parties of transaction and document should be allowed – for example implementation of the support of the Session Initialization Protocol (SIP). The application executing the logic should present the status/availability of parties involved in transaction and the connection between parties should be established on demand. The example is Skype system.
- Integration with cryptocurrency (e.g. Bitcoin) and the use of these currencies in the implementation of the various types of transactions [15].
- The development and implementation of the concept of Block Chains [16] to build confidence in transactions (documents without the electronic signature) and the use of the concept of distributed databases,
- The use of electronic documents (form ebForm) as so called Smart Contracts with the integration with elements of the Internet of Things.
- The development and implementation of electronic forms integrated with the use of the concept of Distributed Autonomous Organization.

It should be highlighted that current implementation of forms in different solutions show the assumptions are correct and further development is promising.

References

1. Wigand, R.T.: Electronic commerce: definition, theory, and context. Inf. Soc. **13**(1), 1–16 (1997)
2. Gray, J.: The Transaction Concept: Virtues and Limitations. Tandem Computers Incorporated TR 81.3 (1981)
3. www.businessdictionary.com/definition/transaction.html. Accessed 3 Mar 2017
4. mfiles.pl/pl/index.php/Transaction. Accessed 3 Mar 2017
5. Wawrzyniak, G., El Fray, I.: An electronic document for distributed electronic services. In: Saeed, K., Homenda, W. (eds.) CISIM 2016. LNCS, vol. 9842, pp. 617–630. Springer, Cham (2016). doi:10.1007/978-3-319-45378-1_54
6. ISO 32000-1:2008. Document management – Portable document format – Part 1: PDF
7. https://www.microsoft.com. Accessed 3 Mar 2017
8. https://tools.ietf.org/html/rfc2821. Accessed 3 Mar 2017
9. http://www.igi-global.com/dictionary/centralised-system/3590. Accessed 3 Mar 2017
10. XML Signature Syntax and Processing. http://www.w3.org/TR/xmldsig-core
11. XML Advanced Electronic Signatures (XAdES). http://www.w3.org/TR/XAdES
12. Extensible Markup Language (XML). http://www.w3.org/XML
13. Namespaces in XML. http://www.w3.org/TR/REC-xml-names
14. Hyla, T., Pejaś, J.: A practical certificate and identity based encryption scheme and related security architecture. In: Saeed, K., Chaki, R., Cortesi, A., Wierzchoń, S. (eds.) CISIM 2013. LNCS, vol. 8104, pp. 190–205. Springer, Heidelberg (2013). doi:10.1007/978-3-642-40925-7_19
15. Narayanan, A., Bonneau, J., Felten, E., Miller, A., Goldfeder, S.: Bitcoin and Cryptocurrency Technologies: A Comprehensive Introduction. Princeton University Press, Princeton (2016)
16. Peters, G.W., Panayi, E.: Understanding modern banking ledgers through blockchain technologies: future of transaction processing and smart contracts on the internet of money. In: Tasca, P., Aste, T., Pelizzon, L., Perony, N. (eds.) Banking Beyond Banks and Money. A Guide to Banking Services in the Twenty-First Century (2016)

Author Index

Printed in the United States
By Bookmasters